FESTIVAL & SPECIAL EVENT MANAGEMENT ESSENTIALS

FIRST EDITION

Johnny Allen

Robert Harris

Leo Jago

In Memorium Ian McDonnell 31.7.1945–25.4.2019

First edition published 2021 by
John Wiley & Sons Australia, Ltd
42 McDougall Street, Milton, Qld 4064

Typeset in 10/12pt Times LT Std
The moral rights of the authors have been asserted.

A catalogue record for this book is available from the National Library of Australia.

Creators/contributors
John Allen (Author), Robert Harris (Author), Leo Jago (Author), Paul Johnson (Author), Eamon D'Arcy (Author)

Wiley
Terry Burkitt (Director, Publishing and Course Development), Kylie Challenor (Senior Manager, Knowledge & Learning Content Management), Beth Klan (Production Editor), Ash Gavin (Product Manager), Emma Knight (Instructional Designer), Tara Seeto (Publishing Coordinator), Rhys Plant (Copyright & Image Research), Delia Sala (Cover Design)

Typeset in India by diacriTech

ABOUT THE AUTHORS

Johnny Allen

Johnny Allen was the Foundation Director of the Australian Centre for Event Management (ACEM) at the University of Technology, Sydney (UTS) from 1999 until 2013, where he taught in the Event Management Program and conducted a series of International Event Management Conferences. Prior to this he was the Foundation Special Event Manager for Tourism NSW from 1996 to 1998, and Event Manager for the Darling Harbour Authority from 1989 to 1996. Johnny has had an extensive career in event management and planning, and is the recipient of an Order of Australia Award for his services to the event industry and event education, and a Lifetime Achievement Award from the Australian Event Awards. He now semi-retired but continues his involvement in the events field.

Dr Rob Harris

Dr Rob Harris has over 25 years' experience in event management research, education and training, including 15 years as the Director of the Australian Centre for Event Management, University of Technology, Sydney. Upon leaving his university position in 2017 he established Event Training Australia as a vehicle through which to continue his work in the field of event management.

Dr Harris has undertaken research projects, or developed and delivered courses for, numerous organisations, including: The United Nations, Bank of China, Cooperative Centre for Sustainable Tourism, Marketing Institute of Singapore, Austrade, Northern Beaches Council and 12 Australian and overseas universities. Additionally, Rob is: the co-author of the widely used texts and handbook *Festival and Special Event Management, Event Management* and the *Regional Event Management Handbook*; a serving judge for the Australian Event Awards; an assessor for Destination NSW's regional event grants; and a member of the editorial board of several international refereed event management journals. Dr Harris presently holds the positions of Adjunct Fellow, School of Business, University of Technology, Sydney and Adjunct Professor, Taylor's University, Malaysia. In 2019 he was appointed a Professional Fellow of the Asia Pacific Institute for Event Management.

Leo Jago OAM

Leo Jago is a Professor in Events at Griffith University and an Emeritus Professor at the University of Surrey in the UK. Over the last 20 years, Leo has been Director of research centres in Australia and the UK including as the inaugural Chief Economist and General Manager of Tourism Research Australia. The focus of his research agenda has been the evaluation of events particularly from economic and social perspectives. He was awarded an OAM in 2016 for contributions to education and the tourism industry.

Paul Jonson

Paul Jonson is a retired academic and lawyer and is now an education and sport governance consultant. He was Head of the School of Events, Leisure, Sport, Tourism and the Arts at the University of Technology Sydney, Australia where he was an Associate Professor. He taught 'Law for Events' as part of both the Undergraduate and Postgraduate Programs at UTS and in the Australian Centre for Events Management professional education courses.

In 1993 Paul received a UTS Teaching Excellence Award; in 1998 an Australian University Teaching prize; and in 2007 and 2009 Faculty of Business Teaching Excellence Awards. Paul is currently the Deputy Chair of The Institute of International Studies; and Governance Consultant to Oceania Rugby Inc. His publications include Thorpe, Buti, Davies and Jonson (2017), *Sports Law* (3rd edition), Oxford University Press, Melbourne.

Eamon D'Arcy

Eamon D'Arcy is one of Australia's most experienced designers both in the cultural and corporate worlds. He trained at the National Institute of Dramatic Art (NIDA) in Sydney and the Motley School in London, and holds a Master of Philosophy Degree (Art History and Theory) from the Power Institute, The University of Sydney. Eamon has also held a number of senior design/creative lead roles in large-scale projects such as the Sydney Olympics Opening Ceremony, Sydney Paralympic Games Opening and Closing Ceremonies, the Winter Olympics Opening Ceremony in Vancouver, the Cisco Pavilion at World Expo 2010 Shanghai and the Asia-Pacific Economic Cooperation (APEC) Sydney. For over twenty years he designed the launch all of Toyota Cars in Australia, as well as their motor show stands.

Between 2009–2012, Eamon was Executive Creative Director for George P Johnston (Sydney Office) where he worked on IBM, Salesforce, Toyota, Lexus and Emirates accounts. In 2000 he was awarded a Centenary Medal by the Australian Government for Services to Design.

BRIEF CONTENTS

CONTENTS

PART 2

PLANNING   89

CHAPTER 5

Strategic event planning   90

CHAPTER 6

Event project management   119

CHAPTER 7

Event financial planning   143

CHAPTER 8

Human resource management and events   165

PREFACE

Festival & Special Event Management Essentials comes at a pivotal time, as the event industry faces its biggest challenge to date. The COVID-19 pandemic in the short term has shut down the industry, and its long-term impacts are expected to be far-reaching and profound. Many believe that it will hasten existing trends, such as the move to video conferencing and the live streaming of music-based festivals as travel becomes more expensive and borders remain closed. What the event industry will look like on the other side of the pandemic is unclear, as many event organising businesses will not have the financial capacity to bounce back, and government and corporate budgets will be heavily trimmed. In the Australian business events sector alone, 96 per cent of events were either cancelled or postponed in 2020, resulting in an estimated loss of some $37.7 billion. This dramatic pause in live events has, nonetheless, provided a powerful reminder of their economic and social value, and while it might take several years, they will return as restrictions are lifted to once again make their vitally important contribution to our lives and society.

As with previous editions, the authors have networked widely with leading event industry professionals to track and capture the developing knowledge base and best practice in the industry. This process also ranged across allied fields such as project management, marketing, environmental sustainability, tourism, financial management and law. The delivery of event courses by the lead authors in a wide variety of countries including Australia, New Zealand, the UK, China, Singapore and Malaysia has also brought a strong international perspective to the book, and this is further reflected in its variety of contributors, and event profiles and case studies.

Unlike traditional textbooks, *Festival & Special Event Management Essentials* is an aggressively concise, high-quality title that gives students the key content they need to succeed in their course and profession. Content is designed around weekly retrieval practice, a pedagogical strategy that is proven to enhance and boost learning. Students are further supported with engaging questions and illustrative examples that provide focus and added clarity.

As an added benefit, this book concludes with a *Future Skills Guide,* which provides practical advice from experts across technology, wellbeing, social intelligence, ethics, skills and development, design thinking and the future of work. The Guide will help students build career-relevant skills and knowledge to complement their specialist knowledge in the field of strategy.

John Allen
Rob Harris
Leo Jago
June 2020

PART 1

THE EVENT CONTEXT AND CONCEPT DEVELOPMENT

The first part of this book looks at the history and development of events, and the emergence of the event industry in Australia. It examines the impacts of events, including their social/cultural, physical/environmental, political and tourism/economic impacts.

CHAPTER 1

An overview of the event field

LEARNING OBJECTIVES

After studying this chapter, you should be able to:

1.1 define special events and demonstrate an awareness of why special events have evolved in human society

1.2 describe the role of special events in Australia and the Australian tradition of special events

1.3 discuss the growth of state event corporations and the emergence of an event industry

1.4 distinguish between different types of special events

1.5 list and describe the components of the event industry

1.6 list and describe the main professional associations in the event industry, discuss the attributes and knowledge requirements of a special event manager and list the types of organisation involved in the delivery of event management training.

FIGURE 1.1   Australian event timeline

Historical events	Celebrations, festivals and events

Arrival of the First Fleet — 1788

First Anniversary Day celebrations

Other states begin to celebrate their own Foundation days

Gold rushes 1850s — 1850

1860

First Melbourne Cup — 1861

Development of country show circuit
Company and trade union picnics
Development of Australian Rules football

Federation — 1901
Inauguration of Federation of Australia, Sydney

World War 1 1914–18 — 1914

1918

Development of surf lifesaving carnivals and test cricket matches; growth of Anzac Day

World War II 1939–45 — 1939

1945

1950

1954 Visit of Queen Elizabeth II

1956 Melbourne Olympic Games

Growth of civic festivals

1959

1960 First Adelaide Festival of the Arts

Australian involvement in Vietnam War 1962–72 — 1970

1971

Early rock festivals

Whitlam Government 1972–75 — 1972 First Tamworth Country Music Festival

1973 Nimbin Aquarius Festival

1974 Sydney Opera House opening

Community arts movement
Multicultural festivals

1978 First Gay and Lesbian Mardi Gras

1979

1980

1981

1982 Commonwealth Games, Brisbane

Australia's Bicentenary
Tall Ships visit
Opening of Darling Harbour, Sydney
Expo 88, Brisbane
First Aboriginal Survival Day concert, Sydney

1980s economic boom

1983

1984 Victoria's Sesquicentenary

1985 First Adelaide Grand Prix

1986 America's Cup defence, Fremantle

1987 First Maleny (later Woodford) FolkFestival

1988

1989

1990

1991 First Gold Coast Indy

1992 Opening of South Bank, Brisbane, and Southgate, Melbourne

1996 Australian Formula One Grand Prix moves to Melbourne

1997 Opening of Crown Casino, Melbourne

Olympic Festival of the Dreaming

1999

2000 New millennium celebrations and Sydney Olympic Games

2001 Centenary of Federation celebrations

2002 Goodwill Games, Brisbane

2003 Rugby World Cup, Sydney | World Masters Games, Melbourne

2004

2005

2006 Commonwealth Games, Melbourne

2007

2008 World Youth Day, Sydney

2009 World Masters Games, Sydney

Global financial crisis

2010 FIFA World Cup Live site, Sydney

2013 First White Night Festival, Melbourne

2014

2015 Cricket World Cup, Australia and New Zealand

2016

2017 Rugby League World Cup, Australia, New Zealand and Papua New Guinea

2018 Commonwealth Games, Gold Coast and Invictus Games, Sydney

2019

2020 Coronavirus (COVID-19) pandemic

Introduction

Today, events are central to our culture as perhaps never before. Increases in leisure time and discretionary spending have led to a proliferation of public events, celebrations and entertainment. Governments now support and promote events as part of their strategies for economic development, nation building and destination marketing. Corporations and businesses embrace events as key elements in their marketing strategies and image promotion. The enthusiasm of community groups and individuals for their own interests and passions gives rise to a marvellous array of events on almost every subject and theme imaginable. Events spill out of our newspapers and television screens, occupy much of our time, and enrich our lives.

As we study the phenomenon of events, it is worth examining where the event tradition in Australia has come from, and what forces are likely to shape its future growth and development. As events emerge as an industry in their own right, it is also worth considering what elements characterise such an industry, and how the Australian event industry might chart its future directions in an increasingly complex and demanding environment.

1.1 Special events as benchmarks for our lives

LEARNING OBJECTIVE 1.1 Define special events and demonstrate an awareness of why special events have evolved in human society.

Since the dawn of time, human beings have found ways to mark important events in their lives: the changing of the seasons, the phases of the moon, and the renewal of life each spring. From the Aboriginal corroboree and Chinese New Year to the Dionysian rites of ancient Greece and the European carnival tradition of the Middle Ages, myths and rituals have been created to interpret cosmic happenings. To the present day, behind well-known figures such as Old Father Time and Santa Claus lie old myths, archetypes and ancient celebrations.

The first Australians used storytelling, dance and song to transmit their culture from generation to generation. Their ceremonies were, and continue to be, important occasions in the life of the community, where cultural meaning is shared and affirmed. Similarly, in most agrarian societies, rituals were developed that marked the coming of the seasons and the sowing and harvesting of crops.

Both in private and in public, people feel the need to mark the important occasions in their lives, and to celebrate milestones. Coming of age, for example, is often marked by a rite of passage, as illustrated by the tribal initiation ceremony, the Jewish bar and bat mitzvahs and the suburban twenty-first birthday.

At the public level, momentous events become the milestones by which people measure their private lives. We may talk about things happening 'before the new millennium', in the same way that earlier generations spoke of marrying 'before the Depression' or being born 'after the War'. Occasional events — Australia's Bicentenary, the Sydney Olympics, the new millennium, the global financial crisis (GFC) and the novel coronavirus (COVID-19) pandemic — help to mark eras and define milestones.

Even in the high-tech era of global media, when many people have lost touch with the common religious beliefs and social norms of the past, we still need larger social events to mark the local and domestic details of our lives.

1.2 The modern Australian tradition of celebrations

LEARNING OBJECTIVE 1.2 Describe the role of special events in Australia and the Australian tradition of special events.

Australian Aboriginal culture had a rich tradition of rituals and ceremonies prior to the arrival of the first Europeans. This rich tradition continues to this day. There has also been a continuing protest at what many see as the invasion of Australia by Europeans in 1788, with an Aboriginal boycott of the centenary celebrations of the arrival of the First Fleet in 1888, and a Day of Mourning protest and conference at the sesquicentenary celebrations in Sydney in 1938. This protest continued at the Australian Bicentenary celebrations on 26 January 1988, when 40 000 people participated in the March for Freedom, Justice and Hope in Sydney, and the first National Sorry Day held on 26 May 1998. Corroboree 2000 took place in Sydney during Reconciliation Week in May 2000 to mark the end of the ten-year official reconciliation process, and the Bridge Walk for Reconciliation and similar events that took place around Australia in the weeks following were collectively the biggest demonstration of public support for a cause that has ever taken place in Australia (National Museum of Australia 2018). Finally, after a long wait, one of the first acts of the newly elected Rudd Labor Government in 2008 was an official apology to the Aboriginal people for the perceived injustices of the past; however, many issues still remain unresolved as witnessed by the ongoing 'change the date' movement with regard to the date of Australia Day.

In the cultural collision between Aboriginal people and the first Europeans, new traditions were formed alongside the old. Probably the first 'event' in Australia after the arrival of the First Fleet was a bush party to celebrate the coming ashore of the women convicts in 1788:

> Meanwhile, most of the sailors on *Lady Penrhyn* applied to her master, Captain William Sever, for an extra ration of rum 'to make merry with upon the women quitting the ship'. Out came the pannikins, down went the rum, and before long the drunken tars went off to join the convicts in pursuit of the women, so that, Bowes remarked, 'it is beyond my abilities to give a just description of the scene of debauchery and riot that ensued during the night'. It was the first bush party in Australia, with 'some swearing, others quarrelling, others singing' (Hughes 1987, pp. 88–9).

From these inauspicious beginnings, the early colonists slowly started to evolve celebrations that were tailored to their new environment, so far from Georgian Britain. Hull (1984) traces the history of these early celebrations, noting the beginnings of a national day some 30 years later:

> Governor Macquarie declared the 26th of January 1818 a public holiday — convicts were given the day off, a ration of one pound of fresh meat was made for each of them, there was a military review, a salute of 30 guns, a dinner for the officers and a ball for the colony society.

This may have been the first festival celebrated by the new inhabitants of Australia. Although 'Anniversary Day', as it was known, was not to become a public holiday for another 20 years, the official celebration of the founding of the colony had begun with the direct involvement and patronage of the government that continues to this day. In contrast to government-organised celebrations, settlers during the nineteenth century entertained themselves with balls, shows and travelling entertainments as a diversion from the serious business of work and survival. The rich tradition of agricultural shows such as the Sydney Royal Easter Show and race meetings such as the Melbourne Cup still survive as major events in their respective cities today.

At the turn of the century, the celebration of Australia's Federation captured the prevailing mood of optimistic patriotism:

> At the turn of the year 1900–1 the city of Sydney went mad with joy. For a few days hope ran so high that poets and prophets declared Australia to be on the threshold of a new golden age . . . from early morning on 1 January 1901 trams, trains and ferry boats carried thousands of people into the city for the greatest day in their history: the inauguration of the Commonwealth of Australia. It was to be a people's festival (Clark 1981, p. 177).

At the beginning of the twentieth century, the new inhabitants had come to terms with the landscape of Australia, and the democratic ritual of the picnic had gained mass popularity. This extended to guilds, unions and company workers, as demonstrated by the following description of the annual picnic of the employees of Sydney boot and shoe manufacturers McMurtie and Company, at Clontarf in 1906:

> The sweet strains of piano, violin and cornet . . . added zest and enjoyment to the festive occasion', said the Advisor. 'Laughter producers were also in evidence, several of the company wearing comical-looking hats and false noses so that even at the commencement of the day's proceedings hilarity and enjoyment was assured.' The enjoyment continued as the party disembarked to the strain of bagpipes, and the sporting programme began . . . The 'little ones' were provided with 'toys, spades, balls and lollies'. The shooting gallery was well patronised, and when darkness fell dancing went on in the beautiful dancing hall. Baby Houston danced a Scotch reel to the music of bagpipes. Miss Robinson sang *Underneath the Watermelon Vine*, and little Ruth Bailey danced a jig.

> At 8 pm, the whistle blew and the homeward journey commenced with 'music up till the last' and a final rendering of *Auld Lang Syne* as the *Erina* arrived at the Quay (Pearl 1974).

However, Australians had to wait until after World War II before a home-grown form of celebration took hold across the nation. In the 1940s and 1950s, city and town festivals were established, that created a common and enduring format. Even today, it is a safe assumption that any festival with an Aboriginal or floral name, and that includes a 'Festival Queen' competition, street parade, outdoor art exhibition and sporting event, dates to this period. Sydney's Waratah Festival (which was later replaced by the

Sydney Festival), Melbourne's Moomba, Ballarat's Begonia Festival, Young's Cherry Festival, Bowral's Tulip Time, Newcastle's Mattara Festival and Toowoomba's Carnival of Flowers all date to the prolific era of local pride and involvement after World War II. Moomba and Mattara both adopted Aboriginal names, the latter word meaning 'hand of friendship'.

Holding such a festival became a badge of civic pride, in the way that building a School of Arts hall had done in an earlier era, or constructing an Olympic swimming pool would do in the 1950s and 1960s. These festivals gave the cities and towns a sense of identity and distinction and became a focus for community groups and charity fundraising. It is a tribute to their importance to their communities that many of these festivals still continue after more than half a century.

Alongside this movement of community festivals was another very powerful model. In 1947 the Edinburgh Festival was founded as part of the post-war spirit of reconstruction and renewal. In Australia, the Festival of Perth (founded in 1953) and the Adelaide Festival of the Arts (founded in 1960) were based on this inspiring model. The influence of the Edinburgh Festival proved to be enduring, as shown by the resurgence of arts festivals in Sydney, Melbourne and Brisbane in the 1980s and 1990s. By the 1970s, however, with the coming to power of the Whitlam Government and then the formation of the Australia Council, new cultural directions were unleashed that were to change the face of festivals in Australia.

The Community Arts Board of the Australia Council, under the leadership of Ros Bower, developed a strategy aimed at giving a voice to the voiceless, and taking arts and festivals into the suburbs and towns of Australia. Often for the first time, migrants, workers and Aboriginal people were encouraged to participate in a new cultural pluralism that broke down the elitism that had governed the arts in much of rural and suburban Australia. Sensing the unique cultural challenge faced by Australia, Bower (1981) wrote:

> In terms of our national cultural objectives, the re-integration of the artist into the community is of crucial importance. Australia lacks a coherent cultural background. The artist needs to become the spokesman, the interpreter, the image-maker and the prophet. He cannot do it in isolation or from an ivory tower. He must do it by working with the people. He must help them to piece together their local history, their local traditions, their folk-lore, the drama and the visual imagery of their lives. And in doing this he will enrich and give identity to his work as an artist. The arts will cease to be imitative, or preoccupied with making big splashes in little 'cultured' pools. They will be integrated more closely with our lives, our history, our unique environment. They will be experimental and exploring forces within the broader cultural framework.

The 1970s involved not only the emergence of multiculturalism and the 'new age' movement, but also the forging of the community arts movement and a new and diverse range of festivals across Australia. Examples of the rich diversity spawned by this period are the Aquarius Festival, which was staged by the Australian Union of Students at Nimbin in northern New South Wales; the Lygon Street Festa in Melbourne's Carlton; the Come Out young people's festival held in alternate years to the Adelaide Festival; the Carnivale celebration of multiculturalism across Sydney and New South Wales; and Sydney's Gay and Lesbian Mardi Gras. Festivals became part of the cultural landscape and connected again to people's needs and lives. Every community, it seemed, had something to celebrate, and the tools with which to create its own festival.

1.3 The birth of an event industry

LEARNING OBJECTIVE 1.3 Discuss the growth of state event corporations and the emergence of an event industry.

Through the 1980s and 1990s, certain seminal events set the pattern for the contemporary event industry as we know it today. The Commonwealth Games in Brisbane in 1982 ushered in a new era of maturity and prominence for that city and a new breed of sporting events. It also initiated a career in ceremonies and celebrations for former ABC rock show producer, Ric Birch, which led to his taking a key role in the opening and closing ceremonies at the Los Angeles, Barcelona and Sydney Summer Olympics and the Turin Winter Olympics.

The Olympic Games in Los Angeles in 1984 demonstrated that major events could be economically viable. The organisers managed to combine a Hollywood-style spectacle with a sporting event in a manner that had not been done before, and that would set a standard for all similar events in future. The production and marketing skills of the television industry brought the Olympics to an audience wider than ever before. Television also demonstrated the power of a major sporting event to bring increased profile and economic benefits to a city and to an entire country.

The entrepreneurs of the 1980s economic boom in Australia soon picked up on this potential, and America's Cup defence in Perth and Fremantle in 1986–87 was treated as an opportunity to put Perth on the map and to attract major economic and tourism benefits to Western Australia. By 1988 there was a boom in special events, with Australia's Bicentenary perceived by many as a major commemorative program and vehicle for tourism. This boom was matched by governments setting up state event corporations, thereby giving public sector support to special events as never before. In Brisbane the success of Expo 88 rivalled the Bicentennial activities in Sydney, and Adelaide managed a coup by staging the first Australian Formula One Grand Prix.

The Bicentenary caused Australians to pause and reflect on the Australian identity. It also changed forever the nature of our public celebrations:

> I would argue that the remarkable legacy of 1988 is the public event. It is now a regular feature of Australian life. We gather for fireworks, for welcome-home marches for athletes and other Australians who have achieved success. We go to large urban spaces like the Domain for opera, rock and symphonic music in our hundreds of thousands. The Sydney Festival attracts record numbers. The Gay Mardi Gras is an international phenomenon . . . Whatever the nature of debate about values, identity and imagery, one certainty is that Australians are in love with high-quality public events that are fun and offer to extend the range and experience of being Australian (McCarthy 1998).

The Bicentenary also left a legacy of public spaces dedicated to celebrations and special events, and of governments supporting events for their perceived social and economic benefits. Sydney's Darling Harbour opened to welcome the Tall Ships on 16 January 1988 and provided the city with a major leisure centre. Darling Harbour incorporates dedicated celebrations areas, tourist attractions, a festival marketplace and the International Convention Centre, all adjacent to the Powerhouse and National Maritime Museums. Likewise, Brisbane's riverside Expo 88 site was converted into the South Bank Parklands, and Melbourne followed suit with the Southbank development on the Yarra River.

Whatever its economic causes, the recession of the late 1980s and early 1990s put a dampener on the party mood and the seemingly endless growth of events — that is, until 4.27 am on 24 September 1993 when International Olympic Committee President Juan Antonio Samaranch spoke those memorable words: 'And the winner is . . . Sydney!'

Many said that the late 1980s recession ended the day Sydney was awarded the Olympic Games of the new millennium. Certainly, it meant the event industry could once more look forward with optimism, as though the recession had been a mere pause for breath. Event corporations formed in the late 1980s and early 1990s started to demonstrate that special events could generate economic benefits. This led to competition between the states for major events, which became weapons in an event war fuelled by the media. Australia approached the end of the century with a competitive events climate dominated by the Sydney Olympics, the new millennium and the Centenary of Federation celebrations in 2001.

This enthusiasm for events has continued well into the first decades of the new century, with the staging of the Goodwill Games in Brisbane in 2001; the World Masters Games in Melbourne and the International Gay Games in Sydney in 2002; the World Rugby Cup in venues around Australia in 2003; the Commonwealth Games in Melbourne in 2006; the World Swimming Championships in Melbourne and the World Police and Fire Games in Adelaide in 2007; World Youth Day in Sydney in 2008; the World Masters Games in Sydney in 2009; the World Cricket Cup in Australia and New Zealand in 2015; the Rugby League World Cup in Australia, New Zealand and Papua New Guinea in 2017; and the Commonwealth Games on the Gold Coast and the Invictus Games in Sydney in 2018.

The corporate world was quick to discover the marketing and image-making power of events, and events became established through the 1990s and the early 2000s as an important element of the corporate marketing mix. By the early 2000s, corporate involvement in events had become the norm, so that sponsorship was perceived as an integral part of staging major events. Companies became increasingly aware of the role that events could play in promoting their image and increasing their market share, but they also became more focused on event outcomes and return on investment. It became common for large companies to have an in-house event team, focused not only on the company's involvement in public events, but also on the internal role of events in company and product promotions, staff training and morale building. Events became not only a significant part of the corporate vocabulary, but also a viable career option with employment opportunities and career paths.

Challenges face the new industry

However, the path of the modern event industry has not always been smooth, and it has faced many challenges in its short history. These include the September 11 terrorist attack on New York; the SARS crisis; the GFC; a major upheaval in the global insurance industry, resulting in escalating insurance costs and in the need for the industry to adopt strategies for managing the risks to events; and the novel coronavirus (COVID-19) in 2020.

As we entered the middle of the first decade of the 2000s, the spectre of climate change began to affect the industry as the world became increasingly aware of the threat of global warming. Environmental sustainability became a key event management concept, with green initiatives adopted to reduce the environmental impact and the carbon footprint of events. Many events were created as models to impart awareness of climate change, and to encourage participants to change their habits and lifestyle. Indicating the development of public awareness of the issue is the remarkable growth of Earth Hour, an initiative of the World Wildlife Fund to switch off the lights in major cities to encourage awareness of climate change, starting in Sydney in 2007 with 2.2 million participants. In 2008, 50 million people participated across 35 countries. By 2018 hundreds of millions of people around the world in more than 7000 cities in over 180 countries were participating in the event (Earth Hour 2018). In 2019 the School Strike for Climate mobilised school children around the world in a massive action that reverberated in the global consciousness and media (Shine 2019).

Much of the rapid expansion of events was fuelled by the longest economic boom in living memory, and, by the end of the first decade of the 2000s, a reality check was long overdue. This came with the global financial crisis sparked by the USA sub-prime mortgage affair in 2008, continuing worldwide into 2009. As the economy worsened, many corporate clients cancelled events, and those that continued them tightened their budgets. The mood switched swiftly to one of austerity, and the events that continued were required to exhibit modesty and thrift — virtues that the event industry now had to practise in order to survive.

Although the GFC had a considerable impact on the event industry, events, now established as an integral part of modern business practice, managed to survive the economic downturn, as they have survived other challenges in the past. A lasting legacy is that event managers have been called upon to deliver more with less, and to tread a thin and careful line between the twin challenges of economic and environmental sustainability.

In the decade since the GFC, events have continued to grow apace and to further entrench their position as a key part of our cultural life. Event managers and producers have sought to produce ever more innovative and attractive events in order to win our hearts and minds, and open our pockets. In 2009 Vivid Sydney was born as a smart light festival headlined by Brian Eno and using the Sydney Opera House as a giant screen for lighting projections. Over the following decade, it has morphed into a giant festival of light, music and ideas, attracting massive local and international visitation and bringing Sydney alive in winter. In the same year Federation Square in Melbourne initiated The Light in Winter project, and other lighting festivals have followed with the White Light Festival in Melbourne, Enlighten in Canberra, the Swan Festival of Lights in Perth and Field of Light at Uluru in the Northern Territory. Food and wine, film and music festivals have also continued to proliferate in cities and towns around Australia.

This veritable explosion of festivals caused Munro (2016) writing in *The Sydney Morning Herald* to ask, 'Have we reached 'peak festival'?'

> . . . between the Sydney Festival, the Festival of Dangerous Ideas, Vivid Sydney, Sydney Writers' Festival, . . . Sydney Design Festival, Laneway Festival, Vibes on a Summer's Day, Sydney Comedy Festival. . . you might start feeling festival fatigue.
>
> There's a festival for every occasion, season and sensation in this city. Could Sydney finally have hit 'peak festival'?

However, Westwood (2017) writing in *The Australian* challenges this assumption:

> Ticket data collated by Live Performance Australia shows that 2.5 million people collectively spent almost $170 million on festivals in 2015, a figure that does not include film and writers' festivals, or the huge attendance at the free outdoor attractions of Vivid Sydney. And there's no sign of enthusiasm waning . . .

In early 2020, the novel coronavirus (COVID-19) pandemic exploded worldwide, fracturing many of the norms and structures of society. With the ban on mass gatherings, countless events were shut down almost overnight in Australia and globally. Despite innovations such as video conferencing and internet delivery of events, the virus had a devastating impact on the event industry, as it did on the whole of society and the economy. At the time of writing, it is impossible to predict how long the crisis will last, or what the event industry will look like on the other side of the shutdown. However, given the importance of events and the crucial role that they play in society, it is likely that the industry will rebound and that events will continue, albeit modified to suit changed circumstances and the new norm.

Vivid Sydney: light, music, ideas

Vivid Sydney started in 2009 as a smart light festival at Sydney Cove. As the festival developed, projections on the sails of the Sydney Opera House, the Sydney Harbour Bridge, the Museum of Contemporary Art and Customs House at Circular Quay helped to define a unique festival precinct. The use of computer mapping technology and high-quality projections brought the iconic precinct to life, supported by a series of innovative and often immersive installations by Australian and international lighting artists and companies to become the Light Walk. Crowds flocked to the festival, which quickly became a signature event for Sydney and a tourism drawcard,
attracting interstate and overseas visitors during the normally quiet winter season. Venues were expanded, including by 2018 the Royal Botanic Gardens Sydney, the Rocks, Barangaroo, Luna Park and Darling Harbour, along with the city's Kings Cross, Chatswood and Taronga Zoo precincts.

Vivid had a strong music component from the beginning, attracting legendary performers including over the first decade Brian Eno, Lou Reed, Laurie Anderson, The Cure, Kraftwerk and Pixies to a program of concerts focused initially on the Sydney Opera House. By 2018 this had expanded to include Carriageworks, the City Recital Hall and a host of music venues across the city, with a wide range of local and visiting performers.

Parallel to this, a festival of ideas was developed which by 2018 had grown to over one hundred workshops, forums and creative events at venues including the Museum of Contemporary Art, the Art Gallery of New South Wales, the City Recital Hall, and the Powerhouse and Australian Museums. Headliners in 2018 included James Cameron, filmmaker of Avatar and Titanic; Dare Jennings, founder of Mambo, Phantom Records and Deus Ex Machina; and Dan Goods, strategist at NASA's Jet Propulsion Laboratory and co-founder of the Museum of Awe.

Ever-increasing crowds led to challenges of congestion and transport for the festival. Organisers responded by extending the duration of the festival to 23 days, encouraging visitors to explore the newer venues and to visit on the less crowded early weeknights, with the Light Walk becoming one-way at peak times.

In 2019 Vivid Sydney set a new record with 2.4 million people attending the festival and contributing over $172 million to the NSW economy (Destination NSW 2020).

However, Vivid Sydney at the end of its first decade was not without its critics, one of whom complained that it is too crowded, too repetitive and has lost its creative mojo (Farrelly 2018):

> Vivid at 10 has proved you can be loud without actually being vivid . . . So, question: has Vivid become the victim of its own success? Has it fallen into that old Sydney trap of substituting quantity for quality? . . . Do we really care about biggest? Whatever happened to best?

Events on the world stage

This brief outline of the history of modern events relates primarily to the Australian situation, but a similar story has been replicated in most post-industrial societies. The balance between more traditional festivals and contemporary corporate events changes according to the nature of the society in a given geographic area.

Nevertheless, there is ample anecdotal evidence to suggest that both the growth of events and the twin challenges of economic and environmental sustainability are worldwide phenomena. In 2017 the International Congress and Convention Association (ICCA) reported a record number of 12 558 international association meetings taking place globally, the highest annual figure ever recorded in its yearly analysis of the immediate past year's meetings data. It had previously identified a 50-year trend of exponential growth in the number of international association meetings, with numbers doubling every 10 years. Although this exponential growth had slowed in recent years, it was still described as a more mature, but still solid growth pattern (International Congress and Convention Association 2018).

Meanwhile in Asia, the staging of the Summer Olympics in Beijing in 2008, World Expo in Shanghai and the Asian Games in Guangzhou in 2010 and the Commonwealth Games in Delhi in 2010 saw these cities use major events to showcase their emerging prominence to the world. This increasing interest in events in Asia is reflected in the establishment of International Festivals and Events Association affiliates in China and South Korea (International Festivals and Events Association 2018).

Australia still retains a degree of prominence in the international events field, with state governments' event corporations and the staging of the Sydney Olympic Games in 2000 being regarded as international benchmarks for best practice in the field.

1.4 Special events

LEARNING OBJECTIVE 1.4 Distinguish between different types of special events.

The term 'special events' has been coined to describe specific rituals, presentations, performances or celebrations that are consciously planned and created to mark special occasions or achieve particular social, cultural or corporate goals and objectives. Special events can include national days and celebrations, important civic occasions, unique cultural performances, major sporting fixtures, corporate functions, trade promotions and product launches. It seems at times that special events are everywhere; they have become a growth industry. The field of special events is now so vast that it is impossible to provide a definition that includes all varieties and shades of events. In his ground-breaking work on the typology of events, Getz (2005, p. 16) suggests special events are best defined by their context. He offers two definitions, one from the point of view of the event organiser and the other from that of the customer or guest:

1. A special event is a one-time, or infrequently occurring event outside the normal program or activities of the sponsoring or organizing body.
2. To the customer or guest, a special event is an opportunity for an experience outside the normal range of choices or beyond everyday experience.

Among the attributes that he believes create the special atmosphere are festive spirit, uniqueness, quality, authenticity, tradition, hospitality, theme and symbolism.

Types of events

There are many different ways of categorising or grouping events, including by size, form and content, as discussed in the following sections. This text examines the full range of events that the event industry produces, using the term 'event' to cover all of the following categories.

Size

Special events are often characterised according to their size or scale (figure 1.2). Common categories are mega-events, hallmark events, major events and local/community events, although definitions are not exact and distinctions can be blurred.

Mega-events

Mega-events are those events that are of such scale and significance that they affect whole economies and reverberate in the global media. They include Olympic Games, the FIFA World Cup and World Fairs, but it is difficult for many other events to lay claim to this category.

Hall (1992, p. 5), defines them as:

> Mega-events such as World Fairs and Expositions, the World Soccer Cup final, or the Olympic Games, are events which are expressly targeted at the international tourism market and may be suitably described as 'mega' by virtue of their size in terms of attendance, target market, level of public financial involvement, political effects, extent of television coverage, construction of facilities, and impact on economic and social fabric of the host community.

Müller (2015) examined the definitions of several researchers in the field and concluded that:

> [m]ega-events are ambulatory occasions of a fixed duration that (a) attract a large number of visitors, (b) have large mediated reach, (c) come with large costs and (d) have large impacts on the built environment and the population.

FIGURE 1.2   Categorisation of events

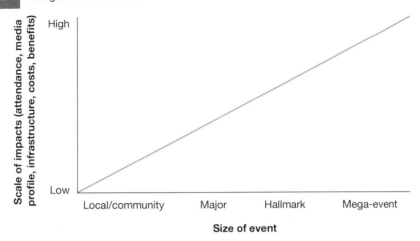

By these definitions, the Sydney Olympic Games in 2000 was perhaps Australia's first true mega-event. The Melbourne Olympics in 1956 belonged to an earlier era of far less extensive media coverage and smaller television audiences, although in relative terms it may qualify as a mega-event of its era. Even Brisbane's Expo 88 was officially a 'B' class World Expo, and events such as the Commonwealth Games in Brisbane in 1982 and the America's Cup defence in Perth and Fremantle in 1986–87 would struggle to meet some of the criteria. More recently, the Rugby World Cup in 2003, the Commonwealth Games in Melbourne in 2006 and the Gold Coast in 2018 may be seen as contenders.

Hallmark events

Hallmark events, sometimes also known as flagship or signature events, are events that become so identified with the spirit or ethos of a town, city or region that they become synonymous with the name of the place, and gain widespread recognition and awareness. The term is often used in relation to tourism, where hallmark events not only serve to attract visitors, but also help to create and support the image and brand of the destination. Tourism researcher Ritchie (1984, p. 2) defines them as:

> Major one-time or recurring events of limited duration, developed primarily to enhance awareness, appeal and profitability of a tourism destination in the short term and/or long term. Such events rely for their success on uniqueness, status, or timely significance to create interest and attract attention.

Classic examples of hallmark events are the Carnival in Rio de Janeiro, known throughout the world as an expression of the vitality and exuberance of that city; the Kentucky Derby in the United States; the Chelsea Flower Show in Britain; the Oktoberfest in Munich, Germany; and the Edinburgh Festival in Scotland. Hallmark events may even relate to whole countries rather than just cities or regions, with some examples being the Tour de France and Mexico's Day of the Dead celebrations. Such events, which are identified with the very character of these places and their citizens, bring huge tourist dollars, a strong sense of local pride and international recognition. Getz (2005, pp. 16–17) describes them in terms of their ability to provide a competitive advantage for their host communities:

> In other words, 'hallmark' describes an event that possesses such significance, in terms of tradition, attractiveness, quality, or publicity, that the event provides the host venue, community, or destination with a competitive advantage. Over time, the event and destination can become inextricably linked, such as Mardi Gras and New Orleans.

Examples in Australia might include the Sydney Gay and Lesbian Mardi Gras, Vivid Sydney, the Australasian Country Music Festival at Tamworth, the Melbourne Cup and the Adelaide Festival, all of which have a degree of international recognition and help to identify the ethos of their host cities. Hallmark events are an important component of destination marketing, which will be discussed further in the chapter on event tourism planning.

Major events

Major events are events that are capable, by their scale and media interest, of attracting significant visitor numbers, media coverage and economic benefits. Melbourne has developed the Australian Open tennis tournament, the Australian Formula One Grand Prix and the White Night Festival into significant annual major events. Perth has staged the Mastercard Hopman Cup in tennis, the Johnnie Walker Classic golf tournament and the Bledisloe Cup in 2019. South Australia has developed the Santos Tour Down Under into the prime cycling event in the southern hemisphere. Cultural events can also be contenders, such as the Adelaide, Sydney and Melbourne arts festivals; the MOFO and Dark MOFO festivals in Hobart; and regional festivals such as Ten Days on the Island in Tasmania and the state-wide Queensland Music Festival.

Local or community events

Most communities produce a host of festivals and events that are targeted mainly at local audiences and staged primarily for their social, fun and entertainment value. Such events can be found in almost every city and town in Australia. Some examples deserving of attention because of their unusual nature or unique setting include the Birdsville Races in outback Queensland, the Henley-On-Todd Dry River Boat Regatta in Alice Springs, and the Deni Ute Muster in Deniliquin, New South Wales. These events often produce a range of benefits, including engendering pride in the community, strengthening a feeling of belonging and creating a sense of place. They can also help to expose people to new ideas and experiences, encourage participation in sports and arts activities, and encourage tolerance and diversity. For these reasons, local governments often support such events as part of their community and cultural development strategies.

Janiskee (1996, p. 404) defines them as:

> . . . family-fun events that are considered 'owned' by a community because they use volunteer services from the host community, employ public venues such as streets, parks and schools and are produced at the direction of local government agencies or non-government organizations (NGOs) such as service clubs, public safety organisations or business associations.

Janiskee also comments that community festivals can become hallmark events and attract a large number of visitors to a community. Janiskee estimates that community celebrations in the United States have been increasing at an annual rate of 5 per cent since the 1930s, and it is reasonable to assume that they have increased at a similar rate in Australia.

Another growing subsection of community events is charity fundraising events, which seek to increase the profile and raise funds for their respective charities. Well-known examples include Community Aid Abroad's Walk Against Want, SIDS' Red Nose Day and Movember, a moustache-growing charity event held during November each year that raises funds and awareness for men's health. Although these events often have key financial objectives, they are generally seen as part of the not-for-profit community sector.

Form or content

Another common means of classifying events is by their form or content. Festivals are a universal form of event that pre-date the contemporary event industry and exist in most times and most societies. Sports events have grown out of similar roots to become a sizable and growing sector of the event industry. Business events, sometimes called MICE (meetings, incentives, conventions and exhibitions) events, are an established arm of the event industry, and generate considerable income for their host cities and, increasingly, for regional centres.

Festivals

Festivals are an important expression of human activity that contributes much to our social and cultural life. They are also increasingly linked with tourism to generate business activity and income for their host communities.

The most common type of festival is the arts festival, which can encompass mixed art forms and multiple venues — such as the capital city arts festivals — or single art forms such as the Queensland Music Festival, the Sydney Biennale or the Melbourne Writers Festival. The most popular form of arts festival is the music festival. Music festivals can range from classical music festivals such as the International Music Festival in Canberra, to jazz festivals such as the Melbourne International Jazz Festival, to folk and blues festivals such as the Byron Bay Bluesfest and the Woodford Folk Festival in Queensland, to rock festivals such as the Falls Festival and Splendour in the Grass.

Another type of festival that has become universally popular is the food and wine festival. These range from large festivals in the capital cities to local festivals showcasing regional cuisine. Other festivals such as the Tropfest short film festival and Groovin the Moo have become multi-state festivals, while festivals such as Floriade in Canberra and the Sydney Gay and Lesbian Mardi Gras approach hallmark status in their respective cities. Regional festivals, too, are a growing phenomenon, with towns both large and small expressing their unique character and distinctiveness through well-honed festivals and community celebrations. Some examples of the tremendous variety and array of regional festivals include the Mount Isa Rodeo in Queensland, the Wangaratta Jazz Festival in Victoria and the Parkes Elvis Festival in New South Wales. Festivals have become a pervasive feature of our cultural landscape and constitute a vital and growing component of the event industry.

Sports events

The testing of sporting prowess through competition is one of the oldest and most enduring of human activities, with a rich tradition going back to the ancient Greek Olympics and beyond. Sports events are an important and growing part of the event industry, encompassing the full spectrum of individual sports and multi-sport events such as the Olympic, Commonwealth and Masters Games. Their ability to attract tourist visitors and to generate media coverage and economic impacts has placed them at the fore of most government event strategies and destination marketing programs. Sports events not only bring benefits to their host governments and sports organisations, but also benefit participants such as players, coaches and officials, and bring entertainment and enjoyment to spectators. Examples of sports events can be readily identified in each of the size categories listed earlier.

Business events

Another long-established component of the event industry is business events, also known as the meetings industry or the MICE (meetings, incentives, conventions and exhibitions) industry. This sector is largely characterised by its business and trade focus, although there is a strong public and tourism aspect to many of its activities. Meetings can be very diverse, as revealed by the definition of the Commonwealth Department of Tourism (1995, p. 3):

> . . . all off-site gatherings, including conventions, congresses, conferences, seminars, workshops and symposiums, which bring together people for a common purpose — the sharing of information.

A study conducted in 2015, 'The Value of Business Events to Australia', found that in the 2013–14 financial year, over 37 million people attended more than 412 000 business events in Australia. These events generated $28 billion in direct expenditure, $13.5 billion in value-added expenditure and generated 179 357 direct jobs (Business Events Council of Australia 2015).

The following examples illustrate the exposure, visitors and economic benefits that major business events bring to their host cities.
- SIBOS, the world's biggest financial services event, was expected to attract 6000 delegates to the International Convention Centre in Sydney in October 2018, delivering up to $37 million in visitor expenditure (Business Events Sydney 2017).
- The world's largest public transport event, The Union International des Transports Publics (UITP) Global Public Transport Summit, was expected to attract 2000 delegates to Melbourne in 2021 and to deliver $9.4 million in economic contribution for Victoria (Melbourne Convention Bureau 2018).

Another lucrative aspect of the business event industry is incentive travel, defined by the Society of Incentive Travel Executives (cited in Rogers 1998, p. 47) as 'a global management tool that uses an exceptional travel experience to motivate and/or recognise participants for increased levels of performance in support of organisational goals'. Australia's colourful and unique locations and international popularity as a tourism destination make it a leading player in the incentive travel market.

Last, but not least, exhibitions are a considerable and growing part of the business event industry. Exhibitions bring suppliers of goods and services together with buyers, usually in a particular industry sector. They can be restricted to industry members, in which case they are referred to as trade shows, or open to the general public. The International Motor Show, the Home Show and the Boat Show are three of the largest exhibitions in Sydney, each generating tens of thousands of visitors. Major convention centres in most Australian cities and many regional centres now vie for their share of the thriving business event industry market.

1.5 The structure of the event industry

LEARNING OBJECTIVE 1.5 List and describe the components of the event industry.

The rapid growth of events in the past decade led to the formation of an identifiable event industry, with its own practitioners, suppliers and professional associations. The emergence of the industry has involved the identification and refinement of a discrete body of knowledge of industry best practice, accompanied by the development of training programs and career paths. The industry's formation has also been accompanied by a period of rapid globalisation of markets and communication, which has affected the nature of, and trends within, the industry. Further, it has been accompanied by an era of increasing government regulation, which has resulted in a complex and demanding operational environment. The following sections describe the key components of the event industry.

Event organisations

Events are often staged or hosted by event organisations, which may be event-specific bodies such as the Sydney Festival, the Adelaide Festival, or the Australian Open tennis tournament organisers in Melbourne. Other events are run by special teams within larger organisations, such as the City to Surf fun run organised by *The Sun-Herald* newspaper in Sydney, the Sydney to Hobart Yacht Race organised by the Cruising Yacht Club of Australia, or the Taste of Tasmania organised as part of the Hobart Summer Festival by the City of Hobart Council. Corporate events are often organised by in-house event teams or by project teams within the companies that are putting on the event.

Event management companies

Event management companies are professional groups or individuals that organise events on a contract basis on behalf of their clients. The Australia Day Council, for example, may contract an event management company to stage an Australia Day ceremony, or Mercedes Benz may contract an event manager to stage the launch of a new Mercedes car model. The specialist companies often organise a number of events concurrently, and develop long-term relationships with their clients and suppliers.

Event industry suppliers

The growth of a large and complex industry has led to the formation of a wide range of specialist suppliers. These suppliers may work in direct event-related areas, such as staging, sound production, lighting, audiovisual production, entertainment and catering, or they may work in associated areas, such as transport, communications, security, legal services and accounting services. This network of suppliers is an integral part of the industry, and their increasing specialisation and expertise assist the production of professional and high-calibre events.

Venues

Venue management often includes an event management component, whether as part of the marketing of the venue or as part of the servicing of event clients. Many venues, such as historical houses, galleries, museums, theatres, universities and libraries, create additional revenue by hiring their facilities for functions and corporate events. Sydney's Unique Venues Association (2018) encompasses a wide range of venues including Taronga Park Zoo, Luna Park, Sydney Town Hall, the State Theatre and Sydney Harbour Islands. Types of venues that commonly include an event management in-house team include hotels, resorts, convention and exhibition centres, sports and fitness centres, sports stadiums, performing arts centres, heritage sites, theme parks and shopping centres.

Industry associations

The emergence of the industry has also led to the formation of professional associations providing networking, communications and liaison within the industry, training and accreditation programs, codes of ethical practice, and lobbying on behalf of their members. Because the industry is so diverse, multiple associations have arisen to cater for specific sectors of the industry. Some are international associations with affiliated groups in countries such as Australia; others are specific to their region or country. Some key industry associations relevant to the interests of event managers include the following.
- Meetings & Events Australia (MEA). MEA is the peak body representing the event industry in Australia. It is dedicated to fostering professionalism and excellence in all aspects of the industry. MEA's mission is to:
  - promote the growth and excellence in the meetings and events sector
  - create business opportunities and facilitate business-to-business relationships
  - encourage better business practices
  - offer professional development and education to build a skilled and informed industry workforce

- develop and manage an accreditation program to enhance the reputation of the industry and increase consumer confidence when dealing with industry professionals
  - expand the meetings and events market by promoting its value
  - advocate on behalf of the industry to raise its profile with government.
- MEA runs an extensive education and accreditation program. It also conducts an annual conference and a national awards program recognising excellence in a range of events and services to the industry (Meetings and Events Australia 2018).
- Exhibition & Event Association of Australasia (EEAA). EEAA is the peak industry association for those in the business of trade and consumer expos and events. It works to ensure industry growth by encouraging high industry standards, promoting the professionalism of members and highlighting the unique business opportunities that exist through exhibitions and their associated events. EEAA's role is to:
  - strengthen the voice of the exhibition and event sector through effective advocacy and research
  - promote exhibitions and events as the most powerful face-to-face marketing channel
  - drive education, training and best practice in the industry
  - nurture young talent and promote careers in the sector
  - recognise achievement and excellence
  - promote sound WHS and ethical practice
  - help members grow their businesses
  - deliver events and networking channels that allow members to build peer-to-peer contacts.
- EEAA conducts an annual conference and awards program and provides significant industry networking opportunities through the annual EEAA Leaders Forum and the Young Stars and Leaders Table. It provides an ongoing program of professional development for members, a jobs board, an Excelling in Exhibitions Program in association with Sydney TAFE and an industry traineeships program in association with TAFE NSW. It also maintains an annual calendar of events run by its members and conducts an extensive research and advocacy program (Exhibition and Event Association of Australasia 2018). The EEAA code of ethics is reproduced in figure 1.3.
- Professional Conference Organisers Association (PCO). The PCO Association represents the interests of Professional Conference Organisers and Event Managers in Australia and New Zealand. It aims to increase the standard of professionalism of its members and promote a better understanding of the roles, functions and contributions of Professional Conference Organisers and Event Managers in the conference and event sector. It runs an annual conference, and a Certified Event Manager (CEM) accreditation program (Professional Conference Organisers Association 2018).

International event associations the International Festivals and Events Association (IFEA) and the International Live Events Association (ILEA), formerly known as the International Special Events Society (ISES), have both had Australian chapters in the past, but are largely inactive there at this time. A useful list of international event associations can be found at the Bizzabo blog (Bizzabo Blog 2018).

FIGURE 1.3   EEAA code of ethics

All members of the Exhibition and Event Association of Australasia (EEAA) have agreed to abide by a code of ethics.
1. Members of EEAA shall abide by all relevant state and federal laws.
2. No member shall offer or promote any exhibition or service by means of explicit or implicit representation which is likely to have a tendency to deceive or mislead prospective clients.
3. No member shall use an exhibition title which is so similar to the title of another event that it is likely to deceive or mislead.
4. No claims, statistical or otherwise which cannot be substantiated, shall be made in relation to any exhibition.
5. Areas of major expenditure over and above those not included in exhibition space/stand costs shall be clearly indicated to exhibitors.
6. Members shall not accept contracts from companies whose legal or ethical status is known to be in doubt.
7. Fairness shall characterise dealings between members, their clients and visitors.

8. Members will not by innuendo or rumour damage the reputation of another member or disadvantage other members by unfair trading practices.
9. Members shall, at all times, be accessible to their clients and visitors.
10. Members shall make every effort to resolve complaints and grievances in good faith through reasonable direct communication and negotiation.
11. Undertakings or promises made by members in all literature shall be adhered to. In the event of necessary changes, notification will where possible be given to actual or potential clients.
12. Adequate insurance in respect to public liability shall be carried.
13. Wherever possible members shall use the services provided by other Association members.
14. In the event of any member's non-compliance with EEAA Code of Ethics, Clause 7 of the Constitution will apply.

Source: Exhibition and Event Association of Australasia 2018.

External regulatory bodies

As noted, contemporary events take place in an increasingly regulated and complex environment. A series of government and statutory bodies are responsible for overseeing the conduct and safe staging of events, and these bodies have an integral relationship with the industry. For example, many local councils now require a development application for the staging of outdoor events. This application may cover regulations governing the erection of temporary structures, traffic plans, noise restrictions and so on. Councils also often oversee the application of state laws governing the preparation and sale of food, and by-laws regarding street closures, waste management and removal. In addition, event organisers have a legal responsibility to provide a safe workplace and to obey all laws and statutes relating to employment, contracts, taxation and so on. The professional event manager needs to be familiar with the regulations governing events and to maintain contact with the public authorities that have a vested interest in the industry.

1.6 Event management, education and training

LEARNING OBJECTIVE 1.6 List and describe the main professional associations in the event industry, discuss the attributes and knowledge requirements of a special event manager and list the types of organisation involved in the delivery of event management training.

As the size and needs of the event industry have grown, event management training has started to emerge as a discrete discipline. In the early years of the industry, leading up to the mid 1990s, the field was characterised by a large number of volunteers. Those few event managers who obtained paid positions came from a variety of related disciplines, drawing on their knowledge gained from that discipline and skills learnt on the job. Many came from allied areas such as theatre and entertainment, audiovisual production and film, and adapted their skills to events. Others came from a background of working for event suppliers such as staging, lighting and sound production companies, having discovered that they could expand and build on their existing skills to undertake the overall management of events. However, as the use of events by government and industry has grown, event budgets have increased, and the logistics of events have become more complex, the need has emerged for skilled event professionals who can meet the industry's specific requirements. Education and training at both vocational and tertiary levels have arisen to meet this need.

Identifying the knowledge and skills required by event managers

In addition to generic management skills, Getz and Wicks (1994, pp. 108–9) specify the following event-specific areas of knowledge as appropriate for inclusion in event management training:

• history and meanings of festivals, celebrations, rituals and other events
• historical evolution; types of events
• trends in demand and supply
• motivations and benefits sought from events
• roles and impacts of events in society, the economy, environment and culture
• who is producing events, and why?
• program concepts and styles

- event settings
- operations unique to events
- management unique to events
- marketing unique to events.

Studies by Perry, Foley and Rumpf (1996), Harris and Griffin (1997), Royal and Jago (1998), Harris and Jago (1999) and Arcodia and Barker (2002) largely confirm the importance of these knowledge/skill areas. The Event Management Body of Knowledge (EMBOK) program identifies five knowledge domains — administration, design, marketing, operations and risk — each with its classes and processes (see figure 1.4). Thus despite occasional differing emphases and nuances, the field generally agrees on the specific body of knowledge of best practice appropriate to the training of professional event managers.

| **FIGURE 1.4** | Event Management Body of Knowledge domain structure |

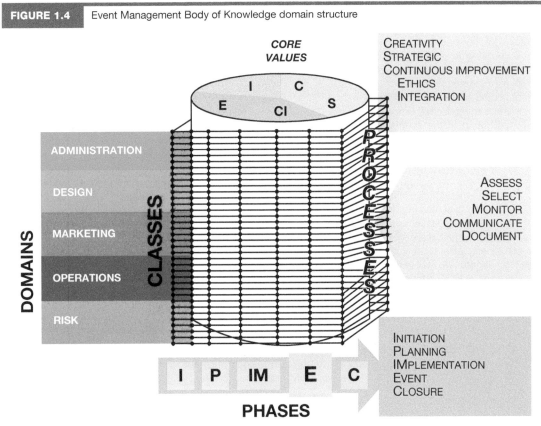

Source: EMBOK 2005.

The content and organisation of this book parallels closely the knowledge domains identified by EMBOK and other researchers in the field. Part 1, the event context and concept development, provides a general background to the event industry, the range of perspectives on events and event impacts. Part 2, planning, deals with the knowledge areas of administration and marketing, while part 3, event operations and evaluation, deals with the knowledge area of operations.

Training delivery

As the industry has grown and the regulatory environment has become more complex, the skills needed for successful event management have also grown exponentially. This has resulted in the availability of a plethora of event management training options, ranging from entry courses to ongoing professional development and advanced event management education. The range of training and education providers includes the following.

- Most event associations provide some form of training, ranging from professional development through seminars, workshops and forums to certificate and accreditation programs (see figure 1.5), sometimes in conjunction with external organisations.
- TAFE and private colleges provide training at certificate, diploma and bachelor levels in a range of event management–related fields.

- Universities provide event management education at both undergraduate and post graduate levels. This may be in dedicated event programs, or as subject components in wider course areas such as tourism, hospitality, leisure, recreation, sports and arts management programs.

In all of the above cases, training may be offered face to face, online or by a mixture of these modes. Many courses also offer an industry internship component, where students are able to gain industry experience under supervision. Intending students are advised to study prospective courses closely, in order to ensure that the course content, mode of delivery, timeframe and cost match their needs.

FIGURE 1.5　The Asia Pacific Institute for Events Management (APIEM)

The Asia Pacific Institute for Events Management (APIEM) is a membership, non-commercial organisation established to contribute to the professionalisation of the events and MICE industry in the Asia–Pacific region. APIEM does this by:
- accrediting as APIEM Centres of Excellence those universities, polytechnics, colleges and training providers that have been audited to demonstrate that they provide an events and MICE curriculum of an international standard
- providing the APIEM Certified Event Manager, Organiser and Planner qualifications that are benchmarked to the United Kingdom National Occupation Standards for the Events Industry
- contributing to the events and MICE academic body of knowledge by publishing the *Asia Pacific International Events Management Journal*, a scientific, international journal
- bringing together events and MICE academics and practitioners at international conferences, meetings and symposiums 29organised by APIEM Events Management Services
- supporting the development of an international standard curriculum in event industry and MICE education through consultancy services to universities, polytechnics and colleges
- 30 organising continuing professional development programs in the Philippines, Taiwan and the United Kingdom for faculty lecturers who teach event industry and MICE subjects.

APIEM offers two main types of membership. Firstly, APIEM individual membership for events and MICE practitioners, faculty and students who wish to be recognised by an international professional organisation for their expertise in events and MICE management. APIEM has individual members in Australia, Polynesia, South-East Asia, Central Asia, Europe, India, Sri Lanka, the Middle East and the United States.

The second type of membership is for education and training organisations that wish to be recognised for providing an events and MICE curriculum that is of an international standard. The APIEM accreditation process to become an APIEM institutional member is based on four criteria: the management and content of the curriculum; teaching and learning standards; resources and learning environment; and welfare and student services.

APIEM has accredited universities, polytechnics, colleges and training organisations as Centres of Excellence in Australia, Indonesia, Malaysia, Philippines and Taiwan.

Source: Hind 2020.

Career opportunities in events

As demonstrated, events are an expanding industry, providing new and challenging job opportunities for people entering the field. Titles and roles in the industry are not yet standardised, and may vary in different sectors of the industry and in different locations. However, the roles outlined in table 1.1 are generally accepted.

TABLE 1.1　**Roles in the event industry**

Title	Role
Event Director	Senior role in charge of a program of events
Event Manager	Person with overall responsibility for the planning and execution of an event
Event Coordinator	Person responsible for a given aspect of an event
Event Assistant	Entry-level position in the industry working under supervision

However, a career in the event industry is not limited to just these roles or to event management companies. There is a vast array of event positions available in different sectors of the industry, including in corporate and government institutions, public relations companies, the media, arts and sports organisations, not-for-profit groups and charities, non-government and community organisations, to name just a few. Inside these and the companies that supply them there is a variety of roles to suit all interests and backgrounds, including project managers, stage managers, technicians, graphic artists, set designers, costume makers, makeup artists, marketers, publicists, photographers, entertainers, comperes, caterers, pyrotechnicians — again, the list is seemingly endless. It is in the nature of the industry that much of this work is freelance and spasmodic, with many event staff working on a short-term contract basis for a series of employers and events.

A successful career in events depends on applicants identifying their own skills and interests, and then matching these carefully with the needs of prospective employers. Areas of expanding activity — such as corporate events, conferences, local government and tourism — may be fruitful areas to examine. Employers often look for a mix of qualifications and experience, so intending job seekers may be advised to consider volunteering and/or taking entry-level positions in order to build their resumes and to gain a foothold in the industry. A satisfying and rewarding career awaits those who apply themselves with vision, passion and perseverance.

SUMMARY

Special events perform a powerful role in society, and they have existed throughout human history in all times and all cultures. Prior to the arrival of the Europeans, the Australian Aboriginal culture had a rich tradition of rituals and ceremonies. The event tradition in modern Australia began in a primitive way with the arrival of the First Fleet, and developed through the late eighteenth and nineteenth centuries as the colony prospered and the new inhabitants came to terms with their environment. The ruling elite often decided the form and content of public celebrations, but an alternative tradition of popular celebrations arose from the interests and pursuits of ordinary people. During the twentieth century, changes in society were mirrored by changes in the style of public events. The post-war wave of civic festivals and arts festivals was strongly influenced by the community arts movement in the 1970s, along with multiculturalism and the 'new age' movement. Notions of high culture were challenged by a more pluralistic popular culture, which reinvigorated festivals and community events.

With the coming of the 1980s, governments and the corporate sector began to recognise the economic and promotional value of special events, and state events corporations spearheaded a new level of funding, profile and professionalism. With the advent of the global financial crisis in 2008, event managers faced a new challenge in balancing the economic and environmental sustainability of events. Events have continued to grow in numbers and complexity in the first decades of the new century.

Events can be classified by size — including mega-events, hallmark events, major events and local or community events — and by form or content — including festivals, sporting events and business events. With increasing expansion and corporate involvement, events have emerged as a new growth industry, capable of generating economic benefits and employment.

Significant components of this industry include event organisations, event management companies, event industry suppliers, venues, industry associations and external regulatory bodies. In response to the requirement for professional event management training, industry associations, universities and other tertiary institutions have developed programs. Intending entrants to the industry are advised to study the industry carefully to match their own interests and skills with those required by prospective employers.

QUESTIONS

1 Why are special events created? What purpose do they serve in society?
2 Why have special events emerged so strongly in recent years in Australia?
3 What are the key political, cultural and social trends that determine the current climate of events in Australia?
4 What do you perceive as the major challenges currently facing event managers in Australia?
5 Identify an event in your city or region that has the capacity to be a hallmark event. Give your reasons for placing it in this category.
6 Examine the structure of the event industry in your area and identify local examples of the components outlined in this chapter.
7 Do you agree with the attributes and knowledge areas required by event managers identified by the studies in this chapter? Create a list of your own attributes and skills based on these listings.

CASE STUDY

THE AUSTRALIAN EVENT AWARDS

The Australian Event Awards is the national awards program for the Australian event industry. It was conceived and first conducted in 1999 with the first awards ceremony being held at the Westin Hotel in Sydney.

The program was developed at a time of significant expansion in many facets of the industry and, at the same time, an increasing fragmentation on the bases of both event type and geography. For example, sporting events were (and to an extent still are) seen as different from business events which were seen as different again from community events. Similarly, the events scene in one city or town was seen as quite separate from that located in another.

The reality for those working in the sector is of course quite different. The same skills of analysing and meeting complex stakeholder needs; developing creative solutions; and balancing the competing challenges of creativity, logistical delivery, limited resources and, recently, security are universal to all event types and they are the core skills of event managers all over Australia (and indeed internationally).

In addition, there remains a real need for Australian event practitioners to come together; great benefit and sometimes commercial opportunity comes from the capacity of like-minded people to share ideas, challenges and solutions and to celebrate those who demonstrate excellence and take events to the next level. It is also true that in any industry there is benefit in 'hunting as a pack', in using the core interests of a significant group to influence public policy, internal organisation and the identification of new opportunities.

Thus, the Australian Event Awards was born with three core aims:

1. to reward the performance of those people, organisations and events that are doing the best work in Australia
2. to encourage ongoing excellence and the further development of a thriving event industry in Australia
3. to unite the Australian event industry.

STRATEGIC CONSIDERATIONS

The Australian Event Awards is not the only awards program available to the event industry in Australia. Others include the following.

- The International Live Events Association (formerly The International Special Event Society) Esprit Awards
- The International Festival and Events Association Awards
- The Meeting and Events Australia (MEA) Awards
- The Exhibition and Event Association Awards
- The Australian Tourism Awards (which has some event-related categories).

The Australian Event Awards differentiates itself from all of these programs by remaining relevant to all Australian events, event managers and support service providers regardless of event:

- type or audience
- size or attendance
- location or association membership.

The awards openly encourage all entrants to enter multiple programs and see significant value in excellence being celebrated at all levels of the industry, culminating in the broad, industry-wide Australian Event Awards.

Another strategic consideration is the significant resources required for entrants to participate in awards programs. In addition to entry fees, there is an amount of staff time and expertise required to enter awards programs and often, for those who do not win, there is the feeling that these resources have been wasted. The Australian Event Awards addresses these issues by:

1. minimising the challenge presented by the entry process — the process is entirely online and limited in the total word count. It aims to be fairly easy to complete while also balancing the need to let entrants show the judges their best performance. The mantra 'easy to enter, hard to win' is synonymous with the Australian Event Awards.
2. ensuring that every entry has access to feedback from the judging panel. This approach means that regardless of how an entry fares, every entrant receives expert feedback — effectively a peer review of their work — as part of the entry process. Often entrants take this feedback away and improve their work which then improves events and the whole industry.

Finally, in the age of the internet, award entrants (and indeed judges and other stakeholders) have a right to expect openness and transparency from those evaluating the work of others. From inception in 1999, the Australian Event Awards has embraced this as a key component of the program. By publishing the awards rules and the detailed judging process on the awards website, and of course by following these documents to the letter, the Australian Event Awards simultaneously enhances its reputation for fairness and heightens the prestige associated with winning.

INDUSTRY INVOLVEMENT

From the beginning, the Australian Event Awards took the view that it has to be interest from the event industry itself that keeps the project alive. Indeed, without the support of the industry, the awards themselves would simply not be possible. Generally, the industry supports the awards by:

1. sponsoring categories. In exchange for cash support, prominent industry companies are permitted to 'own' an Australian Event Awards category. By so doing they guarantee themselves exposure as part of the marketing campaign, and an opportunity to present the awards and say a few words at the ceremony about their support of the industry.

2. providing goods and services in-kind. The Australian Event Awards' 'project delivery partners', of which there are about 20, are able to showcase their products and services to the industry and to show their support in the most practical way. From lighting to sound to fireworks, entertainment, AV and effects, the project delivery partners treat the industry to a spectacular ceremony to highlight the achievements of the industry over a year.
3. judging the awards. There are over 40 industry experts involved in the judging of the Australian Event Awards. These judges give their time on a voluntary basis to sift through hundreds of awards entries each year and evaluate them according to the published judging process.
4. entering. Of course, no awards program can exist without entrants and it is in this area that the vast majority of participants get involved.
5. attending. There are also industry players that simply attend the awards to meet and network with their fellow events players and to show support for those who are doing outstanding work and demonstrating excellence.

The awards program itself is regularly reviewed by a small advisory panel of partners, judges, entrants, finalists and winners to ensure that the program meets the needs and expectations of the industry and remains relevant.

CHOOSING A HOST DESTINATION

One of the bigger challenges facing any national event in Australia is the process by which a destination (state, city, venue) is chosen. With significant competition between destinations at all levels to host the Australian Event Awards and showcase regions to the event industry, the Awards has adopted a triennial bid process which it calls its 'Search for a Home'. Every third year starting in 2010, the Awards invites proposals from any state, city, venue or joint venture thereof to host the awards ceremony for the following three years. This has yielded the following host destinations:

- 2009: The Westin Sydney, NSW
- 2010: Sydney International Aquatic Centre, NSW
- 2011: Allphones Arena, Sydney, NSW
- 2012: ANZ Stadium, Sydney, NSW
- 2013: Doltone House Hyde Park, Sydney, NSW
- 2014: Doltone House Darling Island Wharf, Sydney, NSW
- 2015: Doltone House Jones Bay Wharf, Sydney, NSW
- 2016: Novotel Twin Waters, QLD
- 2017: The Event Centre, Caloundra, QLD
- 2018: Novotel Twin Waters, QLD
- 2019: Perth Optus Stadium, WA
- 2020: Adelaide Entertainment Centre, SA.

CATEGORIES, CRITERIA AND QUESTIONS

The Australian Event Awards consists of 23 categories; these are divided into 11 'best event' categories, eight 'achievement' categories and four 'headline' categories. Each category has its own distinct weighted judging criteria and questions designed to lead the entrants to address the criteria and provide as much information to the judges as they can within the word limits.

Broadly, the criteria address the following areas:
- overall quality
- the use of 'best practice' techniques
- identification of stakeholders and meeting of their needs
- degree of difficulty with regard to scale, challenges and complexity
- sustainability
- the backing of claims in the entry with evidence.

Entrants are encouraged to provide photos and video to communicate their achievements to the judges.

JUDGING — CONFERRING THE AWARDS

The judging process for the Australian Event Awards is in three parts. The 'first round' is performed 'blind' by judges who score each entry against each criterion without reference to each other or to other entries. That is, each entry is scored against the criteria and entirely on its own merits. The scores are compiled, moderated for bias and the top four entries in each category become finalists.

The judges are then informed of the finalists and a 'finalist review' process is undertaken whereby any judge that believes that an outstanding entry that they judged has been overlooked can nominate that entry for a review by the co-chairs of the judging panel. If approved, an entry nominated in this way can become a fifth finalist in its category.

At this point all non-finalist entries receive their judges' feedback and often a certificate of commendation. All finalists are provided with a logo kit and public relations kit to assist in celebrating their achievements.

Following the public release of the finalist list, the second round of judging takes place. In this round an entirely new group of 10–12 judges, led by the co-chairs of the judging panel, examines all the finalist entries and votes anonymously for the winner of their choice. The entry with the most votes becomes the winner.

THE AWARDS NIGHT

The Australian Event Awards ceremony is held each year between September and November and celebrates finalist events and achievements that occurred between July 1 the previous year and June 30 in the year of the awards. The ceremony includes a three-course meal and showcase performances from industry entertainers. The awards category partners present the category that bears their name and each winner is permitted a few words of thanks. Typically, the ceremony is live streamed on the Australian Event Awards website, disseminated through social media and reaches an audience of well over 1000 people.

EXPANSION — THE AUSTRALIAN EVENT SYMPOSIUM

In recent years, the Australian Event Awards Ceremony has been held in conjunction with the Australian Events Symposium, a two-day conference and exhibition for event industry professionals staged by the awards team on the days surrounding the awards ceremony. Each symposium has theme and topics that reflect that theme.

The aims of the symposium are aligned with those of the awards, and are to:
- drive industry growth and development
- ensure Australia remains on the leading edge of the event industry worldwide
- foster unity and advancement within the event industry
- create networking and collaborative opportunities across all sectors of the industry.

The content of the symposium is focussed on professional development for industry representatives and on delivering strong take-away value for delegates.

The addition of the Australian Event Symposium has allowed the Australian Event Awards to grow into the industry's annual key gathering point drawing hundreds of professionals for three days of festivities, education and celebration of the national event industry.

Prepared by Ian Steigrad, Director, Australian Event Awards

QUESTIONS

1 What benefits and/or value does the Australian Event Awards provide to entrants and to the event industry?

2 What are the benefits to the Australian Event Awards of changing the host destination every three years?

3 What does the Australian Event Awards do to try to remain relevant to all events regardless of size, location or type of event?

REFERENCES

Arcodia, C & Barker, T 2002, 'A review of web-based job advertisements for Australian event management positions', in *Events and place making: proceedings of International Research Conference held in Sydney 2002*, eds L Jago, M Deery, R Harris, A H & J, Australian Centre for Event Management, Sydney.

Bizzabo Blog 2018, 'Directory of event planning associations', https://blog.bizzabo.com/event-planning-associations, viewed 25 April 2020.

Bower, R 1981, 'Community arts — what is it?', *Caper,* vol. 10, Community Arts Board, Australia Council, Sydney.

Business Events Council of Australia 2015, 'The value of business events to Australia', www.businesseventscouncil.org.au, viewed 25 April 2020.

Business Events Sydney 2017, 'NSW looks to huge schedule of business events', www.besydney.com.au, viewed 25 April 2020.

Clark, M 1981, *A History of Australia,* vol. 5, Melbourne University Press, Melbourne.

Commonwealth Department of Tourism 1995, *A national strategy for the meetings, incentives, conventions and exhibitions industry*, Australian Government Publishing Service, Canberra.

Destination NSW 2020, 'Vivid Sydney', www.destinationnsw.com.au/events/vivid-sydney, viewed 25 April 2020.

Earth Hour 2018, 'What is Earth Hour', www.earthhour.org, viewed 25 April 2020.

EMBOK 2005, 'EMBOK Model', www.embok.org, viewed 30 June 2020.

Exhibition and Event Association of Australasia 2018, www.eeaa.com.au.

Farrelly, E 2018, 'Kind of tacky: Sydney's Vivid has lost its mojo', *The Sydney Morning Herald,* 8 June.

Getz, D 2005, *Event management and event tourism*, Cognizant Communication Corporation, New York, pp. 116–17.

Getz, D & Wicks, B 1994, 'Professionalism and certification for festival and event practitioners: trends and issues', *Festival Management and Event Tourism,* vol. 2, no. 2, pp. 108–9.

Hall, CM 1992, *Hallmark tourist events: impacts, management and planning,* Belhaven Press, London.

Harris, R & Griffin, T 1997, *Tourism events training audit*, Prepared for Tourism New South Wales Events Unit, Sydney.

Harris, R & Jago, L 1999, 'Event education and training in Australia: the current state of play', *Australian Journal of Hospitality Management,* vol. 6, no. 1, pp. 45–51.

Hind, D 2020, Pers. Comm.

Hughes, R 1987, *The fatal shore,* Collins Harvill, London.

Hull, A 1984, 'Feasting on festas and festivals', Paper delivered to the Association of Festivals Conference at the Caulfield Arts Centre, Victoria.

International Congress and Convention Association 2018, 'ICCA releases 2017 statistics with another record number of association meetings', www.iccaworld.com, viewed 25 April 2020.

International Festivals and Events Association 2018, 'IFEA global affiliates', www.ifea.com, viewed 25 April 2020.

Janiskee, R 1996, 'Historic houses and special events', *Annals of Leisure Research,* vol. no. 2, pp. 398–414.

McCarthy, W 1998, 'Day we came of age', *The Sun-Herald*, 25 January, p. 46.

Meetings & Events Australia 2018, 'About', www.meetingsevents.com.au, viewed 25 April 2020.

Melbourne Convention Bureau 2018, 'Melbourne wins world's largest event in public transport sector', www.melbournecb.com.au, viewed 25 April 2020.

Müller, M 2015, 'What makes an event a mega-event? Definitions and sizes', *Leisure Studies* vol. 34, issue 6, pp. 627–42.

Munro, P 2016, 'Have we reached "peak festival"?', *The Sydney Morning Herald*, 30 November.

National Museum of Australia 2018, 'Walk for Reconciliation', www.nma.gov.au, viewed 25 April 2020.

Pearl, C 1974, *Australia's yesterdays*, Reader's Digest, Sydney.

Perry, M, Foley, P & Rumpf, P 1996, 'Event management: an emerging challenge in Australian education', *Festival Management and Event Tourism,* vol. 4, pp. 85–93.

Professional Conference Organisers Association 2018, www.pco.asn.au.

Ritchie, JRB 1984, 'Assessing the impact of hallmark events: conceptual and research issues', *Journal of Travel Research,* vol. 23, no. 1, pp. 2–11.

Rogers, T 1998, *Conferences: a twenty-first century industry,* Addison-Wesley Longman, Harlow.

Royal, CG & Jago, LK 1998, 'Special events accreditation: the practitioner's perspective', *Festival Management and Event Tourism,* no. 5, pp. 221–30.

Shine, R 2019, 'National School Strike for Climate sees students across the country planning to skip school', *ABC News,* 20 September, www.abc.net.au/news/2019-09-20/national-climate-strike-students-across-australia-skip-school/11528100, viewed 25 April 2020.

Sydney's Unique Venues Association 2018, 'List of venues', www.suva.com.au.

Westwood, M 2017, 'Festivals bring hot times to the old towns', *The Australian*, 23 May.

ACKNOWLEDGEMENTS

Photo: © Kathy Dorsey / Getty Images

Photo: © Taras Vyshnya / Shutterstock.com

Figure 1.3: © Exhibition and Event Association of Australasia

Figure 1.4: © The International Event Management Body of Knowledge (EMBOK) by International EMBOK Executive. Licensed under a Creative Commons Attribution 4.0 International Licence (licence available at www.creativecommons.org/licenses/by/4.0/legalcode). Figure has been redrawn.

Perspectives on events

After studying this chapter, you should be able to:

2.1 list the range of roles that governments play in events

2.2 describe the nature and function of government event strategies

2.3 discuss the use of events by governments as tools for economic regeneration and development

2.4 discuss the use of events by the corporate sector and describe the role that events play in integrated marketing strategies

2.5 list and describe methods used by the corporate sector in measuring the return on investment (ROI) of events

2.6 discuss the benefits that can result to communities from the staging of events

2.7 list the range of strategies available to event managers to promote community engagement in events and discuss the implications for event managers of differing perspectives on events in the event planning process.

Introduction

Events take place across the full spectrum of society, leading to differing contexts, goals and objectives. This chapter looks at events from the perspectives of the three major sectors — government, corporate and community — and examines how these perspectives vary and the implications of this for event managers.

Governments play a leading role in events, and increasingly employ event strategies in order to guide their involvement, priorities and decision-making. In recent years, many governments have created dedicated celebration spaces for the staging of public events, and some have consciously used events in tandem with other policies and strategies as tools for urban regeneration and development.

The corporate sector is a major player in events, using them regularly in the course of business administration, staff motivation and training, and as a significant element of the integrated marketing mix in the sale and promotion of goods and services. Companies also sponsor public events in order to demonstrate product attributes, build brand awareness and reach target markets effectively.

Events have long played a universal and enduring role in communities, whose prime focus is on their direct entertainment, social, cultural and sporting benefits. In planning events, event managers need to devise and incorporate appropriate strategies for community ownership, participation and engagement.

2.1 The government perspective

LEARNING OBJECTIVE 2.1 List the range of roles that governments play in events.

All levels of government, national, state and local, make frequent use of events both in conducting the affairs of government and as part of their service delivery. Executive offices of all three levels of government — for example, the departments of the Prime Minister and Premier, or the office of the Mayor — are often involved in the conduct of civic events such as official visits, national days and citizenship ceremonies. They will often combine in the celebration of significant national anniversaries and events, as was seen in Australia with the nation's bicentenary in 1988 and the centenary of Federation in 2001.

National government

However, it is the national or federal government that usually has the prime carriage of these major celebrations of national significance. It will then work closely with other levels of government to augment related programs at state and local levels.

National governments are also increasingly involved with hosting and organising major international political and economic gatherings; for example, the G20 Summit, the Commonwealth Heads of Government Meeting (CHOGM) and the Asia–Pacific Economic Cooperation forum (APEC). Such events present increasing logistic and security challenges, but confer significant prestige on their host governments. National governments also make significant use of cultural events in the promotion of trade through their foreign affairs departments, as was seen in the lead-up to the Beijing Olympics by the Year of Paris in Beijing and the corresponding Year of Beijing in Paris.

The staging of major sporting and cultural events on home soil is more the province of state and city governments, although, the International Olympic Committee has stated that the Olympic Games will not be awarded in future to cities that do not have the express underwriting and support of their national governments.

State government

State governments play a major role in bidding for and staging major events of economic and tourism significance, often setting up event corporations and convention and visitor bureaux for this purpose, as we saw in the overview of the event field chapter. Most state government departments are involved in staging or assisting events as part of their portfolio — for example, arts ministries with major festivals, sports ministries with major sporting competitions, ethnic affairs ministries with events celebrating ethnic diversity, or tourism ministries with flagship tourism events. They may sponsor or be involved in events that carry messages relevant to their charters. For example, the Victorian Health Ministry, in partnership with the Transport Accident Commission (TAC), has sponsored the Wangaratta Festival of Jazz in order to promote 'don't drink and drive' messages (Wangaratta Jazz Festival 2009). Almost all government departments make extensive internal use of events in order to train staff, develop networks and communicate with the public.

Local government

Local governments are also increasingly involved with events, seeing them as an important means of creating quality of life for their constituents, and attracting tourism and economic benefits to their regions. Local government in Australia is now one of the biggest players in the event field, with almost every local government body employing an event manager or team, and with most providing funding and support for a wide range of local events. These may include events specifically designed to support tourism visitation and expenditure, and to increase the profile of the destination as an attractive place to visit or to do business. They may also include events whose primary focus is the local community, thus increasing their entertainment, cultural, leisure or sporting options. Increasingly, local governments aim to support and encourage business events such as conferences, meetings and exhibitions that attract visitors from the business sector.

The role of government in events

Governments commonly perform a wide and complex variety of roles in events, particularly in the arena of public outdoor events and festivals. The extent and scale of these roles will vary according to the size and level of governments, and to the degree of their resources and commitment. However, the roles listed below and the issues that arise from them are common to most governments, and provide the impetus for them to form event departments and create strategies in order to delineate and implement their role in events.

Venue owner/manager

Governments are often the owners of parks, playing fields, streets, town halls, and sports and community centres where events are staged. They are responsible for the development and maintenance of these assets, as well as managing them on a day-to-day basis. They therefore need to employ staff to run them, and set and administer policies and charges for their use.

Consent authority and regulatory body

Governments also set and administer many of the laws and policies that govern the staging of events in matters such as the creation of temporary structures, the sale of food, noise restrictions, street closures and traffic and parking requirements. Local councils often work closely with other government agencies such as road and traffic authorities, health departments and police in the drafting, implementation and monitoring of rules and regulations governing these areas. For large events, councils may require a formal development application addressing issues such as environmental impact, traffic management and safety, while smaller events may simply require the issue of a licence or permit.

Service provider

Many of the services required by events are provided by governments on a cost recovery basis. These can include cleaning, waste removal and traffic management. For larger events with the involvement of state governments, these services can extend to the provision of public transport, police and emergency services. In the case of major events, central government may play a coordinating role across a range of government-related services and agencies (see figure 2.1). In some cases, government services may be provided gratis in lieu of the perceived value of the event to the local economy. For example, in Sydney, events defined as having hallmark status may be provided free government services such as police and traffic assistance.

FIGURE 2.1   NSW Event Operations Group

The NSW Event Operations Group (EOG) is a best practice example of government coordination of major events. It is an interagency group led by the Department of Premier and Cabinet, and is part of the NSW Government's strategy to enhance the safety and enjoyment of events for the community and visitors.

Senior operational personnel from over 30 NSW Government and non-government agencies, along with event organisers, meet monthly to share information, identify unresolved issues, and conduct debriefs in order to continually improve event effectiveness, efficiency and safety. EOG is a conduit for events such as New Year's Eve and the City2Surf to communicate with government agencies about the possible impacts

▶

---

of events on government infrastructure and operations. It was a legacy of the Sydney Olympic Games and remains an ongoing asset for New South Wales in the government coordination and servicing of major events.

Participating agencies include:

- NSW Police Force
- NSW Ambulance
- Fire and Rescue NSW
- NSW Roads and Maritime Authority
- Transport for NSW
- Sydney Trains
- State Transit Authority
- Harbour City Ferries
- City of Sydney
- Botanic Gardens and Centennial Parklands
- Sydney Opera House
- Property NSW
- Destination NSW.

Source: Willett 2018.

Funding body

Governments often establish funding programs that aim to develop and assist events. This may be at a community level, where assisting events is seen as part of the overall provision of services to the community. In such cases, the scale of funding is likely to be modest, and guidelines are likely to focus on community/cultural services and outcomes. In other cases, governments may support events because of their perceived economic and tourism benefits, and will seek to fund and develop events that match this agenda. Clear funding criteria and guidelines need to be established, and procedures put in place for the monitoring of event implementation and the reporting and measurement of event outcomes.

Event organiser

Governments may also themselves be event producers or host organisations. This may involve the organisation and protocol of official visits and ceremonial events, or the celebration of national days and important anniversaries such as Anzac Day and Australia Day. Governments may also choose to mount a program of local events and celebrations in order to animate civic spaces, to enhance the quality of life of residents or to attract visitors.

Event/destination marketer

Governments may assume some responsibility for the compilation and promotion of an annual calendar of events, both as a service to residents and as part of the overall tourism promotion of the city or destination. Such event calendars may be supported by a communications strategy, with highlight events the subject of individual campaigns. The use of events as part of destination marketing strategies will be discussed further in the event tourism planning chapter.

2.2 Event strategies

LEARNING OBJECTIVE 2.2 Describe the nature and function of government event strategies.

Increasingly governments are developing event strategies in order to coordinate their overall involvement in events, to plan the use of resources and to improve and measure the outcomes of programs and services. Such strategies ideally dovetail with other policies and strategies in the areas of urban planning, community and cultural services, economic development and tourism. They also establish strong links with agencies at other levels of government, and the private sector.

Event strategies seek to delineate government objectives in the events area, and to identify the appropriate policies, infrastructure, resources, staffing and programs needed to achieve them. They often include the development of a portfolio or annual program of events designed to reflect the particular characteristics and needs of a city or region. Such a portfolio may include a broad range of events, including signature or flagship events that are intended to promote the destination, and other events designed to serve particular cultural, sporting, economic or tourism goals and objectives. Event portfolios may involve both existing events, and the sourcing of new events by bidding for suitable event properties or by developing events from the ground up. Event strategies provide a framework for the appraisal of proposed new events in order to determine their fit with strategic objectives.

An event strategy will often include the creation of a 'one-stop shop' for event organisers in order to bring together and coordinate various government departments and services related to events. This will greatly assist in the efficient planning and delivery of events, and create an 'event friendly' culture and working environment that will strengthen the role of events and the outcomes of the strategy.

Different cities and countries all have their own unique blends of brand, history, assets, strengths and challenges, requiring different event strategies tailored to their needs. The following strategies reflect Scotland at a pivotal time in the development of its event culture, and Singapore looking to further develop an already mature MICE events strategy in order to maintain its competitive edge.

Scotland Events Strategy

In 2009 VisitScotland produced 'Scotland the perfect stage: a strategy for the events industry in Scotland 2009–2020' (VisitScotland 2009). Building on an earlier event strategy created in 2002, this document addresses the changed events landscape in Scotland due to the securing of the Commonwealth Games and the Ryder Cup in 2014, and the advent of Homecoming Scotland in 2009. It was reviewed in 2014, and its timeframe extended to 2025, after which it will be reviewed every five years. The key elements of the strategy are outlined below (VisitScotland 2018a).

Vision and mission

The vision contained in the strategy is: 'To establish Scotland as the perfect stage for events'. Flowing from this, the mission is: 'To develop a portfolio of events that delivers impact and international profile for Scotland'.

Assets

In order to fulfil this mission, the strategy aims to utilise assets that make Scotland 'the perfect stage' for events. Assets identified in the strategy include:

- *cultural identity and heritage* — including Scotland's rich history, its food and drink, its reputation in the fields of education and innovation, and its iconic poets, artists, writers, musicians and vibrant contemporary culture
- *people* — including a strong business community with good international links and large numbers of people across the world who have an affinity for Scotland
- *natural environment* — including dramatic landscapes ranging from mountains to lochs, beaches and islands
- *built facilities* — Scotland has a long architectural history and tradition, including castles, public buildings and cityscapes, as well as iconic buildings, in which to stage events, and quality facilities being designed to house the Glasgow 2014 Commonwealth Games
- *signature events* — Scotland already has a range of iconic signature events to build upon, including Edinburgh's Festivals, the Glasgow Commonwealth Games, the Ryder Cup in 2014 and Homecoming Scotland in 2009.

The strategy plans to further develop its events portfolio by adding new events on a major scale, and by developing Scotland's own events to stand alongside these.

Rationale

The strategy identifies seven areas of event impacts that can be used to evaluate the level of impact of new events, and to determine whether they should receive public sector support, and whether this should be at a national or local level. The impact areas are:

- tourism and business
- image and identity as a nation
- media and profile
- participation and development
- environment
- social and cultural benefits.

These key areas can also be used in post-event assessment, and in defining return on investment of public funds.

Priorities

In investing its allocated budget in events, VisitScotland will give priority to:
- those events whose estimated economic impacts demonstrate a return on investment of at least 8:1
- events where media is the prime driver for investment, a media index of 8, 9 or 10/10
- demonstrated levels of funding by other partners of at least 1:1.

Its main emphasis is on economic and media benefits, with a focus on events of national and international significance, complemented by other events that are supported at the local level.

Principles

Three core principles will guide the work of VisitScotland:
- VisitScotland will work in partnership with event organisers, deliverers and funding partners.
- VisitScotland will support work that has national significance in terms of the seven impacts, and will aim to support events in every local authority area over each four-year period, ensuring that the benefit reaches all of Scotland.
- VisitScotland's input will bring additionality by using funding to add value to existing events, or by securing an event that would not otherwise come to Scotland.

Operational functions

VisitScotland will play a leadership role in events in Scotland in the following areas:
- developing strategy
- developing and measuring impact and methodology
- gathering best practice examples and information
- evaluating and sharing the impact of events on other key policy areas
- building international reputation and expertise in events
- capitalising on opportunities, including the development of new and upgraded facilities offered by events such as Homecoming Scotland 2009, The Commonwealth Games and the Ryder Cup in 2014
- coordinating public sector support
- identifying and maximising event legacies
- assessing which events should be supported and at what levels
- monitoring and evaluating supported events
- establishing partnerships to ensure high-quality delivery of events.

Operational practice

VisitScotland will assess all events supported or considered for support using the seven impact areas previously listed, including a pre-event assessment of potential economic and media benefits. It will operate support programs to deliver against 'the perfect stage', and the range and scope of these programs will be reviewed regularly to ensure maximum outcomes. VisitScotland will also coordinate input from other public agencies, and seek to engage the business community in events.

It will not normally consider support for conferences, as this function is undertaken by the Business Tourism Unit of VisitScotland. Exhibitions may be considered, using the event evaluation framework.

In the area of sports events, VisitScotland aims to balance three categories:
1. fixed events held annually in the same location in perpetuity
2. recurring events held annually in the same location for a number of years
3. one-off events, usually subject to the bid process for a single staging.

One-off events selected must fit the UK and Scottish priorities for the sport, be winnable, and be able to be delivered in existing facilities with available resources.

The approach to cultural events will differ somewhat, as few cultural events are subject to the one-off international bid process. Many fixed cultural events will be treated in the same way as sports events, by providing additionality in order to help them grow. Specific events that have growth potential, and where the ambition to grow is shared by event organisers and other partners, will be the subject of a long-term and proactive approach by VisitScotland. It will also research and seek cultural events that can be attracted to Scotland or bid for.

In both sports and cultural events, a key role of VisitScotland will be to gather international intelligence and engage proactively with the copyright holders of international events prior to the bid process. VisitScotland will also take a proactive role in the training, development and networking of the event industry, including the staging of a national events conference.

Legacy

The strategy places strong emphasis on delivering both long-term and short-term benefits from events. It acknowledges the importance of not only resourcing events, but also of core funding for the building of event facilities, and the need for allocating resources for developing event legacies. It further acknowledges the importance of planning for legacy at the outset of events, of government agencies agreeing on common objectives, and of developing methods of evaluating legacy. Event legacy might include economic benefit, facilities, and an increase in personal and community capacity. Legacy goals and results should be explicit, and will be communicated to the wider Scottish community as a key aim of 'the perfect stage'.

What will make Scotland 'the perfect stage'?

The strategy envisions the events scene in Scotland in 2020 will be characterised as follows:
- Scotland will be recognised as a leader in the development of events.
- Events will take place in Scotland across the calendar year and throughout the country.
- The event industry will be a significant contributor to the Scottish economy.
- An events portfolio of core events unique to Scotland, covering all aspects of Scottish culture, will be delivered annually.
- The portfolio will be complemented by a range of high profile one-off and recurring events attracted by Scotland's unique appeal and international event reputation.
- The roles of public, private and voluntary agencies will be clearly identified and working in partnership will be a recurring theme.
  In order to achieve this, it identifies several critical factors:
- successful delivery of the identified event impacts
- the ability and credibility of VisitScotland to lead the implementation of the strategy, and the expertise and network of key contacts of its staff
- the credibility and capacity of Scottish and UK event partner agencies and their staff
- the engagement and support of the business community
- a high level of political support for events
- positive national and international media coverage delivering the desired messages
- the vision to anticipate market changes, and the ability to adapt plans and practices
- resources that match the level of ambition
- a well-trained and motivated volunteer workforce
- a successful track record at international, national and local levels
- international standard venues
- the ability to identify, develop and utilise Scotland's unique selling points.

These critical success factors will be reviewed and reported on by VisitScotland in its annual report (VisitScotland 2018a).

Strategy review

The strategy was reviewed in 2014, extending it from 2015 to 2025 (VisitScotland 2018b).

The review identified three key areas to be addressed over and above the expressed need for political and financial support for events, with these three pillars developed further with associated themes under the following headings.
1. Developing events
   - Portfolio of events
   - Event impact
   - Investment and support
2. Developing the industry
   - Partnership and collaboration
   - Education and knowledge sharing
   - Quality, organisation and delivery
3. Developing Scotland
   - Infrastructure and services
   - Reputation
   - Visitor economy.

Measuring and reporting the impacts of events was identified as fundamental to the success of the strategy and a critical area for future planning. The five key impact areas identified were:

1. economic — tourism and business
2. brand, identity and reputation
3. media and profile
4. social and cultural
5. sustainability.

The eventIMPACTS methodology, developed in 2010, enabled these five areas to be assessed according to the criteria in table 2.1.

TABLE 2.1   The key event impact areas identified in VisitScotland's strategy

Key impact area	Strategic goals
Economic — tourism	• Net additional spend in the host economy • Gross value added • Equivalent jobs created/sustained
Economic — business	• Number and value of contracts issued by event organisers; number and value of these to Scottish and local businesses • Number of businesses engaged, including Scottish and local breakdown • Supported by case studies • Ability to export business skills and knowledge
Brand, identity and reputation	• Familiarity of the audience with a brand • Familiarity with brand values • Fit with national strategies
Media and profile	• Amount of coverage • How media coverage contributed to the event's objectives • Impact of social media coverage (both pre-event and mid-event marketing) and post-event evaluation
Social and cultural	• Number of volunteers • Number of new volunteers • Volunteer hours • Number of attendees from local authority area • Percentage of attendees from local authority area • Sense of wellbeing in host community • Sense of wellbeing in attendees • Case studies of interventions
Sustainability	• Against British Standard BS 8901:2007 on sustainable event management • Meeting Scottish legal requirements • Undertaking Scotland's Resource Efficiency Pledge

Progress of the strategy will be reviewed annually, with the option to review the strategy before 2025 if this is considered necessary or advantageous (VisitScotland 2018b).

The Scotland event strategy can be considered a best practice example of the strategic planning of events at government level. It illustrates the complexity of factors that must be taken into account, and the unique circumstances that each event strategy needs to address. It also demonstrates that a clear vision, accompanied by the right skills and resources, can contribute greatly to the successful event outcomes of both cities and nations.

Singapore MICE strategy

Singapore has long featured a strong MICE industry, and the MICE 2020 Road Map developed by the Singapore Tourism Board (STB) with the participation of major industry players in 2013 reflects this. It is the culmination of a year-long process of consultation involving interviews with over 200 MICE decision-makers and business event visitors. The road map places emphasis on strengthening Singapore's existing competitive advantage, and aims to strengthen industry standards through training and partnerships in order to improve business competitiveness, and create new strengths to generate greater value for visitors and MICE companies. The key aspects of the strategy are outlined below (Singapore Tourism Board 2014).

Challenges

The road map identifies the following as major challenges for the industry.

- *Growth limitations.* We see some events going directly to the source markets. However, our small domestic market need not limit our growth as Asia's business hub, if we can continue to tap on regional opportunities.
- *Limited pool of biddable events.* Of the 4200 world rotating association congresses, only a limited number have a Singapore member. This is a challenge we need to address as most of these association events require a strong local host to bid for the events.
- *The incentive game.* Cost is an increasing concern and clients are looking for value-for-money destinations. Our competitors are offering aggressive incentives to attract MICE events. We need to operate beyond the incentive game and create highly-customised solutions that will deliver the 'wow' factor.
- *Rising customer expectations.* In a world where the customer is always asking for more to extract greater value from organising and attending business events, we need to create more innovative content and user-centric experiences.
- *Associations in a nascent stage of development.* There are enthusiastic associations in Singapore who want to be part of the MICE growth story, but often lack the time and resources to create, bid or manage business events.

Insights from market research studies

A Business Events Visitor Needs Study interviewing 120 business visitors in 2013 indicated that as a business destination, Singapore has done well in getting the basics right, such as safety, convenience, transport and accessibility. However, the value proposition needs to go beyond delivering the basics in two key areas: delivering innovative events with inspiring content and creating deeper, lasting connections with business visitors.

A MICE perception study was commissioned in 2013 to understand the considerations by MICE organisers when selecting destinations for business events, and Singapore's current ability to meet their needs. More than 120 decision-makers and key influencers in the MICE industry from 12 cities were interviewed. Singapore scored highly in hygiene factors which were most important to organisers, signalling strengths in the areas of safety and accessibility.

Three areas of focus

Research for the road map identified three major areas for development, with an analysis of the current state of affairs and strategies to move forward.

1. Connected city

The goal of the 'connected city' strategy is to develop Singapore into a smart MICE city that enables visitors to get to where they want and do what they want seamlessly.

- Convenient and seamless wi-fi connectivity within MICE venues
  - *Where are we now?* The mobile wi-fi age demands connectivity anytime, anywhere. Intermittent and unreliable wi-fi connectivity is a bane, in particular for business visitors, who today are increasingly digital-savvy and often plan their itineraries on the move. While the current lack of seamless connectivity is not unique to Singapore, there is need for Singapore's infrastructure to evolve to support a convenient and stable wi-fi connection that only requires a simple one-time login to enjoy a transformative digital experience.
  - *Where are we going?* A seamless mobile experience accords the time-pressed business visitor the effortless ability to mix work with leisure. A business visitor will arrive at their meeting venue assured that they will be able to access seamless wi-fi coverage wherever they may be on the premises. The access to a world of information allows them to multitask, from sending emails, to finding the best deals on post-meeting drinks, to buying the perfect gift and doing a flight check-in.
  - *How do we get there?* What's unique about Singapore is its strong public–private partnership. Working together with key MICE venues, precinct stakeholders and telcos, expanding wi-fi-covered areas in MICE-centric precincts could be a possibility.

- Big data analytics
  - *Where are we now?* The world is standing at the edge of a big data revolution today. There is awareness of the potential that big data can bring, but businesses are grappling with the ability to make meaningful sense of the avalanche of data available. Today, the use of big data analytics to customise the business visitor experience is in its infancy. As part of Singapore's bid towards being a Smart Nation, there needs to be greater understanding and industry efforts in applying big data analytics to the MICE business, so that its potential can be fully realised.
  - *Where are we going*? With wider and more seamless wi-fi coverage comes the ability to collect and aggregate huge amounts of data, and more importantly to make business sense out of these insights. Embracing the use of big data analytics means that MICE businesses can now understand the needs and wants of their target audience and create customised value propositions. Capability needs to be built up to understand and anticipate visitor needs — before, during and after event hours, from MICE venues to lifestyle precincts.
  - *How do we get there?* With strong partnerships. As a first step, by partnering StarHub to test-bed an essential application for visitors, Goru, designed to combine information, content and experiences across different travel applications that will provide visitors with a seamless interface to discover the best of Singapore. StarHub's big data platform, SmartHub, can also be used to harness the power of big data to improve the user experience, content relevancy and commerce effectiveness. By collaborating with the SmartHub team, businesses in the hospitality industry can fine-tune their offerings to engage our visitors more effectively. Beyond this, more stakeholders and partners can come together to create other collaboration opportunities for the region.

2. Singapore MICE experience

The objective of the 'Singapore MICE experience' strategy is to develop Singapore into an inspiring destination with experiential events and authentic local character.

- Experiential events and destination immersion
  - *Where are we now?* Singapore is currently known for being efficient, safe and convenient and is the go-to MICE destination for business events that run smoothly from start to end. However, it is still important to ensure that at the end of each event, visitors leave with more than just an efficient meeting experience. They need to bring back emotive memories of the event and Singapore.
  - *Where are we going?* Business visitors are increasingly looking for experiential learning. They want to be engaged not only intellectually, but emotionally as well. This experience should be conveyed throughout their business visit, inside the event and outside of it at the destination level. The Singapore MICE experience is about both mixing business with leisure, and making business itself an inspiring, fun and personalised experience. At every possibility, these business events will connect to businesses and the local community to create better value for all.
  - *How do we get there?* With software, hardware and 'heartware'. Skills in experience creation are a key part of this software to future-ready our MICE industry. The experience development series (EDS) was created with the aim of equipping the tourism industry with tools and methodologies for experience creation, thus enabling stakeholders to move towards delivering memorable and personal experiences to differentiate themselves and drive higher value business. We will also 'wrap the city around the business event', where precinct-wide activities and campaigns are centred around major events. For a start, we have identified three 'B2B2C' and lifestyle-centric clusters to test-bed innovative experiences — TravelRave, Singapore Design Week and Singapore Media Festival, and we invite you to come on board with us. Through the innovative use of technologies across the event life cycle — from planning, on-site discussions, to networking and sharing information, every step of the way can be an awe-inspiring one. Together, Singapore will become more than just a MICE destination: it will become an unforgettable experience.

3. MICEHQ.SG

The third key focus area of the road map is to promote Singapore as Asia's MICE resource capital: home to skilled talent, knowledge, strong MICE companies and associations.

- Centre for MICE thought leadership
  - *Where are we now?* Today, Singapore is already considered a strategic location for companies to set up their regional headquarters and engage in business activities. However, we can do so much more to evolve ourselves as a regional leader. This is especially so in view of the less than ideal state of MICE data and standards available to meet the needs of MICE companies and clients who are interested to engage with the region.

- *Where are we going?* Imagine a nerve centre where MICE companies, associations and delegates defer to for information. Imagine a research and development base enriched with a myriad of MICE resources. Imagine a leader which establishes standards that others benchmark themselves against. Singapore desires to be this thought leader.
- *How do we get there?* STB will invest and lead research that aims to move our MICE industry up the value chain. Recognising the potential that environmental sustainability can contribute towards our MICE value propositions for instance, work has begun to guide sustainable practices in our MICE ecosystem. An inaugural Singapore MICE sustainability report will soon ensue to lead the industry forward. Industry players will also be given grants to undertake more R&D works that will benefit the industry. Research findings will be made readily available through an e-portal, so that as an industry, we all become more informed and knowledgeable to better engage our businesses.
- Building strong MICE companies
  - *Where are we now?* While Singapore can continue to upgrade our MICE hardware such as venues and facilities, it is the software — the quality of our industry players — that will distinguish us from our competitors.
  - *Where are we going?* Knowledge is power and we aim to equip our MICE players with the know-how to build stronger MICE companies, raise professionalism, drive innovation and spur productivity.
  - *How do we get there?* A MICE talent development framework has been established by the Singapore Association of Convention and Exhibition Organisers and Suppliers (SACEOS) to look at developing the talent of the MICE industry in a holistic manner, from talent attraction to talent retention. STB will also lead a MICE job profiling study to identify the talent gaps in the industry. This will better match the education and training curriculum to the needs of the industry. More can be done to expose our MICE companies to international best practices so as to enhance their business competitiveness and create business development opportunities.
- Building strong Singapore-based associations
  - *Where are we now?* Our local MICE associations have played a vital role in attracting a number of world congresses to Singapore. Many of these are championed and led by passionate and influential professionals based in Singapore. However many other associations are also in a nascent stage, managed by volunteers and lack adequate resources to effectively create, bid and organise conferences.
  - *Where are we going?* We will boost the capabilities of these associations by enhancing their resources and ability to bid for and manage events.
  - *How do we get there?* Forging partnerships with international MICE leaders will continue to be a critical strategy. This provides learning opportunities for our associations. Apart from imparting them with a global overview, trends and best practices, these initiatives aim to boost our associations' competencies in the areas of conference management and biddings. STB recently secured a partnership with the Chicago-based Professional Convention Management Association (PCMA) to organise the first PCMA Meetings Advisory Forum in Asia. More of such initiatives would be organised to upgrade the competencies of our Asian associations. We would also continue to enhance our network of advocates, through our Conference Ambassador Programme for instance, to strengthen the impact that our associations can make in profiling and connecting Singapore to the international market place (Singapore Tourism Board 2014).

Singapore's road map is a good example of the use of an event strategy applied to a specific event area in order to provide a strategic advantage in the marketplace. Taken with Scotland's 'Scotland, the perfect stage', the two examples illustrate the role of government in leading event industry development in order to improve outcomes for all stakeholders.

2.3 Governments creating celebration spaces and precincts

LEARNING OBJECTIVE 2.3 Discuss the use of events by governments as tools for economic regeneration and development.

The relationship between entertainment and commerce has a long history that dates back at least to medieval times, when town markets and fairs attracted not only traders and their customers, but also a colourful bevy of minstrels, jugglers and acrobats. Indeed, the origins of the street theatre of today can be traced back to the bazaars and marketplaces of the ancient world.

Many cities and towns now consciously set out to create civic areas and public celebration spaces that perform much the same function as the traditional city square or village green. A seminal example in the 1960s was the development of the Inner Harbor of Baltimore in Maryland, USA. Initially a community celebration was held in order to promote cultural diversity in a derelict downtown area that had been the site of riots in the city. This ultimately inspired the regeneration of the Inner Harbor shores, with a festival marketplace, museums and hotels transforming the rundown area into a lively urban precinct. This, in turn, became the model for similar waterfront precincts in other parts of the world, including Darling Harbour in Sydney, Cape Town in South Africa, Yokohama in Japan, Fisherman's Wharf in San Francisco and the Singapore riverfront.

In Sydney, the celebration of Australia's Bicentenary in 1988 became the catalyst to transform the derelict railway goods yards adjacent to the city into the modern tourism precinct of Darling Harbour. A combination of festivals, community events and street theatre was used to attract visitors to the precinct, and to position it as 'Where Sydney Celebrates'.

The Bicentennial celebrations were also the catalyst for the Newcastle Foreshore Development, again transforming a disused rail yard on the city's edge into a prime harbour-side recreation space for the city and its visitors. In Brisbane, the Expo 88 site across the river from the city would eventually become South Bank Parklands, a popular urban leisure park and centre for festivals and events. In Melbourne, the Southbank precinct along the Yarra River began a transformation of the city that has continued with the construction of Federation Square to mark Australia's centenary of Federation in 2001.

The transformation of the Sydney waterfront continued with the development of the Barangaroo project, again transforming a disused maritime area into a modern business and leisure precinct.

Town councils and urban planners everywhere were influenced by these ideas, with waterside areas at Kiama, Nelson Bay and The Entrance in New South Wales serving as just a few examples of the creation of public recreation and celebration spaces that have become widespread in Australia and other Western nations. Festivals, concerts, markets, public art programs and street theatre are tools commonly used to animate these spaces, and to make them congenial spaces for people to congregate in and enjoy.

Events and urban development

Governments have increasingly come to see events as potential tools for urban regeneration and renewal. They can provide the impetus for development, and become catalysts for the commitment of public funds and the investment of private capital needed to secure it. Integrated with other strategies such as town planning, commercial development, arts and cultural development and tourism, they can become powerful drivers in changing the image of destinations and in bringing new life and prosperity to communities.

An early example in Australia was the hosting of the America's Cup by Fremantle, Western Australia, in 1986–87. An icon of the sport of yachting with one of the world's oldest sporting trophies, the race had been dominated for most of its long history by North American yachting teams. When in a surprise coup a West Australian syndicate led by Perth entrepreneur Alan Bond snatched victory, tradition decreed that the team's home city would host the next event.

The port city of Fremantle, which had suffered a long economic downturn due to the slow decline of the shipping industry, had been the subject of various government regeneration and improvement proposals. The momentum of hosting the America's Cup was used to fast-track these proposals, and to attract finance and the will to transform the city. Motivated by the promise of a tourism bonanza and the stimulus that 'the eyes of the world will be on Fremantle', an enthusiastic wave of refurbishment and new building transformed the sleepy working-class port into a popular tourism destination. While some of the visitor predictions ultimately proved an exaggeration, the city of Fremantle emerged with a greatly improved image and higher self-esteem, although arguably at the expense of its original working-class character and values (Hall and Selwood 1995).

The spell of the Americans having been broken, the America's Cup was hosted by Auckland, New Zealand, in 1999–2000 and 2002–03. The somewhat dilapidated Auckland harbourside was transformed into an upmarket restaurant precinct, with positive urban redevelopment and tourism outcomes for the city.

The UK example

Perhaps nowhere has the use of events as tools for urban regeneration been as striking as in the United Kingdom. From having been the leader of the industrial revolution, by the mid-twentieth century many of the UK's major industrial cities, particularly in the north of England and in Scotland, were in an advanced state of decay. Typically, the inner-city urban areas where industrial plants had congregated were subject to high levels of unemployment, high rates of crime, substandard housing and low self-esteem.

With strong initiative and ingenuity, the UK tackled this problem to become a pioneer in urban regeneration and the use of event-based strategies. A series of five National Garden Festivals during the 1980s and early 1990s in Liverpool, Stoke-on-Trent, Glasgow, Gateshead and Ebbw Vale were used to transform derelict sites into attractive housing estates and parkland (Shone 2001). The Glasgow site now houses the Glasgow Science Centre and a digital media village on the banks of the River Clyde. Glasgow went on to use the accolade of European City of Culture in 1990 and the UK City of Architecture and Design in 1999 to transform its image from that of a decaying industrial city into that of a dynamic centre with a strong arts and tourism base.

Probably the most outstanding example of the use of events in urban regeneration in the UK is that of the Manchester 2002 Commonwealth Games.

Background: Manchester in decay

By the 1990s Manchester, once known as 'the workshop of the world' during the industrial revolution, had been in a period of steady decline for several decades (Commonwealth Games Legacy Manchester 2002; Hughes 1993). With the economic recessions of the 1970s and 1980s, it lost 60 per cent of its employment base. Between 1981 and 1991 the resident population fell by 11.5 per cent, leaving a demographically unbalanced population with heavy concentrations of the old, the young, ethnic minorities and the economically disadvantaged. By August 1992, unemployment had risen to 17.5 per cent (compared with a UK average of 9.9 per cent), and more than a third of the population received income from social security. An IRA bomb explosion in 1996 led to the further demoralisation of the city.

Government strategies for urban renewal

In the 1990s a comprehensive and integrated approach was established to regenerate the city (Manchester City Council 2005). The area was identified as one of 17 national pathfinders under the New Deal for Communities (NDC) Initiative in 1998. The East Manchester Plan, Beacons for a Brighter Future, was the first successful NDC scheme in the country, securing funding of £51.7m. Its key themes were tackling crime and the fear of crime; improvements to housing and neighbourhood management; the provision of positive open space; an emphasis on education, skills and training to help local people take advantage of employment opportunities; capacity building within the community to increase confidence and promote sustainability; and projects aimed at promoting the health and wellbeing of the community. Subsequently, complementary UK government funding from the Single Regeneration Budget of £25m enabled the activity and benefits from the NDC to be rolled out across the wider area.

East Manchester was also identified as one of three pilot urban regeneration companies in the UK, with New East Manchester Limited set up by the government in 1999 to provide an integrated and coordinated approach to regeneration. Formed as a partnership between the City Council, English Partnerships, the North West Development Agency and the local communities covering the wider East Manchester area, its charter was to prepare and implement a strategic framework for the area, secure additional funding, take the lead on particular development projects, secure inward investment and coordinate the range of initiatives in East Manchester.

The Commonwealth Games serve as a catalyst

An important strategic initiative of the regeneration program was to utilise the hosting of major events as a tool for urban regeneration and economic development. The City of Manchester bid unsuccessfully for the 1996 and 2000 Olympic Games, and was finally awarded the 2002 Commonwealth Games in 1995. The staging of the Games became a catalyst to inspire commitment and fast-track much of the planned regeneration and development. The building of venues was used to rejuvenate East Manchester, and to upgrade the transport and accommodation infrastructure of the city. The successful hosting of the Games not only brought visitors and media attention to the city, but also attracted further business investment and support. The final Games report (Commonwealth Games Legacy Manchester 2002) stated that over the following 15 years New East Manchester was expected to secure more than $2 billion in public and private funding, with the New Business Park development expected to create more than 6000 jobs, and a new retail centre, four-star hotel and new housing developments expected to create 3800 jobs for the people of East Manchester.

The legacy continues

Manchester has continued to pursue a major events strategy, with a Five Year Regional Events Strategy drawn up by the North West Development Agency in 2004. Manchester City Football Club, as the new resident in the City of Manchester stadium, draws 40 000 people to the streets of East Manchester for each of its home games. Concerts by U2 and Oasis in the summer of 2005 attracted 360 000 music fans. In 2005 Manchester Event Volunteers, an outgrowth of the Games, had a database of over 2000 volunteers taking part in a wide range of events including the Salford Triathlon, the Great Manchester Run and the World Paralympics event.

The final Games report (Commonwealth Games Legacy Manchester 2002) concludes that:

> This event had to be about more than municipal ego. More than an opportunity to bathe in the reflected glory of a world event successfully staged. Manchester was always explicit in its intention. In bidding for the Commonwealth Games its aim was not only to deliver a world-class event but also to create a lasting legacy for Manchester and the region. A unique and innovative approach was taken to the legacy of the Manchester Games. Any city or organisation would expect the successful delivery of such a huge event to deliver benefits to tourism, sporting infrastructure and measurable commercial gains. Manchester went further.

> The aim was for the hosting of the Games to provide the catalyst for the whole scale regeneration of a large area of the city.

London Olympics 2012: The Regeneration Games

The notion of using major sporting events as catalysts for urban regeneration was carried over from the Manchester Commonwealth Games in 2002 to the London Olympic and Paralympic Games in 2012.

The regeneration of the East End of London was established by The London Olympic Board as one of five key priorities for the legacy of the London Games (Sportcal 2018):

1. Making the UK a world-leading sporting nation.
2. Transforming the heart of East London.
3. Inspiring a new generation of young people to take part in volunteering, cultural and physical activity.
4. Making the Olympic Park a blueprint for sustainable living.
5. Demonstrating the UK is a creative, inclusive and welcoming place to live in, visit and for business.

The vision for the regeneration of east London was further elaborated on in the official Games report (The London Organising Committee of the Olympic Games and Paralympic Games n.d.):

> The Olympic Park will be created in the Lower Lea Valley, 13 km east from the centre of London. This area is ripe for redevelopment. By staging the Games in this part of the city, the most enduring legacy of the Games will be the regeneration of an entire community for the direct benefit of everyone who lives there. The Olympic Park will become a hub for east London, bringing communities together and acting as a catalyst for profound social and economic change. It will become a model of social inclusion, opening up opportunities for education, cultural and skills development and jobs for people across the UK and London, but especially in the Lea Valley and surrounding areas. The new facilities in the Olympic Park will be open to the whole community, not just elite athletes. This will lead to more opportunities for everyone to participate in sport and physical activity. This will create a more inclusive, more active community, leading to a fitter society and reducing health inequalities.

This vision presented an enormous challenge. East London is an area of over 300 square kilometres encompassing seven London boroughs, with a population in 2004 of 1.5 million. It suffered badly as a result of deindustrialisation when the Docklands area was unable to compete with new container ports in the 1960s and 1970s. The Docklands area underwent a major transformation that was completed in 1998, including the establishment of a secondary financial district, the Docklands Light Railway and the City Airport.

The Thames Gateway project extended the regeneration further east to a 64-kilometre segment of the Thames estuary with a focus on sustainability, using existing Brownfield sites and regenerating deprived populations in 'linked communities' with affordable housing. London's successful bid to host the 2012 Olympic Games has helped to kickstart regeneration programs in the area.

The Lower Lea Valley in the Newham Borough was chosen as the Olympic Park site. It was designed to host the Olympic Stadium with a capacity of 80 000 spectators, the Olympic Village accommodation for athletes, the Aquatics Centre and the Hockey Centre. The Docklands Light Railway was to be extended to the site, with much of the Olympic Village to be converted into affordable housing after the Games, with a total of 9000 new homes to be built in the vicinity. Five of the new sports venues were to remain for use by the local community, and to be available to all people, irrespective of age or disability (Geography Teaching Today 2009). The sheer scale of the project led to the London 2012 Olympics being dubbed 'The Regeneration Olympics'.

So how successful were the Games in achieving this ambitious legacy program? A post-Games evaluation report prepared for the Department of Culture, Media and Sport in 2013 examined evidence-based progress in the regeneration of east London. Under the subtheme of transforming place, it made the following observations (Department for Culture, Media and Sport 2013).

- *Olympic Park remediation and development.* The program of land acquisition, remediation and development of the Olympic Park delivered a number of positive outputs including the:
  - remediation and clean-up of 2.5 km^2 of Brownfield land
  - demolition of more than 200 buildings
  - undergrounding of 52 power pylons
  - creation of a new utilities network to provide power, water and sanitation to the site
  - reuse or recycling of 98 per cent of materials generated through the demolition process
  - creation of 100 hectares of greenspace
  - planting of 4000 semi-mature trees
  - creation of the Athletes' Village (which in legacy will be transformed into 2818 homes)
  - creation of permanent sporting venues in East London including the Olympic Stadium, the Aquatics Centre, the Velodrome and associated cycle tracks, the Handball Arena, hockey pitches and tennis courts
  - creation of 80 000 m^2 of business space through the International Broadcast Centre/Main Press Centre (IBC/MPC)
  - building of more than 30 bridges and connections across the Olympic Park.
- *Post-Games transformation and venues.* The transformation of the venues and the Olympic Park itself are currently well underway with some of the key legacy outputs beginning to become apparent from as early as mid-to-late 2013. The first of these will be the conversion of the Athletes' Village into 2818 apartments and town houses — 1379 of which will be social housing with the remaining 1439 being private homes, the majority being private rental. This will be followed by the conversion of the Athlete's Health Centre into a community health centre and the conversion of Olympic Park Operations Centre into a new academy, Chobham Academy. Together, this activity will see the creation of 'East Village' and the first new community in the park.

  Significant progress has also been made since the end of the Games:
  - the transformation works have now commenced and are currently on schedule
  - all permanent venues now have permanent operators with the announcement of West Ham United FC as the operator of the stadium
  - planning consent was granted in September 2012 for the Legacy Communities Scheme.

  While there were emerging plans for the redevelopment of Stratford prior to the Games, it can be concluded that without the Games the largely derelict, polluted and inaccessible site that ultimately became the Park would have remained as it was for the foreseeable future, the new Olympic venues would not have been constructed and the Olympic Park would not exist. Therefore, it is possible to conclude that these outputs are wholly attributable to the Games as is the evidence of their impact.
- *Public transport improvement.* Another key component in the transformation of East London as a place has been the improvement of public transport in the area. A number of important transport improvements have been implemented that can be attributed to the 2012 Games. The influence of the Games has largely been catalytic, with plans brought forward significantly as a result of the demand provided by the Games and the additional funding which helped to unlock planned investments. Alongside this, the availability of new additional investment also resulted in a number of improvements that would not have happened in the absence of the Games.
- *Public realm improvements.* To maximise the impact of the Olympic Park and to better integrate it into East London more widely, a program of public realm improvements was delivered in and around the host boroughs. Between 2009 and 2012 the original five host boroughs implemented a joint program of public realm capital schemes, valued at £190 million. While much of this activity was part of larger and longer term development schemes, they would most likely have been on a smaller scale or at a later date, with some projects, such as the live sites and walking routes, considered wholly additional and attributable to the Games. The Games had an important catalytic effect in bringing forward a significant amount of public realm improvements that have undoubtedly made a positive contribution to the transformation of East London as a place.
- *Wider public and private sector investment in the area.* The Games have leveraged wider private sector benefits, the most notable of which is the role that they played in bringing forward the Westfield Development at Stratford City — and all the employment and economic benefits associated with it —

by between five and seven years. The Games have also played an important catalytic and/or influencing role on a number of others including Lendlease's investment in the International Quarter and the Strand East project in Stratford being developed by Inter IKEA.

It appears that the Games have also played an indirect role in attracting higher education institutions to the area. Birkbeck (with a new campus in Stratford's cultural quarter) and Loughborough University (with a new campus to be located in iCITY) both state that the decision to locate in East London was not made directly because of the Games. But, given the Games' influence on transforming Stratford and making it a first-class location, the Games have clearly had a notable indirect influence.

As a result of this activity, parts of East London, particularly those around Stratford already look, feel and function differently to how they did before London was awarded the right to host the Games, and perhaps more significantly to how they would have done had London not been awarded the right to host the Games.

The report also examined other legacy subthemes including transforming communities, transforming prospects and convergence in some detail, concluding that many impacts had either been caused or accelerated by the staging of the London 2016 Olympic Games and Paralympic Games. However, the study concluded that while change is already apparent, the true legacy impact of the Olympic Park and its associated venues will not be fully realised for a number of years (The London Organising Committee of the Olympic Games and Paralympic Games n.d.).

The regeneration of East London is not without its detractors, with the gentrification of the area, the perceived lack of consultation with locals and the failure to live up to expectations being just some of the many criticisms levelled at the project. What is not debatable, however, is that the area has been transformed beyond recognition, and that the London 2012 Summer Olympics have been a major catalyst in the process.

2.4 The corporate perspective

LEARNING OBJECTIVE 2.4 Discuss the use of events by the corporate sector and describe the role that events play in integrated marketing strategies.

Events have a unique ability to bring people physically together, and to inspire and communicate with them in ways that cannot be easily duplicated by other means and media. This has been recognised by the corporate sector, which, as we saw in the overview of the event field chapter, increased its use of events rapidly in the 1990s, establishing a trend that continued into the first decade of the new millennium. This trend reflects the recognition of the power of events by the corporate sector, and its increasing use of events as tools both to improve company morale and business procedures, and to increase profitability and income.

Kline (2005) summarises this trend:

> We have seen a significant shift in the way companies are allocating funds — moving their dollars from extensive advertising toward the development of event-focused integrated marketing programs. Corporations are investing money in their events and in their people. Special events are seen as opportunities to motivate and educate their work force in an effort to be more successful at reaching their audience and goals. Consumer lifestyle events are created that bring relevance, influence behaviour and present new choices to the public.

Corporate use of events

Silvers (2007) describes corporate and business events as 'any event that supports business objectives, including management functions, corporate communications, training, marketing, incentives, employee relations, and customer relations, scheduled alone or in conjunction with other events.'

The use of events by companies and businesses may be focused internally, aimed at their own business practices and staff, or may be focused externally, aimed at their customers and clients (see table 2.2). The common thread is the demonstrated ability of events to deliver results in terms of business objectives, and therefore to provide a return on investment.

Internal events

Internally, companies make significant use of events such as management meetings and staff training in the day-to-day conduct of their business. Given the modern corporate environment, major internal company events such as annual general meetings (AGMs), corporate retreats and board meetings are often treated as significant occasions deserving of dedicated organisation and meticulous attention to detail. Other internal events such as staff social events, team building, incentives and award nights are seen as valuable tools to inspire and motivate staff, and as contributing to the development of a successful corporate culture. Sales conferences and product seminars are used to extend this culture further to company representatives and dealer networks. Many companies contribute considerable resources towards ensuring that such events are perceived as part of their corporate identity and style, and that they are conducted with high standards of professionalism and presentation.

TABLE 2.2   Corporate use of events

Internal	External
Annual general meetings (AGMs)	Grand openings
Corporate retreats	Product launches
Board meetings	Sales promotions
Management meetings	Media conferences
Staff training	Publicity events
Team building	Photo opportunities
Staff social events	Exhibitions
Incentive events	Trade missions
Award nights	Trade shows
Sales conferences	Client hospitality
Dealer network seminars	Event sponsorship

An example of an internal corporate event was the 2013 Woolworths National Conference in Melbourne organised by cievents. The week-long event for more than 3200 delegates kicked off with a three-and-a-half-hour interactive session that involved more than 100 actors and a series of tailor-made videos presented on six LED screens. During the conference, cievents literally made history with a successful bid to break the Guinness World Record for the largest ever fitness circuit class, when more than 2000 people took part in the biggest class the world has ever seen. Another highlight of the week was the Big W Fashion Show — a 20-minute performance designed to showcase Big W's new line of soft goods, fashion and accessories for spring and summer 2013. Two themed lunches were provided, which each saw more than 3000 square metres of the main foyer of the Melbourne Convention and Exhibition Centre turned into a grassy outdoor picnic area overnight, followed later in the week by the South Wharf Promenade being transformed into a giant pop-up street festival (cievents 2018).

External events

Externally, events are highly valued for their ability to communicate corporate and sales messages, and to cut through the clutter of advertising and media to reach customers and clients directly and effectively. As detailed in table 2.2, grand openings, product launches, sales promotions, media conferences, publicity events and photo opportunities are just some of the wide variety of events that are used to gain the attention of potential customers, and to create a 'buzz' around new products and services. Companies also use exhibitions, trade missions and trade shows to reach distribution networks, and to maintain a company presence in selected markets.

An example of the use of events to promote a corporate image and launch new products is provided by the official midnight launch of the PlayStation 3 (PS3) console by Sony Computer Entertainment Australia (SCEA) in March 2007. Teaming up with SCEA for the event, the department store Myer set up a big viewing space outside its store with a free screening of *Casino Royale*. The film was played directly from a PS3, and gamers were given the chance to play the PS3 on the big screen and to win PlayStation-themed giveaways (Ramsay 2007).

Another growing corporate use of events is the entertaining of clients in order to build and nourish business relationships with them. This can take the form of hosted cocktail parties, dinners or receptions, or hospitality at company-sponsored public events. Often the sponsorship of events can bring many of these aspects together, enabling companies to reach event attendees and demonstrate product attributes through associating their product with the event, while at the same time hosting clients in a convivial atmosphere.

Another corporate-related use of events touched on in the overview of the event field chapter is that of conferences and business meetings. A large and growing number of professional, academic and industry associations use meetings, congresses and conferences to communicate with their members, to explore relevant issues and to disseminate information to their respective audiences. These can be local, national or international in scope, with many international associations maintaining a structure and bidding process similar to that of major sporting bodies. An important aspect of these events is the opportunity provided by participants to keep abreast of developments in their professional fields, and to network with colleagues and associates. There has been recent speculation in the industry that the fragile economic climate, increasing environmental impacts, travel costs and security issues, coupled with the increasing technological capacity for online meetings and video conferencing, will slow the growth of the industry. However, the advantages of direct networking and face-to-face contact still provide a powerful incentive for live meetings, and association conferences continue to be held worldwide albeit with reduced budgets and, in some cases, declining numbers.

2.5 Return on investment

LEARNING OBJECTIVE 2.5 List and describe methods used by the corporate sector in measuring the return on investment (ROI) of events.

The growth in the use of events by the corporate sector has been accompanied by an increasing desire and need to evaluate their outcomes. With the increasing amount spent on events, companies understandably want to know what their events are achieving, and their effectiveness and return on investment (ROI) compared with other marketing tools and strategies. This has led to a greater emphasis on the establishment of measures, or metrics, to benchmark events and to quantify their outcomes.

However, many of the benefits and outcomes of events are difficult to quantify in monetary terms, and different companies will use different measures and yardsticks. Myhill (2005) maintains that the ROI for meetings and training events can be calculated by the use of careful data planning and analysis, using the Phillips ROI methodology developed in the 1970s. The methodology uses five levels of evaluation, leading to the full numerical calculation of return on investment.

1. Reaction and planned action — measures attendee satisfaction, usually by the use of generic questionnaires. While important, attendee satisfaction does not in itself guarantee the acquisition of new skills, knowledge or professional contacts.
2. Learning — uses tests, skill practices, group evaluations and other assessment tools to ensure that attendees have absorbed the meeting material and know how to use it properly. However, it does not guarantee that what has been learnt will be used on the job.
3. Job applications — used to determine whether attendees applied what they learnt from the meeting on the job. While a good gauge of the meeting's success, it still does not guarantee a positive business impact for the organisation.
4. Business results — focuses on the results achieved by attendees as they successfully apply what they learnt from the meeting. Typical measures include output, sales, quality, costs, time, and customer satisfaction. However, this still does not provide a measure of the financial value of the meeting or event.
5. Return on investment — compares the monetary benefits gained from the meeting with the costs. A numerical ROI percentage can be obtained using the formula:

$$\frac{\text{Meeting benefits} - \text{Meeting costs}}{\text{Meeting costs}} \times 100$$

This formula can be used to compare the ROI of meetings and events with alternative events and strategies. However, Myhill suggests that it is not appropriate to conduct such a study on all meetings and events. She recommends that only five to 10 per cent of events should be taken to ROI, with the most suitable being those linked to the operational goals and/or strategic objectives of the organisation, and which incur significant costs and staff/participant time.

Events aimed at external stakeholders are typically measured by attendance numbers, sales leads obtained, or changes in attitude or perception. It is often as much about brand awareness and enhancement as it is about actual sales or measurable outcomes. Kline (2005) comments:

ROI is very important, but it is measured differently by each client. The return could be measured by the number of people attending the event, how the event looked and was perceived, or how each attendee felt as they left the event. We believe that ROI of events can be somewhat intangible, but the true value resides in that moment when the brand achieves relevance and preference to the audience, and that is what we focus on.

2.6 The community perspective

LEARNING OBJECTIVE 2.6 Discuss the benefits that can result to communities from the staging of events.

Most public events are either community events or major events that take place in host communities that have a particular interest in and attitude towards the event. Thus the community is a major stakeholder in events, and it is incumbent on event managers to consider the community perspective and to include this in the event planning process.

Community events

As discussed in the overview of the event field chapter, some form of festivals and events can be identified in every human society and in every age. They are part of how we interact as humans, and form part of the social fabric that binds our communities together. This can be seen in many country town and regional festivals, where the main social event of the year is often the town festival. The myriad social interactions that go into creating the festival — the committee meetings, the approaches to local businesses for support, the involvement of local arts and sports groups, the contacting of service groups and volunteers — all help to create social capital and community wellbeing. In many cases, these festivals provide an annual opportunity for local clubs and societies to fundraise and recruit new members, which is crucial to their survival. Communities, of course, are not always heterogeneous, and festivals can provide the stimulation for healthy disagreement and debate about their priorities and identity. In many very real ways, therefore, these festivals help to create and strengthen a sense of community and belonging. For this and related reasons, they are often supported by local governments and other government agencies concerned with maintaining and supporting healthy communities.

EVENT PROFILE

Parkes Elvis Festival

Parkes has a population of 12 000 and is located in the central west of NSW 365 kilometres west of Sydney.

In 1993 a local couple who ran Gracelands Restaurant decided to host a dinner to celebrate the birthday of Elvis Presley on 8 January. To their surprise, roughly two hundred people attended the sell-out event, and the Parkes Elvis Festival was born. Over the next 10 years more events were added to the program and the Festival became a two-day event, but still with only a small audience. Then with the vision and efforts of new committee members, the Festival experienced a surge in popularity in 2004 and 2005, with word quickly spreading across Australia about this fun and quirky event. 2009 saw 9500 people attend the event, and in 2018 more than 26 000 visitors attended, with the festival enjoying a worldwide media audience of 60 million with fans around the globe (Parkes Elvis Festival 2018).

The Parkes Elvis Festival is held every year in the second week in January, coinciding with Elvis Presley's birthday, with over 150 events across five days from Wednesday to Sunday. Officially endorsed by the estate of Elvis Presley, Elvis Presley Enterprises Inc. in Memphis, Parkes Elvis Festival hosts a number of live entertainments including the official Ultimate Elvis Tribute Artist Contest (the winner representing Australia in Memphis, US), a feature concert series starring a special guest artist, a street parade, renewal of vows ceremony, the Miss Priscilla Dinner, and many free live concerts, competitions and prizes.

The Elvis Express train between Sydney and Parkes is an annual highlight for Festival visitors. The Festival experience begins even before visitors arrive in town, as they are serenaded by Elvis impersonators all the way from Sydney.

While Parkes was previously best known as the home of the CSIRO Radio Telescope due to the release of the Australian Film 'The Dish', Parkes is now widely recognised as the 'Elvis Capital of Australia', with the festival having firmly cementing Parkes as a tourism destination (Handley 2015).

Regional festivals as community builders

Gibson and Stewart (2009) surveyed 480 regional festivals and events from a database of 2856 festivals in New South Wales, Victoria and Tasmania. They found that the most common types were sporting, community, agricultural and music festivals, which together made up three-quarters of the festivals surveyed. Country, jazz, folk and blues festivals accounted for over half of the music festivals, despite the popularity of styles such as rock in the wider recorded music retail market. Sixty-seven festivals (15 per cent) had been running before 1900 — mostly gardening and flower festivals and agricultural shows; 24 per cent were established between 1900 and 1980; and 61 per cent after 1980, with music, food and wine festivals the most common in this group,

The average attendance of the festivals surveyed was 7000, although there was a wide variation in attendance, and 11 festivals (2 per cent) had an attendance of more than 50 000. Attendees across all festivals were 58 per cent local, 11 per cent from the state capital, 21 per cent other intrastate, 8 per cent interstate and 1 per cent international.

The average duration of the festivals was 3.3 days, and the average number of stalls including food, clothing and merchandise was 67. Seventy-four per cent of the festivals were run by nonprofit organisations, with only 3 per cent run by profit-seeking private companies. The majority of festivals were linked to the interests and passions of the organising committee, or had cultural goals, such as building community, rather than income generation. Nevertheless, the researchers concluded that regional festivals were a sizable industry in a cumulative sense, with the surveyed festivals generating total ticket sales of $550 million annually, as well as considerable related economic activity.

The researchers noted the community-building aspect of regional festivals (Gibson and Stewart 2009):

> It is a truism to say that festivals build community — but it is worth highlighting the extent and functions of festivals in local communities, and especially in small places... Festivals are pivotal dates on the annual calendars of towns and villages, they support charities and provide opportunities for high schools and Rotary clubs to raise funds; they bring together scattered farm-folk, young and old and disparate subcultures; they blend attitudes, expand social networks and encourage improvements in social cohesion... Festivals provide rural communities with coping mechanisms at times of drought and economic hardship, and catalyse community in the name of fun.

The individual perspective

From the perspective of community members, their requirements and expectations of community events are often very simple and direct. They want to participate and be entertained — to have a social and enriching experience beyond their everyday reality. They may want to participate as a family, so that they can enjoy the experience together and so that children are provided a special treat at an affordable cost. They may want to showcase their creative talents in the case of arts or cultural festivals, or to enjoy friendly competition in the case of sporting events. In some cases they may want the satisfaction and achievement of being involved as organisers, or the social contact and recognition of being involved as volunteers. They may have some awareness of the larger role of the event in their community, but are likely to be more interested in the social and cultural benefits than the business and economic outcomes of the event.

Major events and the community

The community perspective changes when we examine major events within the community that attract many visitors. Community members may still look forward to enjoying the event as participants or spectators. However, as the event organisation becomes larger and more professional, much of the event planning is often taken out of the hands of members of the host community. They are now more likely to be concerned with the wider impacts of the event, which may include a sense of pride in their community, economic and job creation benefits, and physical impacts such as traffic restrictions and crowd congestion. Their relationship with the event is likely to be less direct, and the media may become the main source of information on the planning of the event and predictions of visitor numbers, media coverage, economic benefits and job creation. Under such circumstances, it is easy for members of the community to become distanced from the event, and to fluctuate in their perceptions and expectations of the event experience and outcomes.

For the event organisers, keeping the host community informed and onside becomes a vital task in the event planning process. Not only is it important to keep the community engaged with the event, but if it becomes disaffected then this attitude is likely to affect the experience and enjoyment of visitors to the event. The protest by Albert Park residents over the alienation of parklands by the Australian Grand Prix in Melbourne and the backlash against Schoolies Week on the Gold Coast are just two examples of the negative impact of community disengagement with events. Event organisers therefore need to develop strategies to involve the host community in the planning of the event, to maintain good community relations, and to monitor the community's perceptions of and attitudes to the event.

The Henry Lawson Festival of Arts at Grenfell, NSW, used a mix of public meetings and local newspaper articles in 2009 to involve the community in a re-evaluation of the festival's priorities and future. Many events use social media such as Facebook, Twitter, Flickr and YouTube to stay in touch with their audiences and to invite feedback from the local community. Federation Square in Melbourne, for example, uses a live twitter feed on screens at outdoor events to incorporate feedback from their audience (Dunbar 2009). A more detailed description of strategies for community engagement follows.

2.7 Strategies for community engagement

LEARNING OBJECTIVE 2.7 List the range of strategies available to event managers to promote community engagement in events and discuss the implications for event managers of differing perspectives on events in the event planning process.

Community perceptions of an event will depend to a large extent on the levels of community engagement, and on the efforts made by event organisers to involve the community in the planning, implementation and evaluation of the event. Appropriate liaison with stakeholders will ensure that the event represents the true values of the community, and will often serve to resolve many of the potential community conflicts and disruptions in relation to the event.

Harris and Allen (2006), in a study for artsACT, examined 22 medium to large-scale public events in Australia and overseas in order to identify strategies employed by event managers to facilitate community engagement. They posited core values for public engagement and participation based on those of the International Association for Public Participation (2010):

- Public participation is based on the belief that those who are affected by a decision have a right to be involved in the decision-making process.
- Public participation includes the promise that the public's contribution will influence the decision.
- Public participation promotes sustainable decisions by recognizing and communicating the needs and interests of all participants, including decision-makers.
- Public participation seeks out and facilitates the involvement of those potentially affected by or interested in a decision.
- Public participation seeks input from participants in designing how they participate.
- Public participation provides participants with the information they need to participate in a meaningful way.
- Public participation communicates to participants how their input affected the decision.

In practice, the study found that the extent and type of community engagement varied widely in the events that they studied, with some events much more proactive than others in seeking to involve and engage the community. Mechanisms for community engagement in the events examined by the study included:
- Participation facilitation
  - Free or discounted transport provision
  - Provision of on-site facilities and services for specific groups, such as marquees for elderly people and creches for young families
  - Radio broadcasts for community members who are housebound
  - Free access to aspects of an event's program

- Discount ticket prices for selected groups, such as the unemployed, pensioners and students and access to free tickets for selected groups
- Provision of specific services and facilities for people with a disability
- Embracing a variety of geographic locations within a community when delivering the event program, or when engaged in outreach activities
• Community input and feedback facilitation
  - Public meetings
  - Community-based 'whole of event' strategic reviews
  - Festival workshops designed to seek input with regard to event design and programming
  - Open calls for membership of an event organising committee
  - Dedicated local radio talkback sessions with event organisers
  - Community advisory committees or consultation groups that serve to provide input into the event, or the inclusion of community representatives on the organising committee
  - Inclusion of a feedback or contact facility on the event website
• Inclusive programming
  - Targeting of specific community groups to deliver, or assist with, one or more aspects of the event program. Such groups included the unemployed, at-risk youth and special interest groups such as environmental organisations
  - Designing program elements with the needs of specific groups in mind (for example, the participation of schools by incorporating an 'education day')
• Incentives
  - The provision of free stall space to nonprofit organisations and charities to raise funds, attract new members, or raise awareness of a particular issue or cause
  - Competitions and contests that serve to encourage involvement by particular community groups such as school children, local artists and sporting groups
• Outreach
  - Profits from the event used to engage in extension activities to specific, often disadvantaged groups in the community
  - Shop fronts that provide an ongoing connection between the event and its community
  - Involvement of schools by seeking inclusion in school curriculum activities or by creating lesson plans for use by teachers that deal with various aspects of events in general
  - Access to event websites for nonprofit organisations so that they may enhance their community presence
  - The use of symbolism to reach out to communities on an ongoing basis (for example, a public installation or sculpture to remind local people of the ongoing connection between the town and the event)
  - Broadening the local community by expanding the footprint of the event into nearby areas.
• Community development and capacity building
  - Internships, traineeships and work experience programs that provide opportunities for young people to learn new skills and knowledge that can be used within their communities on a paid or voluntary basis
  - Provision of volunteering opportunities, training sessions and volunteer social events that facilitate the creation of new networks within the community, and may result in new business and other opportunities for volunteers
  - Enhancement of the community's capacity to deal with a specific issue or problem
  - Channelling financial resources from an event into the development of various nonprofit community organisations in order to progress a community's development efforts
• Friends of the event/event alumni associations
  - The creation of 'friends' or 'alumni' groups to integrate an event further with its community.
• Local business engagement
  - Encouragement of attendee expenditure at local businesses through the creation of special incentives tied in with the event
  - Giving preference to local businesses for the supply of services.

This study is primarily an exploratory one, and more research needs to be devoted to identifying community engagement mechanisms, and their relative effectiveness. Nevertheless, for the event manager, it indicates that there is a broad range of initiatives available to engage the involvement and participation of host communities in events. However, considerable care must be taken to ensure that the particular strategies chosen are best suited to the particular community and its needs, and are most likely to achieve results. This will reap rewards in terms of a greater sense of community ownership of the event, and a more positive perception of its benefits and impacts.

SUMMARY

This chapter examined a number of important perspectives that have implications for event managers in the planning and delivery of events. From the government perspective, a number of disparate roles and functions in events are often integrated through the use of event strategies, as illustrated by the Scotland and Singapore events strategies. Governments may also create dedicated celebration spaces, and use events as tools for urban renewal. Event managers need to be aware of government regulations and requirements, and to see governments as key stakeholders and potential partners in events. The corporate sector uses events to achieve both internal and external goals and objectives, as well as sponsoring public events in order to obtain commercial benefits. Event managers need to be aware of corporate objectives, and of the increasing need of companies to identify the return on investment (ROI) of events. From the community perspective, community members are often focused on the direct impacts and benefits of events on them personally and on the community in general. Managers of public events need to carefully choose and implement appropriate mechanisms for communication and engagement with the community.

QUESTIONS

1 Does the local government in your area have an event strategy? Analyse the roles that your local government plays in the regulation and coordination of events.
2 Can you identify a dedicated celebration space in your city or region? How is the space managed, and what role does it play in the life of the community?
3 Identify a corporate event in your city or region. What were the objectives of the event, and how did it fit with the overall marketing strategy of the company?
4 Analyse the corporate sponsorship of an event and identify the main benefits that were obtained.
5 Choose a community event with which you are familiar, and identify the benefits to individuals and to the community from the staging of the event.
6 Identify a local community event that you are familiar with. Analyse and describe any strategies that the event has for engagement with the local community, and how it contributes to community building.
7 Discuss the implications for event managers that arise from the analysis of the government, corporate and community perspectives on events.

CASE STUDY

EDINBURGH: 'THE WORLD'S LEADING FESTIVAL CITY'
'This is a city of shifting light, of changing skies, of sudden vistas. A city so beautiful it breaks the heart again and again' (McCall Smith 2006).

Overview

Scotland's capital city Edinburgh is a must-see contemporary European cultural capital city, known as 'the world's leading festival city'. The city has a dynamic and vibrant cultural life with 11 major annual international festivals creating global awareness of the destination. The Edinburgh International Festival, Edinburgh Festival Fringe and Edinburgh International Film Festival each celebrated their 70th anniversary in 2017, creating global awareness of the destination, with the Edinburgh Festival Fringe being the world's largest arts festival with 2.8 million tickets issued in 2018. In addition to the six high-profile summer festivals — the Edinburgh International Festival, the Festival Fringe, Edinburgh Jazz & Blues Festival, Edinburgh International Book Festival, Edinburgh Arts Festival and the Royal Edinburgh Military Tattoo — there are five other major festivals at other times of the year including Edinburgh's Hogmanay (December/January); Edinburgh Science Festival (April); Edinburgh International Children's Festival (Imaginate; May/June); Edinburgh International Film Festival (June); and the Scottish International Storytelling Festival (October).

In 2017 Edinburgh attracted over 2 million international visitors (Ottewell 2018), making the city the UK's second most popular destination for international visitors after London.

The city's impressive natural beauty and built environment, with 4.46 square kilometres of the city centre (the medieval 'Old Town' and the 18th and 19th century 'New Town') a designated UNESCO World Heritage site, creates a distinctive visitor experience. In 2004 the city was designated as UNESCO's first 'World City of Literature' in recognition of its rich literary credentials past and present. Harking back to Edinburgh's leading role in the 18th century Age of Enlightenment, the city remains a thought leader in many fields of research, academia, business and cultural endeavour, with a diverse and resilient economy and a growing population of over half a million people — a vibrant and dynamic 21st-century city.

An often asked question of city stakeholders is: 'What is the secret of Edinburgh's success as an events tourism destination and the longevity of its major festivals?' The reality is that there is no single characteristic of the Edinburgh destination experience that defines its success, but rather a coming together of a distinct combination of factors including the nature and profile of Edinburgh's citizens; the nature and form of the city's built and natural environment which creates a 'perfect stage' with a special atmosphere and ambience, the scale and compactness of the city; dynamic cultural institutions; a developed visitor and cultural infrastructure; professional capacity and capability within the event industry; and the creativity, innovation and strategic global perspective adopted by the key stakeholders involved in festivals and events in the city.

In this case study the focus will be on the exemplar strategic and collaborative approach adopted since 2006 by Edinburgh's stakeholders to advance the destination's position as 'the world's leading festival city'.

Longevity and sustainability of Edinburgh's festivals and cultural tourism experience

In 1947 when the first Edinburgh International Festival took place, the objective was to provide a platform for the 'flowering of the human spirit and enrichment of the cultural life of Scotland, Britain and Europe', utilising the power of culture and the arts to rebuild relationships between peoples and nations, a philosophy at the heart of Edinburgh's Festivals 70 years later (Festival Calendar n.d.). The changing tenure of the Director's role at the Edinburgh International Festival also ensures regular refreshing and refocusing of the festival programming; for example, the current director has experimented with new programming elements targeted on millennials (the future generation of festival audiences).

The concentrated nature of Edinburgh's 'Summer Festivals' also unleashes an extraordinary, creative and artistic firmament (and 'buzz') that defines for performers, audiences and residents the Edinburgh festival experience. Edinburgh's summer festivals have been identified by the national events agency VisitScotland in 'Scotland, the perfect stage: Scotland's event strategy 2015–2025' as a leading signature event in Scotland's event portfolio.

The ethos of the Festival Fringe remains 'uncurated' programming where 'anyone with a story to tell and a venue willing to host them' (The Edinburgh Festival Fringe n.d.) can participate. This philosophy nurtures inclusiveness and fosters creative expression, a strong customer focus and makes it truly cutting edge. The significance of this experimental characteristic is also reflected in the fact that the Fringe is equally important as an industry showcase for spotting new talent as it is about entertaining audiences.

A defining characteristic of Edinburgh's festivals is that they are honest to their roots and their locality; the Science Festival, for example, draws on Edinburgh's distinguished heritage of scientific discovery and research, while the International Book Festival draws on Edinburgh's rich historic and contemporary literary credentials. Festivals Edinburgh's impact studies consistently demonstrate that over two-thirds of Edinburgh's citizens actually attend the festivals (Festivals Edinburgh 2016). The Festivals put a strong emphasis on the live experience which resonates with current consumer aspirations for the experiential. There is also strength in Edinburgh's festival mix that ensures durability, with each festival being a world leader within its own festival genre and applying a 'lead ethos' in programming that remains relevant to changing audiences and refreshes the festival experience, while in the city there undoubtedly exists a critical mass of professional event industry capability and capacity.

Adopting a strategic perspective: 'Thundering hooves'

'Edinburgh is a small city but its festivals put it onto the world stage' (Festivals Edinburgh 2015, p. 2).

A new collaborative ecosystem among the 11 major festivals and key stakeholders, where all partners feel they have ownership of a common agenda and are working towards a collective and shared set of goals, is a defining outcome of the 2006 strategic review report 'Thundering hooves' (Festivals Edinburgh 2006). Most important was the creation of the Festivals Forum made up of key stakeholders and the umbrella partnership of Festivals Edinburgh with a team of permanent and professional staff. The strategy was revisited in 2015 in 'Thundering hooves 2.0: a ten year strategy to sustain the success of Edinburgh's Festivals', and fostered further new collaborations and innovations.

The umbrella partnership and organisation Festivals Edinburgh has a mission to 'support Edinburgh's Festivals in sustaining and developing their position as the world's leading festival city through development and delivery of collaborative projects and initiatives which support growth, product development, leadership and audiences; acting on behalf of and representing the collective strengths of the Edinburgh Festivals' (Festivals Edinburgh n.d.).

Over the past 12 years, Festivals Edinburgh has consolidated collaborative working between the major festivals and partnerships with key stakeholders such as the Scottish government and its agencies, the tourism sector, British Council, cultural industry and the local community. Concurrently, Festivals Edinburgh has been advancing initiatives, innovations and interventions that for over a decade have undoubtedly driven the nature and form of Edinburgh's collective festival offering, helping to extend the event lifecycles of the portfolio of major festivals, assisting sustainability, helping to create a competitive advantage, and strengthening the global perspective and positioning of the festivals and Edinburgh as a world-class visitor destination. The 2015 report states, 'This next ten years is about capitalising on [Edinburgh's festivals'] reputation and advantage; finding new ways of experiencing and investing in one of Scotland's greatest assets... The city needs to be confident and bold in its ambition to take its world leading festivals forward' (Festivals Edinburgh 2015, p. 2).

In 2015 there was recognition by the Festivals Forum and Festivals Edinburgh of the need to review festival strategy in light of the global financial crisis; critical macro drivers being identified as part of the ongoing development of the digital economy and the rise of new technologies; and significant political and cultural changes in Scotland. Part of the review was a situational analysis profiling Edinburgh with Montreal, Austin, Venice and Manchester. 'Thundering hooves 2.0' identified six major themes for Edinburgh's Festivals going forward (Festivals Edinburgh 2015):

1. The festival city (evolve the city's infrastructure and operations to provide an unrivalled experience)
2. Deep and wide engagement (collaboration to support educational aims and social justice through participation, learning and belonging)
3. National and global positioning (strong international partnerships, branding and marketing linked to the 70th anniversary year to give the nation a voice on the world stage)
4. Digital ways and means (embrace new technologies to offer new ways to experience the festivals, and means of creation and international brand building)
5. Investment and enterprise (innovation in programming, enterprise and investment and exploration of new sustainable business models and funding through engagement with the tourism sector and business community)
6. Developing and delivering (adaptation of the leadership by the Festivals Forum based on an open, collaborative and engaged approach and evolution of partnerships and structures).

Alongside the strategic review work, Festivals Edinburgh has led on impact research and the 2015 festivals impact study demonstrated that Edinburgh's festivals attracted an audience of 4.5 million, putting them on par with the FIFA World Cup, and generated over £280 million worth of additional tourism revenue for Edinburgh (up 19 per cent on 2010) and £313 million in total for Scotland (up 24 per cent on 2010; Festivals Edinburgh 2016). Key findings from the impact study also show that Edinburgh's festivals:

- position the city region as a leading international destination with 94 per cent of respondents stating that the festivals are part of what makes Edinburgh special as a city
- present unique cultural experiences with 92 per cent of respondents stating that the festivals were must-see events that gave them the chance to see things they would not otherwise see
- play a crucial role in year-round audience development, with 68 per cent of respondents stating that attending the festivals made them more likely to attend another cultural event
- create a sense of civic pride with 89 per cent of local festival-goers agreeing that the festivals increased their pride in Edinburgh as a city
- deliver quality professional Festivals, with satisfaction ratings of 95 per cent — being the highest rated outcome in the entire study (Festivals Edinburgh 2016).

There is a danger that mature festivals become complacent, with the event lifecycle leading to the danger of terminal decline. Critical to the sustained development of Edinburgh's Festivals and their longevity is awareness by festival stakeholders of the challenge of being market leaders. The importance of establishing, tracking and communicating the economic, social and cultural importance and environmental impacts of Edinburgh's Festivals is represented in their regular impact studies (Festivals Edinburgh 2005; Festivals Edinburgh 2011; Festivals Edinburgh 2016), which continue to provide hard evidence of the value and contribution of Edinburgh's festivals for Edinburgh, Scotland and globally, and are effectively used for advocacy purposes with and by stakeholders to secure ongoing support of and investment in Edinburgh's festivals.

Not only is 'the world's leading festival city' the brand for Edinburgh's festivals but it also forms the basis of the framework for the way Festivals Edinburgh identifies and approaches strategic activity. Festivals Edinburgh's strategic themes in the autumn of 2018 are listed below.

- World ensuring global reach/relevance — issues and opportunities relating to Visas (especially for African and Asian artists)/Brexit/hostile environment
- Leading through invention/internationalism — issues and opportunities around digital (all about the live experience)/Edinburgh positioning itself as a SMART city/environmental issues
- Festival by focusing on the experiential (tourism/the visitor experience) — issues and opportunities around managing growth
- City through engaging with the local community/people of Edinburgh and Scotland — issues and opportunities around engagement (ownership/experimentation) one in every two audience members is Scottish. Each of the Festivals individually is a leader in their own sector.

As part of this ongoing impact assessment in 2018, two major research projects were undertaken by Festivals Edinburgh investigating the cultural impact of the festivals on Scotland's cultural and events ecosystem (talent development and profiling) including through work commissioned under the Scottish Government's Expo Fund and Made in Scotland initiatives, and looking at the 'network effect' (that is, networking, training, business development and capacity building) of the festival. In 2016–17, for example, the festivals collectively spent £10.5m on event production (89 per cent of which was spent with Scottish Companies) and £9.3m on creative talent (56 per cent of which was spent on Scottish-based individuals and organisations; Festivals Edinburgh 2018).

Festivals Edinburgh has led the way, working with the 11 festivals in helping to enhance local engagement with the wider community in Edinburgh through the Platforms for Creative Excellence (PLACE) initiative which has two strands, 'Programme' and 'Community', and will focus for example on supporting new program partnerships and skills development. The PLACE program is linked to a Scottish government funding pledge of £3m a year for five years as a legacy from the 70th anniversary year in 2017 and in response to recommendations in the 'Thundering hooves 2.0' report recommending additional funding for the festivals against the backdrop of austerity funding pressures.

Innovation has been a significant work strand for Festivals Edinburgh since the 2006 'Thundering hooves' report. For example, Festivals Edinburgh has embraced the use of the media and new technologies for the distribution of product and engagement with customers and audiences. Achieving extended global media coverage for the festivals was a recommendation of the report and from 2006 onwards led to greater proactive engagement with UK and International media. Festivals such as the Royal Edinburgh Military Tattoo have built on their audience awareness globally to present the festival in North America, Australasia and China (Festivals Edinburgh 2006).

Conclusions

A critical factor of Edinburgh's sustained success as the 'world's leading festival city' is a heightened understanding among festival and destination stakeholders (including politicians) of the collective responsibility to guard against complacency, which potentially comes from being a mature brand and market leader, coupled with a recognition of the value of collaboration and the need to support continuous innovation to extend competitive advantage.

The strength of leadership through the Festivals Forum and Festivals Edinburgh partnerships represents a model of best practice. Festivals Edinburgh's program of ongoing research provides robust and longitudinal evidence of (and advocacy for) the cultural, social, economic and environmental impacts and benefits of the festivals. Edinburgh's festival experience proves the added value, and force for innovation, that can be gained from collaborative working across the cultural and tourism sectors. In the city there is a spirit of 'cultural entrepreneurship' exemplified by the work of Festivals Edinburgh, the 11 major festivals, and the creative and cultural industry players in the city. There is an awareness of the evolution in customer expectations, the importance of enhancing the visitor experience across the customer journey. The value of the Edinburgh brand is now more fully understood, while creativity and culture most definitely define and drive the brand: 'Edinburgh — the world's leading festival city'.

Prepared by Kenneth Wardrop BA (Hons) MBA FTS, Visiting Research Fellow, Business School, Edinburgh Napier University

QUESTIONS

1 What evidence supports the claim in the title of the case study that Edinburgh is 'The World's Leading Festival City'?

2 What characteristics of Edinburgh have enabled the city to build such a strong festival culture?

3 What steps has Edinburgh taken to develop and capitalise on Edinburgh's festivals that might be a useful model for other cities?

REFERENCES

cievents 2008, 'Woolworths National Conference', www.cievents.com.au.

Commonwealth Games Legacy Manchester 2002, 'The XVII Commonwealth Games 2002 Manchester: Regeneration/Legacy', www.gameslegacy.com.

Department for Culture, Media and Sport 2013, 'Report 5: Post Games evaluation', https://assets.publishing.service.gov.uk/government/uploads/system/uploads/attachment_data/file/224181/1188-B_Meta_Evaluation.pdf, accessed 5 May 2020.

Dunbar, P 2009, 'Using Social Media for Events Promotion', address given to Australian Events Master Class on Social Media Marketing for the Events Industry in Sydney on 8 October 2009.

Festival Calendar n.d., 'Festival info: Edinburgh International Festival', www.festival-calendar.com, viewed 5 May 2020.

Festivals Edinburgh 2005, 'Edinburgh's year-round festivals 2004–2005: economic impact study', SQW Limited & TNS Travel and Tourism, www.edinburghfestivalcity.com, viewed 5 May 2020.

Festivals Edinburgh 2006, 'Thundering hooves: maintaining the global competitive edge of Edinburgh's festivals', AEA Consulting, www.edinburghfestivalcity.com, viewed 5 May 2020.

Festivals Edinburgh 2011, 'Edinburgh Festivals 2015 impact study: technical report', BOP Consulting, www.edinburghfestivalcity.com, viewed 5 May 2020.

Festivals Edinburgh 2015, 'Thundering hooves 2.0: a ten year strategy to sustain the success of Edinburgh's festivals', BOP Consulting, www.edinburghfestivalcity.com, viewed 5 May 2020.

Festivals Edinburgh 2016, 'Edinburgh Festivals 2015 impact study', BOP Consulting, www.edinburghfestivalcity.com, viewed 5 May 2020.

Festivals Edinburgh 2018, 'The network effect: the role of the Edinburgh festivals in the national and cultural events sector', BOP Consulting, www.edinburghfestivalcity.com, viewed 5 May 2020.

Festivals Edinburgh n.d., 'About Festivals Edinburgh', www.edinburghfestivalcity.com, viewed 5 May 2020.

Geography Teaching Today 2009, 'Urban regeneration in East London — geography explained' fact sheet, www.geographyteachingtoday.org.uk.

Gibson, C & Stewart, A 2009, *Reinventing Rural Places: The extent and impact of festivals in rural and regional Australia*, Australian Centre for Cultural Environmental Research, Wollongong.

Hall, C & Selwood, J 1995, 'Event tourism and the creation of a postindustrial portscape: the case of Fremantle and the 1987 America's Cup', in *Recreation and tourism as a catalyst for urban waterfront development: an international survey*, eds SJ & M Fagence, Praeger Publishers, Westport, Connecticut.

Handley, K 2015, 'Becoming the Elvis capital of Australia', *ABC Central West NSW*, 7 January, www.abc.net.au, viewed 5 May 2020.

Harris, R & Allen, J 2006, 'Community engagement and events: a study for artsACT', unpublished report by the Australian Centre for Event Management, Sydney.

Hughes, H 1993, 'Olympic tourism and urban regeneration', *Festival Management and Event Tourism*, vol. 1, no. 4, pp. 157–62.

International Association for Public Participation 2010, 'IAP2 Core Values', www.iap2.org.

Kline, J 2005, 'Jeff Kline, guest room: Jeff Kline on TBA going global', www.specialevents.com.

Manchester City Council 2005, 'Regeneration in Manchester statement: regeneration initiatives — East Manchester', www.manchester.gov.uk.

McCall Smith, K 2006, in Shennan R 2020, '15 quotes about Scotland: the most inspiring words about Scotland from the country's actors, writers and sports people', *Edinburgh Evening News*, 7 April, www.edinburghnews.scotsman.com, viewed 1 May 2020.

Myhill, M 2005, 'Return on investment: the bottom line', *MeetingsNet*, 1 September, www.meetingsnet.com.

Ottewell, D 2018, 'The Scottish cities where tourism is booming', *Insider.co.uk*, 23 July, www.insider.co.uk viewed 5 May 2020.

Parkes Elvis Festival 2018, 'Festival history', www.parkeselvisfestival.com.au, viewed 5 May 2020.

Ramsay, R 2007, 'Sony unveils official Aussie PS3 midnight launch event', *Gamespot*, www.gamespot.com, viewed 5 May 2020.

Shone, A 2001, *Successful event management*, Continuum, London.

Silvers, J 2007, 'Event management body of knowledge project', www.juliasilvers.com, viewed 5 May 2020.

Singapore Tourism Board 2014, 'MICE 2020 roadmap report', www.stb.gov.sg.

Sportcal 2018, 'London 2012 Legacy Vision Presented to International Olympic Committee', www.sportcal.com.

The Edinburgh Festival Fringe n.d., 'Chair of board of trustees', www.edfringe.com/uploads/docs/About_Us/Fringe_Society_Chair.pdf, viewed 5 May 2020.

The London Organising Committee of the Olympic Games and Paralympic Games n.d., 'London 2012 Olympic Games Official Report Volume 1', https://stillmed.olympic.org/Documents/Reports/Official%20Past%20Games%20Reports/Summer/2012/ENG/2012-RO-S-London_V1_I_eng.pdf, viewed 27 April 2020.

VisitScotland 2009, 'Scotland, the perfect stage', www.visitscotland.org/events.

VisitScotland 2018a, 'The National Events Strategy', www.visitscotland.org.

VisitScotland 2018b, 'New National Events Strategy', www.visitscotland.org.

VisitScotland 2019, 'Key facts on tourism in Scotland 2018', www.visitscotland.org/binaries/content/assets/dot-org/pdf/research-papers-2/key-facts-on-tourism-in-scotland-2018-v2.pdf, viewed 30 July 2020.

Wangaratta Jazz Festival 2009, www.wangarattajazz.com, viewed 5 May 2020.

Willett, J 2018, Pers. Comm.

ACKNOWLEDGEMENTS

Photo: © ChameleonsEye / Shutterstock.com
Photo: © Alf Manciagli / Shutterstock.com
Extract: © International Olympic Committee
Extract: © International Association for Public Participation www.iap2.org.

CHAPTER 3

The event planning context

LEARNING OBJECTIVES

After studying this chapter, you should be able to:

3.1 identify challenges and opportunities linked to the social, political, legal and regulatory, economic and environmental contexts that might need to be addressed or exploited through the event planning process

3.2 discuss the legacy dimension of events and how to plan for these legacies.

Introduction

It is important at the outset of the event planning process that event organisers understand both the diversity of roles events perform in communities, as well as the many factors that can condition their actions or require responses. Without this understanding, organisers will lack the ability to see their event in its broader societal context and to navigate the complexities this context presents. This chapter seeks to provide this understanding by examining social, political, legal and regulatory, economic and environmental roles events perform, and the challenges and opportunities event managers face within these different settings. Additionally, this chapter explores event legacies, the form these take and how best to ensure their achievement.

3.1 Contexts of event planning

LEARNING OBJECTIVE 3.1 Identify challenges and opportunities linked to the social, political, legal and regulatory, economic and environmental contexts that might need to be addressed or exploited through the event planning process.

Social and cultural context

Many types of events have a direct social and cultural effect on their participants, as well as in some instances, their wider host communities (Hall 1989; Getz 2005). This effect may be as simple as the enjoyment attendees have in the sharing of an entertainment experience with others, or it might extend to the intense feeling of community pride felt by the residents of an area when it hosts a major sporting or cultural event. The euphoria in the city of Newcastle, New South Wales when it became the first regional city to host the A-League Grand Final in 2018 is an example of the latter. In this instance locals reacted to this situation by showing support for their home team (Newcastle Jets) through various actions, including painting their lawns in team colours, dying their hair, renaming their pets in honour of their favourite players and conducting a march through the city (Notzon 2018). This same sense of pride and excitement can be seen when Adelaide was successful in bidding for a leg of the Formula One competition, with researchers noting: 'The Grand Prix in 1985 set Adelaide alive . . . The spirit infected all of us, including large numbers of people who in "normal" times might be expected to be against the notion of this garish, noisy, polluting advertising circus' (Arnold et al. 1989, p. 187). This same 'feel good' factor can be seen more recently in the immense sense of pride demonstrated by the people of China in hosting the Beijing Summer Olympics in 2008, and the people of England in hosting the London Summer Olympics in 2012. The value of this 'feel good' factor of events, particularly large-scale events, can also result in the acceptance by communities of the temporary inconvenience and disruption that can result from them. This acceptance is sometimes made easier by the expectation that longer term benefits such as improved facilities and increased ongoing tourist visitation that may result from an event.

Events also have the power to draw attention to social issues and to aid in their solution. A series of reconciliation marches around Australia in 2000 as part of the National Sorry Day initiative, for example, served to express community support for reconciliation with Aboriginal Australians, and to bring this issue powerfully to the attention of the media. In Sydney, the march took the unprecedented step of closing the Sydney Harbour Bridge, providing a powerful symbolic statement of bridging the gap between Aboriginal and wider Australian communities. The Croc Festival, which was held in multiple locations throughout Australia, sought to perform a similar function, acting to bring young Aboriginal and white Australian youths together with the aim of building partnerships and celebrating youth and traditional culture (Jago et al. 2002). Other more recent examples of events being used in this context include the various climate change marches that have taken place around the world that have sought to focus attention on this issue and stimulate community debate, and the use of events to revitalise communities by helping them heal through bringing residents together and stimulating local economies after the tragic season of bushfires in Australia in 2020 and the ongoing drought which affected many areas. As regards this last issue, the Queensland state government recently announced the Premier's Outback event grants 2019–20 as a way of assisting communities seeking to use events for these purposes. Other positive social roles events can play in community settings include building social capital through such means as deepening and establishing community networks, serving as an outlet for community creativity, expanding cultural perspectives, introducing a community to new and sometimes challenging ideas and assisting in the general development of cultural industries (Hall 1989). An example of the latter is the use of the 2018 Gold Coast Commonwealth Games in Queensland by the Gold Coast City Council to accelerate its efforts at developing the city's cultural industries. The City of the Gold Coast sees arts and culture as 'a key economic driver', and the $30 million associated Cultural Festival 2018 is part of a wider strategy to develop local creative industries in the area (Smith 2018).

The effects on communities of events, however, are not always positive. Arnold et al. (1989), for example, identified 'the hoon effect' in relation to the previously cited 1985 Australian Formula One Grand Prix in Adelaide, when the number of road accident casualties in the five weeks around the event rose by 34 per cent compared with the number in the same period for the previous five years. Accounting for the rising trend of road accident casualties over those years, the researchers calculated that about 15 per cent of these casualties were unexplained, and suggested these could be due to people's off-track emulation of Grand Prix race driving. These community 'spillover' effects can also extend to noise, traffic congestion, crowding and cost inflation in periods leading up to events which can impact housing markets (Getz 2005).

Communities can also find themselves dealing with death and injuries flowing from events. In the Australian context, the tragic drownings during the Sydney to Hobart Yacht Race in 1998, the death of a young rock fan in the mosh pit at the Big Day Out music festival in Sydney in 2001, the death of a competitor in the Southern 80 water skiing competition at Echuca in 2017 and injuries to some 70 people resulting from a crowd crush at the Falls Festival in Lorne in 2016, are all examples of this.

Anti-social behaviour in the form of drunken, rowdy and potentially life and property threatening behaviour by event attendees, is another area where some events present challenges not only for organisers but also their host communities. These problems can be quickly amplified by the media, with subsequent damage to an event's reputation, and can bring about a reappraisal by communities of the benefits of hosting events. Organisers of events as diverse as the Australasian Country Music Festival at Tamworth in New South Wales, Sydney's New Year's Eve celebration, the Australian Motorcycle Grand Prix at Phillip Island in Victoria, Falls Festival (Lorne), the Woodford Folk Festival in Queensland and Schoolies Week on the Queensland Gold Coast have had to develop strategies to handle such behaviour in order to protect their reputation and future viability, as well as maintain their relationship with their host community. While the types of social issues that can arise at individual events will differ it is worth exploring here how several of these events have sought to deal with these challenges.

Schoolies Week began at Surfers Paradise on the Queensland Gold Coast in the 1970s as a celebration marking the end of high school, and a 'rite of passage' for young people entering the adult world. It has since become an Australian tradition and expanded to include other major holiday destinations in most Australian states, as well as Bali, Fiji and Vanuatu. As the event has grown, significant problems have arisen because of the behaviour of its participants, as well as others attracted by the staging of the event. These issues have included alcohol and drug abuse, sexual health problems, sexual assault, drug spiking, participation by cults and evangelists, and suicide. Additionally, host communities have faced problems associated with noise, litter, vandalism and damage to accommodation and other property, and simply being 'crowded out' of their own towns. The original home state of this event, Queensland, which does not promote participation in Schoolies Week, has nonetheless responded to the influx of tens of thousands of young people with the Safer Schoolies Initiative. This initiative is a partnership between various government agencies, community organisations and councils with the intent of both minimising disruption to communities as a result of the event and encouraging safe and responsible behaviour by school leavers. Actions taken as part of this initiative include a highly visible police presence; additional emergency services; improved coordination between council areas affected, volunteers and community organisations; a centralised hotline for complaints and feedback; an official Schoolies Week website; and educational awareness programs in schools. Funding has also been made available for organisations coordinating safety responses during the event to minimise local risks, issues and problems. This funding covers measures such as registration and wrist banding to identify Schoolies; the recruitment and training of volunteers to give advice and support; the provision of free transport; and Schoolies-only activities in alcohol and drug-free environments (Queensland Department of Communities 2010; Queensland Government 2020).

Another example of modifying anti-social behaviour at events is the action taken by the Falls Festival which takes place in four locations in Australia (Byron Bay, Marion Bay, Lorne and Fremantle). In 2018 the organisers of this event sought to counter the incidence of sexual assaults. Following independent research conducted at the Byron Bay iteration of the festival in 2017, its organisers decided to introduce sexual assault counsellors at all sites the following year. Their role was to provide immediate crisis care, introduce victims to local support services for short- and long-term help, and to guide them through the various processes should they want to engage with police. At the same time organisers increased the number of CCTV cameras and security officers in their campgrounds, and trained selected senior staff in psychological first aid, as well as ensuring all staff were aware of how to deal with reports of sexual assault or harassment. These new initiatives joined others that were already in place including a 24-hour attended Patron Safety Hotline, a behavioural guide made available on screens at the event and via the event app, on-site medical services, and the presence of Red Frogs (patron safety volunteers) and PASH, a sexual health consortium (Eliezer 2018). The intent of these actions was summed up by the event's co-producers, Jessica Ducrou and Paul Piticco (as cited in Williams 2018):

> Falls has a zero tolerance policy with regard to dangerous and irresponsible behaviours, the safety of our patrons is our foremost concern . . . We work year-round to bring together incredible events, at some of Australia's most iconic locations — we want everyone to feel free and safe in our spaces . . .

It should also be noted that the broader societal context in the form of customs, traditions, religious beliefs and general social trends has the capacity to affect the way events are planned and delivered and as such event organisers need to be responsive to these factors. The global push towards more environmentally sustainable business practices, the need in some instances to accommodate religious observances (for example, Ramadan) and to be aware of changing cultural attitudes to specific groups within a society (for example, LGBTIQA+ individuals and women) are but a few examples. As regards this last point, it can be seen from the extract below that a failure to embrace changing societal norms can be catastrophic to an event's future (Prynn 2018):

> . . . 360 men at the black-tie Presidents Club Charity Dinner — described as 'the most un-PC event of the year' — were entertained by 130 'hostesses' in short dresses and high heels at The Dorchester . . . many were groped or harassed at a drunken after-party. . .

> . . . two beneficiaries of the event . . . said they were 'shocked' and would return all previous donations . . .

The political context

Politics and politicians are an important part of contemporary event management. Ever since the Roman emperors discovered the power of the circus to deflect criticism and shore up popularity, shrewd politicians have had an eye for events that will keep the population happy and themselves in power. No less an authority than Count Niccolo Machiavelli (1515), adviser to the Medicis in the sixteenth century, had this to say on the subject:

> A prince must also show himself a lover of merit, give preferment to the able and honour those who excel in every art . . . Besides this, he ought, at convenient seasons of the year, to keep the people occupied with festivals and shows; and as every city is divided into guilds or into classes, he ought to pay attention to all these groups, mingle with them from time to time, and give them an example of his humanity and munificence, always upholding, however, the majesty of his dignity, which must never be allowed to fail in anything whatever (Machiavelli 1962).

The British Royal House of Windsor took this advice to heart, providing some of the most popular public events of the past century, with the coronation of Queen Elizabeth II, the fairytale-like wedding of Prince Charles and Princess Diana, and more recently the Queen's Diamond Jubilee, and the weddings of Prince William and Catherine Middleton, and Prince Harry and Meghan Markle. Successive Australian politicians have continued to use the spotlight offered by different events to build their personal profiles and gain political advantage. A former South Australian Premier, Don Dunstan, used the Adelaide Festival, for example, to create an image of Adelaide as the 'Athens of the South' and of himself as a visionary and enlightened leader. Former Prime Minister Bob Hawke bathed in the glory of Alan Bond's America's Cup victory in Fremantle, while a past Victorian Premier, Jeff Kennett, used events such as the Australian Formula One Grand Prix to create an image of himself as a 'winner' — and of former New South Wales Premier Bob Carr as a 'loser' — as he sought to position his state capital, Melbourne, ahead of Sydney as Australia's event capital.

Governments internationally have realised the capacity of events to raise the profile of politicians and the cities and states that they govern. Events gain media coverage and notoriety, and at the same time they attract visitors and therefore create economic benefits and jobs. This potent mixture has prompted governments to become major players in bidding for, hosting, staging and supporting events. Reflective of this last point are the various grants and support services that federal, state and local governments now provide for events (see the chapter on event tourism planning).

This increasing involvement of governments in events has, to a degree, politicised the public events landscape. As Hall (1989) notes:

Politics are paramount in hallmark events. It is either naïve or duplicitous to pretend otherwise. Events alter the time frame in which planning occurs and they become opportunities to do something new and better than before. In this context, events may change or legitimate [sic] political priorities in the short term and political ideologies and socio-cultural reality in the longer term. Hallmark events represent the tournaments of old, fulfilling psychological and political needs through the winning of hosting over other locations and the winning of events themselves. Following a hallmark event some places will never be the same again, physically, economically, socially and, perhaps most importantly of all, politically.

Arnold et al. (1989, pp. 191–2) is of a similar view:

Governments in power will continue to use hallmark events to punctuate the ends of their periods in office, to arouse nationalism, enthusiasm and finally, votes. They are cheaper than wars or the preparation for them. In this regard, hallmark events do not hide political realities, they are the political reality.

Events also have a role to play in promoting international cooperation, as is evidenced by the co-hosting of the Soccer World Cup by Japan and Korea in 2002, and the combined entry of the North and South Korean teams into the stadium at the Opening Ceremony of the PyeongChang Winter Olympics in Korea in 2018. They can also serve to showcase emerging nations and economies, as was the case with the Beijing Olympic Games in 2008 and the Commonwealth Games in Delhi in 2010. Events can also stimulate action by governments around issues of national and international importance. The watershed United Nations Conference on Environment and Development ('The Earth Summit') in Rio de Janeiro in 1992, and the subsequent conference in Paris in 2015 leading to the Paris Climate Agreement are examples of where events can serve this role. On the other hand, it should also be pointed out that events can have a more sinister political overtone, as was the case with the use of the Nuremberg Rallies by Adolf Hitler in Nazi Germany, and of the many political rallies that have been, and still are, conducted in Russia, China and North Korea by their leaders which are designed to stir nationalist sentiment.

The legal and regulatory context

Event organisers need to operate within the legal and regulatory context. As such they must be aware of the multitude of the laws and operational requirements to which they must adhere. These can extend to areas such as equal opportunity, disability discrimination (see figure 3.1), health and safety at work, data protection, requirements for staff working with young people, alcohol licensing and regulations around food hygiene, gas and electrical equipment and temporary structures. Additionally, organisers may need to adhere to conditions imposed on them by police or public authorities when using public spaces or closing public roads. As this aspect of event management can be very complex, various guides have been produced by government agencies that include coverage of legal and regulatory issues (for example, NFP Law, see w ww.nfplaw.org.au/events). A detailed discussion of legal aspects of conducting events appears in the legal considerations in event planning and management chapter.

FIGURE 3.1   Excerpt from Equal Access's fact sheet on accessibility in public events

Accessibility in public events

This information has been prepared by Equal Access to provide guidance on access requirements to all parties involved in the festival and event industry.

According to a 2009 survey by the Australian Bureau of Statistics there are four million people in Australia with a disability, which equates to 18.5% of the population.

It is clear from recent complaints made to the Australian Human Rights Commission that accessible features in events continue to be misunderstood and overlooked. Failure to successfully plan for the needs of people with disability presents a significant risk to event organisers if not carefully considered at all stages of an event. There is however little guidance material available to provide advice on how these risks can be reduced and how compliance with applicable legislative requirements can be achieved.

On 1 May 2011 the Commonwealth Disability (Access to Premises — Buildings) Standards 2010 (Premises Standards) were introduced and adopted into the Building Code of Australia as well as state based legislation, including the Victorian building regulations.

The objectives of the Premises Standards are to ensure that 'dignified, equitable, cost-effective and reasonably achievable access to buildings, and facilities and services within buildings, is provided for people with a disability'.

The Premises Standards applies to new buildings and existing buildings being altered and sets out clear parameters for access requirements. However, as access is improved within the built environment it is also reasonable for members of the community to expect that good access is provided to events, festivals and temporary structures (such as marquees, event tents, exhibition spaces etc.).

If an event organiser fails to acknowledge accessibility as a critical component of their event plan it will present a major risk to the organisation under the *Commonwealth Disability Discrimination Act 1992*. A person with a disability could make a complaint to the Human Rights Commission under Section 23 Access to Premises, or Section 24 Goods, services and facilities. There have already been a number of such complaints made to the Commission which have been resolved through a conciliation process.

It is therefore important for all parties involved in events to consider accessibility in the early stages of event planning. This will not only reduce risk but increase the potential for increased attendance rates and the overall success of an event.

Access considerations:
When preparing an event plan, the following must be considered to provide equitable and dignified access:
- Choosing the right venue
- Providing information about the event
- Travelling to the event
- Arriving at the event
- Entering the event
- Moving around the event
- Accessing goods and services within the event
- Using facilities within the event
- Obtaining further assistance
- Emergency management

Where to get help:
Equal Access are perfectly positioned to assist with providing access advice for festivals and events. We are one of Australia's leading Accredited Disability Access Consultancies and are registered with the Association of Consultants in Access Australia. For a number of years we have provided a specialist consulting service to enhance the built environment and to provide 'Equal Access' for members of the community with disability.

Equal Access has also prepared an Event Access Checklist.

Source: Equal Access n.d.

Environmental context

Events in some instances can be leveraged to showcase, through the media and other means, the unique characteristics of a host environment. Selling the image of a hallmark event commonly includes marketing the intrinsic properties of the location where it is taking place. The 2018 Gold Coast Commonwealth Games, for example, provided a significant opportunity to enhance international awareness of the tourism attributes of the state of Queensland and of Australia more generally. This opportunity was taken up by Tourism and Events Queensland, Destination Gold Coast and Australia's tourism promotion body, Tourism Australia (Tourism Australia n.d.). This same event demonstrated how events can be used to bring about change in the environmental practices of organisations, such as suppliers and sporting organisations associated with it, as well as in its staff and attendees (Gold Coast 2018 Commonwealth Games Corporation 2018). Further examples of how events can be leveraged for environmental sustainability purposes can be found in the chapter on sustainable event planning.

In the staging of large events, the provision of infrastructure is often a costly budget component, but this expenditure can result in an improved physical environment and facilities for their host communities. There are a number of examples of this in the Australian context. Brisbane, for example, benefited from the transformation of its Expo 88 site into the South Bank leisure and entertainment precinct, while the Sydney Olympic Games left a substantial built legacy of sporting facilities and transport infrastructure, along with a much cleaner environment, at, and around, Sydney Olympic Park. Overseas examples of similar outcomes can also be easily identified. The America's Cup in Auckland in 2000 and 2003, resulted in the transformation of the Auckland waterfront into an up-market restaurant precinct, while Manchester's 2002 Commonwealth Games, London's 2012 Olympics and Glasgow's 2014 Commonwealth Games, all of which took place in run-down areas, generated significant urban renewal outcomes. That said, it must be acknowledged, as Getz (2016) has observed, 'The world is full of over-sized, "white-elephant" arenas and stadia', and as such thorough cost–benefit analysis is required by communities before committing to host such events.

Each event will vary in terms of its potential environmental benefits and costs. The size and complexity of large-scale events may demand formal impact assessment studies, while smaller venue bound events may only need to consider several issues such as waste management, noise and traffic that effective communication with suppliers, attendees and local authorities can go a long way towards addressing. Irrespective of the scale or type of event involved, it is now the case that the issue of planning for more environmentally sustainable outcomes has become a requirement of event production. Reflective of this is the establishment by the International Organization for Standardization of a standard for sustainable event management — ISO 20121 — and the emergence of organisations engaged solely in this area (for example, a Greener Festival, Sustainable Event Alliance) and various event industry initiatives (for example, Event Industry Council Sustainability Initiative).

Other environmental considerations of relevance to events are the increased variability in weather patterns, and the emergence of viruses that can quickly move between countries and have devastating and relatively long-lasting impacts on the ability of event organisers to host events. The novel coronavirus (COVID-19), for example, has led to unprecedented cancelling of events both large and small. At the time of writing, for example, the following cultural events had been cancelled or suspended in the United States: South by Southwest Festival (Austin, TX), Ultra Music Festival, New York City Half Marathon, NCAA basketball conference championship.

Economic context

The strong growth of the festival and special event sector is part of a general economic trend away from an industrial product base to a more service-based economy. Traditionally, communities and governments have staged events for their perceived social, cultural and/or sporting benefits and value. This situation began to change dramatically in the early 1980s when major events in many parts of the world became regarded as desirable commodities for their perceived ability to deliver economic benefits through their capacity to generate visitor expenditure, create employment and leave an infrastructure legacy.

Mules (1999) dates this change in attitude in Australia to around 1982–86, with the staging of the Commonwealth Games in Brisbane (1982), the Formula One Grand Prix in Adelaide (1985) and the America's Cup defence in Fremantle (1986–87). He notes that state governments began around this same time to become aware of the economic potential of events, aided by studies such as that of the Adelaide Formula One Grand Prix (Burns, Hatch and Mules, cited in Mules 1999), which established that the income generated by the event exceeded the cost of staging it to the South Australian Government. Not surprisingly, Australian state governments began to pursue vigorous event strategies after this time, building strong portfolios of annual events and aggressively bidding for the right for their state to host major one-off events. Apart from interstate rivalry and political kudos, what motivates and justifies this level of government involvement in what otherwise might be seen as largely commercial enterprises? According to Mules (1999), the answer lies in what he terms the 'spillover effects' of events. While many major events might make an operational loss, they produce benefits for related industry sectors such as travel, accommodation, restaurants, hirers and suppliers of equipment and so on. They may also produce long-term benefits such as an enhanced destination image that can stimulate post-event visitation. As a single organisation or business type (for example, accommodation providers) cannot capture the wide range of economic benefits events provide, and cannot afford to independently underwrite them, governments are often called upon to play a role in funding or supporting them so that these generalised benefits might be obtained.

By stimulating activity in the host economy, expenditure associated with events can also have a positive effect on employment. Employment multipliers measure how many full-time equivalent (FTE) job opportunities are supported as the result of conducting an event. However, it is easy to overestimate this number as the jobs created by major events tend to be short term in nature and employers often meet this demand by using their existing staff more (through overtime), rather than employing new staff members. Nonetheless, major events can generate substantial employment. For example, a comparison of economic impact studies of recent Commonwealth Games revealed the following statistics on FTE jobs created (Duc Pham et. al 2018):

- Manchester 2002 — 6300
- Melbourne 2006 — 13 600
- Glasgow 2014 — 2100
- Gold Coast 2018 — 16 440.

Events can also provide their host communities with a strong platform for showcasing their expertise, hosting potential investors and promoting new business opportunities. During the Sydney 2000 Olympics, for example, the New South Wales Government spent $3.6 million on a trade and investment drive coinciding with the event (Humphries 2000). This effort led to more than 60 business-related events, board meetings of international companies, briefings and trade presentations being held in Sydney at the time of the Olympics. Additionally, 46 international chambers of commerce were briefed on business opportunities, and more than 500 world business leaders, Olympic sponsors and New South Wales corporate executives attended four promotional events. State treasurer at the time, Michael Egan, was quoted as saying, 'We'll be benefiting from the Games well after we think the benefits have worn off and in ways that will never show up in statistics' (Humphries 2000). Similar business development strategies accompanied the staging of the World Rugby Cup in Australia 2003, the Melbourne Commonwealth Games in 2006, the World Swimming Championships in Melbourne in 2007 and the Gold Coast Commonwealth Games in 2018. It is noteworthy, however, that little research has been done on analysing such strategies and quantifying the amount of business that they generate. One such effort, *The Australian Olympic Caravan*, a book by Cashman and Harris (2012), sought to examine the involvement of Australian businesses and individuals that 'cut their teeth' on the Sydney 2000 Olympic Games in some 13 subsequent large-scale events around the world, and while not quantifying these outcomes, were able to identify the businesses that had benefited along with the products and services that they provided to these events.

While the economic impacts of major events on their host cities are generally well documented, the effects of local events are not as well researched, although many such events have in recent years sought to quantify these outcomes as a means of maintaining or gaining government support. One of the few studies in this area is that of Gibson and Stewart (2009). They examined regional festivals in New South Wales, Victoria and Tasmania, and found that although festival organisers themselves may make little or no direct profit, festivals benefit many functionally related local small businesses such as cafes and restaurants, hotels and motels, pubs, sound and lighting suppliers, printers, advertising agencies, legal services, catering companies and petrol stations. They also found that the majority of inputs (for example, staff, catering and staging) were sourced locally thus limiting the leakage of event-related expenditure to outside areas.

Another, often overlooked, economic benefit of events is knowledge transfer and the development and enhancement of professional, business and researcher networks that result from the conduct of business events. Specifically, these events allow delegates to share research and ideas, build relationships that lead to grant and research collaborations and set agendas for their disciplines (Foley et al. 2013). Additionally, they expose their delegates to cutting edge knowledge, techniques and technologies from around the globe, that can then be implemented in their workplaces, often to the benefit of the broader community. Further, business events attract global talent, catalyse industry sectors, drive innovation and social change, and serve as an effective meeting place for academics and practitioners where partnerships can be forged that are critical for innovation and knowledge economies (Edwards et al. 2017). These benefits are increasingly profiled through websites such as The Iceberg (www.the-iceberg.org) and Business Events Sydney (www.besydney.com.au). Indeed, as Edwards et al. (2017) point out, conferences have played a role in some of the most significant global discoveries of the last 50 years. These types of outcomes raise the issue of how events can be designed to leverage this potential. The International Convention Centre in Sydney, for example, has given this issue some thought and has developed several initiatives in this area. For example, its Innovators and Entrepreneurs program aims to provide NSW entrepreneurs and startups with exhibition space and communication platforms at conferences so they can connect with relevant delegates.

3.2 Event legacies

LEARNING OBJECTIVE 3.2 Discuss the legacy dimension of events and how to plan for these legacies.

In recent years the emphasis of governments seeking to host events has shifted from short-term to long-term outcomes (often referred to as the legacy of events). Thus an event with an operational balance sheet that reflects a loss — that is, its costs outweigh its income — may nonetheless be supported as it has the capacity to generate a long-term positive legacy in the form of improved infrastructure, transport and communication facilities, urban regeneration and increased awareness of the host destination.

As yet there are very few longitudinal studies that are able to trace the long-term benefits of mega-events, and over time, the influence of other mitigating factors obscures them, making such benefits difficult to trace. For example, tracing the long-term tourism impacts of the Sydney 2000 Olympics would involve separating out the negative counter-impacts of events such as the September 11 attacks, the SARS epidemic and the 2008–09 global financial crisis — a difficult, if not impossible, task.

Nevertheless, the legacy of events has become a significant factor in event planning, influencing the thinking of governments, and the philosophy and approach of organisations such as the International Olympic Committee (IOC). This organisation, for example, requires bidding cities for their summer and winter Games, to address the legacy issue and actively promotes the various legacies that have emerged from its past events. As an example of the types of legacies an individual event might be leveraged to produce, when hosting the 2018 Gold Coast Commonwealth Games, the Queensland Government created the Embracing 2018 Legacy Program. This program included among its legacy aspirations: enduring jobs and powering economic growth; accelerating the Gold Coast to a world-class boutique city; and active, engaged and inclusive communities. Further, it sought 31 benefits and opportunities across eight themes including:

- economic growth and tourism
- inspiring games
- sport and healthy lifestyles
- trade
- Aboriginal and Torres Strait Islander initiatives
- engaged and inclusive communities
- art and culture
- supporting Queensland business.

Additionally, the program included mechanisms for delivering and measuring its achievements. The final legacy report for the event demonstrated that it had been successful in achieving the vast majority of the outcomes sought. In the context of the event's economic legacy, for example, the event was estimated to have resulted in a $2.5 billion boost to Queensland's Gross State Product (GSP), after considering the state's $1.34 billion investment. To generate economic and other types of legacy outcomes, as Thomson et al. (2009) point out, it is important that, as was the case with this event, a strategic management approach is taken to legacy promises and planning. A key aspect of this approach should be, as Foley, Edwards, Jasovska and Hergesell (2019) note, the establishment of legacy objectives at the outset of the planning process.

SUMMARY

The event planning process requires an understanding of the context in which events operate. This context has multiple dimensions — societal, legal and regulatory, political, economic and environmental. Event organisers need to establish how these factors might influence their specific circumstances so that they can avoid any pitfalls (for example, changing cultural mores), appreciate how various stakeholders might view their events, be alert to those things their planning must embrace, and identify the opportunities inherent in their event and how these might be exploited or leveraged. This chapter has also highlighted the potential some events hold to generate a range of legacies, largely of a social, economic or environmental nature. To achieve these outcomes, it has emphasised that legacy considerations must be part of an event's overall planning process, with specific objectives used to focus and drive the results sought in this area.

QUESTIONS

1 Discuss, giving examples, how events can draw attention to social issues and aid in their solution.
2 Identify an event that you know has been marred by social problems or bad crowd behaviour. As the event manager, what would you have done to manage the situation and improve the outcomes of the event?
3 Explain why customs, traditions, religious beliefs or general social trends should be a consideration for an event organiser.
4 For what political purposes might governments, or individual politicians, seek to leverage events?
5 Select, and discuss, one area of the law that might affect the event planning process.
6 List and describe what you consider to be the main reasons why governments support events.
7 What does legacy planning involve, and why has it become so integral to the event planning process for larger scale events?

CASE STUDY

CAMPAIGNING AGAINST CLIMATE CHANGE

One day in late August, activist Tamsin Omond was struck with a brilliant idea. She was at the Climate Camp at Kingsnorth and reading a book about the Suffragettes. In it, she noticed a date: 13 October 1908. It was the day the Suffragettes rushed Parliament, when more than 60 000 people rallied in Parliament Square and groups of Suffragettes tried to force their way past police lines. Thirty-seven people were arrested. It got her thinking. What if, to mark the centenary of the rush, there were to be a protest in Parliament Square, this time to lobby for climate action rather than women's rights. And so the idea for the Climate Rush 2008 was born. Time was ticking, though: there were only two months to go before October.

As a member of the protest group Plane Stupid and one of the so-called 'Commons Five' who scaled the roof of the Houses of Parliament in February 2008, Tamsin is no stranger to radical antics — although the bail conditions that arose from her subsequent arrest made a return to Parliament a risky one. Then there were the nuts and bolts of putting the event together. Spotting a ripe opportunity for a protest is one thing — actually pulling it off is another. On 8 October 2008 more than 1000 people turned up in Parliament Square. It made for an extraordinary scene. Many wore Edwardian costume, hundreds wore Suffragette-style red sashes emblazoned with the slogans 'Climate Code Red', 'No Airport Expansion', 'No New Coal' and 'Reform Climate Policy'. One banner read 'Well-Behaved Women Never Made History'.

After hearing speeches from the likes of veteran feminist and sustainable food champion Rosie Boycott and Green MEP Caroline Lucas, a group broke police lines, lightly vaulted makeshift barriers and rushed towards the doors of Parliament. Fists banging against closed doors they chanted 'Deeds Not Words'.

What began as a single event has now grown into a high-profile environmental activist group inspired by the actions of the Suffragettes. The Climate Rush has since staged the infamous Edwardian picnic at Heathrow Terminal 1 and more recently the No New Coal Awards, among other acts of 'peaceful civil disobedience'. You've probably read about them in the press. The events tend to get coverage because of their innovative nature. More imaginative than protest marches, they blend costume, humour and entertainment with a strong environmental message. They're planning an event a month until Copenhagen in December.

Like anyone who is clued into the science and urgency of climate change Tamsin realises that we need to get things moving more quickly and that we need more people shouting louder for change. And that there is power in numbers. 'At Parliament Square nothing would have happened if there were 100 people,' she says. 'It's this thing of critical mass. Everyone sort of knew that it was celebrating the 100th anniversary of when the Suffragettes rushed Parliament and that at 7.30 they might be expected to rush. It's about creating a context wherein something that is ostensibly legal, like standing in Parliament Square, becomes something where so much more can happen just because of a collective group.'

The Climate Rush, intended to be a one-off event, evolved into an ongoing campaign group. 'There was an unexpected amount of support for it,' says Tamsin. 'We had loads of women saying, "We love this and we really want you to do something else." They liked the creative, inclusive thing about it.'

One of the aims of Climate Rush is to make direct action more accessible and engage average people who would never have thought of themselves as activists. 'We need to wake up a lot of people to the fact that this really is the defining issue and is going to be hugely impactful on all our lives,' she says. And for those people who are awake it gives them something they can do that is more than simply changing their lightbulbs or individual way of life, but maybe less than getting involved in a more covert group where you know you may get arrested. At a Climate Rush event you can go along and think 'maybe if I do something I might get arrested but actually I can just stand back and watch it happen.'

Following the Parliament Square Rush, newly recruited climate Suffragettes didn't have long to wait for the next event: 'Dinner at Domestic Departures' on 12 January. The mission? To protest against Heathrow expansion plans and domestic flights. The method was inspired and the resulting scene memorably absurd: 250 Climate Rushers were briefed beforehand to enter Terminal 1 under the guise of normal travellers but to wear turn-of-the-century-style clothing underneath their coats ('think Mary Poppins for style'). In their carry-on wheelie cases were picnics, tea and cake, blankets, cushions, foldout chairs and tablecloths. At 7 pm, when the string quartet played its first note, picnic blankets reading 'No Domestic Departures' and 'Climate Chaos — It's No Picnic' were rolled out and sat on. Picknickers then tucked into cucumber sandwiches, samosas and cloudy lemonade. After dinner began the dancing — a conga round the terminal.

The police were 'somewhat bemused — and out in their hundreds' but ultimately, as the protest was peaceful, what could they do? There was no disruption to flights. The picnic at Heathrow was widely covered in the media, which Tamsin sees as a useful tool. 'If the climate movement had the same advertising budget as Coca-Cola then we'd be fine. Everyone would want to be green. But in a way the coverage we get is our form of getting the message out there for free. The media is our loudspeaker.'

In March, the Climate Rush organised the No New Coal Awards — an event designed to 'highlight the ridiculousness' of the UK Coal Awards Ceremony due to take place in a swanky London hotel. 'The absurdity at having an awards ceremony for the coal industry at a time of climate crisis . . . We want to draw attention to the issue of coal being the dirtiest way to produce electricity.'

Rushers were invited to 'dress formally for cocktails' in the Landmark Hotel's Winter Garden, where the awards were due to take place. The idea was to schmooze with the industry and challenge them. 'What I love about the Rush is that it's people you can relate to and who could be your daughter or wife or mother — or whatever boy version. So you've got a 19-year-old about to go to university asking you, "Why are you being so self-congratulatory? Can you at least be a little bit ashamed?"'

As it turned out, unbeknown to the Rushers, the coal industry had done a crafty change of location. Unperturbed, the mock awards went ahead as planned, giving out six papier-mâché canary-shaped awards, representing the birds used to detect lethal gas in coalmines. 'They also represent the arctic ice caps, which are the canaries of our world. They have started melting — a warning sign to us.' Categories included Best Supporting Role, which went to 'the biggest climate coward' Gordon Brown, and UK Coal Personality of the Year, which went to the CEO of E.ON for outstanding services to greenwash (while plotting to build Kingsnorth).

Spirited and strategic, it's a form of protest that does things creatively and yet is still challenging. 'One of the reasons why our generation is protesting in this way is because we are the anti-Iraq-War-march generation,' Tamsin says. 'We understand the Government's reaction to marches.' This year, however, she thinks the feeling of disempowerment seems to be turning, what with the Obama frenzy. People are realising 'they can make things happen and put the right people in the right place — but you have to get a bit more involved'. Tamsin has a refreshing faith in people power: 'Every individual is as powerful as he or she realises themselves to be. Just divert your being into it.'

What's the bravest thing she's ever done? 'I don't know. I think I'm mostly reckless rather than brave.' Reluctant to appear like some kind of heroine she instead shifts the conversation to the wider cause. 'It's the thing with the Suffragettes again: 100 000 women were prepared potentially to risk prison because there was this huge issue. That's the thing that really inspires me to act — that and the knowledge that how the future is going to look is so much defined by our actions now.'

Source: Adapted from Laura Sevier 2009, 'Case study: campaigning against climate change', *The Ecologist*, 1 May, originally published at www.theecologist.org/2009/may/01/casestudy-campaigning-against-climate-change.

QUESTIONS

1 What role are events being used to perform in this case study?

2 What are the potential dangers of conducting these types of events, most particularly to the causes they are seeking to draw attention to?

3 Why have the events documented here been successful in drawing attention to the issues they are focused on? How important has 'creativity of concept' been in their success?

REFERENCES

Arnold, A, Fischer, A, Hatch, J & Paix, B 1989, 'The Grand Prix, road accidents and the philosophy of hallmark events', in *The planning and evaluation of hallmark events*, eds. GJ Syme, BJ Shaw, DM Fenton & WS Avebury, Aldershot.

Cashman, R & Harris, R 2012, *The Australian Olympic caravan from 2000 to 2012: a unique Olympic events industry*, Walla Walla Press, Petersham, NSW.

Duc Pham, T, Xin Jin, C, Naranpanawa, A, Bandaralage, J & Carmignani, F 2018, 'The economic impacts of the 2018 Gold Coast Commonwealth Games', www.embracing2018.com/sites/default/files/gc-2018-economic-benefits-griffith-uni-report.pdf, viewed 10 February 2019.

Edwards, D, Foley, C & Malone, C 2017, *The Power of Conferences: Stories of serendipity, innovation and driving social change*, UTS ePress, Sydney, doi.org/10.5130/ 978-0-6481242-0-7.

Eliezer, C 2018, 'Falls Festival announces more initiatives to protect patrons against sexual assault', *The Music Network*, 18 August, www.themusicnetwork.com/falls-festival-announces-more-initiatives-to-protect-patrons-against-sexual-assault, viewed 18 March 2020.

Equal Access n.d., 'Accessibility in public events', www.disabilityaccessconsultants.com.au, viewed 19 March 2020.

Foley, C, Edwards, D, Jasovska, P & Hergesell, A 2019, 'Business event legacies: JMIC case study project report', http://hdl.handle.net/10453/135365, viewed 7 May 2020.

Foley, C, Schlenker, K, Edwards, D & Lewis-Smith, L 2013, 'Determining Business Event Legacies Beyond the Tourism Spend: an Australian case study approach', *Event Management: An International Journal*, vol. 17 (3), pp. 311–22.

Getz, D 2005, *Event management and event tourism*, Cognizant Communication Corporation, New York.

Getz, D 2016, 'Revised event portfolio models', https://donaldgetzprofessor.files.wordpress.com/2016/10/donald-getz-event-portfolio-paper-oct-2016.pdf, viewed 7 May 2020.

Gibson, C & Stewart, A 2009, *Reinventing rural places: the extent and impact of festivals in rural and regional Australia*, Australian Centre for Cultural Environmental Research, Wollongong.

Gold Coast 2018 Commonwealth Games Corporation 2018, 'Post-Games sustainability report', www.gc2018.com/sites/default/files/2018-08/Sustainability%20Report%20-%20Post%20Games%20(Final).pdf, viewed 19 March 2020.

Hall, C 1989, 'Hallmark events and the planning process', in *The planning and evaluation of hallmark events*, eds. G Syme, B Shaw, D Fenton & W Avebury, Aldershot.

Humphries, D 2000, 'Benefit to economy is unseen', *The Sydney Morning Herald*, 23 August, p. 8.

Jago, L, Chalip, L, Brown, G, Mules, T & Ali, S 2002, 'The role of events in helping to brand a destination' in *Events and place making: proceedings of International Research Conference held in Sydney 2002*, eds. L Jago, M Deery, R A Hede & J Allen, Australian Centre for Event Management, Sydney.

Machiavelli, N 1962 & 1515, *The Prince*, trans. L Ricci, Mentor Books, New York.

Mules, T 1999, 'Estimating the economic impact of an event on a local government area, region, state or territory', in *Valuing tourism: methods and techniques*, eds. K A Allcock, T Frost & L Johnson, Bureau of Tourism Research, Canberra.

Notzon, N 2018, 'A-league grand final fever in Newcastle as Jets bid for glory', *ABC News*, www.abc.net.au/news/2018-05-03/finals-fever-newcastle-in-the-grips-of-the-a-league-spell/9722388, viewed 18 March 2020.

Prynn, J, Bentham, M, Moore-Bridger, B & Murphy, J 2018, 'City sexists at Presidents Club Charity Dinner told "your time is up" after undercover sting shames raucous behaviour', *Evening Standard*, 24 January, www.standard.co.uk/news/london/city-sexists-told-your-time-is-up-after-undercover-sting-shames-raucous-presidents-club-charity-a3748261.html, viewed 19 March 2020.

Queensland Department of Communities 2010, 'Safer Schoolies Initiative', www.communityservices.qld.gov.au.

Queensland Government 2020, 'Safer Schoolies Initiative', www.saferschoolies.qld.gov.au, viewed 15 March 2020.

Sevier, L 2009, 'Case study: campaigning against climate change', *The Ecologist*, 1 May, www.theecologist.org/2009/may/01/case-study-campaigning-against-climate-change, viewed 19 March 2020.

Smith, A 2018, 'How the Gold Coast games transformed a resort region into a city', *The Conversation*, 13 April, www.theconversation.com/how-the-gold-coast-games-transformed-a-resort-region-into-a-city-94877, viewed 19 March 2020.

Thomson, A, Schlenker, K & Schulenkorf, N 2009, 'The legacy-factor: towards conceptual clarification in the sport event context', in *The proceedings of The International Event Management Summit held in Surfers Paradise in July 2009*, ed J Allen, Australian Centre for Event Management, Sydney.

Tourism Australia n.d., 'Gold Coast 2018 Commonwealth Games', www.tourism.australia.com/en/about/our-campaigns/past-campaigns/gold-coast-2018-commonwealth-games.html, viewed 19 March 2020.

Williams, T 2018, 'Falls Festival Announces New Safety Measures, Following Alleged Assaults', *Music Feeds*, 15 August, www.musicfeeds.com.au.

ACKNOWLEDGEMENTS

Photo: © ArliftAtoz2205 / Shutterstock.com
Figure 3.1: © Equal Access
Case study: © Laura Sevier / *The Ecologist*. All rights reserved. Reproduced by permission.

CHAPTER 4

Conceptualising the event

LEARNING OBJECTIVES

After studying this chapter, you should be able to:

4.1 identify the range of stakeholders in an event and describe and balance the overlapping and sometimes conflicting needs of stakeholders

4.2 describe the different types of host organisations for events and discuss trends and issues in society that affect events

4.3 understand how to engage sponsors as partners in events

4.4 understand the role of the media in events

4.5 identify the unique elements and resources of an event

4.6 understand the process of developing an event concept and understand the importance of designing the event experience

4.7 apply the screening process to evaluate the feasibility of an event concept.

Introduction

A crucial element in the creation of an event is the understanding of the event environment. The context in which the event is to take place will play a major role in determining the event concept. In order to understand this environment, the event manager must first identify the major players — the stakeholders who are the people and organisations likely to be affected by it. The event manager must then examine the objectives of these major players — what each of them expects to gain from the event, and what forces acting on them are likely to affect their response to the event. Once this environment is understood, the event manager is then in the best position to marshal the creative elements of the event, and to shape and manage them to achieve the best outcomes for the event. Here, design will play a key role in shaping the experience to be provided for event participants. This chapter examines the key stakeholders in events, and outlines some of the processes that event managers can use to devise creative and successful event concepts.

4.1 Stakeholders in events

LEARNING OBJECTIVE 4.1 Identify the range of stakeholders in an event and describe and balance the overlapping and sometimes conflicting needs of stakeholders.

As discussed in the previous chapters, events have rapidly become professionalised and are increasingly attracting the involvement and support of governments and the corporate sector. One aspect of this growth is that events are now required to serve a multitude of agenda. It is no longer sufficient for an event to meet just the needs of its audience. It must also embrace a plethora of other requirements, including government objectives and regulations, media requirements, sponsors' needs and community expectations.

People and organisations with a legitimate interest in the outcomes of an event are known as stakeholders. These will include internal stakeholders, such as the host organisation, staff and volunteers, and external stakeholders, such as media, the host community and regulatory bodies. The successful event manager must be able to identify the range of stakeholders in an event and manage their individual needs, which will sometimes overlap and conflict (figure 4.1). As with event impacts, the event will be judged by its success in balancing the competing needs, expectations and interests of a diverse range of stakeholders. For example, the media organisation doing a live broadcast of an event may require it to be held in prime time, which may not be suitable for participants and attendees. When questioned on the reasons for the success of the Sydney Summer Olympics, chief executive of the Sydney Organising Committee for the Olympic Games (SOCOG) Sandy Hollway attributed the effective coordination and management of a large and diverse range of stakeholders (Hollway 2002).

| FIGURE 4.1 | Key stakeholders in events |

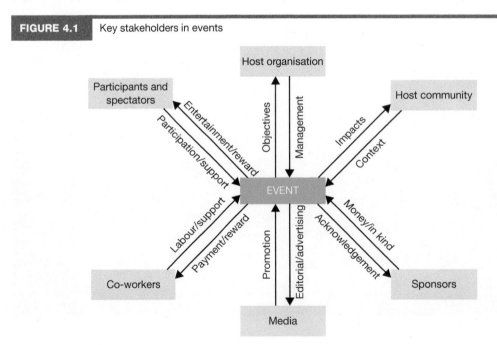

Mal Hemmerling (1997), architect of the Australian Formula One Grand Prix in Adelaide and former chief executive of SOCOG, describes the task of the contemporary event manager as follows:

> So when asked the question 'what makes an event successful', there are now numerous shareholders that are key components of modern major events that are looking at a whole range of different measures of success. What may have been a simple measure for the event organiser of the past, which involved the bottom line, market share, and successful staging of the event are now only basic criteria as the measures by other investors are more aligned with increased tourism, economic activity, tax revenues, promotional success, sustained economic growth, television reach, audience profiles, customer focus, brand image, hospitality, new business opportunities and investment to name but a few.

4.2 The host organisation

LEARNING OBJECTIVE 4.2 Describe the different types of host organisations for events and discuss trends and issues in society that affect events.

As we saw in the chapter on the event planning context, events have become so much a part of our cultural milieu that they can be generated by almost any part of the government, corporate and community sectors (see table 4.1). Governments create events for a range of reasons, including the social, cultural, tourism and economic benefits generated by events. These events are often characterised by free entry and wide accessibility, and form part of the public culture. Government bodies often have a mixed role including not only the generation of events, but also their regulation and coordination, as was discussed in detail in the perspectives on events chapter. The corporate sector is involved in events at a number of levels, including staging their own events, sponsoring events in order to promote their goods and services in the marketplace, and partnering with other events that have a common agenda. These events, although they may still offer free entry, are often targeted at specific market segments rather than at the general public.

These sectors often interact, with public events providing opportunities for corporate sponsorships and hosting.

Within the corporate sector, there are also entrepreneurs whose business is the staging or selling of events. These include sports or concert promoters who present ticketed events for profit, and conference organisers or industry associations who mount conferences or exhibitions for the trade or public — for example, wine shows, equipment exhibitions or medical conferences. Media organisations often become partners in events organised by other groups, but also stage events for their own promotional purposes or to create program content. Examples are radio stations promoting their identity through concerts, newspapers promoting fun runs, or television networks presenting Christmas carol programs live to air.

Other events emanate from the community sector, serving a wide variety of needs and interests. These may include local sporting events, service club fundraisers, car club gatherings, local art and craft shows — the spectrum is as wide as the field of human interest and endeavour. All of these sources combine to create the wonderful tapestry of events that fill our leisure time and enrich our lives.

TABLE 4.1 Event typology

Event generators	Types of event
Government sector	
Central government	• Civic celebrations and commemorations — for example, Australia Day, Anzac Day • State visits and hosting of international government meetings, for example, Association of Southeast Asian Nations (ASEAN)
Event corporations	Major events — focus on sporting and cultural events
Public space authorities	Public entertainment, leisure and recreation events
Tourism	Focus on events that attract visitors, including festivals, special interest and lifestyle events, destinational promotions
Convention bureaus	Meetings, incentives, conventions, exhibitions
Arts	Arts festivals, cultural events, touring programs, themed art exhibitions

(continued)

TABLE 4.1 *(continued)*

Event generators	Types of event
Ethnic affairs	Ethnic and multicultural events
Sport and recreation	Sporting events, hosting of state, national and international championships
Economic development	Focus on events with industry development and job creation benefits
Education	Training and educational events, academic conferences
Local government	Community events, local festivals and fairs
Corporate sector	
Companies and corporations	Promotions, product launches, image-building sponsorships, staff training and incentive events
Industry associations	Industry promotions, trade fairs, conferences
Entrepreneurs	Ticketed sporting events, concerts and exhibitions
Media	Media promotions — for example, concerts, fun runs, appeals
Community sector	
Clubs and societies	Special interest group events
Charities	Fundraising and profile-building events
Sports organisations	Local sporting events

Types of host organisation

Whether events emanate from the corporate, government or community sectors will determine the nature of the host organisation. If the host is from the corporate sector, it is likely to be a company, corporation or industry association. The event manager may be employed directly by the host organisation, or on a contract basis with the organisation as the client. If the host is from the government sector, the host organisation is likely to be a government or council department. Again the event manager may be a direct employee, or a contractor if the event is outsourced. If the host is from the community sector, the host organisation is more likely to be a club, society or committee, with a higher volunteer component in the organisation.

Whatever the host organisation, it is a key stakeholder in the event, and the event manager should seek to clarify its goals in staging the event. These goals will often be presented in a written brief as part of the event manager's job description or contract. Where they are not, it will be worthwhile spending some time to clarify these goals and put them in written form as a reference point for the organisation of the event, and a guideline for the evaluation of its eventual success.

The host community

All events have a specific host community that impacts greatly on the success or failure of the event. This can be the geographical community where the event is located, or a community of interest from which the event draws its participants and spectators. Many researchers (Getz 2005; Goldblatt and Perry 2002; Jago et al. 2002) have recognised the importance of the host community being involved in and 'owning' the event, which in turn emits positive messages to visitors. An example quoted by Jago et al. (2002) is the Gold Coast's Indy Carnival during the lead-up to the Indy 300 race day, where community events helped to create a local atmosphere that contributed to the destination's brand. In another example, a 'My Family's Olympics' competition conducted in China during the Beijing Olympics included a group of children from a mountainous area who organised their own torch relay using sticks of corn as torches, which was filmed by an internet user and broadcast on CCTV.com (Wang 2008).

Many community members actively participate in events in their communities, and act as advocates on behalf of the event to potential participants. The Sydney Gay and Lesbian Mardi Gras and Nimbin's Mardi Grass are examples of events that are fuelled by social activists committed to the goals of the event. Local participation and ownership of events are perhaps most visible in the many local and regional events that continue to exist only because of the committed input of dedicated volunteers. Strategies for community engagement in events were discussed in the perspectives on events chapter under community perspectives on events.

The host community may also include residents, traders, lobby groups and public authorities such as council, transport, police, ambulance and fire brigades. The event manager should aim to identify and involve representatives of these groups, and to consult them in the planning of the event. As discussed in the event planning context chapter, councils may have certain requirements, such as parade and catering permits. Often police and councils will combine to form a 'one-stop shop' for such matters as street closures, special access and parking arrangements. If the event is large enough to impact significantly beyond the boundaries of the venue, a public authorities' briefing may identify innovative ways to minimise the impact and manage the situation. Major events in Sydney such as the New Year's Eve fireworks, Vivid and the City to Surf fun run have been adapted and refined over many years by working in close association with the NSW Event Operations Group (see profile in the perspectives on events chapter).

In addition to formal contact with authorities, the event manager should be aware of the all-important local rumour mill that can often make or break the host community's attitude to the event.

Music festival organisers know only too well the power and impact of word of mouth on festival attendances. The success of music festivals such as the Falls Festival and Splendour in the Grass in recent years has largely been driven by their reputations, making it imperative for the organisers to keep their programs current and in tune with their audiences. The Port Fairy Folk Festival in Victoria and the Woodford Folk Festival in Queensland both sell out with minimal expenditure on publicity, but only because their organisers jealously guard and protect the reputations of their festivals. The effort and cost of maintaining the quality of these events are rewarded by exceptional word of mouth.

General trends in the host community

Event managers need to have a good grasp and understanding of the broad trends and forces acting on the wider community, as these will determine the operating environment of their events. The mood, needs and aspirations of the community will determine its receptiveness to event styles and fashions. Accurately gauging and interpreting these are basic factors in the conceptualising of successful events.

A major factor currently impacting on events is climate change, and the resulting worldwide interest and commitment to sustainability and the protection of the environment. This has given rise to specific events that aim to mobilise public opinion and action. The School Strike for Climate in September 2019 galvanised school children around the world in a mass protest that reverberated in the global media. Earth Hour, which was celebrated in more than 7000 cities in over 180 countries in 2020, encourages people to turn out their lights for an hour in order to show their support for the environment (Earth Hour 2020). The summer bushfires in Australia in 2020 were a dramatic example of the impacts of climate change, causing events to adapt and resulting in the creation of many events as fundraisers for the victims of the fires.

The sustainability issue has also given rise to a wide range of initiatives to green events and reduce their carbon footprint, such as the use of environmentally sustainable products and services, the use of green electrical power, and catering with food sourced from the local district, as will be discussed in more detail in the chapter on sustainable event planning.

Other significant forces currently acting on the community are globalisation and technology, which are combining to make the world seem both smaller and more complex. These forces affect almost every aspect of our lives, including events. As international travel, trade and communications increase, national boundaries and local differences are increasingly subsumed into the global marketplace. The novel coronavirus (COVID-19) pandemic, unfolding as this book went to print, is a graphic example of the impacts and vulnerability resulting from globalisation on international health and the world economy.

This process is accelerated by technology and the media, which have the power to bring significant local events to a worldwide audience, overcoming the barriers of geographic boundaries and cultural differences. This is exemplified by the global television coverage of major sporting events. World championships and mega-events such as the Olympics and World Cup Soccer are beamed instantly to live audiences throughout the world, giving them previously unimagined coverage and immediacy.

As global networks increasingly bring the world into our lounge rooms, the question arises of how local cultures can maintain their own uniqueness and identity in the face of global homogenisation. International arts festivals increasingly draw from the same pool of touring companies to produce similar programs. Local festivals and celebrations must increasingly compete with international products and the raised expectations of audiences accustomed to streamlined television production. The challenge for many events is how to function in this increasingly global environment while expressing the uniqueness of local communities and addressing their specific interests and concerns.

Globalisation also influences corporate events as companies increasingly plan their marketing strategies, including their event components, with potential global audiences in mind. This has resulted in some local Australian event companies being bought out by overseas companies in an attempt to create networks that can serve the international needs of their clients. This approach sometimes comes unstuck as different markets in, say, New York, Sydney and Hong Kong reflect different event needs and audience responses. However, the forces of globalisation are likely to lead to increasing standardisation of the corporate event product and market.

Simultaneously, the all-pervasive internet and advances in information technology are increasing the availability and technological sophistication of events. Event participants now use the internet and mobile phone technology to research events prior to their attendance, to augment the event experience, and to relive the highlights after the event. During the Beijing Olympics, online broadcasts in China far exceeded conventional television broadcasts in terms of total hours. CCTV.com broadcast the Games in cooperation with eight domestic websites, with 6.329 billion page views and 138 million unique visitors per day, greatly outnumbering the 65 million television viewers per day. The general manager of CCTV.com (Wang 2008) commented:

> Different types of media have their own strengths in presenting the Olympic experience: television highlights the feeling of being present at the scene; newspapers and magazines provide in-depth coverage that lasts over time; the Internet delivers instant information and interactivity; mobile TV is portable and is regarded by users as a kind of companion. People select different combinations of media according to their preferences and changing demands.

The use of virtual reality has the power to transform events. In its bid to host the 2022 World Cup, Japan proposed beaming matches directly onto pitches in stadiums throughout the world. This was to be made possible by placing 200 8K Ultra-HD TV cameras around the stadium. This 360-degree coverage would record live matches and provide images to be shown on massive flatbed screens laid on the pitch of 400 stadiums across 208 countries (Tanimoto 2012, as cited in Robertson et al. 2015). More recently, the Adelaide Symphony Orchestra in Australia partnered with the company Jumpgate Virtual Reality to offer virtual reality experiences for audience members. By wearing headsets, the audience was able to mingle with musicians on stage, as well as stand next to the conductor (Keen 2015, as cited in Robertson et al. 2015).

Technology had impacted not just on how audiences receive events, but also on how they are created and delivered. Event managers must be aware of this trend and learn to operate in the new global environment. Event software programs and templates can reduce the planning time of events, and enable event managers to work on several events simultaneously. Social media such as Twitter can be used to track popular trends in the 'Twitter Universe', which can then be incorporated into the theming and content of events. However, despite the increasing technological sophistication, the opportunity that events provide to mix and interact with other people in a live situation remains one of their enduring strengths. Paradoxically, live events may increasingly become the means by which communities affirm their own sense of place, individuality and cultural uniqueness.

4.3 Sponsors

LEARNING OBJECTIVE 4.3 Understand how to engage sponsors as partners in events.

In recent decades, there has been an enormous increase in sponsorship, and a corresponding change in how events are perceived by sponsors. There has been a shift by many large companies from viewing sponsorship largely as a public relations tool generating community goodwill, to regarding it as a primary promotional tool in the marketing mix. Successful major events are now perceived as desirable properties, capable of increasing brand awareness and driving sales. They also provide important opportunities for relationship building through hosting partners and clients. Corporations invest large amounts in event sponsorship, and devote additional resources to supporting their sponsorships, to achieve corporate objectives and sales goals.

In order to attract sponsorships, event managers must offer tangible benefits to sponsors, and effective programs to deliver them. Large corporations such as Coca-Cola and Telstra receive hundreds of sponsorship applications each week, and only consider those events that have a close fit with corporate objectives and a demonstrable ability to deliver benefits.

Sponsors as partners in events

It is important for event managers to identify exactly what sponsors want from an event and what the event can deliver for them. Their needs may be different from those of the host organisation or the event manager. Attendance numbers at the event, for example, may not be as important to them as the media coverage that it generates. It may be important for their chief executive to officiate or to gain access to public officials in a relaxed atmosphere. They may be seeking mechanisms to drive sales, or want to strengthen client relationships through hosting activities. The event manager should take the opportunity to go beyond the formal sponsorship agreement and to treat the sponsors as partners in the event. Some of the best ideas for events can arise from such partnerships. Common agendas may be identified that support the sponsorship and deliver additional benefits to the event.

Countrylink, which runs country rail services to regional New South Wales, sponsors the Parkes Elvis Festival each January by running an Elvis Express train between Sydney and Parkes for the festival. Elvis impersonators entertain passengers on the journey, and the mayor and councillors greet the train in Elvis costumes. The opening of ticket bookings is awaited eagerly each year by Elvis fans, and the available tickets sell out within hours. As a quirky news item, the Elvis Express generates enormous publicity for the festival, and promotes Countrylink as supportive of the local community.

For the FIFA World Cup in Germany in 2006, German Railways provided free domestic rail travel for 6000 overseas media representatives for the duration of the tournament. The selection of the Escort Kids (McDonald's), the Ball Crew (Coca-Cola) and the Flag Bearers (adidas) provided further evidence of the commitment of the official partners and suppliers to staging attractive promotions in partnership with the event (Niersbach 2006). The role of sponsors in events, along with techniques for identifying, sourcing and managing sponsorships, is explored further in the chapter on marketing and sponsorship planning.

4.4 Media

LEARNING OBJECTIVE 4.4 Understand the role of the media in events.

The expansion of the media, and the proliferation of delivery systems such as cable, satellite television and the internet, have created a hunger for media product as never before. The global networking of media organisations and the instant electronic transmission of media images and data have made the global village a media reality. When television was introduced to Australia in time to cover the Melbourne Olympic Games in 1956, the world still relied largely on the physical transfer of film footage to disseminate the images of the Games interstate and overseas. Australia's Bicentennial celebrations in 1988 featured an Australia-wide multidirectional television link-up, which enabled Australians to experience the celebrations simultaneously from a diverse range of locations and perspectives, seeing themselves as a nation through the media as never before. The opening ceremony of the Winter Olympic Games in Nagano in 1998 featured a thousand-member world choir singing together from five different locations on five continents, including the forecourt of the Sydney Opera House. Global television networks followed New Year's Eve of the new millennium around the world, making the world seem smaller and more immediate. When the 2000 Olympics began, a simultaneous global audience estimated at two and a half billion people was able to watch the event tailored to their own national perspectives, with a variety of cameras covering every possible angle. As might be expected, the Beijing Olympic Games attracted the largest global television audience ever, with 4.7 billion viewers — or 70 per cent of the world's population — tuning in over the period of the Games (Nielsenwire 2008).

A good example of how technology can expand exponentially the audience for a local event is Tropfest, which began with a small local audience at a Sydney coffee shop in 1993, and by 2009 was being screened simultaneously to a crowd of 150 000 people in Sydney, Melbourne, Canberra, Perth, Brisbane, Hobart and Adelaide (Conroy 2009). Despite weathering financial challenges and changes in sponsors and venue, Tropfest has been staged in places as far afield as New York, Abu Dhabi, Penang and New Zealand, and in 2018 managed to again reach audiences around Australia through a partnership with the Australian Broadcasting Commission (Tropfest 2018).

Mobile phone applications enable sports fans to access the latest results and news as it happens for a range of sports from their mobile phones. For example, the Optus Stadium app designed for the new Perth Stadium enables attendees to access the stadium event calendar and book tickets, plan their journey to and find their way around the stadium, explore food and drink options and access unique offers and promotions (Optus 2018).

Social media, including Facebook, Twitter, YouTube, Flickr, Instagram, Tumblr and LinkedIn, have made events more personalised in their communication and more interactive. Many events now incorporate social media into their websites, enabling patrons to feed back their comments and opinions, exchange views with other event participants, and even participate in the design and programming of events.

The combination of the event website, social media applications (apps) and social media channels enables event managers to encompass the complex communication needs of the event, and to bring attendees closer to the event, enabling them to become co-creators and to contribute user-generated event content (Inversini and Williams 2017).

This revolution in the media has, in turn, revolutionised the conduct of events. Media innovations such as YouTube have created new forms of virtual events, such as the YouTube Symphony Orchestra, with musicians from 30 countries selected from 3000 musicians by open audition on YouTube, leading to a live performance in Carnegie Hall in April 2009 and available for viewing on YouTube (Nichols 2009). The Portable Film Festival enabled phone owners to participate in a short film festival with selected films downloaded to their phones (Portable Film Festival 2010).

Events now have a virtual existence in the media at least as powerful, sometimes more so, than in reality. The live audience for a sports event or concert may be dwarfed by the television audience. Indeed, the event may be created primarily for the consumption of the television audience. Events have much to gain from this development, including media sponsorships and the payment of media rights. Their value to commercial sponsors is greatly increased by their media coverage and profile. However, the media often directly affect the way events are conceptualised and presented, as in the case of One Day Cricket and Super League, where the competition formats have been modified in order to create more appealing television product. So far, sports events have been the main winners (and losers) from this increased media attention.

The available media technology influences the way that live spectators experience an event. The wiring of the modern stadium allows for digital television and enables every spectator to have a unique seat with personalised communication services. Increasingly, spectators' viewing capabilities are technologically enhanced to parallel those of people watching at home.

Media interest in events continues to grow as their ability to provide saleable product and to attract commercial sponsors is realised. Sporting events, parades, spectacles, concerts and major public celebrations are areas of strong interest to the media, where the imperatives of television production are likely to continue to influence the direction and marketing of events. The role of the media can vary from that of media sponsors to becoming full partners — or even producers — of the event.

Whatever the role of the media, it is important for the event manager to consider the needs of different media groups, and to consult with them as important stakeholders in the event. Once the media are treated as potential partners, they have much to offer the event. The good media representative, like the event manager, is in search of the good idea or unusual angle. Together they might just dream up the unique approach that increases the profile of the event and, in turn, provides value to the media organisation. The print media might agree to publish the event program as editorial or as a special insert, or might run a series of lead-in stories, competitions or special promotions in tandem with sponsors. Radio or television stations might provide an outside broadcast, or might involve their on-air presenters as comperes or special participants in the event. Mobile phone companies and internet providers might integrate their products with the promotion and delivery of the event. This integration of the event with the media provides greater reach and exposure to the event, and, in turn, gives the media organisation a branded association with the event. New media developments and increasingly innovative technologies continue to expand the media dimension of events, and to provide additional opportunities for collaboration between event organisers and the media.

Co-workers

The event team that is assembled to implement the event represents another of the key stakeholders. This team will include not only paid staff members, but often unpaid volunteer workers also. For any event to be truly effective, the vision and philosophy of the event must be shared by all of the team, from key managers, talent and publicist, right through to the stage manager, crew, gatekeepers and cleaners. No matter how big or small, the event team is the face of the event, and each member a contributor to its success or failure.

Goldblatt (1997, p. 129) describes the role of the event manager in this process:

> The most effective event managers are not merely managers, rather, they are dynamic leaders whose ability to motivate, inspire others, and achieve their goals are admired by their followers. The difference between management and leadership is perhaps best characterised by this simple but effective definition: *managers control problems, whereas leaders motivate others to find ways to achieve goals.*

Most people have experienced events that went well overall, but were marred by some annoying detail or shortcoming. There are different ways of addressing such problems, but good teamwork and management are always crucial factors in handling them. The Disney organisation, for example, has a system in which roles, such as performer, cleaner and security, are merged so that staff members consider themselves to be one team looking after the space. The roles tend to ride with the needs of the moment — when the parade comes through the theme park, it is all hands on deck. The daily bulletin issued to all staff members reminds them that customers may visit Disneyland only once in their lives, and their impressions will depend forever on what they experience that day. This is a very positive philosophy that can be applied to all events.

Participants and spectators

Last but not least are the 'punters' on the day — the participants and spectators for whom the event is intended and who ultimately vote with their feet for the success or failure of the event. The event manager must be mindful of the needs of the audience. These include their physical needs, as well as their needs for comfort, safety and security. Over and above these basic requirements is the need to make the event special — to connect with the emotions of the participants. A skilled event manager strives to make events meaningful, magical and memorable. Hemmerling (1997) describes the criteria by which spectators judge an event:

> Their main focus is on the content, location, substance and operation of the event itself. For them the ease with which they can see the event activities, the program content, their access to food and drinks, amenities, access and egress etc., are the keys to their enjoyment. Simple factors such as whether or not their team won or lost, or whether they had a good experience at the event will sometimes influence their success measures. Secondary issues, such as mixing with the stars of the show, social opportunities, corporate hospitality and capacity to move up the seating chain from general admission to premium seating are all part of the evaluation of spectator success.

Current technologies can assist the event manager in involving and servicing event participants, as was discussed earlier with the use of contemporary stadium technologies to enhance the audience experience, and the use of the internet to extend the reach and access to events.

By understanding how the nature and make-up of the event audience influence the event concept, event managers can tailor their events more adequately to meet the needs of participants. As discussed in greater detail in the chapter on marketing and sponsorship planning, this understanding also helps to accurately direct the marketing efforts by using channels specific to the audience — for example, the marketing of Schoolies' Week on the Gold Coast through secondary schools in New South Wales, Victoria and Queensland.

4.5 Sourcing events

LEARNING OBJECTIVE 4.5 Identify the unique elements and resources of an event.

Events are usually obtained or generated from one of the following sources:
- in-house events
- pitching and tendering for events
- bidding for events
- franchising events.

In-house events

Many events are conducted in-house by corporate, government, education, charity and community organisations. In such cases, the management of the event may be a part of the job description and responsibilities of a staff member. For example, the event manager of a company may be responsible for its annual conference, Christmas party or client function. An event manager working in local government may be given the responsibility of organising a local festival, tourism event or school holiday program. In each case, the event manager may inherit existing events, each with their own history and established venues and formats. Alternatively, they may be given the task of initiating new events, which have to be created from scratch with no previous history of precedents.

In some instances companies are set up whose entire function is the conduct of an event; for example, The Australian Tennis Open or the Sydney Festival. Other companies are set up whose business is the staging of events for profit. This is common in the entertainment industry, with specialist companies staging theatrical shows and touring concert performers and bands.

Pitching and tendering for events

Many corporate events are subject to the process known as pitching for events. In this instance, the company or organisation intending to stage the event will invite a number of event management companies to present or 'pitch' their creative concepts for the event. Prior to formulating their ideas, a company pitching for an event will usually research thoroughly the aims of the client and the context of the event. They will then brainstorm a creative concept for the event, and prepare a presentation including a detailed description of the event, often supported by sketches, storyboards and a detailed breakdown of the event costs including the event management fee. The pitch will usually involve a live presentation providing an opportunity for the event management company to 'sell' their event concept, and to strike a rapport with the client. Often the detail involved in the presentation is such that, should the pitch be successful, much of the basic planning and costing of the event will already have taken place.

The tender process is similar to pitching in that a formal public invitation is issued seeking proposals from companies or individuals interested in managing an event. The tender is often advertised, and tender documents issued outlining the terms of the tender and the parameters of the event. Companies intending to respond may be given the opportunity to meet with and question the client in order to clarify any aspects of the tender. Formal tenders are then lodged, and the successful company appointed to manage the event. The tender process is often employed by government organisations where an open and transparent selection process is required.

Bidding for events

There are many existing events that are 'footloose' in the sense that they are seeking cities or organisations to host them, and that may be obtained through the competitive bidding process. This is particularly true of major sporting events and conferences, which typically move between cities on a regular, often annual basis. These events are usually controlled by a national or international body that is the 'owner', or copyright holder of the event. Permission to stage the event locally must be obtained by successfully bidding for the right to host the event.

There are usually three parties involved in the bid process:
1. the local chapter of the event owning body; for example, a sporting or industry association
2. a government body that backs and supports the bid; for example, an event agency such as the Victorian Major Events Company, Destination NSW, Queensland Events Corporation or EventsCorp Western Australia, or a convention bureau such as the Melbourne Convention and Visitors Bureau or Business Events Sydney
3. tourism and event industry suppliers, such as event management companies, hotels and airlines, whose involvement is often coordinated through the event corporation or convention bureau.

Considerable research, effort and, often, cost need to be committed to the bid process, which is described in more detail in the chapter on strategic event planning.

Although the basic format of the sporting event or conference will usually already be established, the host city or organisation will contribute greatly to giving the event a local context and creative flair. No two events are ever exactly the same. The Commonwealth Games, for example, will take on a different image and flavour according to whether it is hosted by Manchester, Melbourne, Delhi, Glasgow or the Queensland Gold Coast. The same industry conference in, say, Brisbane will vary greatly if it is staged in Cairns, Hobart or Adelaide, or for that matter in Shanghai, Singapore, Kuala Lumpur or Hong Kong.

Once the bid has been won and the event obtained, the successful sporting or industry association will appoint a committee and event management team to develop a creative concept and plan the event.

Franchising events

A variation on bidding for events is franchising, where the core concept of the event is developed by an organisation that then permits or sells the rights for the event to be developed in other locations. An outstanding example is the Rock Eisteddfod Challenge, which began in 1980 as a New South Wales Arts Council sponsored event featuring a handful of Sydney high schools. In 1988, the New South Wales Health Department came on board, seeing the Rock Eisteddfod as an opportunity for delivering their 'Quit for Life' anti-smoking message to secondary school students in New South Wales. The event spread rapidly so that by 2009 nearly 300 Australian schools and 25 000 students took part in shows in 17 regions across Australia. More than 1 million students have now performed on stages from Belfast to Albany, Johannesburg to Thursday Island, and Aberdeen to Auckland as part of Global Rock Challenge. Sadly, due to funding constraints, the last Rock Eisteddfod was held in Australia in 2012, though the event lives on elsewhere around the world (Rock Eisteddfod Challenge 2009; Rodley 2015).

Another example of an event concept spreading globally is that of Taste Festival — food festivals whose title is usually prefixed by the brand 'A Taste of'. From an initial festival staged in London in 2004, the concept had spread by 2016 to 22 cities around the globe, including London, Paris, Hong Kong, Sydney and Melbourne, with over half a million foodies enjoying the delights of Taste Festival (Dublin Taste Festivals 2016).

4.6 Creating the event concept

LEARNING OBJECTIVE 4.6 Understand the process of developing an event concept and understand the importance of designing the event experience.

In all of the above instances, a core task of the event manager or team will be to create a strong concept for the event, or to update an existing concept and apply it to the particular context and circumstances of the event. Deciding on the basic idea or concept of an event creates the foundation on which the whole event creation process will later be built. It is crucial therefore to identify a sound and robust concept, based on a good understanding of the full context of the event and its stakeholders. The concept must be capable of achieving the event's purpose, flexible enough to serve the full range of stakeholders, and achievable within the available resources.

Identifying an appropriate event concept will require considerable research, insight and creativity. However, getting the concept right will greatly increase the potential for a successful event outcome.

Defining the purpose of the event

The first step in creating the event concept is to define the purpose of the event, which ideally should be outlined in the event brief supplied by the host organisation. For corporate events, this is sometimes known as the business case, or the justification for holding the event. This in turn will drive the major decisions regarding the development of the event, including the choice of theme and elements and the key corporate messages that the event needs to deliver.

If the purpose of the event is not clearly expressed in the event brief, then the event manager will need to interact with the client in order to clarify and articulate it. Likewise, for public events, the event manager should clarify with the host organisation the purpose of holding the event. The purpose may be multi-faceted — for example, to provide a leisure activity for residents, to attract visitors and to create economic benefit. Identifying the purpose, fully and accurately, will provide a sound starting point for determining the event concept.

Identifying the event audience

The next important question to clarify is who will be attending the event. For corporate events, knowledge of factors such as the age and gender of attendees, their levels of seniority in the participating organisation, and their experiences and tastes will be of great assistance in tailoring the event concept to the needs of the audience. The event needs and expectations of a group of senior executives and clients will differ greatly from those of younger staff members or middle management. Often, the audience will encompass a wide range of ages and backgrounds, which, in turn, will influence decisions about the event concept. It will be useful to inquire about what previous events the company has conducted, and what concepts worked for them. This will provide insights into their corporate culture, and help to avoid repeating ideas or themes they have experienced previously.

For public events, it is important to know whether the event is directed at the whole community, or to one or more segments within it; for example, teenagers, young singles, couples, families with children or seniors. Their age range, income levels and lifestyle interests will all help to determine the event concept. Studying the history of a repeat event may reveal what has been done before, what was successful and what could be improved. For new events, it may be worth searching the internet to identify other events that are similar in style or content.

Deciding the timing of the event

Important decisions need to be made about the duration of the event, and about the season/time of year, day/s and time/s when the event will be held. For corporate events, the business cycle may influence the timing; for example, the avoidance of a particularly busy time of the year for the company, or to coincide with the launch of a new product. A similar logic will determine an appropriate day of the week and time of the day; for example, a product launch may best be held on a weekday when clients and the media are available to attend, or a company celebration may best be held on a Friday night isolated from the business week and providing time for recovery.

The timing of public events may be determined by favourable seasons — for example, spring and autumn are likely to provide temperate weather for outdoor events, though this may lead to increased competition with other events in the marketplace. A family event may best be held on the weekend when all family members are available, or a seniors' event may best be held on a weekday morning to suit the needs of participants. Account should also be taken of global events such as Christmas, New Year, Easter and so on which influence attendance patterns and the availability of attendees. The football grand final weekend may not be the best time to conduct a sporting or community event. Government elections and school holiday periods may also affect the availability of audiences, depending on the nature of the event.

Choosing the event venue

The location of the event will be another important factor in developing the event concept. The venue must meet the needs of the event, not only catering for the number of attendees, but also contributing to the desired style and atmosphere. A formal event, such as an awards night or a black-tie ball, will have different needs to an informal event, such as an office party or a rock concert. The venue must be able to meet the operational needs of the event in terms of access, catering, staging and facilities. It will need to fit inside the budget, including the costs of decoration, theming, and the provision of adequate power, water and staging facilities if these are not provided. Lastly, it will need to meet the needs of participants including transport, parking and convenience.

Scanning the event environment

Before developing the event concept, it will be useful to apply some deep thought and research into the environment in which the event is to take place. Consideration should be given to current trends and fashions that will impact on the audience and their response to the event. Issues such as the environment, the 'Me Too' movement and sensitivity to cultural differences need to be taken into account. If media coverage is important to the event, it will be necessary to consider likely media interest in the subject matter, and to highlight and promote those aspects likely to attract the media.

For some events, competition in the market place will be important. Are there similar events in theme or concept, and are there other events in the same timeframe? If so, what is the point of difference of your event, and how can this be promoted?

Developing the event concept

Once the basic parameters of the event have been identified, the task is to develop an event concept that best meets the needs of the event. Firstly, a decision will need to be made about the overall format of the event. If it is a corporate event, should it be a product launch, a training seminar or a media conference? Is a cocktail party appropriate, or is a formal sit-down dinner required? For a public event, it may be a concert, a festival, an exhibition or a parade. Should it be indoors or outdoors? How large should it be?

A widely used and rewarding technique employed by many event managers for developing event concepts is brainstorming (see figure 4.2). This involves first bringing a group of people together that may include stakeholders, other work colleagues and interested people. The group should then be briefed on the context and parameters of the event, and encouraged to participate in a free and associative flow of suggestions and ideas for the event concept. The only rule is that 'there are no rules', with participants invited to express whatever enters their minds, no matter how outrageous or impractical it may seem. It is useful to record ideas as they are expressed on a whiteboard or butchers' paper. Often the ideas tend to come in waves, with one person stimulated and inspired by the ideas of another until that particular wave is exhausted. Then, after a pause, another idea will start the process again. The brainstorm should be allowed to continue until the waves have subsided and the process is exhausted. Then the ideas can be reviewed and evaluated. At this stage, some ideas may be dismissed as marginal or impractical. Elements of some may be combined with others to form a single concept. If good fortune prevails, one idea may resonate so strongly that it emerges as the chosen event concept. Otherwise the ideas should be prioritised and carried forward for further consideration and development. In some instances the brainstorming process can be conducted over several sessions, or a single session can be used as the basis for identifying ideas that the event manager or team will continue to develop and refine.

FIGURE 4.2	The brainstorming process

- Define the parameters of the event
- Form a group of event stakeholders and colleagues
- Brief them on the event context and the parameters of the event
- Brainstorm a wide range of event concepts and ideas
- Identify the ideas that best serve the needs of the event
- Evaluate and prioritise these ideas
- Choose and refine an event concept

Choosing an event theme

Another issue closely related to the event concept is that of the theme. Theming is an integrated approach to the design of the event so that all aspects of promotion, presentation and staging are coordinated around a single look or theme. For a corporate event, this may simply be the corporate colours of the company, or a smart contemporary look and feel. The message that the event is required to deliver may suggest a theme that amplifies and supports the message. An event for a company wanting to project an innovative image, for example, might require a futurist theme with sophisticated staging involving high-end technology.

Goldblatt (2011) suggests that event themes are often derived from three main sources:

1. the destination, for example, Bali, Paris, New York, Australia
2. popular culture, including books, movies and television, for example, *Mad Men, Harry Potter*
3. historical and current events, for example, Art Deco, the 1950s, the New Millennium.

It will be useful to peruse books, fashion and style and magazines, which can often stimulate ideas for theming. State of the art work by other event managers can be tracked via websites such as BizBash (www.bizbash.com).

Silvers (2012) emphasises the importance of incorporating the senses in developing the event theme:

A theme should incorporate all five senses throughout the event design, including sight, sound, taste, touch and smell. The more senses affected by the environment the more memorable the event will be . . . The sensory cues in an event environment include the following:

- **Sight** — setting, props, floral arrangements, color fabrics, food presentation, lighting, attire
- **Sound** — ambient noise (good or bad) soundscaping, musical entertainment, dialogue, dining sounds (i.e. glasses clinking, crunchy foods etc.)
- **Taste** — food, beverage, atmospheric and olfactory aftertaste
- **Touch** — surfaces, fabrics, furnishings, food texture, visual textures (that stimulate a tactile sensation)
- **Smell** — food aromas, flowers, fuels (cooking and power generation), scented candles/incense/oils, ambient aromas (natural scents and malodorous smells).

A well-chosen theme will help to strengthen the event and to unify and provide inspiration for the other creative elements and program. Whatever theme is chosen, it is essential that it matches the purpose and needs of the event.

Designing the event experience

Some writers (Silvers 2012; Berridge 2007) approach events as experiences, and note the role and importance of such experiences in contemporary lifestyles and the modern economy. Futurist Alvin Toffler wrote that 'Consumers [will] begin to collect experiences as consciously and passionately as they once collected things' (as cited in Silvers 2012). People seek and embrace experiences that enrich their lives, and that resonate with their images of themselves and of their desired or imagined lifestyles. Thus lifestyle events that cater to people's tastes in music, fashion, leisure, food and wine become part of how they define themselves, and how they construct their identity and social networks. Companies also create events that enable their clients to experience the personality and attributes of their brands and products.

From an event manager's viewpoint, an event can be seen as a designed experience, consciously created in order to achieve a given purpose or objective. The task of the event manager is, then, to formulate a clear vision of the event experience, and to identify and design the elements needed for the experience to be realised. Silvers (2012) writes:

> Remember that you are packaging and managing an experience. This means that you must envision that experience, from start to finish, from the attendees' point of view. Imagine every minute of their experience. Identify elements that will build on previous successes, elements that will take advantage of opportunities and strengths, and elements that will mitigate challenges, weaknesses and threats.

Seen from this perspective, the role of design in events involves much more than just the invitation, sets, costumes and table settings. The design process involves a myriad of decisions and choices that contribute to the overall experience of the event attendees. It includes elements such as the site layout, flow of guests, performance program, catering, security, site decoration and atmosphere. Berridge (2007) suggests that the design process can also be applied to the senses, interaction (such as trying out products and sampling services), the emotions and even the meaning and significance that participants take away from events. The total effect of these decisions will determine the nature of the event experience, and how it is received by individual participants or guests. Berridge (2007) emphasises the importance of this wider concept of the design process to events:

> The most important part of any understanding of design is to recognise that it is a planned process, and one that leads onto a pre-conceived outcome from an original idea and one that can be estimated and produced and that this applies to any number of applications. In an event there is a clear intention to firstly identify a set of features and then to see them translated into a (temporary) reality (or fantasy) that others can then experience, and therefore the role of design should be regarded as of fundamental and central significance to this process.

Summarising the process of creating the event concept

Goldblatt (1997) suggests that the process of creating an event concept can be summarised by asking five key questions that he terms the 'five Ws' of the event.

1. *Why* is the event being held? There must be compelling reasons that confirm the importance and viability of holding the event.
2. *Who* will be the stakeholders in the event? These include internal stakeholders, such as the board of directors, committee, staff and audience or guests, and external stakeholders such as media and politicians.
3. *When* will the event be held? Is there sufficient time to research and plan the event? Does the timing suit the needs of the audience, and if the event is outdoors, does it take the likely climatic conditions into account?
4. *Where* will the event be staged? The choice of venue must represent the best compromise between the organisational needs of the event, audience comfort, accessibility and cost.
5. *What* is the event content or product? This must match the needs, wants, desires and expectations of the audience, and must synergise with the why, who, when and where of the event.

Exploring these key questions thoughtfully and fully will go a long way towards identifying a strong event concept tailored to the specific context and needs of the event, which can then be built upon to create a unique and memorable experience. Remember that the event concept is only the basic idea for the event, which will be fleshed out and elaborated later in the event creation process. However, the identification of the event concept is a crucial decision on which the ultimate success of the event will depend.

EVENT PROFILE

WEBSTOCK '15

New Zealand's capital city Wellington is home to a vast number of hugely successful information and communications technology (ICT) businesses. From established, high-flying companies such as Silverstripe, Xero and Intergen to individuals who are starting up, Wellington has the highest concentration of web-based and digital technology companies per capita in New Zealand.

We love the supportive and collaborative nature of Wellington, it is super connected and its size lends itself to an excellent environment where it is easy to share ideas, do business and to build reputation and credibility.

An innovative culture thrives in this vibrant city, including the ICT sector which is flourishing three times faster than in any other region in the country. Together with Wellington's positive synergy between developers, designers, government and entrepreneurs the boutique city is an ideal location for web design and development conference Webstock. With

attendees coming from America, Canada, UK, Australia and across New Zealand, Wellington's schedule of regular international and domestic flights and a transfer time to the airport of just fifteen minutes proved another draw for organisers.

Webstock first began in February 2006 as the brainchild of Natasha Lampard, Mike Brown, Deb Sidelinger and Ben Lampard; a small group of web professionals who've taken it upon themselves to promote raising the standard of websites in their own backyard (and abroad). Now in its ninth year the conference has grown from 500 delegates to more than 800 and is renowned for bringing business and creative minds together to connect, inspire and educate. Webstock runs over five days, which includes a two-day web design and development conference and three days of pre-conference workshops. It combines the internet with creativity, arts and social change and each year it continues to attract a stellar line-up of speakers.

Natasha Lampard says: 'Wellington's technology community seems to be growing all the time while still retaining the "collegial feel" that has welded Webstock to the city. People know each other in Wellington and they share stuff and want to help each other.'

In 2015 Webstock chose to return to the two Positively Wellington Venues (PWVs) which successfully hosted the 2014 event; the St James Theatre was used as the anchor venue and the Michael Fowler Centre (MFC) for pre-conference workshops. Not only are both venues within walking distance of each other, but also to Wellington's central business district, hotels, restaurants, shops and galleries. The after party was held at Wellington's prestigious Embassy Theatre.

The character, heritage and state-of-the-art technology in each venue fit perfectly with Webstock's selection criteria. The St James Theatre's stunning 100-year-old auditorium was used for the main conference with plenary for 800 delegates. The theatre's facade and dramatic showbiz elegance provided the perfect paradox between the building's history and heritage and the cutting-edge ideas shared on stage. The setting was a suitable backdrop to the sometimes eccentric and always entertaining personalities of the presenters.

Together with Webstock's sponsors and organisers, the team at PWV worked behind the scenes with their food and beverage partners, Restaurant Associates (RA), and the technical and production team at Multi-Media Systems, to give the conference a trademark Wellington twist.

RA works closely with the region's top food and beverage producers to deliver tailored dining experiences. Webstock delegates were given a taste of Wellington, from chic canapés to a stand up 'walk & fork' lunch served in noodle boxes. Wellington-based organic coffee roaster People's Coffee were on hand to provide delegates with their caffeine fix of freshly roasted coffee throughout the day. The Greengrocer served delegates fresh cold-pressed juice for a healthy boost, and Garage Project, a start-up Wellington craft beer brewery, fuelled delegates' creativity kick at afternoon tea. Wooden Spoon, a boutique Wellington freezery, cooled down delegates with 'all you can eat' artisan ice-cream.

Multi-Media Systems turned the theatre into a state-of-the-art presentation centre by fitting out the theatre boxes on the side of the stage with screens that acted as electronic billboards and used this to create multifaceted presentations. The massive projector screen on the centre stage was fitted with a purpose-built giant frame used in the various presentations. A gauze screen behind it was lit up to bring in new elements, which included a live band.

Webstock 2015 was a 'sell-out' and a fitting celebration of the web — the creativity, the magic, the craft and everything in between.

Delegates said: 'The event is world-class and hosting it in Wellington brings big ideas into a contained and connected environment that celebrates all things digital. Webstock brings together a collection of digitally-minded dreamers looking for enlightenment, learning and growth. The content sits beyond the pragmatic and makes you think laterally about what digital represents both now and in the future. And the quality speakers are not only entertaining, but inspire you to think beyond convention.'

Source: Business Events New Zealand 2015.

4.7 Evaluating the event concept

LEARNING OBJECTIVE 4.7 Apply the screening process to evaluate the feasibility of an event concept.

Once the event concept has been decided and an initial scoping of the event completed, it is essential to examine whether the event can be delivered successfully within the available timeframe and resources. This process is known as a feasibility study, and may be conducted internally or, in the case of larger events, contracted to an external body (see also the section on feasibility analysis in relation to bidding for events in the chapter on strategic event planning). On the basis of the feasibility study, a decision will be made as to whether or not the event will proceed. Shone and Parry (2004) describe what they refer to as the 'screening process' to examine the feasibility of the event. This involves using three screens to determine whether the event concept matches the needs and resources of the event. The three screens are:

1. the marketing screen
2. the operations screen
3. the financial screen.

The marketing screen

The marketing screen involves examining how the target audience of the event is likely to respond to the event concept. To determine this, an environmental scanning process needs to be conducted. This will help to determine whether the event concept resonates with current tastes and fashions, and whether it is likely to be perceived as innovative and popular or as boring and predictable. A good barometer will be the media response to the concept. If media representatives consider it to be of current interest, they are likely to become allies in the promotion of the event. If the media response is poor, then it will be difficult to promote interest and engage the audience.

For much of this assessment, event managers will need to rely on their own instincts and on testing the response of friends, co-workers and stakeholders to the concept. An alternative, particularly if a large investment is involved in the event, is to undertake some form of market research. This can be done within the resources of the event management company or by employing marketing professionals to conduct a market survey or focus group research. Such research may reveal not only the likely market acceptance of the concept, but also additional information, such as how much the target audience is prepared to pay for the event, or how the event concept may be adapted to meet market expectations or requirements.

A further factor in the environmental scan will be to examine the competition provided by other events in the market. This step will examine whether there are other events on a similar theme or in a similar timeframe, or major events and public holidays that are likely to impact on the target market. An investigation of the competition through a 'What's on' in the city listing, tourism event calendars and so on will assist the event manager to identify and hopefully avoid direct competition with other events in the marketplace.

The operations screen

The operations screen will consider the skills and resources needed to stage the event successfully, and whether the event manager has these skills and resources or can develop them or buy them in for the event. Specialised technical skills, for example, may be needed to implement the event concept. The event manager will need to consider whether event company staff members have these skills, or whether an external supplier needs to be engaged to provide them. Special licences, permits or insurance may be needed in order to implement the concept. If the event concept is highly innovative and challenging, the event manager may need to consider the degree of risk involved. It may be desirable to deliver an innovative event, but costly and embarrassing if the event is a failure because the skills and resources available to stage it are inadequate.

Another major consideration, as part of the operations screen, is staffing. This step will examine whether the event company has sufficient staff available with the right mix of skills and at the right time, place and cost to deliver the event effectively. If the event needs to rely heavily on volunteers, the operations screen will examine whether sufficient numbers are likely to be available, and whether the right motivation, training and induction procedures are in place.

The financial screen

The final screen suggested by Shone and Parry (2004) is the financial screen. This screen examines whether the event organisation has sufficient financial commitment, sponsorship and revenue to undertake the event. The first step in this process is to decide whether the event needs only to break even, which may be the case if it is being staged as a company promotional event, or whether it is required to make a profit for the host organisation.

The next step will be to undertake a 'ballpark' budget of the anticipated costs and income of the event. Breaking the event down into its component parts will allow an estimate to be formed of the costs for each component. A generous contingency should be included on the cost side of the ledger, as at this stage of the event there are bound to be costs that have been underestimated or not yet identified. Calculating the income may require deciding on an appropriate pricing strategy and identifying the 'break-even' point of ticket sales. Other key revenue items to take into account may include potential government grants or subsidies, merchandising income and sponsorship support, both in cash and in-kind. It is important not to overestimate the sponsorship potential, and professional advice or a preliminary approach to the market may be required in order to arrive at a realistic estimate.

Cash flow is an important aspect of the financial screen often overlooked by inexperienced event managers. It is important not only to have sufficient funds to cover the expenses of the event, but to have them available when they are required. If, for example, a large part of the revenue is likely to be from ticket sales on the day, then it may be necessary to chart out the anticipated expenditure flow of the event, and to consider whether credit arrangements need to be made.

Once the event concept has been screened and evaluated from the marketing, operations and financial aspects, the event manager is in a position to make an informed decision with regard to the conduct of the event. If the result is a 'go' decision, then the process of refining the event concept and developing the all-important event strategies and plans can begin.

Remember that the event concept is only the basic idea for the event, which will be fleshed out and elaborated later in the event creation process. However, the identification of the event concept is a crucial decision on which the ultimate success of the event will depend. The elaboration of the event concept and its implications for theming, venue, programming, performance, props and decoration, catering and staging will be discussed in detail in the chapter on event design and production.

SUMMARY

Events are required to serve a multitude of agenda, due to the increased involvement of governments and the corporate sector. The successful event manager needs to be able to identify and manage a diverse range of stakeholder expectations. Major stakeholders include the host organisation staging a particular event and the host community, as well as the various public authorities whose support will be needed. Both sponsors and media are significant partners, and can make important contributions to an event of support and resources beyond their formal sponsorship and media coverage. The members of the event team should share the same vision of the event and understand the philosophy behind it, and the contribution of the team members should be recognised. Ultimately, it is the spectators and participants who decide upon the success or failure of an event, and it is crucial to engage with them on an emotional level to create the event experience.

Events can be sourced or generated in a number of different ways. However, once the event has been obtained, the creation or updating of the event concept is a crucial step in the event management process. This begins with identifying the objectives of the event, and researching its history and participants. The next priority is to brainstorm ideas with stakeholders so that a shared vision for the event can be shaped and communicated. All aspects of events need to be designed, so that a total event experience is created, serving the needs of all stakeholders. The screening process then needs to be applied to the chosen concept to determine whether it is feasible given the limited resources available to the event. No event is created by one person, and success will depend on a collective team effort.

QUESTIONS

1 Who are the most important stakeholders in an event, and why?
2 Give examples of different events staged by government, corporate and community groups in your region and discuss their reasons for putting on these events.
3 Name a major event that you have attended or in which you have been involved, and identify the prime stakeholders and their objectives.
4 Focusing on an event that you have experienced first-hand, list the benefits that the event could offer a sponsor or partner.
5 Identify an event that uses social media to engage participants in the event. List the media that it uses, and describe how they are utilised in the event.
6 What are the means by which an event creates an emotional relationship with its participants and spectators?
7 What events can you think of that demonstrate a unique event concept or idea? What are the aspects or qualities that you consider to be unique?
8 Choose one of the events that you identified in the previous question, and discuss how the design process has been applied to choosing and implementing all aspects of the event.
9 Imagine you are planning a tourism event in the area where you live in order to promote the area as a tourism destination. What are the unique characteristics of the area, and how might these be expressed in the event?

CASE STUDY

SCHOOL OF ROCK

Event type	Conference, team building and party
Number of guests	340
Client	UK-based consumer payments company

BRIEF

To provide a full event package including a morning conference and a creative team-building challenge that leads into an evening party. The team-building challenge and party should have continuity and run seamlessly into each other with an emphasis on fun, competitive spirit and interaction.

The whole company, with a broad range of ages and job roles from sales and customer service teams to finance and management.

WHAT WE DELIVERED

The venue:

The venue, Heythrop Park Resort, Oxfordshire, was selected because of its location (with easy transport links from most of the company's nationwide offices), conference facilities (tiered conference theatre to seat 400), large event spaces and breakout rooms (perfect for the team building), and capacity for all guests to have accommodation on-site.

The conference:

We kept the conference simple utilising the in-house resources but bringing in our own experienced team to run the AV on the day. Subtle use of brand colours through lighting, carefully selected music and high-impact visuals ensured a captivating presentation.

Team building:

At the end of the conference our team of actors/mentors took over the stage to introduce the next part of the event. All 340 delegates were about to be enrolled in a School of Rock. In just one afternoon they were drilled (in teams of 25) by our professional musicians, choreographers and directors to prepare for a performance that evening in a battle of the bands meets X Factor–style stage show. Each group had just three hours to learn their song, perfect choreography as well as direct, star in and edit their own intro video which would be shown at the start of their performance later in the evening.

At the end of rehearsals teams had to head to the pop-up costume and make-up studios we built to prepare for their performance. Our professional costumiers and make-up artists were on hand to ensure they looked the part.

Each team had their own band manager and tour manager (actors and event managers), producer (band member/musician) and choreographer (professional dancer) who steered them through the whole experience. We provided each group with their own rehearsal studio complete with sound system, lyric sheets, props and instruments. Each group then had their own dedicated costumier to help them into full costumes all pre-designed to suit their band and song as well as a make-up artist and accessories for the finishing touches.

Teams were also provided with their own professional video recorders and brief for creating their video. We had a team of professional editors ready to work with the teams to ensure a slick video with sound effects and special effects was delivered.

The event:

Guests had a fun and informal street food–style dinner while they mingled with other groups as anticipation for the evening's performance built.

While the teams had been rehearsing in the afternoon, our set-building and production team had been busy transforming the conference theatre into a stadium fit for rock stars. A bespoke giant speaker stage set, huge sound system, gig-style lighting and special effects were all rigged by our team making the space unrecognisable from the morning conference.

Bespoke posters and flyers around the whole resort added to the build-up and excitement.

The evening's show was run like a live X Factor episode with guest judges who commented on each performance, pre-recorded voiceovers, stunning lighting personalised to each performance and a live rock band that each team performed with. We also created bespoke visual content which was played on a huge screen behind the band as the groups performed. In addition, a live video feed captured the performances and was combined with the bespoke visuals. We wanted each team to have a fully immersive experience of being a true rock star, performing at a live stadium and taking part in a live TV show all at once.

Our live rock band also performed high-impact performances of rock and roll favourites while the judges deliberated. Usherette staff delivered ice-creams and drinks to the guests throughout the show to encourage everyone to participate and support the other acts.

At the end of the show a winner was selected and invited back on stage for an encore with the live band being showered in gold confetti and handed awards by the CEO of the company. An afterparty with a DJ, cocktails and rock and roll vibes was then organised in a separate part of the resort.

THE FEEDBACK

The team-building challenge was inclusive of everyone and although some staff seemed reticent at first about the performing element, there was a real feeling of togetherness and fun which was reassuring.

The evening show was hugely engaging, and a majority of participants found the evening to be exciting, unique and a truly memorable experience. The team-building challenge and party rolled seamlessly into each other and the whole event built in momentum throughout the day. The CEO loved the concept and, with the competitive fun spirit that it evoked, he has opted to repeat the event going forward, building on the theme and adding different twists to the performances and theme.

Prepared by Becky Handley, Director, Theme Traders, London

QUESTIONS

1 What factors did the event management team have to consider when deciding on the venue?

2 What key difficulties do you think the team faced when planning and executing this event?

3 What do you think the event managers in this study were most concerned about in terms of risk and how would you deal with these issues?

4 What are your ideas about potential development of the event in the future?

REFERENCES

Berridge, G 2007, *Events design and experience*, Butterworth-Heinemann, Oxford, Burlington, MA.

Business Events New Zealand 2015, 'Webstock '15', www.businessevents.newzealand.com/en-au/help-and-support/conference-case-studies/webstock-%E2%80%9914/, viewed 7 May 2020.

Conroy, S 2009, 'He who dares, wins', *Virgin Blue Voyeur*, July 2009 issue, Text Pacific Publishing, Sydney.

Dublin Taste Festivals 2016, 'Taste Worldwide', www.dublin.tastefestivals.com/taste-worldwide, viewed 7 May 2020.

Earth Hour 2020, www.earthhour.org.au.

Getz, D 2005, *Event management and event tourism*, Cognizant Communication Corporation, New York.

Goldblatt, J 1997, *Special events — best practices in modern event management*, Van Nostrand Reinhold, New York.

Goldblatt, J 2011, *Special events: a new generation and the next frontier*, John Wiley & Sons Inc, Hoboken, New Jersey.

Goldblatt, J & Perry, J 2002, 'Re-building the community with fire, water and music: the WaterFire phenomenon', in *Events and place making: proceedings of international research conference held in Sydney 2002*, eds L Jago, M Deery, R Harris, A Hede & J Allen, Australian Centre for Event Management, Sydney.

Hemmerling, M 1997, 'What makes an event a success for a host city, sponsors and others?', Paper presented to The Big Event Tourism New South Wales Conference, Wollongong, New South Wales.

Hollway, S 2002, Keynote address delivered to Events and Place Making Conference, Australian Centre for Event Management, University of Technology, Sydney, 15–16 July 2002.

Inversini, A & Williams, N 2017, 'Social media and events' in *Events Management: An International Approach*, Ferdinand, N & Kitchin, P, SAGE Publications, London.

Jago, L, Chalip, L, Brown, G, Mules, T & Ali, S 2002, 'The role of events in helping to brand a destination', in *Events and place making: proceedings of International Research Conference held in Sydney 2002*, eds L Jago, M Deery, R Harris, A Hede & J Allen, Australian Centre for Event Management, Sydney.

Nichols, M 2009, 'YouTube orchestra prepares for Carnegie debut', http://uk.reuters.com.

Nielsenwire 2008, 'Beijing Olympics draws largest ever global TV audience', http://blog.nielsen.com.

Niersbach, W 2006, FIFA World Cup Germany 2006, News 15 An XXL World Cup for the media, www.fifaworldcup.com.

Optus 2018, 'Here's what you can do with the new Optus Stadium app', www.yescrowd.optus.com.au/t5/Blog/Here-s-what-you-can-do-with-the-new-Optus-Stadium-app/ba-p/387928, viewed 7 May 2020.

Portable Film Festival 2010, www.portablefilmfestival.com.

Robertson, M, Yeoman, I, Smith, K & McMahon-Beattie, U 2015, 'Technology, society and visioning: the future of music festivals', *Event Management*, vol. 19, pp. 567–587.

Rock Eisteddfod Challenge 2009, www.rockchallenge.com.au.

Rodley, C 2015, 'The 40 greatest moments in the history of Rock Eisteddfod', *Buzzfeed*, 21 September, www.buzzfeed.com, viewed 7 May 2020.

Shone, A & Parry, B 2004, *Successful event management*, Thomson Learning, London.

Silvers, J R 2012, *Professional event coordination*, John Wiley & Sons, Hoboken, New Jersey.

Tropfest 2018, www.tropfest.org.au/images/Tropfest2018_Event_Program.pdf.

Wang, W 2008, 'The internet and the Beijing Olympic Games', www.china.org.cn.

ACKNOWLEDGEMENTS

Photo: © MauxArts / Shutterstock.com
Extract: © Business Events New Zealand 2015
Photo: © Robert CHG / Shutterstock.com

PART 2

PLANNING

Planning in an event context takes a variety of forms. Depending on the nature of any single event, planning efforts may extend to matters linked to strategy development, project management, marketing and sponsorship, tourism, risk management, finance, human resources and environmental sustainability. In this section of the book each of these areas, plus the matter of legal considerations in event planning and management, are explored from the viewpoint of how they link to the task of achieving an event's stated objectives.

CHAPTER 5

Strategic event planning

LEARNING OBJECTIVES

After studying this chapter, you should be able to:

5.1 discuss the function of the strategic planning process in the context of event management companies, host locations and individual events

5.2 describe the stages in the strategic planning process for mobile, new and existing events and develop a basic strategic plan for an event organisation.

Introduction

This chapter provides an overview of strategic planning as it applies to the field of event management. It begins by discussing the importance of strategic planning and then moves on to describe its application in the contexts of event management companies, host locations (cities, towns, regions) and individual events, with an emphasis on the latter. While the steps involved in the process of strategic planning vary within these different contexts, its intent, to identify a desired future and to work towards it, remains the same.

5.1 What is strategic planning?

LEARNING OBJECTIVE 5.1 Discuss the function of the strategic planning process in the context of event management companies, host locations and individual events.

In its simplest form, strategic planning can be defined as a systematic process by which a desired future is envisioned and then progressed through a sequence of steps. Actions directed at achieving this future are in turn guided by the development of clear vision, mission and value statements, along with associated goals and objectives. In other words, the strategic planning process is concerned with end results and the means to achieve those results.

The value of strategic planning is reflected in the following conversation between the Cat and Alice in Lewis Carroll's famous children's story *Alice's Adventures in Wonderland*:

> 'Cheshire Puss, … Would you tell me, please, which way I ought to go from here?'
>
> 'That depends a good deal on where you want to get to,' said the Cat.
>
> 'I don't much care where —,' said Alice.
>
> 'Then it doesn't matter which way you go,' said the Cat.
>
> '— so long as I get SOMEWHERE,' Alice added as an explanation.
>
> 'Oh, you're sure to do that,' said the Cat, 'if you only walk long enough.' (Carroll 1977, p. 87)

This quotation, in a somewhat humorous way, emphasises the point that if an organisation — for example, a community committee responsible for the planning and conduct of an event, an event production company or a local council that delivers multiple community events — does not have a clear direction that it is seeking to pursue, its subsequent actions will lack purpose. Without a stated purpose, organisations will struggle to set priorities, allocate resources and gain commitment from their employees and other stakeholders as there exists no common understanding of what is intended to be achieved.

While the power of strategic planning in facilitating progress towards a desired outcome(s) has been acknowledged by numerous writers (see Bryson 2011; Pearce and Robinson 2014; Grant 2015; Rothaemel 2017; Lynch 2018), actually engaging in it involves a measure of discipline on the behalf of the organisation concerned. As Sir John Harvey-Jones, a past chairman of Imperial Chemical Industries in the UK, notes, 'Planning is an unnatural process: it is much more fun to do nothing. The nicest thing about not planning is that failure comes as a complete surprise, rather than being preceded by a period of worry and depression' (*Economist* 2012).

While key to the success of event organisations, it must be kept in mind that the process of strategic planning is one that, at its base, should serve as a means of organising discussion, processing information and developing a consensus around what direction(s) an organisation should take (Grant 2015). If viewed this way, the potential 'pitfalls' associated with its use can more easily be avoided, including:
- overplanning and becoming obsessed with detail as opposed to overall strategic considerations
- viewing plans as one-off exercises rather than active documents to be regularly consulted and adapted in the light of such considerations as experience, new technological developments and changed market conditions
- seeing plans as conclusive rather than directional in nature (Grant 2015; Johnson and Scholes 2018).

The strategic planning process and event organisations

Nuances exist in the application of the strategic planning process in different event-related settings. A traditional organisational strategic planning framework (figure 5.1), for example, would likely apply in the context of an event production company, while cities, towns or regions seeking to strategically develop their portfolio of events for tourism purposes would approach the task of strategy development in a similar, but slightly different way (see the chapter on event tourism planning). Organisations wishing to attract geographically mobile events through the bidding process (for example, professional associations, sporting bodies), or create new events (for example, entrepreneurs, community groups), would also differ to some extent in their approach (see figure 5.2). Irrespective of these differences, the essence of strategic planning remains the same in that it serves to structure discussion by moving managers through sequential and interrelated steps that require the analysis of information and the development of a consensus around what actions should be taken.

FIGURE 5.1   Event production company strategic planning framework

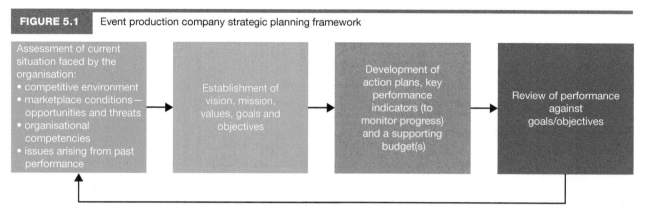

FIGURE 5.2   Stages in the strategic planning process for new and geographically mobile events

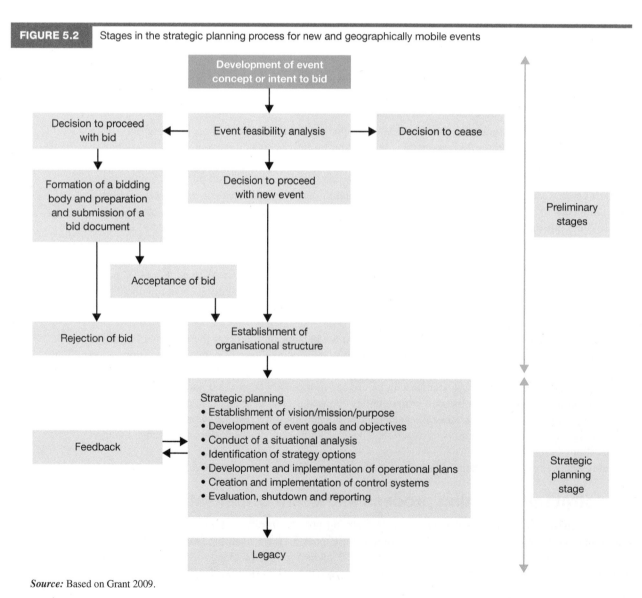

Source: Based on Grant 2009.

5.2 Strategic planning process for new and geographically mobile events

LEARNING OBJECTIVE 5.2 Describe the stages in the strategic planning process for mobile, new and existing events and develop a basic strategic plan for an event organisation.

To demonstrate how the strategic planning process works in practice, the example of new and geographically mobile events has been used in the following section. It should be noted, however, that in the case of the former it is assumed that the intention is for there to be future iterations of the event.

Preliminary stages

Event concept or intent to bid

In the context of proposed new events, this stage in the strategic planning process involves developing an initial event concept and refining it, often in consultation with relevant stakeholder groups. Depending on the event, these might include tourism bodies, local Chambers of Commerce, police, local communities, telecasters, potential suppliers, and government agencies and departments. Emerging from this process will be a much more 'concrete' event concept with matters such as duration, timing, program elements and likely target market(s) having been further clarified. This in turn will allow the proposed event to be subjected to a more detailed analysis in the form of a feasibility study.

In instances where bidding is involved, an event must first be identified for which a bid can be made. Commonly, the event owner (for example, a corporation, sporting body, association or professional body) asks for bids by a specific date for the conduct of their event at a specified future time. In the context of business-related events, such as conferences, convention and visitors' bureaux play a major role in identifying events that can be attracted to their city/town through the bidding process. Once an event is identified, these bodies act to encourage and facilitate bids by those organisations that are potentially in a position to host it. These organisations, depending on the event, might be the local chapter of the international association, society or professional body that owns the event. Single or multisport governing bodies (for example, national Olympic committees) and state-based major event agencies also engage in the bidding process from time to time, seeking to attract international, national or state athletic competitions, or other large scale events (for example, Formula One, world expositions). Once an event is identified, it is common for a preliminary assessment to be made as to its 'fit' with the capabilities of the potential event organising body and/or proposed host destination. This assessment is often made easier by criteria supplied by the event owner (see the example in figure 5.3). Events deemed worthy of further investigation after this initial assessment are often, but not always, further assessed by being the subject of a feasibility study.

FIGURE 5.3 Local Government NSW Annual Conference 2019 criteria for expressions of interest

Local Government NSW Annual Conference 2019 criteria for EOIs to be host destination in a Sydney metropolitan area

Councils wishing to host the LGNSW Annual Conference are invited to submit an expression of interest (EOI). EOIs must be received by 4 May 2018 and address the following criteria:

a) Threshold criteria
- Hotel rooms for up to 900 (delegates, sponsors, guests, staff) for three nights maximum
- An auditorium that seats 900 people theatre-style
- A trade exhibition space for at least 45–50 booths of 2 metre x 3 metre space and catering space

b) Detailed criteria
1. Write a statement about why your council area should host the conference and what your destination will add to the conference experience of attendees.
2. Accommodation
   Provide details of at least three accommodation provider(s) and the prices applicable for the duration of the Conference.
   - Accommodation: minimum 3.5-star standard, private facilities in each room.
   - No more than 30 minutes' drive from the main conference venue.
   - Some rooms will be required for speakers etc. as part of the overall 900 room requirement, preferably within a single hotel. Speakers' accommodation must be connected to or very close to

▶

the conference venue (max. 5 minutes' walk). LGNSW will work with the accommodation supplier to confirm and pay for the rooms allotted and used and will release rooms back by agreed dates where relevant.

– No price gouging — LGNSW hosts conferences in non-CBD areas in recognition of the economic and reputational benefits a significant conference brings. A region's accommodation providers may see the conference as an opportunity to increase their normal room charges. While some changes are acceptable to cover additional costs due to an influx of delegates, price gouging (increases greater than 10% over normal published rack rates) is unacceptable. Councils bidding to host a conference are advised to lock in accommodation pricing at the time of submitting their bid.

– Caravan parks will not be considered.

3. Auditorium

The auditorium must:

– hold up to 900 people seated theatre-style
– allow on-site catering for morning tea, lunch, afternoon tea, delegate networking etc.
– provide disabled access and amenities (access, egress and toilets, hearing loop)
– have adjustable air conditioning
– have adjustable lighting
– have adequate parking and easy access to amenities
– have, in addition to the main auditorium, 2–3 smaller rooms for meetings/breakout sessions for up to 200 pax each and a conference office with 3 desks, 6 x chairs, access to a high-speed photocopier and printer
– have mobile telephone reception
– deliver free WiFi access for delegates and attendees (LGNSW will appoint the audiovisual and staging company)

4. Conference support facilities

Facilities must also include:

– a medium space suitable for use as a media room (with internet and telephone)
– a large space adjoining the conference venue for a trade display area (capacity of at least 45–50 trade exhibition booths of approximately 2 x 3 metres with space for catering for approximately 900 delegates and guests)
– easy access to load in and load out for suppliers
– other smaller meeting spaces close to the main venue
– on-site parking or parking close by
– good public transport access

5. Social events

A bidding council must identify:

– a suitable venue to host the main conference dinner, for up to 900 persons, a maximum of 30 minutes' drive from the main conference venue
– a suitable venue for a Welcome Reception that may or may not be at the main venue. Both social events should showcase what is unique about the destination
– buses, if required, to transfer delegates from the conference venue to social events

6. Childcare facilities

Councils must be able to provide childcare facilities during all conference sessions and functions or arrange childcare. Demand is usually low (e.g. no more than 5 children).

7. Motor vehicles and drivers

Bidding councils must be able to supply a vehicle and driver if needed — e.g. to pick up/transfer speakers and special guests.

8. Ecologically sustainable development principles and the Conference

All bidding councils must work with the LGNSW Events team to ensure the conference reflects the LGNSW Principles and Guidelines for Event Sustainability.

Important information

The process

Following the closing date for EOIs, responses will be assessed against the threshold criteria and then the secondary criteria. This review may require a site visit. A final decision is expected in June 2018.

The role of LGNSW and the host destination

The ownership of the conference remains with LGNSW, and LGNSW maintains overall control of running the conference. In Sydney, LGNSW will deal directly with venues and suppliers as required. LGNSW will assume the financial risk of attending delegates including underwriting the income from delegate fees, meeting sponsorship targets. LGNSW will run the budget, registration and reconciliation processes. The host council will provide support and advice in planning and arranging the social program.

LGNSW expects all aspects of the conference to be executed to the highest possible standards, and that professional events staff working within the host council will assist LGNSW. Association staff will work with the host council at each stage as part of effective conference planning and management. Further details of the role of the host council (and LGNSW) are as follows:

Council's responsibility	Association's responsibility
Advising on the social and partners' program in conjunction with the association and assist in planning the local event aspects of these activities	All venue logistics including catering, security, staffing, in-house audiovisual and social events
Suggesting business session and social program venues	Quality control of all facets of the conference and final decision-making
Securing accommodation and arranging bookings	Arranging the content of the conference including business sessions, timeframes, speaker management and business papers
Determine community involvement and volunteer assistance as required; leaving a legacy	All financial aspects of the conference and arranging trade displays and sponsorships
Compliance with LGNSW's sustainability policy	The running orders and programming of the conference
Security arrangements at the request of the association (e.g. security guards)	Preparing and distributing business papers
To provide the skilled resources necessary to adhere to LGNSW's timelines for delivery	All design and printing requirements and brand management of the conference
Provide local flavour and innovation where possible	On-site registration on the day, delegate fulfilment (e.g. satchel, gifts, conference papers), on-site information desk
To communicate and meet regularly with LGNSW and have a dedicated event team	To communicate and meet regularly with the council and have a dedicated events team

Source: Local Government NSW 2018.

Feasibility analysis

To assess the potential an individual event has for success, it is sound practice to objectively (perhaps via the use of an external organisation or consultant) engage in a formal analysis of this potential. Conducting this assessment, commonly called a feasibility study, involves taking multiple factors into consideration. These may include, depending on the event, likely budget requirements; managerial skill needs; venue capacities; host community and destination area impacts, both economic and non-economic; availability of volunteers and supporting services (for example, equipment hire firms); projected visitation/attendance; infrastructure requirements; availability of public/private sector financial support (for example, grants; see figure 5.4); availability of sponsorship; level of political and community support; and the track record of the event, if it is not being conducted for the first time, in terms of matters such as profitability. It should be noted that the level of detail and complexity associated with these studies will vary. An event such as an Olympic Games, for example, would involve a more lengthy and detailed analysis than a state sporting championship or an association conference.

FIGURE 5.4   Extract from 'Northern Beaches Council Events Grants 2018/19'

Northern Beaches Council, Sydney Event Grants

Program overview

The Events Grants Program has been developed in line with the Northern Beaches Events Strategy. It seeks to provide funding to eligible organisations for events taking place within the Northern Beaches Local Government Area (LGA).

The Events Grants Program aims to build the skills and resources of the community to deliver a rich and diverse calendar of local events that promote community participation and celebrate the unique social and cultural fabric in our villages and town centres. The outcome from the program will see enhanced

▶

economic, social, environmental and/or cultural benefits to the Northern Beaches community. The focus is on new and innovative events and others that add value and benefits to our local villages and town centres across the Northern Beaches. Council has $210 000 available in 2018/19 to fund events across three funding streams. No recurring funding will be offered during this round.

Funding stream	Max. funding	Total funding available	Opening date / Closing Date
Local event or place activation	$5000	$60 000	28 June 2018 / 6 August 2018
Signature/regional events	$10 000	$50 000	28 June 2018 / 6 August 2018
Major events	$20 000–$50 000	$100 000	Open all year round

Local event or place activation
Grants of up to $5000 are available for events that:
- activate local town or village centres and places
- are supported by local businesses, community groups and organisations
- contribute to social and community outcomes
- have local media promotion
- are vibrant and diverse activations.

Regional event — Northern Beaches wide
Grants of up to $10 000 are available for events that:
- attract large numbers of people
- are supported by local businesses and organisations with the potential to be a major event in the future
- contribute to economic, social and community outcomes
- have local and metropolitan media promotion.

Major events
Grants between $20 000 and $50 000 are available for events that:
- attract significant visitor numbers
- are supported by state agencies and/or national/international organisations
- demonstrate measurable economic, social and community outcomes
- provide metropolitan, national and international media promotion
- demonstrate a plan for being self-sufficient into the future.

The major events stream is open to applications any time between 28 June 2018 and 30 May 2019 or until the funding has been allocated.

Objectives
Northern Beaches Council's Events Grants Program aims to address Council's vision and values outlined in the Community Strategic Plan by supporting events that:
- provide an opportunity for measurable economic, social, environmental and/or cultural benefits to Council and the Northern Beaches community
- provide opportunities for the community to participate in and contribute to activities/events in the Northern Beaches LGA
- promote the Northern Beaches and contribute to its reputation as a great place to live, visit, work and invest.

Priority areas for funding
Funding priority will be given to events that:
- add value to our villages and town centres and provide a range of community benefits
- are new, innovative, exciting and engaging
- promote environmental sustainability
- support local businesses and boost the local economy
- promote and celebrate our diversity and are inclusive of all people
- promote effective transportation and connectivity for people to get to and from events.

Source: Northern Beaches Council 2018.

Decision to proceed or cease

In the case of both mobile events and new events, while the outcomes of a feasibility study are a key input into the decision to proceed or not, it must be kept in mind that their role is to inform the decision-making process rather than to make a recommendation in this regard.

Formation of a bidding committee and bid preparation

In the case of mobile events, once it has been decided to proceed with a bid, a committee will need to be established to prepare a formal bid document. This committee will commonly comprise individuals from within the bidding organisation; however, it might also include people from outside the organisation with expertise in specific areas. Advice and support for bidding committees is often provided, in the case of business events, by convention and visitors' bureaux (see the chapter on event tourism planning).

The bidding process commonly involves several steps:

- developing a timeline for the preparation and presentation of a bid document to the owners of the event
- responding to each of the bid criteria set by the event owners (see figure 5.3)
- identifying the key elements of past successful bids to ensure these elements are dealt with fully in the bid document
- preparing a bid document
- presenting and/or submitting a bid to the owners of the event
- lobbying in support of the bid
- evaluating reasons for bid failure (if necessary).

It should be remembered that the bidding process is likely to commence some years prior to the date an event is scheduled to take place. It is also not uncommon for organisations seeking to host an event to go through the bidding process on several occasions before they are successful, if indeed they do succeed.

Establishment of an organisational structure

Once a decision is made to conduct an event, an organisational structure will need to be established through which the event can be delivered. Such structures serve to:

- indicate decision-making power and communication channels
- establish formal relations between departments/committees/individuals
- provide a visual representation of how tasks will be grouped, so that the task of organisational coordination and job design becomes easier
- link activities and people with associated expertise so that events can be conducted effectively and efficiently
- define lines of reporting (Hill, Schilling and Jones 2016).

There are several organisational structures commonly used by event organisations, with the decision as to which structure is most appropriate depending on the characteristics and needs of the event itself.

Functional structures

As the name suggests, a functional structure is based upon the main tasks or functions that an organisation needs to perform to fulfil its mission. These tasks commonly emerge from the work breakdown structure process discussed in the chapter on event project management and will vary from event to event. As an example, the Roskilde Festival (see figure 5.5), a large Danish music festival, has placed several key tasks in the hands of its general management team, as well as identifying eight key functions to which additional managers have been assigned. Completion of these tasks, in turn, will require the engagement of group leaders, working area managers and volunteers.

The more complex an event the greater the number of tasks that need to be embraced within a function-based organisational structure. Figure 5.6 shows the complex organisational structure used to deliver the 2006 Commonwealth Games in Melbourne, Victoria. This structure also serves to highlight the diversity of tasks associated with large-scale events. In this instance, tasks extend from those of a commercial nature to construction, overall project management, risk management, venue, financial, sport and human resource management, ceremonies and broadcasting.

A range of benefits can be attributed to the use of a function-based organisational structure within an event context. Central among these is that individuals can specialise, and so make use of their pre-existing expertise in a specific area as well as further develop this expertise. This is particularly the case when employees or volunteers are placed into functional teams where they can learn from others (Lynch 2018). Additionally, when task areas are identified, and responsibility given to groups or individuals to carry them out, consideration can be given to the amount of work involved within each task so that it can be realistically performed within the time available. The Sweet Pea Festival, Montana, for example, is an event run entirely by time-constrained volunteers, which accounts for the large number of task-based committees within its structure (figure 5.7). By breaking down an event into task areas, functional structures also reduce the possibility of inefficiencies resulting from overlapping areas of responsibility.

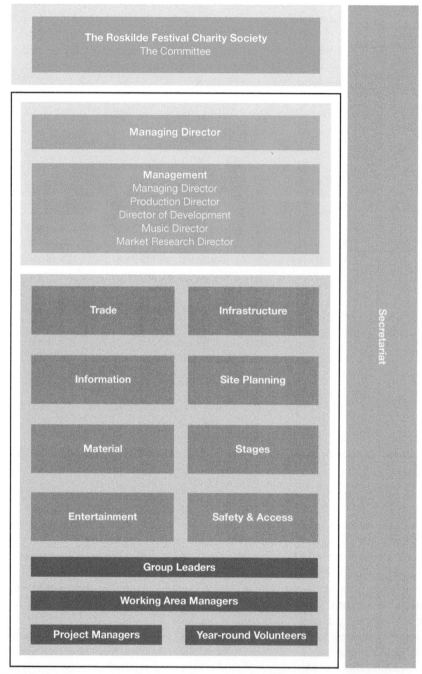

Source: Roskilde Festival 2010.

Finally, as events tend to build their organisational structures quickly, and to tear them down even faster, this structure offers their organising bodies the ability to quickly add, subtract or expand the number of functional areas based on their needs. This capacity is particularly useful when it is necessary to functionally 'evolve' event organisational structures as an event moves from its planning phase through to its delivery.

While functional structures are a widely used approach to organisational design in event settings, there are nonetheless potential limitations to this method. These include problems of coordination, due partly to a lack of understanding by staff in individual functional areas of the responsibilities of people in other task areas, and the possibility of conflict between functional areas as each seeks to protect what it considers its interests (Hill, Schilling and Jones 2016). Various techniques can be identified that go some way to preventing these problems. These include employing multi-skilling strategies that require the rotation of staff through different functional areas, regular meetings between the managers of all functional areas, general staff meetings, and communications (such as newsletters) that aim to keep those engaged on the event aware of matters associated with its current status, such as the passing of milestones (for example, registration numbers, ticket sales, site build completions).

FIGURE 5.6 2006 Commonwealth Games organisational structure

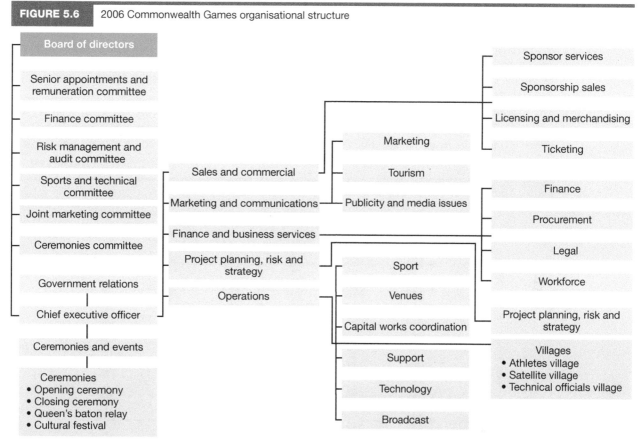

Source: Office of Commonwealth Games Coordination 2006.

FIGURE 5.7 Sweet Pea Festival organisational chart

Outside Counsel Legal Counsel Accounting	Staff Executive Director Office Coordinator	Executive Board President Vice-President Secretary/Treasurer	Nominating Committee						

Admissions Division	Children's Activities Division	Exhibitions Division	Grants & Special Projects Division	Human Resources Division	Merchandising Division	Performing Arts Division	Physical Arrangements Division	Special Events Division	Long Range Planning
Design Committee	Children's Activities Committee	Arts & Crafts Committee	Grants Committee	Publicity Committee	Poster Graphics Committee	Dance Committee	Food Concessions Committee	Bite of Bozeman Liaison	
Festival Sales Committee	Children's Volunteers Committee	Art Shows Committee	Historical Committee	Public Relations Committee	Merchandise Festival Sales Committee	Family Entertain Ment Committee	Off-site Services Committee	Chalk On The Walk Liaison	
Head-quarters Committee		Ball Committee	Park Committee	Schedule Of Events Committee	Merchandise Post-sales Committee	Music Committee	Park Services Committee	Church Service Liaison	
		Flower Show Committee		Volunteer Recruitment Committee	Merchandise Pre-sales Committee	Theatre Committee		Children's Run Liaison	

Source: Sweet Pea Festival 2008.

Program-based matrix structures

Matrix structures group activities by function as well as by project (Hill, Schilling and Jones 2016). In an event context, such structures are often used in instances where multiple venues are involved, and result in staff having two reporting lines. For example, all staff associated with competition programming for a sporting event may be required to report to a competition programming manager, but these same staff may also be assigned to different venues where they are also required to report to the venue manager.

Matrix structures often emerge out of functional structures in multi-venue events as their delivery date approaches. The organisational structure of the 2000 Sydney Olympic Games, for example, moved from a functional structure to that of a venue-based matrix structure as the event date neared (figure 5.8) (Toohey and Halbwirth 2001; Sloman 2006). The reason for this movement lies in the need to 'push' functional expertise (for example, security, event programming, ticketing), which had been developed centrally, out to venues where these tasks need to be undertaken. By acting in this way, decision-making bottlenecks are largely avoided, as are communication problems that might have occurred if an event was to maintain its centralised functional structure.

FIGURE 5.8	Sydney 2000 Olympic Games matrix organisational structure

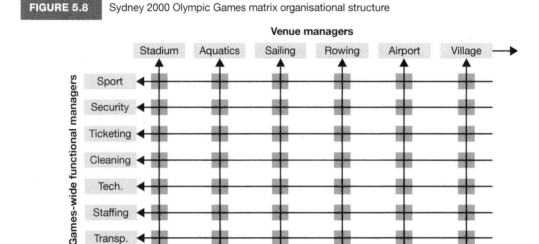

Source: Sloman 2006.

While there is much to recommend the use of a matrix structure when large multi-venue events are involved, if the event is to be presented as a unified whole, a high value must be placed on coordination across the various venues by senior management. Additionally, as staff located in venues effectively have two bosses, issues can arise around communication, reporting and lines of authority.

Multi-organisational or network structures

Most specialist event management companies are relatively small (fewer than 20 people), yet many conduct quite large and complex events. This is possible because these organisations enlist the services of a variety of other firms (see figure 5.9). In effect, they create 'virtual' organisations that come together quickly and are disbanded shortly after an event is concluded. Central among the benefits of employing this structure is its ability to allow the event management organisation to specialise in the 'management' function and so become increasingly capable in this area. This structure also avoids the need to maintain a large staff with multiple skills which, for periods between events, would have little or nothing to do. Other advantages of a network structure include: its ability to contract specialist businesses with current expertise and experience; greater accuracy in the event costing process as supplier expenses can be established via the contracting process; and quick decision-making as the 'core' management group is made up of only a few people or one individual.

As with the other structures previously discussed, there are also possible disadvantages to be considered. These include concern over quality control and reliability that arise from the use of outside contractors, and the associated potential difficulties involved in developing an integrated 'team' to deliver the event. Nevertheless, network structures can be very effective for certain kinds of events (for example, corporate events), and their use is supported by contemporary management thinking on downsizing, sticking to core activities and outsourcing.

FIGURE 5.9   A network structure

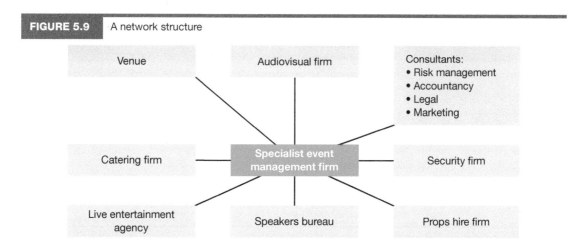

Strategic planning stage

Once established, an event organisation's first task is to engage in the formal strategic planning process. This involves moving through a number of sequential steps. The first involves the development of an event's vision, mission and values which will serve to guide its subsequent actions. In the case of those events for which successful bids have been made, it should be noted that these might already exist. Next, clear event goals and objectives need to be set to focus the event's management team on how it is to progress the event's vision and mission, engage with its values and benchmark its performance. An understanding of the internal and external factors that might impact on the event and shape its actions is then required before strategic options can be explored, a course of action determined and supporting operational plans developed. Systems and processes will also be needed to monitor and control progress, and to allow outcomes to be evaluated and reported on so that future event iterations can be improved upon. It should also be noted that, if appropriate, the issue of generating and managing legacies from the event (for example, physical infrastructure) will need to be embraced as part of the strategic planning process.

Vision, mission and organisational values

Vision statements describe what the organisers of an event are seeking to achieve through its conduct in the longer term. In doing so they serve to: build a sense of commitment by those involved with it to a specific future direction; create a sense of the event's identity; and communicate its aspirations to its various stakeholders (for example, attendees, sponsors, granting bodies and local community) (Thompson et al. 2016). In constructing such statements, consideration needs to be given to ensuring that they are distinctive and specific, and that they avoid being overly general in nature. For example, statements such as, 'to be the best Food and Wine Festival in Australia' offer little real guidance to those charged with the management of such an event.

When the first edition of this book was published some 20 years ago, few events could be identified that had sought to reflect on their long-term intent through the development of a vision statement. Today, such statements are not uncommon, and can be found on the websites of many public and corporate events. Examples of these statements are provided in table 5.1.

TABLE 5.1   **Selected event vision statements**

Event	Vision statement
National Folk Festival, Canberra	The National Folk Festival will be a nationally recognised, annual exposition and celebration of folk culture.
Ann Arbour Arts Festival, Michigan	The Anna Arbour Arts Festival aspires to be a nationally recognised arts festival and enduring local treasure — a widely anticipated hub of community and creative energy.

(continued)

TABLE 5.1 *(continued)*

Event	Vision statement
Global Privacy Assembly	An environment in which privacy and data protection authorities around the world are able effectively to act to fulfil their mandates, both individually and in concert, through diffusion of knowledge and supportive connections.
Britt Music and Arts Festival, Oregon	Britt Music and Arts Festival will be a nationally recognized, financially sustainable arts campus destination that embraces artistic risk-taking through exploration, collaboration and creation that intentionally integrates education and performance.
Silicon Valley Jewish Film Festival, Silicon Valley	Silicon Valley Jewish Film Festival will be regarded as a central, unifying event across Silicon Valley that drives the connectivity with and within the Jewish, multi-generational and increasingly diverse community.

Source: Ann Arbour Arts Festival 2010; Britt Music and Arts Festival 2020; Global Privacy Assembly 2020; National Folk Festival 2017; Silicon Valley Jewish Film Festival 2018.

While a vision statement seeks to be inspirational and guide an event's future direction, a mission statement is descriptive and aims to identify its present nature and purpose (Thompson et al. 2016). This being the case, such statements should make it clear why the event exists; how it intends to progress its purpose; and who the event seeks to serve — its beneficiaries and/or attendee groups. Examples of effective event mission statements are provided in table 5.2.

TABLE 5.2 **Selected event mission statements**

Event	Mission statement
World Dairy Expo	World Dairy Expo serves as a forum for dairy producers, companies, organizations and other dairy enthusiasts to come together to compete, and to exchange ideas, knowledge, technology and commerce.
Peel Music Festival	The Peel Music Festival aspires to unite and enrich the communities in the Peel Region by providing a platform for the competitive performance of music and speech arts. Established and maintained by local teachers, the festival strives to create and nurture an appreciation for these arts by providing students with further education through exposure to professional adjudication and performances by their peers.
Governor's Hurricane Conference	The Governor's Hurricane Conference (Conference) was established in order to provide a vehicle to present lessons learned and other important information about hurricanes to public and private officials, especially local emergency management professionals and those involved in preparedness, planning, response and recovery at all levels of government, industry and private interests.
Pride in London Festival	Be fully inclusive of all sections of the LGBT+ community, free at the point of access. Provide a celebration of LGBT+ life and a platform to continue the fight for equality and to challenge prejudice. Establish Pride in London on a sustainable footing and grow the festival over time to serve better the needs of London's LGBT+ community and promote London as a beacon to the world.
Gasparilla Festival of the Arts, Florida	To produce an annual, premier juried outdoor art festival for the enjoyment and education of our patrons, artists and guests and the enhancement of the Tampa Bay area's cultural arts.

Source: Gasparilla Festival of the Arts 2020; Governor's Hurricane Conference 2020; Peel Music Festival 2020; Pride in London 2020; World Dairy Expo 2020.

Some event mission statements also incorporate a set of core values; however, these are increasingly finding expression in separate value statements. These statements comprise those beliefs, traits or behaviours that the event organisation has determined should condition how it goes about pursuing its vision and mission. The core values, for example, of Canberra's National Folk Festival (2017) are as follows:

- *Respect* — for our traditional and contemporary folk culture; for one another
- *Inclusiveness* — openness to diverse participation, respecting personal contribution and effort

- *Teamwork* — common goals, different roles, collaborative action, shared accountability and rewards
- *Professionalism* — good governance and management, honesty, integrity and transparency.
  A similar set of values has been developed by the Oregon Shakespeare Festival (2020):
- *Excellence* — We bring the best possible version of ourselves to our work onstage and to the organization, holding ourselves to high artistic, professional and personal standards.
- *Inclusion* — We include a diversity of people, ideas and cultures in our work, enriching our art, our relationships with each other, our audiences and our community.
- *Company* — We sustain a safe and supportive workplace where we rely on our fellow company members to work toward excellence with trust, respect, compassion and accountability.
- *Stewardship* — We make wise, efficient and responsible use of all the resources entrusted to us, sustaining our long-standing financial stability, the legacy of our organization's 80-year history, and the health of our planet.

Goals and objectives

Once an event's vision, mission and values have been decided, the next task is to establish its goals and objectives. These serve to guide an event's organisers in their efforts to progress its vision and mission, and provide a means of assessing progress towards them. It should be noted that while the terms 'goals' and 'objectives' are often used interchangeably, they are nonetheless distinct concepts. Goals are broad statements that seek to provide direction to those engaged in the organisation of the event, and as such have no time criteria attached to them or any form of quantification (Wheelen and Hunger 2012). Examples of event goals are provided in table 5.3.

TABLE 5.3 Selected event goals

Event	Goals
SFFILM Festival	• Artist and Art-Form Impact: through innovative partnering structures with individuals and foundations we will create new sources of support for filmmakers, ensuring their work is made, seen, and appreciated. • Education: through national online programs we will contribute to a fact- and information-based society and provide more context for young people and education professionals to shape ideas about the world. • Systems: by investing in systems we provide the tools to empower staff to assume leadership in their individual roles and enable better and more data-driven decision-making. • Partners and Venues: through partnerships with key cultural institutions in San Francisco, we will help drive continuous improvement in cultural best practices, elevate the role of film in the civic culture and create a stable venue configuration for the San Francisco International Film Festival. • Tech/New Media: by effectively engaging with the technology communities of the Bay Area, we provide a portal for other cultural organizations to find common cause with the leading changemakers on the planet. • Audience/Community Impact: experimentation with audience development and growth, through new and refined programs for youth and adults, will inspire the formation of a more tightly bound community of people interested in film.
Kalamazoo Poetry Festival	• Strengthen the economic sustainability of KPF • Increase diversity on the KPF board of directors • Grow the Kalamazoo Poetry Festival's offerings to meet demand • Strengthen engagement in our community.
American College of Surgeons, Quality and Safety Conference	• Provide a professional forum to discuss and apply the most recent knowledge pertaining to national, international, and local quality and safety initiatives in the field of surgery. • Present methods used to analyse data from ACS Quality Programs and demonstrate practical ways to use the data for quality improvement. • Assist hospitals and providers in managing, analysing, and interpreting data by providing education on proven methods that will empower hospitals and centres to make a positive impact at their facilities. • Enhance the learning experience by offering breakout sessions that educate attendees on the topic areas of their choice and with consideration of their level of programmatic experience.

(continued)

TABLE 5.3 *(continued)*

Event	Goals
Regina Folk Festival	• We will host high-quality music and arts events. • We will manage our resources to ensure sustainability and return to a break-even point by 2021 using our surplus to maintain what we are doing. • We will build and maintain a festival and a volunteer base that are reflective of the communities we serve. • We will build and maintain appropriate and effective relationships over the next 3–4 years.

Source: American College of Surgeons 2020; Kalamazoo Poetry Festival 2016; Regina Folk Festival 2017; SFFILM 2017.

Objectives are used to quantify progress towards an event's goals. In practice they serve to focus an event's management, provide a means of tracking performance and act to motivate staff (Thompson et al. 2016). Useful criteria that can be applied to the establishment of objectives are summed up by the acronym SMART, which refers to the fact that objectives should be:

• *S pecific* — focused on achieving an event goal
• *M easurable* — expressed in a way that is quantifiable (when at all possible)
• *A greeable* — agreed on by those responsible for achieving them
• *R ealistic* — in terms of the event organisation having the human, financial and physical resources to achieve them
• *T ime specific* — to be achieved by a specific time (ChangingMinds.org 2020).

Events will vary in terms of the objectives they establish; however, common areas include those given in table 5.4.

TABLE 5.4   Categories of event objectives

Type of objective	Examples
Economic and tourism	• Percentage return on monies invested or overall gross/net profit sought • Dollar and in-kind value of sponsorship attracted/merchandise sold/grants won/donations made • Percentage of income to be raised from fundraising activities • Level of event-related spending by out-of-area visitors • Number of full-time-equivalent local jobs resulting from event • Length of stay by out-of-area attendees • Percentage of goods/services purchased locally by organiser • Number of local traders
Attendance/participation	• Total attendance/participation by specific groups (for example, seniors, the socially disadvantaged, young singles, local versus out-of-area teams) • Size of event in terms of stallholders/exhibitors/performers/teams/attendees/registrants • Number of local versus international artists/speakers/teams • Level of repeat attendance/participation
Quality	• Level of attendee/exhibitor/participant/vendor/sponsor/volunteer satisfaction with event components/outcomes • Number of complaints from attendees/participants/vendors/sponsors/exhibitors/volunteers • Number of injuries, arrests and evictions
Knowledge/attitudes/behaviour	• Percentage of attendees that have changed levels of knowledge or intend to alter their behaviour • Percentage of attendees that have altered attitudes towards a specific matter/issue
Human resources	• Percentage of staff/volunteer turnover during an event's planning cycle • Percentage of volunteers retained from previous year • Ethnic diversity/gender composition of leadership team

Administration	• Percentage reduction in cost to revenue ratio • Level of outsourcing
Marketing	• Changes in marketplace perception of event/host destination/product/service • Changes in level of product/service brand awareness • Level of growth in target market attendee/participant numbers, exhibition stand sales, vendor spaces sold and so on • Percentage increase in market share (if the event is competing directly with other similar events) • Sales made/leads obtained • Level of effectiveness of promotional activities (for example, number of social media engagements, enquiries linked to media advertising)
Community	• Number of community groups/charity partners involved • Extent of community benefits (for example, changes in levels of community pride, social cohesion, appreciation/awareness of different art forms, opportunities for fundraising by local community groups) • Percentage of an area's cultural/ethnic groups represented in a program • Provision of professional development opportunities for local artists
Environment	• Energy/water usage levels • Waste generated • Attendee use of public versus private transport • Level of enhanced awareness/understanding of environmental issue(s) • Level of pre- or post-event involvement in environmental projects

Situation analysis

When establishing goals and objectives, along with the strategy an event will use to pursue them, consideration must be given by its management to its internal environment — for example, financial situation, staff expertise, technological capacities — and to its external environment — for example, number and type of competing events, legislative changes impacting event operations, community attitude to the event or events in general, and the impact of climate change. An analysis of these factors often takes the form of a SWOT analysis (strengths, weaknesses, opportunities and threats). Such an analysis will likely involve referring to a range of existing information sources, including data collected by the event on its performance (assuming the event has taken place previously); information on the performance of similar events; census data; and general reports and studies on relevant matters such as trends in leisure behaviour or the industry or professional field that it seeks to serve. On occasion it may be necessary to commission studies to fill information gaps or to update the event organisation on specific matters. A deeper understanding of the needs, wants, motives and perceptions of current or potential customer groups, for example, may be deemed necessary before dramatically altering an event's program in an effort to increase attendance. (For a more detailed discussion of this aspect of strategic planning, see the chapter on marketing and sponsorship planning.)

Identification of strategy options

Events may pursue any number of strategies depending on their vision, goals and objectives. Many of these strategies may not be of a business nature and concern matters such as community capital building, cultural development or environmental enhancement of the location where they take place. While acknowledging this, most events that seek to be ongoing require a business strategy(ies) that will allow them to progress their vision and associated mission. The discussion here focuses on these types of strategies.

Growth strategy

Many event organisations have a fixation on event size and, as such, seek to make their events bigger with each iteration or larger than similar events, with growth being expressed in terms of more revenue, more event components, more participants or delegates, or a bigger market share. Bigger, however, is not necessarily better, as some event managers have discovered. For example, the Sydney Festival, a cultural festival that takes place each year in that city in January, had on one occasion adopted a growth strategy, acting to absorb selected events taking place in Sydney at the same time and describing them as 'umbrella' events. Some critics observed that by doing this the festival seemed to be losing its focus. A subsequent festival director responded to this criticism by concentrating the festival around the Sydney Harbour foreshore areas and decreasing the number of event components but increasing their quality.

It is important to recognise that an event does not necessarily have to increase in size for its participants to feel that it is better than those iterations of the event that preceded it — this can be achieved by dedicating attention to quality enhancement and improved planning. Nonetheless, a growth strategy may be appropriate if historical data suggest there is a growing demand for the type of event concerned, or when a financial imperative necessitates increasing revenue. The annual Woodford Folk Festival in Queensland, for example, expanded the focus of its program a number of years ago by including contemporary rock acts in order to appeal to a market segment with a strong propensity to attend music events. The increased revenue gained in this way was then directed at repaying the festival's debt.

Consolidation or stability strategy

In certain circumstances it may be appropriate to adopt a consolidation strategy — that is, maintaining attendance at a given level. Strong demand for tickets to the Port Fairy Folk Festival, an annual event in Victoria, for example, has allowed this event to sell tickets well in advance, cap attendance numbers and further enhance the quality of its program. By capping ticket sales in a climate of high demand, this event also created a situation in which it had greater pricing freedom. The Woodford Folk Festival, mentioned previously, has also employed a similar strategy in recent years (*Music Feeds* 2017).

Retrenchment strategy

An ongoing event's situational analysis may suggest that an appropriate strategy is to reduce its size. This strategy can be applicable when the operating environment of an event changes. Retrenchment can seem a defeatist or negative strategy, particularly to long-standing members of an event committee, but it can be a necessary response to an unfavourable economic environment or major change in the sociocultural environment. The management of a community festival, for example, may decide to delete those festival elements that were poorly patronised and focus only on those that have proven to be popular with its target market. Likewise, an exhibition company that had previously conducted a conference in association with one of its major exhibitions may cease to do so due to falling registrations. Resources freed through these means can be used to add value to those elements that remain, and in so doing strengthen its capacity to increase attendance in future.

Combination strategy

As the name suggests, a combination strategy includes elements from more than one of the previously cited generic business strategies. An event manager could, for example, decide to cut back or even delete some aspects of an event that no longer appeal to their event target market(s), while concurrently growing other aspects.

Strategy evaluation and selection

To identify which strategic option(s) is likely to be most successful in progressing an event organisation's vision and mission, some form of analysis is necessary. In this regard, Lynch (2018), while acknowledging that each organisation will approach this task in their own way, identifies six general criteria that can be used for this purpose.
1. *Consistency with vision, mission and goals.* If a strategic option does not meet an organisation's vision, mission and goals there is a strong case for dismissing it.
2. *Suitability.* A strategy, when viewed within the context of the environment in which an organisation is operating and its available resources, needs to be seen as appropriate.
3. *Validity.* Any assumptions, for example, the likely future demand for the type of event upon which a strategy is based, need to be well supported by appropriate research.
4. *Feasibility of options.* A proposed strategy must be able to be carried out. Areas where possible constraints might arise need to be considered by an event's management, including the following.
   (a) *Organisational culture, skills and resources.* Will an event organisation have the financial capacity or expertise necessary to pursue a strategy?
   (b) *Constraints external to an organisation.* Will an event's customer base be accepting of a strategy? Will competing events adapt quickly and restrict the ability of an event organisation to pursue its chosen strategy? Will government or other regulatory bodies allow a strategy to be progressed?
   (c) *Lack of commitment from management and employees.* There must be acceptance of whatever strategy is selected by an event's management and staff if it is to have a reasonable chance of success.

5. *Business risk.* Strategic options bring with them various levels of risk. Such risks need to be identified and assessed in terms of how acceptable they are to the event organisation. For example, an exhibition company that is thinking of doubling the size of one of its major exhibitions would need to establish what potential impact such a growth strategy would have on its cash flow and borrowing requirements. As part of this analysis it would need to work through various scenarios around different cost structures, levels of demand, and exhibitor and entry fees.

6. *Attractiveness to stakeholders.* Whatever strategy is chosen needs to have some appeal to an event organisation's major stakeholders. This may be difficult to achieve at times. For example, the organisers of a major city-based festival may wish to pursue a retrenchment strategy due to overcrowding and associated traffic congestion that they view as compromising the experience of attendees, as well as creating problems for residents around the event site. Major sponsors, on the other hand, may be against such a strategy as it might reduce the number of people exposed to their promotional efforts.

Operational planning

Once a strategy(ies) has been agreed upon, the event organisation needs to develop a series of supporting operational plans. The application of project management practices and techniques (see the chapter on event project management) is particularly useful at this point in the strategic planning process.

Operational plans will be needed for all areas central to the achievement of an event's goals and objectives. Areas for operational planning will vary depending on the nature and scale of the event concerned. In the case of a large festival, for example, operational plans would likely be needed in the areas of finance/budgeting, marketing, administration, staging and site management, research and evaluation, security and risk, sponsorship, environmental management, programming, transportation, merchandising and staffing (paid and volunteer).

Each area for which an operational plan is developed will require: a set of objectives that are linked to the achievement of the overall event organisation's strategy; action plans and schedules; monitoring and control systems; and an allocation of resources (financial, human and supporting equipment/services).

Given that many festivals, exhibitions and events are not one-off but occur at regular intervals — yearly, biennially or, in the case of some major sporting events, every four years — standing plans can often be used in operational areas. Standing plans are made up of policies, rules and standard procedures and serve to reduce decision-making time by ensuring similar situations are handled in a predetermined and consistent way. Policies can be thought of as guidelines for decision-making. An event might, for example, have a policy of only engaging caterers that meet particular licensing criteria. Policies, in turn, are implemented by following established detailed instructions known as procedures. In the case of the previous example, procedures may require the person responsible for hiring caterers to inspect their licence(s), check that they are current, and obtain copies for the event's records. Rules are statements governing conduct or action in a particular situation. An event may establish rules, for example, regarding what caterers can and cannot do with the waste they generate on- site, or on what they can or cannot sell.

In some instances, particularly in the context of large-scale sporting events, the capacity of selected operational plans to work in practice may be tested through the conduct of test events. Test events also provide a 'real world' training opportunity for staff and assist in the development of greater coordination between the various 'teams' involved in event delivery.

Control systems

Once operational plans are implemented, mechanisms are required to ensure that actions conform to plans, and to provide information to event organisers so that they can adjustment their operational plans in line with changed circumstances. These mechanisms take the form of systems that allow performance to constantly be compared to operational objectives. The establishment of performance benchmarks and milestones, such as tickets sold or sponsorship received by specific dates, for example, can indicate progress towards these objectives. Meetings and reports are also central to the control process, as are budgets which allow actual costs and expenditure to be compared and updated against those that were originally projected for the various operational areas.

Event evaluation and reporting

For many events, evaluation remains a neglected aspect of their strategic event planning process; yet, it is only through evaluation that event organisations can determine how successful or otherwise their efforts have been in achieving whatever goals and/or objectives they have set. The information that is captured allows reports to be prepared not only for the management of the event itself, but also for stakeholders such as granting bodies, sponsors and permissory bodies (for example, police, local councils). Additionally, problems and shortcomings in current event planning and delivery processes can be identified and recommendations made for change. In table 5.5, an example is given of how one event (the National Folk Festival, Canberra) has used evaluation practices to determine how successful it has been in achieving its stated goals.

TABLE 5.5   **Extract from National Folk Festival, Strategic Plan 2017–2020**

Goals What are we trying to achieve?	Strategy The actions we undertake to deliver the goals.	Key deliverables How will we know if we have achieved our goals?
ARTISTIC Present an artistically engaging and exciting festival.	• Maintain a high-quality program of activity reflecting both traditional and contemporary folk culture. • Ensure a program mix of established artists, festival favourites, community groups and new and emerging performers, over a range of genres. • Create a dynamic environment that actively promotes access and participation in the folk arts within the festival.	• Artistic programming is balanced, diverse and attractive to all festival participants. • Industry and folk community critical feedback is positive. • Participant surveys reflect positive festival experiences. • Box Office targets are achieved. • Venues are full and vibe of the festival is good.
FINANCIAL Strong financial resilience.	• Responsibly manage the financial affairs of the National Folk Festival (NFF). • Ensure stable financial reserves. • Maintain informed and responsible budgeting. • Continually review all business and income streams utilising new technologies such as online and cashless point of sale. • Diversify income sources. • Invest in the business.	• A minimum of 25% of generated surplus has been reinvested to targeted projects such as staffing, set design, office and production technology and equipment. • A minimum of 25% of generated surplus has been invested in folk communities. • The budget target for an annual surplus of $100 000 has been realised. • There is an annual contribution toward the targeted cash reserve of $1 million. • We have conducted an annual review of income streams to reflect current costs and adjusted accordingly. • Annual external financial audit is unqualified. • Ticket income increased by 2% annually. • Diverse commercial opportunities have been reviewed and implemented including: sponsorship for venues; variable stall rates; Festival Shop sales; and year-round merchandise. • Effectively implemented cashless transactions for the NFF. • Income from sponsorships and grants is at 10% of revenue. • A minimum of one new partnership or sponsorship has been added annually to support our financial base.

MARKETING & COMMUNICATION Innovative marketing and promotion.	• Raise the profile of the NFF nationally, in Canberra and the region. • Develop brand recognition through innovative marketing strategies. • Develop and implement appropriate marketing, promotion and media strategies. • Develop and expand positive relationships with relevant media and promotional partners. • Develop and refine our patron database to promote the festival and attract new audiences.	• Implemented clear brand recognition including consistent messaging and signage. • Increased volume and improved quality of media activity. • Strengthened the NFF website and social media presence across all platforms. • Implemented analysis of ticketing data and participant survey information to understand our audience and measure patterns including sales history and demographics. • Feedback from comprehensive patron surveys is considered in delivery of future festivals. • New marketing options and relationships have been explored.
BUSINESS Good business, and an efficient organisation.	• Undertake effective economic and sustainable business practices. • Maintain computer and office systems that are fit for purpose, effectively supporting administration, financial and other record keeping as required. • Establish collaborative alliances and positive relationships with key stakeholders. • Maintain continual engagement with our service providers and contractors. • Maintain and develop partnerships with national cultural institutions.	• Procedures and practices have been subject to continual review reflecting a dynamic organisation. • Post-festival debrief by board and staff updates the Strategic and related Business Plans. • Consistent and engaging positive relationships are maintained with key stakeholders particularly ACT Government and other users of EPIC. • Commercial relationships with service suppliers have been developed. • All commercial suppliers' schedules and contracts have been regularly reviewed. • The NLA Folk Fellowship has been delivered. • New presenter partnerships with national cultural organisations are delivered.
PEOPLE A motivated flexible team.	• Continue to implement ethical, responsible and supportive employment practices. • Maintain a high level of trust and goodwill with our artists, their agents and managers, staff and volunteers. • Attract, retain and train qualified and engaged personnel, both paid and volunteer throughout the year and at the festival. • Ensure there are appropriate personnel in critical areas to mitigate against staff fatigue. • Develop effective succession plans to ensure retention of corporate knowledge.	• All staff have clear duty statements, employment contracts, and have undertaken an annual performance review. • Workplace collaborations and efficient practices that support a positive and productive work culture have been identified and implemented. • Open and fair negotiations have been maintained with all artists and their agents who acknowledge the NFF as the festival of choice at which to perform. • We have retained experienced volunteers while also recruiting new volunteers.

(continued)

TABLE 5.5 *(continued)*

Goals What are we trying to achieve?	Strategy The actions we undertake to deliver the goals.	Key deliverables How will we know if we have achieved our goals?
		• Coordinator and volunteer roles have been documented, understood and implemented by all relevant parties. • We have identified and implemented opportunities for skills development for staff, volunteers and coordinators. • Online volunteer coordinator resources are continually reviewed and provide essential information for all.
GOVERNANCE Effective and sustainable governance.	• Ensure an effective board with strong strategic leadership and governance appropriate for a not-for-profit cultural organisation. • Ensure the NFF operates and complies with contemporary governance practices. • Conduct an annual board review. • Operational policies and procedures are regularly reviewed and updated.	• Board membership reflects NFF core values. • The board maintains a strategic profile. • The board has exercised strategic oversight for financial and operational risk assessment and ensured that reporting systems are maintained. • Policies and procedures have been updated and implemented with appropriate board member oversight to reflect the needs of the NFF. • Governance training for board and staff has been undertaken. • The NFF Annual Report has been published and reflects the good governance of the Company.
OPERATIONS Smooth, efficient operations and a safe, environmentally aware festival.	• Ensure participants are welcomed to the NFF with behaviour consistent with the NFF core values. • Participant experience at all levels of engagement in the festival is positive. • Design and provide a festival site that is welcoming, accessible and safe. • Consolidate the NFF site design and signage. • Pursue ethically sourced supplies and implement environmentally sustainable practices. • Engage with independent contractors to enable reuse of production material. • Provide event production personnel with appropriate resources to deliver the festival. • All personnel continue to work in a safe and appropriately managed worksite at all times.	• Attendee surveys reflect ongoing positive experience. • Attendee surveys and NFF monitoring identify improvements in people movement on the festival site. • Where possible and viable all supplies have been ethically sourced. • The NFF continues to be recognised by participants and industry as an environmentally aware festival. • All relevant external regulatory bodies approve compliance. • Required resources have been identified, scheduled and delivered for implementation of the festival. • The NFF was safe for participants and staff and had conformed to all regulatory standards to mitigate the risk of on-site incidents. • The NFF continues to implement a low energy footprint.

Source: National Folk Festival 2017.

Legacy

Some events have the capacity to generate legacy outcomes for the locations in which they take place. For this reason, national, state and local governments seek to attract selected events through the bidding process, create new events, or act to support the efforts of other bodies wishing to do so through such means as grants. The potential outcomes that events can generate are many and varied, and will depend on the scale and nature of the event concerned, but can include: infrastructure improvements, ongoing increases in tourism visitation, enhanced industry capacities, improved workforce skills, environmental enhancement and improved local economic conditions.

To secure event legacies some writers (see Kearney 2006) suggest that a separate legacy program be created as part of the overall strategic planning process, and that, in the case of large-scale events, a senior level management position be built into their organisational structure with this specific responsibility. While few events have yet to act in this way, the issue of legacy is nonetheless a major consideration for the owners of large scale events, along with those host destination-based organisations that act to deliver them. The body responsible for infrastructure development and event delivery for the 2022 Qatar FIFA World Cup, for example, carries the title of 'The Supreme Committee for Delivery & Legacy' (2020), while the International Olympic Committee has an active program designed to assist Olympic Games organisers with legacy planning (International Olympic Committee 2020).

Strategic planning for existing events

While the preceding discussion has concentrated on new events, or events for which bids have been made, many event organisations will be responsible for the conduct of recurring events such as annual festivals or conferences. In such situations, the event organisation concerned would begin by reviewing the validity of the event's current vision and mission, before going on to assess its current situation, review its organisational structure and assess the effectiveness of its present strategy. This process is likely to result in minor changes or refinements or, occasionally, major revisions. Nonetheless, event managers need to keep in mind — as Mintzberg, Quinn and Voyer (1995) point out — that the strategic planning process tends to encourage incremental change, when what might be needed is a complete rethink of the current strategy.

SUMMARY

The strategic planning process provides an event organisation with a systematic approach to the challenge of planning and delivering successful events. Its preliminary stages involve seeking clarity around the likely viability of an event in terms of the outcomes that are being sought through it. Feasibility studies are key in this regard. If an event proceeds, an appropriate organisational structure is needed, with the nature of the event dictating the use of a functional, matrix or network framework. Once established, an event organisation faces the challenge of developing a detailed strategic plan, which involves sequential steps commencing with the establishment of vision, mission and value statements and ending with the plan's evaluation. The information gained at this final stage in then used to refine, or significantly revise, subsequent strategic planning efforts.

QUESTIONS

1 Briefly discuss the role of vision, mission and value statements, goals and objectives in event settings.
2 Choose an event type (for example, festivals), identify four events of this type that have established mission statements and compare these to the criteria given in this chapter.
3 Conduct an interview with the manager of an ongoing festival, conference or exhibition to identify the key external environmental factors that are impacting their strategic event planning.
4 When might an event employ a retrenchment strategy or a growth strategy? Can you identify any specific event where one of these strategies is in evidence?
5 Select a hallmark or mega-event and discuss the ways in which the event plans for legacy outcomes.
6 What problems can arise with the use of functional and network organisational structures, and how would you overcome these.
7 Outline the role of a feasibility study in the strategic event planning process.
8 Briefly explain the functions of policies, procedures and rules within operational plans.
9 Identify, and briefly discuss, three business strategy options that are available to event organisations.
10 Critically examine the strategic planning process of a selected event in the light of the process discussed in this chapter.

CASE STUDY

ST KILDA FESTIVAL MULTI-YEAR OPERATIONAL PLAN 2016–18

The following plan resulted from a review of the St Kilda Festival in 2014. Its intent was to develop an understanding of its current situation and to propose a three-year action plan to ensure its future sustainability.

Introduction

Since its inception in 1980, the St Kilda Festival has grown to become a unique and iconic event that brings together a broad community through shared experience and gathering together. A flagship event for the City of Port Phillip, the festival is a Melbourne tradition and rite of passage; at once an invitation, a celebration and an annual re-establishing of St Kilda as the beating cultural heart of the city. The St Kilda Festival stakes its claim to notoriety in a number of ways, including being Australia's largest free music festival, and engaging more Australian musicians than any other. Alongside that and in its heart it is unique to St Kilda as a place; celebrating not only a heritage of music and culture, but a community as famous for its diversity and eclecticism as for its welcoming nature and acceptance of all. The St Kilda Festival delivers on key objectives of the Council Plan and City of Port Phillip Events Strategy, in particular to showcase and promote the area as a destination; providing economic growth, profile and tourist visitation. In coming years, the festival will also have a key role to play in facilitating St Kilda's new spaces as they change and grow, including changes to Acland St, Fitzroy St and, most prominently, the Triangle Site. In this context, the festival represents an opportunity to activate and program these spaces in line with their strategic objectives: showcasing their potential, highlighting their value and leading by example.

Mission statement

To promote Australian music, the local music scene and support emerging Australian musicians and artists through a premier event that provides valuable opportunities for musicians and artists to reach new audiences.

To provide a large-scale outdoor celebration that encourages and engages the community with access to a broad variety of music and culture; to create an event that promotes the City of Port Phillip as a cultural hub and establish iconic branding for St Kilda in tourism to benefit local traders for a sustainable economy.

Festival objectives

In 2014, Council undertook a strategic process through which it was resolved that the St Kilda Festival's key purpose is to achieve the following objectives:

1. Iconic branding that showcases the City of Port Phillip while specifically promoting St Kilda and increasing visitation rates of tourists. It is a brand that is known to the local community, wider Melbourne and internationally.
2. A commitment to live music which is a vehicle to promote vibrancy as well as specifically supporting local, young and emerging musicians.
3. Longer term sustainable economic benefit for local traders.
4. Community engagement for local and wider communities which contributes to the City of Port Phillip as a cultural hub.

Alongside these key objectives the St Kilda Festival is committed to public safety as the highest priority, while ensuring costs are contained, continuous improvement and the festival is delivered at a reasonable cost to City of Port Phillip ratepayers.

What is the value of the St Kilda Festival?

- *An accessible event* — with an average of 58% attendees noting they have not attended any other festival in the previous twelve months
- *Welcoming* — with an average of 82% of attendees noting that being at the festival has made them feel part of a local community
- *Valuing the arts* — with an average of 120 musicians/bands employed each year (more than 500 musicians)
- *Assisting local businesses* — with an economic impact of $23 million to St Kilda and $19.7 million to Victoria in 2015
- *Popular* — with attendance between 350 000 and 420 000 on Festival Sunday alone
- *Locally loved* — with 83% of both residents and traders in the municipality answering in 2014 that they wanted the St Kilda Festival to continue
- *A year-round invitation* — with 94% of attendees being 'likely' or 'very likely' to return to St Kilda (not including St Kilda residents)
- *Diverse* — with more than 250 performers featured alongside music, including dancers, children's performers, volleyballers, motorcycle stunt men, footballers and giant teddy bears
- *Community focused* — with an open-access policy to community groups that wish to participate
- *Ephemeral and transformative* — with everyday spaces becoming gathering places, then returning again

Why do we need a three-year St Kilda Festival strategy?

The Festival has a strong reputation as a safe and free event that promotes and celebrates Australian live music, generating economic benefit for the municipality and the state. While the bulk of this benefit is reaped through Festival Sunday, the event comes at a significant cost, with budgeted expenditure of $2.5 million in 2015. Although significant amounts of sponsorship are sought and other revenue sources including site fees are earned, City of Port Phillip ratepayers financially underwrite the event and in 2015 the budgeted net cost of the festival to Council is $1.4 million, including core staff costs of $231 000. Planning for the following year's event begins the day after the festival finishes. This leaves insufficient time to implement significant format changes, to procure or add value to larger components (major sponsors or programming partners), and results in a lack of confidence to proceed with initiatives that may require multi-year implementation to be successful. Annual decision-making for the event also precludes stability and confidence for external partners, discouraging long-term sponsorships or development.

This strategy recommends key directions and actions that will deliver on Council's objectives for the festival while not compromising public safety or financial sustainability over a three-year period. This will enable:

- initiatives that require planning and implementation over a longer timeframe than is possible in between each annual festival
- actions that require a phase-in over the three-year period before full benefits will be realised
- agreements and relationships with suppliers that can be locked in over a multi-year period.

What will we do differently?

1. Reposition the branding of the festival, targeting national and international audiences, increasing value and longer term opportunities for major sponsorship, tourism and destination promotion, including St Kilda's assets for the whole Summer period — consistent with Council's Festival and Events Strategy objectives.
2. Develop the festival's reputation as a live music icon that attracts and supports the Australian live music industry by developing a multi-year program that allows for artist development, long-term programming options and increased benefit for participating artists.
3. Engage local traders and community in a program to raise public donations/contributions and encourage re-visitation to the City of Port Phillip year-round.
4. Seek operational efficiencies and maximum value from festival infrastructure, while maintaining and continually improving safety and access.

How will we do it? A three-year action plan:

Objective: iconic branding

Actions:

- Iconic branding that showcases the City of Port Phillip while specifically promoting St Kilda, increasing visitation rates of tourists. It is a brand that is known to the local community, wider Melbourne and internationally.
- Reinforce the festival as Australia's largest free music festival, a unique and iconic Melbourne event showcasing Australian bands.
- Seek Victorian Government investment, in recognition of the economic benefit to the state of Victoria, including support for an expanded marketing campaign that profiles the festival to a national and international audience.
- Market and promote the festival within the wider context of St Kilda — its places, spaces and people.
- Increase awareness of the full scope of the festival, including Live N Local and Yalukit Wilum Ngargee.

Measure	Baseline 2014/15	Year 1 target	Year 2 target	Year 3 target
Number of interstate and international visitors to the festival	Interstate 3%, 12 300 International 32 800	Interstate 13 350 International 36 080	Interstate 14 880 International 39 700	Interstate 16 370 International 43 670
Number of attendees that note they intend to return to St Kilda in the following 12-month period	91% likely or very likely	91% likely or very likely	92% likely or very likely	92% likely or very likely
Victorian government investment into festival promotion	No investment	Investment made	Investment made	Investment made
Attendance at Live N Local and Yalukit Wilum Ngargee	Yalukit Wilum Ngargee 8000 Live N Local 10 000	Yalukit Wilum Ngargee 8800 Live N Local 11 000	Yalukit Wilum Ngargee 9680 Live N Local 12 100	Yalukit Wilum Ngargee 10 650 Live N Local 13 300

Objective: commitment to live music

A commitment to live music which is a vehicle to promote vibrancy as well as specifically supporting local, young and emerging musicians.

Actions:

- Maintain programming of live Australian music as a priority for all components of the festival.
- Maximise development of new and emerging artists, facilitating pathways from Live N Local, the New Music Stage and Push Stage onto major stages.

- Seek Victorian Government investment in recognition of the development opportunities for young and emerging artists through festival pathways.
- Expand the series of professional development opportunities for musicians, providing unique career development opportunities within live music in Australia.
- Develop a database of local artists, to assist in programming of local venues and other City of Port Phillip events.

Measure	Baseline 2014/15	Year 1 target	Year 2 target	Year 3 target
Number of bands/musicians programmed within the Festival	120	125	125	125
Numbers of acts progressing from emerging positions at the festival through to performances on the major stages	3	5	6	7
Attendance at the artist professional development series	300	330	360	400
Percentage of industry partnerships within the professional development series	57%	64%	70%	77%

Objective: longer term sustainable economic benefit for local traders

Actions:
- Provide further opportunities for extended trading, facilitating increased exposure for traders to visitors and attendees.
- Provide further opportunities for trader promotion within festival marketing.
- Maximise trader participation in the Live N Local program.
- Regularly consult with trader representatives to maintain communication about festival direction.

Measure	Baseline 2014/15	Year 1 target	Year 2 target	Year 3 target
Number of traders taking part in festival opportunities	29	32	35	38
Number of traders participating in Live N Local	18	20	22	24
Percentage of attendees that make a purchase at a local-trader premises during the festival	Not measured	40%	45%	50%

Objective: community engagement

Community engagement for local and wider communities that contributes to the City of Port Phillip as a cultural hub.
Actions:
- Maximise awareness of expressions of interest program for community group participation.
- Maximise access and opportunities for engagement with not-for-profit groups within the festival.
- Maintain accessibility to festival attendance for the wider community.

Measure	Baseline 2014/15	Year 1 target	Target year 2	Target year 3
Number of community groups participating in the festival	5	7	8	10

(continued)

(continued)

Measure	Baseline 2014/15	Year 1 target	Target year 2	Target year 3
Number of charity partners participating in the festival	3	3	3	3
Number of small businesses participating in activations at the festival (through call for entries program)	20	22	24	26
Percentage of attendees who respond that being at the festival makes them feel part of the local community	80%	82%	84%	86%

Objective: maximise public safety at the event and operational efficiencies

Actions:
- Review temporary contract staffing model to seek maximum efficiency and minimise cost.
- Review vending operations model to seek maximum efficiency and minimise cost.
- Procure non-exclusive sponsorship brokerage that will assist Council's efforts to secure major sponsorship for the festival.
- Steadily grow sponsorship investment in the festival, including benefits that extend beyond the event itself.
- Contribute to planning and development of key areas within the precinct, such as the Triangle Site, to ensure the sustainability of holding the festival and other events by minimising temporary infrastructure costs, and ensure alignment.
- Collaborate with emergency service agencies to ensure best practice public safety and emergency management procedures are in place.
- Continuous improvement through implementation of achievable recommendations in debriefs with the Emergency Management Committee and Traffic & Transport Management Committee.

Measure	Baseline 2014/15	Year 1 target	Year 2 target	Year 3 target
Operational expenditure increases of no more than CPI annually (excluding project, development or safety costs)	N/A	CPI increase only	CPI increase only	CPI increase only
Percentage of charity partners participating in the festival	N/A	10%	10%	10%
Number of Emergency Management Committee meetings held with emergency service agencies each year	3	3	3	3

Source: 'St Kilda Festival draft multi-year operational plan', City of Port Phillip 2015.

QUESTIONS

1 Why is the St Kilda Festival seeking to reposition itself in the market?
2 How is the St Kilda Festival acting to improve its community engagement efforts and how is it measuring its outcomes in this area?
3 Why is it suggested that the St Kilda Festival move away from an annual strategic planning model?
4 Would you describe the St Kilda Festival as a successful event even though it is currently being underwritten by council ratepayers for $1.4 million?
5 Do you believe the objectives (and their associated measures) that have been set for the event are realistic? If so, why?
6 Visit the St Kilda Festival website (www.stkildafestival.com.au). Given the event seeks to develop 'iconic' status, do you think this will be possible based on what you can determine from its website?

REFERENCES

American College of Surgeons 2020, 'Conference objectives', www.facs.org/quality-programs/quality-safety-conference/objectives, viewed 6 April 2020.

Ann Arbour Arts Festival 2010, 'Strategic plan', https://a2sf.org/wp-content/uploads/2016/02/Strategic-Plan-2015.pdf, viewed 6 April 2020.

Britt Music and Arts Festival 2020, 'Mission and vision statement', www.brittfest.org/missionandvision, viewed 6 April 2020.

Bryson, J 2011, *Strategic planning for public and non-profit organisations* (4th ed.) Wiley, San Francisco.

Carroll, L 1977 (first published 1865), *Alice's adventures in wonderland*, Puffin Books, London.

ChangingMinds.org 2020, 'SMART objectives', www.changingminds.org/disciplines/hr/performance_management/smart_objectives, viewed 6 April 2020.

City of Port Phillip 2015, 'St Kilda Festival draft multi-year operational plan', www.portphillip.vic.gov.au/E57190_15__St_Kilda_Festival_draft_Multi_-_Year_Operational_Plan.pdf, viewed 6 April 2020.

Economist 2012, 'Planning and procrastination', www.economist.com/schumpeter/2012/10/06/planning-and-procrastination, viewed 6 April 2020.

Gasparilla Festival of the Arts 2020, 'Mission statement', www.gasparillaarts.com/about-the-festival/festival-mission, viewed 6 April 2020.

Global Privacy Assembly 2020, 'Mission and vision', www.globalprivacyassembly.org/the-assembly-and-executive-committee/strategic-direction-mission-and-vision, viewed 6 April 2020.

Governor's Hurricane Conference 2020, 'Mission of the Governor's Hurricane Conference', www.flghc.org/mission-statement, viewed 6 April 2020.

Grant, R 2009, *Contemporary strategy analysis*, Malden, Blackwell, Melbourne.

Grant, R 2015, *Contemporary strategy analysis* (9th ed.), John Wiley, Brisbane.

Hill, C, Schilling, M & Jones, G 2016, *Strategic management: theory: an integrated approach*, Cengage, Boston.

International Olympic Committee 2020, 'Olympic legacy', www.olympic.org/olympic-legacy, viewed 6 April 2020.

Johnson, G & Scholes, K 2018, *Exploring corporate strategy* (8th ed.), Prentice Hall, Hemel Hempstead.

Kalamazoo Poetry Festival 2016, 'Strategic plan 2016–20', www.kalamazoopoetryfestival.com/wp-content/uploads/2018/05/KPF-Strategic-Plan-2016-2020-FINAL.pdf, viewed 6 April 2020.

Kearney, A 2006, *Building a legacy — sports mega events should last a lifetime*, Kearney Inc., www.atkearney.com, viewed 12 August 2018.

Local Government NSW 2018, 'Local Government NSW annual conference 2019 criteria for EOIs to be host destination in a Sydney metropolitan area', www.lgnsw.org.au/files/HOSTING%20the%20ANNUAL%20CONFERENCE%202019%20Criteria.pdf, viewed 25 October 2018.

Lynch, R 2018, *Strategic management* (8th ed.), Pearson, Harlow.

Mintzberg, H, Quinn, J & Voyer, J 1995, *The strategy process*, Prentice Hall, New Jersey.

Music Feeds 2017, 'Woodford Folk Festival capping attendance this year for the first time', www.musicfeeds.com.au/news/woodford-folk-festival-capping-attendance-year-first-time/#cTyqGo03g28vhhMs.99, viewed 18 August 2018.

National Folk Festival 2017, 'Strategic plan 2017–2020', www.folkfestival.org.au/wp-content/uploads/2017-20-Strategic-Plan.pdf, viewed 6 April 2020.

Northern Beaches Council 2018, 'Event grants 2018/19', www.northernbeaches.nsw.gov.au/sites/default/files/event-grants-guidelines.pdf, viewed 11 August 2018.

Office of Commonwealth Games Coordination 2006, 'Organisational structure', internal document.

Oregon Shakespeare Festival 2020, 'Our values', www.osfashland.org/en/company/mission-and-values.aspx, viewed 6 April 2020.

Pearce, J & Robinson, R 2014, *Strategic management: planning for domestic and global competition* (14th ed.), McGraw-Hill Irwin, New York.

Peel Music Festival 2020, 'Mission statement', www.peelmusicfestival.ca/Mission.aspx, viewed 6 April 2020.

Pride in London 2020, 'Our Mission', www.prideinlondon.org/about-us, viewed 6 April 2020.

Regina Folk Festival 2017, 'Goals and key actions', www.reginafolkfestival.com/about-rff/strategic-plan, viewed 6 April 2020.

Roskilde Festival, 'Roskilde Festival's organizational structure', www.roskilde-festival.dk, viewed 9 February 2010 (no longer accessible).

Rothaemel, F 2017, *Strategic management: concepts* (3rd ed.), McGraw Hill, New York.

SFFILM 2017, 'Festival strategic plan 2018–2020', www.sffilm.org/about, viewed 6 April 2020.

Silicon Valley Jewish Film Festival 2018, 'About the Silicon Valley Jewish Film Festival', www.svjff.org/about.shtml, viewed 13 August 2018.

Sloman, J 2006, *Project management and events* (course notes), Major Event Management Program 9–14 June, Sport Knowledge Australia, Sydney.

Supreme Committee for Delivery and Legacy 2020, 'About', www.sc.qa/en/about, viewed 6 April 2020.

Sweet Pea Festival 2008, 'Organisational structure', www.sweetpeafestival.org/media/Divisions_Overview.pdf, viewed 13 August 2018.

Thompson, A, Peteraf, M, Gamble, J & Strickland, A 2016, *Crafting and executing Strategy: the quest for competitive advantage: concepts and cases* (21st ed.), McGraw Hill, New York.

Toohey, K & Halbwirth, S 2001, *The Sydney Organising Committee of the Olympic Games and Knowledge Management: learning from experience*, presented at the SPRIG, Manchester, England, p. 4.

Wheelen, T & Hunger, D 2012, *Strategic management and business policy: toward global sustainability* (13th ed.), Pearson, Boston.

Word Dairy Expo 2020, 'Mission statement', www.worlddairyexpo.com/pages/Mission-&-Vision-&-History.php, viewed 6 April 2020.

ACKNOWLEDGEMENTS

Photo: © Hero Images / Getty Images

Extract: © Carroll 1977 (first published 1865)

Figure 5.2: © Grant 2009

Figure 5.3: © Local Government NSW 2018

Figure 5.4: © Northern Beaches Council 2018

Figure 5.5: © Roskilde Festival 2010

Figure 5.6: © Supplied courtesy of the Commonwealth Games Federation, London

Figure 5.7: © Sweet Pea Festival 2008

Figure 5.8: © Sloman, J 2006, Project Management course notes, Major Event Management Program 9–14 June, Sports Knowledge Australia, Sydney

Extract: © National Folk Festival 2017

Table 5.3: © San Francisco International Film Festival 2017

Table 5.5: © National Folk Festival 2017

Case study: © City of Port Phillip 2015

Event project management

Introduction

This chapter examines how the process of project management can be employed in event settings. In doing so it identifies and describes the sequential stages through which event projects move from concept to their conclusion: initiation, planning, implementation, control and monitoring, and shutdown and review. In examining these stages, those project management tools relevant to each will be identified and discussed. Key among these are work breakdown structures, Gantt charts, production schedules, run sheets and checklists. Additionally, the role of the event manual as a key reference document is explored. The chapter concludes with commentary on the use of software as a means of facilitating the event project management process, and a case study showcasing how a failed event — Fyre Festival — would have benefited from a stronger engagement with this process.

6.1 What is a project and what is project management?

LEARNING OBJECTIVE 6.1 Define key concepts associated with project management.

Projects can be defined as 'a temporary endeavor undertaken to create a unique project service or result' (Project Management Institute 2017). Events meet this definition as they are not ongoing; each is unique (even if it is repeated in different locations and at different times) and they are intended to have a defined outcome (that is, an event of a particular type, length, with specific characteristics). Events also share with other types of projects: the need for independent, but related, tasks to be coordinated within a schedule; a defined set of financial and other resources; and the requirement to identify, and take into account, factors with the capacity to impact the project (for example, client expectations, availability of required resources, legal/regulatory issues, weather).

Project management is the application of processes, skills, knowledge and experience with the intent of achieving whatever project objectives have been set within the resources and timeframe that have been allocated. In event settings it offers many advantages, including:

- allowing resource requirements (for example, staff, equipment) and costs to be determined
- providing a systematic means by which core elements of an event can be identified and broken down into actionable activities that can then be tracked, monitored and updated
- building organisational understanding, communication and learning that enhances future event deliveries, while also avoiding the risk that the success of an event relies on any one person
- facilitating the development of a system with agreed documentation, processes and manuals that enhance organisational efficiency and effectiveness
- encouraging the use of common terminology, the development of clear roles and responsibilities and the facilitation of timely communication across accountable teams responsible for different event tasks (O'Toole and Mikolaitis 2002).

These advantages are evident in the case study of the popular car-based event, Summernats, which is conducted in Canberra annually, that has been provided in the following event profile.

EVENT PROFILE

Summernats introduces project management

Now in its 34th year, Summernats is a car festival staged every January in Canberra that celebrates Australia's love of noisy engines, powerful horsepower and all things automotive. The event was originally managed by a founding owner with a small team of full-time staff supplemented by hundreds of casual short-term staff and contractors employed during the week of the event. In the late 2000s the event was sold to a new ownership group that were looking to streamline and modernise its management systems to bring them into line with the expectations of all event stakeholders, particularly customers, government and sponsors. At the same time, the new owners were seeking to run additional aligned events under the Summernats brand, and needed to make more efficient use of staff, processes and resources in order to do so.

An initial study was commissioned into the event's current level of project management applications through a desktop documentation review and interviews with stakeholders, including key staff and contractors. The study found that individual employees, operational departments and contractors were employing widely varying documented and undocumented (informal) practices, and that much of the event's intellectual property (IP) rested with long-term employees who had developed their own approaches to completing tasks. Additionally, when the matter of running additional events was raised with full-time staff members, they were of the view that they could not cope with any additional work as they were already struggling with their current workload. It was also found that supervision was lacking for short-term casual staff, and that this group lacked training and access to instruction manuals that in turn had resulted in high staff turnover and lost IP. Further, it was discovered that some contractors and senior event staff were reluctant to share information as they wanted to ensure that they were viewed as essential to the event's conduct. There was also evidence that departments were acting as silos. This was acting to limit communication and cooperation between them which was impacting the quality of event delivery and causing some key tasks to 'fall between the cracks'.

With these insights in hand, project management processes and techniques were introduced across the event with the intent of saving time and costs, lessening dependence on key people/contractors, improving communication across functional areas and with stakeholders, and building organisational capacity for continuous learning and improvement. Specifically, these involved:

- development of position descriptions for full-time and casual management staff, as well as clear statements as to their area(s) of responsibility
- distribution of detailed information to departments that made clear management expectations, along with their roles and responsibilities across the event
- establishment of time management processes including work in progress (WIP) meetings, a master timeline of annual milestones in the event delivery journey, bump in and bump out build schedules and detailed run sheets covering the four days of the event inclusive of milestones, times and responsible persons
- development of contractor management tools including clear statements as to the scope of their responsibilities, a requirement for pre-event costings/estimates and the use by the event of purchase orders to manage contractor performance and costs
- introduction of new, time-saving software systems for rostering, exhibitor management and site planning.

The use of these project management systems served to standardise operating practices across the event which greatly increased the efficiency and effectiveness of the event organisation. Additionally, the new events developed under the Summernats brand were able to be conducted without a significant boost in overall staff numbers.

Prepared by Noel Landry, CEO, Summernats

6.2 Considerations when applying project management in event settings

LEARNING OBJECTIVE 6.2 Discuss the benefits and limitations of the use of project management in event settings.

While event organisers have been relatively quick to see the value of a project management approach with its associated advantages, there are nonetheless considerations that need to be taken account of when used in event settings. Specifically, it can be difficult to quantify the work required in project managing events and to forecast all tasks that need to be undertaken. This is because many events are one-off and as such have no prior organisational history. Some can also be very complex because of the many elements and considerations involved including programming, infrastructure construction, the need to adhere to laws/regulations and the requirement to engage with multiple stakeholders, some of which might have conflicting agendas. Additionally, unlike with many other projects (for example, building projects), an event's delivery date is essentially fixed requiring that all tasks are completed prior to a venue/site being opened to attendees. This characteristic can create major issues for event organisers if adherence to schedules is not maintained. Budget certainty is another matter that sometimes confronts organisers, most particularly those that need to generate income through ticket sales and so on. It might be necessary, for example, if initial budget estimates are not met, to undertake changes to the way some tasks, activities or event elements are undertaken to cut costs. Event organisers might also need to ensure that their project management efforts embrace requirements imposed by the organisation for whom the event is being delivered. For example, if an event (for example, an association conference or sporting event) has been acquired through the bidding process there are likely to be criteria to be adhered to contained in the bid document. Finally, there are the inherent trade-offs that all project managers face between time, cost and scope/quality (see figure 6.1).

FIGURE 6.1 The project management triangle

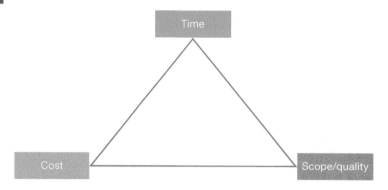

6.3 Skills and knowledge required by event project managers

LEARNING OBJECTIVE 6.3 Identify and discuss the skills and knowledge required of event project managers.

The task of project managing an event will be performed in different ways depending on the scale and nature of the event concerned. In smaller events it is common for the event organiser to take responsibility for this task. In larger events, an in-house event project manager might be used due to the increased complexity involved. In still larger events, such as an Olympic Games, specialist project management companies will often be employed either as consultants or contractors. They will then be attached to the event organising team and/or specific functional areas such as infrastructure or programming. Irrespective of an event's scale, the core competencies associated with project management in event settings remain essentially the same as those in other contexts, and can be summarised as the ability to:

- lead and manage teams — to motivate and mediate as required
- communicate — to understand and be understood and ensure stakeholders have the information they require when they require it
- schedule — to keep an event on track for its delivery date
- manage tasks — to create, assign and manage tasks
- manage costs — to control costs so they are aligned with budget estimates
- manage risks — to identify, establish and employ risk treatments
- negotiate — to manage relationships, establish contract agreements and deal with conflicts
- think critically/problem solve — to analyse, evaluate and develop responses to situations/issues that arise during an event's planning and delivery
- use technology — to enhance the efficiency and effectiveness of project management practices.

6.4 Event project management stages

LEARNING OBJECTIVE 6.4 Describe each of the five stages of event project management and employ project management techniques and tools in the planning and delivery of events.

Events, like other projects, move through a series of sequential stages. These stages are:
- initiation
- planning
- implementation
- monitoring and control
- shutdown and review.

While the specific tasks associated with each of these stages will differ between events depending primarily on their type and scale, the following discussion seeks to provide a general overview of the activities involved in each stage.

Initiation

This first stage of event project management involves a range of tasks. In the case of new events a concept will need to be developed and refined. This will require decisions to be made on matters such as an event's vision/mission/goals/objectives, theming, duration, scale, program, market and proposed venue/site. These decisions, when made in the context of corporate events, are often guided by a client brief (see the chapter on conceptualising the event) or tender document. In other instances (for example, sporting events, association conferences), a bid document (see the strategic event planning chapter), with its associated criteria, may condition many of these decisions. If there is uncertainty around the potential of a new event, a feasibility study (see the strategic event planning chapter) might be required to underpin, and guide, decision-making in this early stage. If an event is pre-existing, this stage will likely involve drawing on prior evaluation outcomes to refine practice in its current iteration. Prior experience, information gleamed from consultations with various event stakeholders and other event organisers will also provide information that will aid in guiding decisions.

Stakeholder (that is, an organisation or an individual who has an interest in an event) identification is also important at this time as their needs and expectations can directly influence how the event project management process proceeds, and what it needs to embrace. Depending on the event, stakeholders can include clients, sponsors, the local community, local government, police, permit granting bodies, contractors/suppliers/vendors/exhibitors, as well as its own organising committee or owner. Failure to identify stakeholders can have major consequences. As an extreme example, two organisers of a series of night-time bike races in Singapore in 2016 failed to identify the country's police and traffic authority as stakeholders in the events and as a result were jailed for seven days and fined $5000 for failing to obtain permission to conduct their events (Chong 2016).

While stakeholder identification is important, so is determining when these groups or individuals need to be engaged. Some might not be involved in this initial stage, while others, such as the police in the case of a large-scale sporting event, might need to be involved in all stages. The form these interactions take also need to be given consideration. For example, councils and granting bodies will require specific documents to be completed before an event can proceed, while an event owner will need regular reports throughout the process. Additionally, an event organiser will need to determine what information or actions they require from stakeholders. For example, event attendees might need to supply personal information to allow them to register for an event, while suppliers will need to provide proof of insurances.

Irrespective of whether an event is new, acquired through the bidding process, or is ongoing, a clear understanding of the 'scope of work' (SOW) required in its planning, delivery and shutdown will be required in this stage. An SOW identifies the tasks that will be required to be performed for an event to take place. In order to determine what these tasks will be, a work breakdown structure (WBS) is commonly employed.

The creation of a WBS involves breaking down an event into logical component parts. By deconstructing an event in this way an event project manager can begin the process of determining an event's resource requirements, costs and timeline. Further, a WBS provides the basis for decision-making as regards the allocation of responsibilities for individual event components and tasks, as well as providing the basis for developing an organisational structure.

The WBS process begins by identifying the major, or level one, task areas based on the volume of their associated work. These task areas are then further broken down into smaller and more manageable components (level two). These smaller tasks can be broken down again (level three) as necessary, and this process can continue until an event organiser believes they have an adequate understanding of the scope of work involved in their event. Figures 6.2, 6.3 and 6.4 show how this process works using the example of a music festival. Additionally, an example of a completed three-level WBS has been provided for a community show in figure 6.5.

For most small to medium-size events, a two or three-level breakdown is often adequate; however, with large-scale events, it will likely be necessary to progress to a fourth or even fifth level. Given the multitude of actions that are likely to be linked to the various identified task areas, a WBS should not be used to capture too much detail. To do so a WBS would become too unwieldy and complex and lose its capacity to provide an overview of the work involved in an event. Other documents, such as Gantt charts, production schedules and run sheets, are employed for this purpose (see later discussion). When creating a WBS it is also sound practice to engage key staff members, and if necessary, other stakeholders such as contractors, to ensure it represents as comprehensive an identification of the task areas involved in the event as possible. Further, it should be kept in mind that there is no one right way to create task groupings; such decisions simply need to make sense to those involved. For example, risk is likely to be assessed as a level one task category in the context of a large-scale sporting event because a multitude of potential risks involved in its conduct; however, in the context of a small-scale conference it might be classified as a level two or three concern.

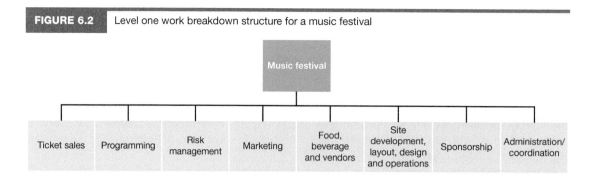

FIGURE 6.2 Level one work breakdown structure for a music festival

Music festival

- Ticket sales
- Programming
- Risk management
- Marketing
- Food, beverage and vendors
- Site development, layout, design and operations
- Sponsorship
- Administration/coordination

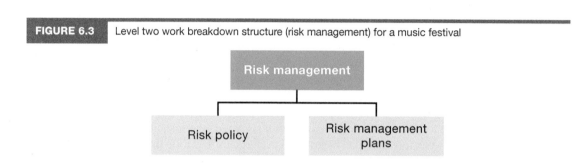

FIGURE 6.3 Level two work breakdown structure (risk management) for a music festival

Risk management

- Risk policy
- Risk management plans

If changes occur in the scope of an event (a process known as scope creep) at any point during the event project management process, due, for example, to the addition of new event elements (for example, a site visit for conference attendees), the implications of these alterations need to be worked through in terms of their impact on resources, costs and schedules. Additionally, if these changes have been requested by a client, communications approving such changes should always be required, and clients must always be made aware of their implications for the event's budget. In this way, later disagreements will be prevented.

In instances where an event is to be conducted by an event management company, a 'statement of work' will need to be agreed upon and this will then become the basis for a subsequent contract. These documents, while utilising the outcomes of a WBS, also commonly include: a statement of the event's goals/objectives; the population to be served by the event; the timeframe in which tasks are to be undertaken; milestones for assessing progress; measurable outcomes; and evaluation approaches. Additional matters addressed in the contract may include cancellation terms, payment schedules, location of governing laws to be employed and indemnification conditions.

Planning

Having established the major work areas and broken these down into their component parts through the WBS process, the next stage is to establish the activities required to be undertaken within these areas. For example, to produce a risk management plan for an event (for example, a community market), it will be necessary to: consult with those able to inform the development of the plan; identify and assess the risks involved; and develop treatment options and processes for their implementation. Once determined, these activities can be linked to the task involved and sequenced within a Gantt chart. This process of identifying actions necessary to complete a task also plays a significant role in clarifying an event's resource requirements and costs, as well as aiding in making decisions as regards what tasks will be the responsibility of the event and what will be outsourced.

Gantt charts list the actions associated with producing a specific event outcome and show when and for how long these actions will occur. This period is commonly represented graphically by a bar, the position and length of which indicate an activity's start date, duration and end date. The use of this scheduling tool, depending on how it is employed, offers a range of benefits, including:

- visually summarising an event schedule so members of the event team can more easily understand the way work on the multiple tasks required to deliver it will flow as the event progresses towards its delivery date
- allowing activities to be sequenced in ways that reduce the potential for overburdening event team members

- making clear interdependencies between tasks; that is, task A must be completed before task B can start
- serving to allocate people/teams to tasks
- assisting in making resource usage more transparent so event organisers can make better use of staff, contractors, equipment and so on
- showing the status of tasks (for example, completed, underway, not started); this can be done by, for example, colouring bars to indicate the status of an activity
- capacity to be employed for individual event elements to overcome the potential problem of having too much information within a single Gantt chart; for example, a conference that includes an exhibition, awards dinner and an optional reception can use different Gantt charts for each event element
- allowing visual markers (symbols with an explanatory key at the bottom of the chart) to be included to show milestone dates by which an activity should have occurred in the context of a specific task area; for example, symbols could be used to indicate, in the context of an event's marketing plan, that tasks such as an event's website, marketing strategy and promotional plan have been completed
- facilitating the sharing of information between staff and event stakeholders in an easily understood form that allows feedback to be obtained on issues such as the appropriateness of the amount of time allocated for tasks and their sequencing. The use of programs such as Google Docs makes this process much easier.

FIGURE 6.4   Level three work breakdown structure (risk management plans) for a music festival

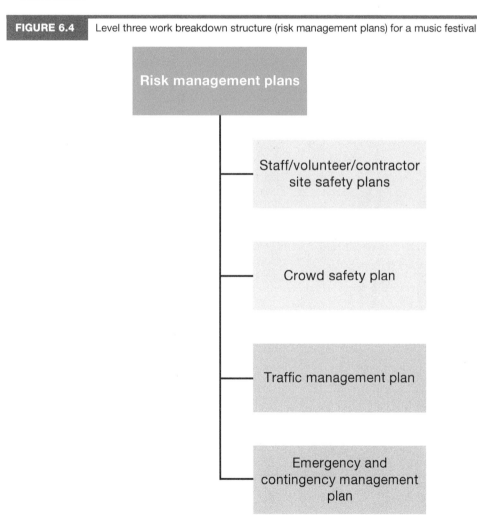

The format Gantt charts take will vary depending on the preferences of the event organiser. The example provided in figure 6.6 shows one approach. You will note from this figure that space has been provided to indicate the person/team responsible for a given task, the current status of that task and any post event actions that might be associated with the task.

FIGURE 6.5 Work breakdown structure for a community show

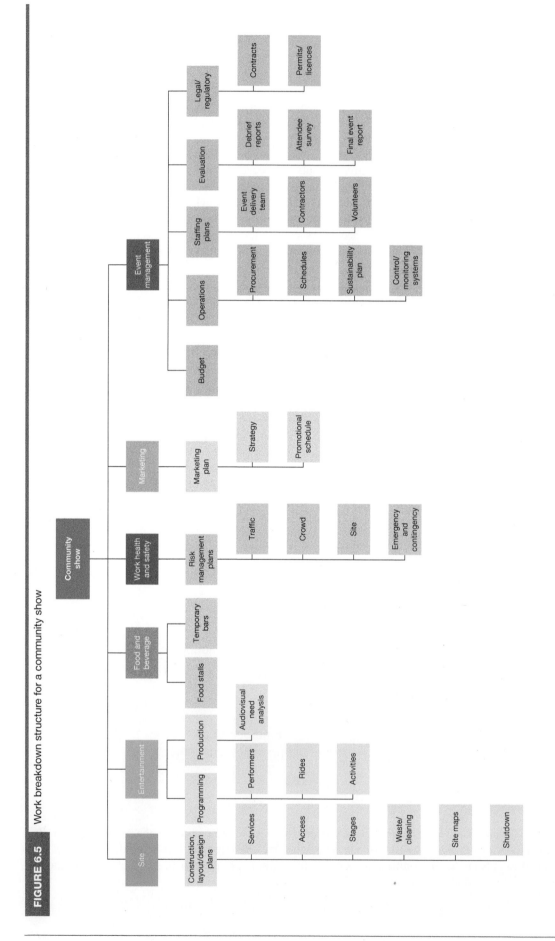

FIGURE 6.6   Sample Gantt chart format

Event: Two-day industry conference
Project manager: Abel Tasman

Task category	Activities	Responsibility	Status	June W/C 01/06	W/C 08/06	W/C 15/06	W/C 22/06	W/C 29/06	July W/C 06/07	W/C 13/07	ETC	Event date	Post-event activities
Venue	Determine event requirements			▓	▓								
	Select					▓							
	Contract (inclusive of catering)						▓						
	Develop venue layout/design plan									▓			
Marketing	Website development and launch					▓							
	Strategy development and finalisation						▓	▓					
	Development of promotional plan and associated schedule								▓				
	Commencement of promotional activities									▓			
Program	Development of program format						▓						
	Identification and contracting of speakers and workshop presenters							▓	▓				
	Program launch									▓			
Audiovisual	Establish audiovisual needs						▓						
	Identify and contract audiovisual company								▓				
Risk	Identification of risks						▓						
	Assessment of risks								▓				
	Development of risk treatments								▓				
	Establishment of risk monitoring and review systems								▓				

Gantt charts, it should be noted, are not once-only exercises. Changes will likely occur through an event's project management process that will require the chart to be revisited to accommodate developments such as changes in the event scope, expanded time requirements for particular tasks, and alterations to sequencing due to the non-availability of equipment or staff.

Determining the amount of time required to complete a task (such as site or venue setup or breakdown) when undertaking it for the first time is not necessarily easy. When confronted with timing uncertainties it can be useful to draw on the experience of other event organisers, as well as suppliers, contractors or venues as appropriate. If a time allocation proves inadequate, it might be necessary to provide overtime payments to staff, employ additional contractors or expedite aspects of the task through other means (for example, using air transport rather than land transport to obtain equipment), all of which can negatively impact an event's budget. This being the case, schedules should be designed in a way that allows some degree of flexibility to cope with time overruns or contingencies such as weather events.

At the same time as estimating the duration involved in completing a task, resource requirements also need to be addressed. An event's WBS, as well as breaking down a task into its component actions, should serve to provide the information required for decisions to be made in this area. Once resource needs have been established decisions can then be made as to where these resources will be sourced from. In some instances events might need to create these resources themselves, or have them specially made (for example, theming material) as they are not commercially available; in others they will need to source them from suppliers (for example, toilets, marquees), contractors (for example, firms specialising in security/risk/waste management), talent agencies (for example, performers), the host community (volunteers) or the venue (for example, audiovisual equipment, catering services). Tempering decisions regarding resources and the quality of their supply will be the event's budget. Another key consideration that should weigh on an event organiser's mind regarding resources is their availability, which can seriously influence scheduling efforts. A useful tool in working through an event's resource requirements is a worksheet such as the one given in figure 6.7.

FIGURE 6.7   Basic task-based resource worksheet

Task	Labour (hours)	Equipment	Materials/ consumables	Source(s)	Cost	Status	Date needed

Prepared by: Date:

Implementation

Once the major task areas associated with an event have been identified, associated actions determined and a schedule in the form of a Gantt chart developed, the next stage in event project management is implementation. In order to operationalise an event's plans an event organiser will need to take various actions, central among which are: establish and manage the event project team(s) (see the human resource management and events chapter); assign resources; develop policies and practices that serve to guide how tasks (for example, procurement, tendering, staffing) are executed; develop detailed scheduling tools (for example, production schedules, run sheets) and checklists to guide event delivery; conduct status meetings with staff and stakeholders; engage in active risk management; and modify plans and schedules (as required) in light of unexpected events/situations. The following discussion explores several of these actions in more detail.

Procurement

The procurement process involves the identification, grouping and pricing of equipment and services required to build, operate and dismantle an event. The specific tasks involved in procurement can extend to venue acquisition/hire, product manufacture (for example, merchandise, signage), equipment hire (for example, portable toilets, fencing, bars, radios) and contracting service suppliers (for example, security firms, audiovisual companies, waste-removal firms). To ensure this function is performed effectively, procurement requirements need to be subject to a scoping exercise to establish an event's precise requirements before going to the market with a request for quotes or a response to tender documents. This may necessitate consulting with people with expertise in specific areas. In this regard, contractors or suppliers are sometimes willing to assist with this task providing they later have an opportunity to quote on the provision of the item(s)/service. An example of the outcomes of such an exercise for the supply of electrical services to an event has been provided in figure 6.8.

Once the scoping process has been completed, the next task is to identify equipment/service suppliers. This can be done in several ways. If an event is run by a local council, for example, use can be made of Local Government Procurement that will communicate tenders through to registered event suppliers and contractors, of which there are a number. There are also other web-based organisations (for example, Australia Tenders) that perform a similar function. In other instances, tenders or requests for quotes can be directed to specific businesses identified through such means as web searches, the use of personal networks and by reference to industry directories (for example, the A List Guide).

FIGURE 6.8   Contractor scope example — electrical services

Scope of work elements	Requirements
Service outline	• The contractor will provide all necessary electrical equipment and services for a bushfire fundraiser event to raise funds for those impacted by fires and to acknowledge rural fire brigades. • The event will be televised live nationally by Network X. • The contractor is expected to provide uninterrupted power supply including all necessary equipment to stage both the live and broadcast components of the event for the duration of the program.

Scope of work elements	Requirements
Event details	• The event will be held at the Rod Laver Arena with 10 000 attendees seeing over 20 domestic and international acts on two stages with rotating acts in operation from 1 pm to 12 am. • Bump in will be from 6 am Friday 13 March and bump out and removal of all equipment to be undertaken from concert close to Monday 16 March at 12 pm.
Specific agreed service and compliance expectations	• UPS capable of covering all broadcast, lighting and production needs for the period of the broadcast. • Back up equipment and spares as required to provide the service outlined. • All equipment and works supplied to be fully compliant with relevant local authority requirements and relevant Australian Standards for the works. • Staff provided to be currently licensed and accredited electricians. • The contractor will seek and obtain all necessary approvals required to provide the service as outlined. • A minimum of three electricians to be on duty during the event period including one stationed at each stage for the duration of the performance.
Equipment required	• The contractor is required to supply all equipment necessary for delivery, installation, operation, maintenance and removal of the attached scope including: – temporary generators – leads, power boards and switchboards – uninterrupted power supplies (UPS) – testing and monitoring equipment – plant and equipment to install the equipment – spares and consumables for the above. Note: truss, rigging, sound, broadcast and general production will be supplied by others.
Resources required	• The contractor is required to supply all labour required for delivery, installation, operation, maintenance and removal of the attached scope. • The contractor's lead project representative is expected to attend a minimum of three site pre-planning meetings and one project debrief. • A list of equipment used is to be provided post-event.

Government-run events most often use formal tenders due to their need for transparency in purchasing exercises. Less bound by regulation, private-sector events tend to use more informal practices that involve negotiating with a small group of trusted contractors and suppliers.

A range of other considerations should also be taken account of when engaging in the procurement process:

- cost-effectiveness of hiring equipment as opposed to purchasing equipment; decisions made need to take account of costs associated with storing and maintaining items
- potential for contractors to include an additional margin into a quote in situations where: a tender or request for a quote contains too little detail; where responses are required quickly thus allowing little time for them to fully understand the scope of what is being requested; and in periods of high demand
- importance of clarity on inclusions and exclusions (for example, delivery, maintenance callouts) when comparing quotes
- quality of supply: contractors and suppliers are integral to overall perceptions of event quality — the wrong choice can significantly impact attendee satisfaction and damage an organisation or event's brand. For this reason, many event organisers will use a few preferred suppliers/contractors who they can trust to engage quickly with the event team and who can be relied upon to provide quality services/items.

Once contracts have been signed with suppliers and contractors, all the information likely to be needed by them — delivery locations, site maps, setup/layout drawings, location of services such as water and electricity, event team contact details and supply timings — must be provided in a timely manner. They should also be consulted when an event's production schedule and run sheets are being prepared so that they can provide feedback on matters such as the adequacy of time allocations for the services or tasks (for example, erection of marquees) with which they are involved. Once provided, a check should also be performed to ensure supply conforms to contract requirements.

Operational policies and procedures

Policies direct how a task or activity is to be undertaken and as such set limits on actions, ensure consistency in decision-making and direct behaviour. (A detailed discussion of the development and use of a policy in the area of environmentally sustainable procurement appears in the chapter on sustainable event planning). They also serve to avoid the need for constant management intervention by allowing control by exception. Policies can emerge as a result of external laws/regulations (for example, health and safety laws, disability discrimination laws) or an organisation's desire to guide action in a specific area (for example, environmental sustainability, employee hiring, procurement). Procedures, on the other hand, provide a series of steps that are to be followed in carrying out a policy. For example, actions might be stipulated to ensure a product conforms to an event organisation's sustainability policy before it is ordered. Whatever policy and procedures are set, they will be rendered useless unless an event organisation's management activity adheres to them and effectively communicates them to their employees and other relevant stakeholders.

Once established, it is also important to monitor policies and procedures to establish if they are serving the purpose for which they were developed. Indicators that they are not can include an increase in the number of accidents/injuries occurring at an event site, time overruns for tasks, increases in reported staff stress levels, poor event evaluations and increasing numbers of staff questions regarding the performance of operational tasks.

Event human resource requirements

The size, makeup and skills of an event's workforce will be determined by factors such as its nature (for example, a sporting event vs conference), program elements, scale and budget. As an event progresses through its implementation stage, it will grow in terms of the staff required as more of the tasks identified in the planning stage need to be activated. This can present a significant challenge, particularly in larger events. In order to deal with this challenge, it is important that: job descriptions are clear; lines of communication and reporting are understood; onboarded staff are adequately trained for roles they are to perform; and that human resource management processes are capable of dealing with the event's expanding workforce. Refer to the chapter on human resource management and events for more detailed information on this topic.

Production and breakdown schedules, run sheets and checklists

Capturing the fine detail associated with particular tasks such as site/venue setup and breakdown, and the activities necessary to deliver an event's program, is not something that can be incorporated into an event's Gantt chart because of the level of detail needed. For this reason, production schedules and run sheets are employed.

Production schedules capture the activities required to be undertaken in the day(s) immediately leading up to the commencement of an event in preparation for the arrival of guests/registrants/ticket holders. In order to construct a production schedule, a clear understanding of these lead up activities is required, along with how they need to be sequenced to ensure that they occur in a logical manner. Additionally, staffing requirements during this period must be established, along with who on the event team will have responsibility for overseeing the various activities that will be taking place. It will also be necessary to communicate the production schedule to suppliers and contractors to ensure they understand exactly when they will be required. A sound practice to employ after distributing information to these groups is to contact them a few days out from when they are needed to remind them of timings and to identify if there are any issues that may force the schedule to change (for example, a weather event impacting delivery times). Once an event is concluded, a breakdown schedule will also be needed which essentially performs the same role as a production schedule but deals with the activities associated with removing equipment and services from a site/venue.

Failure to adhere to a production or breakdown schedule can have significant consequences. Delays in setting up a venue or site, for example, can result in attendees being inconvenienced as they are forced to wait in long queues before they can enter, which might attract unwarranted media attention. Not being able to return a site or venue back to its pre-event state by the contracted time can also attract a financial penalty.

The format of production schedules will differ slightly between events. Nonetheless, these documents commonly include the following information:

- task start and end times
- the activity (for example, delivery of fencing, installation of electricity supply)
- location of the activity/service provision — this is particularly important if the site/venue is large and entry needs to occur at specific gates or zones.
- supplier/contractor name/contact, and if relevant for security purposes, vehicle registration number
- ordered items (for example, 200 chairs) — allows a check to be made on arrival
- explanatory notes/comments — as required.

A basic production schedule template for an outdoor event involving a multi-day setup has been provided in figure 6.9.

FIGURE 6.9	Sample production schedule template for an outdoor event

Start	End	Activity/location/ supplier/contractor/ ordered items or services	Supplier/contractor contact and vehicle registration	Event team member with oversight responsibility	Notes
		Day 1			
		Day 2			
		Day 3			
		Day 4			

While production schedules establish the 'flow' of event activities prior to its commencement, a run sheet (sometimes called a show flow or schedule) is used to capture and schedule activities during an event. The time intervals in a run sheet are generally smaller than those in a production schedule, and in the case of, for example, a televised event, can be down to the second.

A run sheet is used to deliver an event's program, and as such shows program elements and their timings (for example, workshop commencement times), as well as other relevant matters germane to the flow of the event. For example, the actions of staff (for example, venue door to be opened, guests to be ushered from the reception room into the main dining area), performers (for example, band to commence playing), venue staff (for example, drinks service to commence, room to be reconfigured for plenary session) and suppliers (for example, buses arrive to transport guests to dinner venue). These documents also indicate who in the event team has responsibility for overseeing the timely conduct of these activities. Other common inclusions: contact details of those involved in various capacities in event delivery; location where an activity is to take place (for example, reception room 1, zone A); radio frequencies in use (if relevant); and space for notes. If events have multiple elements (for example, a festival might have multiple stages, a children's activity zone and an area where presentations/workshops take place), then it will be necessary to have run sheets to control each area. Some event organisers also attach appendices to a run sheet, such as site/venue maps, staffing schedules, room diagrams and lists of matters for attention (for example, placement of microphones for questions from the floor). In the case of simple events it is possible to construct a combined run sheet and production schedule, as has been done in figure 6.10.

Once a run sheet has been developed it should be communicated to all those involved in the event's delivery. As changes can occur close to the date of an event, as well as during an event, it is important to include version numbers on run sheets, indeed most event documents, in case they need to be modified and resent to stakeholders. It should also be kept in mind when constructing run sheets that timings need to be realistic and adhered to ensure the flow of the event.

FIGURE 6.10 Combined production schedule and run sheet

Contacts

Event manager	Jade Davis: 0400 000 000
Client	Joanne Rossiter: 0400 000 001
Chef	Justin South: 0400 001 000
Venue	Tory Summ: 0400 002 000
Floral styling	Nicholas Connell: 0400 003 000

Bump in

Time	Action	Who
16:00	EM, Client on-site	Jade Davis, Joanne Rossiter
16:00–16:20	Bump in glassware	BEA
16:15–16:45	Bump in tableware (crockery, napery, cutlery etc.)	Justin South
16:30–17:00	Bump in floral	Nicholas Connell
16:30–17:00	Set table settings	Justin South
17:00–18:30	Food prep	Justin South
18:30	All bump in/prep complete	

Event

Time	Action	Who
18:45	All on standby for early arrivals	Waitstaff
19:00	Guest arrival, pre-dinner drinks and canapes in casual seated/kitchen space	Guests
19:30–19:40	Kelly to invite guests to be seated — per table seating plan and personalised name cards • Drinks topped • Amuse-bouche served	Kelly, waitstaff

Bump out

Time	Action	Who
22:15	Pack down commences	
22:15–22:45	Clean/clear kitchen	Waitstaff
22:30–23:00	Pack down tableware	Waitstaff

| 22:30–22:45 | Pack down floral | Nicholas Connell |
| 23:00 | Collection of tableware (return to hirer tomorrow) | Jade Davis |

Checklists are another major tool used during an event's implementation stage. They act to ensure consistency and completeness in carrying out a policy, procedure or activity and can be employed in a variety of areas. In developing checklists care should be taken to clearly identify the policy, procedure or activity for which the checklist is to be prepared. For example, disability access, on-site sustainability practices, venue selection, volunteer site induction or the carrying out of a specific task (for example, inspections of vendor conformity to electricity and gas safety requirements). Additionally, the focus of a checklist should be researched to ensure all relevant factors have been included. In this regard, feedback should be sought from experienced team members, contractors/suppliers, or other event managers to reduce the potential for items being omitted. To make checklists more user friendly, employing category headings and placing related items under these is good practice. For example, a venue selection checklist might include the following headings: access, audiovisual, sustainability policies/practices, food and beverage, health and safety, power and electrical, security, staging, wi-fi, location, contract conditions/charges, on-site facilities, and quality of furnishings and fittings. This approach to constructing a checklist is evident in the example provided in figure 6.11, which is an extract from a much longer risk assessment/safety checklist.

The event manual

Compiled progressively through the implementation stage, the event manual serves as the major operational reference document. It also serves as an event's project management 'history' which can, post-event, be reviewed with the intent of making changes/modifications for subsequent event iterations. The content of an event manual will vary depending on the type of event and its scale/inclusions. A listing of possible inclusions appears in table 6.1. Upon event completion, event manuals should be finalised by the inclusion of evaluation data, photographs of the event, incident reports and stakeholder (for example, venue, suppliers, council, caterers, police, sponsors) debrief outcomes so their role as a record of the operational aspects of the event is complete.

TABLE 6.1 **Potential event manual inclusions**

General	Venue/supplier/contractor/trader/performer
Event Details — description, organisational chart, reporting structure and list of key contacts	Venue/supplier/contractor/trader/performer contracts
Operational procedures and policies	Venue/supplier/contractor/trader/performer contacts
Licences/permits — site use permit, alcohol licence, live and recorded music licence	**Staffing**
Communication plan: event command and control, radio channels and protocol	Staff/volunteer position descriptions and responsibilities
Templates/forms, for example, incident reports, property damage report	Staff and volunteer rosters
Insurance documents	**Sustainability**
Event program	Environmental management plan — waste, noise, carbon footprint

(continued)

TABLE 6.1 *(continued)*

General	Venue/supplier/contractor/trader/performer
Site/venue	**Risk**
Site/venue maps/room configurations	Work, health and safety plan
Signage plan	Crowd management plan
Transport and traffic management plans	Contingency plans
Access plans	Emergency management plan
Road closures	Alcohol management plan
Site services plan — lighting, water, electricity	Children and vulnerable persons protection plan
Toilets amenities management plan	Security plan
Security deployment map	**Sponsors**
	Sponsor agreements and associated deliverables
Schedules/checklists	**Other**
Production schedule/run sheet(s)/breakdown schedule	Media plan
Checklists	VIP and protocol plan

Monitoring and control

The monitoring and control stage of event project management runs in parallel with the implementation stage. Monitoring is concerned with collecting information on how planned outcomes, and the activities underpinning them, align with the schedule that has been set and serve to ensure the event's readiness for its commencement date. The information provided during this stage allows an event organiser to determine what (if any) schedule variances exist, and to take corrective actions as required.

Various practices can be used to monitor the performance of an event against its project plan. One key means of ensuring an event remains on schedule is to conduct regular meetings between project team members to: assess progress in their respective areas; identify issues that have arisen that might impact on the tasks for which they are responsible; and discuss how the issues that have been identified can be dealt with. At these meetings (or at other designated times) status reports are commonly presented so progress in specific areas can be monitored. When conducting meetings reference to milestones, which show progress towards completion of a task, can provide a valuable focus for discussion. For example, an event's website going live might be a milestone in its overall marketing planning efforts, or the completion of an event's resource analysis might be a milestone in its operational planning. It is important to establish a meeting schedule early in the event project management process and to include dates in the event's planning timeline so staff and other relevant stakeholders can schedule their attendance and be prepared with any relevant information they are expected to input or review. It is also imperative that meeting minutes are taken that show the decisions that have been made and any follow-up actions that are to be taken and by whom. These minutes should then be distributed to participants and the actionable items reported on in subsequent meetings.

Budgets can also be used as a monitoring tool, with income received from event revenue streams, and expenditures made by specific dates providing information on an event's financial health. Observation is another technique that can be employed during an event's build period and prior to its commencement using pre-established checklists. For example, checklists can be used to: establish if particular tasks have been completed as planned (for example, room setups); identify risks that need to be dealt with (for example, trip hazards, untagged electrical cords or gas bottles, or failure to install weights on marquees); and determine if supply is as per contract (for example, have 200 chairs been delivered or only 150). Observation can also be used during an event to report on delivery issues such as unacceptably long entry queues or the emergence of attendee behavioural problems.

FIGURE 6.11	Extract from a risk assessment/safety checklist

Amenities			
Sufficient toilets and hand washing facilities for expected number of attendees	☐	☐	
Adequate amenities provision for people with disabilities	☐	☐	
Adequate drinking water available for attendees	☐	☐	
Power			
USC approved electrician used for electrical set up	☐	☐	
All portable electrical equipment/tools, leads and power boards tested and tagged as required	☐	☐	
No daisy chaining of extension cords and power boards	☐	☐	
Leads connections etc are protected from weather or any other liquid	☐	☐	
All leads secured	☐	☐	
Leads/cables not to be placed across thoroughfares	☐	☐	
Generators, if used, safely positioned and access to area restricted — Location approved by USC Fire Safety Advisor (FSA)	☐	☐	
Slips trips and falls			
Pathways and thoroughfares kept free of trip hazards	☐	☐	
Site assessment/inspection to identify trip hazards — plan set up to avoid trip hazards	☐	☐	
Signage where necessary	☐	☐	
Noise			
Noisy activities are planned for time of least disturbance of other activities	☐	☐	
People who may be affected by nuisance noise have been alerted to time and duration of noise	☐	☐	
Security			
Security have been kept informed about event	☐	☐	
Any activity which may produce smoke, fire or dust has been reported to Security prior to the event	☐	☐	
The requirement for additional fire fighting equipment has been communicated to Security/Facilities Management (FM)	☐	☐	
Waste management			
Adequate bins have been provided	☐	☐	
Increased bin emptying has been arranged through FM	☐	☐	

Source: University of the Sunshine Coast n.d.

Information gained through the monitoring process is fed through to an event's management team so that the implications to such areas as scheduling (that is, production schedules, run sheets), quality of event delivery, risk management and conformance to permit/licence conditions can be identified and appropriate controls employed. These controls will vary based on the issues identified; however, controls employed in the lead up to, and during an event, can include:

- implementation of contingency plans
- increased allocation of staff/resources
- improvements in staff/volunteer training
- enforcement of contracts
- alterations to existing operational activities/practices/procedures
- implementation of risk treatments.

Event organisers can be proactive in the way they approach the task of project control by anticipating issues that may arise and seeking to prevent them from occurring. For example, large-scale sporting events use trial events to identify shortcomings in operational systems prior to the main event occurring, while it is common practice in many events to employ rehearsals and engage in equipment testing before an event's commencement. Contract specifications can also be used to avoid problems occurring. Equipment standards, or types, can be stipulated, as can a requirement that all licences, insurances, permits, proof of training (for example, food handling certificates) and engineering sign offs be provided by set dates or during the event build period. Prior scenario planning can also be employed in areas such as budgeting and risk management, to establish clear strategies should specific circumstances arise. Prior assessments of suppliers/contractors/performers can also be undertaken by attending events where they are present, or by requesting feedback from other event organisers.

A major means by which event organisers can reduce their need to invoke control practices is by employing learnings from prior events to refine/change the way they approach the event project management process. Through this means, events may effect changes to any number of current practices/processes, such as:
- supplier contracts/selection processes
- event delivery systems
- financial management procedures
- security/crowd management practices
- signage/way finding/queue management
- risk management planning
- marketing practices.

Shutdown and review

An event's shutdown stage should be embraced as part of its overall project planning efforts. This being the case, the tasks associated with it should be identified and then incorporated into a schedule. Too often this stage is given little thought, and actions necessary to complete it are rushed and not well planned or executed. This creates potential problems for staff/supplier/contractor safety, the orderly flow of equipment from the venue/site and the ability of event organisers to refine future practice. Failures at this point can also have cost implications as noted earlier. Further, theft can also be an issue if insufficient security is maintained at this time. Considerations during this stage embrace both the breakdown of the site/venue itself and a range of post-event activities. These two areas are best dealt with through separate schedules that allocate responsibilities for identified activities to specific staff members and contractors (for example, traffic management and audiovisual companies). Additionally, the risks during this stage need to be identified, and treatments developed and implemented as required. A list of some of the major activities that might need to occur (depending on the event concerned) in these two areas has been provided in table 6.2.

It is also at this stage that the event organiser should reflect on the overall project management process, the degree to which it served to achieve the event's goals and objectives, and what future changes might be necessary to better align the process with the outcomes that were sought. Information needed for this purpose should emerge from attendee and staff feedback, as well as from debriefs conducted with key stakeholders.

TABLE 6.2   Event shutdown activities

Event site/venue shutdown activities	Post-event activities
Management of attendee departure, and transport, away from the venue/site	Compensation of suppliers for breakages/damage to supplied equipment
Return, and sign off, of equipment supplied to staff (for example, hand-held radios, uniforms)	Provision of incident reports to insurance companies in support of claims (if necessary)

Scheduling the removal of equipment, disconnection of services, and dismantling of structures (for example, exhibition stands, stages, marquees)	Debriefs with staff/volunteers/suppliers/contractors/sponsors and other stakeholders as needed
Resource recycling	Grant acquittal (if necessary)
Venue/site cleaning and handback	Acknowledgement (for example, letters of thanks, functions) of the contribution of staff/volunteers and other stakeholders to the event's success
Security staff rostering	Making agreed contributions to charities/community services (for example, Rural Fire Service) for assistance provided during the event
	Sale or auction of equipment that has no ongoing use
	Checking final invoices to ensure any changes that might have occurred during the event's planning and implementation stages are reflected, and paying contractors/suppliers
	Finalisation and audit (if required) of the event budget
	Preparation of video content, keynote speeches and blog posts for distribution to attendees
	Sale of a conference's proceedings (ongoing)
	Preparation of a final event report (see the chapter on event evaluation and research)
	Finalisation of the event manual
	Conduct of attendee surveys (see the chapter on event evaluation and research). This task might be undertaken post-event or immediately prior to close.

6.5 Project management software for events

LEARNING OBJECTIVE 6.5 Discuss the benefits and limitations of event management software systems.

The uptake of time- and cost-saving software systems to aid efforts at event project management has increased dramatically over the past 10 years. This growth has been fuelled by such developments as improvements in the capacity of mobile technology, cloud-based storage and the emergence of programs specific to events. Event organisers have exploited these developments to varying degrees depending on their assessment of such factors as ease of use of software packages, capacity for customisation, efficiency benefits and cost. At one end of the use spectrum, event organisers are employing generic spreadsheet software, such as Google Docs, and within these tools developing work breakdown structures, schedules, budgets, risk management plans, site/venue maps and so on. These electronic documents can be shared easily between event team members and stakeholders as required and can be updated to reflect changes or show the current status of various tasks. Additional to these tools are a myriad of other generic software programs (for example, SmartDraw) that provide customisable templates or tools that facilitate the creation of site/venue plans, Gantt charts, run sheets and other documents such as checklists. There are also integrated generic project management software programs that can be adapted for use in event settings (for example, Trello, Microsoft Projects). Another form of software that is commonly in use in the events field is that of cloud-based video, audio and chat conferencing platforms, such as Zoom and Microsoft Teams, that facilitate collaboration between event project team members including the sharing of documents.

While many event organisers find they can use or customise generic software programs sufficiently to meet their needs, an increasing number are turning to event-specific programs. These programs can be significantly more expensive than generic programs, and often require users to commit to their use for a set period via a contract. That said, they can prove very cost effective in that their integrated nature greatly enhances organisational efficiency and effectiveness. The wide variety of tasks handled by these programs extend to areas such as eCommerce, scheduling, website creation, attendee management, procurement and contract management, venue sourcing, ticketing/registrations, abstract management, exhibitor management, marketing, staff and volunteer management, venue management, team communication, talent management, risk management, reports, budgeting, surveys and catering. Figure 6.12 provides an example of the functions of one such program used in the festivals area, FestivalPro.

Commonly, event project management software programs are designed with specific types of events in mind (for example, conferences, exhibitions, festivals) and this is reflected in their various features. It should also be noted that there are many software programs that deal with only specific aspects of overall event project management, rather than seeking to provide a comprehensive solution. For example, there are many programs that deal only with ticketing or registrations (for example, Aventri, Hubspot) and there are an increasing number that focus on risk management (for example, RiskSense101).

FIGURE 6.12   Features of FestivalPro event management software system

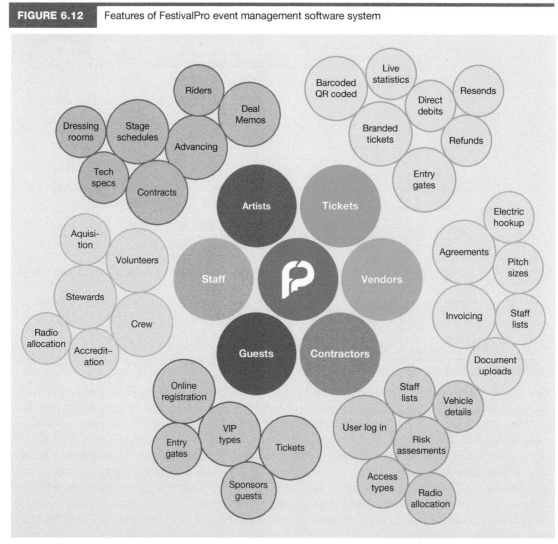

Source: FestivalPro 2020.

The decision to use, or not to use, event project management software requires an event organiser to seek answers to a range of questions, central among which are the following:
- Does its use save staff time, and to what degree are the savings in staff time, and associated salaries, offset by upfront licence fees, ongoing use charges, and training requirements and costs?
- What are the costs of implementation likely to be in terms of interruptions to existing processes and systems, the need for equipment upgrading, and staff stress levels and motivation?
- What training is required, how long will this take and how will staff respond to the need to learn a new system?

- Should it be necessary to terminate the user contract, are there exit fees? If so, how much are these fees?
- To what degree does a purpose designed event project management software program impact efficiency and cost compared with the use/adaptation of a generic software program?
- How easy is the program to use for staff, and other stakeholders, that will need to interact with it?
- Which tasks, and to what extent, will it automate/streamline, and what degree of customisation is possible?
- How compatible is it with the other software systems and processes currently in use?

SUMMARY

Events can be viewed as projects, and as such the discipline of project management has much to offer the practicing event organiser. Specifically, it provides a structural overlay to the event planning and delivery process, encouraging event organisers to view events as projects comprising a logical sequence of stages — initiation, planning, implementation, monitoring and control, and shutdown and review — and suggests a range of tools that can be used to guide them through these stages to their delivery date. Key among these tools are work breakdown structures, Gantt charts, production schedules, run sheets and checklists.

In order to facilitate how the event project management process occurs in event settings, the use of a variety of generic and event specific software programs were briefly discussed. Decisions as regards their use, however, needs to be subject to seeking responses to a range of questions, including their ability to reduce costs, create time efficiencies and their compatibility with other software programs used by an event organisation.

QUESTIONS

1 What role does project management play in the planning and conduct of an event?

2 What are the limitations of using project management practices in event settings?

3 Why is stakeholder management a key aspect of managing event projects?

4 What role does the monitoring and control stage play in event project management?

5 What is a work breakdown structure and what function does it perform in overall event project management?

6 Interview a music festival director or conference organiser to determine what project management tools, techniques and processes they currently employ. Identify the positions of the various staff that are responsible for their development and implementation.

7 What specific features do you think you would want in an off-the-shelf event project management software system if you were conducting small to medium-sized conferences?

8 What is an event manual and what role does it play in event project management?

9 Explain the key differences between an event work breakdown structure and a production schedule.

CASE STUDY

10 PROJECT MANAGEMENT LESSONS FROM THE FYRE FESTIVAL

The best thing that can be said about the Fyre Festival fiasco is that it provides a teachable moment in how not to manage large-scale creative projects. The doomed 'luxury musical festival' that was a social media laughing stock in 2017 and is now the focus of brand-new documentaries on Hulu and Netflix features all the elements of a project manager's nightmare — poor planning, blown budgets, lack of accountability and unrealistic and unmet expectations are just the start. Whether you're planning a major event or a new product launch, you can learn from where festival organizer like Billy McFarland and rapper Ja Rule went wrong. Here are 10 key project management lessons we can learn from the disaster that was the Fyre Festival.

1. Be careful what you promise

What raised the stakes on delivery was an epic promotional video used to build interest for the Fyre Festival. It opens with a shot of a deserted island, with a voiceover saying, 'The actual experience exceeds all expectations', while images flash of private jets and the world's top supermodels. Not only was this image impossible to live up to, it made the gap between the eventual reality and the expectation more embarrassing when organizers didn't deliver. Smart project managers keep a tight handle on stakeholder expectations from the start.

2. Listen to your people

Chloe Gordon worked on the festival and says everyone around the leaders saw it was going to fail. 'It was clear to most of us that nothing was going to come together at this rate', she later wrote for *The Cut*.

'I cannot explain how or why the bros running this festival ignored every warning sign they were given along the way. The writing was on the wall. I saw it firsthand six weeks ago.' Multiple people in the documentaries warned organizers, but they refused to listen, and now they're paying the price. If someone on your team raises a red flag about an aspect of a project, take the time to assess their concerns.

3. Keep communication open

According to the Netflix documentary, the owner of the private island organizers intended to use wanted to rebrand the island and asked them not to mention the rumour that it was once owned by drug kingpin Pablo Escobar. That very sentence showed up in their promo video, which got them kicked off the island. If proper approval and communication channels had been set up, they would have been able to keep the original, promised location.

4. Money can't solve everything

A big budget is nice, but it can't buy you more than 24 hours in a day. About a month before the festival, according to *VICE*, '[Organizers] were running low on cash and the festival lacked fundamental necessities — toilets and showers, for example — and they were running out of time. One supplier told *VICE News* that when they were contacted by the festival in April, they told the organizers that all the money in the world wouldn't get trailers for toilets and showers past customs in time, because that takes weeks to process.' Organizer Billy McFarland thought angel investors could grant wishes, but that just wasn't true.

5. Know when to cut your losses

When the timeline became too tight, Gordon says staff realized 'the best idea…would be to roll everyone's tickets over to 2018 and start planning for the next year immediately'. They had a meeting with the Fyre execs to deliver the news. A member of the marketing team said, 'Let's just do it and be legends, man'. They are legends, but not for the right reason.

6. Make a budget and invest in fundamentals first

McFarland went so strong on paying to promote the event that he seemed to forget about the costs of the event itself. According to *VICE*, in a meeting McFarland had with a potential investor, he 'intimated that Fyre had spent several million dollars on celebrity endorsements and marketing and now needed cash to pay vendors staffers, and artists'. Don't spend so much on the icing that you forget about the cake.

7. Don't promise the impossible

As long as McFarland was bringing in ticket sales, he didn't care about anything else. According to the Netflix documentary, he invented new packages, like cabanas that didn't exist, to sell before they were ready. Deliver what you originally committed to doing before upselling the client and/or adding new challenges to your team's plate.

8. Don't surround yourself with yes people

It wasn't just that McFarland didn't listen to his people, he got rid of those saying things he didn't like. According to *VICE*, 'The organizers … cycled through several production teams, after firing some for saying the job was impossible'. Good project managers understand the value of critical feedback and constructive conflict.

9. Respect your team

For a festival that was supposed to be an amazing time, it seems like everyone around McFarland was miserable. He didn't pay his workers or his vendors, he didn't treat his creative staff with respect, and he certainly didn't seem to care about the concert-goers. If you don't treat your team with respect and work to motivate them in a positive way, don't expect them to go the extra mile for you.

10. Own your failures

The day that Fyre Festival was supposed to happen, McFarland sent out a message that said, 'due to circumstances out of our control, the physical infrastructure was not in place on-time and we are unable to fulfill on that vision safely and enjoyably for our guests'. An employee on the Netflix documentary said it was entirely under their control. If they had owned their mistakes, they might not have had so many people gleefully mocking them to the world on social media. Take ownership of any project failings instead of trying to pass the buck and step up with a plan for how you'll make things right for your client.

While the mistakes of Fyre Festival seem obvious in hindsight, it can often be difficult even for experienced project managers to spot when things are going wrong in real time and make the necessary course corrections. If you keep these 10 lessons in mind, however, you can minimize the risk of your next big creative project imploding in such spectacular (and public) fashion.

Source: Workgroups DaVinci n.d.

QUESTIONS

1 Why is it important to 'respect your team' when project managing events?
2 How would a comprehensive work breakdown structure and a detailed Gantt chart have improved this event's project management?
3 Discuss the implications of the differing levels of emphasis placed on marketing as compared to project management in this case.
4 Time is a finite resource. Do you think the event organisers in this instance understood this?
5 Why should a 'tight lid' be kept on stakeholder expectations? Was this done in this instance?

REFERENCES

Chong, E 2016, 'Jail and fine for duo behind illegal bicycle races', *The Straits Times*, 5 October, www.straitstimes.com/singapore/courts-crime/jail-and-fine-for-duo-behind-illegal-bicycle-races, viewed 10 April 2020.

FestivalPro 2020, 'Features', www.festivalpro.com, viewed 10 April 2020.

O'Toole, W & Mikolaitis, P 2002, *Corporate event project management*, John Wiley and Sons, New York.

Project Management Institute 2017, *Project Management Body of Knowledge — PMBOK Guide* (6th ed.), Project Management Institute, Newtown Square, Pennsylvania.

University of the Sunshine Coast n.d., 'Risk assessment and safety checklist', www.usc.edu.au/media/1083076/usc-event-risk-assessment.pdf, viewed 7 April 2020.

Workgroups Davinci n.d., '10 Project Management Lessons from the Fyre Festival Fiasco', www.workgroups.com/resources/blog/10-project-management-lessons-from-fyre-festival, viewed 10 April 2020.

ACKNOWLEDGEMENTS

Photo: © SFIO CRACHO / Shutterstock.com
Figure 6.11: © University of the Sunshine Coast n.d.
Figure 6.12: © Festivelpro 2020
Case study © Workgroups DaVinci n.d.

CHAPTER 7

Event financial planning

LEARNING OBJECTIVES

After studying this chapter, you should be able to:

7.1 describe and discuss the financial management process in the context of income-generating and fully funded events

7.2 employ selected financial management tools.

Introduction

Event organisers approach the challenge of financial management from a range of different perspectives. Some events are solely profit driven (for example, an entreprenerd music festival), while for others generating a surplus is one of several objectives. Association conferences, for example, seek to connect their attendees with the latest developments, technologies and practices in a particular field, while at the same time generating revenue for the association itself. It is also the case that some events aim to merely recoup costs. Many community-based events fall into this category. For still other events, there is no intention by their organisers of recouping associated expenses, the focus being on post-event outcomes such as increased sales or raised levels of awareness. Product launches, for example, are of this nature. Irrespective of the outcomes sought through an event's conduct, it is still the case, as Sounder (2004, p. 137) notes, that all events need to meet or exceed certain financial performance objectives and as such require responsible financial management.

This chapter explores how the money resource can be efficiently and effectively used to achieve an event's predetermined financial outcomes. It begins by examining the financial management process as it applies to both income-generating and fully funded events. It then moves on to describe key financial concepts and practices that serve to inform or guide this process. The final part of this chapter briefly overviews selected issues that are aligned with effective financial management.

7.1 The event financial management process

LEARNING OBJECTIVE 7.1 Describe and discuss the financial management process in the context of income-generating and fully funded events.

Events fall into two broad categories from a financial management perspective: those that are fully funded; and those that seek to generate an income to partly or fully offset their costs, or produce a surplus. Given that the latter types of events are more complex from a financial planning perspective, these are dealt with first here.

Income-generating events

The starting point for financial planning for an event that is required to generate an income will depend on whether it is a new event or one that is ongoing. If the event is new, a feasibility study might be required (see the chapter on strategic event planning) to establish its potential viability from various perspectives, including that of its capacity to generate income. If this study concludes that an event does have the potential to meet its objectives, inclusive of those of a financial nature, a more detailed business plan can then be developed to guide its establishment and development. These initial steps are obviously not required in the context of existing ongoing events, instead the process of financial planning would commence by taking into consideration feedback from the prior iteration of the event, along with changes in the business environment in which it operates (for example, levels of competition, the broader economic situation). This information would then be used to refine current financial objectives and the event's associated budget.

The financial objectives that events set can be quite varied. Some events (for example, community-based events) might seek to recoup some or all (break-even) of their costs, while others aim for a targeted net profit figure or a specific return on monies invested (for example, entreprenerd music festivals, association conferences, exhibitions). In the case of some types of new events, it can also be appropriate to adopt a staged approach to becoming revenue positive, with decreasing loss-making objectives set for the first few years of operation as they develop a marketplace position and grow demand before progressing to profitability. In these instances, an event will need to be underwritten by the organisation conducting it, or by some other means (for example, a loan). Community-based festivals, for example, sometimes receive financial support in the form of grants from local councils until they become self-supporting.

Once financial objectives have been established, a budget needs to be developed that will serve to deliver on them, and by so doing forecast the event's desired financial future. In performing this role budgets force event organisers to engage in a detailed analysis of costs and revenue, and to acknowledge any assumptions that underpin these (for example, inflation rates, perspectives on the current or future economic environment). These assumptions can be particularly significant in instances where events are scheduled to take place at a time some years into the future, as is the case with many association conferences and major sporting events. Budgets also make clear to those responsible for managing an event's expenses and revenue-specific financial targets that they must operate within or seek to achieve. Related to this role is the educative value of budgets in forcing a systematic and rigorous examination of how costs and revenues are behaving. Further, they provide the means by which the inflow and outflow of the money resource can be monitored and controlled as the event moves through its planning cycle. Finally, budgets serve as an evaluation tool as event organisers seek to review forecasted financial performance against actual results.

Event expenses

Accurately determining event expenses is key to preventing cost 'blow-outs'. This can be achieved in several ways including obtaining quotes from suppliers; going out to the market with tenders for specific services; or drawing on insights from an event's past budgets. As regards quotes, it is common practice for three or more to be sought from potential suppliers. In assessing quotes, it is important to keep in mind that they need to be carefully reviewed to ensure they are based on the provision of exactly the same service/item. For example, a venue may quote a lower amount than others but might not include add-ons such as wi-fi and audiovisual equipment which the other quotes do. When these factors are accounted for the lesser quote may not represent better value for money. Additionally, consideration should be given to the benefits of working regularly with a limited range of suppliers as opposed to always going out to the market for quotes. These benefits include the ability of suppliers to quickly integrate into an event organiser's planning and delivery processes due to their prior experience(s) and the potential willingness of suppliers receiving regular work to assist at short notice if required.

When working through the expense side of their budgets, event organisers should always be looking for ways to minimise costs, while still ensuring that the quality of the final event experience aligns with attendee and/or client expectations. In this regard various practices can be employed depending on the event, including:

- shifting event dates/timings to periods of lower demand when venue/supplier charges might be less. For example, conducting an event in winter at a seaside location may significantly reduce venue charges
- negotiating with venues and suppliers with the goal of having them lower their quotes
- identifying items for which sponsorship, or in-kind contributions, might be sought (for example, catering, speakers)
- using volunteers to reduce labour costs
- exploring ways by which catering costs can be reduced while still meeting attendee expectations. Such practices include the use of standup or buffet lunches rather than sit down meals, limiting drink offerings and bar opening times and selecting venues that do not require additional kitchen equipment to be hired and brought in
- reducing promotional costs by making greater use of social media
- eliminating printing costs by transferring material such as programs and tickets into electronic form
- reducing waste management costs by restricting what can be brought into an event site by suppliers, or by making suppliers responsible for their own waste
- selecting venues that are within walking distance of each other when multiple venues are in use to reduce transport costs.

In small-scale events it is likely the event organiser themselves will be responsible for determining costs; however, in larger events individuals in charge of various program elements (for example, entertainment, site operations, food and beverage provision) will often be asked to provide input into the process before a master budget is developed. By engaging key staff in this way, there is also the likelihood that there will be greater buy-in to the budgeting process as expenditure targets won't be viewed as being imposed from above without consultation.

Every event will have its own specific expenses, and it is important that these are all identified and included in an event's budget to avoid overspending (see a generic listing of event costs in figure 7.1). Overspending can be a problem in instances where short planning timeframes are involved, and expenditure commitments are made prior to any exchange of paperwork. To ensure these commitments are captured, rather than coming as a 'surprise' later in the event budgeting process, they should always be noted and the amount remaining for the item concerned adjusted accordingly in the budget. It is also a reality for some events that it can be extremely difficult to identify all costs associated with them because of their unique nature, in which case this needs to be recognised at the outset and an adequate contingency amount put aside.

FIGURE 7.1 | A generic listing of event costs

Marketing	Ticketing/registrations/invitations	Program	Staffing
• Advertisements — online, print, outdoor • Public relations • Website development, hosting and management • Development of social media tools and their management • Email marketing • Banners and signage • Postage • Logo creation and artwork	• Ticketing and registration costs resulting from third party usage (for example, Ticketek) or the need to develop internal systems for this purpose • Processing costs (for example, credit card charges) • Name badges and badge printing	• Speaker, performer and/or master of ceremonies (MC) fees • Speaker, performer and/or MC travel and accommodation costs • Speaker, performer and/or MC gifts • Riders — food, drink and special requests • Event app production • Filming (if required) • Attendee transport — coach/car hire • Event streaming/broadcasting/podcasting production costs • Tours and other off-site activities	• Permanent and casual staff labour costs • Staff training • Staff travel and accommodation • Event management fee (if outsourced) • Staff subsistence • Volunteer-related expenses • Donations to not-for-profit organisations (for example, Rotary) or community groups for the supply of services

Venue/site	General administrative expenses	Contingency	Other
• Room(s)/site hire • Early access/late access fees • Décor/theming hire • Audiovisual equipment hire • Wi-fi and network connections • Rigging costs • Furniture/tent/marquee hire and setup/breakdown • Linen and table cover hire • Food and beverage • Permits and licences • Parking • Security/crowd management • Staging and lighting equipment hire • Exhibition booth hire and set-up costs • Fencing and barriers • Toilet hire • Water tank hire and installation • Trackway • Site/venue office expenses (for example, leased photocopier, printer, scanner and other equipment) • Waste management charges	• Event management software costs • Accounting fees • Insurances • Legal fees • Consultancy fees • Stationery and office supplies • Printing costs • Courier costs • Taxes imposed on sales (for example, GST) • Petty cash expenditure • Communication costs	• Percentage of total expenses/designated amount	• Delegate kits • Gratuities • Photographer and/or videographer services • Awards/gifts

Event revenue streams

As with expenses, income sources for events can be many and varied and will depend on the specific event concerned (for a generic listing of potential revenue sources see figure 7.2). A common mistake made by event organisers is not spending enough time identifying and exploring the viability of potential income streams. For example, are there grants that might be applied for, or does the event lend itself to seeking sponsorship or engaging in merchandising? In answering such questions, it is important that realistic assessments are made of any new potential source of income based on the financial return it is likely to produce. Additionally, current revenue streams should be scrutinised to determine what they are contributing to an event's bottom line once expenses associated with them have been accounted for — their contribution margin (see later discussion). For example, some event organisers who see sponsorship as a potential revenue stream might be surprised to find that once they total the costs involved there is little or no return. These expenses can include: the direct costs involved in providing a sponsor with the benefits that have been agreed upon (for example, signage, advertising, exhibition space, free tickets/registrations/parking); staff time involved in developing and selling sponsorship packages and engaging with sponsors prior to, at and post the event; and any sponsorship evaluation–related costs. A range of other factors can also come into play when assessing the revenue potential of a specific income stream, such as:

- market price sensitivities — what can realistically be charged for registrations, stallholder fees, tickets and sponsorships, and so on
- degree to which (if at all) an event is unique or special and therefore able to leverage this by increasing its ticket/registration/sponsorship charges; for example, the only conference of its type to take place in the southern hemisphere in a particular year
- extent to which various forms of discounting will be employed; for example, early bird rates, group discounts
- characteristics of the competitive environment in which an event operates
- market place trends — is the demand for the specific event type rising or falling?
- market feedback on charges from previous event iterations — what capacity (if any) exists to increase registration/ticket prices, or stallholder/exhibitor fees, for example
- changes in the economic environment — exchange rates, inflation and the overall state of the economy
- period covered by the event's planning cycle — an event may take place at a time several or more years into the future in which case changes in costs over this period will need to be accounted for.

FIGURE 7.2	A generic listing of potential revenue sources for events

Income stream	Description

Registration fees/tickets	Some events charge a single price for attendance, while others offer different prices based on a range of criteria, including:
	• advance purchase — tickets purchased a designated time out from the date of an event might attract a discounted rate (for example, early bird discounts)
	• audience characteristics — reduced rates might be offered to individuals possessing specific characteristics based on:
	  – age (for example, seniors, children)
	  – membership of selected organisations (for example, professional bodies, automobile associations)
	  – employment status (for example, employed/unemployed, student)
	  – personal characteristics (for example, people with disabilities)
	• duration of attendance — in the case of multi-day events, rates might be offered for attendance on specific days, or after stated times
	• experience characteristics — some events have the capacity to offer differentiated experiences. Some music festivals, for example, offer VIP tickets that include catering, parking, access through special entry gates and cordoned off seating areas. In live music/theatre events seating location can also be used as a means of pricing attendance with those seats closer to the stage being priced higher
	• ticket reservation — the capacity to pay to reserve a seat at an event that otherwise offers unrestricted entry
	• group size — volume discounts involving groups of a certain size or above.

(continued)

(continued)

Income stream	Description
Advertising	Advertising space can be sold on an event's website, social media sites, app, in its programs or at the event site/venue.
Exhibition space	A major source of revenue for exhibitions is the sale of allocated spaces to exhibitors. These spaces are often of different sizes and locations within a venue and are priced accordingly. It is also not uncommon for conferences to sell space to exhibitors in common areas such as those immediately outside plenary rooms.
Commissions on accommodation and airline services	Some event organisers have integrated into their structure travel agency services that allow them to capture commissions on delegate airline and accommodation bookings.
Alcohol and food	While alcohol and food sales can be significant revenue streams for events, it needs to be kept in mind that licences will be required and that certain standards must be adhered to in areas such as food preparation, hygiene and responsible service of alcohol. Given these considerations it is often (but not always) more efficient for event organisers to contract out food and alcohol provision to businesses with expertise in these areas.
Sponsorship	Many events provide an opportunity for organisations to directly access and communicate with specific groups of people of interest to them (for example, buyers of their services or products). This opportunity, in turn, can be monetised through the sponsorship process.
In-kind contributions	In-kind contributions take the form of services/products/equipment that an event would otherwise need to pay for. In return for these contributions, events provide benefits such as promotional opportunities (for example, advertising) or the sole right to sell a product at an event. An example of the latter would be a wine company agreeing to supply wine for free at a pre-event party for the media in exchange for the rights to sell their product at the event.
Grants	Event-specific grants are sometimes available from government and non-government sources. In the case of the former, national (for example, Festivals Australia), state (for example, tourism promotion bodies) and local government offer a range of grants for both public and business events. Grants are also available from other sources, such as private foundations. A useful starting point when searching for potential grants is The Grants Hub (see www.thegrantshub.com.au). It should also be kept in mind that granting bodies often require an event's previous and current budget as part of the information they need prior to providing funds.
Donations	Some individuals, particularly high wealth individuals, will provide funding for specific projects, including events. Arts-based events are often the beneficiaries of such income. Donors commonly receive benefits in the form of free tickets and invitations to openings and other special events, the costs of which need to be accounted for when determining the net benefit of this income stream. Philanthropy Australia (see www.philanthropy.org.au) is a useful starting point for events seeking to explore opportunities in this area.
Broadcast/streaming rights	Some events, particularly large-scale sporting events and music festivals, lend themselves to the sale of broadcast or online streaming rights. Negotiating such rights is a complex process and is best dealt with by hiring legal professionals with expertise in the area. An entry point into the streaming space that some events currently use is that of YouTube Live. Through this free platform, an event can run advertisements while live streaming. It is also the case that the use of such services enhances the potential value of sponsorships as the event is exposed to a wider audience.
Concessions/sale rights	Fees or commissions are often charged by event organisers to allow individuals/organisations to sell products or services (for example, alcohol, food, arts and crafts) at an event site.

Merchandise sales/licensing	Attendees at some events, particularly those with strong brands, often wish to purchase a memento of their attendance. This desire can be leveraged to create branded merchandise (for example, T-shirts, posters, cups). Events have the option of producing such material themselves (and taking the risk that sales revenue will exceed the cost of manufacture) or of using a merchandising company and receiving a commission on their sales or a flat licensing fee. It should also be noted that some events operate either a physical and/or online store that sells branded material on a year-round basis (for example, Edinburgh Fringe Festival).
Raffles/competitions/auctions	Opportunities exist during the delivery of some events to raise additional revenue through the conduct of raffles (a licence might be required), competitions, or auctions of often donated items.
Parking and camping fees	Some events, such as multi-day outdoor events, have the capacity to make available, as part of attendee packaged ticket prices or as separate offerings, camping and recreational vehicle spaces or parking.
Crowdfunding	A relatively new funding source commonly used by start-up events. Crowdfunding sites such as Chuffed allow hopeful event organisers to propose a new event to a targeted audience offering them unique benefits. These benefits might include, in addition to tickets, T-shirts, masterclasses, behind the scenes tours, and access to mini-events prior to the main event that are intended to create further interest and word of mouth. A key aspect of using this funding source is that a target figure must be set along with information on how the amount raised is to be spent. Should the target figure not be reached, all monies are returned to contributors by the crowdfunding site.
Add-on experiences	Business events, such as conferences, sometimes offer tours or site visits to delegates at an additional charge. These activities are frequently arranged through tour companies with the event receiving a commission on sales. Additionally, some events, such as exhibitions, offer add-ons to their main programs (for example, seminars) for which a fee is charged separate to any registration or entry fee.

Establishing an event budget

Once an event has identified its expenses and revenue streams, it then needs to embrace these within a budget. Commonly, event budgets take the form of an Excel or Google spreadsheet making such documents easy to manipulate and share as required. The option also exists for budgets to be developed within one of the growing numbers of integrated financial (for example, Xero) or cloud-based event management software packages (for example, iVvy). It should be noted that various free event budget spreadsheet templates are available online. These include those provided by EventMB Studio Team (2019, p. 43) and Eventbrite (n.d.).

Events use line-item budgets that list revenue sources and expenditure items on individual lines, grouping the latter under broad headings, such as marketing, catering and audiovisual. A sample line item budget for a conference incorporating a trade show has been provided in figure 7.3. It is noteworthy that this example includes three columns — likely, pessimistic and optimistic. The benefit of constructing budgets in this way is that decisions can be made as to how the organiser will adapt to specific financial scenarios as an event unfolds. This avoids the pitfalls of making decisions on the run when their consequences might not be able to be thoroughly thought through. It is also sound practice to design budgets in ways that can easily be understood by all those involved in using them. In this regard the ability of software to translate figures into pie charts or bar graphs can be particularly useful (see figure 7.4). It is also important to keep in mind that it is likely that unexpected costs (for example, casual staff labour costs exceeding initial estimates), or a failure of one or more income streams to meet its expected target, will occur. For this reason, a contingency amount should be built into budgets. This amount will differ between events depending on the degree of certainty/uncertainty the organiser feels is inherent in their initial calculations, often this figure is in the 5–10 per cent range.

| FIGURE 7.3 | Sample budget based on a conference (incorporating a trade show) and using scenario planning |

Conference name:
Start date:
Finish date:

Revenue	Estimate (realistic)	Estimate (pessimistic)	Estimate (optimistic)
Early bird registration revenues	$ -	$ -	$ -
Registration on day of registration	$ -	$ -	$ -
Revenue from registrations for part of conference only	$ -	$ -	$ -
Discounted registration revenues (students/members of associations)	$ -	$ -	$ -
Sponsorship	$ -	$ -	$ -
Revenue from trade show lease of space	$ -	$ -	$ -
Trade show revenues from percentage of total trade show sales	$ -	$ -	$ -
Conference facilities and accommodation revenues	$ -	$ -	$ -
Other revenue (for example, parking, advertisng, merchanise sales)	$ -	$ -	$ -
	$ -	$ -	$ -
Total revenue	$ -	$ -	$ -

Expenditure

Conference marketing:

Publicity: promotions & advertising			
Printing — brochures	$ -	$ -	$ -
Posters & signage to advertise conference, venue & exhibitors	$ -	$ -	$ -
Website development (if required)	$ -	$ -	$ -
Website hosting	$ -	$ -	$ -
Social media	$ -	$ -	$ -
Sub-total	$ -	$ -	$ -

Conference facilities

Facility hire	$ -	$ -	$ -
Signage inclusive of stands and signs	$ -	$ -	$ -
Communications: telephone & network connections at facility	$ -	$ -	$ -
Trade show costs	$ -	$ -	$ -
Photocopier/printer/scanner/other equipment lease	$ -	$ -	$ -

Sub-total	$ -	$ -	$ -
Conference trade show			
Exhibitors floor space — power and other services	$ -	$ -	$ -
Security and other services specific to exhibitors requirements	$ -	$ -	$ -
Sub-total	$ -	$ -	$ -
Conference administration	$ -	$ -	$ -
Registration — administration fees	$ -	$ -	$ -
Credit card booking expenses	$ -	$ -	$ -
Printing and binding of conference proceedings	$ -	$ -	$ -
Program printing	$ -	$ -	$ -
Online abstract/conference paper submission/review	$ -	$ -	$ -
Key-note speaker payments/gifts	$ -	$ -	$ -
Videotaping of keynote speakers	$ -	$ -	$ -
Delegate Conference Kit	$ -	$ -	$ -
Courier charges	$ -	$ -	$ -
Sub-total	$ -	$ -	$ -
Catering, transport, entertainment			
Meals: Conference morning and afternoon tea, lunch and dinner	$ -	$ -	$ -
Welcome reception	$ -	$ -	$ -
Conference entertainment	$ -	$ -	$ -
Pre-conference site visit	$ -	$ -	$ -
Delegate airport transport	$ -	$ -	$ -
Cleaning	$ -	$ -	$ -
Security	$ -	$ -	$ -
Sub-total	$ -	$ -	$ -
Labour costs	$ -	$ -	$ -
Permanent staff	$ -	$ -	$ -
Casual staff	$ -	$ -	$ -
Volunteer expenses	$ -	$ -	$ -
Sub-total	$ -	$ -	$ -
Other expenses (please specify)			
Item 1	$ -	$ -	$ -
Item 2	$ -	$ -	$ -
Sub-total	$ -	$ -	$ -

(continued)

(continued)

Revenue	Estimate (realistic)	Estimate (pessimistic)	Estimate (optimistic)
Contingencies	$ -	$ -	$ -
Total expenditure	$ -	$ -	$ -
Total revenue – Total costs = Net surplus/loss	$ -	$ -	$ -

Source: Based on University of Western Sydney n.d.

FIGURE 7.4 Sample event budget incorporating the use of graphics

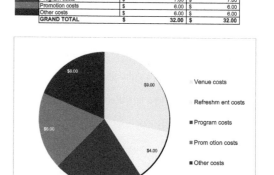

Expenses	Estimated Cost	Actual Cost
VENUE		
Room/venue hire	$ 1.00	$ 1.00
Electricity	$ 1.00	$ 1.00
Staff (security, check-in staff, etc.)	$ 1.00	$ 1.00
Furniture rentals	$ 1.00	$ 1.00
Equipment rentals (speakers, microphones, etc.)	$ 1.00	$ 1.00
Decorations	$ 1.00	$ 1.00
Signage	$ 1.00	$ 1.00
Other	$ 1.00	$ 1.00
Other	$ 1.00	$ 1.00
Total Venue	$ 9.00	$ 9.00
REFRESHMENTS		
Food	$ 1.00	$ 1.00
Drinks	$ 1.00	$ 1.00
Other	$ 1.00	$ 1.00
Other	$ 1.00	$ 1.00
Total Refreshments	$ 4.00	$ 4.00
PROGRAM		
Presenters	$ 1.00	$ 1.00
Performers	$ 1.00	$ 1.00
Presenter / Performer travel	$ 1.00	$ 1.00
Presenter / Performer accommodations	$ 1.00	$ 1.00
Photographer / Videographer	$ 1.00	$ 1.00
Other	$ 1.00	$ 1.00
Other	$ 1.00	$ 1.00
Total Program		
PROMOTION		
Physical Advertisements(flyers, stickers, etc.)	$ 1.00	$ 1.00
Web Advertisements(paid Facebook/Instagram ad	$ 1.00	$ 1.00
Printed agendas/programs	$ 1.00	$ 1.00
Swag (stickers, keychains, etc.)	$ 1.00	$ 1.00
Other	$ 1.00	$ 1.00
Other	$ 1.00	$ 1.00
Total Promotion	6.00	6.00
Other		
Other	$ 1.00	$ 1.00
Other	$ 1.00	$ 1.00
Other	$ 1.00	$ 1.00
Other	$ 1.00	$ 1.00
Other	$ 1.00	$ 1.00
Other	$ 1.00	$ 1.00
Total Other		
GRAND TOTAL	$ 32.00	$ 32.00

Expense Breakdown	Estimated Totals	Actual Totals
Venue costs	$ 9.00	$ 9.00
Refreshment costs	$ 4.00	$ 4.00
Program costs	$ 7.00	$ 7.00
Promotion costs	$ 6.00	$ 6.00
Other costs	$ 6.00	$ 6.00
GRAND TOTAL	$ 32.00	$ 32.00

Source: Eventbrite n.d.

Once budgets have been established, they will likely need to be approved by, in the case of corporate events, the client, or in the case of other types of events, the body with ultimate authority for them, such as an organising committee. Subsequent changes to the budget also generally require approval and such approval should be documented to avoid any arguments.

Continued engagement with the budget as an event moves through its planning cycle is key to ensuring, to the extent possible, that its financial objectives are met. With this goal in mind, event organisers have a variety of control mechanisms available to them, including:

- regularly updated statements of expenditure and/or income prepared by individuals/committees responsible for aspects of an event (for example, ticketing, marketing). These statements should show the total spent and the budgeted amount remaining, or the income received as a percentage of that forecast for the revenue stream concerned (see figure 7.5)
- limiting responsibility for updating and managing an event's budget to a single person, such as the event's financial controller or manager. If authority is delegated for particular expenditure areas to an individual, or committee, they need to be instructed as to the level of budgetary control they have and any restrictions to which they need to adhere
- purchase orders confirm to a supplier exactly what is required, and provide delivery dates, locations and contact details. These documents provide a checking mechanism when passing invoices for payment so it can be established if the services supplied equate with what has been invoiced for

- use of financial ratios (see later discussion)
- scheduled regular budget meetings involving key staff/committee chairs designed to review actual expenditure and income vs projected expenditure and income
- comparisons with expenditure or income from previous years' events so deviations can be quickly identified, investigated and actions taken as required such as reducing costs or seeking to grow revenue through increased marketing.

FIGURE 7.5 Live event budget — summary

	INCOME	1. Projected	2. Income to date	3. Variance (1–2)
1	Ticket sales	$	$	$
2	Sponsorship	$	$	$
3	Merchandising	$	$	$
4	Concession fees	$	$	$
	Etc.			
	Total income	$	$	$
	EXPENDITURE	**1. Projected**	**2. Expenditure to date**	**3. Variance (1–2)**
1	Marketing	$	$	$
2	Venue	$	$	$
3	Audiovisual	$	$	$
4	Catering			
	Etc.			
	Total expenses	$	$	$
	Plus contingency amount	$	$	$
	Total expenses plus contingency	$	$	$
	Total income – Total Expenditure = Net surplus/deficit	$	$	$

Source: Based on VisitScotland 2019.

Upon an event's completion, a final budget is needed showing actual expenditure and income. This expenditure can then be benchmarked against projections with the difference (or variance) being shown as a percentage. Those items showing a meaningful divergence from that predicted can then be explored in detail to establish why this occurred. This practice can also highlight issues in the projection process itself if significant areas of over or underspend are identified, or if income streams have performed below or above expectations. This information can also be used to: redirect expenditure at future events; aid in making the argument for tighter budgetary controls; and to support alterations to an event's current business model. Additionally, if an event is ongoing, this process will establish its financial position going forward. It should be kept in mind that some event stakeholders, such as granting bodies and the tax office, might require detailed budgets and other financial documents, such as a profit and loss statement (see later discussion) once an event has concluded. They can also sometimes reserve the right to carry out an audit post an event. Given these possibilities, it is always best practice to keep appropriate, and transparent, financial records.

While budgets play a key role in guiding the financial future of an event, it should be kept in mind that there might be times when they will need to be adapted to changed circumstances. For example, it might be necessary to shift financial resources within a budget because of a change in the event's operating environment or the event might need to reduce its original estimates as regards income from a particular revenue stream. The case study at the end of this chapter, which deals with music festivals in the UK, provides examples of the type of real-world financial challenges that need to be responded to when conducting events.

Figure 7.6 summarises the previously discussed process of financial management for events where income generation is an objective. This figure is based on a new event, and therefore assumes a feasibility study and business plan will be necessary.

FIGURE 7.6 Event financial management process from the perspective of a new event

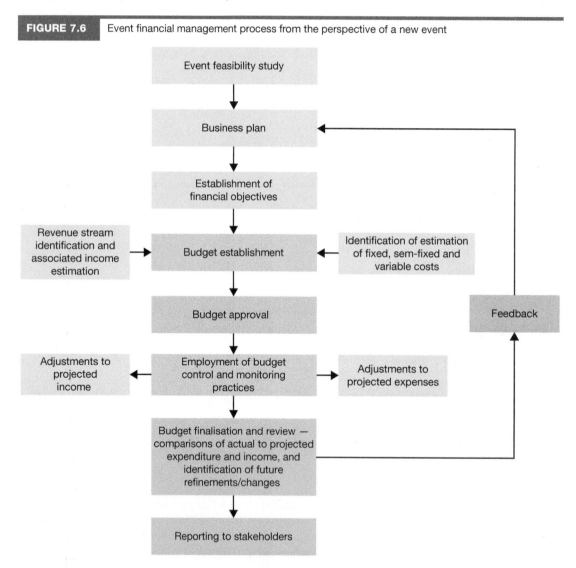

Fully funded events

In instances where an event is fully funded by an organisation, event organisers need only concern themselves with the management of expenses and ensuring these (inclusive of their own management fees) align with the budget that they have created for it. While there are differences in how the financial planning process works in events of this type, they generally involve the event organiser establishing event costs, developing an expenses budget, monitoring and controlling it, and producing a final expense report. To illustrate how the financial management process works in this context, the example of a product launch has been used in this section.

Companies wishing to conduct product launches initiate contact with event organisers through sending them a client brief. This document provides key details regarding the event they wish to conduct (for example, objectives, audience size, nature of product(s), information on prior launches) along with a proposed allocation of funds (although this may not always be included). Based on this information, the event organiser then develops a concept for the event and an associated budget, inclusive of their management fee, both of which are then sent to the potential client. As regards the management fee that is charged, this is generally in the range 15–20 per cent of the event's total budget. Some companies, it should be noted, prefer to charge a lump sum or a per hour rate. Whatever pricing approach is taken, however, event organisers should be conscious of the need to avoid underpricing their services. While this can increase the volume of business conducted, it can also lead to stretched resources; limited capacity to reinvest in the business (for example, equipment, staff training); staff departures due to overwork; declines in event quality; and ultimately a spiral of ever declining business (see figure 7.7).

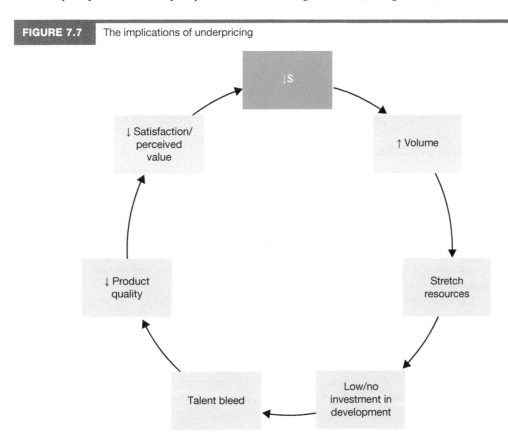

| FIGURE 7.7 | The implications of underpricing |

While multiple event companies are often asked to make submissions based on the same brief, only one company will be selected to proceed. The company that is selected and contracted might also be required to make refinements to its concept/budget. Once finalised and agreed upon, the budget is then overseen by the event organiser to ensure that actual expenditure aligns with that forecasted as any cost overruns become their responsibility. Should the client make changes during the planning cycle that impact the budget, these changes must be documented and signed off on to prevent issues arising later as regards expenditure exceeding that which was originally agreed. At specific times (as per the contract) in the event planning cycle payments are made to the event organiser to cover event expenses, and so ensure the event company is not funding the event out of their own financial resources. Once the event has been delivered, the budget showing actual versus forecast expenditure is presented to the client. This triggers the final payment to be made to the organiser. A summary of this process has been provided in figure 7.8.

7.2 Useful tools, practices and concepts aligned with best practice event financial management

LEARNING OBJECTIVE 7.2 Employ selected financial management tools.

To be effective managers event organisers need an understanding of a range of financial tools, practices and concepts. This section identifies and discusses the most significant of these.

FIGURE 7.8   Corporate event company budgeting process (product launch)

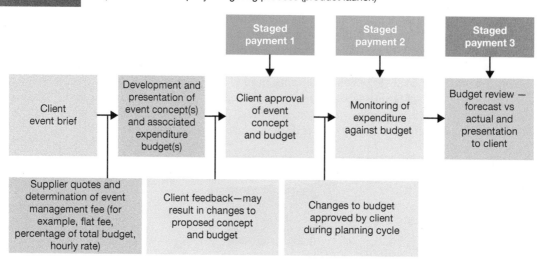

Fixed, variable and semi-variable costs

Fixed costs are those that do not change with the number of people in attendance at an event. These expenses will vary depending on the event concerned, but might include, for example, venue hire, loan costs, marketing, the event organiser's management fee, licences and permit charges, freight charges, signage, audiovisual equipment hire, site layout and theming costs, insurance, accounting and legal fees, speaker/performer fees, costs associated with the establishment of ticketing/registration systems and staging and fencing. Variable costs, on the other hand, change with the number of people attending an event. In the case of a conference, for example, these would include catering and attendee-related print material and satchels.

In addition to fixed and variable costs, some costs can be seen to be fixed for a given level of attendance but become variable after this number is exceeded, and as such are described as being semi-variable (also sometimes referred to as semi-fixed costs). For example, festival organisers may initially develop and cost their security plan assuming a specific number of attendees. If more tickets are sold than expected they might be required to add additional security staff at a ratio predetermined in their operating licence. This ratio can vary but is commonly one security guard per 100 attendees. A similar situation exists with such inputs as toilets, seating, first aid stations and water stations, and so on. In the case of a conference, additional attendees may mean there is a need to hire additional break-out rooms or buses to transport people between venues.

The relatively high fixed-cost commitments associated with the conduct of many events mean that organisers that are seeking to profit from them need to be assured that they will meet their financial objectives as early as possible. Should revenue inflows not reach targeted levels there is a risk cash flow issues will arise (see later discussion) as venue and supplier deposits come due, and promotional and general operational costs build. To avoid this situation events will often offer discounts (for example, early bird rates) or added incentives (for example, giveaways) for early payment.

In instances where events are likely not to cover their costs, there are three options available to their organisers. Firstly, the event can be cancelled, and the costs incurred up until that point absorbed. Secondly, a decision might be made to proceed if it is determined that by doing so a smaller loss will be made than would be the case if it were cancelled. This decision would be based on the income that had been received/is projected to be received and its capacity to partly offset 'sunk' costs (for example, marketing, venue deposits). Lastly, the organiser might make the decision to proceed based on a desire to protect their, their client's or the event's, brand. In this case the issue of seeking to generate a perception that the event has been successful arises. A commonly used strategy in this situation is to 'paper the house', a theatrical term referring to instances where tickets/registrations are heavily discounted, or given away, in order to fill a venue. Should this occur, it needs to be done in a targeted fashion so as not to engender discontent among those who have paid. It should also be kept in mind that event organisers that have decided to proceed knowing they will face a loss need to avoid cost-saving actions that will meaningfully reduce the event's capacity to meet attendee expectations. To do so runs the risk of having a similar effect to cancelling the event, that is, damage to the event's, event organiser's or client's reputation (EventMB Studio Team 2019).

Break-even analysis

By knowing what an event's fixed, variable and semi-variable costs are, an event organiser can determine its total cost at various levels of attendance. To establish the point (the break-even point) at which these costs are met by the income an event generates, event organisers need to estimate how revenue will grow over its planning cycle. This is not necessarily an easy task as events can have multiple revenue streams and forecasting how they will perform both individually and collectively requires making assumptions. These assumptions are generally based on experience (if the event has been conducted before), and research into those factors likely to impact its revenue-raising efforts. These factors can include, as noted previously, the availability of grants/sponsorship; level of competition from other events; and the general economic environment.

Break-even points can be calculated under various cost and income scenarios using spreadsheets, but to explain how the concept works in practice, a diagram has been used here (see figure 7.9). For simplicity, this figure assumes that an event has only one revenue source, registration/ticket sales. The first step in the process is to calculate fixed costs. As previously noted, these do not vary by the number of people in attendance and as such are represented in the diagram by a straight line parallel to that of registration/ticket sales. Variable costs begin to be incurred as soon as sales are made and rise with the number of attendees. Together variable and fixed costs comprise the total cost of conducting an event at various registration levels. In the diagram, the line representing total costs is always parallel to that of the variable cost line as it is simply shifted upwards by the fixed cost amount.

As an event sells registrations the revenue line rises until (hopefully) it reaches a point where it crosses that of the total cost line. The point at which the two lines cross is an event's break-even point. Once sales go beyond this point the event begins to make a profit, prior to that it is losing money. In instances where semi-variable costs are incurred, the effect is simply to cause the total cost line to jump up at the number of registrations at which this expense take place. This then results in the break-even point moving up and along to reflect the fact that more sales will be required to reach this point.

FIGURE 7.9 Break-even point graph

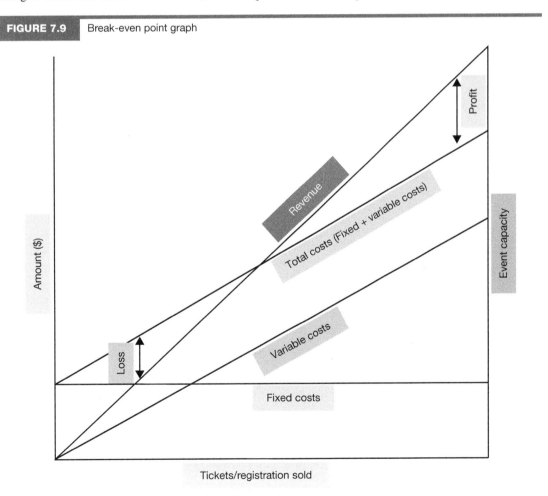

Ratio analysis

A range of ratios can be used to establish the financial health of an event. The relevance of these will depend on the nature of the event concerned, however, commonly used ratios include the following:

- Return on investment: net revenue divided by the investment made. This ratio in particularly relevant when an event is being conducted primarily with the intent of generating a profit (for example, an entreprenerd music festival), and its owner, or those investing in it, seek clarity around its projected or actual ability to generate a return sufficient to warrant the financial risk associated with its conduct.
- Liquidity ratio: current assets divided by current liabilities. This ratio establishes an event's capacity to meet its short-term liabilities from its cash reserves. A ratio below one can signal that it has cash flow difficulties that need to be promptly addressed.
- Debt ratio: total debt divided by total assets. Ongoing events, most particularly those that own and operate their own site/venue, and have significant investments in event-related equipment, need clarity around their capacity to meet their ongoing financial commitments. A debt ratio of less than one would signal that its ability to quickly raise money through a loan, or from an investor(s), could be limited.
- Net profit margin: net profit divided by total sales. This ratio determines what percentage of an event's ticket sales/registrations have been turned into profit after all related expenses have been considered. The resulting percentage can be used to compare an event to other similar events, or to other profit-making opportunities.
- Contribution margin: the price of an item minus its associated variable costs. From this ratio the capacity of a given revenue item to contribute to fixed costs and to profit can be determined. If this ratio is low or negative it can highlight that the item concerned, for example, a category of sponsorship, might need to be eliminated or increased in price in future. It also identifies those items that are contributing most to profitability and as a result should be given more prominence in marketing activities.

Cash flow

As part of their financial planning efforts, event organisers need to monitor inflows and outflows of cash to ensure they have enough money on hand to meet their short-term financial commitments. To achieve this, a cash flow statement is commonly used. In its initial form this statement will be based on a forecast, however, as contracts are signed and dates on which payments are required become known, this forecast will be adjusted. As an event progresses through its planning cycle and income begins to be received and costs are incurred, it needs to constantly update its cash flow statement to reflect its actual cash situation. An example of a generic cash flow template for an event has been provided in figure 7.10.

As significant expenditure is often required in the initial phase of event planning (for example, website development, venue deposits, promotional activities) prior to any income being received, the task of cash flow management can be challenging. There are, however, various ways of potentially dealing with this issue. These include: having a client organisation pay in full at the time of signing a contract or by instalments ahead of when funds are required; funding the initial shortfall from an event organiser's own financial reserves; having another organisation underwrite an event until it reaches a cash flow positive position; accessing grants from government agencies payable early in an event's planning cycle; use of borrowed funds; and negotiating the timeline for supplier and venue payments so as to push payments to a time when the event will have sufficient cash reserves available. It should also be kept in mind that it can be problematic if registration and ticketing revenue is used to fund expenses prior to a decision being made to proceed with an event as this money will need to be returned if it is cancelled. If an event organiser is using an online ticket agency, it is also the case some of these companies will not provide access to ticket revenue until after an event has been conducted.

Event organisers have available to them various ways of stimulating cash flow should this be an issue, these include: early bird ticket/registration discounts; incorporating early payment requirements into sponsorship agreements; and putting in place effective credit control procedures that minimise late or non-payment by attendees, sponsors, granting bodies, exhibitors and so on.

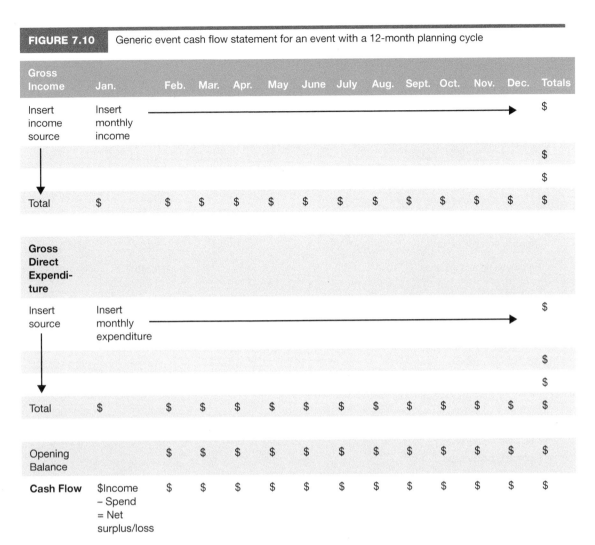

FIGURE 7.10 Generic event cash flow statement for an event with a 12-month planning cycle

Gross Income	Jan.	Feb.	Mar.	Apr.	May	June	July	Aug.	Sept.	Oct.	Nov.	Dec.	Totals
Insert income source	Insert monthly income											→	$
													$
													$
Total	$	$	$	$	$	$	$	$	$	$	$	$	$

Gross Direct Expenditure													
Insert source	Insert monthly expenditure											→	$
													$
													$
Total	$	$	$	$	$	$	$	$	$	$	$	$	$

Opening Balance		$	$	$	$	$	$	$	$	$	$	$	$
Cash Flow	$Income – Spend = Net surplus/loss	$	$	$	$	$	$	$	$	$	$	$	$

Source: Based on VisitScotland 2019.

Profit and loss statements

Profit and loss (P&L) statements serve to summarise an event's revenues and expenses, and are commonly prepared post an event, although for large-scale ongoing events they might also be prepared periodically (for example, quarterly) to track financial performance. In figure 7.11, the profit and loss statement for the Australian National Folk Festival has been provided. It can be observed from this figure that broad categories of revenue (for example, sales) and costs (for example, operational costs) are used rather than individual line items. Once totalled, these figures allow an event's net profit/loss before any income tax to be established. By including data from the previous year, as has been done in this statement, it is also possible to judge how the event has performed against its previous iteration.

Other financial considerations

Cash handling

If cash is needed during an event for till floats or petty cash, this amount should be arranged in advance with an event's bank, along with the denominations required. Additionally, when cash is being used on-site, consideration needs to be given to: the safety of those staff/volunteers responsible for it; storage facilities; and the training of those that will have oversite of it, or who will be directly handling it. Event organisers should also ensure their insurance policies cover cash-related issues. In order to avoid these types of concerns many events are moving to pre-purchased coupons and cashless payments facilitated through the provision of tap and go card systems and wristbands that can be loaded up with credit and used in a similar fashion to tap and go cards.

National Folk Festival Limited
ABN 96 058 761 274
Statement of Profit or Loss and Other Comprehensive Income
For the Year Ended 30 June 2018

	Note	2018 $	2017 $
Sales revenue	4	2 299 415	2 203 782
Other revenue	4	56 048	40 628
Depreciation and amortisation	8.1.	(23 097)	(24 056)
Employee benefit expense		(530 407)	(562 505)
Finance costs		(4 147)	(3 336)
Marketing expenses		(74 104)	(77 035)
Occupancy costs		(19 487)	(15 151)
Operational costs		(1 087 054)	(1 029 570)
Other expenses		(105 633)	(108 622)
Performance costs		(389 718)	(364 623)
Profit before income tax		121 816	59 512
Income tax expense		–	–
Profit for year		121 816	59 512
Other comprehensive income		–	–
Total comprehensive income for the year		121 816	59 512

Source: National Folk Festival Limited 2018.

Asset register

Events commonly purchase a range of equipment, the larger the event the more equipment it is likely to acquire and need to store. It is good practice to create an asset register to keep track of such equipment to save on replacement costs. Such a document should include:
- a description of each asset
- purchase price and date of purchase
- where the asset is located
- contact details of the person holding the asset.

SUMMARY

Events, from a financial planning perspective, fall broadly into two categories: those that are required to raise revenue and those that are fully funded. In the case of the former, organisers are faced with the challenge of both accurately forecasting costs and revenue, a process that requires a range of factors to be taken into account. These factors can encompass concerns external to the event itself, including the prevailing economic environment, as well as matters more directly linked to the event itself, such as its prior budgetary performance. To allow for variability in forecasting an event's financial future, it is useful to work through different possible financial scenarios at the outset of the budgeting process in order to reduce the risk of making ill-considered decisions later in its planning cycle. It is also the case that organisers need to carefully monitor and control inflows and outflows of money, a process that requires, among other things, the constant updating of an event's budget. In the context of fully funded events, the financial management process, while less complex, still requires that costs are accurately determined and embraced within a regularly updated budget in order to ensure actual and projected expenditure align.

The later part of this chapter examined selected concepts, tools and practices that result in best practice financial management, including cash flow management, break-even analysis and ratio analysis. Additionally, the issues of cash and asset management were briefly overviewed to highlight the need to consider these matters as part of an event's overall financial planning efforts.

Finally, event organisers will find the following words of John Aitken (2006), a former General Manager, Events and Marketing, of the Sydney Royal Easter Show, worthwhile keeping in mind as they approach the financial management challenge:

> Successful events are big business, requiring leaders who understand the importance of profit making. Consumers demand innovation and quality. Innovation and quality cost big bucks. If you don't offer what your customers want then your competitor will. Profits mean success, confidence and influence. Leisure and the arts are not immune to such market trends.

> Money will always get in the way, but the more money you have, the less painful your problem is! It's easier to manage the threat of compromising your artistic integrity for commercial imperatives than explaining to your investors that you've planned for their demise.

> Producing events is a serious business. If your strength is about inspiring and creating, then you may find yourself too busy and (most probably) by nature unable to focus on maintaining the level of discipline, attention to detail and tough decision making that the business of events requires. Don't try to do it all, play to your strengths and weaknesses by developing the team around you. A call to the best accountancy firm in town may prove to be your best investment!

> So long as you understand that profit equals success, continuity and strength, then you'll be on the right track. With money in the bank you have options and opportunities. The alternative of operating at a loss is that your event will struggle, your ability to influence your financiers will be eroded and if the problem persists, your position and your event, or both, will perish. Some of your peers may wish to challenge your decision making with cries of 'too commercial' or 'sold out for the almighty dollar', but at least you'll be around to take heed of such criticism and reassess the balance of your business, artistic and strategic intent.

> No matter how engaging, wholesome and humanistic your ideology or creativity may be, if you don't possess a robust business plan centred on the discipline of good decision making and wise investment of your available resources — including meticulous assessment of the risk elements of your adventurous plan — then your position or your event will be short-lived. All that you stood for, sought to achieve, your artistic endeavour and uncompromised beliefs and, perhaps more tragically, the countless hours you and your loyal followers invested will result in nothing but heartache. You owe it to yourself, your investors, your followers and believers, including financial backers, staff, volunteers, sponsors and attending public, to make as much money as you can to enable the business of your event to grow and prosper.

> Please disregard all of the above if money grows on trees in your neck of the eventing woods.

QUESTIONS

1 Identify and briefly discuss the key steps in the financial planning process for revenue-generating events.

2 What approaches can event organisers employ to reduce the risk of cost 'blowouts'?

3 What roles do budgets perform?

4 Why is cash flow of such importance to event financial management?

5 What effect does a change in the semi-variable costs associated with an event have on its break-even point?

6 Why are return on investment and liquidity ratios useful in event financial management?

7 Briefly discuss the major differences between revenue generating and fully funded events from the perspective of their financial management.

CASE STUDY

THE COST OF STAGING A MUSIC FESTIVAL: 'WE SPENT £30 000 ON THE WASTE'

As you hike in through the gates of whichever festivals you attend this summer, you might survey the scene — a miniature city, centred around stages, with its own infrastructure — and imagine that the £170 or so that you and tens of thousands of others have paid is going to make quite a lot of people quite a lot of money. You'll be paying for the bands, of course, but you'll also be ensuring the promoter's bank balance looks an awful lot healthier. Right? Hardly.

The economics of festivals are finely poised. These events wobble on a knife-edge between glorious success and ignominious bankruptcy and looking at where the money goes is a sobering undertaking. The first thing to remember is that a chunk of money has been taken from what you paid for your ticket even before the promoters and bands take their shares. There's an automatic deduction of 20 per cent in VAT, and 3 per cent goes to PRS, which collects the money owed to songwriters for performances of their songs. That means the promoter is down by almost a quarter of their gross from ticket sales before they've so much as booked a band or installed a portable loo.

That miniature city (or, in the case of Glastonbury, Reading and Leeds, Isle of Wight or T in the Park, not-so-miniature-city) doesn't pay for and build itself, either. The promoter has to pay to hire the site, put up the fencing, build the stage, lay on water, electricity and waste management, sort out security — and more. 'For a 10 000-capacity festival, your power will cost you between £60 000 and £100 000', says Gareth Cooper, co-founder of Festival No 6. 'We would spend up to £30 000 taking the waste away.'

And the bigger the audience, the greater those costs are. 'At the Isle of Wight festival, between security and police, it costs £1m', says John Giddings, the event's head. He has to employ around 5000 people to ensure he can lay on all the necessary amenities and a greenfield site isn't immediately fit for a festival just because you've made it fine for campers and live entertainment. Giddings says he spent £250 000 building roads into the site's car park. 'Parking cars on grass', he says with the weary voice of experience, 'is not the best idea in the world'.

As Jon Drape, managing director of outdoor event production company Ground Control, puts it: 'Most festival sites are, literally, green fields. There are no utilities there. There is very stringent legislation that festival organisers need to meet to stage a festival. A lot of the expenditure is around very unsexy items — sanitary provision, showers, toilets, waste management, power, site lighting. All those utilities need to be brought in.'

Even after you have made that investment, it can all disappear. This year's T in the Park festival, running this weekend, has had to move to a new site at Strathallan Castle, having been forced out of its 18-year home in Balado owing to issues caused by an oil pipeline running under the site. 'We are the fifth biggest town in Scotland when T in the Park is on, with all the issues that come with running a major town', says festival director Geoff Ellis, who estimates the running costs over the years at £1m. Now he has to start from scratch on a new site and get it up to the standard it took nearly two decades to reach at its old location. And even then, there is no guarantee he will get planning permission for T beyond the initial council-approved three years.

So, you've splashed out all that money. How do you get it back? It's not just from the ordinary punters who are paying no more than the ticket price and bringing their own tent. As with football, they might be the bedrock of the festival, but they also provide the atmosphere that turns a festival into an experience for those with more money to spend. Among them are a group that hardened festival goers' despair of, but who bring in a load more money — the 'glampers'. '[We] probably sell more boutique camping per head than any other festival', says Bradley Thompson, festival director of Festival No 6. 'It's around 15 per cent of people.'

There is a growing demand for it — glamping enclosures often have their own toilets and showers, and phone-charging tents — and festivals are mustard-keen to provide it. Chris Carey, CEO of Media Insight Consulting, spells it out in harsh fiscal terms. 'Against the backdrop of a lot of festivals coming into the market, the big ones are doing a much better job of monetising people on site', he explains. At Latitude next weekend, you can get an Airstream caravan for between £2150 and £2750 — and a chunk of what you pay for your glamping goes back to the festival promoter.

Aligned to this is sponsorship. 'Sponsorship is like a safety net that helps cover the cost of putting on the event', Giddings says. But it is not just a case of taking the money and running. Sponsors want to be more directly involved, seeking to do 'experiential marketing' on the site. Some festivals believe, if done right, this can improve the event for attendees. Others face bigger moral quandaries. 'Finding ethical sponsors is never straightforward, so we have never relied on sponsorship', explains Womad director Chris Smith. 'If we were approached by a car manufacturer, it wouldn't work for us at all. You have to make sure it's the right motivation behind it.'

Others don't have the luxury of saying 'no' to sponsors — simply because they are too small to attract other offers. 'We are interested in sponsorships, but one of our problems is our size', says Marina Blake, director of the 1000-capacity Brainchild, which takes place at Bentley Country Park in East Sussex this weekend. 'But just reaching 1000 people is not very exciting for a lot of sponsors.'

You've got your glampers and your sponsors. Now you need to work out how to get money from the caterers. Food and drink are a major means by which festivals to recoup money, either by selling it themselves or bringing in external companies and charging them rent (or sometimes running on a profit split). Graeme Merifield, director of Wychwood, estimates that ticket sales only go to pay for 60 per cent of running his festival. 'The other 40 per cent is made up from pitch fees from traders and caterers, sponsorship money and our bar profits as we run our own bars', he says. 'If we didn't have any of those other incomes, then we wouldn't be able to run a festival.'

Hugh Phillimore, festival director of Cornbury, suggests that he would charge a trader between £300 and £400 to have a stall at the festival. 'You have to be careful', he cautions, 'that you don't have too many as then none of them will do any business'. Get it right, though — enough stalls to cater for everyone without massive queues, offering good food and drink — and your food can become an attraction in itself.

Even if your overheads are skeletal, ever-present meteorological risk can be unforgiving. In the wet summer of 2012, a number of smaller festivals went out of business as the costs of addressing flooding or dealing with cancellations were beyond them financially. 'When it rains, you have to pay a lot of extra money for straw to go on the mud', Giddings says. 'When the sun shines, you have to pay a lot of money to give away water for free.'

Cooper puts it more bluntly. 'You plan for a year and it could all be washed away. That's not a sensible business. It's a reckless business.'

Inclement conditions can also affect 'walk-up' sales (people buying a one-day pass on the day itself). Phillimore said that, in 2013, Cornbury sold 1200-day tickets, but the year before, because of rain, it only sold 200 — equivalent to a shortfall of around £80 000. Not every festival can sell out in advance, so walk-ups can mean the difference between disaster and success.

Making the numbers add up is going to become incrementally more difficult as musicians steadily hike up their appearance fees, as a means of offsetting declining income from record sales. Some festivals see that as an inevitable byproduct of market forces while others are refusing to be washed along with such demands since their margins are already wafer thin. 'Not only are artists demanding more money, they can command it with the sheer number of festivals out there', says Drape. For many of the biggest events, it becomes a financial arms race as a handful of headline-level acts know they can play rival festivals off against each other to secure the highest fee possible.

Merifield says Wychwood will not allow the romance of securing big names to overtake financial pragmatism. 'We have an idea in our heads for how much we are going to spend on the headliner and, if people ask for more than that, then we just walk away', he says. 'Years ago, we put on an act that cost us more than we had ever spent before, thinking it would have a golden effect. But it had no effect at all.'

It is a sobering thought this summer — as you prop up the organic cider stalls, pondering which stage to go to next — to remember you are standing in the middle of one of the highest-risk businesses in the world.

'If festival promoters were better business-people, they wouldn't be in festivals', says Cooper.

So, why do it? The possibility of making a fortune coupled with the thrill of taking a massive patch of grass and magically transforming it into a mini city where, hopefully, tens of thousands of people will have the best three days of their summer, still holds plenty of appeal for some. While you are having fun, spare a thought for the organiser, sitting in their portable building and sweating over their spreadsheets.

Source: Forde, E 10 July 2015, 'The cost of staging a music festival: "We spent £30 000 on the waste"', *The Guardian,* 10 July, www.theguardian.com/music/2015/jul/09/cost-of-staging-music-festival.

QUESTIONS

1 What types of operational costs do music festivals need to take account of as they seek to determine their financial viability?

2 Other than the potential for cost 'blowouts' what other risks do music festivals face?

3 What issues surround the development of sponsorship as a revenue source at music festivals?

4 What types of revenue sources are available to music festivals, and what can impact these?

5 Why are music festivals often 'mustard-keen' to provide glamping experiences?

6 What are some of the challenges music festivals face when seeking to book performers?

REFERENCES

Aitken, J 2006, General Manager, Events and Marketing, Sydney Royal Easter Show, Royal Agricultural Society of New South Wales, personal communication to Bill O'Toole, June.

Eventbrite n.d., 'The event budget template you need to keep on track', www.eventbrite.com.au/blog/academy/event-budget-template, viewed 13 February 2020.

EventMB Studio Team 2019, 'Event budget: 60 tips, templates and calculator for 2019', 29 July, www.eventmanagerblog.com/event-budget, viewed 13 February 2020.

Forde, E 2015, 'The cost of staging a music festival: "We spent £30,000 on the waste"', *The Guardian*, 10 July, www.theguardian.com/music/2015/jul/09/cost-of-staging-music-festival,viewed 12 February 2020.

National Folk Festival Limited 2018, 'Financial Statements for the Year Ended 30 June 2018', p. 8, www.folkfestival.org.au/wp-content/uploads/National-Folk-Festival-Ltd-Financial-Statement-year-end-30-June-2018.pdf, viewed 13 February 2020.

Sounder, M 2004, *Event entertainment and production*, John Wiley & Sons, New York.

VisitScotland 2019, 'Budgets and financial statements', *Event Management Guide*, pp. 41–55, www.visitscotland.org/events/advice-materials/management-guide, viewed 16 April 2020.

Western Sydney University n.d., 'Conference Policy Budget Template', https://policies.westernsydney.edu.au/document/associated-information.php?id=190, viewed 16 April 2020.

ACKNOWLEDGEMENTS

Photo: © teekid / iStockphoto

Figure 7.3: © Western Sydney University n.d.

Figure 7.4: © [2019] Eventbrite, Inc. Used with permission.

Figures 7.5 and 7.10: © Published by VisitScotland / EventScotland in 2006. Co-authors Marie Christie and Lesley McAteer.

Figure 7.11: © National Folk Festival Limited 2018

Extract: © John Aitken 2006

Case study: © Eamonn Forde / *The Guardian*. All rights reserved. Reproduced by permission.

CHAPTER 8

Human resource management and events

After studying this chapter, you should be able to:

8.1 describe the human resource management challenges posed by events

8.2 list and describe the key steps in the human resource management process for events

8.3 discuss approaches that can be employed to motivate event staff and volunteers

8.4 describe techniques for event staff and volunteer team building

8.5 state general legal considerations associated with human resource management in an event context.

Introduction

Effective planning and management of human resources are at the core of any successful event. Ensuring an event is adequately staffed with the right people, who are appropriately trained and motivated to meet its objectives, is fundamental to the event management process. This chapter seeks to provide an overview of the key aspects of human resource planning and management with which an event manager should be familiar. It begins by examining considerations associated with human resource management in the context of events. It then moves on to propose a model of the event human resource management process and to discuss each of the major steps in this model. Selected theories associated with staff/volunteer motivation are then described, followed by a brief examination of techniques for staff and volunteer team building. The final part of this chapter overviews legal considerations associated with human resource management.

8.1 Considerations associated with human resource planning for events

LEARNING OBJECTIVE 8.1 Describe the human resource management challenges posed by events.

The context in which human resource planning takes place for events can be said to be unique for two major reasons. First, and perhaps most significantly, many events have a 'pulsating' organisational structure (Raj, Walters and Rashid 2013; Hanlon and Jago 2000; Hanlon and Cuskelly 2002). This means their organisational structures grow rapidly in terms of personnel as an event approaches and contracts even more quickly when it ends.

From a human resource perspective this creates potential challenges. These include:
- obtaining paid staff given the short-term nature of the employment offered
- working to short timelines to hire and train staff
- attrition due to the pressure of working to tight deadlines
- shedding staff quickly once an event is over.

Secondly, as volunteers, as opposed to paid staff, can sometimes make up a significant proportion of an event's workforce, or indeed, on occasions, can comprise its entire workforce, matters specific to the management of this labour source need to be understood (see later discussion).

8.2 The human resource management process for events

LEARNING OBJECTIVE 8.2 List and describe the key steps in the human resource management process for events.

Human resource management for events should not be viewed simply in terms of several isolated tasks, but as a series of sequential interrelated processes and practices. If an event seeks to grow in size and attendance, for example, it will need a human resource strategy to support this growth through such means as increased staff recruitment (paid and/or volunteer) and an expanded (and perhaps more sophisticated) range of training programs. If these supporting human resource management actions are not in place, problems such as high staff/volunteer turnover due to overwork, poor quality service delivery and an associated declining marketplace image may result. Events will differ in terms of the level of sophistication they display in the human resources area. Contrast, for example, a local community festival that struggles to put together an organising committee and attract volunteers to a mega-event such as the Olympic Games. Nonetheless, it is appropriate that the 'ideal' situation is examined here — that is, the complete series of steps through which an event organiser should proceed when undertaking the human resource management task. By understanding these steps, and their relationships to one another, event organisers will give themselves the best possible chance of managing human resources in a way that will achieve their event's goals and objectives.

While a number of general models of the human resource management process can be identified, the one chosen to serve as the basis of discussion in this chapter is that proposed by Getz (2005), specifically for events (see figure 8.1).

FIGURE 8.1 | The human resource management process for events

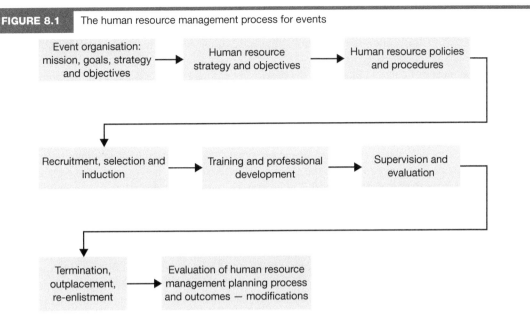

Source: Based on Getz 2005, p. 221.

Event organisation

An understanding is required at the outset of planning in the human resource area of an event's mission/purpose, goals and associated objectives along with the strategy(ies) it is, or that it is seeking to, pursue. The importance of this can be seen in the following examples that show how human resource management is impacted by organisational decisions in selected areas:

- cost containment — improved staff/volunteer productivity, reduced absenteeism and decreased staff numbers
- improved quality — better recruitment and selection processes, expanded employee and volunteer training, improved contractor/supplier selection processes, increased staff and volunteer numbers, and improved staff financial rewards and volunteer benefits
- improved organisational effectiveness — better job design, changes to organisational reporting and communication practices, and improved relations with employees and volunteers
- enhanced performance regarding event environmental sustainability outcomes — improved staff, volunteer, contractor and supplier training, and development of a dedicated sustainability team inside the event.

Additionally, if an event has been conducted previously, an understanding of its current human resources strategy, along with processes and practices in this area, will be needed.

Human resource strategy and objectives

Once an event's overall strategy, and the current status of its human resource management efforts, have been determined (if it has been delivered previously), focus can shift to establishing guiding strategies and objectives, and the decisions flowing from them. Key among these decisions is that of the number of staff (paid and volunteer) the event will require and the nature of the jobs they will perform with the latter requiring the tasks of job analysis, job description and job specifications to be undertaken.

Staffing

Event organisers need to make decisions concerning how many staff/volunteers are needed to deliver an event, what mix of skills/qualifications/experience is required, and when in the event management process these staff and volunteers will be needed (for example, the event start-up stage only). The starting point for these decisions should be an event's work breakdown structure (WBS; see the event project management chapter), as it identifies the tasks associated with its planning, delivery and shutdown. In performing this role, the WBS also allows event organisers to begin thinking through which of these tasks will be contracted out and which will be undertaken in-house by event staff and/or volunteers. Also, by placing the tasks identified in the WBS into a Gantt chart (see the event project management chapter), an event manager can start to determine when staff and volunteers will be needed, how many will be required and the skill/knowledge sets that they will need.

Perhaps the most difficult undertaking in the previously outlined process is that of determining exactly how many people will be needed to perform the various identified tasks, particularly if the event is new. Managerial judgement is often cited as the most common approach (Armstrong 1999; AIHR Analytics 2020) used in business to answer this question. There are, however, more sophisticated processes that employ modelling to aid decisions in this area which have applicability in large-scale event settings (National Academy of Sciences, Engineering and Medicine 2007). While acknowledging this, the former approach is the one most encountered in the event industry. Essentially, this involves the event organiser, or various functional managers if the event is large enough, acting to estimate how many, and what type, of human resources are needed to meet their objectives. In making such estimations, they are likely to base their decisions on such factors as their own experience; demand forecasts for the event; the number of venues/sites involved; skill/expertise requirements of the event workforce; previous instances of similar (or the same) events; the degree of outsourcing possible; the availability of volunteers; and the human resource strategies adopted by the event. It should be noted that it is not uncommon in the context of large-scale events for initial estimates of workforce size to grow as an event's delivery date draws closer. The Manchester Commonwealth Games, for example, first estimated (via a consultant's report) its core workforce requirements at 262. This number was revised upwards to 660 as the organising committee gained first-hand experience of other major sports events and their workforce requirements (Manchester Commonwealth Games 2003).

In the case of some tasks associated with the conduct of events, it is possible to estimate staffing needs by engaging in some basic arithmetic. The number of people who can pass through a turnstile per hour, for example, can be easily calculated by dividing the processing time for an individual into 60 minutes. Assume the figure generated in this way is 240 — that is, 240 people can be processed in an hour through one turnstile. Next, an estimate of event attendance (including peaks and troughs in arrivals) is required. Now assume total attendance for the event has been largely consistent at 5000 over the past three years, with 80 per cent (4000) of people arriving between 9.00 am and 11.00 am. If this number of people is to be processed over a two-hour period, about eight turnstiles would need to be open (4000 attendees divided by two hours (= 2000 per hour), divided by 240 transactions per hour per turnstile). Based on these calculations, eight turnstile operators would be required for the first two hours; after this time, the number of operators could be dramatically decreased. Calculations such as this could also be used in other areas of event delivery. For example, it should be possible to estimate with a fair degree of accuracy the number of staff required to prepare, plate and serve a given number of meals within a particular time period, or the number required to process a given number of on-site registrations at a conference/exhibition.

Job analysis

Job analysis is an important aspect of this stage of the human resource management process. It involves defining a job in terms of specific tasks and responsibilities and identifying the abilities, skills and qualifications needed to perform that job successfully. According to Stone (2014), questions answered by this process include the following.

- What tasks should be grouped together to create a job or position?
- What skills, knowledge, abilities and personal characteristics should be looked for in individuals applying for identified jobs (for example, capacity to work in team environments)?
- What will be the scope of the job (for example, what are the human, financial and material resources that will be required to be managed)?
- Where will the job fit in the organisational structure?
- What tasks should form the basis of performance appraisal for an individual in a specific job?

The level of sophistication evident in the application of the job analysis process will differ between events. Some small-scale events that depend exclusively, or almost exclusively, on volunteers may simply attempt to match people to the tasks in which they have expressed an interest. Even under such circumstances, however, some consideration should be given to experience, skills and physical abilities. Another approach in common use is the undertaking of interviews and the use of questionnaires with current job holders and their supervisors.

Job descriptions

Job descriptions are an outcome of the job analysis process. Specifically, a job description is a statement identifying the purpose of a job, the activities that are required to be performed, the context in which they will take place and the performance standards that must be met (Stone 2014).

Job descriptions commonly include the following information:

- the location of the job in the organisational structure, its associated reporting requirements and the authorities invested in it (for example, capacity to hire or dismiss staff)
- the primary role(s) of the position, along with duties and responsibilities
- performance requirements — what is expected to be achieved, behavioural expectations (for example, be a team player) and how performance will be measured
- key knowledge, qualifications, skills, abilities (for example, high-level problem-solving capacity) and personal characteristics needed by the position.

An example of a well-developed job description for a Festival Manager has been provided in figure 8.2.

While job descriptions for paid positions often involve most, if not all, of the information noted previously, voluntary positions are often described in far more general terms. This is because they frequently (but not always) involve tasks of a less complex nature. This is evident from table 8.1, which provides job descriptions for voluntary positions at the World Confederation of Physical Therapy Congress.

FIGURE 8.2 Cambridge Literary Festival — Festival Manager job description

Festival Manager

About Cambridge Literary Festival

Staging three festivals each year with additional events in between, Cambridge Literary Festival showcases the best in contemporary writing and thinking from across the world. We attract hundreds of acclaimed novelists and poets, cultural thinkers, comedians, politicians and scientists to engage, provoke and entertain our audiences in some of the most historic buildings in Cambridge and around.

Job description

Job title: Festival Manager
Location: Central Cambridge
Reports to: Festival Director
Key relationships: Festival Assistant, Box office, venues, volunteers, production team

The role

Reporting to the Festival Director, the Festival Manager is responsible for the delivery of all festivals and individual events as necessary including:

- Event production and management including monitoring the budget
- Supporting the Festival Director with the Children's Programme
- Overseeing volunteer recruitment and scheduling
- Working with the Associate Director on funding applications.

Responsibility for

Festival volunteers, Festival staff e.g. Production Manager, Stage Manager.

Key responsibilities

As part of the small team that runs the festival year-round, the festival manager works closely with the Festival Director to ensure that all elements of the festival are in place on time and within budget. The role is varied with a focus on logistics and delivery but with creative or development opportunities for the right candidate.

Event production, management and delivery

- Work with existing partners and build new relationships as necessary to ensure that venues for all our events, whether indoor or outdoor, are of a high standard, suitable and safe.
- Plan for and manage the on-site logistics including AV/tech, queuing and seating, Box Office, branding and signage, arrangements for book signing etc.
- Be the main point of contact for the Box Office in the run up to the festivals and any other events to ensure that programme is available on the website and tickets are on sale on time.
- Responsibility (with the Festival Assistant) for ensuring that accommodation and any other special arrangements are made for authors and their events.
- Recruit and manage the delivery team which includes production manager, stage manager, freelancers and volunteers.

▶

- To re-evaluate and improve upon processes where possible in all areas of work as a matter of course.
- Organise and coordinate Festival debriefs as appropriate.

Marketing

To support the Festival Director in developing the marketing strategy and to work with the Festival Assistant to reach as wide an audience as possible for all events including:
- support the Festival Director in preparing print and digital output
- social media: support the Festival Assistant with social media activity (Twitter, Instagram, Facebook) and preparation of e-bulletins in order to implement the Festival's digital marketing strategy
- support PR and media initiatives.

Programming

- Assist the Festival Director to develop the children's programme.

Financial management

- Monitor the festival budgets to ensure that spending is controlled.

Office support

To support the work of the Festival Assistant with regard to the smooth running of the office which will include:
- Support with data management — ensuring that audience data, volunteer lists, mailing lists and other contact information are kept up to date. Ensuring that data complies with DP regulations, and information is protected and backed up.
- Keeping track of invoices and payments received.
- Helping out with member scheme management as necessary.
- General contribution to running the office — answering phone/email enquiries, sorting post, filing, ordering stationery, managing and maintaining existing office systems.

Person specification

You will be a well organised self-starter and problem solver, able to take personal responsibility for your own work as well as contributing to the team.

With excellent communication skills you will have the ability to establish robust partnership and working relationships and a strong commitment to quality and excellence.

Relevant experience is essential. You should have a keen interest in the work of the festival.

Summary of terms and conditions
Contract

This is a four day per week position but with some adjustment related to the festivals. Hours of work will vary according to current priorities, but generally will be 32 hours per week. Additional hours may be required as necessary for the successful performance of the job, particularly while the Festival is running.

Remuneration

In the region of £25 000 per annum (pro rata) which will be paid by BACS transfer monthly in arrears. The Festival Manager will be required to work all festivals and one-off events unless previously agreed in advance with the Festival Director.

Source: Cambridge Literary Festival 2017.

TABLE 8.1   **Volunteer job descriptions, World Confederation for Physical Therapy Congress, Singapore**

Job title:	General Meeting — Credentialing/Registration Assistant
Job description:	Assist WCPT staff with on-site registration of General Meeting delegates
Responsibilities:	• Ensure delegates know which credentialing desk they should use • Assist WCPT staff with checking delegate registrations and distributing delegate packs • Answer general queries related to the General Meeting
Job title:	General Meeting — Hospitality/General Assistant
Job description:	Welcome delegates to the General Meeting: • meet and greet approximately 300 delegates • provide general assistance • assist with setup.

Responsibilities:	• Ensure that any event signage is in place • Greet delegates and direct them to their seats • Provide assistance with new member organisations • Provide any general assistance required, carry out errands and generally assist with the smooth running of the meeting • Possibly assist with set up of the area prior to the meeting
Job title:	Gala Dinner — Registration/Hospitality Assistant
Job description:	Welcome delegates to the Gala Dinner Assist WCPT staff with on-site registration of Gala Dinner delegates
Responsibilities:	• Possibly assist with set up of area prior to event • Ensure that any event signage is in place • Meet and greet approximately 500 delegates • Greet delegates, take tickets at door to event, and maintain an accurate participant count. Ensure only invited guests gain admittance. • In the event that a delegate has misplaced his or her ticket, verify their name on the Attendee List • Lead or direct delegates to event area • Provide assistance with VIPs and award recipients • Provide any general assistance required • Once dinner begins, update delegate list to indicate who has attended (using ticket stubs) • Police re-entry to the event during dinner
Job title:	Pre and Post Congress Courses — Registration Assistant
Job description:	Assist Congress registration staff with the on-site registration of delegates attending Congress Courses
Responsibilities:	Delegates will visit the registration desk to sign in to the course. Volunteers will: • greet delegates • check delegates off a list • check if there are any outstanding fees • distribute the (pre-prepared) name badges and delegate packs/bags • answer general enquiries from delegates.

Source: World Confederation for Physical Therapy Congress 2015.

Job specification

A job specification is derived from the job description, and is often incorporated within it, as it has been in figure 8.2. Essentially, it states the experience, qualifications, skills, abilities, knowledge and personal characteristics needed to perform a given job.

Policies and procedures

Policies and procedures are needed to provide the framework in which the remaining tasks in the human resource management process take place: recruitment and selection; training and professional development; supervision and evaluation; termination, outplacement, re-employment; and evaluation. According to Stone (2014), policies and practices serve to:

- reassure all staff that they will be treated fairly — for example, an event's policy might be to promote from within whenever possible
- help managers make quick and consistent decisions — for example, rather than a manager having to think about the process of terminating the employment of a staff member or volunteer, they can simply follow the process already prescribed
- give managers the basis upon which to resolve problems and defend their positions — for example, an event manager who declines to consider an application from a person with a criminal record may point to a policy on employing people with such a record if there is a dispute.

Human resource practices and procedures for events are often conditioned or determined by those public or private sector organisations with ultimate authority for them. A local council responsible for conducting an annual festival, for example, would probably already have in place a range of policies and procedures regarding the employment of staff and the use of volunteers. These policies and procedures would then be applied to the event. Additionally, a range of laws influence the degree of freedom that the management of an event has in the human resource area. Laws regarding work health and safety, privacy, holiday and long service leave, discrimination, dismissal and compensation all need to become integrated into the practices and policies that an event adopts.

If an event organiser goes to the time and effort to develop policies and procedures, he or she also needs to ensure these are communicated and applied to all staff. Additionally, resources need to be allocated to this area so the 'paperwork' (for example, policy/procedure manuals and staff records) generated by those policies and procedures can be stored, accessed and updated or modified as required.

Again, the larger (in terms of number of staff and volunteers) and more sophisticated (in terms of its management) the event, the more likely it is that the event organiser(s) would have acted to develop a comprehensive set of human resource–related policies and procedures. Nonetheless, even smaller events will benefit in terms of the quality of their overall human resources management if some attempt is made to set basic human resource policies and procedures to guide their actions in this area.

Recruitment, selection and induction

The recruitment of paid and volunteer employees is essentially about attracting the 'right' potential candidates to the 'right' job openings. Successful recruitment is based on how well previous stages in the human resource management process have been performed, and involves determining where qualified applicants can be found and how they can be attracted to the event organisation. It is a two-way process, in that the event is looking to meet its human resource needs at the same time as potential applicants are trying to assess whether they meet the stated job requirements. Figure 8.3 represents the recruitment, selection and induction process in diagrammatic form.

How event managers approach the recruitment process depends on the financial resources they have available to them. With large events, a budget is likely to be set aside for this purpose, designed to cover costs such as recruitment agency fees, advertising, the travel expenses of non-local applicants and search fees for executive placement companies. The reality for most events, however — particularly those relying heavily on volunteers — is that they will have few resources to allocate to the recruitment process. Nonetheless, many of the recruitment strategies listed below are still able to be utilised by smaller, resource-constrained events.

- Partnering with employment websites such as SEEK (see figure 8.4 for an example of such a partnership in the context of the Gold Coast Commonwealth Games).
- Using stakeholders (for example, local councils, community groups, sponsors and event suppliers) to communicate the event's staffing needs (paid and volunteer) to their respective networks. McCurley and Lynch (1998), in the context of volunteers, call this approach 'concentric circle recruitment' because it involves starting with the groups of people who are already connected to the event or organisation and working outwards. It is based on the premise that volunteers are recruited by someone they know — for example, friends or family, clients or colleagues, staff, employers, neighbours or acquaintances such as members from the same clubs and societies.
- Negotiating sponsorship agreements in a way that requires the sponsor, as part of their agreement with the event, to provide temporary workers with particular skills such as marketing.
- Identifying and liaising with potential sources of volunteers/casual staff. Universities and colleges, for example, often require event management students to complete workplacements/internships, and to take advantage of this, some events (see Australian Chamber Music example in figure 8.5) have created programs for this group. Other sources include job centres, religious groups, service clubs (such as Lions and Rotary), senior citizen centres and retirement homes, Chambers of Commerce and community centres. Some event industry associations (for example, Exhibition and Event Association of Australia and Meetings and Events Australia) maintain internship/employment 'banks' on their websites where events can list opportunities.
- Seconding staff. This is a common approach in the context of large publicly funded events such as the Olympic Games and Commonwealth Games where individuals with specific skills and knowledge sets are accessed from government or private sector firms, returning after the event's conclusion.
- Government employment schemes — in some instances event organisers can engage with government schemes that seek to incentivise the employment of selected groups (for example, youth, long-term unemployed and older workers).

- Determining the make-up (for example, age, sex, occupations) and motivations of existing volunteers — this information can then be used as the basis of further targeted recruitment.
- Gaining the assistance of local and specialist media (for example, radio, television, newspapers, specialist magazines) in communicating an event's human resource needs. This process is greatly assisted if one or more media organisation(s) is in some way (such as through sponsorship) associated with an event.
- Targeting specific individuals within a community who have specialist skills (for example, project management, legal, accounting skills).
- Registering with volunteer agencies. In Australia, these agencies include Volunteering NSW/ACT/South Australia/Queensland/Tasmania.
- Conducting social functions at which, for example, existing volunteers or staff might be encouraged to bring potential candidates, or to which particular groups or targeted individuals are invited.

FIGURE 8.3 The recruitment, selection and induction process for paid and voluntary staff

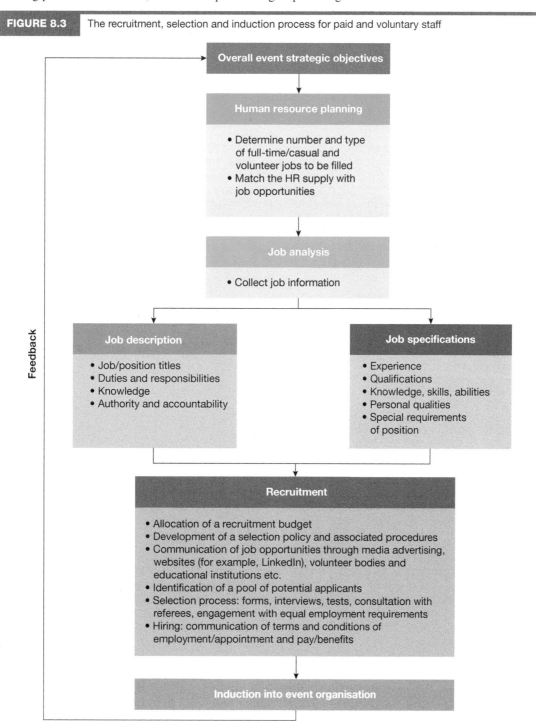

To successfully recruit over 40 000 staff for the Gold Coast 2018 Commonwealth Games (GC2018), the Gold Coast 2018 Commonwealth Games Corporation (GOLDOC), in partnership with SEEK developed a bespoke in-house recruitment strategy that focused on six key principles.

Chances are, if you meet one of the 40 000 officials at GC2018, you won't be able to distinguish whether they are a contractor, volunteer or paid member of staff. This is because they are all 'Games Shapers', enlisted to roll out an event that will see over 6600 athletes from 70 nations compete in 25 sports held at 18 competition venues.

It was never going to be an easy feat recruiting such a volume of staff and it took Anthea O'Loughlin, former HR Operations Manager at GOLDOC nearly three years to refine what she describes as an in-house recruitment model that 'was leveraged off the unique opportunities and challenges presented by the Games'.

Underpinned by a strong partnership with SEEK, the bespoke model focused on six key principles.

1. Attract
Inspired by the 2012 London Olympic Games, GOLDOC and SEEK designed a dedicated GC2018 website that covered everything relating to working at the Games. This website, and subsequent advertising, ensured the messaging showcased the breadth and depth of roles required for the Games.

'Everyone wanted to work at the pool or on the track, so we targeted advertising to draw people into areas they traditionally didn't want to work in,' O'Loughlin said.

2. Stand out
Such diverse roles meant that it was important to have 'super standout job ads' with job descriptions that were unique and attractive to candidates, particularly in areas not in high demand.

'We had really unusual job titles,' O'Loughlin said. 'We had roles such as "C3 Readiness Coordinator", and I thought "where on earth do I put that on SEEK?" so there were lots of conversations about where was the best place to put these ads because they weren't recognisable to anyone.

'It was really about creating a balance to ensure that the obscure roles were highlighted, and that people understood what that job was.'

Case study videos of workers and volunteers from previous games were also created to connect with prospective candidates.

3. Engage
The majority of roles were no longer than twelve weeks, so GOLDOC ensured that people understood all the challenges, expectations and opportunities of being part of a temporary workforce. This was largely achieved through information and articles posted on the SEEK website.

To engage a diverse workforce that reflected the egalitarian values of the Games, GOLDOC also partnered with job network agencies, recruited a Diversity and Inclusion Coordinator and convened an intern program.

4. Educate and excite
To build anticipation, GOLDOC also set up a Games Recruitment Centre for volunteers and paid staff that shared snippets of life at the Games, 'but to also let staff know what a huge achievement it was getting to the final stage of the process,' O'Loughlin added.

5. Manage
To streamline processes, GOLDOC used SEEK Video Screen to get a snapshot of prospective employees and their motivation for working at the Games and applicant tracking system Job Adder to track their progress. Knowing that there would be natural attrition given recruitment started in early 2017, GOLDOC also worked hard to keep the 'silver medallists' (those who missed out on initial roles) warm and engaged throughout the process.

6. Outplacement
GOLDOC and SEEK developed support structures for all the staff, including a series of educational tools to help candidates harness their Games experience to build their SEEK profile and a Virtual Career Fair that facilitated people to connect with potential employers and put their resumes online.

'This really helped to alleviate some of the fear that people were facing and offered support around next steps,' O'Loughlin said.

Source: SEEK n.d.

FIGURE 8.5 The Australian Festival of Chamber Music's internship program

Festival Internships

Students will gain invaluable work experience in the arts industry with one of Australia's most prestigious music festivals!

The Australian Festival of Chamber Music, an international chamber music festival held annually in Townsville, is seeking applications for Intern placements. The Internship Program will run from the end of March through to early August 2021. The Intern Positions are targeted at Music, Creative Arts, and Business/Marketing students.

The Internship Program will endeavour to benefit the student in the following ways:

- Provide valuable experience in planning, conducting and reviewing a Festival
- Development of verbal and written communication
- Development of organisation skills necessary in a working environment
- Development of administration skills
- The ability to work in a busy, small team office environment
- Individual project ownership intended to further career development.

Source: Australian Festival of Chamber Music 2020.

The application process will vary based on the needs of the position, the number of applications anticipated and the resources of the event organisation. In cases where a large number of applications are anticipated, it may be appropriate to consider screening applicants by telephone by asking a few key questions central to the position's requirements — for example, 'Do you have a qualification in event management?' Those individuals who answer these questions appropriately can then be sent an application. In the case of volunteers, applicants for positions in small-scale events may be asked to simply send in a brief statement indicating what skills/qualifications they have, their relevant experience and the tasks they would be interested in doing. For larger events, volunteers may be asked to complete a registration form (increasingly online) such as that developed by the Earth Frequency Festival (see figure 8.6).

FIGURE 8.6 Earth Frequency Festival volunteer application form

Volunteering Experience *

- Select a value -

Volunteering Experience Description

Please specify any previous experience as an event volunteer or employee - including the role/position, name of event and year worked.

Relevant Qualifications

- ☐ **Administration**
- ☐ **Customer Service**
- ☐ **Food Preparation**
- ☐ **Open Driver's Licence**
- ☐ **Blue Card For Working With Children**
- ☐ **White Card For Work In Construction Sites**

Let Us Know 'Why You' In 100 Words Or Less *

Tell us a bit about yourself and why you would be a suitable choice for volunteering at this event.

Source: Earth Frequency Festival 2020.

However basic, application forms for paid employees generally seek information on educational qualifications, previous employment and other details deemed relevant to the position (for example, possession of a driver's licence). The names and contact details of referees who can supply written and/or verbal references are also normally required. Additionally, a curriculum vitae (CV) is generally appended to these forms. Once received, applications allow unsuitable applicants to be culled; those applicants thought to be suitable for short-listing can then be invited to attend an interview. It is often the case with volunteers that selection is based only on the information supplied on their application/registration form, with successful applicants being contacted and asked to attend a briefing session.

Once an appropriate pool of applicants has been identified, the next step is to select from among them those applicants that best fit the available positions. It is important to approach this process systematically, employing appropriate tools, to avoid the costs (financial and otherwise) that come from poor selection (increased training time, high turnover of staff/volunteers, absenteeism, job dissatisfaction and poor performance).

A useful starting point in the selection process is a selection policy. In constructing such a policy, thought needs to be given to:

- approaches to measuring the suitability of candidates — for example, simple rating scales based on set criteria
- sourcing people — for example, will the event organisation promote from within where possible?
- the decision-makers — who will have the final decision on who to engage?
- selection techniques — for example, will tests be employed? Will decisions be made after one interview or several?
- the event's business objectives — for example, do the candidates selected have the qualities and qualifications to progress the event's objectives, such as rapid growth?
- how the event organisation intends to comply with equal employment opportunity legislation.

When selecting applicants, Robertson and Makin (in Beardwell and Holden 2001) suggest considering the following factors.

- The use of past behaviour can be employed to predict future behaviour. That is, the manner in which a person completed a task in the past is the best predictor of the way that person will complete a task in the future. Biographical data (obtained from the curriculum vitae or application form), references and supervisor/peer group ratings are commonly the major sources of such information.
- Employing techniques to assess present behaviour, including:
  - tests, which may be designed to measure aptitude, intelligence, personality and basic core skill levels (for example, typing speeds)
  - interviews (see later discussion)
  - assessment centres, which conduct a series of tests, exercises and feedback sessions over a one to five-day period to assess individual strengths and weaknesses
  - portfolios/examples of work, which are used to indicate the quality/type of recent job-related outputs. An applicant for the position of a set designer for a theatrical event, for example, may be asked to supply photographs of his or her previous work.
- If appropriate, interview information can be supplemented with observations from simulations to predict future behaviour. If the position is for a sponsorship manager, for example, applicants can be asked to develop a sponsorship proposal and demonstrate how they would present this proposal to a potential sponsor. Another common approach, according to Noe et al. (2003), is to ask managerial applicants to respond to memos that typify problems that are commonly encountered. This will provide the potential employer with insights into the problem-solving abilities of applicants, and how they are likely to respond to the challenges offered by the position.

Interviews are likely to be the most common means of selection used by event organisations, so it is worthwhile spending some time looking at how best to employ this approach. A well-designed set of interview questions will enable an assessment of the strengths and weaknesses of applicants to be made and assist in matching them to the needs of the position.

Interviews

According to Noe et al. (2003), research clearly indicates that the interviewing process should be undertaken using a structured approach so all relevant information can be covered and candidates can be directly compared. With this goal in mind, Mullins (2005) suggests using a checklist of key matters to be covered in the interview process. A sample checklist for a paid position with an event is shown in figure 8.7.

Checklists should also be used if interviews are to be conducted for volunteers. Responses from volunteers may be sought to questions regarding the relationship between the volunteer's background/experience and the position(s) sought, reasons for seeking to become involved with the event, the level of understanding about the demands/requirements of the position(s) (such as time and training), and whether applicants have a physical or medical condition that may have an impact on the types of position for which they can be considered (keeping equal employment opportunity legislation in mind). Such checklists will enable volunteer(s) to be matched with the position(s) that best suits their interests and abilities, resulting in better outcomes for the event organisation and increased volunteer satisfaction and retention.

FIGURE 8.7 Sample interviewer's checklist

Interviewer's checklist

Position title: _____ Candidate's name: _____

Date: _____

Interviewees: _____

Interview
1. Qualifications held
2. Employment history
3. Extent to which applicant meets essential criteria for the position
4. Extent to which applicant meets desirable criteria for the position
5. Organisational fit
   (a) To what extent will the position result in personal satisfaction for the applicant?
   (b) To what extent does the applicant identify with the organisation's values and culture?
   (c) Can the applicant's remuneration expectations be met?

Assessment
Summary rating of applicant based on the above criteria. A simple scale of 'all, most, some, none' may be used for criteria 3 and 4. Additionally, some relevant summary comments may be made on each applicant.

Action
Follow-up action to be taken with applicant — for example:
• Advise if successful/unsuccessful.
• Place on eligibility list.
• Background/reference check.
• Arrange pre-employment medical check.

Applicant responses flowing from the interview process need to be assessed in some way against the key criteria for the position. One common means of doing this is a rating scale (for example, 1 to 5). When viewed collectively, the ratings given to individual items lead to an overall assessment of the applicant in terms of how he or she fits with the job, the event organisation and its future directions.

Interviews may be conducted on a one-on-one basis or via a panel of two or more interviewers. The latter has some advantages in that it assists in overcoming any idiosyncratic biases that individual interviewers may have, allows all interviewers to evaluate the applicant at the same time and on the same questions and answers, and facilitates the discussion of the pros and cons of individual applicants.

Once the preferred applicant(s) has been identified, the next step is to make a formal offer of appointment, by mail or otherwise. In the case of paid event staff, the short-term nature of many events means any offer of employment will likely be for a specific contracted period. The employment contract generally states what activities are to be performed, salary/wage levels, and the rights and obligations of the employer and employee.In the case of volunteers, a simple letter of appointment, accompanied by details regarding the position, may be all that is necessary. It is also appropriate to consider supplying volunteers with a statement about their rights and those of the event organisation regarding their involvement in the event (see figure 8.8). Once an offer has been made and accepted, unsuccessful applicants should be informed as soon as possible.

FIGURE 8.8 Rights and responsibilities of volunteers — Midsumma Festival

Your rights as a volunteer:
- To be respected and treated as a co-worker and to not be exploited
- To have access to training sessions where appropriate and possible
- To have on-the-job supervision provided by a designated member of staff or Team Leader volunteer
- To have the necessary support and direction in order to carry out designated duties
- To be entitled to take breaks from their volunteer work, when appropriate
- To be able to contact the Volunteers Coordinator at any time during the festival with concerns, questions or indeed anything to do with being a part of the festival
  In order to enhance the festival, volunteers will:
- start at the scheduled time, and be dressed and groomed appropriately
- wear the festival T-shirt and accreditation when on shift
- be asked to carry out specific duties to the best of their ability
- respect the authority of, and decisions made by, Midsumma CEO and staff
- contribute to the continuous improvement of the festival
- be honest and reliable
- adhere to and follow policy, procedure and guidelines
- not smoke or consume alcohol while in your festival T-shirt
- be conscious of the sustainability of our environment.

Source: Midsumma Festival 2020.

Induction

Once appointees (paid or voluntary) commence, a structured induction program designed to begin the process of 'bonding' the individual to the event organisation needs to be conducted. In this regard a range of matters should be considered for inclusion in such a program, including:
- general information about the event organisation (for example, mission, objectives, stakeholders, budget, program, values, organisational structure)
- a detailed explanation of the role, its responsibilities, relationships to other positions within the event, reporting structure and approaches to performance evaluation
- work health and safety information
- general employment conditions (for example, grievance procedures, absenteeism, sickness, dress code, security, holiday/leave benefits, superannuation, salary and overtime rates, and other benefits such as car parking and meals)
- introduction to other event staff (or at least those in their work area)
- expectations regarding professional behaviour
- information on policies germane to the position.

The induction process can be facilitated by the development of an induction kit for distribution to each new staff member or volunteer. Such a kit might contain:
- the event's annual report
- a message from the organising committee chairperson/chief executive officer welcoming staff and volunteers
- a statement of event mission/vision, goals and objectives
- an organisational chart
- human resource manual (containing policies and procedures)
- a name badge
- a staff list (including contact details)
- a uniform (in the case of volunteers)
- a list of sponsors
- a list of stakeholders
- any other appropriate items — for example, work health and safety information.

A central outcome of the induction process should be a group of staff and volunteers that are committed to the event, enthusiastic and knowledgeable about their role in it, and aware of what part their job plays in the totality of the event. It should also serve to orient the staff and volunteers to the culture of the organisation, and in so doing provide an introduction to its work practices and environment. This will assist in hastening their adaptation to their new work/team environment.

Training and professional development

According to Stone (2014), training and professional development are both concerned with changing the behaviour and job performance of staff and volunteers. Training focuses on providing specific job skills/knowledge that will allow people to perform a job or to improve their performance in it. Professional development, on the other hand, is concerned with the acquisition of new skills, knowledge and attitudes that will prepare individuals for future job responsibilities.

Both training and professional development are significant in driving the success of an event, acting to underpin its effective delivery. For small and mid-sized events, much training is on-the-job, with existing staff and experienced volunteers acting as advice givers. This approach, while cheap and largely effective, has limitations. The major one is that it is not often preceded by an assessment of the event's precise training needs and how best to meet them within resource limitations.

A formal approach to training needs assessment serves to determine whether training taking place is adequate and whether any training needs are not being met. Additionally, such an assessment generates suggestions about how to improve training provided by the event. These suggestions may result in:

- sending, or requesting stakeholder/government support to send, staff/volunteers on training programs dealing with specific skills/knowledge (for example, risk management)
- identifying individuals associated with the event who would be willing to volunteer to conduct training sessions
- commissioning consultants/external bodies to undertake specific training
- encouraging staff/volunteers to undertake event-specific, or more general, training courses in areas such as project management or environmental sustainability practices in return for certain benefits (for example, higher salaries, appointment to positions of greater responsibility/satisfaction).

When trying to identify what training is required to facilitate the effective delivery of an event, the central consideration should be to determine if a gap exists between the current performance of staff and volunteers and level of performance desired by the event organisation. This can be achieved by:

- performance appraisals of existing staff/volunteers — what training management/supervisory staff identify as being required to make the existing workforce more productive
- analysis of job requirements — what skills/knowledge the job description identifies
- surveys of staff and volunteers — to establish what skills/knowledge employees and volunteers state they need to better perform their roles.

The types of training provided by events themselves, as opposed to training they might commission or request staff to undertake independently, will vary; however, it is not uncommon for them to provide a level of general training for all staff in areas such as occupational health and safety and first aid, as well as training designed to provide position-specific skills and knowledge.

Supervision and evaluation

Generally, the bigger and more complex the event, the greater the need is for staff and volunteers to perform a supervisory function. This function may be exercised through a variety of means, including having would-be supervisors understudy an existing supervisor, developing a mentoring system or encouraging staff to undertake appropriate professional development programs.

One of the key tasks of supervisors and managers is that of performance appraisal. This task involves evaluating performance, communicating that evaluation and establishing a plan for improvement. The ultimate outcomes of this process are a better event and more competent staff and volunteers. Stone (2014) proposes a dynamic performance appraisal program (see figure 8.9) based on goal establishment, performance feedback and performance improvement.

According to Stone (2014), goals should be mutually arrived at by a supervisor and a volunteer or staff member. These goals, while specific to the particular job, can concern technical skills and knowledge, problem-solving/creativity, planning and organising, interpersonal skills, decision-making, commitment to quality and safety, the achievement of designated results, attitudes and personality traits, reliability/punctuality, and professional development. It is important that measurements of progress towards goals are established, otherwise there is little point in setting goals in the first place. A person charged with overseeing waste management for an event, for example, might be assessed in large measure based on specific outcomes, such as the percentage of material recycled from the event, levels of contamination in waste, the percentage of attendees (as determined by a survey) that understood directions regarding the placement of different types of waste in specific containers, and the level of complaints regarding matters such as full bins.

FIGURE 8.9 Dynamic performance appraisal program

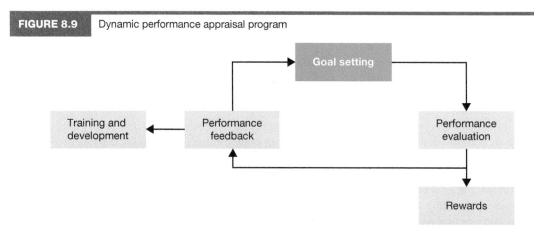

Source: Based on Stone 2014.

Performance, in terms of progress towards established goals, can be assessed in a variety of ways, including performance scales. According to Wood et al. (2004), irrespective of what assessment measures are used, responses to the following questions must underpin any efforts at assessing job performance: What does the job require? What does the employee/volunteer need to do to perform effectively in this position? What evidence from how work is undertaken would indicate effective performance? What does the assessment of evidence of performance indicate about future actions required?

Once an appraisal has been conducted, there should be a follow-up review discussion in which the supervisor/manager and the staff member mutually review job responsibilities, examine how these responsibilities have been performed, explore how performance can be improved, and review and revise the staff members short-term and long-term goals. The interview process should be a positive experience for both parties. To this end, it is worthwhile considering providing training to the managers/supervisors involved in this process so they adhere to certain basic practices such as preparing for the interview by reviewing job descriptions, reviewing previous assessments, encouraging discussion and being constructive, not destructive. As regards this last point, it should be kept in mind that negative feedback on performance can have a demotivating effect, and as such there are benefits in focusing more on the guidance and support needed to achieve the next level of performance than what has happened in the past (Bratton and Gold 2017).

Integral to the appraisal system are rewards that paid staff receive in the form of salaries, bonuses, profit sharing, promotion to other jobs (for example, from Event Coordinator to Event Manager), and benefits such as cars and equipment use (for example, laptop computers). Rewards can also be employed to acknowledge performance and encourage them to return. These can include training in new skills, free merchandise, promotion to more interesting volunteer positions in subsequent event iterations and free tickets/event registration.

The 'flip side' to rewards — that is, discipline — also requires managerial consideration. It is useful to have in place specific policies and practices that reflect the seriousness of different behaviour/actions, and these should be communicated to all staff (paid and voluntary). These policies and practices are likely to begin with some form of admonishment and end with dismissal. Many of the approaches to disciplining paid employees (such as removing access to overtime) are not applicable to volunteers. Instead, approaches that may be applied to this group include re-assignment, withholding of rewards/benefits and suspension from holding a position as a volunteer.

Termination, outplacement and re-enlistment

Whether employing staff on contract or as permanent employees, event managers are occasionally faced with the need to terminate the services of an individual. This action may be necessary in instances where a staff member or volunteer breaches their employment contract/agreed statement of responsibilities. This need may also arise when economic or commercial circumstances of the organisation conducting the event require it to shed staff (such as when there is insufficient revenue due to poor ticket sales).

Various legal issues surrounding termination need to be understood by those involved in event management. In Australia, these issues relate to unfair or unlawful dismissal/termination and are spelt out in the *Fair Work (Registered Organisations) Act 2009* (Cwlth), as well as the Small Business Fair Dismissal

Code (applies to businesses of fewer than 15 employees). It should also be noted that on occasions events will need to 'dismiss' volunteers. In this regard Getz (2005) suggests a variety of approaches. These include making all volunteer appointments for fixed terms (with volunteers needing to re-apply and being subjected to screening each time the event is conducted) and using job descriptions and performance appraisals to underpin any 'dismissal' action.

Outplacement is the process of assisting terminated employees (or indeed volunteers), or even those who choose to leave the event organisation voluntarily, to find other employment. By performing this role the event organisation is providing a benefit to employees for past service, as well as maintaining and enhancing its image as a responsible employer. Even volunteers who are no longer needed can be helped into other positions by being put in contact with volunteer agencies or other events.

With recurring events, such as annual festivals, opportunities often exist to re-enlist for paid or voluntary positions. To maintain contact with potential volunteers and past staff between events, a variety of approaches can be employed, including newsletters and personal contact by telephone.

Event organisers should also keep in mind that staff will often leave of their own accord. The involvement of such staff in exit interviews can provide valuable information that could be used to fine-tune one or more aspects of an event's human resource management process. A study of volunteers at a jazz festival (Elstad 2003), for example, found the main reasons (in order) that volunteers quit were:

1. their overall workload
2. a lack of appreciation of their contribution
3. problems with how the festival was organised
4. disagreement with changing goals or ideology
5. wanting more free time for other activities
6. a lack of a 'sense of community' among volunteers
7. family responsibilities
8. the festival becoming too large
9. the inability to make decisions regarding their own position
10. a dislike for some of their responsibilities
11. lack of remuneration
12. moving out of the festival's geographic area.

Evaluation of process and outcomes

As with all management processes, a periodic review is necessary to determine how well, or otherwise, the human resource management process is operating. To conduct such a review, it is necessary to obtain feedback from relevant supervisory/management staff, organising committee members, and paid and voluntary staff. Such a review might examine aspects such as the staff induction process, adequacy of training and supervision, regularity and effectiveness of work reviews, work conditions and salaries. It might also examine issues such as staff satisfaction levels and the retention rate of staff/volunteers. In visitor surveys of the event, it is worthwhile to canvass the opinions of visitors on issues such as staff/volunteer friendliness, helpfulness and the adequacy of responses to requests for information. It might also be worthwhile to survey volunteers in order to discover what motivated them to volunteer, what the experience was like for them, and their suggestions for improvements in areas such induction, training and supervision. Once a review is complete, revisions can be made to the process for subsequent events.

8.3 Motivating staff and volunteers

LEARNING OBJECTIVE 8.3 Discuss approaches that can be employed to motivate event staff and volunteers.

Motivation is a key, if implicit, component of the human resource management process. It is what commits people to a course of action, enthuses and energises them, and enables them to achieve goals, whether the goals are their own or that of the event organisation. The ability to motivate other staff members is a fundamental component of an event organisers repertoire of skills. Without appropriate motivation, paid employees and volunteers can lack enthusiasm for achieving an event's corporate goals and delivering quality service, or can show a lack of concern for the welfare of their co-workers or event participants.

In the context of volunteers, pure altruism (an unselfish regard for, or devotion to, the welfare of others) may be an important motive for seeking to assist in the delivery of events. Although this proposition is supported by Flashman and Quick (1985), the great bulk of work done on motivation stresses that people, while they may assert they are acting for altruistic reasons, are actually motivated by a combination of external and internal factors, most of which have little to do with altruism. As Moore (1985, p. 1) points out in the context of volunteers, they 'clearly expect to obtain some reward for their participation and performance'.

Researchers from a variety of disciplines have done much work over many years on what motivates people, particularly in the workplace. Perhaps the most relevant and useful of these studies within the context of festivals and events are content theories and process theories.

Content theories

Content theories concentrate on what things initially motivate people to act in a certain way. As Mullins (2005, p. 480) points out, they 'are concerned with identifying people's needs and their relative strengths, and the goals they pursue in order to satisfy these needs'. Figure 8.10 represents the essential nature of theories of this type.

| FIGURE 8.10 | The basis of content theories of motivation |

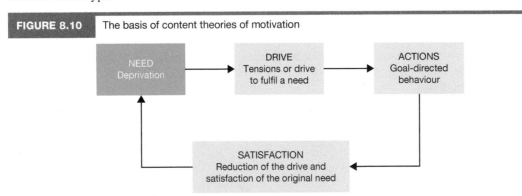

Source: Peach and Murrell 1995.

Content theories assert that a person has a need — a feeling of deprivation — which then drives the person towards an action that can satisfy that need. Maslow's (1954) hierarchy of needs, illustrated in figure 8.11, popularised the idea that needs are the basis of motivation.

| FIGURE 8.11 | Maslow's hierarchy of needs |

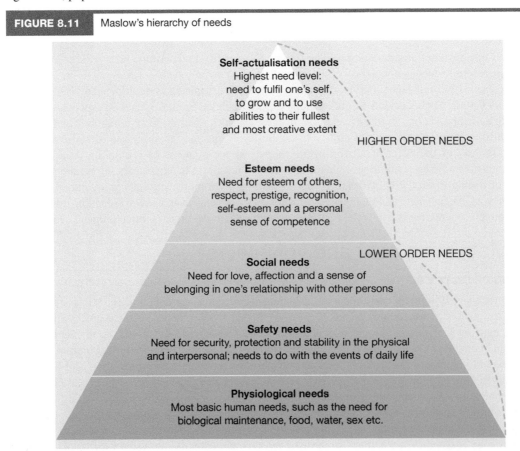

Source: Wood et al. 2004.

Maslow's theory proposes that lower order needs must be satisfied before people are motivated to satisfy the next, higher need. That is, people who are trying to satisfy physiological needs of hunger and thirst have no interest in satisfying the need for safety until their physiological needs are satisfied. The first three needs identified by Maslow are perceived as deficiencies; they must be satisfied to fulfil a lack of something. In contrast, satisfaction of the two higher needs, he argues, is necessary for an individual to grow emotionally and psychologically.

Although little empirical evidence exists to support Maslow's theory, it can give insights into the needs people may be seeking to fulfil through employment. Some research, for example, indicates a tendency for higher level needs to dominate as individuals move up the managerial hierarchy.

Another researcher who falls within the ambit of content theory is Herzberg (1968). He argues that some elements, which he calls hygiene factors, do not of themselves motivate or satisfy people. Among these factors are pay levels, policies and procedures, working conditions and job security. However, the absence or perceived reduction in these items can stimulate hostility or dissatisfaction towards an organisation. Herzberg further argues that other factors, which he calls motivators, of themselves lead to goal-directed behaviour. These elements include achievement, recognition and interesting work. Herzberg's theory is illustrated in figure 8.12.

FIGURE 8.12 Herzberg's two-factor theory of motivation

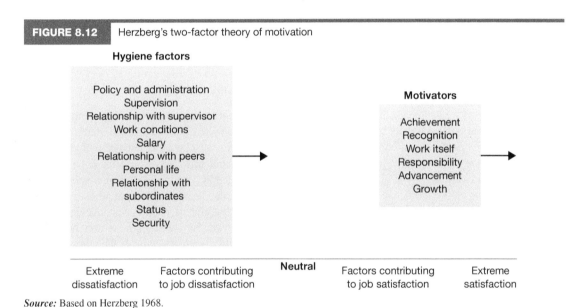

Source: Based on Herzberg 1968.

Herzberg's theory suggests event managers can motivate staff and volunteers by:
• instituting processes of recognising achievement
• empowering staff so they can take responsibility for the outcomes of their part of the event
• providing opportunities for them to grow in skills, experience and expertise.

It also suggests event managers need to be conscious of certain hygiene factors that can act as demotivators. These might include attitudes of supervisors, working conditions such as the length of meal/coffee breaks and hours of work, quality of food provided, the status of one job compared with another (for example, waste management officer versus publicity coordinator), and policies such as the type/quality of uniforms provided to staff versus volunteers.

Content theories, such as those of Herzberg and Maslow, provide event managers with some understanding of work-related factors that initiate motivation; they also focus attention on the importance of employee needs and their satisfaction. They do not, however, explain particularly well why a person chooses certain types of behaviour to satisfy their needs (Wood et al. 2004). Process theories, the subject of the next section, take up this challenge.

Process theories

Representative of process theories of motivation are Adams's (1965) equity theory and Vroom's (1964) expectancy theory.

Equity theory

Equity theory is based on the reasonable premise that all employees (or, for that matter, volunteers) expect to be treated fairly. This being the case, if one employee or volunteer perceives a discrepancy in the outcomes that he or she receives (for example, pay or type of work allocated) compared with those of other employees or volunteers, that employee or volunteer will be motivated to do more (or less) work (Wood et al. 2004). This situation is represented in the following equation.

$$\frac{\text{Individual rewards}}{\text{Individual inputs}} \overset{comparison}{\longleftrightarrow} \frac{\text{Others' rewards}}{\text{Others' inputs}}$$

What an employee or volunteer perceives as fair in terms of compensation (monetary or non-monetary) is subjective. The best way of maintaining an awareness of what an individual is thinking in this regard is to develop and maintain open lines of communication. If inequity is perceived and goes unnoticed, several outcomes are possible, including a reduction in effort, pressure to increase remuneration and departure from an event organisation.

Expectancy theory

Expectancy theory holds that an individual's motivation to act in a specific way comes from a belief that a particular outcome will result from doing something (expectancy). This outcome will result in a reward (instrumentality). The rewards for accomplishing this outcome are sufficiently attractive/desirable to justify the effort put into doing it (valence). Motivation, under this theory (in its most simplistic form), can therefore be expressed as:

$$\text{Motivation} = \text{Expectancy} \times \text{Instrumentality} \times \text{Valence}.$$

This being the case, whenever one of the elements in this equation approaches zero, the motivational value of a decision is dramatically reduced. Event organisers need to be aware of this and, therefore, try to maximise all three motivational components. In other words, there must be a clear 'payoff' if employees and volunteers are to perform at a high level. To understand what this 'payoff' needs to be for each staff member and volunteer is difficult; however, the chances of doing so are greatly increased if lines of communication are kept open and if a genuine effort is made to understand each individual.

As an example of how expectancy theory works, take the situation of people who decide to work voluntarily on their local community festival. They may believe they will gain certain new skills (*expectation*), which will, in turn, enhance their future employability (*instrumentality*). The jobs they will subsequently be able to apply for/request to be appointed to are ones they believe will be more rewarding (*valence*) either in the context of the event or outside it.

While the focus in this section has been on the individual, it should not be forgotten that as events often involve a number of functional area teams, rewards for collective performance need also to be considered.

8.4 Building effective staff and volunteer teams

LEARNING OBJECTIVE 8.4 Describe techniques for event staff and volunteer team building.

As noted at the outset of the chapter, event organisations often come together quickly and exist only for relatively short periods of time. This being the case, one of the greatest challenges faced by an event manager is creating effective team(s) capable of achieving an event's objectives. In the case of small-scale events, such as corporate product launches or hospitality-based events, the event manager will often create a single team comprising members of their own company's staff and those of a range of suppliers (the venue, A/V hire firms, caterers and so on). To develop a sense of 'team' within such a group, the event manager will often rely solely upon one or more 'team' briefings/meetings, supported by detailed event production schedules indicating the roles to be performed by all involved. What simplifies this process in many instances is the ongoing (as opposed to one-off) use by event managers of a given set of contractors, who, over time, come to increasingly understand how best to integrate their activities with those of the event production firm. In the case of larger events where there are many function-based teams, and where the teams that are created exist for longer periods, creating effective teams becomes a more complex issue. In this regard, event managers need to give significant thought to such matters as:

- clearly establishing team tasks
- choosing team members with due regard to personality traits, skills/knowledge and availability (for the period of the event)

- providing adequate support in the form of training, information, resources, opportunities for team building, and designing processes to monitor team performance and provide feedback (Mullins 2005).

Most events are conscious of the significance of the creation of effective teams to their success, with some developing creative responses to facilitate their formation. The Manchester Commonwealth Games, for example, in their efforts to integrate volunteers and paid staff conducted a pre-event 'celebration'. This event, attended by The Earl and Countess of Wessex and hosted by a well-known television presenter, included motivational videos, live sketches, singing and other entertainment. Staff and volunteers attending this function were seated by the venue team and were greeted by their respective venue's management as part of the event's overall efforts at strengthening team bonds. Among other things, this event also sought to:

- inspire and motivate staff
- transfer key messages about what to expect and what was expected of staff and volunteers
- educate staff and volunteers about the global nature of the event and participating nations.

There are a range of models which set out approaches to building effective teams (for example, the GRPI Model, the Katzenbach and Smith Model, and the T7 Model of Team Effectiveness). Looking at these various models collectively, common attributes can be identified, including the following.

- *Goals and objectives* — teams should have clearly defined goals and objectives and performance expectations.
- *Skills and attributes* — care and attention is paid to selecting people with the right combination of skills, personality, communication styles and ability to perform.
- *Processes* — clear decision-making processes and work procedures need to be established.
- *Accountability and collaboration* — team members should be mutually accountable to one another, and be proactive in their efforts at cooperation and communicating information.
- *Team size* — teams should be of a manageable size, often given as between five and 12 (Wharton University of Pennsylvania 2006).
- *Support* — teams require the necessary resources, information, support and training to perform the tasks with which they have been charged. Additionally, access to a coach or mentor when issues arise, and a supportive organisational culture are important.
- *Leadership* — leaders should be chosen that 'fit' the team, and be capable of motivating and building positive staff relationships.
- *Recognition* — teams need to be recognised and rewarded for their performance.

Once teams are in place and operating effectively, an event organiser should monitor their performance and productivity by observing their activities and maintaining appropriate communication with team leaders and members. If deficiencies are noticed during the monitoring procedure, then appropriate action can be taken in terms of training, team structure changes or the refinement of operating procedures in a climate of mutual trust.

8.5 Legal obligations

LEARNING OBJECTIVE 8.5 State general legal considerations associated with human resource management in an event context.

Event managers need to be mindful of laws and statutes that have an impact on the employee and employer relationship, some of which have previously been noted in this chapter (see also the legal considerations in event planning and management chapter). Areas covered by these laws and statutes include work health and safety, discrimination, employee dismissal, salaries/wages, and working conditions (for example, holiday and long service leave, superannuation and workers compensation). As this area of the law is dynamic in nature, it is necessary for event organisations to remain abreast of any developments by contacting such bodies as:

- Safe Work Australia (for occupational health and safety matters)
- Fair Work Ombudsman (workplace relations and compliance with workplace laws)
- Australian Human Rights Commission (for discrimination matters)
- state/territory and national bodies charged with overseeing industrial relations, safety at work and discrimination legislation.

SUMMARY

Event managers should approach the task of human resource management not as a series of separate activities, but as an integrated process involving a sequence of interrelated steps. These steps begin with an appreciation of an event's mission, strategies and goals, and then progress through a series of tasks that require the development of a human resource strategy and objectives; human resource policies and procedures; recruitment, selection and induction processes; training and professional development programs; supervision and evaluation approaches; termination, outplacement and re-enlistment practices; and evaluation and feedback techniques. Each of these stages in the human resource management process, it has been argued here, hasapplication in the context of both paid and volunteer staff, as well as to events of varying size and type. This chapter has also dealt with the issue of motivation, examining two broad theoretical perspectives on the matter, process and content theories. The final sections of this chapter explored mechanisms for developing effective teams and provided an overview of legal considerations associated with human resource management.

QUESTIONS

1 Interview the organiser of a business or public event and ask what legal/statutory requirements impact their human resource management processes and practices.
2 In the context of a specific event, identify the various areas in which it has established human resource management–related policies and procedures.
3 Develop a job specification for a management position within a business or public event.
4 Construct an interview checklist for candidates seeking a supervisory position within a business or public event.
5 Discuss one theory of motivation and indicate how an event organiser might draw on this theory to motivate their paid and volunteer staff.
6 Identify an event that makes significant use of volunteers and critically assess its approach to recruiting, selecting, managing and motivating this component of its workforce.
7 Propose an induction program for staff commencing employment with either an event production company or a large-scale business or public event.
8 Reflect on your experiences working in a team context, and identify what attributes linked to effective teams described in this chapter were present or absent.
9 Identify human resource challenges specific to events and suggest how you would go about dealing with them.
10 Suggest practices you would consider using in order to encourage volunteers to remain with an event over multiple iterations.

CASE STUDY

THE PEOPLE MATRIX OF THE WOODFORD FOLK FESTIVAL: BUILDING A PASSIONATE TEAM

The internationally acclaimed Woodford Folk Festival (established in 1986) is one of Australia's biggest and longest running cultural events. The festival is produced by a not-for-profit incorporated association, Woodfordia Inc (WI). The festival, which runs over six days and nights and attracts an aggregate audience of around 120 000 patrons, is organised and managed by over 3000 volunteers with a core of 25 full-time paid staff.

The enormity of the human resources task undertaken in producing the festival can be appreciated by examining its organisational structure. The task of recruiting, communicating with, resourcing, training, motivating, supervising and recognising this team of passionate and dedicated people is something we have spent many years developing and improving. The success of our mission can be measured by our team member retention rate and we believe it is also reflected in our patron visitation return rate: average volunteer return rate — 60 per cent; department head retention rate — 90 per cent; average patron return rate — 65 per cent.

'Engage passionate people' is one of the best pieces of business advice we have received. The Woodford Folk Festival has never been short of passionate people; the key to the success of our human resources philosophy has been in empowering those people, and recognising, rewarding and maintaining their energy, year to year.

The Woodford Folk Festival is a multi–art form community celebration. Our challenge is to build a temporary township to house and service a population of over 20 000 people for six days and nights. In addition to this, 2300 artists are scheduled to perform across 25 stages (performing on average three shows each). This organisational feat is accomplished by 25 permanent staff, 240 (mostly volunteer) department heads and 'key offsiders', 200 contractors and 2800 volunteers (undertaking over 280 unique roles). The strength and success of the festival lies in our ability to regroup this team year after year, while maintaining their energy and passion for the festival.

The seven critical areas we identify and address in striving for high volunteer satisfaction and retention levels are as follows.

1 *Recruitment*. We ensure that the volunteer undertaking the job has been correctly selected for the position (for example, a 'people person' is in a public relations position).

2 *Communication*. We ensure that the person knows exactly what the job entails (for example, a clear and detailed job description, including expected hours, is available).

3 *Resourcing*. We ensure that the person is given the relevant resources to undertake the role (for example, appropriate equipment).

4 *Training*. We ensure that appropriate training is delivered for the position (for example, inductions in specific tasks such as Responsible Service of Alcohol training).

5 *Motivation*. We ensure that the volunteer is motivated to do well (for example, we aim to match the values of the person with the values of the organisation).

6 *Supervision*. We ensure that the person is given supervision and feedback on their work and has clear a communication path for problem solving.

7 *Recognition*. We ensure that people are appropriately recognised for their contributions.

Delivering these seven fundamental elements in job fulfilment to 2800 volunteers is a challenging task. Achieving an appropriate ratio of supervisors (festival department heads and key offsiders) to volunteers is critical to achieving success in job satisfaction. The perfect ratio for us is between 10 and 12 volunteers to each department head. We have found more than 12 volunteers per department head results in a depersonalised environment where it is harder to deliver each of the fundamental elements listed. We apply the same ratio (1:12) between area managers and department heads and measure the success of our management of department heads by their retention rate, which sits at over 90 per cent annually.

The organisational structure of the festival (as a business of the WI) provides some insight into how the task of maintaining a group of dedicated staff and volunteers each year is accomplished. The structure consists of a series of layers as shown in figure 8.13.

FIGURE 8.13   Organisational structure of the festival

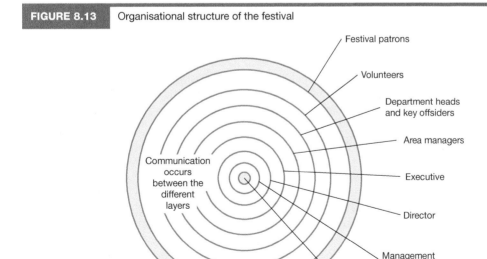

At the centre of this concentric structure are the grassroots members of the WI who annually appoint a Management Committee, which has statutory and fiduciary responsibility for the organisation and its

activities. From here each new layer is appointed by the former layer; for example, the Executive Director appoints the General Manager who in turn engages the permanent staff and appoints a team of 25 Festival Area Managers and so on. The concentric structure highlights the flatness of our organisation (for example, the lack of unnecessary hierarchy or middle management) and the chain of communication.

The management of the Woodford Folk Festival is divided into many small departments (this number reaching 180 departments in 2017) and a department head is appointed to each area. Key offsiders are appointed to assist managers of departments with over 12 members. Area Managers (generally full-time staff members) work with department heads to facilitate the supply of services and resources needed to undertake their roles. A permanent full-time Volunteers' Manager supports department heads in recruiting and managing their team of volunteers to deliver their department's services at the festival.

The success of this system is in large part due to the autonomy each festival department enjoys. Department heads are given a high level of discretion and independence to plan and carry out their work. In our experience this autonomy empowers the department head to build a team and create a culture within their department. It also enables individuals to engage their personal management attributes in order to achieve greater department success and job fulfilment. Over the years, departments have developed unique identities within the greater festival team. This is most clearly evident in the humorous naming of most festival departments; for example, the toilet cleaning department is called the 'Intergalactic S-Bend Warriors' and the fencers are 'The Ministry of Da Fence'. And while there is no uniform for volunteers, many departments also identify themselves by wearing particular colours or by costuming; for example, 'Infology' team members wear purple clothing during their shifts and the 'Lettering House' dress as posties. It's this sense of fun and ownership that greatly contributes to volunteers' sense of belonging and their experiencing the festival as a 'home'. Critically, almost 100 per cent of WI paid staff began their career as a volunteer at the Woodford Folk Festival. Succession planning is also essential to the Woodford people matrix. Department heads are empowered to appoint their own key offsiders (who are generally sourced from returning volunteers) and are encouraged to identify and train their replacement.

The result for WI and the festival is a consistent preservation of corporate knowledge through very high staff retention. Recognition of individuals' contributions (both paid and volunteer) to our organisation and the festival can be both complex and simple. It is complex in that the recognition should be relevant, timely and attractive, and simple in that a personal 'thank you' from the right person at the right time can convey sincere appreciation. In exchange for their time, Woodford Folk Festival volunteers receive a festival entry ticket, a distinctive handmade volunteer medallion, an invitation to the volunteers' party, access during the Festival to a volunteers' lounge with complimentary facilities and a certificate of appreciation.

Over the years we have had many different types of gatherings to bring the team together, some in multi-day conference format, some working bees and some just parties. Our gatherings have now emerged into what we call Citizen Days and there a two of them each year. Our Citizens are people who are part of what we are doing at Woodfordia, whether it be a festival or a regeneration project. The aim of our gatherings is to build on the community ownership of Woodfordia and the engagement of people in all the projects at all levels of decision-making. Citizens Day is one of the most useful tools for building capacity within the organising group by creating awareness across departments and projects, increasing confidence and validating the skills set of individual department heads and putting particularly focus groups together on issues that need to be addressed. Most importantly, it takes place in a social setting where people come together and work as a community. More information can be found on our Citizens program at www.woodfordia.org.

Our human resource philosophy is further supported by systems including our online volunteer management tool. This tool, called 'VENUS', enables department heads to undertake volunteer management online and streamlines the business/data reporting end of management with the object of releasing valuable time for personal interaction. It also enables volunteers to move between departments in a common system. The system is used by both volunteers and department heads for applications, screening, role description, organisational and safety inductions, rostering, ticketing and agreements, contact detail management and communication history, reassignments and evaluations.

The success of our human resources philosophy, together with an organisational structure that enables people to move organically through the layers, has proved highly successful for the Woodford Folk Festival. Visitors to the Festival are often heard asking, 'who runs this place?' One hundred and eighty departments work together side-by-side to deliver services to what is ultimately a township with a daily population of 20 000 people. This people culture is the foundation of the organisation and its ongoing health is central to all current and future successes.

Prepared by Amanda Jackes, General Manager Woodfordia Inc and Deputy Festival Director, Woodford Folk Festival

1 What do you think are the main reasons for the success of the human resources strategy of the Woodford Folk Festival?

2 What are some of the advantages of the flat management style employed by the festival?

3 How does the festival motivate and reward its volunteers?

REFERENCES

Adams, JS 1965, 'Inequity in social exchange', in *Advances in experimental social psychology*, ed. L Berkowitz, Academic Press, New York.

AIHR Analytics 2020, 'Case study: how we determined optimum staffing levels', www.analyticsinhr.com/blog/case-study-determined-optimal-staffing-levels, viewed April 15 2020.

Armstrong, M 1999, *A handbook of human resource management practice*, 7th edn, Kogan Page, London.

Australian Festival of Chamber Music 2020, 'Internship program', www.afcm.com.au/education/internships/, viewed 30 April 2020.

Beardwell, I & Holden, L 2001, *Human resource management: a contemporary perspective*, 3rd edn, Pearson Education, London.

Bratton, J & Gold, J 2017, *Human resource management*, 6th edn, McGraw-Hill, Boston.

Earth Frequency Festival 2020, 'Submit a volunteer application', https://www.earthfrequency.com.au/volunteer_application, viewed 22 July 2020.

Elstad, B 2003, 'Continuance commitment and reasons to quit: a study of volunteers at a jazz festival', *Event Management*, vol. 8, pp. 99–108.

Flashman, R & Quick, S 1985, 'Altruism is not dead: a specific analysis of volunteer motivation', in *Motivating volunteers*, L Moore, Vancouver Volunteer Centre, Vancouver.

Getz, D 2005, *Event management and event tourism*, 2nd edn, Cognizant Communication Corporation, New York.

Hanlon, C & Cuskelly, G 2002, 'Pulsating major sport event organisations: a framework for inducting managerial personnel', *Event Management*, vol. 7, pp. 231–43.

Hanlon, C & Jago, L 2000, 'Pulsating sporting events', *Events beyond 2000: setting the agenda: proceedings of conference on event evaluation, research and education*, eds J Allen, R Harris, LK Jao & AJ Veal, Australian Centre for Event Management, Sydney, pp. 93–104.

Herzberg, F 1968, 'One more time: how do you motivate employees?', *Harvard Business Review*, vol. 46, no. 1, pp. 361–7.

Manchester Commonwealth Games 2003, 'Manchester 2002 The XVII Commonwealth Games — Post Games Report, volume 3', www.thecgf.com/sites/default/files/2018-03/Operations.pdf, p. 10.

Maslow, A 1954, *Motivation and personality*, Harper & Row, New York.

McCurley, S & Lynch, R 1998, *Essential volunteer management*, 2nd edn, Directory of Social Change, London.

Midsumma Festival 2020, 'Volunteer with us', www.midsumma.org.au/support/volunteer-with-us, viewed 16 April 2020.

Moore, L 1985, *Motivating volunteers*, Vancouver Volunteer Centre, Vancouver.

Mullins, L 2005, *Management and organisational behaviour*, 6th edn, Financial Times/Pitman Publishing, London.

National Academy of Sciences, Engineering and Medicine 2007, *Staffing standards for aviation safety inspectors*, eds. W Howell & S Van Hemel, The National Academies Press, Washington.

Noe, R, Hollenbeck, J, Gerhart, B & Wright, P 2003, *Resource management*, 4th edn, McGraw-Hill, New York.

Peach, E & Murrell, K 1995 'Reward and recognition systems for volunteers', in *The volunteer management handbook*, T Connors, John Wiley & Sons, New York.

Raj, R, Walters, P & Rashid, T 2013, *Events management: principles and practice*, Sage, London.

SEEK n.d., 'The six principles of the Commonwealth Games recruitment strategy', www.seek.com.au/employer/hiring-advice/the-six-principles-of-the-commonwealth-games-recruitment-strategy, viewed 16 April 2020.

Stone, R 2014, *Human resource management*, 8th edn, John Wiley & Sons Australia, Brisbane.

Vroom, V 1964, *Work and motivation*, John Wiley & Sons, New York.

Wharton University of Pennsylvania 2006, 'Is your team too big? Too small? What's the right number?', https://knowledge.wharton.upenn.edu/article/is-your-team-too-big-too-small-whats-the-right-number-2, viewed 17 April 2020.

Wood, J, Chapman, J, Fromholtz, M, Morrison, V, Wallace, J, Zeffane, R, Schermerhorn, J, Hunt, J & Osborn, R 2004, *Organisational behaviour: a global perspective*, 3rd edn, John Wiley & Sons Australia, Brisbane.

World Confederation for Physical Therapy Congress 2015, 'Volunteer job descriptions', www.wcpt.org/sites/wcpt.org/files/files/wpt15/WCPT2015-Volunteer_Job_Descriptions-5Jan15.pdf, viewed 16 April 2020.

ACKNOWLEDGEMENTS

Photo: © wavebreakmedia / Shutterstock.com

Figure 8.1: © Getz, D. 1997, Event Management and Event Tourism, Cognizant Communication Corporation, New York

Figure 8.2: © Cambridge Literary Festival 2017

Table 8.1: © WCPT. Reprinted with permission of World Physiotherapy WCPT.

Figure 8.4: © SEEK. The six principles of the Commonwealth Games recruitment strategy. Retrieved from https://www.seek.com.au/employer/hiring-advice/the-six-principles-of-the-commonwealth-games-recruitment-strategy [online resource]. Reproduced by permission.

CHAPTER 9

Marketing and sponsorship planning

LEARNING OBJECTIVES

After studying this chapter, you should be able to:

9.1 define the concept of marketing and state the questions that it seeks to provide answers to

9.2 discuss the characteristics of event experiences and their marketing implications

9.3 describe the strategic marketing planning process and its application in event settings

9.4 define the concept of sponsorship and discuss the benefits sponsoring organisations seek through the use of this promotional tool

9.5 discuss influences on the decision by event organisers to seek or not to seek sponsorship

9.6 describe the stages in the development of an event sponsorship strategy.

Introduction

This chapter deals with marketing and sponsorship management in event settings. It begins by examining the nature of marketing along with those characteristics of events that impact decision-making in this area. The steps in the strategic event marketing process are then identified and discussed, with significant coverage being given to the marketing mix elements that are key to this process. Approaches to keeping an event's marketing planning efforts on track are then described along with how best to approach the task of evaluating the success or otherwise of an event's marketing efforts.

The second part of this chapter focuses on the development of sponsorship as an event revenue stream. It first addresses the benefits events and sponsors seek through establishing sponsorship partnerships, and the importance of events being guided by a policy when seeking funds from this source. The process of establishing a sponsorship strategy is then discussed, along with how agreements in this area should be managed and evaluated. The chapter concludes with a case study exploring current practices in event marketing.

9.1 What is marketing?

LEARNING OBJECTIVE 9.1 Define the concept of marketing and state the questions that it seeks to provide answers to.

Marketing has been variously defined (for example, Elliott et al. 2018; Baines and Fill 2014; Armstrong and Kotler 2013), but essentially it can be thought of as a process through which organisations create, communicate, deliver and exchange products or services that have value for their customers. To guide this process, organisations commonly employ the strategic marketing planning process which provides a logical decision-making framework that can significantly reduce (but not eliminate) the potential for an event to fail. Application of this framework aims to answer a number of key questions, including the following:

- How are an event's internal and external environments likely to influence its capacity to create value for its attendees?
- Who should comprise an event's target market(s) and what are the needs of this market(s)?
- What should an event's marketing objectives be?
- What overarching strategy should an event employ in pursuit of its marketing objectives?
- How should an event position itself in the marketplace relative to other similar events?
- How should an event's experience offering best be designed to align with the needs of its target audience(s)?
- How much should an event charge, and how should it go about providing access to its tickets/registrations?
- What type of marketing communication tools will be most cost-effective and when should these be employed over an event's planning cycle?
- How should an event improve and refine its strategic marketing process over time?

It is also the case that, as many events occur in a highly competitive marketplace, a considered strategy, rather than one developed in an ad hoc fashion, is more likely to allow an event to deal effectively with competitor actions. Additionally, events seeking to attract sponsors, and to apply for grants from government agencies, will find that being able to demonstrate that they have a strategic marketing plan in place will enhance their ability to access revenue from these sources.

9.2 The characteristics of event experiences

LEARNING OBJECTIVE 9.2 Discuss the characteristics of event experiences and their marketing implications.

Before examining the stages in the event strategic marketing planning process, it is useful to make some general observations about the nature of event experiences and the implications of these for event marketers. Specifically, these relate to:

- *intangibility.* Potential attendees cannot 'test drive' events (or other types of experiences for that matter) before committing to purchasing/engaging with them. This being the case, there is arguably a higher sense of risk or uncertainty associated with their purchase. This, in turn, means that event marketers are faced with the challenge of convincing potential attendees that their commitment of time and/or money will result in the outcomes they seek. This situation can be contrasted to, for example, the purchase of a product, such as an item of clothing, which can be examined and 'trialled' before a purchase is made.

This issue of perceived risk has been addressed in various ways by event marketers. Some events, for example, leverage their association with high-profile sponsors and/or the involvement in their programs of performers/speakers/celebrities with a high level of recognition/credibility among potential attendees. Others choose venues (for example, Sydney Opera House) with strong brands, employ testimonials from past attendees with credibility among the markets they target or use endorsements from professional bodies/high-profile individuals. Still others emphasise the length of time the event has been operating or provide video and picture galleries on their websites from past events to make the experience they offer more 'concrete' and so easier to assess.

- *ownership*. Unlike products, attendees do not derive ownership of an event experience through the purchasing process. Nonetheless, it is common for individuals to want to reflect on their experience at an event, make their attendance at it known to others or merely have some form of association with it for reasons such as elevating their social standing. Many events commercially exploit this desire through such means as making available for sale photographs of attendees taken by a contracted photographer, souvenir programs and merchandise (for example, T-shirts, CDs, videos). The availability of these items in some instances is not limited to the event itself, with some events, for example, the Adelaide Fringe, operating online shops through which purchases of event-related merchandise can be made throughout the year (Adelaide Fringe 2020).

- *involvement of attendees in event delivery*. Event attendees need to understand their role in an event's 'production' process if they are to maximise the value they receive from it or reduce the potential that their engagement with it might impact the enjoyment of others that are also present. One way of seeking to ensure this role is understood is through the provision of 'scripts' that serve to ensure a quality experience is had by all attendees. These scripts may include, for example, 'rules' relating to alcohol/drugs, entry/exist processes, noise, dress, waste disposal, camping etiquette and parking procedures. These scripts can be communicated in various ways including through programs, event apps, or via electronic notice boards and signs. Event marketers also need to be conscious of the potential for groups with varying needs to impact each other in event settings. In recognition of this, some festivals, for example, create zones for different groups (for example, family camping zones) or for people seeking spaces away from activities (for example, chill out areas).

- *engagement with event staff, volunteers and vendors*. It is common for staff, volunteers and vendors to interact with attendees at various 'touchpoints' (for example, registration desks, food outlets, merchandising stalls and information booths) during the event delivery process. These interactions can impact the quality of the attendee experience positively or negatively. This being the case, event marketers need to assure themselves that staff/volunteer training and selection processes are adequate and that appropriate processes/policies/standards are in place to guide service delivery by vendors.

- *events can't be inventoried*. Events are perishable (except those that are recorded). This means that any unsold capacity results in income that is forever foregone. This limitation can be dealt with in several ways. In instances where spare capacity is projected to exist at certain times, selected markets can be targeted to boost demand during these periods by offering lower entry prices. Making projections as to the demand for an event over its delivery period, and therefore the need to take such actions, is much easier if historical records are available. The Royal Easter Show in Sydney, for example, offers discounts to price-sensitive groups (for example, seniors) on a day when it knows, based on past experience, that attendance is relatively low, in order to stimulate demand on that day. Another approach that is commonly used is the 'storing' of demand by using registrations, RSVPs and ticketing systems so that delivery capacity (and associated costs) can be better matched to attendee numbers. This avoids unnecessary expenditure being made on items such as food and transport which would potentially go unused.

- *simultaneous production and consumption*. Most types of events take place in real time, and as a result any shortfalls in their delivery systems, staff/volunteer training, venue layout/design and so on, cannot, in many instances, be easily dealt with. Therefore, event marketers need to be concerned with the ability of an event's operational systems and processes to deliver the type, and quality, of experience that they have communicated to potential attendees. A mismatch in this area can impact future attendance and damage an event's brand among attendees and the broader community. One recent example of this involved a Sydney event company that promoted a 'secret maze' event, combined with an after party (see figure 9.1).

- *events are open to external influences*. Events can suffer from a variety of external influences including health issues in attendee markets (for example, the novel coronavirus COVID-19); economic fluctuations (for example, changes in exchange rates); developments in the physical environment (for example, volcanic eruptions, floods); and political unrest. This being the case, event marketers can find themselves needing to adapt their strategies by, for example, reorienting promotional activities away from some markets and towards others, or in extreme circumstances, shifting their focus entirely when an event is cancelled to one of keeping an event's brand 'alive' until it can be brought to market again.

FIGURE 9.1 An example of the consequences of not delivering on promotional messages (extract)

Punters demand refunds after Sydney secret maze event fails to deliver

Organisers of an arts event have been slammed by punters for failing to live up on a promise to take them 'through a maze in a secret location in Sydney'.

As news.com.au reports, ticketholders, who also received entry to the after party for $45, arrived at The Curious Labyrinth party on Saturday to find that the 'secret location' was in fact the same venue where the after party was being held.

Though the event suggested attendees will 'get lost to find music, food, drinks and crazy characters amongst the hedges', the actual event, held at Jam Gallery in Bondi Junction, was described as 'fake greenery in a bad nightclub'.

Some of the people who did go along to the event have reportedly claimed there was no maze and that fake vines were hung along the walls of the Jam Gallery instead.

The Underground Arts Party deleted The Curious Labyrinth event page on Facebook after hundreds of people complained and demanded refunds.

'I seriously doubt so many people would have bought tickets if they knew it would be a themed club night at a bar in Bondi Junction,' one punter said.

'At one point I heard one girl say to someone that she had been watching people walk in and out of the dancefloor room saying, 'Is this it?'.'

An organiser has since told news.com.au that 'some people were disappointed with the maze' and that anybody who had messaged the event page have been refunded.

Source: Handshake Media Pty Ltd 2017.

These previously cited characteristics of event experiences create many potential challenges for event marketers, and these challenges need to be kept in mind as the discussion in this chapter moves to exploring the process of strategic marketing planning in event settings.

9.3 Strategic marketing planning

LEARNING OBJECTIVE 9.3 Describe the strategic marketing planning process and its application in event settings.

Strategic marketing planning is the process used by event organisations to align their marketing resources with their assessment of the internal and external environments they face in order to both create value for attendees and achieve marketing objectives (for example, growth in attendance). While this process is used by many events, it can be observed that a number (particularly those run by volunteers and that are small scale) still have no formal marketing planning process in place. This situation, however, often changes as events grow and the demands for a more sophisticated approach to marketing become increasingly obvious (Tribe 2016).

The sequential steps involved in strategic marketing planning are given in figure 9.2. As is evident from this diagram, the process takes its direction from an event's overall strategic planning process. It progresses from there to establish a clear understanding of the context in which the event is currently operating and the markets to which it might seek to appeal. This information then feeds into decisions as regards: marketing objectives; target market selection; marketing strategy(ies); and the marketing mix elements (event experience, price, distribution, process, people, physical evidence and promotion) that support this strategy(ies). As with all business processes, it is subject to review, with the information gained being used to refine or change future actions. The various stages in the process are expanded upon in the following sections.

FIGURE 9.2 Strategic event marketing planning process

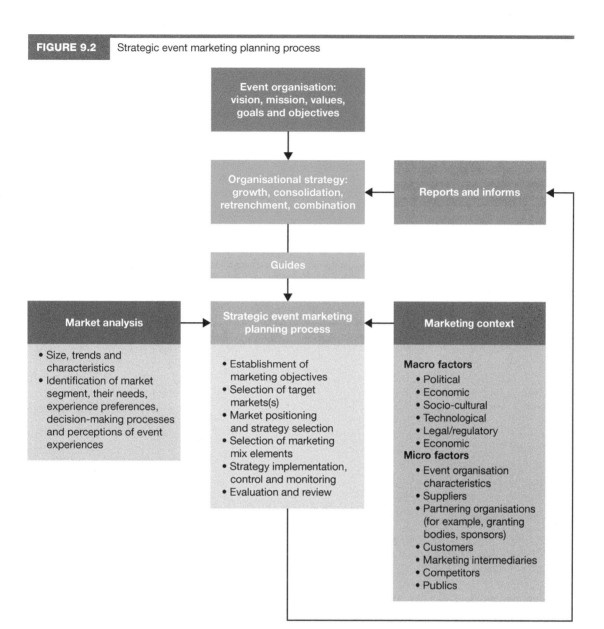

Marketing context

Macro environment

The macro environment refers to external factors with the potential to impact an event's marketing efforts (see the strategic event planning chapter for a discussion of these). Specific factors within these environments that are of relevance to event organisations at any given time can be identified by consulting information sources such as government statistics and reports (for example, reports from the Australian Bureau of Statistics; national, state and local tourism agency market studies); media coverage (for example, industry magazines, blogs); academic papers; national and international event industry association reports and newsletters; and industry websites and consultancy services that regularly report on trends and new developments in specific sectors of the event industry (for example, Ibisworld). In addition to these secondary data sources, events can conduct their own research to fill information gaps they identify. This can be done through such means as interviews or surveys with event practitioners, public sector event agencies, academics and industry thought leaders. This process of gathering and interpreting information on an event's external environment is sometimes called a PESTLE analysis — political, economic, social, technological, legal and environment.

Micro environment

In addition to developing an understanding of the macro environment in which they operate, event organisations also need to ensure they have a clear understanding of those factors in their immediate environment that have the capacity to impact their marketing efforts. These factors include internal factors within the event organisation itself, competitors, attendees, partnering organisations, suppliers/vendors, intermediaries and publics. These are discussed below.

Event organisation

An understanding of an event organisation's internal environment will provide information on matters including its financial status, the capabilities of its staff (skill sets and knowledge) and the efficiency and effectiveness of its current systems, processes and planning efforts. Any shortcomings that are identified through this means can then be worked through and/or acknowledged as constraints that will need to be accommodated in the marketing planning process.

Competitors

Direct competitors (that is, those events that offer essentially the same type of experience) and indirect competitors (that is, events or other activities that are different in nature but that might satisfy the same potential attendee need) should be identified. There are many conferences, seminars and music-based events for example, that compete for the same target groups. This means event organisers need to find a way of differentiating the experience offered by their event in such a way as to give it a competitive edge. Potential attendees can also on occasion find themselves making a decision between attending an event or another type of experience capable of satisfying a specific need(s). For example, the need for entertainment could be met in any number of ways, including by attending a concert, going to a movie or visiting an art exhibition. Understanding which types of alternative experiences enter a potential attendees choice set and the influences on their decision to choose one experience over another (for example, cost, timing, location) can be important in tilting the balance away from indirect competitors to the event concerned.

Attendees

Event organisers require a deep appreciation of their attendees so they can continue to meet their requirements through developing or refining their experience offerings. This appreciation, as will be discussed later, is achieved through directed efforts at seeking feedback.

Partnering organisations

Events can have a range of partnering organisations, including sponsors, granting bodies, media organisations and tourism agencies. Each partner will have specific requirements that will need to be met, some of which will have marketing implications. These must be identified, understood and embraced. For example, tourism bodies providing grants will require recipients to target out-of-area visitors through their promotional activities, and to collect data on how successful they have been at attracting such visitors. Another example would be a newspaper that might offer its support in return for a festival agreeing to conduct joint promotional activities in a local community so it can raise its profile and expand its readership.

Suppliers

The quality of event inputs provided by suppliers and vendors directly impact the experience of attendees. Food, in particular, is an area where events can quickly find themselves being criticised if attendee expectations are not met. The selection of suppliers and vendors, therefore, needs to be made carefully if an event is going to protect its brand and generate positive word of mouth.

Intermediaries

Intermediaries sometimes exist between events and their attendees and play a valuable role in providing convenient access to tickets/registrations, as well as in some instances aiding an event's promotional efforts. In return for their services, these organisations commonly charge a fee that can be incorporated into a ticket/registration price or charged separately. While intermediaries are often used by large festivals, concerts and sporting events to provide market access, they are also being increasingly employed by business, small-scale and even free events as the service they provide can be very cost-effective. Ticketebo, for example, is one such company that operates in this area. Events using this service are not charged for establishing a booking page on its website, nor any ongoing fees. Instead, it charges purchasers a booking fee (with the exception of free events for which it does not charge a fee). Ticketek, Eventbrite and Ticketmaster are further examples of companies that perform this role for events in Australia.

Publics

A public is essentially any group with an actual or potential interest in, or the capacity to impact, an event organisation. Event marketers have an interest in identifying these groups as they can have a negative or positive effect on how an event operates, as well as its brand image. For example, the media (for example, newspapers, television and radio stations, magazines) is one public that event organisations often seek a relationship with as it can act to create a positive narrative around the experience they offer and increase awareness of it. An event's local community is another major public that might need to be actively engaged with as it seeks to enhance its marketplace position or manage issues that sometimes arise (for example, noise, traffic, alcohol/drug abuse) that can damage this position.

Identifying publics that can be of concern to an event can be difficult as circumstances sometimes arise that suddenly cause a group that previously had no discernible interest in an event to develop such an interest. For example, a festival that unknowingly employs an artist that has expressed racist views in the past might suddenly find human rights activists conducting a social media campaign encouraging people not to attend the event.

SWOT analysis

Once an analysis of an event's macro and micro environments has been completed, a summary document can then be developed that identifies its key strengths, weaknesses, opportunities and threats (SWOT) from a marketing perspective (see discussion in the strategic event planning chapter). With these factors in mind, an event marketer can then make informed decisions as to the marketing objectives that they can realistically pursue, and the strategy that will best allow these objectives to be achieved.

Market analysis

Understanding who constitutes an event's market, along with the needs that individuals within it seek to satisfy, is key to successful marketing. This information allows event marketers to, among other things, establish an appropriate pricing structure, target market communication efforts, craft promotional messages that its market will find relevant and design an experience that will be appealing to potential attendees. To achieve this understanding both qualitative (for example, in-depth interviews with attendees, observation and focus groups) and/or quantitative research (for example, attendee and non-attendee surveys) can be used. These techniques are discussed in detail in the event evaluation and research chapter. Emerging from this research should also be an appreciation of how event attendees are making the attendance decision and which market segment(s) offer an event the best opportunity to achieve its marketing objectives.

The attendee decision-making process

Understanding how attendees make the decision to attend an event is important as it provides insights into where in the process an event marketer can intervene. In this regard, there are a variety of factors that can be considered.

- *Who makes the decision to attend?* The answer to this question might seem straightforward: the attendee. This, however, might not be the case. For example, in a family setting, is it the parents or a child who makes the decision for the family to attend a community event? In the context of a conference, is it the individual who decides or is it their manager? If this information can be determined, it allows marketing communication messages to be developed that are more likely to be appealing to the decision-maker concerned.
  - Influencers — there may be individuals or groups that play a significant role in influencing the attendance decision (see figure 9.3). Bloggers or social media influencers, for example, can hold significant sway over those that follow them. These individuals, who include celebrities and experts in particular areas, can be paid, or in some instances simply requested, to carry information concerning specific events to their followers. A quick web search will often identify social media influencers operating in a given area, with lists and contact details being readily available. The endorsement of some types of events by industry associations/government agencies/large corporations can also play an influencing role which is why these endorsements often appear on promotional material for business events.

What is Fyre Festival?

Marketed as the social event to be seen at in 2017, Fyre Festival was advertised as a highly luxurious, super exclusive music festival on an idyllic island in the Bahamas. However, with a lack of proper management and operational guidelines, the event quickly turned into a 24-hour catastrophe. Nonetheless, while the founders were evidently at fault for failing to deliver what was communicated in marketing materials, their influencer marketing campaign was regarded as a success. The founders kickstarted the influencer campaign by working with 10 supermodels to create the vision of an uber-luxury experience of a lifetime. In totality, the supermodels boasted millions of fans and by engaging them, the team was able to spread the festival's message in the widest scope possible.

How Fyre Festival started a #wildfyre

To jump-start the campaign, Fyre Festival's founders flew a band of high-profile supermodels to the Bahamas for a glamourous photo and video shoot. What followed were visually stunning behind-the-scenes Instagram posts by models like Bella Hadid, Kendall Jenner and Emily Ratajkowski to announce the upcoming event. This worked in the founders' favour to build curiosity and trigger conversations online. So much so that media outlets and the supermodels' fans were all pining to know what the supermodels were working on while in the Bahamas. As highlighted in the word cloud below generated by Meltwater's Media Monitoring tool, topics covered in digital publications in the early stages largely hovered around the private island, potential music acts, VIP access and mentions of the supermodels promoting the event.

Considering this was a first-time music festival with tickets upwards of US$1500, this was a great way to generate buzz. Once that hype built up across the supermodels' legion of following, the founders widened their net by engaging 400 celebrity and macro influencers. Each one of them then uploaded a simple orange tile on Instagram in a coordinated move using the hashtag #FyreFest. Spreading like 'wildfyre', this unified influencer effort on a single day and at a specific time was powerful enough to sell out general admission tickets for the event.

Impact of engaging influencers

Ultimately, Fyre Festival's well-constructed influencer campaign proved to be highly effective for a couple of reasons.

1. It drove a significant increase in mass awareness

If executed well with the right influencers, a coordinated move to promote a brand or product could reap tremendous results. In Fyre Festival's case, according to a pitch deck, the team claimed to have reached 300 million impressions in 24 hours when the orange tile push kicked off. Additionally, Kendall Jenner's post announcing the first headliner, G.O.O.D Music Family, claimed to have amassed 6 million unique impressions within 5 days.

2. It reached the relevant target audience

Thanks to the team's clever selection of aspirational influencers, they managed to drive immense desire among their followers, mainly millennials with the capacity to spend. This goes to show it's not enough to only consider if an influencer is a good fit for your brand. It's just as important to identify if their followers are the target audience you want to reach.

3. It boosted ticket sales rapidly

For any campaign, the biggest indicator of success is often seen through conversion. For Fyre Festival, conversion through the coordinated campaign resulted in 5000 people purchasing tickets worth US$4000 within minutes. For a new and unknown event, selling out tickets in that speed was a mean feat. Unfortunately for Fyre Festival, the reality did not match the lavish vision marketed. One lesson to learn here: before embarking on any campaign, always ensure there is a true product to promote.

Source: Kaur 2019.

- *Why are people attending?* The answer to this question underpins the development of the event experience and allows messages to be crafted that speak to these reasons. Common reasons for attending festivals that appear in many studies (for example, Backman et al. 1995; Crompton and McKay 1997; Uysal, Gahan and Martin 1993) include:
  - socialisation or external interaction — meeting new people, being with friends and socialising in a known group
  - family togetherness — seeking the opportunity to be with friends and relatives and doing things together to create greater family cohesion
  - escaping from everyday life, as well as recovering equilibrium — getting away from the usual demands of life, having a change from daily routine and recovering from life's stresses
  - learning about, or exploring, other cultures — gaining knowledge about different cultural practices and celebrations
  - excitement/thrills — doing something because it is stimulating and exciting
  - novelty/ability to regress — experiencing new and different things and/or attending an event that is unique (for example, medieval festivals, historical re-enactment events, Star Trek conventions).

  In the case of business events, reasons that are often cited for attendance include access to current information/developments; networking; easy access to distributors/suppliers; and personal development. It should be kept in mind that any given event will likely have different attendee groups with different sets of motives, and as such, event marketers will need to craft the experiences they offer, along with the messages they create, accordingly.
- *Effectiveness of the types of mediums (for example, brochures, websites, television ads, social media sites) currently in use and the information needs of attendees.* The former is important as it assists in directing promotional efforts and so reduces the potential for promotional expenditure to be wasted. The latter is significant as information requirements associated with attendance at different types of events will not be the same. For example, a decision to attend a nearby weekend organic market would likely involve acquiring basic information such as opening and closing times, location and the types of stalls that will be present, and as such could be classified as a relatively 'low involvement' decision. Contrast this situation with attendance at a major international conference in another country. The significant commitment of time and money involved in this decision would likely require detailed information on its program, social/networking functions, likely attendees, accommodation options, airline partner, registration fees and any applicable discounts (for example, early bird rate), pre and post tours, and so on. The decision to attend in this instance could be seen as 'high involvement' and because of this, an event marketer would need to ensure that these extensive information requirements are met so as to not delay, or act as a barrier to, the decision to attend.
- *Barriers to attendance.* Identifying factors that serve to prevent the decision to attend being made can have a major impact on attendance at an event. For example, an adult lifestyle event was concerned several years ago that its female audience was below that which it had anticipated. When this issue was explored with female non-attendees, it was found that the event, while of interest to them, was seen as having a program that was too male-oriented. Armed with this information, organisers incorporated a ladies-only day into the program for the event's next iteration. They also installed a creche, as the issue of what to do with children while attending the event was raised by a number of respondents. The result of these changes was a 30 per cent increase in female attendance. Other factors that are sometimes noted as barriers to event attendance are inadequate facilities (particularly toilets), lack of shade, travel time and a perception of risk because of reported poor attendee behaviour (for example, drunkenness) in the past.
- *Choice criteria.* Understanding the key determinates (for example, overall program, specific speakers/performers, event location, networking opportunities, price) that a potential attendee will employ in making decisions to attend an event allows an event marketer to ensure these factors are taken into account and feature strongly in promotional messages.
- *Choice set.* As noted previously, understanding which other events, or non-event alternatives, sit inside a potential attendee's choice set will allow an event marketer to make explicit efforts to differentiate their event experience from these, and also craft their promotional efforts in ways that will 'push' potential attendees towards their offering.
- *Past experience.* For past attendees to an event (often a significant market), the decision to attend an event again is likely to be based in large measure on their prior experience. This being the case, event marketers need to ensure they do not over-promise and underdeliver, and that they work with those responsible for an event's delivery to ensure it aligns directly with the messages that have been communicated to the

market (as figure 9.1 made clear). Ongoing events that are successful in meeting attendee expectations can significantly reduce the money they spend on promotion as word-of-mouth communication will go a long way to performing this role for them. There are numerous examples of events that have built up such a strong reputation that they regularly sell out (for example, Woodford Folk Festival, Queensland; Port Fairy Folk Festival, Victoria; Burning Man, Nevada) with little promotional effort on behalf of their organisers.

Segmenting event markets

The market segmentation process is concerned with breaking up a market into smaller groups based on relevant criteria. Depending on the event concerned, these criteria might include age, gender, income, location, repeat purchases vs first time purchases, interests, lifestyle, occupation, needs, price sensitivity and behaviour. Once markets have been broken into segments, specific groups (target markets) can then be identified that offer the most potential from the viewpoint of an event's objectives and overarching business strategy. The event experience, its pricing and marketing communication efforts can then be optimised for these targeted group(s). Some of the approaches to segmentation noted previously are discussed in more detail below.

- *Geographic segmentation* — a commonly used method based on the place of residence of potential event attendees. Depending on the nature of the event concerned, attendees might be drawn from an event's immediate area, surrounding region(s), a state(s), a country or multiple countries. Contrast, for example, a local festival versus a large-scale international sporting event. Governments (local, state and national) are particularly interested in events that draw attendees from outside their boundaries as any expenditure these individuals make represents 'new money' coming into that area and therefore a boost to its economy (see the event evaluation and research chapter). For this reason, they sometimes assist events through the provision of grants or by aiding their efforts to bid for events (see the strategic event planning chapter).
- *Demographic segmentation* — relies on identifying characteristics of individuals such as their age, gender, occupation, income, education and ethnic or cultural group, as these characteristics have an impact on purchasing behaviour. Some events, for example, target-specific occupations (for example, engineers, doctors), others are largely gender-specific (for example, wedding expos, car shows), while still others focus on particular age groups (for example, under 18 discos, retirement lifestyle and travel expos). Regarding age, it is common for marketers to use generational labels when segmenting markets (for example, baby boomers (1946–1964), generation X (1965–1980), Y (1980–2001) and Z ($\geq$2001) and to attribute certain behaviours and product/service preferences to them. For example, baby boomers are deemed to have: high levels of disposable income; more free time (as many are retired, or are close to retirement, and their children no longer live with them); and to place a premium on the consumption of experiences (such as events) rather than products. Caution is required, however, as these types of categorisations are very broad.
- *Psychographic segmentation* — involves dividing a market into segments based on personality traits, interests and motives. In the Australian context, Roy Morgan Research, for example, has broken up the national market into 10 different groupings, including visible achievers, the socially aware and young optimists. These segments have often been used to develop and promote new products and services aimed at one or more of these groups (Elliott et al. 2018). It is difficult, however, to accurately measure the size of lifestyle segments, which breaks one of the cardinal rules for market segmentation — that segments must be measurable in order to judge if it is worthwhile engaging with them. Nevertheless, this type of segmentation can offer a better understanding of the types of experience that different groups seek and can provide further insight into the likely appeal of varying types of events to individuals from within these groups. It is possible to develop customised psychographic profiles for individual events, or a particular category of event, and there are some examples of where this has been done. One study of attendees to a film festival identified three psychographic attendee groups: socially indifferent, film lovers and enthusiasts, each with different needs from a programming perspective, including the value they placed on complementary activities (for example, workshops, networking; Báez and Devesa 2014).
- *Behavioural segmentation* — based on actual purchase and/or consumption behaviour. Aspects of this approach to segmentation that can be useful in event settings include the following.
  - Benefits segmentation — what benefits are expected from an event (for example, information, professional network expansion, family bonding)? Understanding the main benefits that are being sought by different target groups can greatly assist in both event programming and in shaping promotional messages.

- Occasion — the decision to attend an event, or to request one to be conducted, can be linked to specific occasions. For example, the decision to attend a retirement lifestyle expo is likely to be linked to the decision to retire in the near future. Being able to identify, and communicate with, individuals in this situation can be significant in stimulating attendance. Seeking partnerships with superannuation funds and advisors, for example, would be one way of doing this.
- Price sensitivity — what is the impact of price on a potential attendee's decision to attend or not to attend an event? For some events, attendees are more value/quality conscious than price-conscious and so a high price may not impact attendance significantly, if at all. In other instances, small changes in price can be a deterrent to potential attendees. Understanding how potential attendees will respond to a price can enhance an events capacity to maximise revenue (this issue is returned to later in this chapter).

- *Business segmentation* — business events (for example, exhibition, conferences, product launches) use business types as a major segmentation tool. In doing so they employ criteria such as geographical scale of operation (local, national, global), size (small, medium or large scale) and industry segments (for example, telecommunication, building products). Again, the outcome of the segmentation process in this context lies in its ability to construct more appealing event programs and to develop more targeted messaging.

Having identified relevant market segment variables, the next task is to combine these into market segment profiles so an understanding of typical groupings of attendees can be developed. For example, an IT conference being conducted in New South Wales may identify four possible segments.

- Segment 1 — senior software developers, aged 35–50, predominately male, located in Australia and in several overseas countries (Singapore, India, Malaysia, USA's West Coast) and seeking networking opportunities that will facilitate the development of international collaborations in software development/design.
- Segment 2 — mid-career software developers, predominately male, 25–35, located in Australia and seeking access to information on new developments in software engineering
- Segment 3 — software developers with less than five years' experience, made up of both males and females in roughly equal numbers, located on Australia's eastern seaboard, seeking to enhance their knowledge and skill base and establish professional networks that they can leverage for career-development purposes.
- Segment 4 — university and TAFE students studying information technology courses, located in New South Wales, and aiming to build on their limited knowledge and skill base and develop networks that can be leveraged for employment purposes.

Once segments have been profiled, the next question becomes one of deciding which of these groupings the proposed event might best be advised to focus on; in other words, which of these segments should comprise its target market(s) (see later discussion). In creating these segment profiles, it should be kept in mind that groupings need to be clearly identifiable, accessible through promotional channels, of a size that makes them worthwhile engaging with (Elliott et al. 2018).

The strategic marketing planning process

Establishment of marketing objectives

Marketing objectives set out the intent of an event organisation's marketing efforts and provide a basis for benchmarking performance. The criteria that should be employed when setting these objectives are that they should be specific, measurable, actionable, reasonable and time-specific. These criteria were discussed in the strategic event planning chapter, along with the types of objectives that might be relevant in event settings. Of the objectives noted there, those that relate to attendance/participation, economic outcomes, awareness/knowledge/attitudes/behaviour, community development, quality and marketplace positioning can be pursued through the marketing process.

Selection of target market(s)

Once marketing objectives have been identified and market segment profiles have been developed, the matter of what target markets are to be the focus of marketing efforts needs to be decided. In the case of events that run on a commercial basis, decisions in this area will likely be conditioned by the revenue potential of market segments; the level of competition the event organisation faces in seeking to attract each segment; and the costs of both developing an experience likely to attract them and of communicating with them. Returning to the IT example cited previously, it might be that its organisers exclude the first segment as the size and budget of their event, and the nature of its program, is not likely to appeal to this segment. The remaining three segments, however, might be deemed realistic targets as they can be relatively easily reached through existing databases, industry associations and educational institutions, and have overlapping needs that can be accommodated within a single event. The event's pricing structure, however, will likely need to reflect the differing levels of price sensitivity between segments 2 and 3, and segment 4 (students).

It the case of some events, target markets are largely a given, and the event marketer's role becomes more one of trying to stimulate attendance by this group(s). For example, a professional body's annual conference would be drawing its attendees primarily from its membership. Nonetheless, there will still likely be different sub-segments with different needs within this broad grouping, and the more these different groups can be identified and their needs established, the more likely the event experience will be to meet the expectations of all attendees.

Market positioning

Positioning concerns how attendees regard a specific event, relative to other events of a similar nature (Elliott, Rundle-Theile and Waller 2012). This being the case, a market position is something that builds over time and, because of this, is not really relevant from the perspective of one-off events. To build a market position that is unique, and so distinct from other event offerings, requires an understanding of both the benefits that are sought by attendees and the associated value they place on various event attributes (for example, venue, networking, atmosphere, program, cost). It is also important to know how an event is currently perceived as performing against these criteria compared to its competitors. This information can be obtained through the use of qualitative and quantitative research. The Tamworth Country Music Festival, for example, has been very successful in positioning itself over time as the premier event of its type in Australia, based on its line-up of performers from Australia and overseas, and the high-quality and unique nature of its other event elements (for example, Golden Guitar Awards, a cavalcade of country and western performers, and the opportunity it provides attendees to perform themselves — Walk up and Sing Tamworth).

A key aspect of the positioning process is the development of a brand that potential attendees can quickly associate with an event, and so link to the (hopefully) positive feelings they have for it. Brands take the form of a logo, name, sign, symbol or a combination of these, and should serve to identify an event and differentiate it from its competitors. Effective branding results in high recognition and significant attendee loyalty, as well as serving to facilitate the sale of merchandise. It can also allow events to engage in brand 'extension' exercises where a powerful existing brand is transferred to a new event to give it instant marketplace credibility. For example, the successful Tamworth Country Music Festival uses a golden guitar (see figure 9.4) as its brand symbol. This symbol is used to brand all music events that take during the festival period, as well as others that take place at other periods during the year. Even the town of Tamworth itself makes extensive use of this symbol.

FIGURE 9.4 An example of event logo use — Tamworth Country Music Festival

Source: Tamworth Country Music Festival 2020.

Generic marketing strategies

In addition to deciding what position an event will seek in a given marketplace, event marketers need to consider how they will support this position and more generally pursue their marketing objectives.

The broad options available to event marketers in this regard are as follows.

- *Differentiation* — requires that an event convince its target markets that its offering is special or unique in some way compared to that of its competitors. This can be achieved in various ways, depending on the event concerned, including emphasising:
  - program design and inclusions
  - atmosphere — while hard to define, some events (for example, Woodford Folk Festival, Queensland and Port Fairy Folk Festival, Victoria), create an on-site culture and atmosphere that serves to bond attendees to the event for many years
  - location/venue, for example, a unique natural setting, use of a historical building or a building of unique design, and selection of a destination with attributes that are likely to appeal to potential attendees, such as a seaside resort town
  - length of time an event has been operating
  - range/type/number of food and beverage outlets/exhibitors/merchandise outlets
  - nature of attendees, for example, largest number of buyers/exhibitors at a specific type of exhibition in the Southern Hemisphere
  - sustainability aspects of the event, for example, carbon neutrality.
- *Market penetration* — involves identifying those existing target market(s) that offer an event significant potential for growth, and then seeking to further develop these through increased promotional efforts, or program or pricing changes. For example, an Australian-based industry conference might seek to grow the presently relatively low number of New Zealand attendees by developing relationships with industry associations in that country and increasing its promotional spend there.
- *Market development* — requires an event to identify new target market(s) and to actively develop these. Some Australian festivals, for example, have identified significant potential for growth in overseas markets, and have sought to reach out to these by partnering with inbound tour operators; working with tourism bodies (for example, Tourism Australia and state-based tourism destination development agencies); forming partnerships with 'sister' events overseas; and through targeted promotional activities.
- *Market focus* — a strategy used in new-event development where an event is built around the needs of a specific market. For example, people with a special interest (for example, wooden boat festivals, security and risk management conferences) or a particular age group (retirement and lifestyle expos) and so on.
- *Reformulation* — occasionally events are faced with the situation where their programs no longer resonate with their target markets. This often happens over an extended period where no refinements/changes have taken place as there has been no, or only a limited effort, to respond to changed attendee needs. Events in this situation need to undertake market research, 'reformulate' their offering and establish a revised marketplace position if they are to survive. There are many examples of events that have failed to appreciate the degree to which a disconnect has existed between themselves and their target market until it is too late.

Selection of marketing mix elements

Having decided on a strategy(ies) to progress, event marketers must then determine how they intend to progress this strategy through the use of the variables over which they have control. These variables have been variously described over time, beginning with the original four Ps of marketing (product, price, promotion and place) proposed by Professor Eugene McCarthy in 1960.

This chapter uses an expanded version of this original framework, and one that is based on that which is often employed in the context of services (see Elliott et al. 2018; Lovelock, Patterson, Patterson and Wirtz 2014):

- *event experience* — the offering that is made by event marketers to its target market(s)
- *price* — the amount of money that attendees must pay to purchase an event experience
- *distribution* — the channels (for example, direct or through ticketing agencies) by which an event experience is made available to potential attendees for purchase
- *people* — anyone (for example, employees, volunteers, performers and other attendees) that can come into contact with an individual event attendee and effect (positively or negatively) their perception of the event experience
- *process* — systems and procedures (both back of house and front of house) used to create, deliver, communicate and exchange the event experience

- *physical evidence* — the physical environment (for example, event site/venue) and other tangible clues (for example, the appearance of staff) that can impact attendee perceptions of the event experience
- *promotion* — those practices that are used to stimulate awareness, interest and attendance.

The event experience

Event marketers can find themselves facing several situations when deciding on the characteristics of an event experience. In the case of an existing event, feedback received from its last iteration might require changes to be made to the experience offered in order to better meet the expectations of attendees (for example, improved on-site facilities, program enhancements). In extreme situations, this might require 'reformulation' of the event's offering (see previous discussion). It might also be necessary, due to competitor actions, to make changes to an event experience to further differentiate it from similar events. In the case of new events, the experience offering will need to be built from scratch, with an eye to ensuring it is differentiated from any similar events and that it aligns with the needs of identified target markets. On still other occasions event marketers might be asked to develop a new event, but they will be constrained, to a degree, by a client brief (see the conceptualising the event chapter) when doing so.

When working through the form an event experience should take, it can be useful to view it as being made up of four distinct parts (see figure 9.5).

| FIGURE 9.5 | The total event experience concept |

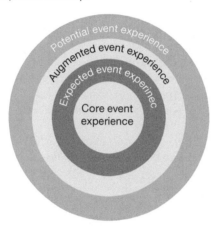

Source: Based on Elliott et al. 2012.

- *The core event experience* — the fundamental benefit(s) sought through attendance at an event. In the case of a conference, for example, this might be current information, skills/knowledge and networking.
- *The expected event experience* — those elements of an event that allow the core event experience to be provided. In the case of a conference, this would be its program of speakers/workshops/site visits and informal (for example, social events) and formal (for example, speed networking events, workshops, interest-based round tables) networking opportunities. Being able to meet experience expectations in ways that are superior to that of competing events will greatly enhance an event's ability to gain a competitive advantage.
- *The augmented event experience* — additional features that go beyond the basic fulfilment of attendee needs and expectations and seek to delight, inspire and energise. Using the example of a conference again, these might include inclusion of virtual and augmented reality elements; live streaming of interviews with thought leaders and experts; development of unique experiences (for example, networking on Ferris wheels, themed venue environments/zones); and inclusion of wellbeing elements (for example, yoga and meditation sessions).
- *The potential event experience* — inclusions that could become part of the expected or augmented event experience. These elements are those that an event marketer might be planning to introduce (based on the availability of new technologies etc.), or that are presently being assessed to determine if they will likely resonate with attendees. For example, a conference could explore the potential for the pre-event use by attendees of facilitated networking through LinkedIn to determine if this is something that would add value to its core experience offering. By acting in this way, event marketers seek to ensure, through innovation, that they remain differentiated from their competition.

Some events offer event marketers the opportunity to package additional services into their experience offering such as accommodation, on-site hospitality, photo opportunities and transport. Service 'bundles' such as these can be put together by the event concerned, or by an appointed external company. For example, Formula 1 works with F1Experiences to offer packages to all its races.

People

Event attendees can come into contact with a number of people that are responsible for delivering various aspects of the event experience (for example, event organisation staff, volunteers, entertainers, vendors, venue staff, security and contractor personal). It should be noted that this process of attendee engagement with people associated with an event can begin even before an event commences, such as during the booking process or when information is being sought. When these interactions occur, attendees have certain expectations as regards service standards and the competence of those people providing the service. To ensure these expectations are met, event marketers should have some input into the processes involved in staff/volunteer selection and training, and performer/speaker/contractor/venue selection. There should also be mechanisms in place (for example, observation and attendee surveys) to gauge the quality of these interactions as they will impact subsequent feedback and the decision to attend in the future.

In addition to interactions between attendees and people involved in aspects of an event's experience delivery, interactions also take place between attendees themselves. At sporting events, for example, unruly fans can significantly impact the enjoyment of other attendees, as can drunk and drug-affected individuals at a music festival. Tactics that can be used to manage these situations include employing adequate numbers of on-site security staff, bag checks, video surveillance and clear communications regarding attendee behaviour prior to an event.

Process

There are a range of processes that can be associated with event experience delivery, including those linked to ticket/registration purchase, entry (security checks), queueing, waste, cleaning, and food and beverage provision. Some processes depend on efficient 'back of house' systems, such as those at a venue that should ensure food is prepared and provided on schedule to attendees at an event. Others are more 'front of house', such as security checks and approaches to queue management. These delivery processes can have significant implications for the attendee experience and need to be designed and managed in line with their expectations. For example, the presence of queues that require waiting times beyond what attendees consider reasonable can be a major irritation and cause for complaints, as can security checks on entry that are not performed efficiently due to poorly trained staff.

Physical evidence

The environment in which an event experience is delivered needs to reinforce the expectations that have been built up through marketing communication efforts and the price charged. The ambience of a five-star hotel, for example, along with the professional appearance of the venue's staff, will provide tangible clues as to the quality of an event. The appearance of marketing collateral (for example, event brochures, tickets, posters) can also provide such clues. For example, a fringe festival might employ a quirky design for its brochure and posters to reflect the 'edgy' nature of its program.

Distribution

Unlike products, which require physical distribution channels to move them from where they are made to where they are consumed, event experiences have no such need. Instead, what they need to be distributed is the opportunity to purchase registration or a ticket. This can be achieved directly by providing an online portal (included as an ecommerce component within an event's website) through which bookings can be made and monies collected. Tickets/registrations can then be sent electronically or mailed to attendees. In other instances, as noted earlier, intermediaries can be used to perform this same function. Some events, it should be noted, allow tickets/registrations to be purchased on arrival, while others are free and as such the distribution task is not one with which they need to concern themselves.

Price

Price plays multiple strategic roles in the event marketing process. It serves to communicate to the market an event's position, and as such creates attendee expectations as regards quality and value. For example, a $3000 registration fee for a two-day conference will result in higher expectations in terms of speakers, food and beverage and its overall look and feel than a $500 registration fee. Price also directly affects revenue and associated profit through impacting demand. For example, it is common for price to be used in ways that exploit differing levels of price sensitivity, and perceptions of value, in order to maximise revenue. Indicative of such uses is that of VIP festival tickets that provide added value (for example, premium viewing area; dedicated entry gate; complimentary drinks/wi-fi/merchandise) but generate higher returns per ticket than the standard offering. Another example of this approach is the different ticket prices charged by theatrical events and concerts based on stage proximity and therefore the quality of the viewing/sound experience.

Discounts are another means of leveraging differing levels of price sensitivity. Multi-day events, for example, sometimes encourage attendance in periods of low demand by targeting specific groups, such as seniors, or offering reduced rates for attendance during particular time periods. The Sydney Royal Easter Show, as noted earlier, provides discounted entry for seniors on a designated day, while also offering discounted entry after 4 pm as a means of topping up demand. Another means that events use to overcome the barrier that price can present for attendance it that of making heavily discounted last-minute tickets available through discount ticket agencies such as Todaytix and Lasttix. Discounts also play a role in managing an event's cash flow (see the event financial planning chapter) through encouraging early payment (for example, early bird rates). Finally, discounts can be employed to stimulate bulk purchases by groups, or to encourage attendance by specific categories of attendees (for example, student attendance at a conference).

Knowing when, or if, to discount is a key pricing decision that event marketers need to make. Information on past attendance patterns, the current economic situation, competitor pricing, an event organiser's financial situation and the level of 'uniqueness' of the event all enter into such decisions. As regards this last point, it is sometimes the case that demand exceeds supply for an event and so discounting is unnecessary. A one-off concert by a popular artist is an example of this. Event organisers can also seek to manipulate the market by indicating supply is limited, such as in instances where a single concert is announced for a popular performer in an effort to sell tickets quickly without the need to discount. Once all tickets are sold, 'amazingly' another concert date(s) is then announced. Another way of limiting supply is to cap attendance numbers (see figure 9.6). While acting in this way can stimulate demand, and encourage early ticket sales, such a decision might also be taken to ensure the attendee experience is not compromised by overcrowding and/or because of health and safety requirements. In some instances where ticket sales are capped, the issue of equity of access can arise. One way of dealing with this concern is through the use of ticket lotteries.

FIGURE 9.6   Ticket sales capping example

Cap to be placed on Woodford Folk Festival attendance for the first time

After the success of The Planting at the end of April, Woodfordia Inc. has announced early bird tickets for this years [sic] Woodford Folk Festival will go on sale this Wednesday.

For the first time in the festival's long history, ticket sales will be capped in an effort to ensure the comfort, enjoyment and safety of festival patrons and to help preserve the Woodfordia site.

Festival Director Bill Hauritz said that after years of unprecedented growth, the decision to limit the number of tickets available, in particular to the festival on New Year's Eve, to the attendance of the 2016/17 event, was necessary.

'Last year was — dare we say it — our 'best' festival,' he said.

'The festival was the cleanest, most respectful, most energetic and beautiful that we've seen. Because of our growing popularity, we've had to make big changes.'

'A lot of work is going into creating a deeper festival experience for our beloved patrons.'

Tickets will be more expensive to buy than in previous years in the hope the not-for-profit can secure a better financial position for the years to come.

Source: Woodford Folk Festival 2017.

While maximising revenue might be the focus for many events, it is not the case for all. Some events might seek to simply cover all or part of their costs, and use grants, donations or direct government funding to make up any shortfall. For example, Vivid Sydney, a major (largely free) public event based on lighting, music and ideas, is partially funded by local (City of Sydney) and state government (Destination New South Wales) as it delivers significant benefits to Sydney and New South Wales in the form of visitation and destination branding. In other instances, events are seen as a social good, such is the case with many community festivals that are conducted by local government. Additionally, some event's that actively seek to generate a surplus, acknowledge that their pricing structure can lead to the exclusion of certain groups in society, and for this reason they quarantine a number of tickets at heavily discounted rates for these types of attendees (see example in figure 9.7) and in the process forego revenue.

FIGURE 9.7   Burning Man Low-income Ticket Program

The Low-income Ticket Program offers over 4500 tickets to people with qualifying applications at $210 each.

Awarded applicants will need to pay for their tickets online between July 20, 2020 and July 26, 2020. They are also eligible to purchase a $140 vehicle pass at the same time if needed. The application will close as soon as we've received as many applications as we can review or on April 15, 2020, whichever comes first. We will not be able to give advance notice of the application closing early so please submit your application as soon as you can.

For more information about the Low-income Ticket Program, please read through the Low-income Ticket page.

Source: Burning Man 2020.

Other factors that can weigh heavy on pricing decisions include the following.

- *Costs* — discussed in detail in the event financial planning chapter, costs (fixed, variable and semi-variable) directly impact the price point at which tickets/registrations are sold if predetermined revenue/profit targets are to be met. Additionally, as events sometimes have multi-year lead times, fluctuations in costs over time need to be accounted for. In instances where performers/speakers or other inputs are being sourced overseas, a strategy (for example, hedging) might need to be put in place to manage the potential for exchange rates fluctuations. Intermediary costs, as discussed previously, need also to be factored into the pricing decision.
- *Potential for subsidisation* — grants, donations or revenue from other sources, such as sponsorship or vendor charges, can be used to either enhance the bottom line of events, or, in some instances, make them more accessible to a wider group of potential attendees, such as when organisers view their offering as more of a social good than a vehicle for profit.
- *Non-ticket/registration costs* — an event's price needs to be seen in context. While registration/ticket prices might not by themselves act as a barrier to attendance, when other associated attendee costs (for example, travel, accommodation and food) are taken into account, the total effect might be to deter attendance. One strategy for dealing with this issue is selecting locations that provide a diversity of accommodation and food options, and to which travel costs are not excessive. Additionally, there is an opportunity cost associated with time away from the workplace, which makes duration a factor in designing particularly business events. Attendees might also perceive 'sensory' costs in the form of crowding (as noted in figure 9.6) or excessive heat/cold. As regards this last point, some events are now discussing, or have acted to (for example, Mission Sunflower Festival, Kansas), move their dates to take account of climate change in order to make attendance a more comfortable experience (Senter 2019).
- *Competition* — if direct competitors exist, event marketers will need to determine if they will seek price parity, or price above or below their offering. To do this they will need to first map competitor offerings (see figure 9.8).

FIGURE 9.8   Example of event price mapping

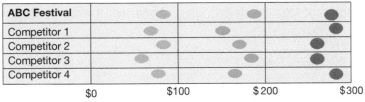

- *Inclusions and exclusions* — ticket/registration prices can incorporate (bundle) a range of potential elements, as noted earlier. For example, a conference's registration fee can include all meals, site visits and the conference reception. Alternatively, some elements might be excluded and treated as optional which would have the effect of reducing its registration fee. The decision to take either action comes down to the degree to which an event's target markets (or some of its target markets) are value- or price-conscious. A medical conference, for example, would probably incorporate all of the previously cited items in its fee, while a conference for charity workers might make some of these elements optional.

Promotion

Promotion is concerned with the creation and maintenance of communication with an event's target market(s). There are four primary communication channels used for this purpose:

1. traditional marketing channels (for example, advertising, public relations, direct marketing, sales promotion, personal selling)
2. the internet (for example, an event organisation's website, online advertising, social media channels)
3. service delivery channels (for example, venue/site communication opportunities, staff/volunteer interactions with attendees)
4. external channels (for example, word of mouth, blogs, social media; Lovelock, Patterson and Wirtz 2014).

In using these channels, an event marketer should always seek to coordinate their promotional efforts in ways that will maximise their communication effect and ensure consistency in the message(s) that are sent. This process is known as integrated marketing communications (IMC). To successfully engage in IMC, an event marketer must seek clarity around a number of questions.

- Who do I need to communicate with?
- What is my promotional budget?
- What should my marketing communication objective(s) be?
- What key message(s) do I wish to communicate?
- What choices do I have regarding promotional channels and tools?
- How do I select the most appropriate channels and tools in order to achieve my promotional objectives?
- How do I organise and schedule the 'mix' of selected promotional tools in each channel to achieve my promotional objectives?
- How will I monitor and evaluate my promotional efforts?

The following discussion provides a measure of insight into how these questions might be addressed.

Target groups

Prior to reaching this stage in the strategic marketing planning process, an event marketer should have clearly identified their target markets (see earlier discussion), and it is to these markets that promotional activities will be primarily directed. In addition to these markets, some events might also seek to communicate with other groups, such as an event's local community, for reasons that will be discussed later.

Promotional budget

Frequently, event promotional budgets are stated as a percentage of an event's total budget or as a percentage of last year's ticket sales/registrations. These approaches can be problematic in that they are not informed by any assessment of what should be done to achieve an event's desired sales targets/attendance levels. Events do not have unlimited promotional budgets, but by approaching this task from this perspective it is possible to group promotional activities into the categories of must do, should do and would like to do, based on their relative estimated effectiveness versus their cost. Guidance as regards this last point can come from previous years' events, or by consultation with other events or consultants in the area. In some instances, an event's promotional budget might be able to extend to a comprehensive set of promotional activities; however, it will most often be the case that some proposed actions will need to be culled. If available funds or resources (that is, staff time) cannot at a minimum allow those actions deemed essential to be undertaken, the event will be placing itself at risk of not meeting its financial and/or attendance targets. There are ways, however, of stretching an event's promotional budget, and these will be returned to later.

Promotional objectives

Depending on an event's overall marketing objectives, the level of competition it faces, the familiarity its target audience(s) already have with it and its current demand situation, a range of possible (and in some instances overlapping) promotional objectives might be pursued:

- creating awareness, interest and/or excitement (particularly important in the case of new events, events targeting new markets and events seeking to penetrate existing markets further)
- creating a perception of difference, and superiority, over competing events or experiences
- reinforcing (or in some instances changing) an event's market position
- encouraging repeat attendance
- reducing perceptions of risk by making the event experience as 'concrete' as possible (for example, through inclusion of images in promotional efforts/on an event's website, and the use of testimonials and endorsements)
- stimulating advance ticket/registration sales

- educating attendees about how best to maximise the value they receive from the event experience (for example, how should they prepare? What should they bring? Where should they park? When should they come?)
- shifting demand from periods when an event is operating at full capacity to periods of lower demand
- creating goodwill towards an event organisation within a community. In instances where an event inconveniences members of a local community (for example, through traffic congestion, noise), ensuring that there is an appreciation of the benefits of hosting the event (for example, economic impact, enhancement of visitation during non-event periods, donations to local service/charity groups, opportunity event provides for entertainment which would not be available otherwise) can reduce community angst regarding these issues.

Consideration should also be given to how performance against promotional objectives will be measured. In this regard, any number of potential measures can be employed depending on the various promotional tools that are being used, including number of enquiries received; website or social media site visits; location where ticket/registration purchasers are from; website visit bounce rates; number of advance/early bird ticket sales; level of repeat patronage; number of registrations/tickets sold to new market segments; increases in ticket sales to existing market segments; changes in attendee perceptions of an event's marketplace position; attendance fluctuations over the duration of an event; and number of local community complaints.

Key messages

Event marketers need to decide what key messages are likely to achieve their promotional objectives. It is these messages that need to be communicated and reinforced through the marketing communication channels that are in use. For example, the following messages were used, and reinforced repeatedly, by a software skills conference with several competitors. This event saw its primary promotional objective as differentiating itself from competitor offerings:

- '. . . the liveliest exchange of the latest ideas and practical skills in software architecture, design and development'
- '. . . where experts gather to learn'
- '. . . set up specifically to circulate know-how, but without the sales bias you get at trade shows, and without the theoretical flavour of some conferences'
- '. . . sessions are interactive — we believe you learn best by doing'
- '. . . an interactive style that clearly distinguishes it from marketing-led, vendor-driven conferences' (Object Technology Conference 2015).

It should be kept in mind that different promotional messages might be needed for different target markets (for example, families vs young singles).

Promotional mix

Event marketers, as noted previously, have available to them four broad types of channels for communication purposes. Decisions as regards how these channels will be employed, the 'mix' of tools that will be used in each, and how these activities should be coordinated in order to maximise desired communication outcomes, are all key to an effective IMC plan.

1. Traditional marketing channels.

Traditional marketing channels include broadcast (TV and radio), print (magazines and newspapers — hard copy and electronic), movie theatres and outdoor media (exteriors of buses and taxis, bus shelter signs, billboards, posters, electronic message boards). Usage of these various channels will depend on how targeted communications need to be. For example, a large festival or sporting event might find television a cost-effective medium because of its substantial, and diverse, target markets. However, a conference for medical specialists would find such a medium wasteful and beyond their budget. Instead, they would likely advertise in specific journals and websites, seek partnerships with relevant medical associations and take action to reinforce their messages through direct communications such as email. It should be noted, however, that small-scale events can sometimes make use of mass media channels by establishing relationships with newspaper and television stations, particularly in regional areas, in return for allowing broadcasting from the site, the provision of tickets that can be used in their promotional activities and so on.

The metric usually applied to advertising effectiveness in these channels is reach and frequency — the number of people in a target market(s) that a promotional message has reached and how many times they have received it. As a general rule, four exposures (frequency) to a message is necessary for it to be effective (Farris et al. 2006). The impact of advertisements in traditional media can be assessed through such means as changes in ticket sales/registrations, click-through rates (if an advertisement is placed in the electronic form of a newspaper, journal or magazine) and attendee surveys (to establish how they became aware of an event).

Public relations. 'Public relations' is a generic term for those promotional efforts used to build positive relations between an organisation and its stakeholders (for example, attendees, local communities, government, staff/volunteers, media). It embraces a wide range of tools and practices, including:

- news releases (see figure 9.9)
- press conferences and interviews with, for example, performers or star players, in the lead up to an event
- special promotional events (for example, holding free lunchtime performances in a central community space to create awareness that an event that will be taking place in the near future)
- electronic and hard copy newsletters distributed periodically through the year to keep past attendees, media and other stakeholders aware of event developments (for example, recently signed performers/speakers)
- establishing relationships with charities/local service organisations, through such means as donations and allowing them to raise funds on-site during an event with the goal of building community goodwill
- obtaining testimonials from individuals that have high credibility/recognition within an event's target markets and using these for promotional purposes
- writing newsworthy articles that link to an event in some way (for example, an article on a new technology in use in civil engineering could be linked to a conference in this area by noting its inventor will be presenting at the event)
- relationship-building efforts with journalists/bloggers through the provision of free tickets/registrations and the creation of media kits. The latter commonly contain background information on the event; the event program; list of sponsors; press releases; free tickets; photographs that can be reproduced in print or online media; and the contact details of the event staff member from whom further details can be obtained.

Public relations can be a very effective event promotional tool, as it is often relatively easy to leverage elements of an event (for example, performers, speakers) to gain media exposure because they have the potential to be of interest to a wide audience. However, marketers must be aware that the media will only use material presented to them, or take advantage of interview offers, if they believe their audience will see it as being of value. This being the case, care should be used in selecting an 'angle' when writing a press release/article or putting forward a speaker for an interview. In the press release example provided in figure 9.9, its angle is the special nature of the event's 2020 program line-up.

FIGURE 9.9   Press release example

International folk legends comprise the line-up for Port Fairy Folk Festival

Hailing from the United States, The Blind Boys of Alabama, John McCutcheon and Patty Griffin will perform alongside Britain's YolanDa Brown, Ireland's Eleanor McEvoy, and Australia's own C.W. Stoneking and The Maes.

'What a line-up we have in store for our 44th festival,' Program Director Caroline Moore says.

'I am delighted to announce these renowned artists for our next festival in March, which will also be filled with special events, family activities, and non-stop musical entertainment. This is a festival for every music lover — from the young to the young at heart.'

On the back of their new album, Work to Do, The Blind Boys of Alabama will bring their sounds of the American south to the Port Fairy stage almost seven decades since the iconic band first began singing together.

Singer, songwriter and multi-instrumentalist, much-loved John McCutcheon will present a special Pete Seeger Session, in addition to his signature concerts which exemplify the folk tradition, and Patty Griffin arrives fresh from her European tour and album release.

British saxophonist YolanDa Brown will bring her sublime jazz-folk rhythms and entertaining children's musical performances to the festival and acclaimed Irish artist Eleanor McEvoy makes a welcomed return to Port Fairy.

The renowned C.W. Stoneking will perform his 1920s pre-war blues sound on his classic guitars and former emerging Port Fairy Artists of the Year 2014 The Maes, featuring sisters Maggie and Elsie Rigby and Monique Clare return from taking Europe and Canada by storm and will play new music from their 2019 self-titled album.

The Port Fairy Folk Festival is on 6–9 March 2020.

Source: Scenestr 2019.

Sales promotion. Sales promotion consists of those activities that use incentives or discounts to increase sales or attendance. Examples of sales promotion include family days at city shows or exhibitions that offer a family discount or free entry for children under a set age; and provision of 'free' merchandise (T-shirts and posters) when purchasing several tickets or more. The Sydney Festival uses this promotional technique in its 'Tix for Next to Nix' promotion. This program involves releasing a limited number of tickets (the number depending upon how popular a show is — the more popular the show, the fewer the number of tickets offered) through an app (TodayTix app) on the day of the performance for a heavily discounted price in order to clear unsold tickets (Sydney Festival 2020).

Personal selling. Personal selling is not a common method of promotion used by events; however, it is employed in some event settings, often when ticket, registration or participation costs are high. The benefits of this approach are that it can be used to respond and adapt immediately to any barriers to purchase that might be presented, the need for additional information, and act to build trust and credibility. Exhibition marketers, for example, often personally contact potential exhibitors with the capacity to purchase large exhibition spaces to try and convince them to spend the often quite significant sums involved. Some organisers of high-cost workshops and seminars also use this approach.

2. The internet

Event organisation's website. A website is an important aspect of an event's promotional mix. Often other promotional efforts will direct potential attendees to an event's website, so its various functions need to be clearly defined. From a marketing perspective, these functions include (depending on the event):

- *selling the event experience* — websites essentially serve to represent the event from a potential attendee perspective. This being the case, they need to reduce perceptions of risk, engage, excite and convince. To do this event websites commonly include, for example, videos, picture galleries, testimonials, detailed program descriptions, and speaker and performer bios (often with links to their respective websites). Additionally, multiple studies have shown that good website design matters, with visitors quickly judging organisations based on visuals alone (EZMarketing 2018).
- *information provision* — key information required by potential event attendees should all be present to maximise the chances that they will book. This includes location, dates, opening and closing times, accessibility, parking, ticket/registration prices, program details, site/venue maps, information to assist attendees in engaging with the event (for example, surrounding accommodation, suggestions to enhance personal comfort/safety while at the event, links to sites providing additional relevant information such as tourist information sites for the area) and links to privacy and legal information (including cancellation and refund policies).
- *media engagement* — press releases, high-resolution photos, event newsletters, videos, images for publication/uploading and the details for the event's media contact person
- *interactive features* — interactivity helps to deepen the event experience and includes links to an event's app and its social media sites; opportunities to hear from, and engage with, speakers and performers; and web polls linked to the event's content
- *communication facilitation* — allows potential attendees to request additional information; ask questions through a toll-free number, contact-us form or live chat; or request to be placed on an event's mailing list. As regards this last point, websites are generally the main means by which events seek permission to send promotional material through to potential attendees.
- *purchase facility* — many events include an ecommerce component to their websites that allows tickets/registrations to be purchased. Additionally, some events, as noted earlier, operate online stores through which merchandise can be bought. This component of an event's website should be easy to locate, simple to use and involve as few steps as possible to avoid losing potential attendees because of the clumsy nature of the purchase process (a common problem with many websites).
- *post-event information* — photos, press coverage, videos of presenters/performers and event proceedings, and so on that will serve to reinforce, and allow attendees to reflect (hopefully positively) on, the experience the event offered.

In addition to the above, websites should be designed so they are mobile-optimised and will load quickly, as mobile devices account for a significant proportion of website visits. Search engine optimisation (SEO) is another matter that needs to be addressed. This requires that event marketers ensure those keywords used by potential attendees when searching for events such as theirs have been incorporated into its website. It can be worthwhile paying a professional to optimise an event website to ensure it appears early in searches (ideally on the first page).

To establish how visitors to an event's website are engaging with its content, tools such as Google Analytics can be linked to it at no cost. These tools provide a number of insights into website visitor use including pages visited; length of visit; date/time of visit; geographic and demographic characteristics of visitors; search engine used; frequency of visits — new vs returning visitors; and sources of visitor traffic.

Online advertising and social networks. Event marketers have two main options when it comes to online advertising: banner advertising or search engine advertising. The former involves the use of an image (banner) that is stretched across the top, bottom or side of a website and can be of a static or animated nature (see example in figure 9.10) This image, when clicked on, takes the internet user to the advertiser's website where additional information can be found and purchases can be made. These types of advertisements are commonly used by events to build awareness, and the key to their success lies in targeting. Options available to event marketers in this regard include keyword targeting; demographic and geographic targeting; website targeting; interest targeting; and targeting individuals that have previously visited an event's website (remarketing). Click-through rates can be very low with these types of advertisements and the emergence of ad blocker technology can limit their effectiveness. It is also the case that their ubiquity has resulted in many people ignoring them. Banner ads can be placed directly with specific websites, or as is commonly the case, placed with online advertising networks such as Google Ads, that will perform the targeting function.

FIGURE 9.10   Banner advertisement example

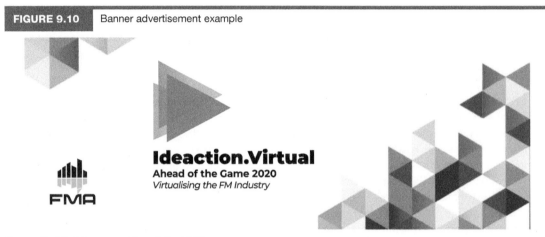

Source: Facility Management Association 2020.

Search engine advertising allows event marketers to create ads and, depending on the keywords individuals use to search the internet, have their ads appear on search listings. As with banners, various targeting criteria can be employed to reduce the potential for wastage. Prices charged for this service are generally on a results basis (pay per click or per phone call), and advertisers can enhance their potential to appear on the first page of searchers by setting a higher amount they are willing to pay per click than their competition.

In addition to paid targeted advertising opportunities available through search engines, social networks (for example, Facebook, Twitter, LinkedIn), video-sharing platforms (for example, YouTube) and photo-sharing sites (for example, Tumblr and Instagram) also offer opportunities to advertise, or to pay for posts/stories to be 'boosted' to increase their visibility to targeted audiences. These sites also facilitate the sharing of information between those involved in them, and allow the creation of content (images, stories, videos) which in turn can also be shared. Many events now have a presence on these sites and seek to build communities around themselves capable of creating greater awareness and interest in the experience they offer.

The effectiveness of online advertising can be assessed through using a variety of metrics (see table 9.1), with these figures being available from the websites that have been used to place ads, posts and so on.

TABLE 9.1   Metrics used for assessing the effectiveness of internet advertising

Metric	Description
Cost per thousand views	The cost of an online advertisement in terms of how many thousands of people see it.
	The cost is known and the number of people visiting a web page on which the advertisement appears is easy to measure. It is impossible, however, to know how many of those visitors saw or paid attention to the advertisement.

Click-through rate	The percentage of people who visited a web page on which the advertisement appears that actually clicked on the advertisement.
	This can be accurately measured and can give an indication of the effectiveness of an advertisement relative to other advertisements. It is still impossible to tell how many people who visited the web page actually saw the advertisement.
Cost per click	This is determined by dividing the total cost by the total number of people who click through.
Conversion rate	This is determined by how many people who clicked through actually completed a marketing transaction. This is the most effective marketing metric in determining the overall outcomes of the advertisement, but does not necessarily allow us to determine why the marketing effort was successful for each customer.
Customer acquisition cost	This is the cost associated with acquiring a new customer. It can be calculated by dividing the total acquisition expenses by the total of new customers.
Unique visitors	This is the number of individuals who have visited the website at least once over a given period of time. Calculations can be based on the IP address and viewed over a 30-day period, or during the campaign.

Source: Elliott et al. 2018, p. 460.

3. Service delivery channels

Events, because of their nature, have the opportunity to engage in promotional activities at venues/sites. For example, signage, posters and staff/volunteer interactions with attendees can be used to draw attention to event-related merchandise that is for sale, optional activities that can be purchased (for example, attendance at workshops, site visits, tours) and encourage attendance at future iterations of an event. Additionally, the look and 'feel' of venues/sites themselves send important messages to attendees as to event quality and the marketplace position of an event.

4. External channels

A range of messages regarding an event come from outside, and as such are not directly controlled by an event marketer. These messages result from word of mouth, tweets, blogs and media coverage. In the case of word of mouth, its extent and content are strongly linked to how satisfied people were with an experience. Events that 'get it right', can significantly reduce their future promotional expenditure, as noted previously, or, as is the case with one-off promotional events such as new product launches, have a major impact on driving awareness, interest and sales among their attendee networks. Getting it wrong, on the other hand, can have a major impact on future demand, with chat groups, online communities and social media sites quickly acting to spread the 'bad news'.

Event marketers can stimulate positive word of mouth through creating experiences people wish to share with others and making the process of sharing as easy as possible by providing photos and videos that can be linked to, or included in, social media messages. Additionally, events can ensure a single hashtag is used across all social media channels; request performers/speakers to use their networks to promote their attendance at an event; and share behind-the-scenes visual content and stories as a way of building engagement and generating a buzz. Bloggers can also be important in stimulating word of mouth as noted earlier, and many events now use Twitter to draw attention to event program developments (for example, the signing of a performer, the announcement of an event's venue) to stimulate interest and discussion by potential attendees as an event approaches, and to remind people of how 'amazing' it was once it is over. Public relations activities also play a major role in stimulating interest in, and discussion about, an event.

Selecting and implementing the promotional mix. Given the array of promotional tools available to event marketers, an effort must be made to identify the 'mix' of these that will be most cost-effective in achieving their event's promotional objectives. This decision is often made in consultation with professionals in the marketing field and/or by referencing past experience. Whatever decision is made, organisers should keep in mind that the mix is likely to change over time as the effectiveness of different mix elements is evaluated, and the promotional objectives that are being pursued are refined or changed. Once determined, promotional mix elements need to be placed within a promotional calendar so that their rollout can be coordinated. A number of templates for such calendars can be found online and can be easily adapted for the needs of a specific event (for example, www.smartsheet.com/free-event-planning-templates). In addition to the use of calendars, there are various social media management platforms available (for example, Hootsuite) that allow this component of an event's promotional mix to be planned and scheduled. In figure 9.11, the Melbourne Comedy Festival has been provided as an example of the characteristics of one event's promotional mix, and how its success in using this mix was measured.

FIGURE 9.11 Melbourne International Comedy Festival's promotional mix

Marketing & media highlights

The Festival aims to engage our existing loyal community and actively develop new audiences for comedy. In 2016 the Festival again produced an impactful marketing campaign with a high visibility spread across a broad marketing mix:
- Printed collateral
- Print, online, radio and television advertising
- Outdoor campaigns
- Meaningful audience engagement, and strong growth, through social channels
- Growth in website functionality and unique users
- Below the line campaigns and cross promotional partnerships
- Targeted tourism advertising

Outdoor

The Festival literally painted the town in yellow for its 30th Birthday, with the Festival brand covering flags, venues, streets and transport. The Festival worked with Adshel and Inlink to deliver outdoor advertising campaigns in key target markets Melbourne, Sydney and Brisbane. The Festival's Melbourne OOH campaign occupied flags and venues across the City of Melbourne, enjoyed a strong presence on Melbourne Airport banners and internal screens, popped up on the Tullamarine and CityLink Freeway and covered the front of Flinders Street Station as well as Melbourne's trains, trams and taxis.

Marketing & media partnerships

Print & online media

Melbourne International Comedy Festival continued to work with the Herald Sun as principal print media partner in 2016. The partnership included:
- Distribution of 400 000 Program Guides state-wide across Victoria, as an insert in the Saturday 27 February 2016 edition of the Herald Sun
- Extensive print and online advertising campaign in the Herald Sun
- Highlight Daily Diaries published during the Festival in the Herald Sun
- Significant digital campaign including dedicating minisite on heraldsun.com.au, an online ad campaign and ads on the Herald Sun mobile optimised site
- Promotional offers including in-paper and member reward giveaways

Television

The Festival produced a 30-second commercial with partner Clemenger BBDO that screened on Network Ten, ONE HD and Eleven, as well as Foxtel's The Comedy Channel, in the lead-up to and during the Festival. The Festival's TVC is also appropriated for the national Melbourne Comedy Festival Roadshow and available for use by all Roadshow presenters / communities.

Festival content was also broadcast to more than 5 million viewers nationally with programming across the year on Network Ten and TenPlay, SBS2 and SBS On Demand, ABC and iView, Foxtel and Foxtel Go and Channel 31 and C31 Live.

Radio outside broadcasts

- ABC 774 — 'Comedy Bites' recorded live from The Comedy Theatre on the eve of the Festival, Tuesday 22 March 2016 (state-wide and online broadcast, recording also available via ABC Soundcloud)
- triple j — 'Good Az Friday' broadcast live from the Main Hall at Melbourne Town Hall on Good Friday, Friday 25 March 2016. Hosted by Matt Okine and Alex Dyson from the triple j breakfast show (national broadcast).
- Nova 100 — 'Breakfast with Chrissie, Sam & Browny' and 'Nova's Hits & Giggles'. Nova's much loved breakfast OB returned to Melbourne Town Hall in 2016 to kick off the Festival on opening morning, Wednesday 23 March. Showcasing up and coming Festival comedians, Nova also held the listener only free event Hits & Giggles on Saturday 9 April at Melbourne Town Hall, sound bites of the event broadcast the following day on Nova 100 and available via online channels.

Marketing & media highlights: online activity

The Festival continues to develop social and online activity to engage and attract domestic and international audiences.

Website activity

For the period from 1 July 2015–30 June 2016 — including the lead-up, pre-sale, launch and 2016 Festival:

- 1 537 065 sessions
- 887 789 unique users (72% of these users also used the website during the Festival period)
- 7.6 million page impressions
- fully optimised website (for desktop, tablet and mobile)
- 60% mobile/tablet users (during the Festival this increases to 65%)
- dedicated 'Visitors Guide' on the Festival website with tourism specific information
- 92% visitors from Australia (74% Victoria, 26% interstate) and 8% from overseas

Social media

The Festival's social media channels continue to see amazing growth, forming an integral part of the marketing mix, including [the] opportunity to engage with Festival fans outside of Melbourne. At the close of the 2016 Festival:

- Facebook:
  - 30 516 likes — up 38% on 2015
  - 17% from interstate
  - 5% from regional Victoria
  - 12% from overseas
- Twitter:
  - 25 854 followers — up 9% on 2015
  - 17% from overseas
  - 31% from interstate
- YouTube:
  - 12 618 subscribers — up 61% on 2015
  - More than 11 million video views (around 49% from international audiences)
- Instagram:
  - 5290 followers — up 106% on 2015

E-news

The Festival's e-news continues to be a key channel to communicate with a growing and loyal group of Festival stakeholders. At the close of the 2016 Festival:

- 101 421 subscribers: 91% from Victoria, 8% from interstate and 1% from overseas
- sent weekly in the lead-up, and twice a week throughout the Festival

Source: Melbourne International Comedy Festival 2016, pp. 15–17.

Implementing, controlling, monitoring and evaluation

Once decisions have been made as regards an event's marketing objectives, target market(s), strategy and promotional mix, the next step is to put the plan into effect, and to control and monitor its rollout. Additionally, the plan must be evaluated to establish its success against the marketing objectives that had been set. The chapter on strategic event planning essentially dealt with these tasks; however, it is worthwhile making a few additional observations here concerning these processes from a purely marketing perspective.

Performance against marketing objectives (for example, ticket/registration sales targets) and associated benchmarks (for example, X percentage of tickets sold by a given date), should be monitored continuously through regular meetings with appropriate staff/contracted marketing firms and periodic reports. Assessment measures should also be in place to gauge the effectiveness of an event's promotional mix elements, many of which have been previously noted, and are also in evidence in the Melbourne International Comedy Festival example in figure 9.11.

It is important to appreciate that the marketing planning process is not a linear one. An event's micro or macro environment might change, promotional messages might need to be altered because of marketplace developments (for example, the emergence of a new competitor), or significant resistance might be experienced to an event's pricing strategy resulting in the need for adjustments. It is therefore important that an event marketer accepts the need to be constantly seeking feedback on the implementation of their marketing plan, and the need for their efforts to be adaptable to changed circumstances. It is also important that summative assessments are made once an event is over to ensure future marketing efforts are refined in the light of feedback that is received.

9.4 What is sponsorship and what benefits do sponsors seek?

LEARNING OBJECTIVE 9.4 Define the concept of sponsorship and discuss the benefits sponsoring organisations seek through the use of this promotional tool.

Sponsorship can be defined as the act of providing money, products/services or other agreed contributions (for example, marketing assistance, provision of expertise) in return for specific benefits. These benefits can be many and varied, and it is important that event organisers identify what they are so that they can align their sponsorship offerings to them. While not comprehensive, the following list provides insights into the types of benefits private sector firms and public institutions might seek from their support of an event:

- access to target market(s) for promotional messages
- association with a specific lifestyle (for example, the surf culture)
- cost-effective means of cutting through promotional clutter in the marketplace — events offer a means of more directly communicating with target markets than most other promotional tools
- goodwill towards the organisation/showing commitment to a community
- brand awareness and acceptance
- opportunity to position/reposition an existing service/product
- client/distributor/supplier/stakeholder entertainment and/or hospitality
- enhanced awareness among attendees of an issue (for example, the need to live more sustainably)
- behaviour change (for example, encouraging attendees to be more active as regards their recycling efforts)
- product/service sales and merchandising opportunities — sponsorship can be based on the ability to sell product or merchandise at an event (for example, a beer company might agree to sponsor an event if it is appointed the sole provider of beer)
- capacity to demonstrate product attributes (for example, Visa, a sponsor of the 2018 Winter Olympics, acted to demonstrate its new tap and pay wearable technology at over 1000 contactless terminals at this event)
- employee rewards and recognition — tickets and other benefits gained through sponsorship can be used to reward and motivate staff (De Pelsmacker, Geuens and Van den Bergh 2004; Geldard and Sinclair 2002).

There has been an increasing push by sponsors to seek deeper engagement with attendees, at the same time as some events have sought to respond to their audiences' concerns about the over-commercialisation of the event experience. The result has been, as figure 9.12 shows, an effort by some sponsors to move towards adding value to the event experience rather than simply being present in the form of signs and logos.

FIGURE 9.12 | Examples of sponsors adding value to the event experience

Adding value: the future of sponsor integration

Sponsors invest significant time and money into your events. They're looking for authentic and memorable interactions with attendees; standard exhibit booths and glossy full-page program ads don't cut it anymore. The future of sponsorships is about looking for ways to make a greater impression by adding value to the overall attendee experience.

SXSW, known for its imbedded creativity and innovation, provided a backdrop for some interesting sponsorship activations and endeavors in 2017. Consider official sponsor Evernote, the cross-platform app for storing notes and files. Evernote took professional notes for 30 sessions in the SXSW 'Workplace Track' and published them online, as well as providing templates and tips for superior note-taking to attendees.

Mobile World Congress knows that networking is central to their event experience, and attendees enjoy comfortable spaces to hang out and make connections. They introduced Networking Gardens throughout the campus, where companies like Adobe, Citi, Twitter, and Visa created branded environments for attendees to network and interact, grab a drink, or just take a break and get some fresh air. Tables could be reserved at specific times for business and client meetings, while open seating provided a comfortable spot to chat and network.

Large consumer events, like music festivals, are ideal settings for true value-add sponsorships — keeping hydrated, charged and in touch with friends can prove tricky in the hectic festival conditions, providing a great in for brands to address and enhance the fan experience. Consider Coachella sponsor Samsung, who had roaming brand ambassadors with fully charged phone batteries ready to swap out with galaxy owners in the crowd. Rather than lugging a portable charger or fighting through crowds and cords at a mobile charging station, fans were able to quickly pop a fresh battery into their phone and go about their fun fully-charged & stress-free.

Source: Sangha 2017.

9.5 Influences on the decision of event organisers to become involved in sponsorship

LEARNING OBJECTIVE 9.5 Discuss influences on the decision by event organisers to seek or not to seek sponsorship.

Despite the financial and other benefits sponsorship can result in for event organisers, it might not be advisable for some events to devote resources to developing this potential source of revenue/cost reduction. In this regard, Geldard and Sinclair (2002) have identified a range of questions that an event organiser should first ask themselves before seeking sponsorship.

- *Does the event have sufficient rights or benefits that can be offered to sponsors?* Organisations must be able to recognise the potential inherent in an event to achieve the objectives they are pursuing through sponsorship. If an event does not offer these opportunities, its organisers are wasting their time in seeking income or other benefits from this source. A better alternative in some instances may be to seek a donation, which, by its nature, does not require marketing benefits to be given in return.
- *Are an event's stakeholders likely to approve of commercial sponsorship, or sponsorship from specific types of organisations?* There can be situations where some members of an event's organising body, or its audience, view commercial sponsorship, or a sponsorship from a specific organisation, negatively. An example of such a situation is given in figure 9.13. In this instance a decision was made to return all monies to the sponsor.
- *Is the event's target market(s) congruent with the target market(s) of the organisation from whom sponsorship is being sought?* For a sponsorship to be able to deliver benefits for an organisation, there must be a high level of congruence between its target market(s) and those of the event. For example, Rip Curl, a designer, manufacturer and retailer of surfing sportswear and associated products, is the naming rights sponsor of the World Surfing League's Bells Beach surfing competition as this event aligns directly with the markets it seeks to serve, and its brand image.
- *Does the event have the resources and skills to engage in the sponsorship process?* A considerable amount of time and effort is required to research, develop and market sponsorships to potential sponsors. Furthermore, sponsorship must be managed after an agreement has been finalised to ensure all promises are fulfilled.

FIGURE 9.13 Example of a sponsorship that created an ethical dilemma for an event

Woodford Folk Festival and the controversial Santos sponsorship: how does a major festival solve an ethical dilemma in sponsorship?

There was a major backlash against Woodford Folk Festival organisers this year after they accepted sponsorship money from mining company Santos. Santos gave the Dreaming $225 000 to be used over three years to support the Indigenous 'Dreaming Festival' at a time when no-one else would give money.

However, Queensland Folk Federation members and festival-goers were hugely upset. There were hundreds of complaints on Woodford's Facebook page and many festival-goers threatened to boycott the event this year.

After a couple of weeks deliberating the issue, organisers decided to hold a forum at Woodford itself, guided by a panel of experts and stakeholders, allowing the public to participate. ABC presenter Mary-Lou Stephens spoke to Woodford Folk Festival director Bill Hauritz about the outcomes of that forum.

He says the taskforce will now seek community opinion on a set of rules or guidelines the festival should adhere to when dealing with sponsorship agreements.

Meanwhile the Santos sponsorship money has been frozen until mid-2012 when the taskforce makes a decision on what to do with it.

Source: Skjonnemand and Stephens 2012.

The value of a sponsorship policy

Grey and Skildum-Reid (2014) strongly recommend that all events seeking sponsorship develop a sponsorship policy to guide their efforts in this area. They suggest that this document should include:

- an event's history of sponsorship and its approach to it, including some definition of what constitutes sponsorship versus grants and donations
- an event's objectives, processes and procedures for seeking sponsorship
- rules for entering into sponsorship and the kinds of companies that 'fit' the event
- a standardised approach to be followed when seeking and managing sponsorships, including the format to be followed in sponsorship proposals and the requirement for a management plan to be developed for each sponsorship
- levels of accountability and responsibility
- a requirement for the policy to be reviewed periodically.

By creating a sponsorship policy, events can avoid the type of situation that occurred in the case of the previously cited Woodford Festival example (see figure 9.13). It should also be noted that many sponsoring organisations have developed their own policies in this area (see example in figure 9.14) that events should consult to establish if these policies impact, or in some cases prevent, their ability to seek sponsorship from them. Some of these policies, for example, exclude certain types of events.

FIGURE 9.14	An extract from an organisation's event sponsorship policy specifying those types of events it will or will not sponsor

Healthway, health promotion sponsorship over $5000 — sport, arts, racing and community events

The Health Promotion Sponsorship Program is focused on four industry areas:

- Arts — Tours, festivals, concerts, exhibitions, structured programs and workshops involving visual arts, craft, fashion design and display, performing arts (theatre, music, dance, comedy, circus, opera and music theatre), film and video, literature and multimedia arts.
- Community Events — Agricultural shows, street festivals and cultural events that encourage community engagement and do not have a substantial arts focus. Community Events do not include sporting events, swap meets, flea markets, seminars or similar activities.
- Sport — Activities that involve a recognised sport or organised active recreation that requires physical exertion and where the primary focus is on human activity.
- Racing — Motor car and motorcycle racing.

Source: Healthway 2017, p. 2.

9.6 Stages in developing an event sponsorship strategy

LEARNING OBJECTIVE 9.6 Describe the stages in the development of an event sponsorship strategy.

Developing an event sponsorship strategy involves progressing through a number of steps, each of which is discussed in this section.

Profiling the event audience

The capacity for an event to obtain sponsorship from an organisation, as noted previously, will be greatly enhanced if it able to provide a clear picture of its actual (or potential) target markets (for example, demographics, socioeconomic status, psychographics). This will allow a potential sponsor to determine the level of congruence between its market(s) and those of the event's, and also to judge whether the size of the event in terms of attendees warrants the money/contra services or products that are being sought.

Establishing potential sponsor benefits

Events will differ in terms of what they can offer potential sponsors; however, common benefits found in event sponsorship proposals include:

- the agreement to purchase product/services from a sponsor (for example, alcohol, transport, food)
- event naming rights
- exclusivity (the capacity to lock out competition within a brand category)
- opportunities for targeted or general networking
- merchandising rights
- distribution of digital and hardcopy promotional material
- ability to directly address attendees at designated times (for example, prior to morning and afternoon teas at a conference)
- media exposure
- online advertising opportunities pre-, during and post-event
- venue signage
- joint advertising designed to allow sponsors to leverage (through association) the positive perceptions attendees have of an event's brand/market position
- capacity to demonstrate products or services
- corporate hospitality opportunities, or the ability for sponsors to create their own on-site opportunities in this area
- tickets/registrations/booths/exhibition space for the sponsor's use.

Once identified, a decision can then be made as to how these benefits will be offered to potential sponsors. Essentially, events have two options in this regard: customised and generic benefit packages. The former involves preparing a sales document that seeks to provide key details (for example, demographics of attendees, proposed program, date(s), prior sponsors) and the spectrum of potential sponsorship opportunities that the event offers. This document then becomes the starting point for discussions, which can also result in additional opportunities being identified that may or may not be acceptable to the event organiser. The latter involves the creation of 'benefit packages', commonly hierarchical in nature. Such packages often begin with naming rights and cascade down through major, gold, siler and bronze sponsorships (see example in figure 9.15).

| FIGURE 9.15 | Example of sponsorship levels for a conference — The Australian Network on Disability's Annual National Conference 2020 |

Sponsorship levels

We have five levels of sponsorship available for the conference.

- Major sponsor — $25 000 + GST.
- Gold sponsor — $15 000 + GST.
- Technology sponsor — $12 000 + GST.
- Silver sponsor — $8000 + GST.
- Exhibitor — $4000 +GST — limited to eight opportunities.

   AND is dedicated to matching sponsor packages to sponsor requirements and, in addition to the packages outlined below, we are happy to discuss a tailored sponsorship solution that meets your organisation's specific objectives.

Major sponsor $25 000 + GST

The Major Sponsor(s) will enjoy unrivalled promotional opportunities, helping to demonstrate their position as a leader and innovator in access and inclusion.

Return on investment:

- Organisation logo displayed and acknowledgement as the Major Sponsor on promotional material. This includes:
  - Event signage
  - Media releases
  - Website articles

▶

- Newsletters
- Holding slides
- Invitations and event reminders
- Conference program and pocket guide
- Organisation logo and 200 word profile to be displayed on the dedicated conference webpage and event app with a link to the organisation's website.
- One full page advertisement inside the conference program (note — program will be published on the event app and website).
- One full page advertisement inside the conference guide (subject to confirmation prior to print deadlines).
- One opportunity to insert promotional collateral into the conference delegate satchels (approx. 250 to 300).
- Opportunity to display branded banners in conference venue foyer and on or near the stage.
- Opportunity for a senior representative to deliver a presentation on sponsor's disability initiatives and/or programs, and talk about the organisation's commitment to inclusion (15min speaking slot).
- Acknowledgement as Major Sponsor by the MC throughout the conference.
- Four complimentary registrations for the full day conference and cocktail event.

Gold sponsorship — $15 000 + GST
Gold Sponsors will benefit from significant promotional opportunities and opportunity to demonstrate their position as a leader in access and inclusion.

Return on investment:
- Organisation logo displayed on promotional material, including:
  - Event signage
  - Newsletters
  - Invitations
  - Conference program and pocket guide
- Organisation's logo to be displayed conference webpage and event app with a link back to the organisation's website. The logo will appear smaller than the Major Sponsor's logo but larger than Silver sponsors' logos.
- One opportunity to insert promotional collateral into the conference delegate satchels (approx. 250 to 300).
- One half page advertisement inside the conference program (note — program will be published on the event app and website).
- Acknowledgement as Silver Sponsors by the MC throughout the conference.
- Four complimentary registrations for the full day conference and cocktail event.

Technology sponsor — $12 000 + GST
Helping to ensure that the event materials can be accessed via cutting edge technology the Technology Sponsor will be able to showcase their innovation in access and inclusion.

Return on investment:
- Organisation logo displayed on promotional material, including:
  - Newsletters
  - Conference program and pocket guide
  - Holding slides
- Organisation's logo to be displayed conference webpage and event app with a link back to the organisation's website.
- One opportunity to insert promotional collateral into the conference delegate satchels (approx. 250 to 300).
- Exhibition space in conference foyer.
- Two complimentary registrations for the full day conference and cocktail event.

Silver sponsorship — $8000 + GST
The Silver Sponsors will benefit from good promotional opportunities and opportunity to demonstrate their position as a leader in access and inclusion.

Return on investment:
- Organisation logo displayed on promotional material, including:
  - Newsletters
  - Conference program
- Organisation's logo displayed under Silver Sponsors section on the conference webpage, with link back to sponsor's website.
- Exhibition space in conference foyer.
- One complimentary registrations for the full day conference.

In the case of larger organisations from whom sponsorship might be sought, it is important to keep in mind that they will often set specific criteria (frequently found on their websites) that must be met before they will entertain a proposal. For example, Westpac requires that any sponsorship proposal they receive must:
- be aligned with the business, brand and marketing objectives, brand vision, mission and values and our social impact framework
- be consistent with our corporate image and identity
- enhance the reputation of the brand in the community
- have the ability to engage our customers and people.
    Additionally, Westpac-specific details are required to be included in such documents:
- A one-page executive summary
- The defined target audience for your event
- A detailed outline of the project/activity plans including start and end dates and locations
- Performance evaluation framework
- Business opportunities
- Confirmation that Westpac will be the only financial services partner
- Cost of sponsorship (Westpac n.d).

Identifying potential sponsors

Determining what organisations might be interested in accessing an event's target audience(s) is key to a successful sponsorship strategy. With this intent in mind, event organisers can act to: identify organisations where target market congruence exists; identify those organisations that have previously sponsored the event concerned or similar events; and review the sponsorship policies of potential sponsoring organisations to establish what types of events they will or will not sponsor (see figure 9.14). Additional to these practices, event organisers can benefit from being attuned (through such means as reading the business press) to organisations that have recently launched, or are about to launch, new services or products, or have particular issues that they are grappling with (for example, a poor market image). These organisations, providing there is market congruence, might be particularly interested in sponsorship opportunities. Once potential sponsors are identified, it can be useful to conduct a more detailed examination of their business and marketing objectives, and the capacity of the event to progress these before sending a proposal or seeking a meeting. This is particularly the case when seeking to develop high-value, customised offerings for potential sponsors.

Identifying the sponsorship decision-maker

In the case of most small and medium-sized enterprises, it is often the person responsible for the organisation's marketing or public relations to whom sponsorship enquiries and proposals should be directed. Larger scale enterprises will sometimes have dedicated staff in the sponsorship area but engaging with them directly can be problematic. As a result, event organisers might find they are limited to sending their proposals, or requests for a meeting to discuss sponsorship opportunities, to an email address and waiting for a reply.

Preparing and presenting sponsorship proposals and opportunities

In instances where generic sponsorship packages are developed, as discussed previously, they need to be incorporated within a formal proposal document. These documents will vary in complexity depending on the cost of the sponsorship and the range and nature of the benefits being provided. A basic proposal document would likely include:

- an overview of the event, including (as applicable) its mission/goals, history, location, current and past sponsors, program, duration, staff, past or anticipated level of media coverage, past or predicted attendance levels, and actual or predicted attendee profile (for example, age, income, sex, occupation)
- the sponsorship package(s) on offer and its/their associated cost
- the proposed duration of the sponsorship agreement (sometimes events offer the option of multi-year agreements and sponsors might welcome this as it can take at least one iteration of an event to establish how best to maximise their value from their association with it)
- a brief discussion of the strategic fit between the event and the business and marketing goals of the organisation from whom sponsorship is being sought
- contact details of the responsible event staff member.

In addition to these elements, event organisers might also benefit from including case studies of past successful sponsorships and specifics on how the event will measure the return on the sponsor's investment (for example, social mentions, sponsor video shares, bar sales for their beverage, sponsor recall by attendees).

Keep in mind that proposals, or invitations to customise a sponsorship opportunity, need to be in the hands of potential sponsors early enough for them to work through how they can maximise the opportunities they present and for them to be considered when sponsorship decisions are being made for the upcoming calendar or financial year. In instances where large-scale events are involved, and the amount of money is significant, this can be several years ahead of when an event is scheduled to take place.

Once sent, it is a useful practice to follow up sponsorship proposals/invitations to sponsor (to the extent possible) within a reasonable period (for example, two weeks afterwards) to determine their status. On occasions, a generic proposal may be of interest to an organisation but they may wish to discuss customising the offering. In this case, event organisers should be cautious of not compromising their ability to sell other sponsorship packages by stripping out key components from them in order to meet such requests.

Placing a value on the benefits promised to sponsors is something that requires considerable thought and involves taking account of a range of factors, including:

- sponsorship fees charged by similar events for similar benefits
- market value of the benefits promised and the costs to the organisation of providing them (for example, staff time). These benefits might include: tickets/registrations, parking, hospitality, advertising, installation and production (if necessary) of sponsor signage, space allocations for sponsors to demonstrate products/services or to provide hospitality to their clients, distribution (in physical or digital form) of promotional material
- opportunity cost of providing exclusivity in a particular product/service category
- uniqueness of the event in terms of the opportunity it provides to connect with a sponsor's target audience, for example, the only medical conference of its type to take place in the Southern Hemisphere in a specific year
- legal fees and travel and communication costs associated with the establishment of a sponsorship agreement
- offsets — any promotional activities, or services, undertaken by a sponsor on behalf of an event should be costed and used to adjust the final sponsorship price
- prevailing economic conditions.

Online tools are now available to assist event organisers in placing a value on their sponsorship assets. Of note is this regard is the 'Sponsorship market rate valuation workbook' (Eventbrite n.d.).

Negotiating event sponsorship contracts

Once an event and a sponsor have agreed on a package of benefits, or a customised sponsorship offering, the next step is to formalise this agreement via a contract. In some cases, contracts can be basic in nature, requiring a sponsor to do no more than tick a box, sign and return a page included at the back of a proposal (see figure 9.16). In other instances, more complex agreements will be required. These often articulate the obligations of both parties (including the schedule of payments); state the rights over the use of trade marks and logos; clarify indemnity, insurance and liability issues; state the duration of the agreement and conditions for its termination; provide a process for dealing with disagreements; state what jurisdiction's laws will apply; and other terms as needed (for example, ambush-marketing protections).

There are numerous sponsorship contract templates available on the internet, and these can be modified as needed by the event or their solicitor. As a general rule, the more money involved in a sponsorship, the more detailed the sponsorship agreement will be required to be.

FIGURE 9.16 The Australian Network on Disability's Annual National Conference 2020 Sponsorship Agreement

SPONSORSHIP AGREEMENT

Please sign your acceptance of this offer and return it by email to info@and .org.au and we will forward an invoice.

I [Print name] _____ on behalf of [print organisation name] _____
agree to provide Sponsorship for the 2020 andAnnual National Conference, as follows (please tick):

☐ Major sponsorship $25 000 + GST

☐ Gold sponsorship $15 000 + GST

☐ Technology sponsorship $12 000 + GST

☐ Silver sponsorship $8 000 + GST

☐ Exhibitor $4 000 + GST llimited to eight opportunities)

Signed:

Name:

Position:

Date:

Source: The Australian Network on Disability 2020, p. 7.

Managing sponsorships

Effective relationships between events and sponsors (like any other relationship) are built on a strong foundation of communication, commitment and trust. If a sponsor believes that their sponsorship has been managed well, there is every likelihood they will consider renewing their contract with an event. In order to assist the process of building such relationships, event organisers should keep in mind the following.

- *Have a single point of contact for sponsors.* One person from the event organisation needs to be appointed as the contact point for a sponsor. The nominated person must be readily available, possess an understanding of the terms of each sponsorship agreement and have the authority to deal promptly with any issues associated with their implementation.
- *Ensure a sponsorship delivery plan is in place for every sponsorship.* Based on the sponsorship agreement, this plan should reiterate what has been promised; indicate when and how these benefits are to be provided; state who is responsible for ensuring they are delivered; and indicate how the sponsorship is to be evaluated. Additionally, this document should include sponsor organisation contact(s); items to be provided by the sponsor (for example, signage, logos); and a schedule showing when these items are required.
- *Under-promise and overdeliver.* Do not promise what cannot be delivered, and where possible, add value to a sponsorship offering (for example, arrange for sponsors to meet artists and celebrities).

Evaluating the effectiveness of a sponsorship

The benchmarks against which the effectiveness of any given sponsorship needs to be assessed are the benefits (or objectives) that were originally set for it. The process of measurement against these benchmarks are a shared responsibility between the event and the sponsor as not all the information necessary to undertake this process will be available to both parties (for example, attendance numbers, number of orders placed as a result of leads generated at an event). Keeping these considerations in mind, table 9.2 lists those areas where objectives are commonly set for sponsorships and the types of measures that can be used in their assessment.

TABLE 9.2   Sponsorship objectives and their associated measures

Sponsorship objective	Measurement tools
Awareness, recognition, image	• Attendee surveys — to establish sponsor recall (aided and unaided) or level of participation in sponsor activities at the venue/site • Radio frequency identification devices — these devices are sometimes used in exhibition settings and can serve to allow sponsors to gather information on individuals (name, organisation, position) who attended their activations, programmed activities and so on which can then be compared to the target markets they were seeking to connect with • Sponsor website engagements resulting from an event (for example, click-throughs from the event's website) • Statistics gathered by an event from its customised app can establish how many attendees engaged with a sponsor's promotional material/videos/podcasts, including clicks and shares • Media coverage — number of times a sponsor appeared in print or electronic media as a result of their engagement with an event • Social media — number of interactions with sponsor messaging (for example, promoted posts) on social feeds; number of comments about a sponsor in a post, and the nature of such comments; hashtag usage; number of shares/likes of sponsor content; increase in sponsor's social media followers
Sales/leads/intent to purchase	• Attendee/exhibitor surveys • Sales made at an event or as a result of leads generated at an event (localised, national or international) • Number of contacts resulting from the event • Number of people who responded to special discount or giveaway offers in the lead up to or during an event
Behaviour/attitude change	• Attendee surveys
Relationship building	• Number of key customers/prospects/stakeholders to whom hospitality/entertainment was provided

SUMMARY

The first part of this chapter sought to provide an overview of the marketing process in event settings. It began by stating the questions that this process should provide event marketers with answers to, and then moved on to address some of the key characteristics of events (for example, intangibility) that have marketing implications. The steps involved in developing a marketing strategy were then examined, with a focus on the marketing mix elements that need to be embraced to deliver an effective strategy — experience, people, process, physical evidence, distribution, price and promotion. The importance of, and practices associated with, the monitoring, controlling and evaluating of marketing efforts were then discussed, with the latter being key to refinements or changes being made to future strategic marketing planning efforts.

The second part of this chapter dealt with the development of sponsorship as a revenue stream for events. It began by identifying the benefits sponsors seek and pointed to the need for events to understand what these benefits are when developing their sponsorship plans. The need for a sponsorship policy was then discussed, emphasising the guiding role these documents play in sponsorship-related decisions and practices. The chapter then moved on to describe the steps involved in working through a sponsorship strategy, and an associated sponsorship proposal. The chapter concluded by discussing the nature of sponsorship agreements and how the outcomes sought through these can be evaluated and reported on. It should always be kept in mind that sponsorship is a two-way relationship — events that realise this have a much better chance of keeping sponsors onboard for future deliveries.

QUESTIONS

1 The terms marketing and promotion are often used interchangeably. Briefly explain your understanding of the difference between the two concepts.
2 What is the difference between a market segment and a target market?
3 Develop a Gantt chart showing the promotional activities you would employ for a small-scale local community festival, and when you would employ them.
4 Briefly discuss three considerations you would keep in mind if you were determining the registration fees for a national conference of engineers.
5 Why is process included here as a marketing mix element for events?
6 Why is sponsorship not an appropriate potential revenue stream for all events?
7 Why should event organisers develop sponsorship delivery plans?
8 If you were asked to provide feedback to a conference sponsor on the success of their sponsorship, what data might you use?
9 What types of information would you consider including in a sponsorship proposal to a potential sponsor of a large-scale music festival?
10 Suggest how you would go about identifying potential sponsors for a regional agricultural show, or a music festival taking place in a regional setting.

CASE STUDY

A DISSECTION OF MODERN-DAY EVENT MARKETING STRATEGIES

If you need a case study into the impact of digital transformation on marketing, events are a great place to start. Printed magazines and billboards were once the joint champions of event promotion. A new, data-driven era is now sweeping into the industry, bringing an increased emphasis on personalization, measurement and, of course, ROI.

If you're running your own events, there are several ways that you can learn from the very best conferences, exhibitions, and private meetings. Let's see how they've been cutting through the noise in 2019.

WHAT IS HAPPENING TO EVENT MARKETING?

If there is one driver of the change we're currently seeing within event marketing, it's data — more specifically, the information used to determine the success of our platforms and strategies. Event marketers are not alone in their pursuit of a more data-led approach. Yet, according to insights from Event Marketer, they seem to be moving quicker than their brand counterparts.

Three quarters (74%) of event marketers use data to inform their marketing strategy, compared to just over half (54%) of brand marketers. A total of 71% use it to track brand awareness (vs 52% of brands), 60% use it to track leads (vs 35% of brands) and 47% use it to justify their marketing budget (vs 28% of brands).

The same research puts this down to two different reasons, namely:

1 Event marketers have a definitive start and endpoint. This makes it easier to use data in quantifying success.

2 Events are a broad channel when it comes to data and insights, meaning there is always information to act on.

The onset of data has triggered a seismic shift in the types of technology used to plan, manage, and promote events. Once viewed as a 'nice to have', data integration between suppliers is vital. That's no mean feat, though, as events have a habit of using tens of different platforms to promote themselves. Multiple technologies also bring the puzzle of multiple dashboards and, in turn, multiple definitions of metrics. This has triggered a shift to platforms with in-built functions for CRM, analytics, email marketing software and more.

The upshot of what we're seeing is:

• Data is vital for demonstrating the success of event marketing

• Events need technologies that can integrate with their other platforms to build a framework for analyzing the performance

• All-in-one solutions provide a workaround, but very few have the required functionality

In any case, a more accountable, data-driven era for events has led them to the door of three main marketing channels. They are as follows.

1. Email marketing/marketing automation

Events are some of the biggest cheerleaders for email software. Their open rates sit at a healthy 20.41%, above the likes of gambling, telecommunications and retail. We've heard that 40% of event organizers list email as their no.1 marketing channel in 2019 and we have seen no reason for their enthusiasm to wane.

One of the bigger updates concerns automation. Rather than spending hours delivering hundreds of 'thank you' messages, you can now queue and send these automatically, post-event, for a quick and timely send-off. Another task for automation lies in the conversion of attendees that have seen their details captured by CRM (for example, web form for free content, newsletter signup) but failed to checkout with a pass. Cart abandonment for event tickets is at a relatively low rate of 30% — far below the 53% reported by fashion retailers, but still representing nearly one in every three visitors.

Events tend to have bigger problems with gradual churn. This is especially the case with annual gatherings, attracting tens of thousands of people, which creates big mailing lists (a positive) and scores of disengaged customers (a positive and a negative). Your re-engagement message should reflect the audience being targeted.

The channel is used frequently as a method of recapturing lapsed sales and customers. And it may as well be called 'marketing automation' for the role that technology has to play here.

2. Influencers

Fyre Festival won't be claiming any awards for its management and attendee experience. However, through its multi-million viral marketing campaign, it produced one of the best case studies into the use of influencers for promoting events. After seeing the likes of Emily Ratajkowski being paid over $200 000 to promote a festival that barely took place, many analysts have highlighted the importance of being transparent over what is being promoted and favoring long-term connections over one-off campaigns.

Thankfully this appears to have carried across to the events themselves, which are deploying influencers in a tactical, resourceful way. Many of our users (both B2B and B2C) have remuneration models for their industry's biggest and most respected figures. They range from extremely basic options like:

• Free products/services

• Free tickets

• Speaking opportunities and sponsorship packages

Events also have influencers working to an affiliate marketing model, where the commission is paid for sales. There are some caveats, though. B2C events can use influencer networks to find good partners and payout structures without too many issues. If you're a B2B pharma conference, you might struggle to find the same.

The use of codes and affiliate models are optional. Nevertheless, by getting to know your analytics and marketing attribution, you can start to use influencers in a way that only sees you paying for results.

3. Paid social

If email is primed for B2B events, then paid social is definitely the weapon of choice for their B2C counterparts. Whether you're looking for ultramarathon contestants or jazz music fanatics, they can often be found amid the hundreds of millions of active users on Facebook, Twitter, and Instagram.

After the decline of organic reach on large pages (a reported 42% on Facebook alone), events have almost been forced into investing in paid social. The good news is that promotion on social media is cheap, effective, and comes with a list of ready-made targeting options.

If you're using Facebook to promote a modern art festival in California, you might want to input:
- Location: California +10km
- Age: 25–34
- Gender: All
- Interests: Art

Another option is to use tools like Audience Finder, Twitter for Business and app Install Campaigns from Google to find people that have certain apps on their smartphone. For instance, if I know my audience has Shazam, Ticketmaster, and StubHub on their device, I can assume their interest in music and live events. We can then funnel that data into paid social and mobile app campaigns.

Within the messaging and creative on social media in general, we find there is always an emphasis on driving sales. Most events have a very short lifespan, which creates little room for extensive brand and awareness-building missions. Take the example of Event Tech Live and its call for exhibitors on Twitter.

It's the same for driving interest around tickets . . .

Good results can be had by retargeting site visitors with tools like Facebook's Custom Audiences. And preferably through ads that instil urgency about 'tickets running low', or something similar.

Is this all a good thing?

Despite the acts of trailblazers, many events remain loyal to traditional, offline methods of promoting themselves. Admittedly, industry magazines still have a good reputation for driving sales and awareness in these circles. But the industry's pursuit of all things data and digital is an amazing piece of progress. It's a sign that we not only want results, but we're willing to take extra steps to achieve them. Event marketing is ushering itself into a data-driven era. And if you really want to get better at audience targeting and measuring ROI, we'd advise you to move in the direction of that particular current.

Source: Bort 2019.

QUESTIONS

1 What issues arise when events use multiple platforms to promote themselves?

2 Use a Google search to look up the following programs and briefly describe the functions they perform and how they might be used to assist events in the promotion task — Audience Finder, Twitter for Business and App Install Campaigns from Google.

3 Briefly explain how influencers can play a role in event promotion.

4 What is meant by the term 'retargeting' and why would an event engage in this process?

5 Given the ability of various internet-based platforms to assist in the targeting of potential event attendees, would you suggest abandoning more traditional marketing communication channels such as print media?

REFERENCES

Adelaide Fringe 2020, 'Merchandise', www.adelaidefringe.com.au/shop/merchandise, viewed 22 May 2020.

Armstrong, G & Kotler, P 2013, *Marketing: An Introduction*, Pearson, New Jersey.

Backman, K, Backman, S, Muzaffer, U & Sunshine, K 1995, 'Event tourism: an examination of motivations and activities', *Festival Management and Event Tourism*, vol. 3, no. 1, pp. 26–34.

Báez, A & Devesa, M 2014, 'Segmenting and profiling attendees of a film festival', *International Journal of Event and Festival Management*, vol. 5, no. 2, pp. 96–115.

Baines, P & Fill, C 2014, *Marketing*, Oxford University Press, Oxford.

Bort, J 2019, 'A dissection of modern-day event marketing strategies', *Clickz,* 26 September, www.clickz.com/modern-event-marketing-strategies/255947, viewed 15 May 2020.

Burke, L 2017, 'Demand for refunds as secret maze turns out to be "fake greenery in a bad nightclub"', *news.com.au*, 24 July, www.news.com.au/lifestyle/food/restaurants-bars/demand-for-refunds-as-secret-maze-turns-out-to-be-fake-greenery-in-a-bad-nightclub/news-story/967abf3968e06eba6ad51e4d3c23f765, viewed 16 May 2020.

Burning Man 2020, 'Low-income Ticket Program', https://tickets.burningman.org/#LowIncome, viewed 4 April 2020.

Crompton, J & McKay, S 1997, 'Motives of visitors attending festival events', *Annals of Tourism Research*, vol. 24, no. 2, pp. 425–39.

De Pelsmacker, P, Geuens, M & Van den Bergh, J 2004, *Marketing communications — a European perspective*, 2nd ed., Prentice Hall Financial Times, Harlow, Essex.

DeSantis, N 2016 in Canal, E 2016, 'Coachella vs. other music festivals: the numbers', *Forbes*, 22 April, www.forbes.com/sites/emilycanal/2016/04/22/coachella-vs-other-music-festivals-the-numbers/#46f879953039, viewed 13 May 2020.

Elliott, G, Rundle-Thiele, S & Waller, D 2012, *Marketing*, 2nd ed., John Wiley & Sons, Milton.

Elliott, G, Rundle-Thiele, S, Waller, D, Smith, S, Eades, L & Bentrott, I 2018, *Marketing*, 4th ed., John Wiley & Sons, Milton.

Eventbrite n.d. 'Sponsorship market rate valuation workbook', www.eventbrite.com/blog/academy/sponsorship-valuation-market, viewed 11 May 2020.

EZMarketing 2018, 'Why good web design is important and why you need it', https://blog.ezmarketing.com/why-good-web-design-is-important, viewed 13 May 2020.

Facility Management Association 2020, 'Ideaction — National FM Conference and Exhibition', www.fma.com.au/ideaction-national-fm-conference-exhibition, viewed 9 May 2020.

Geldard, E & Sinclair, L 2002, *The Sponsorship Manual*, 2nd ed., The Sponsorship Unit, Melbourne.

Grey, A & Skildum-Reid, K 2014, *The sponsorship seeker's toolkit*, 4th ed., McGraw-Hill, Sydney.

Healthway 2017, 'Health promotion sponsorship over $5,000 — sport, arts, racing and community events', www.healthway.wa.gov.au/wp-content/uploads/Over-5000-Sponsorship-Guidelines.pdf, viewed 1 May 2020.

Handshake Media Pty Ltd 2017, ''Punters demand refunds after Sydney secret maze event fails to deliver', *The Music*, 24 July, https://themusic.com.au/news/punters-demand-refunds-after-sydney-secret-maze-event-fails-to-deliver/wuDV1NfW2dg/24-07-17,viewed8July2020.

Kaur, T 2019, 'The power of influencer marketing: the Fyre Festival case study', *Meltwater*, 19 April, www.meltwater.com/au/blog/the-power-of-influencer-marketing-fyre-festival-case-study, viewed 15 May 2020.

Lovelock, C, Patterson, P & Wirtz, J 2014, *Services marketing*, 6th ed., Pearson Education Australia, Sydney.

Melbourne International Comedy Festival 2016, 'Summary festival report', www.comedyfestival.com.au/files/resources/MICF%202016%20Summary%20Festival%20Report.8c79.pdf, viewed 13 May 2020.

Object Technology Conference 2015. Resource no longer available online.

Sangha, V 2017, 'Adding value: the future of sponsor integration', *Sparks*, 18 October, https://wearesparks.com/blog/adding-value-future-sponsor-integration, viewed 15 May 2020.

Scenestr 2019, 'Port Fairy Festival 2020 first line-up', *Scenestr*, 22 August, www.scenestr.com.au/music/port-fairy-folk-festival-2020-first-line-up-20190827, viewed 9 May 2020.

Senter, J 2019, 'Mission merchants move annual Sunflower Festival to October to avoid August heat', *Shawnee Mission Post*, 9 August,www.shawneemissionpost.com/2019/08/09/mission-merchants-move-annual-sunflower-festival-to-october-to-avoid-august-heat-81695, viewed 4 May 2020.

Skjonnemand, U & Stephens, M, 2012, 'Woodford and the controversial Santos sponsorship', *ABC News*, 3 January, www.abc.net.au/local/stories/2012/01/03/3401395.htm, viewed 9 May 2020.

Sydney Festival 2020, 'Tix for Next to Nix', www.sydneyfestival.org.au/tix-for-next-to-nix, viewed 9 May 2020.

Tamworth Country Music Festival 2020, www.tcmf.com.au, viewed 22 May 2020.

The Australian Network on Disability 2020, 'Sponsorship proposal', www.and.org.au/data/2020_Conference/AND_Conference_2020_Sponsorship_Proposal_accessible.pdf, viewed 11 May 2020.

Tribe, J 2016, *Strategy for Tourism*, 2nd ed., Goodfellow Publishers Limited, Oxford.

Uysal, M, Gahan, L & Martin, B 1993, 'An examination of event motivations', *Festival Management and Event Tourism*, vol. 1, pp. 5–10.

Westpac n.d., 'Sponsorship requests', www.westpac.com.au/help/community/sponsorship-requests, viewed 16 May 2020.

Woodford Folk Festival 2017, 'Cap to be placed on Woodford Folk Festival for the first time', 15 May, http://blog.woodfordfolkfestival.com/cap-to-be-placed-on-woodford-folk-festival-attendance-for-the-first-time, viewed 2 May 2020.

ACKNOWLEDGEMENTS

Photo: © pcruciatti / Shutterstock.com

Figure 9.1: © Handshake Media Pty Ltd. Staff writer, 24 July 2017, 'Punters demand refunds after sydney secret maze event fails to deliver', *The Music*, viewed 8th July 2020. Retrieved from https://themusic.com.au/news/punters-demand-refunds-after-sydney-secret-maze-event-fails-to-deliver/wuDV1NfW2dg/24-07-17/ [online resource].

Figure 9.3: © Tarandip Kaur / Meltwater. Reproduced by permission.

Figure 9.4: © Tamworth Regional Council. Toyota Country Music Festival Tamworth 2021, www.tcmf.com.au

Figure 9.5: © John Wiley & Sons Inc. Elliott, et al. 2012. *Marketing*, 2nd ed.

Figure 9.6: © Woodfordia Inc

Figure 9.9: © Eyeball Media Enterprises Pty. Ltd. 'Port Fairy Folk Festival 2020 first line-up', written by Staff Writers Tuesday, 27 August 2019. Retrieved from https://scenestr.com.au/music/port-fairy-folk-festival-2020-first-line-up-20190827 [online resource].

Figure 9.10: © Facility Management Association of Australia

Table 9.1: © John Wiley & Sons Inc. Elliott, et al. 2018. *Marketing*, 4th ed.

Figure 9.11: © Melbourne International Comedy Festival. 30th Melbourne International Comedy Festival — Summary Festival Report. Reproduced with permission.

Figure 9.12: © Vikram Sangha / Sparks Marketing Corp. Reproduced by permission.

Figure 9.13: Ursula Skjonnemand, Mary-Lou Stephen. 'Woodford and the controversial Santos sponsorship', dated 3 January 2012. © ABC. Retrieved from https://www.abc.net.au/local/stories/2012/01/03/3401395.htm [online resource].

Figures 9.15 and 9.16: 'Sponsorship proposal - The Australian Network on Disability's Annual National Conference 2020: Reached capacity the last 3 years'. © Australian Network on Disability

Case study: © Jose Bort / ClickZ.com. Reproduced by permission.

CHAPTER 10

Event tourism planning

LEARNING OBJECTIVES

After studying this chapter, you should be able to:

10.1 discuss the major steps involved in event tourism planning

10.2 conduct an event tourism situational analysis

10.3 describe the range of goals that a destination might seek to progress through an event tourism strategy

10.4 list and describe organisations that might play a role in a destination's event tourism development

10.5 describe generic strategy options available to organisations seeking to develop event tourism in a destination

10.6 list and discuss approaches to the implementation and evaluation of event tourism strategies.

Introduction

Many destinations (cities, towns, regions, states or countries) have identified events as a significant contributor to their economic development because of their ability to stimulate growth in tourist inflows. This chapter explores the process by which destinations can seek to leverage events primarily for this purpose. It begins with an overview of government involvement in event tourism, before moving on to discuss a strategic approach to planning for event tourism. This approach involves a range of steps, beginning with a situational analysis, and the establishment of goals and objectives. It then requires the establishment of an appropriate organisational structure through which to develop and implement an event tourism strategy. Once instituted, this strategy then needs to be monitored and evaluated against the goals and objectives that have been set for it so that refinements/changes can be made over the period in which it operates. Each of these steps is examined in this chapter.

10.1 Government involvement in event tourism

LEARNING OBJECTIVE 10.1 Discuss the major steps involved in event tourism planning.

The willingness of governments to support, and actively direct, event tourism development has become increasingly evident over the last two decades. Both within Australia, and internationally, this involvement has taken a variety of forms including the creation of specialist bodies charged with event tourism development; funding, underwriting or creating new events; developing event-specific infrastructure such as convention and exhibition centres and stadia; and participating in partnerships with private sector firms to plan and deliver events. To guide the actions of government (local, state and national), it is now common for towns/cities/regions/states/nations to have in place event strategies that have at their core the leveraging of events for tourism purposes. It must be stressed, however, that this is not the only outcome of significance sought by locations seeking to position themselves as event tourist destinations. While some of these other outcomes are linked to tourism development more broadly, such as reducing the impact of seasonality and destination image development/enhancement, others are not. These additional outcomes can be quite diverse, and can include:

- showcasing an area's innovation, culture and expertise to external audiences
- urban renewal
- access to new ideas/technologies/knowledge
- attracting investment/funding
- enhanced destination 'liveability'
- establishment of networks/partnerships/collaborations in areas such as research and business
- improved local infrastructure provision
- enhancement of a sense of community belonging and pride
- increased participation in sporting and cultural pursuits
- environmental improvement
- stimulation of interest in a destination as a place to live, work and study.

Responsibility for developing and implementing event tourism strategies varies from destination to destination. In China, for example, provincial governments have been particularly active in this area, with 29 of the 31 provincial governments having set objectives and associated actions for the development of their meetings, incentives, conference and exhibition (MICE) sector in their five-year plans (Wu and Xiao 2012). National plans, developed by government or industry bodies, are also increasingly in evidence, with Scotland (VisitScotland 2015), Wales (Welsh Assembly Government 2010) and Australia (Business Events Industry Strategy Group 2008), for example, having developed such documents. As regards Australia, it can also be observed that state and territory governments have event tourism plans in place, as do many local councils (see Tourism and Events Queensland 2017; Georges River Council 2018).

The event tourism strategic planning process

As a means of maximising a destination's capacity to access the many potential benefits events can provide, a strategic approach to event tourism development offers significant benefits. These benefits lie primarily in the areas of coordination and in the building of an event tourism capacity that offers the best strategic fit with a destination's overall tourism efforts. The timeframe in which event tourism strategic plans operate will vary from destination to destination, but three to 10-year planning horizons are common. For example,

Events Tasmania, the government agency responsible for the development of the event sector in that state, employs a five-year rolling strategy; and Tourism and Events Queensland's strategy extends to nine years (Events Tasmania 2015; Tourism and Events Queensland 2017). When these plans are examined, it can be observed that they all move through a similar series of sequential steps (see figure 10.1).

FIGURE 10.1 Event tourism strategic planning process

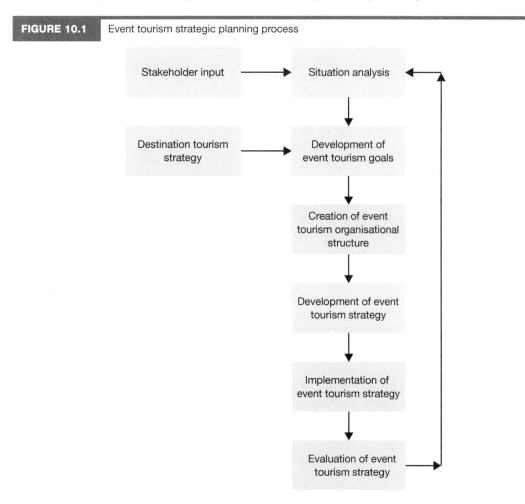

10.2 Situational analysis

LEARNING OBJECTIVE 10.2 Conduct an event tourism situational analysis.

A detailed situational analysis should underpin decisions as to what event tourism goals are set for a destination. This analysis should reflect the various perspectives of key stakeholders in the events area. These stakeholders may include major tourism and event industry firms, individual events, event tourism bodies, event industry associations, the destination's community, and government departments with responsibility extending to areas such as economic development, arts, culture and sport. When developing the 2015–25 events strategy for Scotland, for example, VisitScotland sought input through a series of roadshows, workshops and a questionnaire, which collectively garnered perspectives from over 100 organisations (VisitScotland 2015).

In addition to understanding the various perspectives that exist on event tourism development, it is also the case that a thorough understanding of factors, both positive and negative, that have the potential to impact strategy development are identified. These factors will vary in line with the type of event tourism involved. As an example, figure 10.2 lists the challenges of note in an analysis conducted by Destination NSW (the agency responsible for tourism and event development in that state), when determining how best to go about developing business event tourism in regional areas. A further example of the types of challenges that can be faced when seeking to develop event tourism can be seen in table 10.1 This table outlines the key issues VisitScotland identified, along with their proposed solutions, as it sought to develop its strategic plan. A useful tool for summarising the outcomes of situational assessments is that of a

SWOT (strengths, weaknesses, opportunities and threats) analysis. Factors that might be examined as part of such an analysis are many and will vary depending on the destination concerned and the types of events that it seeks to embrace through its strategy. In figure 10.3 some of the key concerns that might feature in a SWOT analysis have been listed.

FIGURE 10.2 Challenges associated with the development of business events in regional NSW

Challenges

Sector challenges

The business events sector as a whole is extremely susceptible to changes in the economy and business confidence. Although the sector has shown some growth due to overall increases in the number of business events, it is facing a long-term trend towards lower delegate attendance numbers and shorter lengths of stay. This in turn has affected yield from visitor expenditure. For Regional NSW other specific challenges include the following.

Pressure on corporate clients to reduce costs

Time-poor workforces, improved virtual meeting capability and low business confidence puts constraints (time and cost) on organisations and their ability to travel to and/or host conferences in regional areas.

Client expectations

Client groups have increasingly high standards and expectations for conference services. The quality of venue, IT and telecommunication access, food and beverage services, audio visual equipment, entertainment and production services are crucial elements — particularly for repeat business.

Value proposition

Clients are savvy and value conscious, seeking innovative and creative options to achieve their conference outcomes. The value of a conference cannot be sold purely on destination assets, such as beach, river or hinterland experiences — the intricacies of the conference experience itself and how it is delivered are key.

Market readiness

Within Regional NSW there is often a misinterpretation of what it means to be a 'business conference destination'. To be a leading business conference destination, the destination must have: high-quality, meeting specific infrastructure; a supply chain of quality service providers including logistics and transport, accommodation, audio visual equipment and operators, entertainment options and quality tourism leisure product; and moderate-to-strong economic diversity and innovation within its region. It must also have reasonable proximity and/or access to its target markets.

To maintain or attract additional business event clients, a leading business conference destination must be able to demonstrate a successful track record in providing quality customer service and outcomes for clients.

Moving from reactive to proactive marketing

During the consultation process to develop this NSW Regional Conference Strategy and Action Plan, many regional operators indicated their approach to promoting and marketing business conferences was purely reactive. Many viewed conferences as a supplementary revenue stream to simply increase utilisation of their tourism leisure product (for example, spa treatments, wine and food tasting, nature tours and other activities) or for accommodation providers to increase occupancy rates of their existing facilities during the mid-week period.

Challenges facing New South Wales

Two overarching challenges need to be addressed in order to return the NSW regional conferencing sector to growth:
1. NSW needs leadership and coordination in terms of regional conference opportunities, and does not currently have a regional conference strategy in place to address challenges and maximise opportunities.
2. The NSW Regional conference sector needs a collaborative framework to encourage innovation and initiate concerted action.
   Throughout Regional NSW the industry also faces very specific operational challenges in:
- identifying potential business conference opportunities
- lack of conference facilities that are equipped to cater for large conferences
- lack of adequate, quality accommodation facilities
- marketing conferences to build delegate numbers
- major regions lacking qualified staff and/or a Convention Bureau to manage sales and bid activities

- developing competitive bids and completing bid documentation
- responding to conferencing RFTs or EOIs
- operational delivery of conferences
- service standards and quality of F&B offerings
- measuring the number and/or economic impact of conferences
- access and cost of some regional airfares.

Source: Destination NSW 2017, p. 5.

TABLE 10.1   Selected issues impacting event delivery in Scotland and their proposed solutions

Variation in regulations and requirements	Standardised and transparent approach to legislation, regulations, H&S, licencing, insurance etc.
Payment for public services such as police and air ambulance	Clear policies on charging which take account of public value of events and are open, transparent and agreed well in advance.
Increase in costs relating to H&S	Cost effective best practice guidelines produced and disseminated.
Variable quality of affordable Food and Drink	Continue work with Food and Drink and Events industries to address this including further developing the food charter based on Glasgow 2014 Food Charter.
Variable engagement with sustainability	Events industry wide recognition of the need for economically and environmentally sustainable events.
Equality and accessibility issues	There should be events that appeal to and are accessible to all that are promoted as such.
Variable quality of event experience	Events should be safe, reflect best practice and provide the best possible experience to all involved.
Cost of entry, catering and merchandise	Need for pricing at events to be inclusive and to represent value for money.
Variable use of technology	Events in Scotland are seen as innovators in the use of technology and the adoption of new technology.
Overall low engagement of business in events	The business community become more engaged, making a significant contribution while achieving increased business and economic benefit.
Lack of single public facing Events Diary bought into by industry	VisitScotland events listing recognised as the single public facing event diary in Scotland and to ensure this meets partners' needs.
Lack of dissemination of best practice knowledge	Comprehensive cross agency programme of insight and research into relevant aspects of the event industry.
Varying levels of event planning and project management	To develop robust event plans that cover all aspects of planning, management and delivery including budgets; business, transport, marketing, project management, risk management and operational plans.
Lack of co-ordination for innovation in technology around events	Creation of dialogue around how technology can be used to develop and enhance event experiences.

Source: VisitScotland 2015, p. 34.

Strengths/weaknesses

Existing stock of events

- Number and type (for example, local, regional, major)
- Quality
- Uniqueness/competitive advantage
- Duration/timing (for example, impact on seasonality, degree of event 'clustering' and its effect on the demand for visitor services such as accommodation)
- Current financial situation of events and level of dependence on government support
- Image/reputation (particularly in visitor markets) of individual events
- Level of current demand from regional, intrastate, interstate and overseas visitor markets
- Level of understanding (developed through market research) in evidence of the needs of visitor markets
- Event economic, social and environmental impacts
- Existing links between events and the destination's tourism industry (for example, level of packaging evident and extent of partnering with tourism industry marketing bodies)
- Stage of individual events in terms of their 'product' life cycle
- Evidence of long-term strategic planning by event organisers

Venues/sites/facilities/supporting services

- Number, type, quality and capacity of venues/outdoor event sites
- Planned (short term and long term) enhancements/increases in venues/outdoor event sites
- Capacity and quality of supporting services (for example, accommodation, restaurants, retail stores, transport companies, equipment hire firms, audiovisual firms and leisure/recreational services) to support various types of events
- Accessibility of services to people with varying disabilities
- Quality of communications infrastructure (for example, internet speeds)

Destination attributes

- Number/type of tourist attractions (natural and man-made)
- Location relative to major potential visitor markets
- Accessibility — by road, rail, sea and air; transport costs and travel times
- Diversity of economic base — existence of universities, research centres and different types of industries that can be leveraged to attract business events
- Climate — may enhance/limit destination attractiveness as a location for events during certain periods

Human resources

- Level of event management expertise
- Staffing levels of event tourism bodies and the associated level of support they can provide
- Capacity of a community to provide volunteers to support event delivery
- Range/type of event-related training conducted in the area, or that are accessible to people from the area

Stage of event sector development

- Existence of organisations such as event industry associations, convention and visitor bureaux and major event agencies
- Strength of partnerships/networks between private sector businesses and government bodies involved in event tourism development

Level of government and private sector support

- Level of available funding (for example, grants) or other assistance (for example, advice, in-kind support) for event tourism development
- Level of private sector support through the provision of in-kind services, direct funding or sponsorship

Potential to link events with overall destination branding efforts

- Strength and nature of existing destination brand
- Capacity of events to reinforce/change existing marketplace positioning

Level of community support

- Prevailing community perspectives on the economic, environmental and social impacts of events
- Degree to which community/special interest groups are presently involved with events (for example, as performers, contractors, suppliers)
- Level of anticipated local patronage for events (often necessary to underpin the economics of many events)

- Level of community willingness to absorb short-term negative impacts, such as crowding and traffic congestion
- Willingness of the community to support events through volunteering, providing access to community spaces and the provision of home hosting services and so on

Opportunities/threats

Potential for partnering with selected organisations to progress one or more event tourism goals
- Possible partnering bodies include:
  - government departments
  - cultural organisations
  - tourism bodies
  - chambers of commerce
  - tourism businesses (to package events)
  - environmental groups (to minimise impacts/maximise environmental outcomes).

Level and type of competition from other destinations
- Direct competition from similar events
- Indirect competition from dissimilar events taking place within the same time period as existing/ planned events
- Standing of destination relative to competition in areas such as event infrastructure, transport assess and environmental attributes and so on

Market tastes/preferences for events
- Ability of an area to respond to changing market needs (for example, food and entertainment preferences) through existing and new events
- Impact on existing/planned events of demographic (for example, community age profiles, patterns of work/retirement) and attitudinal changes in such areas as health/wellbeing and so on

Local cultural/environmental attributes that have the potential to be leveraged for event purposes
- Capacity of an area's flora or fauna, indigenous culture, history, ethnicity, architecture, local agricultural pursuits and so on to be embraced within an event context

Presence of local chapters/bodies with affiliations to parent organisations that regularly conduct events
- Ability of local sporting/business/cultural organisations to bid for and host events owned by their respective parent bodies. These may include national/international conventions, annual industry trade fairs and state/national/international sporting competitions

Environmental and social impacts
- Capacity of a destination to absorb event tourism impacts without negative environmental or community outcomes. These impacts may be linked to waste generation, anti-social behaviour, crowding and the inability of local area infrastructure to cope with large, temporary population increases.

General prevailing and projected economic conditions
- Employment levels
- Interest rates
- Inflation
- Consumer confidence levels

Other
- Changes in weather patterns due to climate change
- Security and health issues (for example, terrorism, virus outbreaks)
- Political climate (for example, the extent to which events involving particular groups or nations will be supported by key stakeholders, such as state or national governments).

10.3 Development of event tourism goals

LEARNING OBJECTIVE 10.3 Describe the range of goals that a destination might seek to progress through an event tourism strategy.

The role that events can play in a destination's tourism development efforts will vary according to the overarching tourism strategy that is being pursued. An understanding of this strategy is important as it provides, for example, the basis for establishing event tourism visitation targets, as well as insights into destination branding and positioning efforts that an event strategy may be required to support. While acknowledging that each destination will seek to leverage events for differing purposes, it is nonetheless possible to identify a number of common tasks that events are used to pursue.

Leveraging events for economic gain

The economic impacts of events can be significant. In the case of the Australian Capital Territory, for example, the events that have been supported through its government's special events fund have attracted, between 2010 and July 2017, an estimated 2.96 million attendees and generated $636 million in economic return (Australian Capital Territory Government 2017). It should be stressed that the economic benefits flowing from events are often not limited to the individual cities, towns or regions where they take place. Edinburgh's 12 major festivals, for example, generated £280 million pounds in Edinburgh itself, and a further £313 million in Scotland as a whole (BOP Consulting 2016). Single events, such as large sporting events, can also have major economic outcomes, which is why destinations often compete to include them in their portfolios. The 2018 Commonwealth Games, for example, is estimated to have generated $323 million in tourism expenditure, as well as a projected $550 million over the subsequent nine years due to its role in promoting the Gold Coast, Queensland and Australia as tourist destinations (Pham et al. 2018).

While cultural and sporting events can generate significant economic outcomes, it is also the case that business events have the capacity to play a major role in contributing to a destination's economy. By way of example, a report by the Business Events Council of Australia (2015) estimated that during the financial year 2013–14, over 37 million people attended more than 412 000 business events (defined as meetings and conventions, exhibitions, or incentive events with at least 100 delegates and exhibition space of over 500 m^2) across Australia. These events directly resulted in $28 billion in expenditure, $13.5 billion in direct added value, 180 000 jobs, and a contribution to taxation of $860 million. The significance of these types of events can also be further demonstrated by taking the example of China where business travellers spent $114 billion (USA) in 2014 on domestic trips to meetings and conventions — second only to the United States (Global Business Travel Association 2015). Accompanying this high level of expenditure was significant growth in the investment by hotel chains in new developments, many with mega exhibition and convention centres attached (Boey 2016).

Given the previous discussion, it is not surprising that goals linked to generating economic benefits feature strongly in event tourism strategies. As an example, Tourism and Events Queensland seeks to use its event strategy to grow the value of its calendar of events from $600 million in 2017 to $1.5 billion by 2025, while also contributing $1 billion in overnight visitor expenditure and generating five million direct visitor nights (Tourism and Events Queensland 2017).

Geographic dispersal of economic benefits flowing from event tourism

When destinations seeking to engage in event tourism are large geographic entities, such as states or countries, it is not uncommon for them to use events as a means of encouraging travel to areas outside their major traditional tourism centres in order to spread the economic benefits of event-related visitation. As one of its strategic goals, the South Australian Tourism Commission (n.d.), for example, seeks to 'encourage visitors to disperse around South Australia through regional events and festivals', while Tourism and Events Queensland (2017) aims to 'support regional Queensland through the Queensland Destination Events Program'.

Destination branding and marketing

A destination's 'brand' can be thought of as the overall impression, association or feeling that its name and associated symbols generate in the minds of consumers. Events are an opportunity to assist in creating, changing or reinforcing such brands, particularly through the media coverage they can attract. According to a study by Jago et al. (2003), efforts at using events for destination branding purposes depend greatly on local community support and on the cultural and strategic fit between the destination and the event(s) conducted there. This study also found, in the context of individual events, that event differentiation, the longevity/tradition associated with an event, cooperative planning by key players and media support were central factors in the successful integration of an event into a destination's overall branding efforts.

The Tamworth Country Music Festival, Australia's largest country music event, is an excellent example of how an event can be used for destination branding and marketing purposes. This event has been extensively leveraged to create a 'brand' for the town of Tamworth where, arguably, none existed before. The town is now firmly established as 'Australia's country music capital', a position it has sought to strengthen through a variety of means. These have included: developing a 'Roll of Renown', which takes the form of giant granite boulders onto which plaques are placed honouring selected country and western artists; building a guitar-shaped tourist information centre and swimming pool; constructing a 20-metre high 'Golden Guitar' at one entrance to the town; incorporating the event's golden guitar logo into its overall destination branding; establishing an interpretive centre that overviews the evolution of country music in Australia; creating spin-off country music events (for example, Hats Off to Country); and erecting memorials to country artists (Harris and Allen 2002; Destination Tamworth 2018).

Another example of destination 'identity' creation through events can be observed in the Scone district of New South Wales. This area brands itself as the horse capital of Australia and conducts multiple events to reinforce this position. These events include rodeos, horse races, long-distance charity rides, as well as its major event, the Scone Horse Festival (Upper Hunter Shire Council 2018).

Many other examples of branding and marketing through events can be identified. The general category of food and/or wine festivals, for example, perform this function for a number of Australian destinations, reinforcing to the broader market their status as a quality producer of these products, while also aiming to stimulate visitation. For example, the Mudgee Wine and Food Festivals, which take place both in Sydney (a major consumer of food and wine products, and a significant source of visitors to the area) and Mudgee itself, have been very successful in aiding the branding efforts of the area (and its products), as well as in generating visitation (Mudgee Vine 2018).

Another aspect of the link between events and destination branding and marketing is their use by tourism bodies as integral parts of broad 'theme' years. In April 2015, for example, the Welsh government announced a series of three themed years, intended to promote key aspects of the Welsh tourism product: Year of Adventure 2016, Year of Legends 2017 and Year of the Sea 2018. Each themed year included events linked to it, with the last involving events associated with beach sculptures, aquatic sports, fishing and seafood (Business Wales 2018). Scotland is another destination that has made significant use of themed years, which began in 2009. It has now extended their use to 2022, in part, because of their role in stimulating the festival/public events sector to develop new events around these themes (VisitScotland 2018). Themed years, and the various events and activities associated with them, have also been used by this same destination to entice business events to take place during these periods.

It is common for event tourism strategies to explicitly acknowledge their intent to use events as destination branding and marketing tools. In the case of Tasmania, for example, its strategy makes clear that it aims to use its major events to 'contribute to Tasmania's culturally vibrant brand and often provide a trigger for interstate visitation' (Tourism Tasmania 2020). A similar outcome is sought by the Australian Capital Territory that aims to use events to 'Bring to life the essence of Brand Canberra: ensuring major events are confident, bold and ready, and enhancing the appeal and reputation of Canberra as an innovation city, a creative city and an arts city' (Australian Capital Territory Government 2017, p. 6).

Creating off-season demand for tourism industry services

Events have the capacity to be scheduled in periods of low tourism demand, thereby evening out seasonal visitor flows. Skiing centres, for example, often use events as a means of generating demand during non-winter periods. Events can also be used as a means of extending the tourist season by conducting them just before or just after the high-season period. When used in these ways, it is possible for events to assist in changing market perceptions of a destination from that of a single-season-only location to one providing year-round leisure opportunities.

The power of events to influence seasonality is evident from Sydney's Vivid, which describes itself as a light, music and ideas festival. This event takes place at the end of autumn/beginning of winter, when the demand for tourism services, such as accommodation, is traditionally at its lowest. The first time this event was conducted in 2009 it attracted just over 200 000 visitors and resulted in an additional $6 million flowing into the Sydney economy. By 2018 the event was attracting 2.3 million visitors and generating some $173 million in international and intrastate visitor spend (Vivid Sydney 2019).

Enhancing visitor experiences

Events add to the range of experiences a destination can offer, and thus increase its capacity to attract and/or hold visitors for longer periods of time (Getz 2005). Events such as the CMC Rocks QLD, Taste Tamworth Festival, Julia Creek Dirt and Dust Festival, the Noosa Eat and Drink Festival, and the Blues on Broadbeach Music Festival are some examples of the diversity of experiences available to visitors through the medium of events.

Catalyst for expansion and/or improvement of infrastructure

Events can provide a significant spur to both public and private infrastructure investment in a destination. Many writers (for example, Liu 2014; Smith 2012; Dickson, Benson and Blackman 2011; Matheson 2010; and Getz 2005) have highlighted this point, particularly in the context of large-scale sporting events where their role in urban renewal, and the subsequent development of their host destination's attractiveness and capacity as a tourism and event hosting destination, has been significant. In the case of the 2018 Commonwealth Games on Queensland's Gold Coast, for example, the event resulted in: the construction of three new sporting venues, one new multi-purpose venue and seven upgraded venues; enhanced transport infrastructure; aesthetic improvements to urban precincts and public domains; and the acceleration of the city's arts and cultural program. These developments now provide Queensland with a significantly greater capacity to attract further international sporting events, as well as providing a more visitor-friendly and engaging physical and cultural environment (Council of the City of Gold Coast 2018). A similar outcome can be observed to have occurred in Melbourne where the Commonwealth Games was staged some 12 years earlier (Sport and Recreation Victoria 2018a).

Progression of a destination's social, cultural and/or environmental agenda

A range of outcomes, as noted previously, can be pursued through the conduct of events, with tourism development being but one of these. These other outcomes can act to condition how event strategies are constructed, or they might be independent of such considerations. In its major events strategy, for example, the Welsh government has identified a range of benefits that it seeks to leverage events for (see table 10.2), only some of which directly link to tourism (Welsh Assembly Government 2010). Evidence of these broader considerations can be found in a number of destination event strategies where reference is made to such outcomes as improving the quality of life of residents; promoting cultural, sporting and artistic pursuits; and enhancing a sense of community (see Australian Capital Territory Government 2017).

TABLE 10.2   Key reasons the Welsh government invests in major events

A prosperous society — major events can stimulate new enterprise and business growth, leading to the creation of quality, long-term[sic] jobs. They also help to showcase and promote tourism in key markets and can support diversification of the rural economy.

Living communities — successful major events engage communities through local voluntary action, through participation and through the live spectator experience in particular as well as through various media platforms.

Learning for life — major events are a dynamic, knowledge-based creative industry, that requires a range of high-quality skills, from project management and finance to marketing, media and communications. Events can enhance the environment for developing the skills to support a modern, creative economy.

A fair and just society — successful major events can help people and communities to achieve their full potential, including outreach programs targeted at hard to reach and minority groups.

A sustainable environment — major events that proactively embrace the sustainable event management agenda can help to raise awareness of sustainability and showcase good practice such as in the use of renewable energy, integrated transport, waste recycling and the procurement of local goods and services.

A rich and diverse culture — major events showcase Wales' unique cultural identity and heritage, are a catalyst for cultural innovation and expression and provide valuable opportunities for our leading artists and athletes to display their talents on the world stage.

Source: Welsh Assembly Government 2010, p. 9.

10.4 Creation of an event tourism organisational structure

LEARNING OBJECTIVE 10.4 List and describe organisations that might play a role in a destination's event tourism development.

To progress a destination's event tourism goals, it is necessary to allocate responsibility for achieving these to one or more organisations. In the case of towns or regions, these responsibilities often lie with the same body charged with overall tourism development. In the instance of cities, states or countries, multiple organisations may be involved with varying levels of responsibility for business, major and regional events. In the Australian context, there has been a move in recent years to combine previously separate government tourism marketing organisations and major event agencies into single entities so as to better leverage efforts directed at growing visitor numbers. This has resulted in Tourism Queensland and Events Queensland becoming Tourism and Events Queensland; Events NSW and Tourism NSW becoming Destination NSW; and Tourism Victoria, Victorian Major Events Corporation and Melbourne Convention Bureau becoming Visit Victoria. Events now feature as a division or area within their organisational structures, as can be seen in the example provided of Tourism and Events Queensland in figure 10.4.

| **FIGURE 10.4** | Tourism and Events Queensland organisational structure |

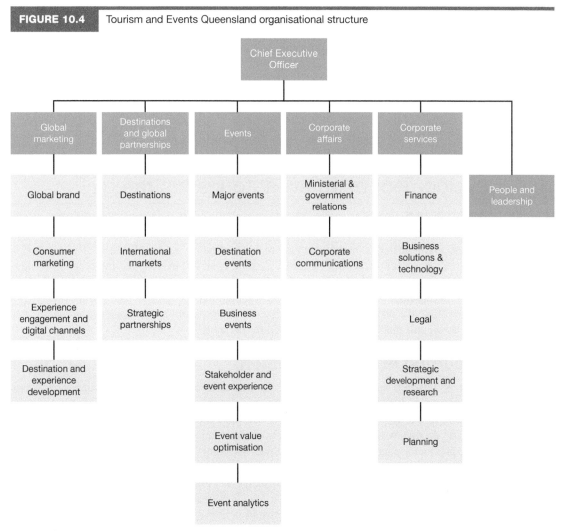

Source: Tourism and Events Queensland 2018.

It should also be noted that private sector industry associations/representative bodies can be considered part of a destination's event tourism organisational structure. In the Australian context these organisations include Exhibition and Events Association of Australia; Meetings and Events Australia; Events Industry Association (Western Australia); Professional Conference Organisers Association; and the representative entities of the Business Events Council of Australia and the Victorian Tourism Industry Council — Events

Policy Committee. These organisations act to provide input into event tourism policies and strategies and play a role in their implementation and review. A summary of the types of organisations that are commonly involved in event strategy development and/or implementation has been provided in table 10.3.

TABLE 10.3   **Organisations involved in event strategy development and/or implementation**

Event advisory boards	The purpose of these bodies, while there is some variation, is essentially one of providing local/state/national governments with event-related strategy and policy advice, as well as encouraging greater coordination within the event sector.
Government event/ tourism/destination development organisations	These organisations perform a variety of event tourism development roles. In some instances, they are responsible for developing and implementing a whole-of-destination event tourism strategy, in others their role may be more limited, such as acting only to promote destination event experiences to tourist markets. Services that these bodies might provide to the event industry include assistance with marketing; provision of operational advice/assistance; funding via competitive grants; and event facilitation through assisting event organisers obtain necessary permissions/licences and to navigate regulatory requirements.
Business event agencies	Variously titled (for example, Convention and Visitors Bureau, Business Events (destination name), Convention and Exhibition Bureau). These organisations are often fully or partly government-supported or government-operated agencies that act to provide advice and assistance directed at acquiring international and national conferences and other forms of business events such as corporate incentive and travel reward programs.
Industry associations and representative bodies	These entities advocate for their specific sector of the event industry in order to influence event tourism strategies and government policies impacting on the area. In performing this role, these bodies will often undertake research in support of their advocacy efforts. Additionally, some of these organisations play a meaningful role in further developing professionalism in their sector of the event industry through training and professional accreditation systems.

10.5 Development of an event tourism strategy

LEARNING OBJECTIVE 10.5 Describe generic strategy options available to organisations seeking to develop event tourism in a destination.

Several strategies are available to destinations seeking to develop event tourism. These strategies concern the development of existing events, bidding to attract existing (mobile) events, and the creation of new events. These three broad strategy options are not mutually exclusive, and it is common for destinations to use several if not all of these options to achieve their event tourism goals. Irrespective of the strategy(ies) selected, it needs to reflect the insights gained through a destination's situational analysis, as well as the broader tourism-related goals that have been established for the area.

Existing/recurring event development

There are a range of possible approaches to using existing events to advance a destination's event tourism efforts, however, it must be kept in mind that picking 'winners' can sometimes be difficult. One option is to identify one or perhaps several events that have the capacity to be developed as major attractions ('hallmark' events), with a view to their use as the foundation for creating/reinforcing a tourism identity/brand. The previously cited example of the Tamworth Country Music Festival is indicative of how events can be used in this way. The Parkes Elvis Festival, in central New South Wales, is another example of an event that has successfully performed this role. A small event initially, it developed (with some local and State government assistance) to the point where it has now created a brand for the town — 'Elvis Capital of Australia', and has been key in increasing visitation to the town and surrounding area (Parkes Elvis Festival 2018).

The event-driven identity/brand of an area can be further reinforced by supporting its hallmark event(s) with smaller similarly themed events that can be conducted at other times of the year, or that can take place under the larger event's umbrella to increase its capacity to both attract visitors and increase the likelihood that they will stay longer. The example of Scone ('Horse Capital of Australia') provided earlier is indicative of how this type of strategy is employed in practice. This event developed the Scone Horse Festival into a hallmark event by placing under its umbrella a number of smaller events, many (but not all) of which were equine related. Another approach to existing event development is to merge smaller events (often of a similar nature) into one larger event with a subsequently greater capacity to attract and hold visitors for longer periods.

It should be noted that a focus on the development of hallmark event(s) can be problematic, in the sense that they might boost visitation for a short period, but do not generate year-long visitor interest in a destination. To avoid this problem, most destinations seek to develop a portfolio of events of different scale and type spread throughout the year (see later discussion).

Event bidding

Many events are 'mobile' in the sense that they move regularly between different locations. Some sporting events (for example, state/national/international sporting competitions), and many business events (for example, association/corporate conferences, exhibitions and incentive-based events) fall into this category. These mobile events can often be formally bid for by organisations affiliated with the owners of these events, such as local sporting bodies and professional associations, frequently with encouragement and assistance from event tourism organisations (for example, national or state-based tourism bodies and/or convention and visitor bureau). This assistance can take a variety of forms as a bid moves through to the point of submission, as can be seen in figure 10.5 in the context of conferences.

| FIGURE 10.5 | Forms of bidding assistance potentially available to a conference bidding body from an event tourism organisation or convention and visitor bureau |

1. Research

Conduct in-depth research to determine, for example, previous conference-hosting locations, possible competition destinations, geographic rotation pattern, reasons prior bids have failed and organisational political factors that might weigh on the selection process. This information can then be made available to the local organising body seeking to host the event (for example, a local chapter of an international professional medical body).

2. Enhancement of local support base

Liaise with government and private-sector interests (as appropriate) to garner support for a bid, and to obtain documentary evidence of this support for inclusion in the final bid document.

3. Plan the bidding strategy

Assist in establishing a clear timeline for the preparation and submission of the bid document and provide advice on how best to address all bid criteria established by the event's owners.

4. Bid document preparation

Undertake the final preparation of the bid document (in association with the local organising body). This document must address all bid criteria in such a way as to make a clear case as to the location's competitive advantages over any competing destination(s).

5. Lobby in support of the bid

Analyse the bid voting process with a view to identifying key decision-makers/influencers and engaging with these individuals to convince them of the merits of the bid.

6. Facilitate destination visits

Arrange and host visits to the destination by representatives of an event's owners (if required) when they are seeking to determine the suitability of a location for their event.

7. Conduct, in association with the local organising body, the final bid presentation prior to voting

If this is required, local organising bodies can benefit significantly from the technical expertise and presentation skills of these supporting bodies.

8. Manage the post-bid relationship

If a bid is successful, planning assistance is often made available including linking local organising bodies to conference organisers and suppliers, and in the form of marketing support.

New event creation

In making the decision to create, or support the creation of new events, reference should be made to the goals that have been established within the destination's overall event strategy. It should also be the case that new events have the capacity to be integrated into the overall destination's event portfolio with due reference to matters such as seasonality of visitor flows and destination image/brand. Exactly what new events are created will vary with the strategic needs of each destination, with the range of generic options including active participant-based events, spectator-based sports events, events with environmental/cultural/heritage themes, music-based events, special interest events and business events. As with the development of existing events, event tourism organisations need to be mindful of the need to ensure new events are adequately resourced if they are to have the best chance of long-term survival. This being the case, it might be desirable for organisations involved in event tourism to limit their support to one, or a few, new events at any one time.

Perhaps the most successful new event in the Australian context in recent years has been Vivid. Initiated by Destination New South Wales in 2009, by 2017 it had grown to become Australia's largest public event with an attendance of 2.3 million. A number of observations can be made about the decision to create Vivid that are germane to the new event creation process. Firstly, the program for Vivid links to, and reinforces, aspects of Sydney's desired brand image, specifically those relating to innovation and being a hub for creative industries and ideas. Secondly, the event has significant spill-over effects to areas outside of Sydney. In 2017 38 000 visitors to Vivid travelled beyond the fringes of Sydney, staying more than 94 000 nights and spending over $16 million in rural and regional economies. Thirdly, the event has resulted in significant international and domestic visitation to Sydney, with 135 841 travel packages sold, 65 491 of which were to international visitors and 70 350 to the domestic market (Destination NSW 2018). Fourthly, Vivid takes place in late autumn/winter, and as a result, serves to significantly boost visitation when there is unused capacity in the destination's tourism industry. Lastly, Vivid highlights the need to give new events scope to evolve rather than being overly concerned with initial outcomes and critiques. In its first iteration it attracted 200 000 people, less than 10 per cent of its current audience. Additionally, during its early years there was some community confusion as to what the event was actually about, but as Fergus Linehan, a former Sydney Festival director observed 'all festivals take time to find their feet. If you look at the history of most events you'll find that they flailed around a little bit as they began to find their identity' (Meares 2014).

Some general considerations in event tourism strategy development

In the context of individual events (existing, new, and events for which bids are proposed), one means of making decisions as to which align best with a destination's event strategy is to rate them against established criteria. For this purpose, a range of inputs can be used (depending on the event) including available event data; data on similar events; and assessments by experts/expert panels. The criteria used will depend on the goals (see previous discussion) the event tourism strategy is seeking to progress. By way of example, a simple 1 (low) to 5 (high) rating system (see table 10.4) could be employed for each criterion, and the result totalled to guide decision-making. A more sophisticated approach would be to weight each criterion to reflect its importance. This would result in the final numeric value for each event being the product of the extent to which it was viewed as meeting each criterion, multiplied by the importance of that criterion (see table 10.5).

TABLE 10.4   New event assessment matrix (unweighted)

Event name	Impact on visitation (1–5)	Impact of seasonality (1–5)	Impact on desired destination brand identity (1–5)	Impact on social/cultural/ environmental agenda (1–5)	Total (20)
A	4	2	3	3	12
B	3	4	5	5	17
C	4	3	3	1	11

In assessing individual events, destinations also commonly think in terms of their 'ideal' portfolio (or mix) of events that will serve the strategic outcomes they seek, and what, if any, gaps exist in their event offerings that might be restricting their ability to achieve these outcomes. For example, a destination may determine it is home to a large number of local and community events but no events of regional or state significance that are serving a branding/identifying role for the location. Additionally, analysing an existing event portfolio might aid in identifying those events with a status that may be most easily altered with additional support. In this regard, events identified as being regional in terms of the area from which they attract attendees are likely to be more easily 'pushed' to hallmark status than those that draw only from their local area.

TABLE 10.5 New event assessment matrix (weighted)

Event name	Impact on visitation (1–5) x (5)	Impact on seasonality (1–5) x (5)	Impact on desired destination brand identity (1–5) x (3)	Impact on social/cultural/ environmental agenda (1–5) x (3)	Total (80)
A	20	10	9	9	48
B	15	20	15	15	65
C	20	15	9	3	47

FIGURE 10.6   Destination event portfolio model

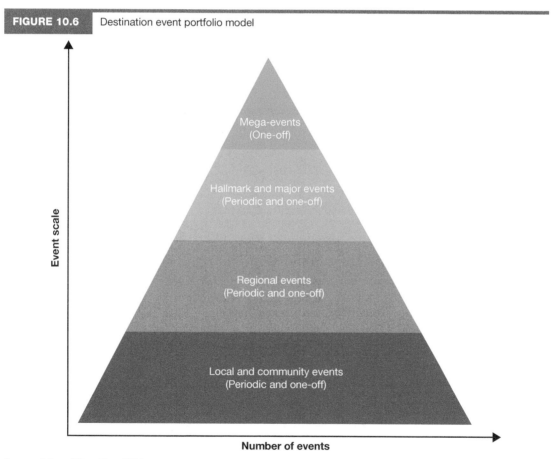

Source: Adapted from Getz 2016.

Visualising a destination's event portfolio can be a useful aid in portfolio decision-making. In this regard Getz (2016) proposes the use of a hierarchical pyramid model. These types of models commonly have three of four classifications or groupings into which events can be placed. The example provided in figure 10.6 has four levels. The first of these is comprised of local and community events such as small-scale festivals/concerts, town parades, small sporting competitions and markets. Events of this type, while having limited capacity to draw attendees from outside an area, nonetheless add to the quality of experience visitors have when they visit an area. The second level is made up of events that, in addition to local audiences, attract visitors from nearby cities/towns/regions. Moving up the hierarchy, the next level comprises hallmark and major events. Hallmark events, as stated in the overview of the event field chapter, are those ongoing events that have become synonymous with the place in which they are held (for example, Tamworth's Country and Western Music Festival, Sydney's Royal Easter Show, Edinburgh's Royal Military Tattoo, Sydney's Vivid, Melbourne's Australian Tennis Open and the New Orleans Mardi Gras). Major events, on the other hand, do not possess this strong association with place and are most often one-off in nature. Examples of these types of events include large international conferences/exhibitions, concerts featuring international artists, single delivery music festivals and large-scale sporting and religious events. Events in this category commonly attract national, and sometimes, international media attention; have a significant economic impact in the town or city where they occur; and attract a considerable number of attendees from interstate and overseas. The final level in the hierarchy is that of mega-events. These events set themselves apart from those in the previous category in a variety of ways. These include high levels of associated international tourism; major requirements for infrastructure investment; substantial global media coverage; and an economic impact that extends to the national level. There are few true mega-events, and they are sought by destinations through the previously discussed bidding process. Examples of these events include World Expositions, Olympic Games (summer and winter), FIFA World Cups, Rugby World Cups and Commonwealth Games.

Hierarchical event portfolio models can also suggest the roles event tourism organisations might effectively play at the various levels. In using these models to aid decision-making, it needs to be kept in mind that the lines between categories can be somewhat blurred, and that the group into which an existing event is placed might change over time as it attracts more attendees or its attendance declines.

10.6 Implementation and evaluation of an event tourism strategy

LEARNING OBJECTIVE 10.6 List and discuss approaches to the implementation and evaluation of event tourism strategies.

Once an event tourism strategy has been established, it then needs to be put into effect. There are a variety of mechanisms that can be employed for this purpose.

Financial support

At the level of individual events, financial support may be provided in the form of grants, sponsorship or equity.

Grants and sponsorships

Grants are a common means of providing support for events that are deemed to have tourism potential, and they can be instrumental in their growth and development (see the event profile on the Julia Creek Dirt and Dust Festival). Destination NSW, for example, operates a Regional Flagship Events program that 'identifies and supports events in regional NSW that have the potential to act as a 'cornerstone' or flagship tourism event for their area by attracting overnight visitation and delivering long term benefits to the region' (Destination NSW 2020). This program is divided into three components and supports both new events and ongoing events:

- Incubator Event Fund — provides seed funding (up to $20 000) for new events to support their first and second years of operation
- Flagship Event Fund — offers grants (one-off annual grants of up to $20 000 and triannual grants of up to $27 500 per annum) to ongoing events
- Event Development Fund — supports (one-off grants of up to $50 000) events that have received their maximum funding under the scheme but can detail a strategy through which they will continue to grow their overnight tourism potential (Destination NSW 2016).

The other Australian states and territories have put in place similar systems through their government tourism and/or event agencies with some slight variations in the events that they seek to target (see table 10.6). When looking to identify potential sources of grants a useful starting point is the online service The Grantshub (www.thegrantshub.com.au).

Julia Creek Dirt and Dust Festival

Grant applications and bulldust don't generally belong in the same sentence.

But in the case of Julia Creek's Dirt and Dust Festival, grants have played a critical part in making it one of Queensland's 'must-go' events.

It all began in 1994 with the unlikely idea of running a triathlon in one of Queensland's hottest and harshest climates. Each year hasseen the addition of new and novel attractions like bull riding, cowpat tossing, tobacco-rolling and a 'best butt' competition, as well as more conventional concerts and cultural events.

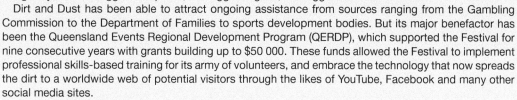

'Getting this far would have been a huge challenge without Grants money,' says Events Manager Margie Ryder. 'A struggle to improve, a struggle to grow, a struggle to attract tourists.'

Dirt and Dust has been able to attract ongoing assistance from sources ranging from the Gambling Commission to the Department of Families to sports development bodies. But its major benefactor has been the Queensland Events Regional Development Program (QERDP), which supported the Festival for nine consecutive years with grants building up to $50 000. These funds allowed the Festival to implement professional skills-based training for its army of volunteers, and embrace the technology that now spreads the dirt to a worldwide web of potential visitors through the likes of YouTube, Facebook and many other social media sites.

A deliberate aim of QERDP's assistance has been to make 'Dirt and Dust' self-sufficient. That goal was achieved in 2010 when it went 'grant-free' for the first time.

So what advice does Margie have for other grant applicants?

'Talk in depth to the body providing the funding; the more you understand what they're looking for, the better you can frame your application,' Margie explains. 'Get a second opinion from colleagues and friends. Value-add every day. Ask the funding body to read and comment on your submission before you lodge it.'

Margie has found them more than willing to help. She has also seen great value in joining with other local attractions and events to promote their region as a whole, receiving ready assistance from Tourism Queensland both financially and in kind, such as providing photographic resources.

As the dust settles after another successful Festival, Margie Ryder knows that funding has been an instrumental part of making this award-winning Festival secure and sustainable for at least the next 50 years.

Source: Tourism and Events Queensland 2011, p. 29.

TABLE 10.6   **State and territory event agencies' event funding targets**

State/territory government event agency	Events targeted through grant funding
Tourism and Events Queensland	Metropolitan and regional events
South Australia's Tourism Commission	New events (targeted through the bidding process), and live music and community events
Tourism Western Australia	Major, large, medium and small-scale regional events.
Events Tasmania	Touring, marketing, championship and one-off events.
Events ACT	Major events, events deemed to have significant visitor growth potential and events that serve to add vibrancy to its events calendar.
The Northern Territory Major Events Company and Department of Tourism and Culture	New and ongoing events; and subsidies based on delegate numbers to business events.

(continued)

TABLE 10.6 *(continued)*

State/territory government event agency	Events targeted through grant funding
Visit Victoria	New and ongoing large, medium and small-scale regional events with demonstrated, or potential, tourism value.
Destination New South Wales	New and ongoing regional events

Sources: Tourism and Events Queensland 2018; South Australian Tourism Commission n.d.; Events ACT 2018; Events Tasmania 2020; Tourism Western Australia 2018; Northern Territory Major Events Company 2018; Northern Territory Business Events 2018; Visit Victoria 2018; Destination NSW 2020.

The criteria used to assess applications by events for grants from government tourism/event bodies often embrace a range of considerations, including:

- potential, or demonstrated capacity, to increase tourist visitation, yield per visitor and length of visitor stay
- relationship between the event and area's overall tourism development strategy, including its branding efforts
- level of evident community/local government/business/tourism industry support
- capacity of event to grow and become self-funding
- event's current tourism packaging efforts or potential for tourism packaging
- timing — does the event occur outside peak visitor seasons when tourism services are already being used at a high level?
- level and quality of business, financial, operational and marketing planning in evidence
- media value associated with the event
- contribution to the vibrancy and diversity of the destination's existing event calendar
- contribution to social, cultural, environmental or economic outcomes sought by the destination
- evidence of processes designed to evaluate the event, particularly its tourism outcomes.

In addition to event tourism organisation grants, a number of other grants can potentially be accessed by individual events, which, while not focused primarily on tourism outcomes, can nonetheless play a role in progressing a destination's event tourism strategy. For example, in the case of Victoria, event funding is available through Sport and Recreation Victoria (2018b), Victorian Multicultural Commission (2020) and Creative Victoria (2018). It can also be observed that local government has been active in the provision of event grants as they seek to progress their respective tourism event strategies. The example of Sydney's Northern Beaches Council provided in the chapter on strategic event planning is but one of the many councils that now support the development of events in their areas, largely, or at least in part, for economic purposes.

At the individual event level, grants often bring with them the need for ongoing reporting regimes. This often time-consuming process can involve: an audit to ensure compliance with grant conditions; regular engagement with the granting body; and a requirement to periodically provide detailed information on how the grant money is being spent. This being the case, costs associated with the grant acquittal process need to be factored into any grant that is received. A useful explanatory document for events seeking to access this source of funding is that of Tourism and Events Queensland's *The Grants Guide* (2011), which deals with the process of grant identification, determining eligibility, grant writing and reporting.

Finally, it should be noted that the terms 'sponsorship' and 'grant' are sometimes used interchangeably by government entities involved in event tourism development. In the case of the City of Sydney, for example, its festivals and events sponsorships have a requirement for acquittal, criteria for their assessment, expected outcomes, maximum funding levels and submission dates, elements that you would also expect to find included in most grant programs (City of Sydney 2020). Tourism Western Australia (2018) also lists avenues for the event funding it provides under the heading of event sponsorships.

Equity and ownership

It is not uncommon for government event agencies to directly invest in new events either through ownership or by taking up equity. Events Management Queensland, for example, is a major event management company wholly owned by Tourism and Events Queensland. This company owns and manages the Gold Coast Marathon and the Pan Pacific Masters Games (Events Management Queensland 2018). Vivid Sydney is a further example of an event developed and delivered by a body (Destination NSW) responsible for its state's event tourism strategy (Vivid Sydney 2018). Additional examples are also in evidence in other Australian states and territories. The decision of event tourism bodies to act in this way is, at least in part, due to the difficulties the private sector sees in planning and delivering major events due to their scale, financial risk and associated organisational complexity.

Bid development and bid support services

As previously noted, bidding for mobile events is one means of adding to a destination's event calendar. Some government event tourism organisations specialise in bidding for specific types of events, such as conference and exhibition bureaux, while others have a wider charter that embrace a range of different event types. For example, the South Australian Tourism Commission (n.d.) has successfully bid for sporting, cultural and large youth events. Indicative benefits of attracting mobile events to a destination are in evidence in the event profile on Melbourne's engineering and scientific sector. Notable outcomes from this event included economic impacts, 'new' money flowing into the destination from overseas participants, spreading of visitation to regional areas and the inward flow of knowledge and expertise. Once a bid is won, event tourism organisations commonly play little, if any, further role other than perhaps assisting to stimulate event attendance or aiding in the creation of an organising committee.

Research

Some event tourism organisations commission or undertake research on a range of event-related matters as a way of providing input into their event tourism strategies. Matters that might be explored include event market trends; relative standings (compared to competitors) in terms of the number and type of events conducted; nature and extent of event legacies; event-specific infrastructure developments in competitor destinations; visitor perceptions of the quality of event experiences (particularly those supported by the event organisation concerned); stakeholder viewpoints on issues associated with the sector's future development; event economic impacts; and constraints on future growth. Events Tasmania is an excellent example of an event tourism organisation that places a high value on research, undertaking studies to identify specific event market segments along with their respective characteristics and economic value. It also encourages event organisers to integrate a research strategy into their long-term planning to assist in making more informed decisions in connection with their future strategic directions. Additionally, Events Tasmania maintains a watching brief on developments in the area of event management research that might have implications for its event's strategy (Events Tasmania 2006). Another example of an event tourism body active in the area of research is that of Melbourne's Convention and Visitors Bureau. It regularly, as do similar bodies in other states, collects data from the events it has assisted (see the event profile on Melbourne's engineering and scientific sector) as part of its efforts to assess the impact of business events on Melbourne and Victoria more generally.

Some event tourism organisations, most specifically those involved in business events, are often members of national and international associations that undertake regular assessments of the business event market. These assessments provide insights into such matters as bids won and lost; delegate numbers, delegate origins (local or international) and estimated spend; and the relative standings of countries and cities. The Australian Association of Convention Bureaus, for example, produces an annual report that allows its members to benchmark their performance on many of these dimensions, while the International Congress and Convention Association provides insights into the relative performance of countries in the international association meeting market (see table 10.7).

TABLE 10.7 **Relative standings of countries in the Asia–Pacific association meetings market in 2018**

Rank	Country	Number of meetings
1	Japan	492
2	China-P.R.	449
3	Republic of Korea	273

(continued)

TABLE 10.7 *(continued)*

Rank	Country	Number of meetings
4	Australia	265
5	Thailand	193
6	Chinese Taipei	173
7	India	158
8	Singapore	145
9	Malaysia	134
10	Hong Kong, China-P.R.	129

Source: International Congress and Convention Association 2018, p. 59.

The absence of research can be a significant limiting factor in progressing an event strategy. In its regional conference and action plan (2017–21), Destination New South Wales, for example, identified that research in the area of regional business conferencing was significantly underdeveloped making planning in the area difficult. In acknowledgement of this, this plan, as one of its key strategic imperatives, required a renewed focus on research (Destination New South Wales 2017).

EVENT PROFILE

Melbourne's engineering and scientific sector on show for 'The 56th IEEE Conference on Decision and Control (CDC)'

The CDC was held in Melbourne during December 2017 at Melbourne Convention and Exhibition Centre (MCEC) connecting an international community of over 1330 researchers, practitioners and students in the field of automatic control. The event is recognised as the premier scientific and engineering conference dedicated to the advancement of the theory and practice of systems and control and is hosted by the IEEE Control Systems Society (CSS).

The state of Victoria is home to a well-established network of small and locally grown technology businesses as well as some of the world's biggest technology companies. Melbourne is also renowned for its capability to deliver a customised event and provide numerous experiences for delegates to explore the city and its regions. These compelling success factors gave Melbourne the competitive edge to win and host a world-class technical program of this calibre. The city served as a platform to discuss new research results, future developments and groundbreaking applications relevant to the sector.

Great minds connecting in Melbourne for a rewarding technical program

The conference incorporated a technical program which included workshops hosted at the University of Melbourne, tutorials and plenary sessions featuring lectures of renowned professors in the field who addressed current and future topics in control systems. The meetings were held across a broad range of topics; from aerospace and automotive controls, healthcare and medical systems, power generation through to smart cities and systems biology. These sessions gave experts in each field the opportunity to connect and discuss relevant matters aligned to the conference objectives, as well as further developing their careers.

Showcasing Melbourne and Regional Victoria

The conference delivered a social program filled with activities focussing on creating opportunities for both leisure and networking for delegates. Commencing with a welcome reception at MCEC, which highlighted an 'Australian Bushland' theme, and incorporated a Welcome to Country ceremony with indigenous performers, the audience was highly engaged from the start.

An awards ceremony and reception also took place at MCEC, and was followed by a gala dinner, in which over 1000 delegates enjoyed an exquisite banquet with Australian first-class produce and wines.

The evening also offered an up-close encounter with native animal wildlife allowing delegates to interact with some of Australia's favourite creatures.

Delegates had the opportunity to explore Melbourne's culture with 'Best of Victoria', Melbourne and regional Victoria tour specialists. Tours incorporated memorable and bespoke experiences showcasing the city and its regions at its best, from the iconic Melbourne laneways and Federation Square to regional immersive experiences such as Phillip Island Penguin Parade and the Great Ocean Road.

A VIP Gala Dinner for 250 guests took place at the Melbourne Cricket Ground, providing guests with an extravagant menu featuring Australian lamb, Wimmera duck and premium Australian wines. Keynote speakers were gifted aged Muscat from premier Victorian wine region, Rutherglen.

The conference concluded with a farewell reception in the main foyer of MCEC, showcasing the Belfast-built, three-masted Polly Woodside ship preserved in Melbourne's South Wharf, where all delegates gathered to enjoy their last night in the city.

Lasting legacies

The CDC 2017 generated over $8 million in economic impact for Victoria, as well as delivering considerable legacy outcomes for the city and sector.

Delivering a highly successful event reinforced Melbourne's expertise in accommodating prestigious international conferences. The city delivered an exceptional program and delegates were highly satisfied with the outcomes of CDC 2017, which set a new standard for IEEE's conferences.

The conference also provided an excellent opportunity for students' professional development by allowing them to connect with the stars of the industry and gain extensive knowledge in their fields. The lectures from respected professors gave the students a once in a lifetime opportunity to learn from the best.

Team Melbourne

Melbourne was chosen as the host destination for its collaborative approach, strong support from Victoria's State Government, City of Melbourne and the world leading facilities at MCEC.

Melbourne Convention Bureau (MCB) secured the 56th IEEE CDC in 2014 and worked closely with IEEE CSS in collaboration with Professor Rick Middleton (University of Newcastle) and Professor Dragan Nesic (University of Melbourne) from bid phase through to delivery. ICMS Australasia was appointed as the professional congress organiser, who ensured the seamless delivery of the event by working closely with all stakeholders.

The CDC 2017 demonstrated the successful 'Team Melbourne' approach to winning and hosting business events, facilitating city-wide collaboration for which MCB is renowned.

MCB partners across accommodation suppliers, attractions, restaurants and retailers were engaged to deliver the best experience delegates could have.

Source: Melbourne Convention Bureau 2018, pp. 1–2.

Training and education

To promote best practice and continuous improvement, and by doing so assist in creating events that are sustainable in the longer term, some event tourism organisations undertake — or commission outside bodies to undertake — training in areas such as event project management, event marketing and general industry best practice. Until recently, for example, Events Tasmania operated a scholarship program whereby selected members of its event industry were able to attend the University of Technology Sydney's Executive Certificate in Event Management program. A number of these organisations have also developed resources that event organisers can draw on for educational/training purposes (for example, Tourism Western Australia 2017; Events ACT 2018). It is also common for these bodies to support industry events, such as conferences, that serve to facilitate the sharing of event industry-specific knowledge, as well as acting as vehicles for upskilling through their associated workshops and seminars.

Coordination, cooperation and facilitation

A range of opportunities exist for event tourism organisations to facilitate the creation and conduct of events. Some event tourism organisations, for example, have created 'one-stop' shops where event organisers can: obtain relevant permissions; seek information/advice on regulatory issues; and gain assistance in coordinating the many stakeholders that are sometimes involved in an event (for example, police, emergency services, transport services, road and traffic bodies). By doing this they aim to facilitate new event development in their destinations. Another example of how this can be achieved can be seen in the services provided by convention and visitor bureaux. These organisations provide a range of services and resources designed to encourage event organisers to select their destination over others, and include: simplifying access to information by developing event planner guides containing information on event-related facilities and services; hosting familiarisation tours and site visits for event organising committees and event planners; providing advice on customs, immigration, venues and suppliers; and assisting with program planning and pre- and post-event tours.

Coordination and cooperation within the event sector can be advanced in various ways. The grants process, for example, can be used by event tourism organisations to encourage the establishment of linkages between events and organisations with the potential to enhance the attractiveness of events to visitor markets, or that can provide access to these markets. This can be achieved by explicitly favouring applications that demonstrate links with tour companies, hotels, transport providers, local tourism organisations and cultural institutions (for example, museums, heritage organisations, art galleries and community arts organisations). Grants can also be used to bring order to destination event calendars by supporting only those events that act to spread visitor demand so that it does not overwhelm existing infrastructure. Additionally, event tourism organisations can put in place practices designed to encourage participation and associated 'buy in' to its event strategy. These practices include the conduct of formal and informal meetings/functions/conferences involving members of the event industry, tourism organisations, other government agencies, the local community and business groups; and the establishment of advisory boards or groups. The Events Tasmania example in figure 10.7 provides an indication of the range of organisations from whom input and cooperation might be sought in event tourism planning.

Event strategy evaluation

Evaluation is fundamental to the success of any event strategy, with the process being based upon the broad goals that have been set, and the associated quantified objectives. Too often strategies are developed, and goals established, without any measures put in place to gauge their achievement. The types of measures that can be used for this purpose include:

- Economic — visitor nights directly associated with event attendance; visitor expenditure; number of out-of-area/region/state/country attendees; economic value of event calendar/portfolio; number of full-time job equivalents resulting from the conduct of events; net contribution of events to town/city/regional/state/national economies
- Visitor experience — number of new events/events of a particular type/scale/duration established; and degree of balance (in terms of types of events) evident in a destination's event portfolio
- Geographic dispersal — extent of rural or regional visitation and expenditure linked to events/or a specific event
- Destination branding and marketing — media (including social media) coverage at the national, local or international level; changed visitor perceptions and/or marketplace positioning of destination
- Seasonality — level of off-season visitor growth attributable to events; and usage levels of tourism services by time of year
- Infrastructure — extent of urban renewal associated with event conduct; improvements of event-specific and community infrastructure linked to the conduct of events; and level of event infrastructure utilisation
- Social/cultural/environmental outcomes — community perception of destination 'liveability' resulting from events; level of social inclusion/diversity evident in event programs and attendees; number of events employing 'best practice' environmental practices as evidenced by ISO 20121 accreditation (see the chapter on sustainable event planning); and degree of enhanced community environmental awareness flowing from the conduct of events
- Event sector development — event management skill/knowledge training/education opportunities; event planning and delivery capabilities of event organisers and their suppliers; user 'friendliness' of destination from the viewpoint of event owners/planners; degree of overall coordination and cooperation evident among key stakeholders in a destination's event strategy; and competitive standing in areas such as number of meetings hosted, income generated and event infrastructure.

FIGURE 10.7 Stakeholders in Event Tasmania's event strategy

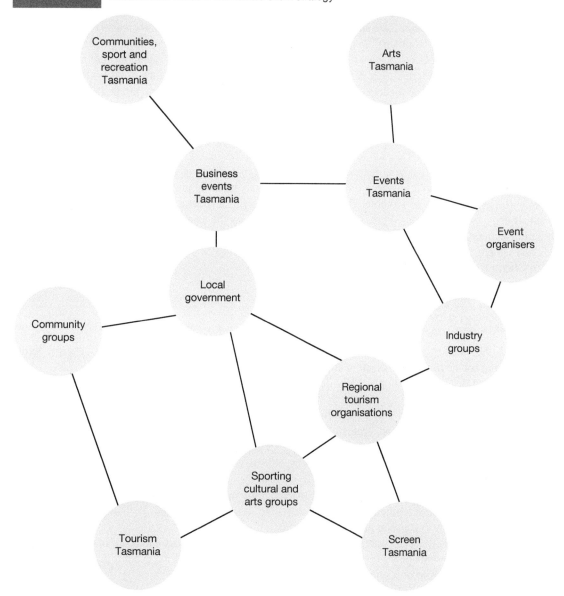

Source: Events Tasmania 2015, p. 8.

SUMMARY

For destinations ranging in size from small towns to countries, event tourism has increasingly become a key component of their overall tourism planning. In this chapter a basic event tourism strategic planning process has been proposed that seeks to bring a measure of structure and discipline to decision-making in this area. This process involves undertaking a detailed situational analysis, which in turn provides the foundation upon which decisions can be made as to the event tourism goals that should be pursued. These goals are then progressed through a body established for this purpose, or one (as has increasingly become the norm in Australia) that has a broader tourism development agenda. Once an organisational structure is in place, strategic options can then be considered, with these options involving decisions as to the mix of existing events, new events or mobile events that best align with the destination's tourism development goals. In pursuit of its selected strategy, a destination may engage in a range of actions including the provision of financial support, providing promotional assistance and undertaking various activities designed to develop the events sector as a whole. How successful these practices are in progressing a destination's event strategy, and its associated goals, needs to be assessed by the establishment of benchmarks in areas including economic performance, seasonality and visitor geographic dispersal. Information gained through this assessment process can then be used to further refine, or in extreme instances, change a destination's event strategy.

QUESTIONS

1 Discuss the value of having a clear understanding of a destination's overall tourism strategy before embarking on the process of creating an event tourism strategy.
2 Identify and discuss three goals that a destination might seek to progress through its event tourism strategy.
3 Discuss the role events can play in dealing with the challenge of visitation seasonality.
4 Briefly discuss the three broad strategic options available to destinations seeking to expand visitation through the use of events.
5 Discuss the value to destinations of establishing objective criteria upon which to assess the outcomes of their event strategies.
6 What types of actions might organisations with event tourism responsibilities consider taking to further their event sector's development?
7 Briefly discuss how events can play a role in branding a destination.
8 Draw a basic event tourism strategic planning model and briefly discuss each step in this model.
9 What role(s) can grants play in progressing a destination's efforts to drive event tourism?
10 Briefly discuss the role of research in event tourism planning.

CASE STUDY

AUCKLAND'S 2011–21 MAJOR EVENTS STRATEGY

Foreword: The Auckland 2011–21 Major Events Strategy, which is reproduced below, was Auckland's first major events strategy. It provided much of the thinking, and the lessons learned from its implementation, that informed the updated Auckland Major Events Strategy 2018–25. Auckland's Major Events Strategy will be reviewed again after 2021.

It is increasingly recognised regionally and nationally that developing the prosperity of Auckland will trigger a chain reaction that can advance the prosperity of New Zealand.

Auckland must, as ever, plan its development and progress in a disciplined and rigorous way. Whilst accepting the role as linchpin in the country's economy, Auckland must balance this responsibility with due commitment to time and public money. Auckland has identified the visitor economy as being critical to the economic success of the country and major events are one of the core pillars of this visitor economy. This strategy, developed by Auckland Tourism, Events and Economic Development (ATEED), sets out a plan for determining the types of major events that are right for Auckland now and in the future, that have the potential to stimulate powerful outcomes for the region.

It applies primarily to major events requiring public sector intervention, and expressly excludes:

- privately funded events
- local and community events managed by Auckland Council and its Local Boards
- business events.

However, the strategy must be implemented within the context of the wider event landscape. The principles and frameworks developed within this strategy can be extended to the wider event population at a later date, if required.

There are a number of funders that support Auckland's broader events programme. The focus of this strategy is on major events that ATEED delivers.

Major events	Regional events	Local events
ATEED	Auckland Council (Governing Body)	Auckland Council (Local Boards)
• Events of national or international interest • Events that are pivotal to Auckland's brand • Can deliver economic and/or social outcomes	• Events that attract regional visitation or participation • Deliver primarily social outcomes	• Events that are driven by and supported by local communities • Deliver primarily social outcomes in a local area

THE OPPORTUNITY

Major events can play a key role in helping cities achieve their long-term economic and social aspirations. This has been recognised by many successful cities around the world. The four main benefit streams associated with events are:
- immediate economic benefits
- city branding
- social wellbeing
- legacy benefits.

Immediate economic benefits

Events can deliver immediate economic benefits by bringing new money into the economy. This can occur through two distinct channels:

1 The event sources some of its income from outside the region and spends it in the region to deliver the event. This results in additional business-to-business expenditure.

2 The event attracts visitors who spend money in the region. This results in additional consumer-to-business expenditure in the economy.

City branding

Hosting major events can have a significant impact on a city and its image, and can be a cost-effective means of promoting the city's brand to a wide audience of potential visitors, investors and immigrants.

Social wellbeing

As well as their short-term benefits, events make cities more vibrant and interesting places to live, bringing people and communities together and giving them a sense of identity and belonging.

Legacy benefits

Elevating the host's global stature and accelerating its economic and social development, major events can be a significant catalyst for change. Cities have used major events to give focus to their priorities such as fast-tracking city infrastructure or developing long-term business and trade connections.

A NEW AUCKLAND

Auckland has a rich major events heritage, having successfully hosted a number of high-profile international events over the past two decades that have delivered significant social, economic and legacy benefits for the region. The city and region are now poised to take the next step.

Auckland's reputation as a major event city was tarnished in the early 2000s due to a relatively thin major events calendar and the loss of some high-profile events to other cities.

However, since 2007 there has been a resurgence in major event activity, with Auckland more aggressively bidding for and securing one-off major events and also increasing capability, co-ordination and resource in preparation for Rugby World Cup 2011.

This resurgence has occurred despite the region's fragmented approach to event attraction and delivery prior to the amalgamation of Auckland's unitary authorities in November 2010.

Auckland Council has articulated a vision with major events as a priority goal. Within Auckland Council's new framework of government, Auckland Tourism, Events and Economic Development Ltd (ATEED) is the entity that has been established to help Auckland achieve its economic potential, supporting both a regional and national growth aspiration.

The recent changes in local governance give Auckland the opportunity to advance this goal and the formation of ATEED marks an exciting step change — it is a first for New Zealand and a first for Australasia. Equally important, this Major Events Strategy presents the first step towards realising Auckland's ambition to be a global events city.

The frameworks and techniques within this strategy are based on considered thinking and evaluation from subject experts and have been peer-reviewed by those in public and private sectors, both locally and internationally.

THE ROLE OF THE PUBLIC SECTOR

Not all events are commercially viable on a stand-alone basis, even if they generate region-wide benefits that exceed the cost of running the event.

An event may generate region-wide benefits that exceed the cost of running it. But it could still fail to be commercially viable if the operator does not secure enough of those benefits to gain a return on investment. So however worthwhile in the wider sense, such an event will fail to find support from the private sector.

This is why a major events portfolio requires public sector investment. But how much? Australian cities offer interesting comparisons, though the following figures often reflect funding between local, state and federal agencies. Nevertheless, there are huge disparities. Auckland's budget is less than a third of South Australia, despite the similarity between their population sizes.

These are funds allocated to annual event programmes. Funding for one-off events, in particular mega events such as the Olympic Games or Rugby World Cup, fall outside of operating budgets.

Funding is only one part of the public sector's role. Auckland must be 'event-friendly' and easy to do business with.

Also required is an event-friendly approach to infrastructure (for example, provision of venues, tourism and transport) and regulatory processes (to avoid red tape and facilitate gaining approvals).

	Baseline funding NZ$ million	Resident population	Funding per capita (NZ$)
Victoria	$71.6	5.55 million	$12.91
Queensland	$18.9	4.52 million	$ 4.18
New South Wales	$51.1	7.24 million	$ 7.06
South Australia	$19.1	1.64 million	$11.66
Wellington	$ 6.0	0.49 million	$12.27
Auckland	$ 6.0	1.49 million	$ 4.03

*Note: Funding amounts as at June 2011.

GLOBAL SCAN

A review of seven comparable cities — Toronto, Sydney, Melbourne, Barcelona, Cape Town, Glasgow and Torino — revealed some common themes.

This strategy highlights the challenge Auckland faces in creating a step-change in the performance of its major event programme — it is competing with other like-minded cities for major events, many of which are better resourced than Auckland and can provide a more compelling commercial proposition. Auckland will therefore need to adopt a more innovative approach to events than other cities if it wants to develop a competitive advantage.

FRESH THINKING

The benefits of an enhanced events economy extend well beyond the immediate social and economic impacts — the bigger picture is an exciting, globally connected city, internationally relevant and therefore with a competitive advantage in retaining and attracting talented people.

In the long-term this will lead to higher quality of life and a more productive and prosperous economy. These outcomes are encapsulated in the following vision statement for Auckland's events portfolio:

ONE	TWO	THREE
They recognise the strategic importance of major events and plan and invest accordingly.	They recognise the importance of balancing social objectives with economic outcomes.	They view mega events as opportunities to transform their social and economic status.
FOUR	FIVE	SIX
They use distinctive major events to promote and enhance their brand.	They host a range of events that are common across cities for example, major sports events, international film festivals, gay and lesbian festivals, visual and performing arts festivals, international comedy festivals and food festivals.	They build their event programmes around between five and ten 'anchor events'.

Events are a cornerstone of the visitor economy and make Auckland a highly desirable place to live and work. Auckland has a portfolio of exciting, distinctive events that make its people proud of who they are and where they live. It understands the positive social and economic outcomes events can deliver, and their impacts on quality of life.

Given the positive link between social wellbeing and long-term economic growth, Auckland needs to strike a careful balance between productive events that result in greater economic activity, and consumptive events that make Auckland a more exciting and attractive place to live. Events that can deliver both simultaneously are highly desirable (for example, Rugby World Cup 2011).

A PORTFOLIO APPROACH TO EVENTS

Both one-off and regular events are currently evaluated based on their individual merits with little consideration given to the outcomes delivered by other events in the programme. This approach has worked reasonably well for Auckland in the past, but now requires a higher level of master planning that would be expected from a global events city. The risks of not working to a master plan include:

- the possibility of competition between events in the programme (for example, two events held at the same time of the year that compete for participation and sponsorship dollars)
- a lack of balance between the productive and consumptive outcomes delivered by the programme
- losing sight of the outcomes the event programme should be achieving for Auckland.

These risks can be mitigated by focusing less on the stand-alone outcomes of an event, and more on how the outcomes of a single event combine with those of other events. This means 'ticking all the boxes' at the programme level, rather than requiring each event to 'tick all the boxes' on a stand-alone basis.

This can be referred to as a portfolio approach to events. Auckland needs to take a portfolio approach to events. To invest optimally in events, Auckland needs to be clear on the outcomes the portfolio should deliver for Auckland, and how they should be measured. These outcomes should be guided by the Council's vision for Auckland.

OUTCOMES

Auckland has determined four key outcomes for its events portfolio:

1 Expand Auckland's economy — inject new money into Auckland and/or minimise leakage out of Auckland — this would be demonstrated by a high Return on Regional Investment (RORI).
2 grow visitor nights in Auckland — attract domestic and international visitors to Auckland and encourage them to extend their stay.
3 Enhance Auckland's liveability — make people proud of who they are and where they live by making Auckland more interesting and exciting.
4 Increase Auckland's international exposure — use events as a platform for promoting Auckland's people, places and way of life to the world.

Attributes

The attributes (characteristics) of individual events are also important because they can have a material impact on the value of the portfolio. The overall performance of the event portfolio therefore depends on both the outcomes and attributes of the events within it; hence careful consideration must be given to each dimension.

1 Extent to which the event is 'distinctively Auckland'
2 Origin of event

3 Event frequency

4 Time of year

5 Extent to which the event can be used to develop local industries

6 Potential for the event to generate long-term legacy benefits

Return on regional investment

This strategy advocates the use of a new measurement and evaluation methodology developed specifically for Auckland called return on regional investment (RORI).

RORI is a useful tool for making investment decisions, as well as measuring and evaluating outcomes and attributes — including those delivered by a major event. Because ATEED is investing in events on behalf of the region, it is appropriate to assess major event return on investment at a regional level.

RORI is calculated as the Gross Domestic Product (GDP) impact caused by the event (the return), divided by the amount of money sourced from Auckland to run the event (the investment). All sources of event income should be considered, including local and central government funding, private sector sponsorship and sales of tickets to local residents and businesses.

Return on Regional Investment (RORI)

Money from outside Auckland − Total regional event investment = True net benefit

CLASSIFICATION SYSTEM FOR EVENTS

A key part of the strategy process has been the development of a simple event classification system that can be used to understand the strengths and weaknesses of Auckland's current major events portfolio. The framework segments the event portfolio across two dimensions: geographic reach (international to local) and scale (large to small).

This segmentation provides a useful framework for describing and analysing a portfolio of events, and can be represented in a simple tabular format as shown below.

On average, economic benefits are likely to grow in an upwards and leftwards direction in the matrix, which have social and community outcomes to the right.

The purpose of this framework is not to strictly or prescriptively order events on the basis of economic impact, but rather to organise them into broad classes that are relevant at a strategic level.

Event classification matrix

Productive ←——————————————→ Consumptive
International ←——————————————→ Local

		TIER A	TIER B	TIER C	TIER D
		Recognised international event; 2 000+ international nights; or strong export focus high international media coverage	Not tier A; and National showcase event; or 10%+ of attendees are visitors; or more than 2 000 visitor nights	Not tier A or B event; and mainly Auckland residents; and regional showcase event; or <80% local participants	Not a tier A, B or C event
Large ↑	LEVEL 1	>50 000 visitor nights	>50 000 attendees	>50 000 attendees	>25 000 attendees
↓	LEVEL 2	10 000 – 50 000 visitor nights	10 000 – 50 000 attendees	10 000 – 50 000 attendees	5 000 – 25 000 attendees
Small	LEVEL 3	<10 000 visitor nights	<10 000 attendees	<10 000 attendees	<5 000 attendees

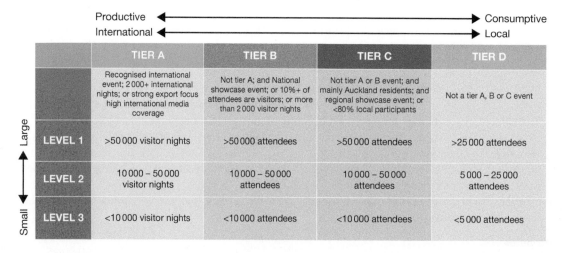

STRATEGIC FRAMEWORK

The event classification matrix can be simplified into the following quadrants:

• mega events — A1

• economic events — A2 and A3

• major social events — B1 and C1

- niche events — B2, B3, C2, and C3
- local events — all Tier D events
- anchor events.

SIMPLIFIED EVENT CLASSIFICATION MATRIX

	TIER A	TIER B	TIER C	TIER D
LEVEL 1	Mega events	Major social events / Major social anchors		Local events
LEVEL 2	Economic events* / Economic anchors	Niche events		
LEVEL 3				

*Economic events also have the ability to deliver social and community outcomes.

ANCHOR EVENTS

Anchor events are the social and economic pillars of a city's event portfolio. They are typically large, regular events with distinctive qualities that cities become known for. It is important to distinguish between social anchors — events that generate significant social capital; and economic anchors — events that attract new ...money into the economy

All anchor events (both social and economic) must have the following properties:

- be distinctively Auckland i.e. they must be consistent with Auckland's brand, or inform the brand
- be regular (ideally annual)
- have mass appeal.

In addition, a social anchor must involve at least 200,000 people (participants and spectators), but is not subject to any economic thresholds. Social anchors will generally be large B1 or C1 events due to their scale, and will therefore have strong consumptive properties. These events will play a key role in enhancing quality of life and make Auckland a more attractive place for talented people to live.

To be an economic anchor an event must generate an immediate Return on Regional Investment (RORI) of at least NZ$5 million. Economic anchors will almost invariably be Tier A events due to the required RORI. Some economic anchors will also deliver significant social benefits (for example, Australia's Melbourne Cup and Boxing Day cricket test), but it will be rare for social anchors to deliver significant economic benefits.

SUMMARY OF CURRENT SITUATION

All anchor events (both social and economic) must have the following properties:

Applying this new framework to Auckland's current major events programme highlights the following strengths and weaknesses:

- Auckland has a good portfolio of major social events, including many of the types of events a global city would be expected to host. Pasifika and Lantern festivals are currently the only major social events that are large enough, and distinctive enough, to be considered social anchors.
- Auckland's current investment in major social events is adequate but not excessive. It would not be feasible to reduce investment in these events without undermining the social benefits they deliver.
- Over recent years Auckland has done well to attract one-off economic events, for example the 2012 Volvo Ocean Race. This proactive approach must continue.
- Auckland's current investment in regular Tier A events is inadequate. Auckland only has four regular major economic events and whilst these are important pillars of Auckland's portfolio, none currently generate sufficient returns to be considered economic anchors.
- Only one-third of the regular events Auckland invests in are currently major social or major economic events — the remainder are niche and local events.

Source: Auckland Tourism, Events and Economic Development Ltd n.d.

QUESTIONS

1 Briefly discuss two of the main 'benefit streams' that the 2011–21 Major Events Strategy has identified as flowing from major events.

2 Briefly discuss the key challenges Auckland faced as it sought to implement the 2011–21 Major Events Strategy.

3 Why did Auckland see the need to develop a classification scheme for its events?

4 What is meant by the term 'anchor events' and what form(s) did these events take?

5 With respect to the 2011–21 Major Events Strategy did Auckland have a balanced portfolio of events? What actions did it propose to reshape its event portfolio?

6 What KPIs did Auckland propose to use to measure the success of its 2011–21 Major Events Strategy, and can you think of any other KPI that might have been relevant for this destination?

7 How did Auckland create an organisational structure capable of ensuring the implementation of the 2011–21 Major Events Strategy?

8 Briefly discuss the role of stakeholder cooperation in the implementation of Auckland's 2011–21 Major Events Strategy.

REFERENCES

Auckland Tourism, Events and Economic Development n.d., 'Auckland's Major Events Strategy', pp. 6–19.

Australian Capital Territory Government 2017, '2025 Major Events Strategy for the ACT', www.tourism.act.gov.au/wp-content/uploads/2017/09/2025_Major_Events_Strategy_for_the_ACT_WEB.pdf, viewed 23 April 2020.

Boey, C 2016 'The goldmine that is China's MICE market', *TTGmice*, 3 June, www.ttgmice.com/2016/06/03/the-goldmine-that-is-chinas-mice-market, viewed 23 April 2020.

BOP Consulting 2016, 'Edinburgh festivals 2015 impact study: final report', www.edinburghfestivalcity.com/assets/000/001/964/Edinburgh_Festivals_-_2015_Impact_Study_Final_Report_original.pdf?1469537463, viewed 23 April 2020.

Business Events Council of Australia 2015, 'The value of business events to Australia', www.businesseventscouncil.org.au/files/View_Report.pdf, viewed 23 April 2020.

Business Events Industry Strategy Group 2008, 'A national business events strategy for Australia 2020', www.businesseventscouncil.org.au/files/BES%20full%20doc%20Nov08.pdf, viewed 8 June 2020.

Business Wales 2018, 'Events calendar 2018', https://businesswales.gov.wales/tourism/events-calendar-2018, viewed 27 August 2018.

City of Sydney 2020, 'Grants and sponsorship program guidelines January 2020', www.cityofsydney.nsw.gov.au/__data/assets/pdf_file/0003/296643/grants-sponsorship-guidelines.pdf, viewed 23 April 2020.

Council of the City of the Gold Coast 2018, 'GC2018 benefits — working draft v.21 June 2018', www.goldcoast.qld.gov.au/documents/bf/gc2018-benefits.pdf, viewed 29 August 2018.

Creative Victoria 2018, 'Touring Victoria', https://creative.vic.gov.au/funding-and-support/programs/regional-development-and-touring/touring-victoria, viewed 2 September 2018.

Destination NSW 2016, 'Regional Flagship Events Program 2017', https://www.destinationnsw.com.au/wp-content/uploads/2016/09/Regional-Flagship-Events-Program-2017-Factsheet.pdf, accessed 23 April 2020.

Destination NSW 2017, 'The NSW regional events strategy and action plan 2017–2021', www.meetinnsw.com.au/sites/default/files/2019-04/The-nsw-regional-conference-strategy-and-action-plan.pdf, accessed 23 April 2020.

Destination NSW 2018, 'Record attendance at Vivid Sydney 2017', www.destinationnsw.com.au/news-and-media/media-releases/record-attendance-vivid-sydney-2017, viewed 1 September 2018.

Destination NSW 2020, 'Regional event fund', www.destinationnsw.com.au/tourism/business-development-resources/funding-and-grants/regional-event, accessed 23 April 2020.

Destination Tamworth 2018, 'Hats off to country', www.destinationtamworth.com.au/Events/Music/hats-off-to-country, viewed 23 April 2020.

Dickson, T, Benson, A & Blackman, D 2011, 'Developing a framework for evaluating Olympic and Paralympic legacies', *Journal of Sport Tourism*, volume 16, no. 4, pp. 285–302.

Events ACT 2018, 'ACT Event Fund 2019, funding round guide for applicants', www.events.act.gov.au/images/assets/documents/ACT-Event-Fund-2019-Information-and-Guidelines.pdf, viewed 2 September 2018.

Events Management Queensland 2018, 'About us', www.goldcoastevents.com.au/about-us, viewed 2 September 2018.

Events Tasmania 2006, 'Role of research in Events Tasmania', www.eventstasmania.com, viewed 3 February 2010.

Events Tasmania 2015, 'Tasmanian Government events strategy 2015–2020', www.eventstasmania.com, viewed 5 May 2020.

Events Tasmania 2020, 'Grants program', www.eventstasmania.com/funding/grants, viewed 23 April 2020.

Georges River Council 2018, 'Events strategy 2018–2020', www.georgesriver.nsw.gov.au/StGeorge/media/Documents/Council/Publications/Event-Strategy-2018-2020-web.pdf, viewed 4 February 2020.

Getz, D 2005, *Event management and event tourism*, 2nd ed., Cognizant Communication, New York.

Getz, D 2016, 'Revised event portfolio models', https://donaldgetzprofessor.files.wordpress.com/2016/10/donald-getz-event-portfolio-paper-oct-2016.pdf, viewed 14 September 2016.

Global Business Travel Association 2015, 'Market assessment of MICE business travel in China', www3.gbta.org/l/5572/2015-10-21/2vkzf2, viewed 23 April 2020.

Harris, R & Allen, J 2002, *Regional event management handbook*, Australian Centre for Event Management, University of Technology, Sydney.

International Congress and Convention Association 2018, 'ICCA statistics report: country & city rankings — public abstract', www.iccaworld.org/dcps/doc.cfm?docid=2321, accessed 23 April 2020.

Jago, L, Chalip, L, Brown, G, Mules, T & Ali, S 2003, 'Building events into destination branding: insights from experts', *Event Management*, vol. 8, no.1, pp. 3–14

Liu, Y 2014, 'Cultural events and cultural tourism development: lessons from the European capitals of culture', *Planning Studies*, vol. 22, issue 3, pp. 498–514.

Matheson, C 2010, 'Legacy planning, regeneration and events: the Glasgow 2014 Commonwealth Games local economy', *The Journal of the Local Economy Policy Unit*, vol. 25, issue 1, pp. 10–23.

Meares, J 2014, 'Vivid Festival's path to success proves illuminating', *The Sydney Morning Herald*, 17 May, www.smh.com.au/entertainment/vivid-festivals-path-to-success-proves-illuminating-20140516-38fee.html, viewed 28 August 2018.

Melbourne Convention Bureau 2018, 'Case study: 56th Institute of Electrical and Electronic Engineers Conference on Decision and Control', www.melbournecb.com.au/blog/post/ieee-cdc-case-study-released, viewed 2 September 2018.

Mudgee Vine 2018, 'Calendar of events', www.mudgeewine.com.au/events-calendar/, viewed 28 August 2018.

Northern Territory Business Events 2018, 'Northern Territory Business Events Support Fund', www.ntconventions.com.au/en/why-the-nt/event-support, viewed 2 September 2018.

Northern Territory Major Events Company 2018, 'Events funding', www.ntmajorevents.com.au/events-funding, viewed 2 September 2018.

Parkes Elvis Festival 2018, 'Festival history', www.parkeselvisfestival.com.au/about/festival-history, viewed 29 August 2018.

Pham, T, Jin, C, Naranpanawa, A, Bandaralage, A & Carmignana, F 2018, 'Economic Impacts of the Gold Coast Commonwealth Games', www.embracing2018.com/sites/default/files/gc-2018-economic-benefits-griffith-uni-report.pdf, viewed 28 August 2018.

Smith, A 2012, *Events and urban regeneration: the strategic use of events to revitalise cities*, Routledge, London.

South Australian Tourism Commission n.d., 'Event funding and support', https://tourism.sa.gov.au/events-and-industry/events-south-australia/event-funding-and-support, viewed 23 April 2020.

Sport and Recreation Victoria 2018a, 'Commonwealth Games legacy', www.sport.vic.gov.au/our-work/events/commonwealth-games-legacy, viewed 29 August 2018.

Sport and Recreation Victoria 2018b, 'Significant sporting events program', http://sport.vic.gov.au/grants-and-funding/our-grants/significant-sporting-events-program, viewed 2 September 2018.

Tourism and Events Queensland 2011, *The Grants Guide*, https://teq.queensland.com, viewed 20 January 2020.

Tourism and Events Queensland 2017, 'Tourism events strategy 2025', https://teq.queensland.com/about-teq-new/plans-and-strategies/events-strategy-2025, viewed 23 April 2020.

Tourism and Events Queensland 2018, 'Organisational structure', www.teq.queensland.com/about-teq-new/our-organisation/organisation-structure, viewed 28 August 2018.

Tourism Australia 2020, 'Major events calendar', www.australia.com/en-in/events/australias-events-calendar.html, viewed 13 February 2020.

Tourism Tasmania 2020, 'Event support', www.tourismtasmania.com.au/marketing/events-support, viewed 23 April 2020.

Tourism Western Australia 2017, 'Resources for event holders', www.tourism.wa.gov.au/events/Event-sponsorship/Pages/Resources-for-event-holders.aspx, viewed 4 September 2018.

Tourism Western Australia 2018, 'Event sponsorship', www.tourism.wa.gov.au/events/Event-sponsorship/Pages/Event-sponsorship.aspx, viewed 2 September 2018.

Upper Hunter Shire Council 2018, 'Scone — horse capital of Australia', www.upperhunter.nsw.gov.au/our-shire/moving-to-our-shire/scone-horse-capital-of-australia.aspx, viewed 28 August 2018.

Victorian Multicultural Commission 2020, 'Multicultural grants', https://www.multiculturalcommission.vic.gov.au/multicultural-grants, viewed 5 May 2020.

VisitScotland 2015, 'Scotland the Perfect Stage: Scotland's Events Strategy 2015–2025', www.visitscotland.org, viewed 27 August 2018.

VisitScotland 2018, 'Scotland's future themed years unveiled — programme extended until 2022', www.visitscotland.org, viewed 28 August 2018.

Visit Victoria 2018, 'How to apply for the Regional Events Fund', https://corporate.visitvictoria.com/events/regional-events/regional-event-fund, viewed, 2 September 2018.

Vivid Sydney 2018, 'About Vivid Sydney', www.vividsydney.com/about-vivid-sydney, viewed 2 September 2018.

Vivid Sydney 2019, 'Five days to glow: Vivid Sydney 2019', www.vividsydney.com/sites/default/files/2019-05/Five-Days-To-Glow_Vivid-Sydney-2019.pdf, viewed 20 January 2020.

Welsh Assembly Government 2010, 'Event Wales: a major events strategy for Wales 2010–2020', https://gov.wales/sites/default/files/publications/2019-06/event-wales-a-major-events-strategy-for-wales-2010-to-2020.pdf, viewed 23 April 2020.

Wu, J & Xiao, X 2012, 'Pattern and Policies of Mainland China's MICE Industry', *Chinese Studies*, vol. no. 2, pp. 5–8.

ACKNOWLEDGEMENTS

Photo: © Derek Trask / Getty Images

Figure 10.2: © Destination NSW

Table 10.1: © Published by VisitScotland / EventScotland in 2015

Table 10.2: © Welsh Assembly Government 2010

Figure 10.4: © Tourism and Events Queensland 2018

Photo: © Genevieve Vallee / Alamy Stock Photo

Extract: © Tourism and Events Queensland 2011

Table 10.7: © The International Congress and Convention Association www.iccaworld.org

Photo: © Gordon Bell / Shutterstock.com

Extract: © Melbourne Convention Bureau. '56th Institute of Electrical and Electronic Engineers Conference on Decision and Control 2017 Melbourne Australia'. Retrieved from https://assets.simple viewinc.com/simpleview/image/upload/v1/clients/melbourne/IEEE_Case_Study_Flyer_FA4_86fc7a0a-4fe1-4fc9-ba37-421883cecd53.pdf [online source].

Figure 10.7: © Events Tasmania

Case study: Auckland Tourism, Events and Economic Development. Reproduced by permission.

CHAPTER 11

Risk management

LEARNING OBJECTIVES

After studying this chapter, you should be able to:

11.1 define the concept of risk

11.2 discuss the importance of risk management in event settings

11.3 discuss approaches to developing a risk management culture in event organisations

11.4 identify and describe each step in the risk management process

11.5 develop a basic risk management plan for an event.

Introduction

Managing risk is a task that all event organisers face. The risk management process is designed to address this issue systematically by providing a means by which risks can be identified, assessed and treated so that they are maintained at an acceptable level. The process also requires that the effectiveness of those strategies employed to treat risks are monitored, and revised/changed if necessary. A level of alertness is also necessary during an event's planning and delivery cycle to ensure unexpected, or new, risks are quickly identified and addressed.

This chapter begins by defining the concept of risk, before moving on to discuss the importance of risk management in event settings. The steps in the risk management process are then identified and described. The chapter concludes with a case study that showcases how the risk management process was employed to deal with a specific risk management challenge at a public festival.

11.1 What is risk?

LEARNING OBJECTIVE 11.1 Define the concept of risk.

Risk is essentially anything that can affect an organisation's ability to achieve its objectives. While risk is often conceived of by event organisers in terms of safety and security, there are a range of additional dimensions to risk. These extend to such matters as financial risk (for example, budget overruns, cash flow problems); reputational risk (for example, negative publicity); compliance risk (for example, failure to adhere to permit conditions); scheduling risks (for example, event site not operational by the event date); legal risks (for example, litigation due to cancellation by headline performer); technological risks (for example, failure of key equipment such as data projectors, software programs or generators) and environmental risks (for example, bad weather or extreme heat). While this chapter focuses on safety and security, it should be kept in mind that event organisers have an obligation to identify, assess and treat all forms of risk as part of their overall planning efforts.

11.2 Risks in event settings

LEARNING OBJECTIVE 11.2 Discuss the importance of risk management in event settings.

Event organisers have a duty of care under Work Health and Safety legislation in Australia, and similar legislation in other countries, to manage the risks to health and safety of everyone (employees, volunteers, suppliers, contractors, sponsors, performers, event attendees) attending a venue or site during an event's setup, conduct and shutdown. This responsibility is shared with that of other organisations that are providing services to an event such as venues and suppliers. By exercising this duty of care, the intent must always be one of reducing risks to as low as reasonably practicable. The consequences of not doing so can lead to significant negative outcomes both for an event and its organisers, and its various stakeholders, as is evidenced in the examples provided in figure 11.1.

FIGURE 11.1	Examples of the consequences of inadequate risk management at events

Food poisoning outbreak at Newcastle Street Spice Festival (UK)

Dozens [of people who were] . . . struck down by food poisoning have received a joint pay-out of over £400 000 following an outbreak at a Newcastle festival. An estimated 12 000 people went to the event between February 28 and March 2 at the city's Centre for Life with over 400 visitors reporting symptoms of gastric illness . . . (extract).

Source: Hutchinson 2017.

Lorne festival victims reach settlement (Australia)

Falls Festival organisers have reached a settlement with six members of a multi-million-dollar class action over a crowd crush at the event in 2016. Ash Sounds Pty Ltd have agreed to payouts for the festivalgoers who were suing for 'significant injury' after a stampede broke out at the Lorne event (extract).

Source: Kolovos and Thomson 2019.

Tent collapse kills 14 (India)

The large tent under which [locals in the Barmer district of Rajasthan] had assembled collapsed . . . killing 14 and injuring 50 others. A local magistrate told Reuters news agency that several people were electrocuted by live electricity wires. . . Rajasthan's disaster management minister questioned why the electrical generators were left on despite the heavy rains (extract).

Source: Watkins 2019.

TABLE 11.1 Examples of potential risks associated with the conduct of events

Compliance	Emergencies	Planning
• Breach of noise restrictions • Failure to adhere to legal/regulatory/permit obligations • Lack of adherence to legal requirements as regards access for people with disabilities • Number of attendees exceeding site/venue limits • Copyright breaches	• Acts of terrorism • Lack of unobstructed access for emergency vehicles • Adverse/extreme weather or events, for example, storms, bush fires and floods • Lack of fire safety precautions and fire-fighting equipment	• Poor financial planning and/or budget forecasting • Inadequate insurance coverage • Absence of contingency/emergency/traffic management plans • Absence of a risk management culture within an event organising body • Reputational damage resulting from poor planning decisions in one or more areas • Unclear responsibilities/lines of communication in the event of a risk occurring

Health and safety	Venue/site design/layout, infrastructure and equipment	Operations
• Lack of cool down/chill-out areas heightening risks from drug/alcohol consumption by attendees • Food poisoning/poor food-handling practices • Absence of high-visibility clothing/equipment necessary for the safe performance of tasks, for example, installation of lighting, traffic directing • Medical emergencies, including drug and alcohol issues, injuries, severe allergic reactions, heat stroke or exhaustion, life-threatening events, and mass casualty incidents, which could overwhelm local health resources • Outdoor site hazards, for example, bites/stings, heat stroke, bush fires and proximity to water bodies and dangerous terrain (cliffs, steep inclines) • Lack of care with hazardous materials • Lack of adherence by stallholders to safety guidelines in areas such as electricity and gas management • Prescribed safe work methods not being adhered to	• Collapse of temporary structures such as marquees, stages or seating areas • Equipment failure, damage or loss • Venue/site damage • Damaging underground services during site setup • Inadequate site services such as toilets, shade, waste management and water impacting health and safety of attendees. • Potential for electrical shocks/electrocution from poorly installed wiring • Gas leaks/explosions • Inadequate site lighting/emergency lighting • Failure of an amusement ride • Lack of storage resulting in equipment/materials being scattered in areas accessible to attendees creating trip hazards • Failure to isolate areas of plant and equipment, or locations where dangerous products are stored • Poor site/venue layout and design leading to 'pinch points' that restrict attendee movement in emergencies	• Inadequate staff identification making it difficult for attendees to identify staff in case of an emergency • Non-arrival of performers/speakers or deliveries of goods • Lost children • Larger than expected crowds and the associated potential for crowd crushes • Electricity outages/surges • Damage or injury resulting from event program elements, for example, fireworks, aerial performances, shows involving vehicles • Poor crowd behaviour, for example, throwing objects on to the field of play/stage invasions, drunkenness • Security breaches, for example, fence jumpers • Insufficient security/police presence for scale of event

(continued)

TABLE 11.1 *(continued)*

Health and safety	Venue/site design/layout, infrastructure and equipment	Operations
• Inability of staff/security staff/volunteers to adequately respond to risk situations due to fatigue/inadequate training • Inadequate staff/volunteer/ contractor training in areas such as emergency management, manual handling and risks inherent in the use of the site/venue	• Absence of signage to highlight dangers/areas off-limits to attendees and emergency exits, and the presence of on-site facilities and services, for example, first aid, water stations	• Communication breakdowns due to cultural/language barriers or communication equipment failures

The effort required to manage risk will depend on the type and scale of the event. Contrast, for example, a large-scale sporting event such as an Olympic Games, with a small-scale conference, wedding or product launch. While acknowledging this, the discussion here seeks to take a comprehensive look at risk in event settings, which can be contextualised as required.

The types of risk events present at different phases in the event planning and delivery process — pre-event, event and shutdown — can be many and varied as table 11.1 shows, and as a result the process of seeking to eliminate, reduce or mitigate risk can be quite complex.

11.3 Developing a risk management culture

LEARNING OBJECTIVE 11.3 Discuss approaches to developing a risk management culture in event organisations.

Without an organisational culture attuned to the need for effective risk management, the effectiveness of efforts in this area are likely to be severely compromised or tokenistic in nature. To develop a risk-aware culture requires a strong managerial commitment reflected in such actions as allocating adequate financial and staff resources to the task of risk management; employing specialist risk manager(s); ensuring risk-related issues are regularly discussed with staff; undertaking staff training in the processes required to manage risk in their areas of responsibility; including safety requirements in contracts with suppliers; requiring the preparation of appropriate risk-related documentation; and placing a high priority on safety in decision-making where conflicting agendas might exist. It is sound practice to underpin, and guide, actions in this area, with an event risk management policy (see figure 11.2).

In addition to developing a risk management culture, effective risk management also requires that a proactive and structured approach is used to guide efforts in this area. Such an approach serves to avoid an over-reliance on subjective decision-making and facilitates efforts at continuous improvement through ensuring insights gained from one event can be incorporated into risk planning in future events. It is to this type of approach, broadly based on the International Standard for Risk Management — 31000:2018 (International Organization for Standardization 2018), that this chapter now turns its attention.

FIGURE 11.2 Sample event risk policy

• We are committed to ensuring the health and safety of all participants in the staging of our event.
• All stakeholders participate through consultation to deliver a safe and successful event, each sharing responsibility for one another.
• We will endeavour to identify and manage all risks/hazards and where possible eliminate them in our workplace.
• We will work with all regulatory and all other authorities to ensure compliance with relevant legislation.
• Where no guidelines exist, we will actively work with our partners and stakeholders to achieve best practices.
• The ultimate goal is to stage a successful event with no harm to people or damage to the environment.

Source: Wynn-Moylan 2017, p. 52.

11.4 The risk management process

The process of risk management, which is outlined in the International Standard for Risk Management (ISO 31000:2018), involves a series of sequential steps: establishing the scope, context and criteria; assessment; risk treatment; and recording and reporting (see figure 11.3). Each step in this process is subject to communication and consultation, along with monitoring and review. The following discussion examines the application of this process in event settings.

FIGURE 11.3   The risk management process

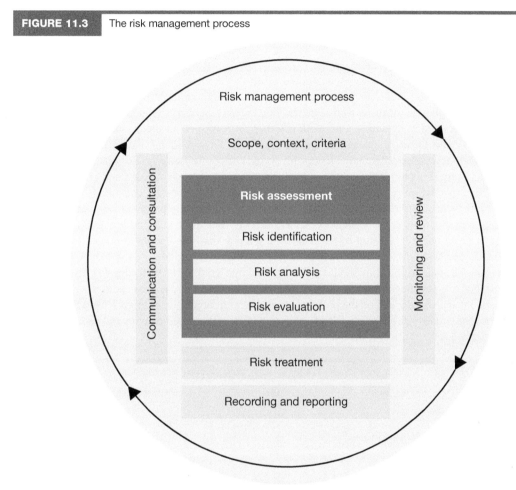

Source: International Organization for Standardization 2018.

Establishing the scope, context and criteria

At the outset of the risk management process it is important that event organisers have a clear understanding of the event for which risk management is being undertaken, including: its mission/purpose and objectives; program elements and activities, when these will be engaged in and by whom they will be undertaken; projected number and characteristics of attendees; proposed location, venue/site; existing event risk management culture and documentation; and financial and other resources that are available that impact the ability to engage in the risk management process. Additionally, external environments need to be assessed (that is, social, cultural, political, legal, regulatory, technological and economic) to establish if they present risk concerns. For example, how does the host community currently perceive the event and how could this impact its conduct? What laws are likely to impact the event? As regards this latter point, there are a multitude of laws and regulations relating to areas such as food handling, gas/electricity safety, work health and safety, dangerous goods, alcohol, fireworks and so on that could potentially be relevant in the context of a given event (see the legal considerations in event planning and management chapter). Event stakeholders also need to be identified and their needs and expectations determined (for example, event attendees/participants, spectators, local community, sponsors, venue/site owner, local/state/national government).

Decisions as to the types of risk that will be the focus of the risk management process need to be considered (for example, health and safety, compliance, reputational, financial). It can also be useful at this initial stage to quantify any specific outcomes that are sought, such as reductions in: levels of drunkenness/drug use; medical treatments/incidents; non-compliance to laws/regulations/contractual obligations by contractors/suppliers; and incidents of violence.

11.5 Risk assessment

LEARNING OBJECTIVE 11.5 Develop a basic risk management plan for an event.

Risk identification

In addition to the consultation process, which should result in the identification of a variety of potential risks associated with a given event, an event organiser should undertake their own independent research. This can be done through such means as web searches, keeping abreast of risk-related matters through trade magazines/newsletters and maintaining a network of other professionals in the events field upon whose expertise they can draw. Other practices that can be employed for risk identification purposes include: brainstorming sessions focused on potential risks with event staff or other stakeholders; reviews of existing event systems and processes to identify areas of weakness that might present risks; and a review of past incident and event evaluation reports. The employment of a risk management consultant, or the hiring of an experienced event safety officer, can also significantly strengthen the process of risk identification. By employing these practices event organisers can avoid costly mistakes, and possibly even legal action should injury or death occur as a result of not considering a risk that was known to others, or that could have been readily identified.

Once risks have been identified, they should then be placed into a risk register. To simplify this process, it is useful to categorise risks under broad headings, as was done in table 11.1. These headings will obviously be event dependent and will depend on the preferences of the event organiser. A large-scale outdoor event, for example, might employ an extensive list of categories due to the range of potential risks their event presents (see figure 11.4).

| **FIGURE 11.4** | Sample risk categories for use in a large-scale, outdoor event risk register |

- Traffic, parking and access
- Bump in/bump out
- Attendees/registrants/participants
- Staff/volunteers
- Contractors/suppliers
- Vendors and performers
- Hazardous substances/dangerous goods
- Alcohol, food and beverage
- Legal/compliance
- Signage
- Amenities
- Environment
- Noise
- Security
- Waste management
- Plant and equipment
- Materials handling
- Site/venue construction
- Field of play
- Amusement devices/rides
- Emergencies
- Power

It must be stressed that the process of risk identification is one that will continue throughout an event's planning and delivery cycle as new risks might emerge, or assessments of existing risks might alter over time due to changed circumstances (for example, changes in the law that impact the conduct of events).

Risk analysis

Once risks have been identified, the next step is to analyse them in terms of their likelihood and consequence. This can be done using qualitative, semi-qualitative and quantitative approaches. Of these approaches, the qualitative approach is the simplest to use as it employs written descriptions and non-numerical values, and it is this approach that is used here. Likelihood refers to the chance that something might happen while consequence is concerned with the resulting outcome(s) should a risk occur. Consequences can be limited in their nature, such as when an attendee requires medical attention for a minor injury, or they might have cascading and cumulative effects such as when food poisoning occurs at an event and results in attendee hospitalisation, negative media coverage, fines and legal action.

The descriptors commonly used when assessing the likelihood and consequences of a risk, range in the case of the former, from insignificant to catastrophic, and for the latter, from almost certain to rare. While there is no definitive way of defining these descriptors in event settings, the example provided in table 11.2, which relates to community-based public events, provides an indication of how to approach this task.

TABLE 11.2 **Consequence rating — qualitative measures of consequence or impact**

Rating	Descriptor	Explanation
1	Insignificant	Negligible financial loss (<$200 or 5% of event budget). No real disruption to event. No injury or first aid only. No impact on morale. No media or political attention. Some local complaints. No breach of legislation. Minor instance of environmental damage. Can be reversed immediately. Interruption to an event — minimal impact to participants/store holders/others.
2	Minor	Minor financial loss ($200–$500 or 5–10% of event budget). Minor financial disruption. Minor variation to budget. Minor medical attention. Negligible impact on morale. Some local media or political attention. Minor community concern. Below 5% of community affected. Minor breach of legislation. Minor impact to environment. Can be reversed in a short timeframe. Minor interruption to event with minor impact to participants/store holders/others.
3	Moderate	Moderate financial loss ($500–$1500 or 10–25% of event budget). Moderate impact to event operations. Moderate variation to budget. Significant injury requiring medical attention. Short term effect on morale. Significant media attention and public interest. Potential for adverse local media attention. 5–40% of community affected. Breach of legislation with penalties. Moderate impact to environment. Localised damage that has potential to spread and reversed with intensive efforts. Moderate interruption to event. Partial Event Emergency Plan action may be needed.
4	Significant	Major financial loss ($1500–$3000 or 25–50% of event budget). Major impact on event operations. Major variation to budget requiring additional funding for event and post event investigations/actions. Serious long-term injury. Temporary disablement. Significant impact on morale and business. Significant adverse media coverage and public interest. Long-term effect on reputation. 40–70% of community affected. Multiple breaches of legislation with penalties. Severe loss of environmental amenity, danger of continuing environmental damage. Major interruption to service delivery. Full or partial Event Emergency Plan action may be needed.
5	Catastrophic	Significant financial loss (>$3000 or 50% of event budget). Ceasing event operation. Significant financial impact during and post-event, major injury/disablement or death. Long-term effect on morale and future staging of the event. Adverse national media attention. Major embarrassment attention. Major breaches of legislation with max penalties. Major loss of environmental amenity — irrecoverable environmental damage. Full Event Emergency Plan action required.

Source: Alexandrina Council 2017, p. 11.

TABLE 11.3   Consequence rating — qualitative measures of consequence or impact

Rating	Descriptor	Explanation
A	Almost certain	Expected to occur at times of normal operations (more than once per year), 95% chance
B	Likely	Will occur at some stage based on previous incidents or in most circumstances (1–2 years), 75% to 95% chance
C	Possible	Not expected to occur but could under specific circumstances. Might occur (2–5 years), 25% to 75% chance
D	Unlikely	Conceivable but not likely to occur under normal operations — has occurred at some time (5–10 years), 5% to 25% chance
E	Rare	Only occurs in exceptional circumstances (>10 years), < 5% chance

Source: Alexandrina Council 2017, p. 11.

Risk evaluation

Once ratings have been established for the likelihood and consequence of the risks that have been identified, the next task is to determine an overall rating for them. This is achieved by using a risk analysis matrix, an example of which appears in figure 11.5. Depending on the rating (low, moderate, high or extreme) that results from this process, different management responses are suggested. These appear in the key at the bottom of figure 11.5. While it is difficult to effectively manage all health and safety risks at an event, event managers should be aware that not having the resources to manage a risk is not a viable defence should it occur under work health and safety legislation.

Risk treatment

Once risks have been identified, analysed and evaluated, treatments need to be developed. The options in this area are as follows.

- *Elimination.* If the risk is deemed too extreme it can be removed prior to an event's commencement.
- *Manage the likelihood of the risk.* Various strategies are available to event organisers to reduce the possibility of a risk occurring and impacting the planning and delivery of an event. These may, for example, involve: making changes to the layout/design of a venue/site; changing work practices or existing operational systems; undertaking staff/volunteer/contractor training; altering the way a performance was planned to take place; using an engineering solution such as installing a guardrail on the edge of a stage; and communicating risk reduction strategies to attendees to lessen, for example, such outcomes as dehydration and sunburn in hot weather.
- *Mitigate the consequences of a risk.* This involves developing responses that lessen the risk should it occur. For example, emergency or evacuation plans lessen the consequences of injury or death from the need to quickly move people out of a venue or site, while providing water and chill-out areas, and enlisting the assistance of volunteer groups such as Red Frogs, can assist in reducing the negative health effects of alcohol consumption.
- *Transfer the risk.* This can be achieved by passing on a risk to a third party. This can be done in several ways.
  - Insurance policies can be used to provide coverage for a number of potential risks, includingpersonal injury to a third party (for example, an attendee); negligence by the event organiser; venue and equipment damage; cancellation due to weather; non-attendance of a performer; and injuries to volunteers.
  - Contracts can be used to require contractors and suppliers to conform to risk management policies and practices, making payment conditional on their doing so.
  - Waivers offer the opportunity to transfer risks to event participants by informing them of the risks involved in an activity (for example, a bike race) and gaining their agreement that they accept these risks. These instruments, however, cannot be used to transfer an event organiser's duty of care to participants.
- *Accept a risk.* It might not be cost-effective to seek to treat or transfer a risk. Weather insurance, for example, can be very expensive and beyond the capacity of smaller outdoor events to afford. Another

example would be a decision not to install a second perimeter fence to deter fence jumpers at a festival. While this would make it easier for security staff to apprehend individuals that act in this way, and would deter such behaviour, the cost of installation when compared to the number of people potentially entering the site through this means might be viewed as having no economic benefit.

| FIGURE 11.5 | Qualitative risk analysis matrix |

Likelihood		Consequence				
		Insignificant	Minor	Moderate	Significant	Catastrophic
		1	2	3	4	5
A Almost certain	5	Moderate	Moderate	High	Extreme	Extreme
B Likely	4	Moderate	Moderate	High	High	Extreme
C Possible	3	Low	Moderate	Moderate	High	High
D Unlikely	2	Low	Low	Moderate	Moderate	High
E Rare	1	Low	Low	Moderate	Moderate	High

Key

Extreme: detailed research and management planning required at senior levels

High: senior management attention needed

Moderate risk: management responsibility must be specified

Low: manage by routine procedures

Source: Alexandrina Council 2017, p. 11.

Recording and reporting

The outcomes of the processes previously described, risk identification, assessment and treatment, underpin the writing of an event's risk management planning documents. Central among these documents are a risk register and a risk treatment plan and schedule. The former commonly groups risks by category and locates risks accordingly. Additionally, the likelihood of the risk occurring, and its associated consequence(s), are described and a rating is provided for each. Treatment options that are currently in place (if any) are also stated and an overall rating of the level of risk is given (see example in table 11.4). Following on from the completion of the risk register, a risk treatment plan and associated schedule are developed. This document identifies the potential treatment options that can be used to deal with each risk, along with which of these are preferred; identifies the overall risk rating prior to treatment and after treatment; states the outcome of the cost–benefit calculation associated with the risk (accept or reject); allocates responsibility for implementing the treatment(s); states when treatment options are to take place; and indicates how the implementation of the treatment(s) will be monitored (see example in figure 11.6).

In addition to a risk register and risk treatment plan and schedule, other documents and associated materials might be required, to ensure an event has a comprehensive risk management plan in place. Depending on the event concerned, these might include:

FIGURE 11.6 Sample risk treatment plan and schedule

Risk category	Risk	Treatment options	Preferred treatment options	Current risk rating	Risk rating after treatment	Cost-benefit analysis Accept/reject	Person responsible for implementation	Control schedule	Monitoring actions
Event infrastructure	Collapse of a marquee during event due to a storm/strong winds	1. Not install marquee 2. Signed certificate of structural integrity obtained from a certified engineer 3. Obtain from installers a wind speed, which once reached requires the marquee to be evacuated	2 and 3	4 + D = High	3 + E = Low	Accept	Site manager	Ongoing after erection	• Wind speed to be monitored during event • Signed certificate of structural integrity to be obtained and placed on file • Twice daily inspection of structure to identify any obvious structural issues, for example, fraying/slack guy ropes
Site services	Faulty electrical equipment and electrocutions of vendors, staffs or public	1. Vendors advised all installations to be in accordance with AS/NZS 3000:2000 Wiring Rules and the Code of Practice temporary installation on building and construction site 2. Only licensed and registered electricians to do installations 3. All leads and appliances to be tested and tagged at event 4. Earth leakage protection fitted and tested	1–4	5 + C = High	4 + D = Moderate	Accept	Site service coordinator in association with contracted electrician	Electrician to complete checklist for each vendor prior to event opening and to inspect all general event wiring and lighting	• Site electrician to conduct two site checks during event to ensure adherence to treatments. Particular attention is to be paid to overhead wiring, cabling and festoon and decorative lighting clearances

- staff/volunteer/contractor site safety induction plans and registers
- traffic and road closure management plan
- crowd management plan — required for larger events and are often best dealt with by professional consultants
- site evacuation/emergency risk management plans — to be developed in consultation, as necessary, with the venue/site owner and police, fire, rescue and ambulance services (see figure 11.7)
- staff identification/accreditation processes to control access to different site/venue areas
- risk-related checklists dealing with, for example, supplier/contractor regulatory compliance; legal/permit/licensing requirements; event zone operations (for example, stage, food area, bars); temporary structures (see example in figure 11.8); and site safety induction checklists/tests (see example in figure 11.9)
- emergency communication arrangements and protocols
- incident procedures and forms
- working with children and vulnerable peoples checks
- wind management plan
- first aid/medical plans
- copies of inspection/compliance certificates and checklists for rides/structures provided by operators/ installers (see temporary structure checklist example in figure 11.8)
- copies of contractor safe work methods statements. These are legal documents that identify the risks involved in high-risk construction work (for example, stage construction, building of backdrops, temporary performance spaces) and the safety measures that have been put in place to control them. Additionally, they must include implementation and monitoring details. An event organiser, or the risk management firm employed by them, has a legal requirement to ensure adherence to these statements
- asset registers — to ensure items such as radios and safety and protective clothing are returned post event.

FIGURE 11.7   Considerations in emergency risk management planning

- Arrangements for dealing with on-site emergencies that do not require outside help
- The notification of ambulance services, and the level of services available during the event
- The notification of local hospitals of the nature of the event, including expected patron profile, and possible medical problems
- Contact details for the officer in charge of the local police station, fire and rescue services, and the services that might be required of them
- Contact details of event managers, promoters and the event management centre
- Effective means of communicating with event patrons that do not rely on potentially overloaded mobile phone networks
- The identification and availability of the types of heavy equipment that may be required in an emergency
- The road network, including access for vehicles to the first aid site
- The official parking areas set aside for emergency vehicles
- The provision of unrestricted entrance and exit routes from the site for emergency vehicles
- A grid-type venue and environs plan, which is made available to all emergency agencies as well as appropriate event staff
- Specific arrangements to hand over control to police and emergency services if required
- An evacuation plan

FIGURE 11.8   Sample checklist for use when assessing temporary structures

The following checklist identifies the elements requiring checking prior to the facility being used.
1. Anchorages are adequate and holding fast.
2. Describe the soil type and identify ground-holding parameters.
3. Wall and roof bracing is installed and adequately tensioned.
4. All ropes or tensioned straps are in good order and correctly fastened.

5. Fabric is tensioned and not prone to ponding.
6. Exits are correctly identified and not obstructed.
7. Exposed ropes and stakes are identified and will not be a hazard to the public.
8. All locking pins and bolts are in place and correctly tensioned.
9. All structural supports are sound:
   – Fabric has no unrepaired tears.
   – Flooring is even and there are no tripping hazards.
   – Walls are adequately secured.
   – Rope and pole tent has its full complement of side uprights, anchor stakes, pulley blocks and guy ropes.
10. Rope and pole tent hoists are secure and can only be released by an authorised person.

Source: Government of Western Australia Department of Health 2009, p. 118.

TABLE 11.4   **Sample risk register document**

Risk category	Risk	Con-sequence	Likelihood	Existing controls	Con-sequence rating	Likeli-hood rating	Level of risk
Event infrastructure	Collapse of a marquee during event due to storm/strong winds	• Injury to attendees/performer-s/staff • Negative news coverage • Legal action	Unlikely	• Employment of a specialist marquee installation company to install marquee	5	D	High
Site services	Faulty electrical equipment	• Potential for electro-cution of vendors, staff or attendees • Negative news coverage • Legal action	Possible	• Vendors instructed pre-event that all installations are to be in accordance with AS/NZS 3000:2000 Wiring Rules and the Code of Practice for temporary installation on building and construction sites	5	C	High

These plans, registers, checklists and so on also serve as proof that a systematic approach to the task of risk management was in place and was being implemented should there be an incident. Event safety officers, appointed by the event organiser, commonly perform much of the oversight role in larger public events to ensure the implementation of an event's risk management plan. Their responsibilities, depending on the nature of the event concerned, extend to:

• the operation of safety elements, equipment and systems including fire suppression equipment, exit signs and emergency lights
• establish a direct communications model for general and urgent notifications
• the establishment and operation of evacuation procedures
• the safety of barriers and exits

- the control of the use of naked flame in theatrical productions
- the exclusion of the public from unsafe areas
- the keeping, testing and storage of flammable material or explosive items and equipment, the ignition of fireworks and the discharge of pistols or other shooting devices in a safe and responsible manner, to the extent that is not required by any other act or regulations
- the availability of specified drinking water facilities
- the location and designation and operation of passageways and exits
- the availability of specified public toilet facilities and the condition of those facilities
- the safe installation of temporary utilities such as power, water, gas and cooking facilities
- the availability of required crowd controllers confirming that relevant documentation is displayed on prescribed temporary structures
- the availability of specified fire suppression equipment
- adequate anchoring of temporary structures including marquees
- the availability of adequate overhead lighting after daylight hours
- access for disabled persons and emergency services
- the availability of specified first aid facilities
- the safe operation of amusement rides
- the availability of specified temporary handrails, balustrades, stairs landings and the like for areas that are more than 1 metre above the surface beneath (City of Greater Geelong 2020).

FIGURE 11.9   Volunteer safety induction questionnaire — Illawarra Folk Festival

Questionnaire

1. As a NEW Volunteer (and you are yet to register and receive your volunteer tag) who should you report to when you arrive at the festival for the first time? HINT: See Page 2 of Emergency Plan *
   - Security
   - Your Team Leader
   - Volunteer Registration tent at the Festival Entry
   - Other Volunteers
2. As a registered Volunteer, who should you report to at the beginning of your working shift? HINT: See Page 2 of Emergency Plan *
   - Security
   - Your Team Leader
   - Volunteer Registration tent at the Festival Entry
   - Another Volunteer
3. If you witness an incident whilst volunteering at the festival, what should you do? HINT: See Page 3 of Emergency Plan *
   - Panic
   - Tell the closest person
   - Report it to your team leader or shift manager
   - Ignore it
4. If you see a fire what would you do? HINT: See Page 3 of Emergency Plan *
   - Call Security
   - Pour a bucket of water over it
   - If skilled, put it out and report it to your team leader, otherwise report it to the shift manager
   - Leave it for someone else to look after
5. What is good practice to reduce the risk of manual handling injuries? *
   - Reduce bending, twisting and/or reaching movements
   - Increase load to get the job done quicker
   - Hold object far away from your body
   - All of the above
6. In response to an incident, how would you identify team leaders or venue managers? HINT: see Page 2 of Emergency Plan *
   - Ask the nearest person
   - Ask Security
   - Ask at the bar
   - Look for a person with blue or red vest

Source: Illawarra Folk Festival 2020.

Consultation and communication

The consultation process is the foundation of risk management. While not all risk management starts with consultation, talking about risk issues is a fundamental step in starting an open and trusting relationship with stakeholders — venue, site owner, suppliers, contractors, police, local councils, insurance companies, government agencies, local communities, staff and so on. This process will help identify and assess risks, allow access to different viewpoints and types of expertise, and assist in ensuring risk planning efforts are constantly reviewed and updated as necessary. Acting in this way also fosters mutual understanding of risk matters among stakeholder groups.

The process of consultation should not stop, as figure 11.3 indicates, with discussions at the commencement of the event risk management process but should continue as required throughout the process. For example, unexpected risks can be identified during the event planning and delivery process that might require further consultation, or induction safety briefings with a supplier or contractor staff may identify issues that their employers had not adequately addressed in their previously submitted risk management plans.

Once the initial process of consultation is complete it is up to the event organiser to make decisions and set directions that will steer their risk management efforts. In large-scale events that present a multitude of risks, consideration should be given to establishing a central command structure comprising the organiser(s) and key response agencies (for example, police, fire and rescue, traffic and ambulance) to facilitate communication when incidents occur.

Once a risk management plan has been developed, it is critical that it be communicated to those individuals/organisations responsible for carrying it out (for example, staff, security/crowd controllers, volunteers, cleaners) so they are clear on their personal roles and responsibilities, as well as those whose cooperation is required for the plan to be successful (for example, contractors and attendees). This can be achieved through such mechanisms as pre-event meetings; direct provision of risk-related information in hard copy or soft copy form; inclusion of risk responsibilities in contracts; placement of electronic notice boards at event venues/sites; and stage presentations directly to an audience.

Monitoring and review

Monitoring

Once implemented, an event's risk management plan needs to be monitored to ensure that risk treatments are being implemented. To ensure this occurs, individuals with responsibilities for this task are noted in treatment plans and schedules (as previously shown in figure 11.6), along with the form monitoring practices are to take. Contractors and others with risk-related responsibilities should also be required to monitor, and report, on their risk management efforts to the event organiser, or event risk manager, as appropriate. Checklists, such as those identified in the previous section, can be particularly useful for this task.

In instances where treatments are not being followed, an event organiser or the event's risk/safety manager, should be immediately advised and corrective actions taken. Such instances should then be recorded so that they can be included in the review process. Additionally, those charged with the monitoring task, should be alerted to, and take appropriate actions when, treatments prove ineffective or where unexpected risks arise that were not foreseen. It should also be kept in mind that where treatments fail, it is often for multiple reasons. For example, let's take the hypothetical example of a young girl who is injured when she is hit by a car participating in a car show that is a component of a multi-day festival. For the purposes of the exercise it will be assumed that the only treatment intended to prevent such an incident was an instruction to drivers that they needed to have their cars parked in a designated area by 8 am. This requirement had been sent in an email but did not require a response. Let's further assume that the incident occurred at 10 am (one hour after the event commenced) when a participant in the car show drove through the crowd to reach the designated area. Under such a circumstance the event organiser could reasonably be argued to be at least partially at fault as they did not have a treatment(s) in place for cars that arrived late, something that could reasonably have been foreseen, and had not had written confirmation from participants that they understood and would comply with the requirement to be parked by 8 am. Further, the event's staff, or security, should have been alert enough to identify the problem and act to stop the driver either before, or shortly after, they entered the site.

Review

Upon completion of the shutdown phase of an event, a time should be allocated for a review of the risk management process. This will involve examining any incident/injury reports (see example in figure 11.10), police statistics (for example, arrests, exclusions, incidents in surrounding areas caused by departing attendees), community complaints (for example, noise, traffic) and damage reports resulting from the event. It will also require the event organiser to conduct debrief meetings with relevant stakeholders (for example, venue, senior event staff, event risk management/safety officer, volunteers, police, security firms, first aiders, contractors, suppliers, local council). Assumptions underpinning the way some risks were rated might also need to be revised. Information gained in this way can be used to refine or alter current practices, create new treatments for unexpected risks that arose and provide feedback and recommendations to stakeholders. Insights gained during this stage in the risk management process should also be used to compile a report for future reference.

FIGURE 11.10 Sample incident report form

Incident details

Incident type

Please refer to the guide to work health and safety incident notification or electrical safety incident notification web page for assistance.

This is to notify of a: ☐ death ☐ serious injury ☐ serious illness ☐ dangerous incident serious electrical incident ☐ dangerous electrical event

Provide an explanation of the type of incident using the categories on the **guide to work health and safety incident notification or electrical safety incident notification web page** *(e.g. a category of 'serious injury' is 'immediate treatment for serious head injury'):*

Incident date, time and location

Date of incident:	Incident address:
Time of incident:	Postcode:

Describe the specific location of the incident *(e.g. aisle 3, plant operation room, tower crane the Elizabeth Street entrance side of the site.)*

Description of the incident *Please provide as much detail as possible, for instance: the events that led to the incident; the work being undertaken when the incident happend; the overall action, exposure or event that best describes the circumstances that resulted in the injury, illness, fatality or dangerous incident; the object, substance or circumstance which was directly involved in inflicting the injury, illness, death or dangerous incident; the name and type of any machinery, equipment or substance involved. Was anyone else involved? Was electricity/electrical equipment involved?*

(Attach a separate piece if paper if necessary)

Did the incident involve licensed work *(e.g. high risk work, electrical work?)*

☐ No ☐ Yes Please provide details of the type of licensed work:

Is the workplace a registered major hazard facility? ☐ No ☐ Yes

Person's injury/illness and treatment details *(if required)*

Title:	First name:		Last name:	

Date of birth:		Contact phone number:	

Residential address:	Unit/Building No.	Street No.	Street Name		
	Suburb/Town/Locality			State	Postcode

Occupation: *(main duties)*

Relationship to the entity notifying

☐ Worker ☐ Self-employed ☐ Member of the public ☐ Labour hire worker ☐ Contractor

☐ Group training apprentice/trainee ☐ Other *(please specify)*:

Description of injury/illness: *(e.g. fracture, laceration, amputation, strain, electrical shock, burn, Q fever)*

Body location: *(e.g. wrist, lower back, internal organs):*

Did the person receive treatment following the injury/illness?

☐ No   Yes Please describe treatment received:

Where was the injured person taken fro treatment?	*(if applicable)*

Legal name of business:	
Trading name of business:	

ABN:		ACN:	

Business address:	Unit/Building No.	Street No.	Street Name		
	Suburb/Town/Locality			State	Postcode

Contact phone number:	Work:		Mobile:	
Business email address:				

Main business activity *(e.g. furniture manufacture, domestic construction, steel warehousing, electrical installation).*

Main industry sector

☐ Accommodation and foof services
☐ Agriculture, foresty and fishing
☐ Construction
☐ Electricity, gas, water and waste services
☐ Health care and social assistance
☐ Manufacturing
☐ Professional, scientific and technical

☐ Rental, hiring and real estate services
☐ Transport, postal and warehousing
☐ Administrative and support services
☐ Arts and recreational services
☐ Education and training
☐ Financial and insurance services
☐ Information media and telecommunications

Mining
Public administration and safety
Retail trade
Wholesale trade
Other services *(please specify).*

Describe any actions taken immediately following the incident to prevent recurrence:

Describe any longer term action proposed to prevent a recurrence:

Notifier's details

Title:	First name:		Last name:	
Position at workplace:		Contact phone number:	
Email:			

Is this the person that should be contacted for further information?

☐ Yes ☐ No If no, please provide the name and contact details of the appropriate person should further infromation be required.

Mr ☐ Mrs ☐ Miss ☐ Ms ☐ First name: | Last name:

Position:		Contact phone number:	

Source: Queensland Government, Office of Industrial Relations n.d.

SUMMARY

Event risk management is a significant responsibility for an event organiser. This task is made more complicated by the number of stakeholders involved; fixed-event delivery date; the use at times of temporary infrastructure; and the presence at the event venue or site during setup, delivery and shutdown of different groups, depending on the event, such as attendees, contractors, suppliers, volunteers, security/police, exhibitors/stallholders, sponsors and performers/speakers.

For the event risk management process to be successful, it requires widespread and open consultation and thorough internal and external research. Additionally, there needs to be a commitment on behalf of an event's organisers to the development of a risk management culture, actively supported by all stakeholders and underpinned by the employment of a systematic process (as outlined in ISO 31000:2018) and associated documentation. This process requires an understanding of an event's scope, context and risk criteria, an assessment of the risks associated with it, the development of risk treatments, and a requirement to monitor, record and review.

QUESTIONS

1 Define the term risk.
2 Briefly explain why managing risk in event settings can be a very complex task.
3 Why should event managers seek to ensure they develop a culture of risk management in their organisations?
4 Define the terms likelihood and consequence and discuss why they are significant when seeking to manage risk at events.
5 Briefly describe the risk treatment options that are available to event organisers.
6 Explain why the consultation process is key to successful event risk management.
7 What types of risk-related documentation do you believe might be required for a small-scale community market taking place in a hotel car park?
8 Why is the review process important in the process of risk management?
9 Discuss the importance of communicating a risk management plan to stakeholders and how this can be achieved.
10 What is a safe work methods statement, and when should an event organiser request one from a contractor?
11 Visit an event and see how many issues you can photograph that you believe should have been addressed in the risk management planning process. Categorise these under broad headings.

CASE STUDY

OPERATIONS AND RISK MANAGEMENT AT THE AUCKLAND DIWALI FESTIVAL — IMPLEMENTATION OF NEW LPG GAS BOTTLE SYSTEM

Introduction

The Auckland Diwali Festival is a free-entry public event to celebrate Indian culture and the Indian community of Auckland. The first official Auckland Diwali Festival was held in 2002, and the event is delivered by Auckland Tourism, Events and Economic Development (ATEED), on behalf of Auckland Council, and in conjuction with founding partner Asia New Zealand Foundation.

A core component of Diwali in Auckland is the authentic Indian vegetarian food on offer, the bulk of which is cooked on-site, with the main fuel used being LPG gas. The vast majority of food vendors (approximately 35 as at 2014) have historically made use of up to four LPG gas bottles.

Inherent in the use of gas is the potential for explosions and/or fire. This risk is compounded by the temporary nature of the kitchens in use and their proximity to one another. The kitchens are located in small 5 m x 3 m marquees with vinyl walls which are provided by the festival. This situation while, initially acceptable, was not deemed to be compliant with a revised set of council guidelines — HS300 Guidelines for Event Health and Safety Plans 2012.

2014 treatment strategy

The event's current approach to risk management at the time was based on responding to an incident(s) should it occur, as well as the employment of some prior mitigation practices including the requirement for vendor supplied fire blankets in all kitchens. Additionally, evacuation procedures were in place, of which vendors and staff responsible for stallholder management were aware. Notification and reminders as to best practice in managing gas bottles for cooking purposes were also provided in communications to vendors at stallholder meetings and by event staff responsible for this aspect of the event.

The responsibility for LPG gas bottle use was in the hands the food vendors with the assumption being that the majority of them were experienced stallholders and as such were well versed in safely managing their own equipment.

The need for change

Following an amalgamation of several councils into a single Auckland council in 2010, it was decided to standardise various practices, including that of regulatory compliance in areas of health and safety. This required, among several other changes, that LPG gas use at festivals and events needed to be revisited.

The new *Health and Safety Guidelines for Event Health and Safety Plans 2014* required that gas bottle quantities used at the event necessitated a minimum separation of 15 metres between users. This was not presently the case, as food providers were grouped together in rows, with some facing each other on opposite sides of a closed road. Further, these new guidelines stipulated that a maximum of two 9 kg bottles could be placed within a vendor's allocated 3 m × 5 m space.

The response
Considerations in developing a compliant risk treatment

For compliance to be achieved in a way that would meet regulatory needs, while also meeting the operational needs of the event, a range of matters had to be considered including:

- compliance against the HS300 guidelines, inclusive of a test certificate for bottles
- minimal loss of vendor cooking time
- logistics and efficiency of any new system within a busy festival environment
- cost and efficiency from a vendor perspective
- vendor expectations.

Consultation was deemed key to the success of any new treatment, and as such expert advice and input were sought from a range of individuals and groups, including:

- the event's production advisor
- senior event staff, including staff responsible for stallholders
- vendors
- certified plumber and gas fitter
- equipment hire company that specialises in hiring and deploying kitchen equipment and services to vendors on-site at other festivals
- Auckland Council Health and Safety Officer.

The process of consultation took approximately four months and multiple treatment options were discussed, assessed, tweaked and discarded before arriving at a workable set of actions (see table 11.5).

TABLE 11.5 Treatment plan

Actions	Notes
Vendor pre-orders required number of 9 kg LPG gas bottles	Extra 9 kg LPG gas bottles can be ordered on-site if required
Vendor pre-pays for LPG gas bottles	Paid direct to LPG gas bottle supplier via the event's LPG Team
LPG Team deploys LPG gas bottle storage cages, spaced out on-site for easy access	LPG gas bottle cages are certified, labelled and only accessible by the LPG Team
Location test certificate assessed and signed off by qualified company	Once confirmed, regulatory signage is deployed
Vendor arrives on-site and sets up kitchen	Stallholder Managers advise LPG Team of vendor arrival
LPG Team connects gas bottles and checks fittings with bubble test	On-site certified gas fitter repairs any connectors as required

Vendor contacts Stallholder Manager when LPG gas bottle runs low. Stallholder Manager radios for LPG Team	LPG Team monitors LPG gas bottle use and intermittently tests the weight of bottles to pre-empt the need for a new bottle
At the end of the night, LPG Team disconnects LPG gas bottles and returns bottle to storage	LPG Team brings refilled LPG gas bottles to site for next festival day

While effective, and compliant, the cost of this treatment proved higher than anticipated. The normal process for the general public to refill a 9 kg LPG gas bottle for a home BBQ averages NZ$39.00. This new festival LPG gas bottle system, with associated administration and crew support costs, resulted in a charge-out rate of NZ$51.00 per bottle. The vendor is charged NZ$45.00 of this amount and the festival organiser absorbs the remainder. Despite this, the team is satisfied with the current model and will continue to work on price coverage over the ensuing years. For this price structure, the festival is fully compliant and the vendors are assured of quality service onsite at the event. The vendor also has less equipment to bring and remove from site.

Source: Adapted from a case study by Eric Ngan, in his role as Event Producer at Auckland Tourism, Events, Economic Development 2014.

This case study was submitted as course work for the Certified Festival and Event Executive (CFEE) program facilitated by the New Zealand Events Association. The risk management for this event continues to be reviewed to ensure ongoing compliance and best practice.

QUESTIONS

1 To what extent does the response to changing regulatory needs in this case conform to the 'best practice' event risk management?

2 How were the risk treatments in this case identified?

3 Why do you think it was important at the outset to identify criteria that revised treatments would need to meet?

4 As the set of treatments that were arrived at resulted in an increase in vendor costs, do you think that this should have caused them to be scrapped and the prior approach reinstated?

REFERENCES

Alexandrina Council 2017, 'Event risk management plan', www.alexandrina.sa.gov.au/__data/assets/pdf_file/0037/194878/Event-Risk-Management-Plan-January-2014.pdf, viewed 24 March 2020.

City of Greater Geelong 2020, 'Places of public entertainment — Safety Officers information', www.geelongaustralia.com.au/popes/article/item/8ce0e9d7f5e7610.aspx#poperesp, viewed 29 March 2020.

Government of Western Australia Department of Health 2009, 'Guidelines for concerts, events and organised gatherings', ww2.health.wa.gov.au/~/media/Files/Corporate/general%20documents/Environmental%20health/Concerts%20and%20Mass%20Gathering%20Guidelines.pdf, viewed 27 March 2020.

Hutchison, L 2017, 'Food poisoning victims paid £400,000 after major outbreak at Newcastle Street Spice Festival', *ChronicleLive*, 28 January, www.chroniclelive.co.uk/news/north-east-news/food-poisoning-victims-paid-400000-12516028, viewed 29 March 2020.

Illawarra Folk Festival 2020, 'Volunteer safety induction questionnaire', www.illawarrafolkfestival.com.au/volunteer-induction, viewed 24 March 2020.

International Organization for Standardization 2018, 'ISO 31000: 2018 — Risk Management', www.iso.org/iso-31000-risk-management.html, viewed 12 May 2020.

Kolovos, B & Thomson, A 2019, 'Lawyer: about 20 Lorne festival victims fall into the significant injury category', *The Standard*, 12 June, www.standard.net.au/story/6212599/falls-festival-settles-six-crowd-crush-claims, viewed 29 March 2020.

Ngan, E 2014, 'CFEE case study: operations/risk management Auckland Diwali Festival — implementation of new LP gas bottle system'.

Queensland Government, Office of Industrial Relations n.d. 'Form 3: Incident notification form', V15.7.19, www.worksafe.qld.gov.au/__data/assets/pdf_file/0020/82505/incidents_form.pdf, viewed 20 July 2020.

Watkins, D 2019, 'India: tent collapse kills 14 at Hindu religious event', *Vatican News*, 24 June, www.vaticannews.va/en/world/news/2019-06/india-tent-collapse-kills-14-rajasthan.html, viewed 29 March 2020.

Wynn-Moylan, P 2017, *Risk and hazard management for festivals and events*, Routledge, Abingdon, Oxon.

ACKNOWLEDGEMENTS

Photo: © Melanie Lemahieu / Shutterstock.com

Figure 11.3: AS ISO 31000:2018 Figure 4. © Standards Australia Limited. Copied by Wiley Publishing with the permission of Standards Australia under Licence CL2906wp

Tables 11.2 and 11.3: © Alexandrina Council 2017

Figure 11.5: © Alexandrina Council 2017

Figure 11.8: © Government of Western Australia Department of Health

Figure 11.9: © Illawarra Folk Festival 2020

Figure 11.10: © Queensland Government. Office of Industrial Relations, Form 3 — Incidence notification form, V15.7.19

Case study: © Auckland Tourism, Events and Economic Development. Reproduced by permission.

CHAPTER 12

Environmentally sustainable event management

LEARNING OBJECTIVES

After studying this chapter, you should be able to:

12.1 define the term sustainable development and discuss its relevance to event production

12.2 employ strategies and practices to reduce the environmental impact of events

12.3 source information concerning the environmental management of events.

Introduction

The societal push towards sustainable development — 'meeting the needs of the present without compromising the ability of future generations to meet their own needs' (Bruntland Commission 1987) — has increasingly impacted the way public and business events have been planned and delivered over the past decade. Initiatives such as the development of an International Standard for Sustainable Event Management (ISO 20121), the establishment of industry standards (for example, Event Industry Council's Environmentally Sustainable Meeting Standards), and the emergence of organisations that serve to support events as they progress down the environmental sustainability path (for example, A Greener Festival and the Sustainable Event Alliance) are all reflective of the progress that has been made in this area. It can also be observed that the owners of events, such as industry associations and sporting bodies, are increasing including environmental sustainability requirements in the conditions they impose on those organisations/cities/nations that are seeking to bid for, and subsequently conduct, their events. Further, event attendees have become more aware of sustainability issues and expect the events they attended to be produced with environmental considerations in mind. It is also the case that government bodies responsible for issuing permits for the conduct of events, along with the corporations that sponsor them, are now much more aware of the potential they possess for creating negative environmental impacts, and the implications should this occur to their community standing and/or brand. This sensitivity can also be viewed as an outgrowth of their own expanded efforts in the area.

While acknowledging that the concept of sustainable development embraces social, economic and environmental components, this chapter will focus only on the latter dimension. The chapter begins by providing an overview of the environmental impacts that can flow from the conduct of events before moving on to discuss approaches to managing these impacts. Event industry responses to the challenge of delivering 'green' events will then be overviewed. This will be followed by a brief discussion of environmental certification programs operating in the events field and approaches to measuring event environmental impacts. To demonstrate how events have sought to be proactive in this area, several examples and case studies have been provided.

12.1 The environmental impacts of event production

LEARNING OBJECTIVE 12.1 Define the term sustainable development and discuss its relevance to event production.

Successful efforts at sustainable event management, as Yuan (2013) notes, require that event organisers integrate sustainability planning into the overall event planning process. Further, he makes clear that engaging an event's various stakeholders is crucial to ensuring that those practices and systems that are put in place to control an event's environmental impacts are effectively implemented. These stakeholders are likely to be many and varied, and depending on the event, might include event owners, event production staff and volunteers, venue owners, transport providers, equipment hire firms, performers, traders, caterers, sponsors, participants and attendees.

The types of environmental impacts that can flow from the conduct of an event will be dependent on such factors as its size, characteristics of its audience (for example, percentage of overseas attendees), type (for example, festival vs a conference) and the location where it takes place (for example, venue(s), greenfield site, city/town). Nonetheless, in general terms, environmental impacts arise from the following:

* consumption of non-renewable energy, and associated greenhouse gas production, resulting from participant travel and an event's power needs
* water use, wastewater production and chemical emissions to water
* solid waste generation (for example, paper, bottles, cans, food waste, construction material)
* noise and light pollution
* habitat and biodiversity impacts at an event site or in its immediate surroundings
* ecological impacts associated with the resources purchased by an event as they move along its supply chain.

To reduce these impacts, event organisers need to develop policies and procedures in a range of key areas, in particular:

* resource purchasing and consumption
* energy use
* waste management and resource recovery
* transport and travel

- water consumption and management
- site use management.

    The following section provides insights into how these areas can be effectively managed.

Sustainable purchasing in event planning

The impact of an event's purchasing behaviour is a major factor in the effectiveness of its sustainability efforts. To align actions in this area with the desire to reduce an event's environmental impact, a sustainable purchasing policy is required. These policies can be used to not only condition an event's own purchasing activities, but also those of third parties that undertake purchases on its behalf, with the latter being achieved through the contracting process. Key questions that event organisers need to seek answers to when involving themselves in sustainable purchasing include:

- What is the product made from, and does it include recycled materials or sustainably produced materials?
- Where did the product come from and how much energy has been involved in its transport?
- Who made the product and were they fairly compensated for their labour?
- What does it come packaged in? Will the manufacturer take packaging back?
- Is the product reusable, more durable than alternatives or can it be repurposed?
- Is any special handling in the product's disposal necessary?
- Does the product conserve energy or water?
- Can the product be recycled, reused, composted or returned to the manufacturer/producer, or will it need to go to landfill at the end of its life?
- Can the claims made for products purchased from suppliers ('eco', 'natural', 'biodegradable', 'fair trade', 'organic', 'green') be substantiated through certification or some other means?

    An effective way of engaging with the concept of sustainable purchasing is to develop a sustainable sourcing code (or sustainable purchasing policy) to guide purchasing decisions. The recent Gold Coast 2018 Commonwealth Games (GCCG) provides an excellent example of an event that developed a sustainable sourcing code to direct the purchasing decisions of its vast network of internal and external stakeholders. The principles set by this document offer inspiration for devising similar sourcing codes for events of any type or scale, and for this reason an extract from this code dealing with the application of its guiding principles has been included here (see figure 12.1).

A key goal of sustainable purchasing policies, which can be difficult to achieve in the context of some purchases, is a circular resource flow of material through recycling, reuse or repurposing leading to a closed-loop process that avoids disposal to landfill. DGTL, an electronic music festival, provides an insightful example of how a circular resource flow can be achieved. This event, held in Amsterdam, does not use the term waste, and considers all residual materials as a resource. As a result, it does not have a waste plan, but rather a resource plan that is designed to ensure event inputs are re-used, recycled, down-cycled, incinerated or otherwise processed rather than sent to landfill. All uneaten food, kitchen scraps and compostable serviceware (that is, biodegradable cutlery and plates), for example, are composted on-site and the resulting compost distributed to local urban gardens. Reusable 'hard' cups are also used to eliminate one-use cups from the 'waste' stream. This event is also experimenting with on-site closed-loop systems with plastic waste (for example, water bottles) being converted back into oil via a process known as pyrolysis, and attendee urine being treated to meet the standard for drinking water (DGTL Festival 2018).

FIGURE 12.1   Extract from the Gold Coast 2018 Sustainable Sourcing Code — Application of Guiding Principles

5. Application of Guiding Principles

This section provides information on how to apply the guiding principles:

- responsible sourcing
- inclusivity and diversity
- minimising embodied and operational impacts.

    The fourth principle, value for money, underpins all of these and it can be seen within the Minimum Requirements such as 'where cost-comparable options exist' or in the preference of hiring versus buying products. Specific obligations in the application of these principles are set out in the Minimum Requirements at section 6. Aspirational outcomes are also tabled. Suppliers are encouraged to achieve over and above the Minimum Requirements. For clarity, the Minimum Requirements and the guidance in this Code apply to all procurement categories. Suppliers should also note that additional requirements

▶

may be included in tender documentation for categories that Gold Coast 2018 Commonwealth Games Corporation (GOLDOC) deem are high impact for sustainability.

5.1 Responsible Sourcing

GOLDOC is committed to ensuring its products and services are sourced and produced under a set of internationally acceptable environmental, social and ethical guidelines and standards. Suppliers agree that GOLDOC may undertake audits or other activity to assess compliance with these requirements. More information is included on audit, complaints and incident management in section 8 and section 9.

5.1.1 Labour Rights

Suppliers must take appropriate steps to ensure that all locations used in the manufacture and supply of products and services to GOLDOC meet the requirements of the core International Labour Organization's (ILO) Conventions and local laws of the country in which the products or services are sourced. This includes manufacturing sites and service centres of sub-contractors or sub-licensees who are engaged by GOLDOC Suppliers. The list of ILO Conventions totals 190 laws which aim to improve the labour standards of people around the world. There are eight fundamental Conventions (on prohibition of forced labour, child labour, the right to organise in a trade union, and suffer no discrimination) which are binding upon every member country of the ILO from the fact of membership, since the Declaration on Fundamental Principles and Rights at Work in 1998. Where the international and national labour rights differ, the more stringent will be adhered to.

5.1.2 Workplace Health and Safety

GOLDOC is committed to ensuring that the GC2018 will be delivered in a safe manner that will protect all Workforce and Constituent Groups, and meet all applicable work health and safety (WHS) legislative requirements. All Suppliers are responsible for their own WHS and the WHS of others, and WHS must be an integral part of how the Supplier does business. Where sourcing items from overseas it is expected that the WHS of workers is assured and relevant ILO conditions relating to health and safety are met.

5.1.3 Food Certification, Animal Welfare and Testing

Suppliers should seek to support high standards of animal welfare particularly in the case of animals involved in the production of food products. Suppliers are encouraged to exceed the Minimum Requirements wherever possible. Where products are likely to have been tested on animals, suppliers should seek advice from GOLDOC before supplying them.

5.2 Inclusivity and Diversity

5.2.1 Local Industry

A Local Industry Participation Plan (LIPP) has been implemented by GOLDOC to support the Queensland Government's Local Industry Policy and Queensland Procurement Policy. The LIPP ensures GC2018 applies full, fair and reasonable procurement processes that provide the opportunity for local industry to participate. GOLDOC is committed to maximising local industry participation in procurement opportunities where local businesses offer solutions that meet GOLDOC's needs, as per the Queensland Charter for Local Content 1. 'Local' suppliers include Australian and New Zealand enterprises as per the Australian and New Zealand Government Procurement Agreement 2. The Industry Capability Network Gateway (Queensland) (ICN Gateway) is being utilised to facilitate the registration of interested parties in relation to GC2018 procurement. All local suppliers are encouraged to register their interest in relevant procurement categories on ICN Gateway. GOLDOC uses this information to inform its Procurement Process.

5.2.2 Opportunities for Aboriginal and Torres Strait Islanders

GOLDOC recognises that GC2018 presents an opportunity to generate awareness and recognise Aboriginal and Torres Strait Island (ATSI) culture and respect for the Traditional Owners of the land. GOLDOC and the Queensland Government in conjunction with Reconciliation Australia are developing a GC2018 Reconciliation Action Plan (RAP) that includes commitments to engage Indigenous suppliers in procurement processes. GOLDOC encourages suppliers to align themselves with the RAP wherever possible.

5.3 Minimising Embodied and Operational Impacts

GOLDOC seeks to minimise the embodied and operational environmental impacts associated with its procurement. This section is organised by product type so suppliers can easily see which focus areas are relevant to their product or service and what GOLDOC expects Suppliers to do to address related embodied impacts.

5.3.1 Timber and Forest Products

Sustainable forestry is an important concern for the health of ecosystems, biodiversity and Greenhouse Gas (GHG) emissions. Unless timber and forestry products are reused or recycled materials they must be certified under an accepted international sustainable forestry management scheme in accordance with the Minimum Requirements

5.3.2 Printed Material

GOLDOC aims to minimise the use of printed materials wherever possible. This includes paper products and signage. Where printed material is required efforts will be made to minimise the environmental impact of the printing processes, substrate material or paper as the case may be.

5.3.3 Refrigerants and Insulation

The Australian Government has progressively phased out Ozone Depleting Substances (ODS) under its Montreal Protocol on Substances that Deplete the Ozone Layer obligations. Under this protocol all chlorofluorocarbons, halons, carbon tetrachloride, methyl chloroform, hydrobromofluorocarbons, bromochloromethane and methyl bromide were to be totally phased out. Hydrochlorofluorocarbons (HCFCs) were to be reduced by 90% by 2015 and totally phased-out by 2020. In the transition to non-ODS refrigerants there has been a significant increase in the use of Hydrofluorocarbons (HFCs). Many synthetic HFCs have very high Global Warming Potential (GWP). HFCs represent 1.5% of total warming potential today and their share of greenhouse gas emissions will rise in the next 30 years if no action is taken. In light of the above, GOLDOC supports the use of natural refrigerants. Common natural refrigerants in commercial equipment include: R170, R290, R600a, R717 and R744.

5.3.4 Electronic Office Equipment

Electronic office equipment (office equipment) includes multifunctional devices, photocopiers, printers, scanners, fax machines, computers and monitors. The key environmental impacts of electronic office equipment include energy use in operation, energy use in manufacturing and disposal/reprocessing.

5.3.5 Temporary Materials, Portable Building and Overlay

A significant amount of temporary materials, buildings and 'overlay' infrastructure will be required for GC2018. These materials are unique in terms of sustainability because their temporary nature leads to different sustainability issues. Due to this, and the large variety of materials that are included in overlay infrastructure, prescriptive guidelines are unlikely to be appropriate. Therefore, in order to guide material selection, the following principles have been adopted to guide decision-making:

- Avoidance or reduction of material use.
- Minimise waste to landfill.
- Minimise embodied energy over the lifetime of the product.

These principles are implemented through a decision-making process which is outlined in the figure below. The term 'material' in the process refers to any form of overlay material or infrastructure component.

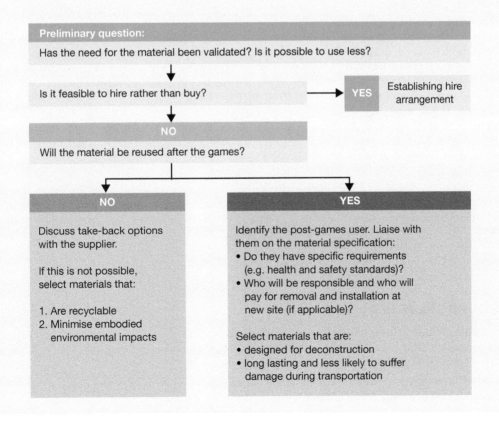

The following further information is provided as accompanying guidance to this decision-making process:

Recyclable materials:

The most easily recyclable materials are in their raw forms. That is, without finishes or composite components that will limit or add costs to the recovery of the raw material in recycling processes.

Minimise embodied environmental impacts:

Environmental impacts may occur across a wide variety of impact categories, from GHG emissions to land and water use. A full life cycle assessment is required to properly account for these impacts across the lifetime of the product. If this information is unavailable it is suggested that the decision maker focuses on GHG emissions as a proxy for overall impacts. Therefore, products that are produced with processes that use less energy than average and/or use less energy in operation should be given preference. Portable buildings represent a specific case within temporary materials and are likely to represent a significant hotspot for embodied and operational environmental impacts, particularly embodied carbon. Portable buildings should therefore be a particular target for hire arrangements.

5.3.6 Furniture, Fixtures and Equipment

As with other temporary materials all efforts will first be made to reduce the need for furniture, fixtures and equipment. Hiring of the goods versus buying of goods will be explored, taking into account legacy opportunities, as the next best option before purchases are made. Where purchasing is required Suppliers will be asked about take-back options.

5.3.7 Cleaning Products and Services

Cleaning has health, safety and environmental implications. GOLDOC has aligned its sustainability requirements for cleaning product and services with the 'Queensland Government Sustainable Procurement Product Guide for Cleaning Services'.

5.3.8 Travel

GOLDOC aims to reduce the carbon impact for the GC2018 event as much as possible. Carbon is our most certain environmental impact and steps we take to reduce that impact have other environmental and social flow on effects. GOLDOC is addressing its carbon footprint by developing a baseline carbon footprint for GC2018 and implementing a Carbon Management Plan to manage and mitigate GOLDOC controlled emissions. GOLDOC encourages all Suppliers to support its responsible carbon goal and choose to offset travel-related emissions.

5.3.9 PVC

Polyvinyl Chloride (PVC) is a plastic formed from vinyl chloride monomer. PVC is mostly used in the built environment for conduit pipes and fittings, flooring, cable and wire insulation and also in the frames of windows and doors. Health and environmental concerns particularly relating to use of chemicals in manufacturing processes and use of additives are well established. Australian Best Practice Guidelines for PVC in the Built Environment have been developed to minimise environmental and health risks.

5.3.10 Paints and Adhesives

Volatile Organic Compounds (VOCs) are organic chemicals consisting primarily of petrochemical solvent-type compounds. Health effects of exposure to VOCs include eye, nose and skin irritation, headache and lethargy.

5.3.11 Packaging

Packaging is any material, or combination of materials, that is used to contain, protect, deliver, handle or present products. Packaging plays an important role protecting products in transport and facilitating distribution to the point of consumption. Packaging is also a significant source of waste and its environmental impacts can outlast the use of the product itself. The waste hierarchy (avoid, minimise, reuse, recycle and dispose) should be used as a guideline for packaging development.

Source: Gold Coast 2018 Commonwealth Games Corporation (GOLDOC) 2016.

Sustainable energy use

Most events require power sourced either from landline 'mains' electricity supply and/or mobile power generators. The impact of power generated through these means is the consumption of fossil (non-renewable) fuel and the production of greenhouse gases. Events have various options available to them to reduce their energy usage and/or curtail their resulting emissions. For example, events held indoors can be conducted at energy-efficient venues (see figure 12.2) that have made a commitment to sourcing renewable energy and to using energy-saving technology (for example, LED lighting, energy-efficient air conditioning systems, room monitoring systems that turn off lighting when spaces are not used).

Event organisers can also influence their own energy consumption at venues by careful production and equipment use planning, and by placing protocols on third party power users such as exhibitors. 'Power diets', for example, can be imposed on large power consumers as a way of trying to reduce their energy consumption. This strategy involves charging for power usage beyond a given amount.

If a venue is not making use of renewable energy, it may also be possible for an event to purchase renewable energy credits or buy 'green power' from an electricity supplier. In Australia, for example, this can be done through GreenPower, a joint initiative of the governments of the Australian Capital Territory, New South Wales, South Australia, Victoria and Tasmania. This initiative acts to guarantee that an event's energy use is displaced with certified renewable energy, which is added to the electricity grid on their behalf (GreenPower 2011).

It should be noted that, in relative terms, the greenhouse gas emissions that directly result from an event's power usage is often far outweighed by those stemming from attendee travel, a matter that will be returned to later in this chapter. Nonetheless, this should not detract from the responsibility event organisers have to act in this area.

Sustainable mobile power supply

Many events use mobile generators to supply power. Most generators run on mineral diesel, a non-renewable and polluting fuel. When looking to reduce energy demand on diesel generators, 'smart' power plans can be put in place. These plans involve, depending on the event, the use of smaller generators that can be switched off completely when not needed and clustering generators so that they can work in sync with one another — this leads to less operating inefficiencies. Actions such as these might require an event to seek external advice, or to work closely with their generator supplier, to maximise their fuel-saving benefits. The value of engaging with these types of energy-saving practices can be seen in the 'Smart Power Plan' that was provided by ZAP Concepts for the Volvo Round the World Yacht Race stopover in The Hague, where it successfully reduced fuel consumption by an estimated 37 per cent on a 'business as usual' scenario (ZAP Concepts n.d.).

Transitioning from fossil fuel to sustainably fuelled generators can significantly reduce greenhouse gas emissions from events. In this regard, biodiesel which is produced from waste oil and fats, or sustainably certified crops, should be used when available. Generators, however, need to be tuned in such a way as to be able to accept these alternative fuels. The push to reduce (mineral) diesel fuel use is nonetheless in evidence in the outdoor event area. This can be seen in the goal set by the UK festival 'think-do tank' group Powerful Thinking which aims to reduce the use of diesel (in all its forms) by 50 per cent (or more) by 2025 (Powerful Thinking 2018).

FIGURE 12.2	Melbourne Convention and Exhibition Centre (MCEC)'s environmental sustainability practices

Our commitment to sustainability

At MCEC we strive to be leaders in sustainable business practice. We are always working to find innovative ideas that provide better outcomes for our community, our customers and our environmental footprint.

For more information please visit mcec.com.au/sustainability

Diverting waste

In 2018–19 we diverted 62 per cent of all waste from landfill using 17 waste streams.

Single-use plastics

We've banned plastic straws and are eliminating the use of over 30 000 straws, 500 000 plastic bottles and 11 000 coffee cups annually.

Community partnerships

74 265 meals (24 755 kilograms of food) was donated to OzHarvest's food rescue program in 2019.

Food waste

Our on-site organic dehydrator processed 44 tonnes of food waste from our kitchens in 2019. That's equivalent to the carbon emissions associated with the electricity consumption of 20 households for one year.

Reducing our carbon emissions

We've reduced carbon emissions per square metre by 22 per cent, and are well on track to achieve our target of a 30 per cent reduction by 2021 against 2015 levels.

▶

Sustainable design

The Melbourne Convention Centre incorporates natural light, sensor lights, low energy escalators and solar capture used for the heating of water.

The Melbourne Exhibition Centre is fitted with an Energy Management System, complete with CO_2 monitoring and variable speed drives, responsible for a 30 per cent reduction in energy use since 2016.

Championing local produce

We source our produce from local, passionate and ethical suppliers to promote the wonderful producers we have here in Victoria and to reduce our venue's environmental footprint.

Leader in water efficiency

MCEC is the regional leader in limiting water use, due to sensor taps and the capture and re-using of water from the Melbourne Convention Centre roof. In 2019 we harvested over 3100 kilolitres of rainwater.

Partnerships: Melbourne Renewable Energy Project

In 2018 MCEC joined 13 other reputable Melbourne organisations to support the development of a wind farm in regional Victoria. This initiative enables us to offset the projected electricity use of our 20 000 square metre expansion space with renewable energy.

Sustainable sourcing

Our coffee supplier The Sustainable Coffee Company (TSCC) is a Melbourne-based roaster and the first Australian coffee company to be 100 per cent carbon offset from tree to cup. As part of their commitment to sustainability, TSCC offer returnable bulk coffee bags.

We've partnered with local company Biofilta to install 36 permanent food cubes in our courtyard. They are made from recycled material and are used to grow herbs and other food for our Goldfields Café & Bar.

Awards and accolades

- The first convention centre in the world to be awarded a 6-star green star environmental rating.
- 'Best Corporate Citizen' at 2018 Exhibition and Event Association of Australasia Awards for Excellence.
- 2018 Premier's Sustainability Award — Government category for Melbourne Renewable Energy Project.
- EarthCheck Gold Certified 2019 seven years in a row.

Source: Melbourne Convention and Exhibition Centre 2020.

Zero emissions power supply

Replacing mineral diesel generators with those powered by biodiesel is one of many options available to outdoor events seeking to reduce or eliminate their carbon footprint. Others include:

- mobile (trailer mounted) solar power generators
- hydrogen fuel cells, used to power temporary lighting towers
- hybrid power generators (HPG) comprising battery banks connected to biodiesel generators.

The latter system is in use by Shambala, a music and arts festival in the UK, which is run on 100 per cent renewable energy. This festival employs a mix of waste vegetable oil diesel generators linked to batteries and solar power. Additionally, it encourages low energy usage among its cafes and traders through the imposition of an energy tariff (Shambala 2020).

As the world accelerates its response to the threat of climate change, there will be more solutions to responsible energy supply available to events. For example, Denmark's Roskilde Festival is now using electric cars to provide a backup energy source at its main food court during peak energy demand periods (Jensen 2019).

Developing a checklist of practices to minimise energy usage

Events differ in terms of their energy needs and the forms of energy potentially available. It is therefore not possible to propose a definitive checklist to guide organisers in this area. Nonetheless, by seeking answers to, and acting on the responses received from, the following questions it should be possible to significantly reduce event energy usage.

- Is the venue(s) powered by renewable energy, is it operated with due regard for energy efficiency and does it have a low energy use rating?
- Are renewable energy credits, or other instruments that facilitate access to renewable energy, available for purchase?
- Are environmentally friendly biofuels or zero-emissions energy sources available at an acceptable cost?
- Can a 'smart power' plan be developed to enable the most fuel-efficient mobile power generator configuration?
- Can demand for power be reduced through energy-efficient equipment and energy conservation actions?

- Does the event context allow power quotas and restrictions to be placed on users such as stallholders, exhibitors and food providers (a 'power diet')?
- Can restrictions be put in place to prevent attendees, stallholders, food providers and so on from using their own power generators thus forcing them to draw down electricity from the event's own sustainably sourced power?
- Can power consumption (mains kWh, fuel use) be measured so future (lower) energy use targets can be set?

In addition to reducing energy usage, the actions described in this section can also serve to showcase practices and technologies to an event's various stakeholders. This may, in turn, have flow-on effects, particularly if they are reported upon and publicised.

Recovering event waste resources

Waste creation can be the most visible environmental impact of an event. There are, however, a range of practices that can be used to maximise resource recovery and to restrict, or eliminate, event inputs finding their way into landfill.

No matter the event size or type, resource recovery efforts are often similar because the bulk of waste results from the same activities — food and beverage, branding, and site bump-in and bump-out operations. The objective of conducting a zero-waste event may seem impossible but setting this as an event's goal can focus its stakeholders on ways to prevent waste being generated in the first place, and to think creatively about how different types of waste can be recycled, reused, repurposed or donated.

Reducing the amount of 'stuff' used at an event can also have an upstream waste-reducing effect as every item used has its own waste-creating legacy as it moves along its path from raw material to its point of consumption. Waste creation also has a direct climate change impact as there is embedded energy in each item that ends up in landfill — a legacy of mining, growing, manufacturing, transporting, consuming and disposing of the item. Further, in the case of biodegradable waste that ends up in landfill, methane gas from its decomposition (that which is not captured for energy production) will ultimately escape and contribute to atmospheric greenhouse gas.

To optimise the likelihood of success, and to plan the most effective resource recovery effort for an event, answers are needed to a range of questions, specifically:
- What types of waste will be generated?
- How can waste be prevented?
- How can bin logistics and signage work to progress efforts at waste management?
- What opportunities exist for eliminating, recycling, salvaging or repurposing waste?
- How is biodegradable and compostable waste best dealt with?
- What practices can be employed to increase the effectiveness of waste management efforts?
- How can the types of waste generated be influenced or regulated?
- What capacity exists in terms of recycling and waste management in the location where the event takes place?

Responses to these questions can be used to inform an event's resource recovery plan; a framework for developing such a plan has been provided in table 12.1. Additionally, an event profile (Concert for the Planet) has been included in this section to show how waste management systems can be employed in event settings.

Key also to successful waste management, and environmental sustainability more generally, is the creation of a 'green team' comprising not only an event's staff and volunteers, but also suppliers, sponsors, venue(s), waste contractors, caterers and so on. This team should then be directed/given responsibilities aligned with the event's overall sustainability plan.

Types of waste produced at an event

Before devising sustainable waste solutions, the types of waste produced must be identified so that plans can be developed to allow it to be adequately managed. Events need to therefore think ahead and identify the types of waste sponsors, traders, exhibitors, workshop creators, performers, athletes, spectators, registrants or fans might generate.

At many events food and beverage provision is often the major contributor to an event's waste stream and comprises items such as drink cans, plastic and glass bottles, paper, uneaten food, packaging and disposable cups. Another major contributor to the waste resulting from events is that linked to their production. Depending on the event, this might involve timber offcuts, plastic pallet wrap, cardboard boxes, scrap metal, plumber's piping, electrical cabling, batteries, plastic sheeting, e-waste, used liquid receptacles and liquid/chemical/paint wastes. Branding overlay (for example, signs), along with waste resulting from the building of bespoke installations, theming and the construction of stage(s) and exhibition stand(s) can also create a large volume of material that presents a significant resource recovery challenge.

Waste prevention

If the types of potential waste likely to result from an event can be pre-identified it becomes possible to put steps in place to minimise or prevent it being generated in the first place, thus reducing the amount going to landfill. Interventions that can be effective in achieving this include:

- hiring, rather than purchasing, equipment and other items that will not be used after an event
- instituting a 'no plastic bag' policy and encouraging traders to sell or give away reusable shopping bags
- eliminating single-use water bottles by providing refillable cups or bottles to ticket holders/registrants/participants
- restricting or eliminating single-serve sachets and straws and discouraging individually pre-wrapped food items
- utilising biodegradable takeaway food packaging only and collecting it for composting
- restricting, or eliminating, the handing out of brochures, show bags, samples and promotional items
- using apps/websites to provide event program information and to distribute sponsor promotional material and conference/meeting proceedings and other information to attendees
- using electronic notice boards on-site to communicate program details and other matters to event attendees
- employing paperless ticketing and registration systems
- incorporating conditions into vendor contracts that require the use of biodegradable containers and cutlery, exclude plastic packaging or single-use plastic items, and require all waste to be removed upon close.

TABLE 12.1 **Resource recovery action plan**

Process steps	Actions
Establish goals	• Achieve [XX] per cent resource recovery rate • Achieve [XX] per cent compliance to waste segregation plans
Identify waste streams	Identify the waste streams that are likely to be generated by the event. As part of this process event stakeholders (for example, stallholders, exhibition stand operators, contractors) will need to be identified along with the potential waste they can generate. Waste resulting from an event can include: • compostable and biodegradable waste — for example, food • plastic — single-use and soft plastics • glass — bottles • metal — cans and scrap • textiles — clothing, soft branding materials • oil — waste cooking oil • electronics — e-waste • timber — pallets, construction offcuts, timber waste from the breakdown of exhibition waste • paper and cardboard • chemicals (paints, thinners, other chemicals, machinery oil) • serviceware — cups, bottles/cans, knives, forks, plates, food containers • event production waste, for example, construction material and packaging. Identify the optimal end-of-life for all waste resources. This might require the event negotiating with its waste management contractor to add (perhaps at extra cost) more waste stream management options to their standard waste services offering.

Plan for waste avoidance/minimisation	• Identify what waste resources can be eliminated from the event (for example, attendee giveaways, hard copy material).
	• Influence, or contract-in, what traders and contractors can bring into an event site (for example, no plastic bags, use of biodegradable serviceware only) and how they must deal with the waste they generate.
	• Replace single-use items. For example, water bottles can be replaced by providing reusable cups/bottles that can be refilled at water stations or by water jugs.
	• Replace waste-creating items that cannot be recycled at a materials recovery centre with ones that can. This may mean ensuring food and beverage providers use only certain types of containers.
	• Utilise reusable serviceware in the form of crockery plates and cups and metal knives and forks.
Engage stakeholders	• Communicate the event's waste management strategy to stakeholders along with their specific responsibilities.
Identify resource recovery options	• Identify what is best practice in resource recovery locally.
	• Identify any existing programs or resources that can be leveraged, or engaged with, to assist with resource recovery.
	• Determine where identified waste resources can be managed locally.
	• Prioritise options that assure local or national processing, rather than overseas processing.
	• Based on research, identify the optimal end-of-life outcome for all waste resources. This may include additional services added to the existing waste or cleaning contractor's offering.
Implement waste management practices and encourage engagement with them	• Ensure staff, volunteers, suppliers, contractors and other stakeholders have a clear understanding of their role in the waste management process. Training may be required, and should be allowed for, in terms of time and cost.
	• Police compliance with contract requirements/policies/regulations such as the use of specific types of serviceware, waste segregation and volume limits and exclusions (for example, no single-use plastics or plastic bags).
	• Decide on the division of roles to be performed by the event's organisers and any contracted waste management company. For example, who will be responsible for bin placement, provision and emptying; sourcing and designing bin signage; and dealing with waste contamination?
	• Ensure all bin options are always available at bin stations throughout a venue/site.
	• Provide staff/volunteers to work in resource recovery roles including decontaminating bins, recovering resources when they observe them at the site/venue and acting as bin stewards to prevent incorrect waste segregation by users.
	• Offer incentives/rewards. For example, deposits on cups, bottles, cans or other large-volume items that are a focus for recovery can significantly reduce the time and costs associated with post-event clean-up.
	• Establish penalties for non-compliance. For example, bonds can be charged and returned only when vendors, exhibitors or attendees are able to show compliance with resource recovery efforts.
	• Pre-sort waste, and correct contamination problems, before it is sent for onwards processing to avoid waste being rejected at the chosen materials recovery centre and sent to landfill.
Performance assessment and review	• Conduct waste audits during an event to assess compliance, along with the general level of effectiveness of the waste management systems that are in place.
	• Measure and report on segregation success, collection volumes, weights per category of waste, total waste avoided through initiatives and waste per person per day.
	• Review waste management systems and their success with the aim of modifying future action.

Bin logistics and signage

Apart from identifying what can be recycled, composted, sent for energy recovery or to landfill, it is important to consider the issue of bin management. In this regard there must be easy access to bins by attendees, they must be of adequate size and they must be emptied on a regular basis to prevent them overflowing. Additionally, and importantly, signage used on bins must be clear and relevant to the nature of waste to be placed in them (see the example in figure 12.3). It is also important to group bins as single bins, irrespective of their labelling, frequently become a place for all waste to be disposed of. If possible, staff/volunteers should be allocated to bin stations to decrease the potential for contamination.

For venue-based events such as conferences and exhibitions, an event's waste system will likely be managed by the venue as part of the services it provides. Where this is the case, event organisers should work closely with cleaning staff to ensure that bins are: in the correct combination; sufficient for the number of attendees; and placed appropriately.

Some venues go beyond simply employing recycling bins and take a very proactive approach to waste management. The RAI Amsterdam Convention and Exhibition Centre, for example, aims to recycle 100 per cent of the waste generated by events conducted at its facilities. To do this, it encourages exhibitors to reduce, reuse and recycle as much as possible so that waste does not need to leave the facility for placement in landfill sites. This is achieved by charging for any waste generated during the setup, conduct and breakdown of an event, and by providing containers, bags and bins that allow for detailed sorting of waste by exhibitors to facilitate later recycling. In addition to resulting in very high levels of resource recovery, this approach to waste management also acts to create a greater sense of responsibility for waste management by exhibitors (RAI Amsterdam Convention and Exhibition Centre 2020).

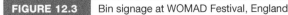

FIGURE 12.3 Bin signage at WOMAD Festival, England

Recycling

While recycling systems of various levels of sophistication exist in most venues, it is also the case that many outdoor events, such as festivals and outdoor markets, have in place resource recovery systems that separate out paper, cardboard, plastic, glass, metals, timber, aluminium and other recyclable items for later processing at a materials recovery facility (MRF). It needs to be kept in mind, however, that these facilities, and their associated technology and infrastructure, are designed to process different types of materials and as such might have specific requirements as to the form these must take. For example, some take plastic drink bottles but not plastic milk bottles; others take only Tetra Pak containers. Additionally, MRFs will commonly not accept plastic bags, and often require waste to be loose rather than bagged. These types of requirements need to be determined prior to an event to ensure an appropriate MRF is selected and that the form the waste is delivered in conforms to its requirements.

Some event organisers work with MRFs to operate on-site resource recovery systems. In New Zealand, for example, the event cleaning company Clean Event NZ offers an on-site back-of-house material recovery service as part of their standard service. This practice overcomes the problem of significant amounts of waste being sent to landfill due to cross-contamination once it arrives at an MRF. Some events have also established their own 'green team' of volunteers with similar intent (Clean Event NZ 2020).

On occasion event recycling efforts can be hampered by those charged with the materials transport and processing failing to process the waste effectively or acting to simply place it in landfill. It is therefore important for an event organiser to establish the credentials of any waste management company they contract. For example, in the 2018 Volvo Round the World Ocean Race, concerns over waste handlers in Hong Kong resulted in the event setting up its own on-site MRF to segregate out glass, cardboard, food waste, hard plastic, soft plastic and metal. Each material processing vendor then picked up directly from the event site and a staff member from the event accompanied the materials to the processing facility to ensure its delivery.

Engaging event attendees in the recycling process is also key to successful resource recovery efforts. This can be done by making regular public announcements during an event aimed at reminding attendees to make correct use of the bins provided and including information on the event's website as to its waste management practices. Some events go as far as to use a performer dressed in recycled materials to wander around the event site with the intent of drawing attention to its efforts at recycling and promoting the effective use of its bin system. Event organisers can also incentivise attendees to engage in the waste collection process by including deposits in the price paid for drinks sold in bottles or cans that can later be recouped for food or drink credits. Additionally, the option exists to reward attendees in similar ways for the collection of designated volumes of waste, or to charge waste bonds upon ticket purchase, with the bond being refunded upon exiting the site with recycling in-hand.

Biodegradable/compostable waste

Food provision at events has the potential to create a large volume of food and disposable packaging waste. Apart from uneaten food, plates, bowls, cutlery and cups, there will also be waste generated through the food preparation process. To capture and treat the biodegradable elements of this waste, separate bins will be needed. These bins, while placed around an event site in association with other waste bins, may need to have a heavier presence near designated food 'zones' and in back-of-house areas in these same locations. Allocating responsibility (often to the event's waste contractor, or to staff from the event's 'green team') for managing this component of an event's waste management efforts is key to its success, as is training catering staff/food service providers and reminding attendees of the need to ensure that waste is placed in the appropriate bin.

Ideally, food waste should be sent to a composting service provider. These facilities vary in terms of what they will take with some taking only food scraps, while others will also accept compostable materials such as paper plates/cups, biodegradable cutlery and serviettes and so on. Meat is another product where variations in acceptance will occur. Consideration can also be given to processing compostable waste on-site for later use as fertiliser, providing the event site is large enough and the appropriate authorities approve. It is noteworthy that some venues have developed a capacity to act in this area. The Adelaide Convention Centre, for example, has been operating a large worm farm for over 10 years as a means of dealing with much of its compostable waste with the resulting compost being used on its own, and local, gardens (Adelaide Convention Centre 2018).

Salvage and repurposing

To engage in salvage, re-use and repurposing, an event must first pre-identify what items can be utilised in these ways and to have a 'home' in mind for them. A system must also be in place to ensure they are captured and not mixed in with the event's general waste stream. As part of any system developed, consideration should be given to establishing a salvage area at an event and to partnering with a recycling centre or organisation (for example, a charity) that will be responsible for removing the material. Surplus food should also be considered a salvageable item as it can be removed by a food charity such as, in the Australian context, OzHarvest or Foodbank. A prior arrangement will need to be made for this to occur and pre-established standards for its handling must be met.

Concert for the Planet

On the 24th March 2018, Climate Wave Enterprises conducted Concert for the Planet, an Earth Hour event held at the Home of the Arts on the Gold Coast, Australia, with a total of 1500 attendees. To deliver a low-waste event, the organisers sought to capture as much of the resources used as possible and to later recycle the material recovered. To achieve this, they employed four bins that separated the event's waste into mixed recycling, compostable serviceware, food waste and general waste to landfill. Additionally, all food vendors were requested to only use compostable serviceware made from bamboo, sugarcane, paper/cardboard or polylactic acid (PLA, a form of plastic derived from renewable resources such as corn starch).

At the end of the event, food waste was sent to a large-scale worm farm to be converted into biological 'tea' and fertiliser for use on local area gardens, while compostable material was delivered to a community composting project (Joan Park Community Gardens). Material that was not recyclable was sent to landfill.

In the case of the compostable serviceware that formed part of the compostable waste stream, a scientific monitoring regime was put in place to determine how effective disposal, by way of a small-scale local composting facility, would be in breaking this waste down. This was done to assess if disposal through this means was possible. If this was found to be the case, it could eliminate the need (and cost) for relatively small-scale events to transport waste long distances to industrial composting facilities, while at the same time providing a community benefit.

To minimise contamination between the four waste streams, a team of 14 volunteer 'Eco Angels' were recruited to assist Climate Wave in educating attendees as to the correct bin in which to place their waste. They also explained the intent of the waste separation process. Unfortunately, during the event, one food trader introduced plastic forks into the waste management system, which corrupted the segregation efforts of all involved. This resulted in a significantly higher than expected hand sorting of waste. The resultant outcomes of the event's waste management efforts are given in the table below.

TABLE 12.2   Outcome: 72 per cent diversion from landfill from an event with 1500 visitors

Type	Litres	Percentage of total waste
Mixed recycling	480	28 per cent
Compostable serviceware	720	42 per cent
Food waste	30	1.75 per cent
Landfill	480	28 per cent
Total	**1710**	
Total diversion		**72 per cent**

As there were no controls on the food and beverage, and its associated packaging, that attendees were able to bring into the event site (it was not a gated event), waste from this source comprised the bulk of the 28 per cent of total waste that went to landfill. Nonetheless, the event was successful in saving 72 per cent of the material it generated from this fate.

The effort to compost materials in the local community composting facility was determined to be only partially successful. Paper compostables took an acceptable one week (napkins) to three months (coffee cups) to compost, while PLA items (forks, knives and plates) did not readily biodegrade in the community composting setting. This being the case, it was concluded that this type of material is not appropriate to send to small scale community garden composting facilities. Instead, it should be sent to a large-scale industrial composting centre. The use of the Eco Angels was assessed as having been key to the event's high level of waste diversion from landfill, as was pre-event engagement with stallholders and checking their compliance with the event's waste management efforts prior to its commencement. It is noteworthy that the latter process identified several stallholderstallholders that were non-compliant. These vendors were required to remove single-use plastic items including straws, utensils and water bottles from their stalls prior to the event's opening. Given the significant contribution of waste to landfill made by attendees in this instance, this case study also highlights the potential value that might exist in engaging attendees prior to an event as to its waste management goals and how they can assist in their achievement.

Source: Climate Wave 2018.

Sustainable transport solutions in event production

Moving people, supplies, equipment and waste to and from an event will likely be the cause of the bulk of its greenhouse gas output, with attendee travel being the largest component. This is particularly the case for those events where travel by plane is involved for a large percentage of those attending, such as is the case with large international conferences. Developing a sustainable travel plan is therefore key to reducing an event's impact in this area. These plans encourage the use of public transport; active travel (for example, walking and the use of push bikes); and shuttle buses in instances where attendees need to be moved between venues/transport hubs. These plans might also call for the offsetting of greenhouse gas resulting from attendee, supplier and event production staff travel. In the case of air travel, some airlines offer this service at an additional charge, or events themselves can link with a carbon offsetting company and seek a voluntary payment for this purpose. It should be noted, however, that there is significant debate around the effectiveness of the offsetting process (Choice 2017). Plans of this nature also need to be communicated to event stakeholders, and resources provided to allow easy engagement. These resources may include local area public transport schedules and related apps, bike route maps and bike access locations, and provision of details regarding how to engage with event offsetting efforts. The checklist provided in figure 12.4 provides a useful starting point for developing a strategy in this area.

FIGURE 12.4 Sustainable transport checklist

Create a year-round travel policy for the event organisation. This might include the use of cycle couriers, travel by hybrid/electric cars when vehicles are needed, requiring ground transport to be used instead of air travel for trips to locations less than a set distance (for example, 300 kilometres) away, and encouraging the use of video conferencing as opposed to meetings that require personal travel. ☐

Choose a venue or site with consideration for sustainable transport access by attendees. ☐

Establish the most convenient/efficient routes and modes of travel for attendees and communicate these. ☐

Arrange shuttles to connect urban transit hubs, or major attendee accommodation locations, to the event site/venue. ☐

Consider providing recharge points at the event site/venue for electric bikes, scooters and cars. ☐

Heavily promote sustainable travel and provide information regarding this on the event's website/app, and through other attendee communication channels. Provide regular announcements concerning public transport and shuttle bus services during the event. ☐

Promote car sharing and recognise, or reward, those that opt in to car-sharing programs. ☐

Ensure event maps contain public transport/shuttle bus pick-up/drop off points and bike parking areas. ☐

Offer bundled tickets for 'show and ride'. ☐

Provide VIP access, priority seats or other incentives to 'green' travellers. ☐

If car parking is available, give priority spots to electric and hybrid vehicles, and for those arriving in full cars. ☐

Dampen enthusiasm for driving by requiring car parking spaces to be booked in advance. Charge a fee for parking that will make public transport more attractive. ☐

Put 'anti-idling' policies in place in delivery areas of the event site. Ensure event security enforce this. ☐

Source locally to reduce product miles — this includes staff and labour contractors. ☐

Provide on-site storage for exhibitors and vendors to prevent many short trips back to their home bases. ☐

Set up wholesalers on-site to service vendors (especially food vendors) to reduce the need for short re-provisioning trips. ☐

If air travel is likely to be involved for a meaningful number of attendees, identify a suitable carbon offsetting project partner and actively promote this to flyers, or suggest airlines that operate offsetting programs. ☐

Offset any flights paid for by the event. ☐

In addition to employing a sustainable travel plan, location decisions made by event organisers can also be significant in reducing the need for attendee travel. For example, venues can be chosen that are conveniently accessible by public transport and that offer in their immediate vicinity (and within easy walking distance) a range of accommodation options; location decisions for 'out of venue' activities (for example, dinners and receptions) can be made with reference to their walking distance from the event's main venue; and cities/towns can be selected to conduct events that have a demonstrable commitment to environmental sustainability including well-developed mass transit systems and bike paths.

Where local transport is required, consideration should be given to the use of electric or hybrid vehicles. Additionally, incentivising the use of bikes by detailing bike routes that can be taken to the event site/venue, providing bike parking facilities, or arranging satellite park and ride locations, can all contribute to reducing private transport use. Thought could also be given to providing priority parking for electric/hybrid cars and ensuring that these types of vehicles are used whenever possible by the event's organisers.

Sustainable water and sanitation for event production

Events will vary in terms of the options available to them for conserving water and managing wastewater. Venue-based events, for example, are limited by the systems that are already in place, although selecting venues that are active in this area, for example, those that employ waterless urinals and auto-shutoff taps should be a consideration in venue choice. Outdoor events face a variety of challenges in this area. Water is used in a range of different ways in these settings including for catering, cleaning, toilet flushing, washing, attendee drinking water provision, misting stations, dust settling, grounds preparation and garden maintenance. If mains water is not available for these purposes, water will need to be trucked in (which will increase an outdoor event's carbon footprint), and/or dams or other storage water storage facilities will be needed. Further, wastewater, in the absence of access to a sewer system, might need to be stored and trucked from the event site periodically to treatment facilities if it cannot be processed on-site.

Greywater (water from showers and other washing operations) can sometimes be absorbed into the ground in soakaway areas or used, depending on the water management systems in place, for non-contact purposes such as toilet flushing and irrigation. It needs to be kept in mind, however, that local government and environmental agency regulations are likely to place restrictions on greywater collection and disposal to ensure contaminants are filtered through the soil before entering any nearby watercourses. Blackwater (that is, sewage and catering sullage) cannot be easily processed on most event sites, although some events (for example, Woodford Folk Festival) that own their own large event site have installed on-site sewerage treatment systems for this purpose. The cost of having waste of this nature transported off-site, along with the environmental consequences of doing so, has given rise to a range of viable alternatives. The use of waterless portable, or fixed, composting toilets are increasingly being used in festival settings. These toilets have been found to reduce the volume of transportable sewage by up to 80 per cent as waste is composted in situ, as well as generating significant water savings. It should also be kept in mind, in the context of toilets, that biological treatment products should be preferred over harsh chemicals as they are much kinder to sewerage systems and break down more readily. Indeed, chemical use at events should be carefully monitored and natural and/or biodegradable products used wherever possible. A checklist to guide sustainable water management has been provided in figure 12.5.

Site use management

Protection of event sites, particularly if parkland is being used, can be a factor that organisers of outdoor events need to consider during the operational phase of their event. The challenges that might be faced in this regard include the need to prevent erosion; soil compaction around trees (which restricts water-reaching tree roots); weather events that can quickly cause grassed areas to become saturated and susceptible to damage; and the need to protect wildlife and wildlife habitat. Various practices can be employed to address these possible concerns, including the use of trackways, roping off areas, limiting vehicle access routes and seeking advice from local wildlife organisations. Events can also play a meaningful role in the environmental enhancement of the sites they use. The Woodford Folk Festival, which, as noted earlier, owns its own site, is acting to:

- establish habitat for butterflies and other invertebrates, as well as wildlife, through planting trees and bushes
- restore soil fertility through distributing compost collected from food stalls during the event
- replace the event site's original flora including fungi, cycads, orchids, palms and ferns
- eliminate areas of erosion (Woodford Folk Festival 2018).

FIGURE 12.5 Sustainable water management checklist

Water conservation

Ensure water-saving devices are on taps, hoses, showers and drinking water standpipes. ☐

Reduce water usage through 'water-wise' grounds preparation and gardening. ☐

Use dust suppressant additives to reduce water volume used on dampening dust. ☐

Capture water and store it in rainwater tanks or dams. ☐

Use waterless urinals and toilets (for example, vacuum or compost toilets). ☐

Reduce water pressure. ☐

Supply water-free hand sanitisers. ☐

Conduct a water conservation campaign to encourage water saving by event attendees and the event's workforce. ☐

Wastewater management

Capture and treat greywater using soakaways, reed beds or mechanical filtering. ☐

Re-use greywater on-site for non-contact uses (for example, toilet flushing). ☐

Emissions to water

Use chemical-free cleaning products. ☐

Use biological toilet treatment products. ☐

Use non-toxic paints. ☐

12.2 Event sustainability policies

LEARNING OBJECTIVE 12.2 Employ strategies and practices to reduce the environmental impact of events.

A sustainability policy will help to focus the efforts of an event's planning and production team around the challenge of reducing its environmental impacts. A comprehensive policy of this nature should provide:

- a statement of commitment by the event and its leadership to sustainable event production and upholding sustainable development principles
- key impact areas it seeks to engage with — for example, energy use, transport, water and effluent management, resource consumption and recovery, plastic use and general site environmental management
- objectives that will be used to measure performance against, along with a clear indication of how monitoring and review will take place
- information on the consultation and engagement process to be employed with stakeholders and staff
- any codes of best practice/standards (for example, ISO 20121 — Event Sustainability Management Systems) or certification schemes (see later discussion) to which the event has committed or plans to commit.

While not common, an increasing number of events, event organisers and locations (for example, local council areas) are acting to develop these guiding documents. Figure 12.6 provides an example of one that has been developed by a local council in Sydney, Australia to guide both the conduct of its own events and those that happen in the area it manages.

FIGURE 12.6 Extract from the Mosman Council Sustainable Event Management Policy

Mosman Sustainable Event Management Policy
Purpose/explanation
To ensure that sustainability principles are applied to the planning, management and implementation of all events within the scope of this Policy. Mosman Council is committed to:

▶

1. reducing Mosman's ecological footprint and minimising impacts on the environment by incorporating the principles of ecologically sustainable development into event planning, management and implementation
2. using current best practice standards
3. applying sustainability principles to the purchasing and procurement of goods and services for events
4. implementing waste avoidance strategies and maximising resource recovery for events
5. ensuring responsible use of natural resources and protecting flora and fauna through appropriate event planning and management
6. implementing efficiency measures to reduce water and energy consumption before, during and after events
7. reducing greenhouse gas emissions through sustainable transport options
8. enhancing environmental awareness and fostering environmentally responsible behaviour in all relevant stakeholders to build their capacity to plan, organise, deliver or participate in a sustainable event
9. striving for ongoing improvement in environmental performance through monitoring and evaluation of sustainable events.

Scope

This Policy is to be implemented in conjunction with the Mosman Guide to Sustainable Event Management. It applies to all events, workshops and meetings of 50 or greater participants coordinated by Mosman Council and/or held on land owned or managed by Council within the Mosman Local Government Area. This includes, but is not limited to:
- internal events
  - special events
  - civic events
  - forums/conferences
  - workshops; meetings
  - Mosman markets
  - Festival of Mosman
- external events
  - minor events
  - major events.

Exemptions

This Policy does not apply to:
- wedding receptions held at the Art Gallery or Rotunda
- small private gatherings of less than 50 participants
- internal Council meetings of less than 50 participants.

Notwithstanding, the organisers of these events are encouraged to consider the environment during their event/meeting, including the purchasing and use of sustainable products, catering, sustainable transport options, waste minimisation and the appropriate disposal of waste and recycling in the bin facilities provided.

Event management requirements and considerations

Sustainability principles should be considered and demonstrated during:
- pre-event planning — to incorporate sustainability into event planning, contract management, procurement and promotion prior to an event
- event implementation — delivering and managing the planned activities during the event, and monitoring to ensure compliance with the Policy.

The following should be considered and actions incorporated, where applicable, into the planning, management and implementation of all events within the scope of this Policy:
- waste avoidance and minimisation
- resource recovery (reuse, recycling)
- energy conservation
- air quality
- sustainable transport
- water conservation
- biodiversity conservation
- animal welfare/ethics
- sustainable purchasing (for example, sustainable products/services)
- social considerations (for example, volunteering, charity)
- economic considerations (for example, local stakeholders, local product, value for money).

Mandatory Inclusions

The Mandatory Inclusions must be complied with for all events within the scope of this Policy.
- Promotional materials are to be printed on recycled paper (80–100% post-consumer recycled content).

- All cups, plates, napkins and cutlery purchased, used and distributed at an event must be made from recycled/recyclable /reusable/biodegradable and/or compostable materials.
- Plastic bags are not to be used and/or given away during events. Alternative products should be used/provided.
- Balloons are not to be released into the environment before, during or after any event.

  Note: Balloons may be used as decoration both at indoor and outdoor events as long as they are adequately weighted and/or secured, and are not released into the environment.

Preferred alternatives

Event organisers are strongly encouraged to consider the following preferred alternatives:

- Where products such as tea, coffee, hot chocolate or chocolate are to be provided at events, the use of Fair-Trade products are preferred.
- Encourage event participants to bring their own reusable water bottle to the event.
- Provide alternative water sources in lieu of giving away or selling plastic water bottles. Alternative water sources could include:
  - providing pitchers of water for meetings/workshops/events
  - water stations set up with water containers or water trailers
  - use of bubblers or water bottle refill stations, if available at the event venue.

  Where there are valid reasons for alternatives not to be used (that is, specific sporting events, safety reasons), the event organiser must ensure that sufficient recycling bin facilities and adequate signage is provided for the appropriate disposal of plastic water bottles for recycling.

Sustainable Event Management Checklist and Plan

Under this Policy, relevant Council staff responsible for the planning and implementation of Council events must complete the Sustainable Event Management Checklist. External event organisers must complete and submit to Council the Sustainable Event Management Plan. Both the Sustainable Event Management Checklist and Sustainable Event Management Plan must demonstrate that the Mandatory Inclusions have been implemented, that the Preferred Alternatives have been considered, and that other sustainability aspects, as provided in this Policy, have been incorporated, where possible. The areas identified in the Checklist or Plan are as follows.

- Mandatory inclusions
- Preferred alternatives
- Venue selection
- Transport
- Water and energy
- Waste management equipment, supplies and products
- Event promotion & materials
- Catering training / awareness.

Compliance

Failure to comply with this Policy and the approved Sustainable Event Management Plan may result in the exclusion of the external event organisers responsible for the non-compliance in any future events hosted by Council, or inform Council's decision to reject a booking on land managed by Council of any future events hosted by the non-complying external event organisers.

Responsibility

The Manager Environment and Services will be responsible for reviewing this Policy, and monitoring compliance and environmental performance in accordance with the Policy. The Venue and Markets Officer will be responsible for ensuring that Mosman Markets stallholders comply with the Mandatory Inclusions and where appropriate the Preferred Alternatives included within this Policy. The Events and Marketing Coordinator and Council Bookings Officer will be responsible for ensuring external event organisers/individuals are aware of this policy and are provided with the documentation to complete and submit the Sustainable Event Management Plan as required. The Rangers will be responsible for monitoring compliance on the day of the event, where possible. All relevant Council staff and external event organisers responsible for planning, managing and implementing events, workshops and meetings (of 50 or greater participants) must be aware of and adhere to this Policy and the accompanying Guide to Sustainable Event Management.

Communication

This Policy is to be communicated to external event organisers through the event booking process and made available on Council's website. The Policy detail is to be communicated to Council staff via internal communication channels and the new staff induction process.

Related information

The existing Special Events Management Policy and Drill Hall Venue Hire Policy and Procedures must be implemented in conjunction with this Policy to ensure sustainability principles are considered and

▶

incorporated into all events within the scope of this Policy. This Policy allows for the provision of a preferred suppliers list for sustainable products, including but not limited to; printing, catering supplies, a preferred suppliers list which can be utilised by internal Council staff and external event organisers to purchase sustainable products/materials for an event within the scope of this Policy.

Source: Mosman Council 2014.

12.3 Measurement, industry initiatives and certification

LEARNING OBJECTIVE 12.3 Source information concerning the environmental management of events.

Measurement

The only way to assess how an event is performing against its environmental objectives or 'key sustainability indicators' is to measure its performance. The following are examples of the quantitative measures that can be used (depending on the event) to assess its environmental performance:

- waste
  - weight or volume of general waste to landfill
  - weight or volume of recycled waste (by material type)
  - weight or volume of biodegradable waste (by type of processing — compost, energy recovery, landfill)
  - weight or volume of salvaged waste (materials that would otherwise have been disposed of (for example, timber, food)
  - waste intensity of the event (by person, square metre of venue size, days or another relevant measure)
- energy
  - landline (mains or grid) power: kilowatt hours (kWh)
  - mobile power generators: litres of diesel, average efficiency by loading rate
  - zero-emissions power: kilowatt hours (kWh)
  - proportion of event power from renewable sources
  - total greenhouse gas emissions (GHG) from event power
  - total GHGs avoided due to conservation or renewable sources
- water
  - volume of water used, by water source
  - volume of greywater and/or sewage produced
- transport
  - production transport
  - ground transport (freight) of infrastructure and goods (distance, by mode, GHG)
  - air freight (distance, weight, GHG)
  - participant travel
  - percentage of event attendees, workforce, talent, contractors and others involved in the event, by each mode of transport
  - average distance travelled for each mode
  - total GHG
- sourcing
  - percentage of sourcing by material type that meets the environmental specifications of the sourcing policy.

While measurement is important in both accessing current performance and in setting benchmarks for future performance, it must be realised that it can take a deal of time and resources, depending on the scale and nature of the event (for example, single venue or multi-venue). Compounding the difficulties associated with measurement is that different units of measurement are involved (for example, kilowatts and litres) which present challenges when seeking to identify which aspects of an event has the greatest impact. In recent years several online event carbon calculators have become available that allow the carbon emissions of events to be assessed, but again they require a commitment on behalf of the event concerned to collect data on its various aspects in order to provide the necessary information. These difficulties notwithstanding, measurement is key to driving future efforts at reducing event environmental impacts. If an event has deep enough pockets it may be able to commission an impact analysis; however, most events will likely not be in a financial position to do this. An alternative approach would be to identify elements of the event with the greatest potential for impacts and for an event to focus on these, gradually moving to embrace other areas in subsequent event deliveries. In any case, building measurement into an event's sustainability plan at the outset, allocating resources to this task, along with responsibility (perhaps to the event's 'green' team), will go a long way to ensuring progress is made in this area.

Industry initiatives

Event industry groups with an environmental focus have emerged in recent years to aid the efforts of events seeking to progress their sustainability efforts. A Greener Festival (a not-for-profit company), for example, is an organisation committed to assisting music and arts-based events seeking to reduce their environmental impacts. It does this by providing information and educational resources, and by facilitating the sharing of ideas among event managers (A Greener Festival 2020). In the case of sporting events, the Council for Responsible Sport provides both resources for events seeking to 'green' their operations along with a path to environmental certification (Council for Responsible Sport 2018). The Sustainable Event Alliance is another organisation that has been active in this area. It comprises an international network of practitioners and stakeholders involved in aiding the events sector develop its ability to create solutions to the sustainability challenges it faces (Sustainable Event Alliance 2020).

Event industry associations can also be observed to have become increasingly active in sustainability matters. The International Festivals and Events Association, for example, has for several years acted to acknowledge the environmental achievements of its members through its annual industry awards. The USA-based Events Industry Council, and its Sustainability Initiative, which is primarily directed at business events such as conferences and meetings, is another example of an industry body actively involved in encouraging more environmentally sustainable event operations. Still another industry association that has been active in this area is the UFI (The Global Association of the Exhibition Industry) that has rolled out several initiatives in recent years designed to reduce the environmental impact of exhibitions. These have included: educational forums; reports on sustainability practices; and an ongoing project on exhibition sustainability impact measurement (UFI 2020).

The actions of individual events and/or their owners in progressing the adoption of sustainable practices should also be noted. In the sports area, for example, large-scale events and their owners — such as the FIFA World Cup, the Commonwealth Games and the Olympic Games — have been particularly active in developing sustainable event frameworks to overlay on their event planning efforts. Some have gone further still, with the International Olympic Committee (IOC), for example, having: established processes to share information on sustainable practices through its network; included sustainability conditions as part of its bid requirements for potential host cities; developed a sustainability and legacy commission to guide its activities in the area; and established a bi-annual conference on sport and the environment which it has conducted since 2004 (International Olympic Committee 2018).

Green event standards and certifications

The event industry's approach to sustainability management has been progressing and maturing over the past decade. In 2012 an international standard was released: ISO 20121 — Event Sustainability Management Systems. This standard requires a systematic approach to the sustainable management of events and helps to embed processes and rigour in the way event organisations implement sustainability practices (International Organization for Standardization 2012). ISO 20121 is not a checklist or performance-based form of certification, rather it provides the basis for auditing events to establish if the systems and processes they have in place are sufficient to conform to the standard and to be certified as such.

There are also environmental certification schemes through which events can seek external accreditation based on their environmental performance. These programs often require events to measure, monitor and make ongoing improvements in a range of key environmental areas such as energy and water use. An example of one such program is that of EventCheck (EarthCheck 2018).

Event sustainability as the norm

While it is difficult to generalise about how events have approached the challenges posed by the need to act in ways that are more environmentally sustainable, it can nonetheless be observed that it is increasingly common for events to be proactive in this area. The establishment of bodies to aid events as they increasingly embrace green practices, the development of an ISO standard, and the creation of certification schemes and awards specific to this aspect of event management, all reflect a growing commitment to reducing event environmental impacts. This commitment is further evidenced by the actions of events of all scales and types, from mega-events such as the Olympics to more modestly sized public and business events.

Resources guiding the actions of events in this area have expanded rapidly. There are now texts (for example, *Sustainable event management: a practical guide* — Jones 2017), government-developed guides (for example, 'Sustainability guidelines for the Singapore MICE industry' — Singapore Tourism Board 2013), aggregations of online material provided by non-government organisations (for example, A Greener Festival and Event Training Australia's online event sustainability resources) and readily accessible information on practices currently in use by events and event owners (for example, Glastonbury Festival 2018; the International Olympic Committee 2018). There are also experts available, such as those involved with the Sustainable Event Alliance, that can assist events to develop and implement their sustainability policies and practices.

SUMMARY

This chapter provided an overview of the environmental impacts of event production. Additionally, it sought to engender an appreciation of best practice approaches to environmental management, and to provide examples of the use of such practices in various event settings. It also overviewed various industry initiatives, standards and certification schemes intended to encourage or facilitate actions designed to reduce event environmental impacts. Further, it highlighted the importance of measurement as a means of encouraging events to strive for improved environmental performance and pointed to the fact that it has increasingly become the norm for environmental sustainability to be embraced within the overall planning process of events. Finally, it drew attention to the extensive range of resources and expertise now available to event organisers as they seek to respond to the challenge of producing increasingly more environmentally sustainable events.

QUESTIONS

1 In general terms, what are the major areas in which events can impact the environment?

2 What functions does an event's environmental policy perform?

3 What types of solutions might be available to events seeking to reduce the environmental impacts flowing from their material usage?

4 Briefly discuss how waste associated with food preparation and consumption at events can be minimised.

5 Select an event that has made a significant effort to engage with the concept of sustainable event production. Identify and discuss the practices it employed for this purpose.

6 How has the event industry responded to the challenge of producing more environmentally friendly events?

7 Identify and briefly discuss approaches that can be employed to reduce energy usage in either a venue-based or outdoor event.

8 Briefly discuss the concept of sustainable purchasing. Why is this concept significant from the viewpoint of sustainable event management?

9 Access either the International Association of Exhibitions and Events website (www.iaee.com/res ources/sustainability-initiative) or A Greener Festival website (www.agreenerfestival.com). Briefly describe the types of information available from your chosen site that might assist an event manager in producing events that are more environmentally sustainable.

10 How would you describe the efforts of the event industry to date as it seeks to meet the challenge of producing more sustainable events?

CASE STUDY

VOLVO OCEAN RACE 2017–18

The Volvo Ocean Race is the world's longest and most competitive professional sporting event. Considered by many as the pinnacle of offshore ocean racing, the event takes place over a period of nine months and involves a series of legs that take its participants around the world. The race is a feat of human endurance and maritime ingenuity and has millions of fans and followers.

The 2017–18 Volvo Ocean Race was its 13th edition (the event takes place every fourth year) and involved stops at twelve host cities. At each host city temporary Race Villages were established that were visited by around 2.5 million people. Given the event's high profile and associated fan base, and its use of the earth's oceans as its racetrack, the event organisers saw the opportunity to leverage it to highlight the related issues of ocean health and plastic pollution. In doing so they aimed to engender lasting impressions and commitments for action by the stakeholders it touched during its nine-month conduct. The event was also cautious to ensure its own operations did not contribute to these problems or to environmental degradation more generally. Its sustainability strategy was therefore based on three pillars: maximise impact, minimise environmental footprint and leave a positive legacy. Its actions were further guided by a sustainability charter that set out the intentions of the 2017–18 race in this area. The event's program of awareness-raising and engagement activities included:

- using entrants to capture and analyse information data on the spread of plastic waste and the impact of the changing climate on ocean health and weather patterns
- running seven Ocean Summits at host cities that were designed to raise awareness and seek solutions to matters linked to ocean health. These events were attended by over 2000 politicians, scientists and business leaders.
- developing an education program that engaged over 100 000 school children in 37 countries, in host cities and online
- operating a cinema in Race Villages that educated 404 000 visitors on matters linked to ocean health
- developing a publication, *Turn the tide on plastic at sporting events — user guide*, to share what the event learnt through its efforts in this area
- developing exhibitions and activities at Race Villages to further engage attendees around ocean health–related issues
- establishing a partnership with the United Nations Environment Programme's (UNEP) Clean Seas campaign (and directly linking with United Nations sustainable development goals) that served to further amplify the event's message as well as offering a platform for public commitments and pledges. As a result of these efforts, some 20 000 people and three countries signed the UNEP Clean Seas pledge during the event.
- using the profile of the event to develop a powerful communications program designed to convey a message in host destinations, as well as globally, of the need to improve ocean health. This involved the creation of online videos and articles, and the use of competitors as media spokespeople and in community outreach programs. The latter also included well-publicised beach clean-up events in each host city.

The event's own efforts at sustainability were also significant. In this regard it sought to:
- utilise the sustainability framework provided by ISO 20121
- source resources from local suppliers and engage in sustainable procurement
- identify, and seek to reduce, the environmental impacts of freight and flight requirements
- use renewal energy (for example, biodiesel) when available
- establish a 'green team' with representatives from all functional areas of the event organisation
- encourage stakeholders to use sustainable means of transport
- partner with recycling companies to develop a resource recovery strategy capable of diverting more than 75 per cent of waste from landfill
- educate Race Village visitors as to the importance of recovering plastic at the end of its life, and the different forms plastics take, along with the recycling options specific to each
- minimise the use of plastic by eliminating single-use plastics, excluding plastic water bottles and plastic food and beverage containers, and installing water bottle refill points in each Race Village
- find solutions for hard-to-recycle forms of plastic and e-waste in host destinations
- use food serviceware, such as plates, cups and cutlery, that were compostable
- collect food waste for later processing into organic fertiliser.

The results of these efforts have yet to be fully reported upon; however, interim results relating to the area of waste are impressive, as can be seen from the figures below:
- 388 207 single-use plastic bottles avoided across the 12 host city stopovers
- 1 000 000 single-use plastic food and beverage serviceware items avoided
- 180 000 single-use cable ties avoided through employing reusable bungee straps
- 67 per cent of all waste resources recovered, recycled or composted
- 10 per cent of typical potable water volume used (when compared with other events of its type and size) in the Race Village in Cape Town through targeted water conservation and non-potable water sourcing
- 17.7 tonnes of plastic collected for recycling — it is estimated 20 per cent of plastic was lost to landfill due to mishandling
- 2.69 tonnes of film (soft) plastic recovered through targeted collection for recycling
- 29.8 tonnes of compostable resources (such as food waste and disposable plates) collected for composting.
- 3 tonnes of high-quality food donated to charity.

Several key factors can be identified in the event's success at awareness raising and impact minimisation. It was very effective at engaging and enthusing its stakeholders, including its partners (both commercial and non-commercial), sponsors, host cities, sailors and its workforce around a potent and tangible issue (ocean health) with obvious links to the sport of ocean racing. This also meant that the event's own sustainability efforts (particularly reducing plastic usage) could be framed within the context of ocean protection, a problem that people were already primed to seek a solution to, and therefore willing to act to address. It can also be said that there was a strong level of commitment, dedication and support from the event's leadership team around the sustainability program which served to drive it forward. This support can be seen in the willingness to create and resource a 'green team' to action the event's sustainability plan. The power of sport to connect with a large audience was also a factor in the success of the event's efforts, specifically its ability to amplify issues that can be linked to it.

In terms of the event's ongoing legacy, the UNEP's Clean Seas campaign has agreed to continue its partnership with the event as it considers it to be a valuable platform to create awareness and empower people around its goal of a plastic-free ocean. Additionally, the event contributed in a meaningful way to ongoing scientific research through its data collection efforts and left millions of people with a deeper appreciation of the urgent need to address the issue of ocean health.

Prepared by Meegan Jones, Sustainability Program Manager, Volvo Ocean Race

QUESTIONS

1 Outline the educative practices engaged in by the Volvo Ocean Race. What other event settings do you believe these practices could be used in?

2 Go to the Volvo Ocean Race website (www.volvooceanrace.com/en/sustainability/news.html) and explore the section dealing with the event's sustainability efforts. Identify and briefly discuss three ways in which it was able to project its message of the need to free the ocean of plastic pollution.

3 Discuss the value of creating a 'green team' for large events, such as the Volvo Ocean Race, with multiple functional areas within its organisational structure.

4 Why can sports be effective vehicles for driving environmental awareness and actions?

5 Identify, and briefly discuss, the key success factors in the event's environmental sustainability efforts.

REFERENCES

A Greener Festival 2020, 'About us', www.agreenerfestival.com/about-us, viewed 22 January 2020.

Adelaide Convention Centre 2018, 'Adelaide Convention Centre cements global sustainability leadership with coveted EarthCheck Platinum Certification', www.adelaidecc.com.au/adelaide-convention-centre-cements-global-sustainability-leadership-with-coveted-earthcheck-platinum-certification, viewed 1 November 2018.

Bruntland Commission 1987, *Our Common Future*, Oxford University Press: Oxford.

Choice 2017, 'Should you but carbon offsets', 16 May, www.choice.com.au/travel/on-holidays/airlines/articles/should-you-buy-carbon-offsets-for-flights, viewed 27 October 2018.

Clean Event NZ 2020, 'Waste management for events', www.cleanevent.co.nz/services, viewed 21 January 2020.

Climate Wave 2018, 'Concert for the Planet', www.climatewave.com/concert-for-the-planet, viewed 28 October 2018.

Council for Responsible Sport 2018, 'What we do', www.councilforresponsiblesport.org/what-we-do, viewed 3 November 2018.

DGTL Festival 2018, 'DGDL presents sustainable game-changers', https://dgtl.nl/dgtl-presents-sustainable-gamechangers, viewed 2 November 2018.

Earthcheck 2018, 'EventCheck', www.earthcheck.org/products-services/certification/eventcheck, viewed 3 November 2018.

Glastonbury Festival 2018, Our Green Policies, www.glastonburyfestivals.co.uk/information/green-glastonbury/our-green-policies, viewed 4 November 2018.

Gold Coast 2018 Commonwealth Games Corporation (GOLDOC) 2016, 'Sustainable Sourcing Code', https://gc2018.com/sites/default/files/2017-11/GC2018_Sustainable_Sourcing_Code.pdf, accessed 23 April 2020.

Greenpower 2011, 'Event overview', www.greenpower.gov.au/events, viewed 28 October 2018.

International Olympic Committee 2018, 'Sustainability essentials', www.olympic.org/sustainability-essentials, viewed 4 November 2018.

International Organization for Standardization 2012, 'Sustainable events with ISO 20121', www.iso.org/iso-20121-sustainable-events.html, viewed 3 November 2018.

Jensen, T 2019, 'Roskilde Festival: electric cars replace generators at food court', *DTU*, 5 July, www.dtu.dk/english/news/2019/07/roskilde-festival-electric-cars-replace-generators-at-food-court, viewed 24 April 2020.

Jones, M 2017, *Sustainable Event Management: A Practical Guide*, 3rd ed., Routledge, London

Melbourne Convention and Exhibition Centre 2020, 'Our Commitment to Sustainability', https://mcec.com.au/about-us/sustainability, viewed 20 January 2020.

Mosman Council 2014, 'Sustainable events policy', https://mosman.nsw.gov.au/file_download/2352/MOSMAN+SUSTAINABLE+EVENT+MANAGEMENT+POLICY.pdf, viewed 20 February 2020.

Powerful Thinking 2018, 'Festival vision: 2025', www.powerful-thinking.org.uk/vision2025, viewed 28 October 2018.

RAI Amsterdam Convention and Exhibition Centre 2020, 'Zero waste', www.rai.nl/en/organising/services/afvalmanagement, viewed 20 January 2020.

Shambala Festival 2020, 'Green Shambala', www.shambalafestival.org/essential-info/sustainability, viewed 22 January 2020.

Singapore Tourism Board 2013, 'Sustainability guidelines for the Singapore MICE industry', www.visitsingapore.com/content/dam/MICE/Global/useful-downloads/sustainability-guidelines-for-mice.pdf, viewed 22 January 2020.

Sustainable Event Alliance 2020, 'Roles', www.sustainable-event-alliance.org/sea-roles, viewed 22 January 2020.

UFI 2020, 'Sustainable development', www.ufi.org/industry-resources/sustainable-development, viewed 3 November 2018.

Woodford Folk Festival 2018, 'Environmental statement', www.woodfordfolkfestival.com/about/environmental-statement, viewed 29 October 2018.

Yuan, Y 2013, 'Adding environmental sustainability to the management of event tourism', *International Journal of Culture, Tourism and Hospitality Research*, vol. 7, issue 2, pp. 175–83.

ZAP Concepts n.d., 'Volvo Ocean Race', www.zapconcepts.com/en/category/volvo-ocean-race-en, viewed 28 October 2018.

ACKNOWLEDGEMENTS

Photo: © spwidoff / Shutterstock.com

Figure 12.1: © Gold Coast 2018 Commonwealth Games Corporation GOLDOC 2016

Figure 12.2: © Melbourne Convention and Exhibition Centre 2020

Figure 12.3: © Angela Hampton Picture Library / Alamy Stock Photo

Figure 12.6: © Mosman Council 2014

CHAPTER 13

Legal considerations in event planning and management

LEARNING OBJECTIVES

After studying this chapter, you should be able to:

13.1 describe the legal structures available to event organisations

13.2 recognise where contractual situations arise when organising events

13.3 state the various forms that intellectual property rights take and the significance of these to event organisers

13.4 describe consumer law protections for event attendees and their implications for event organisers

13.5 discuss the duty of care principle and its relationship to risk management and insurance in event settings

13.6 identify and describe those laws and regulations of relevance to the conduct of events and those licences and permits that may be required for an event to proceed.

Introduction

The impact of the law on event planning and management is both immense and diverse. That is, almost all activity connected to the preparing for and staging of an event will be affected by some aspect of the law.

All events are owned and managed by a legal entity. There will be a multitude of contracts entered by the owners and organisers of an event, most of which will be in writing, some made verbally — both of which are equally binding. There will also be intellectual property rights that an event's owner, and its various stakeholders such as sponsors and performers, will possess and that will need to be acknowledged and protected. Additionally, when promoting events care will need to be taken not to infringe these rights and to ensure that activities in this area take place with due reference to consumer protection laws.

Event organisers also have a particularly onerous duty of care to both employees (work health and safety) and patrons (negligence). In addition to observing the relevant regulations, there is the need to engage in risk management, a key aspect of which is identifying and taking out appropriate insurances. Coupled with these actions is the need to acquire numerous licences and permits depending on the event type, its location and the nature of services that are to be provided to attendees.

The foregoing legal issues will be discussed in this chapter with the intent of making event organisers aware of their legal responsibilities, and how these responsibilities influence the way their events are planned and delivered. In many instances it will be prudent to seek legal advice when navigating these responsibilities. For much of the time, however, it is a case of simply being mindful of these legal considerations and ensuring that they are observed. Remember, ignorance is no excuse in the eyes of the law!

Event organisers need to be mindful of the fact that Australia is a federation and as such both Commonwealth laws, that relate to the whole of the country, as well as individual state/territory laws that relate only to their jurisdiction, need to be taken into account when planning and conducting events. It is beyond the scope of this chapter to cover all laws from all these jurisdictions with possible implications for event organisers; instead the focus here is on those general legal principles and commonly shared laws with most relevance to the event context.

13.1 Legal structures for event ownership and management

LEARNING OBJECTIVE 13.1 Describe the legal structures available to event organisations.

All events have in law an owner/s and an organiser. They may or may not be the same person(s) or company — that is, there may be different legal entities that own the event and who plan and manage it. So, for example, an industry association's annual conference, which is held at a different location every year, might assign (through a contract) the management of the event to a different conference-organising firm each year based in its chosen destination. In other instances, an event, such as a privately organised, annual music festival, will be owned and managed by the same organisation. In either situation, legal entities need to be established as vehicles through which the event can be conducted.

Legal entities

There are fundamentally four types of legal entity that are typically used for the ownership of an event, or by those charged with its planning and management:

1. *sole proprietor*: one person; unlimited personal liability
2. *partnership*: two or more persons; joint and several personal liability
3. *company*: a separate legal entity to those that own the company; limited personal liability; governed by the *Corporations Act 2001* (Cth)
4. *association*: relevant only to not-for-profit organisations. If unincorporated the members have unlimited personal liability (that is, legal responsibility) similar to that of sole proprietors and partners. If incorporated, the members and the committee have limited personal liability like that of a company. Associations are governed by the various state or territory associations incorporation Acts.

There are other types of legal entities, such as trusts; however, the choice of entity is based on both legal (for example, liability concerns) and tax considerations. It will also depend on the specific characteristics of the event concerned. Is it a one-off? Is it being conducted by a not-for-profit organisation? Are there a number of persons involved and are they wanting to operate together? When selecting between these options it is wise to seek advice from a lawyer (and possibly an accountant) to determine which legal entity best suits an event's specific circumstances and those involved with it.

Whichever type of business structure is chosen, there must be a legal entity in existence. In order to establish such an entity several formalities need to be observed, in particular the business must have either an ABN (Australian business number) or an ACN (Australian company number) and a business name. These are attained through the Australian Securities and Investments Commission (ASIC).

13.2 Contracts

LEARNING OBJECTIVE 13.2 Recognise where contractual situations arise when organising events.

There is no more fundamental feature of doing business in relation to an event than the contract. A contract is essentially a legally enforceable agreement between two or more legal entities (typically referred to as 'parties'). A contract can be in writing or verbal (except contracts in relation to land which must be in writing and signed). Almost every provision of a service or a good will be based on a contract: the talent; food and alcohol supply and service thereof; entry/seating tickets; sponsors; risk management plan; security; venue hire; marketing; and broadcasting, to name but a few.

Formation of a contract

To form a contract, there are six elements.
1. There must be an intention to enter a legal relationship.
2. There must be an agreement. This is best understood as a meeting of the minds. That is, all parties to the contract must agree on exactly the same things.
3. There must be an exchange. This is formally referred to as 'consideration'. It means something must be given for something. Typically, it will be a good or service in exchange for money. It is not necessary for money to be involved. For example, a provider of goods (such as food or alcohol) may accept in exchange the promotion of their brand and product at an event, along with tickets to attend.
4. The parties to the contract must have the 'capacity' to enter a legally binding agreement. This is particularly relevant when dealing with minors, that is, children under the age of 18. Unless it can be shown that the contract was for the benefit of the child, then the contract may be unenforceable. The meaning of benefit in this context will generally refer to the provision of the necessities of life and employment. Other persons who lack the capacity to enter contracts include those who are mentally ill or so intoxicated that they did not understand to what they were agreeing.

    It is worth noting that an unincorporated association, such as a local community not-for-profit group, has no legal status and therefore has no capacity to enter a contract. In such a circumstance the contract should be entered into with a specific person(s).
5. The terms of the contract must be 'certain'. The terms of the contract are all the provisions (promises) in the contract. If there is ambiguity as to the term of a contract then the term may be deleted from the contract or in some cases the whole contract could be unenforceable, depending on the nature of the term. Ambiguity around money terms will usually render the contract void.
6. A contract must be for a legal object. Hence any element(s) of an event, that is outside the law is fundamentally flawed. This does not mean all contracts related to the event are void, only those which are illegal themselves. For example, a performer who agrees to perform an illegal act will not be able to enforce a contract between themselves and an event organiser in order to obtain their payment.

One oft-found term in a contract, which is potentially unenforceable, is that which seeks to restrain a person from plying their trade. So, for example, if the event organiser seeks to create some exclusivity in relation to the talent, they may include a clause in the contract, which states that the talent will only perform at the organiser's event while in Australia and not for some fixed time before and after their performance at the event. This is described as a 'restraint of trade'. Great care needs to be taken with such clauses as unless the restraint is deemed to be reasonable (essentially based on for how long, where and for how much money), it will be removed from the contract and the talent will be able to perform whenever and wherever they want outside of their obligation to perform at the organiser's event.

In a similar vein, a performer cannot be compelled to perform. If the talent for any reason refuses to perform, the only remedy available to the event organiser is to seek compensation. Enforcing performance would be tantamount to slavery and hence is not acceptable.

Terms of the contract

All contracts are made up of terms. These are the promises that are made by the parties to the agreement and comprise the clauses in a contract. As noted in the previous section, it is important for terms to be clear and unambiguous. Furthermore, it is important to appreciate that not all terms are equal. The critical terms of a contract are known as 'conditions', while the less important ones are known as 'warranties'. The importance of this distinction is the different rights that arise upon their breach. If a condition or a 'fundamental term' is breached, then the other party has the option to terminate the contract and/or obtain compensation for any loss suffered. If, however, a warranty is breached, the other party may only obtain compensation — they cannot elect to terminate the contract.

While only necessary for contracts related to land — which therefore includes the leasing of an event's venue/site — the importance of having a written contract cannot be overstated. This is particularly important to ensure that what has been agreed to has been accepted and understood by all parties. Often there are negotiations preceding a finalised contract. During these discussions various representations will be made. Typically, it is only those representations, which are included in the written contract that are going to be enforceable. Moreover, having any representations in written form provides added certainty to what has been agreed. While it is better to have a contract signed as this provides proof that the other party intended to enter into it and to be bound by its terms, it is not necessary unless the contract relates to land. Having said that, it should be noted a verbal contract is just as enforceable as a contract in writing be it signed or unsigned.

One very important type of clause in a contract is the 'exclusion clause' (also known as a waiver or disclaimer). These are clauses, that seek to absolve one of the parties of legal responsibility even if they breach the law. Typically, these clauses relate to acts of negligence by one of the parties. In essence if, for example, an event organiser commits an act of negligence which causes injury to a patron of the event and there is an exclusion clause on the ticket — such as: 'we will not be responsible if any patron falls and suffers injury whether or not it is due to the acts of the event organiser or any of its employees' — then the patron will be unable to gain any compensation for any injury or loss suffered as a result of such a fall. Exclusion clauses are therefore very effective in protecting event organisers from being successfully sued, particularly for any acts of negligence. However, such clauses must be carefully worded and are best done so by a lawyer.

Performance of the contract

Contracts must be performed exactly as they are agreed, unless the parties mutually agree to vary the term(s) or, the contract itself allows for variation. For example, if the alcohol supplier for an event provides a wine of superior value and quality (and price!) to that which was agreed without seeking any increased payment, this may only be done with the consent of the event organiser.

An issue, that often arises in relation to an event is where some external factor renders it impossible for it to take place, or if it does proceed, its form is such that it is so different as to be effectively a changed experience. This is known as 'frustration' and is usually referred to as due to a 'force majeure' or 'act of God', that is, a circumstance over which neither of the parties to the contract had any control, such as a major weather event. A current example is the novel coronavirus (COVID-19) pandemic, which has seen many events cancelled due to government health and travel restrictions. Where a frustration to the performance of a contract occurs, the law states that it is only for those services, which have been provided up to the point of frustration (the governmental decrees) that payment needs be made. Any money paid for services not provided must be refunded. Hence if a person had a ticket to a show that did not happen because of government prohibitions then they would be eligible to receive their money back in full. If, however, one of the parties to a contract wilfully, or indifferently, fails to fulfil their promise(s) in the contract (for example, an event organiser replaces the headline act at a concert with a band covering the act's songs) then there are various remedies that the other party may pursue, as discussed in the following section.

Remedies for breach of contract

The most obvious remedy for a breach of a contract is, arguably, 'termination'. However, as indicated above, this is only available where the term breached was fundamental or essential. Hence termination should be a last resort and should be exercised carefully.

Other remedies include 'specific performance', which will require a party to the contract to do what they promised in the contract to do (excepting as stated above, to perform physically, such as to entertain). A party may also be stopped from ongoing breaches by way of an 'injunction'.

The most common remedy for breach of contract is monetary compensation or 'damages'. The aim of damages in a contract is to return the affected party to the position in which they would have been in if the breach had not occurred and the contract was performed as promised. Of particular relevance to the event industry are damages for 'loss of enjoyment'. These damages are awarded for the mental distress, injured feelings or disappointment a party suffers due to the breach of a contract where the object of the contract is to provide entertainment, enjoyment, pleasure or relaxation. The significant point about damages for loss of enjoyment is that the amount awarded by the court can be greater than the price of the contract. In one legal case, an event organiser was to supply a horse and carriage to take the bride to the church and, later, the newly married couple to the reception for £250. The carriage failed to appear. As a result, the new bride and groom hastily put a ribbon on a car and arrived at the reception very late. The resultant court case saw the event organiser being required to pay £3500 in damages for the disappointment suffered.

Selected considerations associated with event stakeholder contracts

There are various nuances associated with event stakeholder contracts of which event organisers need to be aware. These are discussed in the context of the major stakeholder groups with which an event organiser is likely to deal.

Entertainers

As well as the specifications for the entertainment contracted (for example, timing, repertoire), a common feature of entertainment contracts is the 'rider', which comprises an agreed amendment or addition to it. For example, hiring a headline performer may necessitate signing a 20–30-page contract. Appended to this agreement may be a rider requiring the event company to provide various goods and services (for example, alcohol, food, pre- and post-event accommodation, transport).

Another clause that sometimes appears in entertainment contracts concerns exclusivity. A headline act, for example, may be the major attraction for a music festival, and if the act were to also perform at a nearby location this could easily detract from the appeal of the event. To prevent this, a clause might be inserted into the contract that prevents the act from performing within a specified geographic radius or area during the event or for a certain number of days prior to or after it. This 'restraint of trade' is also discussed above under 'Formation of a contract'.

Contracts in this area should also include a clause to cover instances where a performer's agent is signing on their behalf, stating that they have written authority to do so. This authority should be made available to the event organiser prior to the contract being signed.

Venue

Venue contracts can be quite lengthy and cover a multitude of factors. Depending on the scale and nature of the event, and its program elements, it can be wise to have these documents reviewed by a lawyer before they are signed. Common inclusions in these documents are:

1. cost — the cost of hiring the venue for the required time. For events such as conferences held in hotels, the venue may charge on a per person per day fee basis that includes all food, beverage and venue hire, rather than separate rates for each element, which reduces the fixed costs of the conference and makes the process of event budgeting easier.
2. security deposit — an amount, generally a percentage of the hiring fee, to be used for any additional work such as cleaning and repairs that result from the event
3. cancellation — often a sliding scale showing cancellation fees as a percentage of the total venue hire fee by time out from the event
4. access — the period from which the event organiser will have access to the venue for setup purposes and the time by which all equipment and so on must be removed and the venue handed back
5. late conclusion — the penalty for the event going over time
6. house seats — the free tickets reserved for venue management
7. additions or alterations — any changes to the internal structures of the venue necessitated by the event, which are commonly required to be removed and the venue returned to its original condition
8. signage — placement locations and characteristics.

To avoid misunderstandings and potential unforeseen costs, it is prudent to ascertain exactly what facilities are included in the venue hire. Just because a piece of equipment, for example, was seen during a site inspection does not mean it is included in the venue hire cost.

Sponsor

The contract with a sponsor would include all that the sponsee promises to deliver — naming rights, signage, distribution of promotional material, complimentary tickets/registrations, pre-event promotional activities and so on — and the fee (consideration) to be paid in return. Details of how and when the payment (cash or contra) is to be made will also be included in the contract. Other matters that might need to be taken into account with this stakeholder group include the level of exclusivity provided by the agreement (for example, the sponsor will be the only sponsor of the conference reception) and how the event will inhibit ambush marketing (most applicable in large-scale events and discussed below).

Broadcast

Broadcast contracts can be very complex due to the large amounts of money involved. Common clauses covered in these contracts include:

- territory or region — the broadcast area (local, state or international) must be defined. If the contract states the region as 'world', the event company must be fully aware of the rights it is bestowing on the broadcaster and their potential value.
- guarantees — a guarantee that the event organiser/owner has the rights to sign for the whole event, because performers' copyright can preclude any broadcast without written permission from their record and publishing companies. Comedy acts and motivational speakers can also be particularly sensitive about broadcasts and recordings, and contracts in this area might require explicit permission from them to broadcast or record their performance.
- sponsorship — this area can present problems when different levels of sponsorship are involved. Sometimes the rights of the event sponsor and the broadcaster's sponsors can clash, which can require delicate negotiations to resolve. This is particularly applicable to sports events, where, for example. the match sponsor's products can clash with an individual team member's sponsorship.
- repeats, extracts and sub-licences — these determine the allowable number of broadcast repeats, whether the broadcaster is authorised to edit or take extracts from the broadcast, and how such material can be used. Other issues that can arise here, that contractual terms need to address, include instances where:
  - an event organiser signs with one broadcaster, and later finds that the rights to cover the event have been sold on, for a much larger figure, to another broadcaster
  - sub-licence clauses have been included that allow a broadcaster to use their own sponsors in broadcasts, which might be in direct competition with the event's sponsors
  - ownership of future broadcasting or recording rights is sought. The diversity of media now available mean such rights need to be very prescribed otherwise significant future revenue could be forgone.
- access — the physical access requirements of broadcasting must be part of the staging and logistic plan of the event. A broadcaster can easily disrupt an event by demanding to interview performers and celebrities. It is therefore necessary to specify how much access the broadcaster may have to performers and at what times.
- credits — this establishes, at the outset, the people and associated event elements that will be listed in the titles and credits.

Event organisers should also be mindful of the potential assistance broadcasters can offer in areas such as lighting and décor as it is in their interests to make the event look as visually appealing as possible.

Suppliers

Event organisers enter numerous contracts for the supply of goods and services. These agreements should specify not only quantity (for example, X number of data projectors) but also quality (for example, brand, projection quality). In some extreme instances in the area of catering, some organisers have included the right to employ their own supervising chef, to oversee the efforts of a contracted caterer to ensure agreed quality standards are met.

There are numerous examples of contracts linked to the stakeholders discussed here available through web searches. These contracts can be a useful starting point for gaining a more detailed understanding of their general inclusions (for example, a sample sponsorship agreement can be obtained for a nominal fee from the Arts Law Centre of Australia website: www.artslaw.com.au/product/sponsorship-agreement).

13.3 Intellectual property

LEARNING OBJECTIVE 13.3 State the various forms that intellectual property rights take and the significance of these to event organisers.

A legal feature of almost every event is intellectual property (IP). These will now be considered as they relate to events. It is important to note that as with all property, IP can be sold and bought, leased and licensed. For events, IP is most often dealt with in the latter ways.

Copyright

To have copyright is to be able to reproduce or publish a written or recorded work — such as a painting/drawing/poster, a song/music or event plan/layout.

What must always be remembered with copyright is that it does not arise until there is actual publication or recording in a tangible medium (which includes digital media). Hence, ideas for an event should be recorded before being communicated to anyone as there is no ownership of an 'idea'. There is no formal requirement to establish or register copyright, although it can be done (Australian Copyright Council 2020).

It is important to note that authorship of an event theme tune or event plan does not necessarily mean ownership. So, for example, an event owner might want to have a distinctive musical theme or song for their event. Accordingly, they engage a musician to compose the tune/song. This does not mean, however, that the event owner has ownership of the IP — the copyright — unless they acquire the ownership of it through the contracting process.

Copyright lasts for the life of the author plus 70 years, and can extend to:
- literary, dramatic, musical works and software programs
- photographs and engravings
- sound recordings
- cinematographic films
- television and sound broadcasts (*Copyright Act 1968* (Cth)).

In the area of performance copyright, it is noteworthy that a new organisation OneMusic Australia has been established to administer both the Australasian Performing Rights Association (APRA) and the Phonographic Performance Company of Australia Limited (PPCA). This body issues licences (and charges royalties) for the performance of their members' works to, among others, event organisers that wish to make use of them (OneMusic Australia 2020). For example, if an event decides to set fireworks to music, and makes use of recorded music to do so, it will likely need to pay a royalty fee to this organisation for its use or it will be contravening the copyright that exists in the work.

It is a well-established legal principle that there are no intellectual property rights in an event. That is, the owner or organiser of an event cannot, for example, restrict the taking of photographs of the event except by contractual agreement or by preventing access to the event. This principle was adopted and expanded in Australia in the case of *Victoria Park Racing & Recreation Grounds Co Ltd v. Taylor* (1937). In that case, a radio broadcasting company erected a platform on a property adjoining the racecourse thereby giving its announcers the ability to provide radio commentary on the races, which they did. The racing company took legal action to prevent the broadcast from proceeding on the basis that it had a proprietary right (that is, ownership) in the races. However, the High Court held that there was no such proprietary right and the radio broadcast could proceed. This decision still represents the law today as it relates to radio broadcasts and photographs of an event or spectacle; however, the law was changed for television.

Under s. 91 of the Copyright Act, copyright subsists in a television broadcast or sound broadcast of an event provided that the broadcast is made from a place in Australia under the authority of a licence or a class licence under the *Broadcasting Services Act 1992* or by the Australian Broadcasting Corporation or the Special Broadcasting Service Corporation. Hence, copyright in a sound or television broadcast of an event arises instantaneously for the broadcaster (unless there is a contractual agreement to the contrary), whether it is recorded or not.

One area of copyright where owners and organisers do need to act is in relation to music broadcasts at their events. Essentially, under the Copyright Act any music that is played in public or broadcast attracts a fee for what is in effect a licence to use the work. This will be discussed further below.

It is also to be noted that no-one has any property rights in their image or personality unless it is used in conjunction with the marketing of a product or service. Hence an event manager or the talent cannot stop the image of the talent or the event itself being used as news or in social media. Given this, what many event managers do is allow access to their events only to accredited photographers and the like.

Trade marks

A trade mark is a distinctive mark or sign, which identifies and signifies products or services. Some famous trade marks are the Nike swoosh, the Apple Inc. partly eaten apple and the five rings of the Olympics. Not every mark or sign used in the course of trade is a trade mark. To be classified as such it must be capable of indicating a relationship between the organisation (for example, the International Olympic Committee) and that organisation's product or services (for example, the Olympic Games). Although, as with copyright, a trade mark can still exist without any formal process, to ensure the best protection for a name, logo or other similar identifying mark associated with an event, or the organisation that owns or manages it, is to register it under the *Trade Marks Act 1995* (Cth).

The importance of registration of a trade mark under the Trade Marks Act is to establish ownership of the mark unequivocally: registration gives the registered owner the exclusive right to use the trade mark or authorise another person to use the trade mark in relation to the goods and services for which it is registered (Trade Marks Act, s. 20). Moreover, the registered owner has the right to obtain relief under the Act if their trade mark is infringed. Very simply, a trade mark is infringed if a person or organisation uses a sign that is substantially identical with, or deceptively similar to, another organisation's trade mark, without consent, in relation to similar goods and services (Trade Marks Act, s. 120).

Confidential information

Whenever organising an event there will be information transferred between the various parties to the event. Names of potential patrons, sponsors, suppliers and so forth may, for example, be provided from the owner of the event to the event organiser. All this information can have significant commercial value. The most effective way to protect the wrongful use of this confidential information is to do so by contract. In the absence of a contract, a legal action for 'breach of confidence' may be brought against someone who uses the information if it can be shown that the secret or confidential information obtained, directly or indirectly, from the owner of the information was used without the consent of its owner. In order for a legal action to be taken in this area, four conditions must exist:

1. the information claimed to be subject to the obligation of confidentiality must be specifically identified (rather than a general description)
2. the information must not be publicly known, but rather have a 'quality of confidence'
3. the circumstances in which the information was provided and received must suggest an 'obligation of confidence'
4. use of the information may be actual or threatened and without the consent of the party who provided the information (*Smith Kline & French Laboratories (Australia) Ltd v. Secretary Department of Community Services and Health* (1990)).

While commercially valuable information includes trade secrets and business information, an important distinction to make is between 'know-how' and confidential information. Know-how, the use of which is not a breach of confidence, is described as 'accumulated experience and knowledge in a particular line of work or field... peculiar to the relevant industry (rather than the employer or particular business)'. Hence information that represents a 'natural increase in skill and aptitude gained in the course of service' can be used elsewhere, while specifically acquired knowledge will be capable of protection as confidential information. For example, an event organiser will likely acquire general skills or know-how while working for an event organisation as well as specific information about the organisation for which they are working, its suppliers and so on. Information of the latter type they would legally be prohibited from passing on to another organisation or using at another event.

Special-purpose legislation to protect intellectual property

The protection of some intellectual property rights for events (especially sport events) is found in legislation that is event or organisation specific (Thorpe et al. 2017). This includes:

- *Olympic Insignia Protection Act 1987* (Cth)
- *Indy Car Grand Prix Act 1990* (Qld)
- *Gold Coast Motor Racing Events Act 1990* (Qld)
- *Australian Grands Prix Act 1994* (Vic)
- *Sydney 2000 Games (Indicia and Images) Protection Act 1996* (Cth)
- *Commonwealth Games Arrangements Act 2001* (Vic)
- *Melbourne 2006 Commonwealth Games (Indicia and Images) Protection Act 2005* (Cth)
- *Major Sporting Events (Indicia and Images) Protection Act 2014* (Cth).

The need for this legislation arises because of shortcomings in intellectual property laws that have been previously discussed, and the highly valued and sought-after intellectual property these types of events possess. As such, organisations involved in these events seek maximum protection for their brand so they can protect their ability to leverage it for revenue-raising purposes (for example, sponsorship).

The general thrust of this event-specific legislation is to protect the use of specified symbols, mottos and other words and phrases, indicia, designs, images, mascots, pictograms, logos and associated images that would suggest a connection with the particular event against their commercial use by unauthorised third parties. The legislation also makes clear who is the owner of the intellectual property and gives them copyright, trade mark and design protection in the various forms of intellectual property.

Business names

It is required to register a business name if the name under which the business trades differs from the full names (or initials and last names) of all the owners or the company incorporated name without other addition. Hence, there is no need to register your business name if it is your own name. No-one can be prevented from using their own name in connection with a business, but you cannot do so in a way that is misleading or deceptive (see later discussion concerning consumer protection).

As noted previously, ASIC conducts a central business name registry pursuant to the *Business Names Registration Act 2011* (Cth). The registration of a company or business name does not of itself give the registered owner of the name any copyright in it. Hence registration of the name 'AAA Event Management' will not necessarily prevent the registration of a similar name (for example, AAA Event Management Australia). This is so for two reasons. Firstly, it is unlikely that the first name (or the second!) would be determined to be an original work in order to establish copyright. Secondly, the primary purpose for the registration of a business name is simply to allow identification of the owner of a business.

While any copyright in a name cannot be given additional protection by the registration as a company or business name, copyright may exist in an invented name for your event, particularly when it appears in a stylised format. Such a name can be given additional protection by registering it as a trade mark.

Domain names

It is permissible to register a domain name as a trade mark, provided that it meets the requirements of the *Trade Marks Act 1995* (Cth). It is generally the unique identifier part of the domain, for example 'HyperFest', that is considered for trade mark registration, rather than the standard address material such as 'http://www' or 'com' or 'org'.

13.4 Consumer protection

LEARNING OBJECTIVE 13.4 Describe consumer law protections for event attendees and their implications for event organisers.

An event marketer is charged with one primary responsibility: attracting an audience to an event. In attempting to do so a marketer will employ various strategies, as discussed in the marketing and sponsorship planning chapter. The main body of law relating to marketing behaviour for events is that which deals with deceptive practices: Australian Consumer Law (ACL), Schedule 2 of the *Competition and Consumer Act 2010* (Cth). However, the laws examined in the previous section regarding intellectual property rights remain relevant here as organisations will sue for breaches of intellectual property rights as well as for deceptive behaviour in connection with the same activity.

The aim of the Australian Consumer Law (ACL) is to protect the public from misleading and deceptive behaviour. So in the event context the law seeks to stop marketers from providing information to consumers that is untrue, or that is capable of misleading a consumer, even if it is factually true. The two sections of most relevance to event marketing are s. 18 and s. 29 of the ACL. It should be remembered that there is no law preventing hyperbole that is very general — what, in law, is termed 'puffery'. Mere puff is, typically, self-evident exaggeration: 'the greatest event', 'the best show', 'the most entertaining festival'. These are not measurable or objective in any way. The courts will give a wide degree of latitude to words which are imprecise, ambiguous, loose, fanciful or unusual (*Farquhar v. Bottom* (1980)).

Section 18(1) of the ACL states: 'A person shall not, in trade or commerce, engage in conduct that is misleading or deceptive or is likely to mislead or deceive.' From an event marketer's perspective, this means that if a court can be convinced that a potential attendee (it does not need to be an actual attendee) of an event could have been misled, or deceived, by an event's promotional strategy, then the promoter may be sued. The upshot is that the marketing of the event needs to be conscious of not giving any impressions that might be misconstrued by anyone who might go to the event.

As regards s. 29 of the ACL, it states (as relevant to events which are part of 'services'):

> A person must not, in trade or commerce, in connection with the supply or possible supply of goods or services or in connection with the promotion by any means of the supply or use of goods or services:
> (b) make a false or misleading representation that services are of a particular standard, quality, value or grade; or
> (e) make a false or misleading representation that purports to be a testimonial by any person relating to goods or services; or
> (f) make a false or misleading representation concerning:
>   (i) a testimonial by any person; or
>   (ii) a representation that purports to be such a testimonial relating to goods or services; or
> (g) make a false or misleading representation that goods or services have sponsorship, approval, performance characteristics, accessories, uses or benefits; or
> (h) make a false or misleading representation that the person making the representation has a sponsorship, approval or affiliation; or
> (i) make a false or misleading representation with respect to the price of goods or services

From this viewpoint of this section, events would be considered services, and as such, event marketers are expressly prohibited from making any false representations about any aspect of their events (for example, performers, speakers, sponsorship, supporters, registration/ticket prices).

Another section of this legislation that should be noted is the restriction imposed by s. 32 that states:

> A person must not, in trade or commerce, offer any rebate, gift, prize or other free item with the intention of not providing it, or of not providing it as offered, in connection with:
>
> (a) the supply or possible supply of goods or services; or
> (b) the promotion by any means of the supply or use of goods or services.

An example of such a breach of this section would be a conference that has promoted a free copy of a speaker's recent book with every registration and then provided only a one-page summary document of such.

ACL requires event marketers to be particularly careful in their activities as its provisions can be far-reaching in that they can punish even quite innocent errors in promotional efforts. Penalties may include fines, civil actions (for example, being sued for damages), injunctions restricting further advertising or a requirement to undertake corrective advertising, all of which can be damaging to an event's reputation.

Ambush marketing

Ambush marketing is the practice of unauthorised association of a brand with an event to give the impression of authorised association. This is a common phenomenon, most particularly in the context of large-scale sporting events, with perpetrators attempting to take advantage of an event's brand, and associated intellectual property rights, without paying to do so. Such actions also seek to avoid any provisions within ACL.

The first modern-day major marketing ambush took place at the 1984 Los Angeles Olympic Games when Nike booked every available billboard in Los Angeles before and during the Games. On these billboards were photographs of athletes competing in Olympic events. There was of course a Nike swoosh, too. The effect was that Nike was believed to be the official sponsor of the USA Olympic Team. The problem for Converse was that it, not Nike, was the official sponsor.

Ambush marketing may be seen as a clever way of avoiding the cost of acquiring the intellectual property or associated rights, while at the same time leveraging off the brand of an event. Its effect, however, is to devalue the commercial investment of official sponsors, suppliers and partners. It also deprives the event organiser of revenue that should have been paid by the ambusher for the connection. It may even cost an event organiser the future support of the authorised sponsor.

The primary actions an ambushed party can take against an ambusher to protect their intellectual property are to enforce their copyright and register their trade marks. Further, they can claim misleading and deceptive behaviour under ss. 4, 18, 29 or 32 of the ACL or draw on common law provisions concerning 'passing off' to argue that such misrepresentations are damaging to their reputation and goodwill under the tort of passing off. In so doing the ambushed party will seek to obtain injunctions to restrain ambush behaviour, and damages to compensate losses from the economic effects mentioned above.

One strategy developed by the lawmakers to meet the ambush marketing challenge is the development of special-purpose legislation. Examples of where this has occurred in the Australian context include the following.

- The *Gold Coast Motor Racing Events Act 1990* (Qld) and *Australian Grands Prix Act 1994* (Vic) contain prohibitions of certain types of advertising within the area surrounding the event as well as unauthorised filming.
- The *Sydney 2000 Games (Indicia and Images) Protection Act 1996* (Cth) was designed to regulate the use for commercial purposes of the indicia and images associated with the Sydney Olympic Games.
- The *Olympic Arrangements Act 2000* (Cth) prohibited aerial advertising around Olympic venues and live sites as well as advertising on prominent buildings and fixtures.
- The *Major Sports Facilities Act 2001* and *Major Sports Facilities Amendment Act 2006* (Qld) contain a general prohibition of any unauthorised advertising, including blimps and sky writing, laser or digital projection, banners on buildings, or attached to aircraft within sight of a major sporting facility during declared event periods.
- *The Major Events (Aerial Advertising) Act 2007* (Vic) prohibits unauthorised aerial advertising within sight of specified venues for specified or declared events. Breach of the Act is an indictable offence with substantial fines and civil remedies.
- *Commonwealth Games Arrangements Act 2011* (Qld) which established the Gold Coast 2018 Commonwealth Games Corporation, regulates the use of references and images associated with the XXI Commonwealth Games and related purposes.
- *Major Events Act 2013* (SA) sets out regulations in relation to declaring a major event and in relation to certain commercial activities (including ticket scalping and ambush marketing), broadcasting, airspace controls and use of logos and titles.
- *The Major Sporting Events (Indicia and Images) Protection Act 2014* (Cth) — this Act regulated the commercial use of indicia and images associated with the Asian Cup 2015, the Cricket World Cup 2015 and the Gold Coast Commonwealth Games 2018.

13.5 The duty of care

LEARNING OBJECTIVE 13.5 Discuss the duty of care principle and its relationship to risk management and insurance in event settings.

A fundamental legal principle is that members of the community are responsible for taking all reasonable care to avoid acts or omissions that could injure someone in any way that is reasonably foreseeable. This is known in law as the 'duty of care'. It is defined by the Legal Services Commission of South Australia (2020) as '[t]he obligation of a person to exercise reasonable care in the conduct of an activity'. Breach of a duty of care which causes damage or loss to another may give rise to an action in tort. A tort is a breach of duty owed to other people and imposed by law and, in this, it differs from the duties arising from contracts, which are agreed between contracting parties. Unlike criminal law, which is concerned with deterrence and punishment, the law of torts is concerned with compensation.

Event organisers must exercise their duty of care by taking actions that will prevent any foreseeable risk of injury to the people who are directly affected by, or involved in, their events. This includes event staff, volunteers, performers, patrons or spectators and the general public in the surrounding areas. As regards this last group, it should also be kept in mind that this duty of care extends to the amenity of an area in proximity to an event site or venue.

In a similar vein, noise from an event (particularly music-based events) is restricted by state and territory Environmental Protection Acts (EPAs). For example, the Victorian State Environment Protection Policy (Control of Music Noise from Public Premises No. N-2) controls the timing and noise level of music coming from non-residential premises. This generally means that police have the power to instruct venues to abate noise after midnight.

Employer requirements (see the risk management chapter), under work health and safety legislation, which encapsulates the concept of duty of care in this setting, is another area where the law sets standards in this context.

Thorpe et al. (2017) in their book *Sports law* give many examples of sport events being sued for lack of duty of care to either competitors or spectators. For example, in the case of *Harris v. Bulldogs Rugby League Club* (2006), Mr Harris was injured by a firework while viewing a match at the Sydney

Showground, the home ground of the Sydney Bulldogs. Mr Harris was watching the game from a terraced area known as Bulldog Hill. Flares had been let off during the game, and about ten minutes before the match finished Mr Harris was hit in the eye by a flare, and consequently lost his sight in that eye. He then sued the club for not taking adequate security measures. The club argued that they had employed Workforce International, who provided 80–90 staff to provide security at the venue. In addition, 47 fee-for-service police officers were deployed inside and immediately outside of the stadium. Further, all spectators' bags were searched before entering the ground. As a result of the efforts made by the club, it was found not to have breached its duty of care as its security measures were deemed to be appropriate (Thorpe et al. 2017, p. 296).

The lesson flowing from this case for event organisers is that if appropriate actions are taken to meet their duty of care they will generally be assessed as having met their legal obligations in this area. Employing professional risk management and security firms that have experience in constructing strategies and practices aligned with legislative requirements, as this case also demonstrates, should also be a consideration.

Insurance

In addition to putting in place actions designed to exercise their duty of care to patrons, staff, volunteers, participants and so on, insurance is central to any strategy of liability minimisation for an event organiser (Tasmanian Department of Premier and Cabinet 2012). By taking out insurance, the event planner and manager passes on the risk of financial loss. The insurance contract is based on the event planner paying a 'premium' to the insurance company in return for the insurance company agreeing to pay for those losses specified in the insurance contract.

Useful suggestions for obtaining appropriate insurance include the following.

- Allow time to investigate the event's insurance needs and to arrange the appropriate insurances. This task will likely include seeking quotes and advice from a qualified insurance broker. The latter will require that the event has identified all potential risks for which coverage is being sought.
- Ensure coverage begins from the outset of the event planning process.
- Check what is included and excluded in the insurance document. For example, if rain insurance is sought, how much rain must fall, and when must it fall, for a claim to be successful? Are event volunteers, or other stakeholders not specifically named on the policy, covered by it?
- Be prepared to give the insurance broker all information concerning the event and the companies involved. They may require a list of possible hazards, such as pyrotechnics.
- Be prepared to record the details of any damage or injury. Photographs and videos are helpful.
- Keep all records, as a claimant has six years to formulate a claim.
- Do not accept the transfer of liability by suppliers to the event's management.
- Are additional stakeholders insured? These are companies or individuals covered by the insurance but are not the named insured. The sponsors and the venue, for example, may benefit from the insurance policy.

There are many types of event insurance policies, including:

- weather
- workers compensation
- personal accident for the volunteer workers
- venue, property, machinery and equipment, including money
- theft and fire
- non-appearance of a performer and event cancellation
- public liability
- force majeure
- directors' and officers' liability.

The choice of insurance cover is determined by the risk management strategy developed by an event organisation (see the risk management chapter). The cost of premiums in all insurance areas is a burden on the event industry and is a particular problem for small-scale community festivals. Given this, a number of strategies can be employed to ease this burden, including:

- *bulk buying*. A number of events and event companies could pool their resources and approach insurance brokers with a large pool of funds in order to negotiate bulk discounts.
- *analysing the activities of the event into levels of risk*. A high premium may be the result of one aspect of the event. By changing or eliminating this from the event program it may reduce the event risk seen by an insurance company.

- *creating a comprehensive risk management procedure.* Many events that previously ignored risk management have now adopted a formal risk management process. This is one positive outcome of the insurance issue. A risk management plan can then be used in discussions with an insurance company, and if necessary modified, to reduce its assessment of the risk presented by the event.
- *capping liability.* Some state governments have enacted maximum levels of payouts for damages sustained at an event. This allows insurance companies to predict their payments and, therefore, lower the premiums for public liability.
- *holding harmless clauses or forfeiting the right to sue.* An attendee can be required to sign a contract with an exclusion clause to the effect that they are voluntarily assuming the risk inherent in the event activity. This is known in law as a 'disclaimer' or 'waiver'. Legal advice should be obtained in their preparation.

Consideration should be given to engaging insurance brokers who have a department that specialises in event insurance. These organisations will often have an online form that can help event managers decide what matters should be covered by their insurance policy and determine what the appropriate level of insurance is for their event. By completing this form, an event organiser can also anticipate the likely risks their event presents, eliminate or minimise these and hence reduce the insurance premium.

Event managers are well advised to consult an insurance broker to ensure that they are not placing the event or themselves in a catastrophic situation where a claim can severely financially damage the event or themselves (see the event profile).

EVENT PROFILE

So you think you have insurance!
Multi-sport is more than just sport. It's an adventure, a journey and a challenge that demands skill, experience, fitness and endurance. It's also eco-sport; taking advantage of the wonderful natural features of our land, with courses set over alpine moors, through majestic forests and down wild rivers. Cross-country skiing, whitewater kayaking, running and mountain biking are just some of the skills demanded to negotiate courses.

There are three major one-day multi-sport events established in Tasmania — the Ben Lomond Descent, the Tasmanian Winter Challenge and the Mersey Forest Descent. The organisers of each are associated through canoeing and are the Tamar Canoe Club, the Tasmanian Board of Canoe Education and Canoe Tasmania respectively.

Operating on the basis of verbal advice obtained from the Australian Canoe Federation when the events were first established, it was assumed that each event had cover afforded through the policy of the ACF which extends to affiliated clubs and associations (an insurance levy is a component of affiliation costs).

In early 1988, the Tamar Canoe Club decided to organise a new multi-sport event in the Launceston area. They were aware that Australian Canoeing Inc.'s (formerly the ACF) insurer had recently changed and thought it best to check the extent of the cover provided for such an event under the new policy.

The reply received was that only canoe events were covered — multi-sport events were not. The Tamar Canoe Club was rightly concerned that such a change had occurred in the cover provided by the new policy and sought clarification from Australian Canoeing Inc. The reply was that multi-sport events were definitely not covered. Further, they had never been covered under previous policies. The original advice had obviously been incorrect. It was indeed fortunate that the events had no need to claim against the 'insurance'.

The lesson is clear — organisers of events should never assume that they have suitable insurance. Always check and, if possible, receive written confirmation from the insurer, or their agent, that cover is provided and that it meets the event's requirements.

Source: Office of Sport and Recreation Tasmania 1999, p. 9.32.

13.6 Regulations, licences and permits

LEARNING OBJECTIVE 13.6 Identify and describe those laws and regulations of relevance to the conduct of events and those licences and permits that may be required for an event to proceed.

There are long lists of legal regulations that need to be adhered to when staging an event. Generally, the bigger and more innovative an event, the greater the number of regulations to which it must adhere, and these regulations may vary from state to state. To avoid inadvertently contravening any legal regulation that governs the conduct of events, it is necessary to undertake rigorous research. Enquiries with events of a similar nature are a good place to start but much more, as shall now be discussed, needs to be done.

It is the responsibility of event organisers to ascertain, and comply with, all pertinent rules and regulations. To establish what these are, it might be necessary, depending on the event concerned, to make inquiries of police, local and state government, Safe Work Australia and state/territory-based work health and safety authorities, food hygiene authorities, liquor licensing authorities and their lawyer, to ensure all relevant regulations are taken into account. Listed below are common permits, licences and regulations which an event may need to have, or with which it may have to comply.

- Liquor licensing and Responsible Service of Alcohol (RSA) — state liquor licensing bodies and local government
- Health and hygiene — state food and health authorities
- Temporary infrastructure — state planning and construction authorities and local government
- Hazard management and fire safety (for example, equipment requirements, use of gas cylinders, use of open fires) — fire and rescue bodies and state planning bodies
- Crowd management and road closures — police and roads and traffic authorities
- Location-specific regulations (for example, public space alcohol consumption restrictions, signage placement, event permits, permissions to use public buildings/spaces) — local councils
- Use of drones and conduct of laser light shows — civil aviation authorities
- Raffles — often permits are not required but event organisers need to adhere to appropriate state-based legislation. In NSW this is the *Trading Lotteries and Art Unions Act 1901* and the *Lotteries and Art Unions Regulation 2014* administered by Fair Trading NSW.
- Noise limitations — environmental protection authorities (EPAs)
- Use of copyrighted music — OneMusic Australia (see earlier discussion)
- Workplace safety — state-based health and safety bodies
- Equal opportunity and anti-discrimination legislation — these laws prohibit discrimination against people on the basis of a 'protected attribute' (protected attributes include a person's impairment or disability, age, sex, race, religious beliefs, status as a parent or carer, pregnancy or breastfeeding status among many other attributes). Some exceptions to the laws apply (Justice Connect 2017).

Many regulations, permits and licences change with each local government area and state, and new regulations and reinterpretations of the old rules are proclaimed regularly. For example, work health and safety (WHS) is a matter for state and territory governments. However, the Commonwealth authority Safe Work Australia is charged with promoting best practice in occupational health and safety, to develop national WHS policy and guidelines, and to promote consistency in legislation produced by state and territory governments (Safe Work Australia n.d.). This means that WHS regulations are now somewhat more uniform than they were. Each state has a department to regulate WHS; for example, SafeWork NSW, SafeWork South Australia, Workplace Health and Safety Queensland, WorkSafe Tasmania, WorkSafe Australian Capital Territory and WorkSafe Northern Territory administer WHS matters in their respective jurisdictions. However, as discussed above under 'The duty of care', it is the responsibility of event organisers to provide a safe and healthy workplace to their staff and volunteers. If in doubt, consult the WHS department in the state or territory in which the event is to be held.

An example of a recent change in the law affecting events is the *Music Festivals Act 2019* introduced by the NSW Government in 2019. This legislation required the preparation of safety management plans for music festivals classified as 'high risk'. This change was not without controversy, as figure 13.1 attests.

FIGURE 13.1 Victory for music festivals as NSW Parliament passes safety laws

The music festival industry has won its battle against the Berejiklian government over a safety licensing scheme ahead of the busy summer season.

The government also claimed victory on Thursday as Parliament voted to reinstate safety measures after they were abolished by the upper house in September following a backlash from festival organisers.

But in a significant concession, the government will be forced to establish a music industry roundtable, with the first to be held next month.

This was included in the new laws through amendments secured by Labor and crossbench MPs in the upper house.

Live Performance Australia and the Australian Festival Association celebrated the outcome, after a year-long dispute with the Berejiklian government over the regulation of festivals.

'We believe it's important that the consultation process is set out clearly in the legislation. We thank the Parliament for supporting the industry's call,' Live Performance Australia chief executive Evelyn Richardson said in a joint statement issued by the two organisations.

It comes after some of the biggest festivals, including Falls Festival and Splendour in the Grass, threatened to leave NSW unless the roundtable was included in the laws.

The first roundtable will be held on December 4, comprising 10 members from the festival sector and 10 government department members, including NSW Police, NSW Ambulance and Liquor and Gaming.

The laws require the roundtable to be held four times a year, with at least one held at a festival site.

This year's summer festival season will be reviewed in April by the roundtable, which will examine the operation of the new safety protocols.

Customer Service Minister Victor Dominello did not mention the roundtable as he took aim at Labor, the Shooters, Fishers and Farmers and the Greens for scrapping the previous licensing regime.

'[They] took away these regulations and replaced them with nothing, putting lives at risk. We put politics aside and delivered on a promise to prioritise safety for festivalgoers,' he said.

'We've reinstated a regime that ensures festival organisers abide by the highest community and health standards.'

The regime will require 'high risk' festivals to submit safety management plans 90 days before the event, which must be developed in consultation with NSW Health, NSW Police and the Independent Liquor and Gaming Authority.

The government opposed the roundtable amendments as they were passed in the upper house on Wednesday, but ultimately accepted them as the bill was passed in the lower house on Thursday.

Labor's music spokesman John Graham, who moved the amendments, said the outcome was a 'victory for common sense'.

'This was an eminently reasonable and common-sense request from the festival industry. It is just mind boggling that the government was so stubborn on this issue,' Mr Graham said.

The new regime will apply to 11 of the more than 90 festivals held in NSW.

Source: Visentin 2019.

This complex area needs the close attention of event organisers. Government agencies may take a long time to respond to requests. It is necessary, therefore, to begin seeking any permits and licences early and to factor delays and difficulties with obtaining them into the timeframe of the event planning process.

SUMMARY

This chapter has provided an overview of the legal entities through which events can be conducted, the development and use of contracts and the merits of securing intellectual property rights. Additionally, it has offered insights into the application of consumer law, the prevention of 'ambush marketing' and the need to ensure that an event organiser exercises their duty of care to all those persons that they can reasonably foresee as potentially being injured by their acts or omissions. The final sections of this chapter dealt with event insurance requirements and selected laws not previously discussed and listed key areas where regulations might apply, and where permits and licences might be needed.

Event management and planning is a challenging task. It is made more so by the legal (including regulatory) issues that arise when doing so. This chapter has sought to create awareness of many of the legal and regulatory challenges event organisers face, and to provide links to sources of guidance and practical assistance. It should always be kept in mind that the law is very unforgiving — and if the laws of a country or state are transgressed, or the legal rights of another member of the community compromised, then there is a risk of becoming embroiled in expensive and stressful legal proceedings. This outcome can be avoided, however, by taking account of the matters addressed here. Always keep in mind that if uncertain regarding a legal or regulatory issue, seek legal advice.

QUESTIONS

1 What legal structure would you advise a not-for-profit organisation to use for their annual fundraising event? What about a one-off event for a private enterprise?
2 What contracts are needed for an outdoor music festival?
3 When dealing with intellectual property, what steps should you take to ensure you are not breaching an owner's rights?
4 Give three examples of how the Australian Consumer Law can impact on the management of events.
5 What are the ramifications of the duty of care principle for event organisers?
6 What types of insurance would you suggest the organisers of a community festival taking place in a public park consider purchasing?
7 Why do organisations such as OneMusic Australia, APRA and PPCA exist?
8 What permits and licences would be required for a country music festival held in a recreation reserve that featured local amateur talent performing cover songs, and at which food and alcoholic beverages would be served?

CASE STUDY

BLUESFEST TICKET FIASCO

The annual Byron Bay 'Bluesfest' has been conducted since 1990. Held in an area off the highway between Brunswick Heads and the popular tourist destination of Byron Bay in northern New South Wales, it runs for five days over the Easter period and features more than 30 musical acts from the past and the present. Each year it attracts in excess of 100 000 patrons, many of whom are 'regulars'.

Patrons are able to buy tickets for the whole event or daily passes. Under the Bluesfest development application approval with Byron Shire Council, parking fees at the festival are included in the ticket price. In February 2018 Bluesfest applied to the Council to amend the conditions of its approval to introduce paid parking at the festival; however, that was rejected. Bluesfest chief operating officer, Steve Romer, explained the festival needed to cover the 'Hundreds of dollars' it cost to provide parking at the festival when fewer people parked at the site. 'About 50 per cent of people either catch public transport, camp or find other ways to attend that don't involve parking at the festival,' Mr Romer told the council (Moore 2019).

Bluesfest applied again in August 2018, describing the proposal as a 'congestion-busting' green strategy to discourage people from driving to the festival. This time the Byron Shire Council approved the introduction of paid parking at the festival in 2019 (Moore 2019).

As with many patrons, Burleigh Waters resident Anthony Donnellan purchased his tickets in the sum of $1200 for the 2019 festival in mid-2018. When the festival announced in December 2018 that it would be charging separate parking fees for the first time, the organisers incurred the wrath of thousands of ticketholders including Mr Donnellan. Coming more than seven months after the tickets for the 2019 event had gone on sale, the measure would have forced patrons to pay up to $250 more to attend the festival. In fact, after the announcement was made in December, many patrons chose to purchase the parking fees separately in advance.

A Bluesfest spokesperson defended the festival's decision to introduce paid parking for the next year, saying organisers had been given 'full approval from Byron Shire Council, the NSW Police and the Roads & Maritime Services to include parking. Paid parking is being introduced due to increased costs in multiple areas of the live music business including artist fees, production, logistics, grounds maintenance and security' (Bibby 2019).

He further said, 'As the last major live music event within the region to introduce a parking fee, Bluesfest understands it imposes a further cost for patrons, however as a business, the company needs to ensure the future of the festival' (Bibby 2019).

Mr Donnellan, who was angry there was no warning paid parking would be introduced before people bought tickets to the festival, took the festival owner, Bluesfest Pty Ltd (which is owned by Peter Noble), to the New South Wales Civil and Administrative Tribunal (NCAT).

The NCAT on March 20, 2019 upheld Mr Donnellan's claim. Bluesfest Pty Ltd, the company which runs Bluesfest, was found guilty of misleading and deceptive conduct over its plan to introduce a $50 per day parking fee, when parking is legally included in the ticket price. It ordered Bluesfest Pty Ltd to immediately refund Mr Donnellan the $1200 he had spent on tickets. The NCAT said it had ordered the refund owing to 'misleading and deceptive conduct' on the part of Bluesfest because of their proposal to introduce paid parking at the 2019 festival after it had already sold tickets (Bibby 2019). The festival organisers also agreed to refund the thousands of payments for parking fees that were paid in advance.

Mr Donnellan said the Tribunal's decision was the outcome he was hoping for. 'I always said that everybody should have the opportunity to get a refund and the NCAT was the only way that I could see we could achieve that. People can now decide whether they want to go to next year's festival knowing that they will have to pay [extra] for parking', he said (Bibby 2019).

Two weeks after the tribunal found that the festival had engaged in 'misleading and deceptive conduct' over the parking plan, the Bluesfest organisers issued a statement in which they apologised to customers but did not mention the NCAT ruling, saying they would postpone charging patrons to park until the following year's (2020) event.

'All 2019 ticket holders [who have already paid for parking] will be refunded [those fees] by 12 April 2019,' a festival spokesperson said. 'Bluesfest apologises for any confusion caused and inconvenience it may have caused ticket purchasers' (Bibby 2019).

Sources: Bibby 2019; Encalada 2019; Moore 2019.

QUESTIONS

1 Who is the owner of the event and what was the type of legal entity used? Why do you think this entity was chosen?

2 What was the contract between the owners and the patrons? What were the relevant terms?

3 What law was used by Donnellan to take the owners to the NCAT?

4 How would you, as an event organiser, have handled the situation:

   a Could you have included an exclusion clause in the contract? What would it have said?

   b Do you think the Tribunal's ruling should have been mentioned in the apology? Why/why not?

REFERENCES

Arts Law Centre of Australia 2020, 'Sponsorship agreement', www.artslaw.com.au/product/sponsorship, viewed 29 April 2020.

Australian Copyright Council 2020, 'Home', www.copyright.org.au, viewed 14 May 2020.

Bibby, P 2019, 'Bluesfest backs down on parking fees plan', *Echo Netdaily*, 28 March, www.echo.net.au/2019/03/bluesfest-backs-parking-fees-plan, viewed 29 April 2020.

Encalada, J 2019, 'Fan's fest blues over parking hit', *Tweed Daily News*, 30 March, www.pressreader.com/australia/tweed-daily-news/20190330/281951724173155, viewed 29 April 2020.

Justice Connect 2017, 'Checklist: to complete when holding an event', www.nfplaw.org.au/sites/default/files/media/Checklist_to_complete_when_holding_an_event_CTH_.pdf, viewed 14 May 2020.

Legal Services Commission of South Australia 2020, 'Legal terms', www.lawhandbook.sa.gov.au/go01.php, viewed 29 April 2020.

Moore, T 2019, 'Bluesfest guilty of "misleading, deceptive conduct" over parking plan', *The Sydney Morning Herald*, 28 March, www.smh.com.au/business/consumer-affairs/bluesfest-guilty-of-misleading-deceptive-conduct-over-parking-plan-20190328-p518hd.html, viewed 29 April 2020.

Office of Sport and Recreation Tasmania 1999, *A sporting chance: a risk management framework for the sport and recreation industry*, OSRT, p. 9.32.

OneMusic Australia 2020, 'Events', www.onemusic.com.au/licences/events, viewed 29 April 2020.

Safe Work Australia n.d., 'About us', www.safeworkaustralia.gov.au, viewed 29 April 2020.

Tasmanian Department of Premier and Cabinet 2012, 'Insurance and risk management (Tasmania)', www.dpac.tas.gov.au/data/assets/pdf_file/0004/228532/5.Insurance.pdf.

Thorpe, D, Buti, A, Davies, C & Jonson, P 2017, *Sports law*, 3rd ed., Oxford University Press, Melbourne.

Visentin, L, 2019, 'Victory for music festivals as NSW parliament passes safety laws', *The Sydney Morning Herald*, 14 November, www.smh.com.au/politics/nsw/victory-for-music-festivals-as-nsw-parliament-passes-safety-laws-20191113-p53a9a.html, viewed 29 April 2020.

STATUTES AND AUTHORITIES

Associations Incorporation Acts (various states and territories).

The Australian Business Licence Information Service (ABLIS), https://ablis.business.gov.au.

Australian Consumer Law (ACL), Schedule 2 of the *Competition and Consumer Act 2010* (Cth)

Australian Copyright Council, copyright.org.au.

Australian Securities and Investments Commission (ASIC), www.asic.gov.au.

Broadcasting Services Act 1992 (Cth).

Business Names Registration Act 2011 (Cth).

Copyright Act 1968 (Cth).

Corporations Act 2001 (Cth).

Legal Services Commission of South Australia, www.lsc.sa.gov.au.

Music Festivals Act 2019 (NSW), www.legislation.nsw.gov.au/acts/2019-17.pdf.

Victorian State Environment Protection Policy (Control of Music Noise from Public Premises) No. N-2, www.epa.vic.gov.au.

Trade Marks Act 1995 (Cth).

CASES

Farquhar v. Bottom (1980) 2 NSWLR 380.

Harris v. Bulldogs Rugby League Club (2006) NSWCA 461.

Smith Kline & French Laboratories (Australia) Ltd v. Secretary Department of Community Services and Health (1990) 17 IPR 545.

Victoria Park Racing & Recreation Grounds Co Ltd v. Taylor (1937) 58 CLR 479.

ACKNOWLEDGEMENTS

Photo: © Nils Versemann / Shutterstock.com

Extract: © Sport and Recreation Tasmania

Figure 13.1: © The Sydney Morning Herald, 'Victory for music festivals as NSW Parliament passes safety laws', Lisa Visentin, 2019

Note: All information contained in this chapter is by way of general instruction and is not intended nor should it be taken as specific legal advice. No responsibility is taken by the authors or the publishers if anyone should act on anything stated herein and thereby suffers any loss or injury.

PART 3

EVENT OPERATIONS AND EVALUATION

This section examines event design and production processes, before concluding with a detailed discussion of the role of evaluation in the strategic event management process.

CHAPTER 14

Event design and production

LEARNING OBJECTIVES

After studying this chapter, you should be able to:

14.1 discuss major influences on event design decisions

14.2 identify and describe common event design elements

14.3 discuss selected event production processes and their significance in event experience delivery.

Introduction

For many event organisers, the 'fun' part of being in the event industry is the opportunity to engage their imagination and creativity through the event design process. The major influence on this process is the purpose of the event itself, as it will condition all subsequent decisions relating to the type of attendee experience that is developed. The tools available to an event designer in creating the attendee experience are many and include furniture and props, lighting, sound, colour, music, staging, food and beverage, talent, and event experience–enhancing technologies. All of these need to be coordinated into a unified whole, commonly coalescing around a chosen theme. Underpinning the ability of event organisers to deliver the experience that they have developed are various event production-related processes, some of which are identified and discussed here, specifically: site/venue selection, layout and design; and queue, transport, communication and site/venue services management. All of these production-related processes are dependent on the ability of an event organiser to put together an effective event production team.

14.1 Key factors influencing event design decisions

LEARNING OBJECTIVE 14.1 Discuss major influences on event design decisions.

The attendee experience

Event attendees are active participants in events, not passive observers. In effect, event organisers are taking people on a journey, just as the writer of a good novel does. And just as a good novel does, the 'story' that is told needs to engage and immerse attendees as it moves from its beginning to its end. Given this, consideration needs to be accorded to what attendees will be doing, thinking and feeling from the time they arrive until the time they leave. Will there be times, or spaces, where they can be active (for example, dancing), passive (chill-out areas), listening (plenary sessions), networking (event receptions), playing (games areas), learning (for example, product demonstration areas), entertained (stage areas) or 'wowed'? In working through answers to these questions (all of which have programming implications), attention should also be paid to how, or if, attendee senses (sight, hearing, smell, taste and touch) can be engaged to deepen the experience that is offered. Scent generators, for example, are sometimes used to positively affect the mood of attendees through their ability to create a pleasant ambient environment, while incorporating interactive screens can better engage people around a particular product or service.

In addition to these considerations, another issue that arises in the context of many events is that of how the attendee experience can be made more memorable or special in some way. If successful in doing so, people will be more likely to share their experience (either in person or via social media) with others, which will then strengthen an event's marketplace position, or that of the brand/product that is its focus. In the context of corporate events, for example, a 'wow factor' is often introduced using theatrical techniques combined with high-tech wizardry. Building a 'wow factor' into an event doesn't have to be expensive. For example, a car company that was launching a new vehicle recently used as its 'wow factor' a man who had only ever bought one car model that they produced for his whole life. He showed photos of all his cars, some with just himself, and some with his family as they grew up. As he showed these images he told the story of how his cars took the family on holidays, drove his boys and their friends to local football matches, and how one had even been the lead vehicle used at his daughter's wedding. In this instance, the 'wow factor' was simply a man talking about his experiences and the emotional connection he had with a car brand.

Event attendees, whether they attend physically or digitally, will also seek to customise their experience depending on what they are seeking from it: information; networking; excitement; fun; or bonding with family, friends and work colleagues. One way to appreciate how this experience might unfold is to create a map that describes step-by-step how they might interact with the event. Marketers refer to this process as service blueprinting (Lovelock et al. 2015). In figure 14.1, for example, two basic demographic profiles have been used, a mother with a teenage boy and a middle-aged man. Each has their own 'map' that marks out what happens at each point of their respective journey. A mother with a son can be anticipated to behave differently to a man walking around the event by himself. If you refer to this figure you can see that the man is at the computer product counter to ask questions and explore software options for his business, while the mother and son are at the event because of the son's school requirements and take the opportunity to ask about 'gaming'. Both these experiences need to be managed, designed and delivered making sure all visitor expectations are met (for example, information requirements, access to products/services and on-site service needs such as food, beverages, shade and seating).

The 'blueprinting' process can also be extended to encompass the total experience of attendees from the time they first become aware of the event (for example, by invitation) until the time they attend and return home. In doing so, matters such as the types of expectations that marketing communications generate (which then need to be met through the on-site experience), transport usage (ease of event access), pathways/routes used (near event signage needs), estimated time on site (site/venue capacity), arrival times and entry points (number of turnstiles/registration staff needed at entry points, projected queuing times, best ticketing options — on-site and/or prior to arrival) can be anticipated and planned for.

FIGURE 14.1 Basic attendee experience map

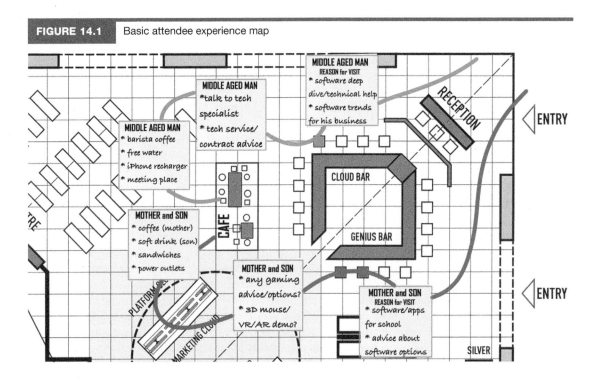

In summary, as Silvers (2004) notes:

> An event experience must be choreographed and blocked out as carefully as any dance or play. The professional event coordinator crafts a plan that takes the attendee or guest through a structured progression of various sights, sounds, tastes, textures, smells, highs, lows, climaxes, diversions and discoveries that delivers the intended impact and message of the event.

Programming

Once the elements of the attendee experience have been identified, concern can then shift to the type of program that is capable of delivering this experience. In its initial form, this document will comprise various ideas and suggestions, and as such is a useful tool for experimentation and innovation. For example, in the context of a conference, consideration might be given to the number of plenary sessions, workshops, networking opportunities to be included; type(s) of entertainment to be provided; and if one or more 'wow' factor moments should be incorporated. As further thought is given to this aspect of event design, and input is received from (depending on the event) the client, event owner and other stakeholders (for example, sponsors, venue, suppliers, permissory bodies), a final program will emerge detailing the 'journey' on which attendees will embark. This program will take two forms: one that is made public, and the other that is used to produce the event and is embraced in its production/running schedule(s) (see the event project management chapter). In developing the latter, a number of issues need to be addressed/considered. Depending on the event, these include:

- number and type of activities (for example, performances, workshops, plenary sessions, site visits, award presentations), and the type of spaces each require (for example, breakout rooms, plenary rooms, specific activity zones for dancing, food and beverage consumption, relaxing, networking)
- duration of activities, and whether activities will be sequential or run in parallel

- audience characteristics (for example, age, gender, number)
- event food and beverage requirements (for example, number and timing of meals, whether dining will be seated or standing, or special dietary requests)
- time requirements necessary to reconfigure rooms/spaces for different uses (for example, to change a room used for plenary sessions to the dinner venue for a conference)
- flow and tempo of the event 'journey' (for example, whether free time should be included, whether the program should lead to a climax)
- staging requirements (for example, the number of stages that will be in operation, the technology/equipment that will be in use)
- activations (for example, whether sponsors will need designated spaces and times for showcasing and engaging attendees with their products/services)
- extent to which a program needs to be differentiated from competing events' programs.

Site/venue selection

Sites/venues come in a variety of forms (see table 14.1) and need to be selected based on their alignment with an event's purpose, planned attendee experience and associated program.

TABLE 14.1 **Examples of potential indoor and outdoor spaces**

Indoor spaces	Outdoor spaces
Landmark buildings	Waterfront areas/islands/beaches
Purpose-built conference/exhibition centres	Public parks and domains
Art galleries	Streets and laneways
Sheds, warehouses and factories	Plazas and malls
Department stores	Backyards
Office building foyers	Car parks
Private/historic houses	Country properties
Empty/unused spaces (for example, military barracks)	Historic precincts
Hotel ballrooms and other event spaces	Theme parks
Nightclubs/restaurants/bars	Rooftops
Museums	Vineyards
Theatres	Disused buildings
Ferries/boats	Botanical gardens
Stadia	Rainforests

Depending on the event concerned, there is the potential for a range of factors to enter into the decision-making process in this area, including the following.
- The characteristics (for example, age, type of disabilities, level of seniority), number and expectations (in terms of facilities/services and their associated quality) of attendees. Contrast, for example, the profile and requirements of attendees to a major international conference to those of attendees to a local community festival.
- Nature of the event (for example, business or entertainment-based, formal or informal, indoor/outdoor, scale and event elements that need to be accommodated — entertainment, décor and theming, breakout sessions and meals).
- Sustainability (for example, does the site/venue have a sustainability policy or are they accredited with an external environmental body such as GreenGlobe? If so, what practices/systems are in place and how can the event link to them? See the sustainable event planning chapter for more information.)

- Location of the site/venue relative to existing destination attractions/business district/other services (for example, restaurants and accommodation). This issue can serve to make the event more or less attractive to certain groups of potential attendees.
- Event's operational requirements (for example, proximity to airports, on-site or near-site parking, access to loading dock areas, ceiling heights, performer dressing rooms, rigging points, door widths, floor weightings, lighting, internet access, level of susceptibility to weather events, ability of venue/site to be customised for theming, branding or message delivery purposes and floor space available for exhibits/displays).
- Brand image of the site/venue (for example, contrast the Sydney Opera House to a local community hall) and its relationship to the event's purpose and audience.
- Use of the site/venue by a client's competitors, or by the client themselves, in the recent past. This might prevent the use of a site/venue in the short to medium term.
- Limitations, conditions and inclusions/exclusions associated with the site/venue's use. For example, how long does the contract allow to load the event into the site/venue and load it out, and will this be sufficient? What facilities, services or equipment are included in the hire price (for example, audiovisual equipment, security services, cleaning, air-conditioning) and what will need to be brought in or paid extra for? Are external contractors (for example, caterers) allowed at the venue or must the venue's services, or those of its contracted suppliers, be used?
- Site/venue's cancellation charges and deposit/bond requirements and when these come into effect.
- History of the site/venue as an event location — types of events previously held, experience/quality of event staff and any issues that have arisen with previous events.
- Nature of any events being hosted at the venue at the same time. For example, if it is discovered that a 'battle of the bands' event is being held on the same date as a proposed business conference, it might be wise to seek an alternative venue as there may be noise issues and the audiences for the two events might not be compatible.
- Site/venue environs. Does the area immediately surrounding the site/venue detract from it in any way? For example, is the area run down or highly industrialised?

From this list of site/venue selection considerations it is evident there can be a vast range of factors impacting decision-making in this area. Given the importance of this decision to the success of an event, it is imperative that all relevant factors are considered and that items are not overlooked. For this reason it is sound practice to employ a checklist (a basic example has been provided in figure 14.2) when carrying out a site inspection. During these visits, site/venue maps/floorplans should be checked to make sure that any that the event organiser had previously obtained are current and are true representations of what exists at the site/venue. A handheld laser and/or tape measure, and a camera/phone to record the visit, can also prove useful. In the context of hotel venues, it is noteworthy that some event organisers even go as far as to stay overnight, making use of the hotel's services in an effort to gain practical insights into the quality of its offerings. In the case of large-scale outdoor events using 'greenfield' sites, it is not unusual for their organisers to have the proposed area independently surveyed with the information gained being used to construct detailed site plans.

When seeking to shortlist possible sites/venues, a variety of sources can be used. Personal connections in the form of fellow event organisers and suppliers can be particularly useful as they often have first-hand experience with venues that are under consideration or with outdoor sites such as beaches and parks on which it can be difficult to get information. Additionally, there are many publications (for example, the A LIST Guide and Best Venues of Australia directories, conference and exhibition bureau venue guides) that list venues and provide details on matters such as the number, size and schematics of their meeting rooms, and on-site services and facilities (for example, number of guest rooms and restaurants). Many venues also have websites (some offering virtual tours) with the capacity to provide much of the information needed by event organisers. It should also be kept in mind that Google Maps can be used to help locate possible venues and sites, show nearby facilities and services, and for some venues, also provide floor plans. Once a shortlist has been developed, site inspections have been carried out and a site/venue has been selected, an event organiser can then turn their attention to site/venue design.

FIGURE 14.2   Basic venue checklist

What to ask

Date

Is the date available? Are the days either side of the event day available for access? ☐

Are there other parties booked that day? If so, are they in close proximity to my event? Will they impact on my event? ☐

Payment

How much of a depositis required, and when is this due? ☐

Are there hidden costs (for example, aservice charge or gratuity)? ☐

Whatare the cancellation policy terms? ☐

What's the final date that we can make changes? ☐

Logistics

How many people can the room/table/venue accommodate? ☐

Are private rooms available? ☐

Is there room for a band? Is there room for a dancefloor? ☐

Does the venue provide sound equipment, or do we need to provide it? Can we rent it from the venue? ☐

Does the venue have disabled access? ☐

Is there sufficient parking? Is parking free? If not, what is the cost to guests ☐

What are the limitations on decorating? For example, can we use candles/electrical equipment? Can we pin decorations to the ceiling and walls? ☐

What time will guests have to leave the venue? ☐

Who is responsible for setting up and taking down the decor, and when will it be completed? ☐

Food and drinks

Do you have set menus or à la carte options? What's the pricing? Is this price inclusive of drinks? ☐

When do you need dietary requirements details by? ☐

What is the cut off date for final numbers? ☐

Can we bring our own alcohol? ☐

If so, do you charge a fee for corkage? ☐

Staff

Who will be our contact person before the event? ☐

Who will be our contact person on the day of the event? ☐

Can we meet with them in advance? ☐

14.2 Event design elements

LEARNING OBJECTIVE 14.2 Identify and describe common event design elements.

As is the case with products, services such as events are also designed, with their designers assembling a range of components into a unified whole to achieve one or more outcomes. These components will depend on the type and scale of the event, but major factors include the overall site/venue layout, theming elements (furnishings and props, lighting, colour, music, sound, stage(s), food and beverage, talent) and experience-enhancing technologies.

Layout

Decisions as regards how an event site/venue should be laid out involve considering a range of factors. Depending on the event concerned, and the characteristics of the site/venue, these might include:

- surrounding area (for example, can the surrounding area be incorporated into the event to create a sense of excitement/curiosity before entering the site/venue?)
- type of activities to be undertaken (for example, networking, presentations, performances)
- desired balance between empty and furnished space
- location of event inputs — services (for example, wi-fi access, toilets, showers, water stations, power, waste facilities), site office, bike storage, fencing, stage(s), backdrops/drapes, props/inflatables, rigging points, barricades, theming elements, furniture (for example, tables/chairs), equipment storage area(s), lighting towers, tents/marquees, camping sites, parking, equipment (for example, sound desks, data projectors), food and beverage (back of house and/or front of house), security staff and first aid positions, signage, registration desk/ticket booths, entry and exit points, restricted areas, performer change rooms, and plenary and breakout rooms
- attendee flow within the site/venue — where best to locate walkways/paths/aisles from the viewpoint of the event's purpose and operational efficiency, and how wide should they be? Should visitor flows be one way or both ways?
- operational flows (for example, how will equipment, materials, staff and performers move between areas once the event commences operation?)
- sightlines
- seating (for example, will seats be fixed or removable? What type of seating arrangement will be in use? See figure 14.3)
- standing room — will there be a need for standing room
- access for people with disabilities and for emergency services
- adherence to fire and safety regulations/event's risk management plan.

FIGURE 14.3   Common seating setup styles

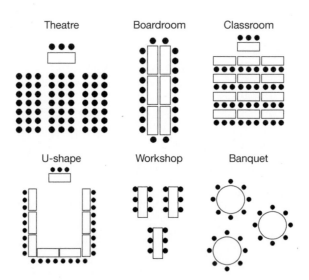

When responding to these matters, it should be kept in mind that while some spaces, such as a park, or a ballroom in a hotel, might seem to be blank canvases from an event design perspective, they nonetheless have their own physical dynamic, and this must be worked with, rather than against. For example, a park might offer a natural amphitheatre in the form of a large depression, a treed area where services and equipment such as generators can be hidden from view, or a large flat area adjacent to a road suitable for parking.

Resulting from consideration of the previously listed factors will be a site/venue map. These commonly take two forms. The first is to scale (see figure 14.4) and is a true representation of what will be found on the 'ground' at the site/venue (also known as the groundplan). A number of versions of these maps are often created as the event organiser explores different configurations until they settle on the one that best meets the needs of their event. In doing so, they will, for example, seek to examine possible configurations that: exploit existing attributes of the site/venue (for example, pre-existing pathways, entry points, lighting positions, electrical services, views); avoid potential site/venue logistical and safety issues; and maximise revenue. The finalised map is then made available to suppliers, vendors, contractors and staff, sometimes in a modified form that only includes those 'need-to-know' elements of relevance to that specific group (for example, setup, drop off or equipment installation locations). Commonly, another version of this map is created for attendees (see figure 14.5) so they can navigate their way around the event site/venue and engage with the event experience. Scale is not so significant with attendee maps, and only those site/venue attributes with which they might need to engage are shown (for example, toilets, food and beverage outlets, stages, parking, entry/exit, exhibitors, activity zones).

The development of site/venue maps is assisted by the use of computer-aided design (CAD) or similar software. In some instances, particularly in the context of larger scale events, the complexity involved in using such software requires the contracting of professionals. With smaller scale events it is possible to use off-the-shelf software designed specifically for events. For example, Vivien Event Designer software (https://cast-soft.com/vivien-event-designer/) allows event organisers to create 2D and 3D scale renderings of their events (see figure 14.6) by dragging and dropping true-to-scale furniture and equipment onto the scaled plans provided by venues (Cast Group n.d.).

Additionally, many of these types of programs, including Vivien Event Designer, can be used to create seating plans, seating allocations and seating charts.

Furnishings and props

Furnishings perform a variety of functions from an event design perspective, they can:
- add balance to a space
- draw attention away from, or to, particular areas of an event site/venue
- hide unsightly aspects of a venue, or reduce the size of a venue to create a more intimate atmosphere, or to partition an event space into zones (for example, through the use of curtains)
- assist in creating a particular mood/style (for example, bean bags vs leather chesterfield lounges, formal vs basic table settings, Arabian style tents vs army-style tents, dark coloured furniture vs light coloured furniture, rustic vs sophisticated vs beach casual style furniture, furniture from a particular era, for example, art deco)
- create 'wow' elements. The use of oversized objects, for example, such as giant chairs, inflatable figures, unusual sculptures or strangely shaped common objects can create a focal/talking) point and remove an event from the 'ordinary' world attendees inhabit day-to-day (see figure 14.7).

Lighting

With advances in LED technologies, lighting is becoming a major element in good event design, but to use it effectively responses to a number of questions need to be worked through, specifically: how intense (bright) should it be? Should coloured lighting be used? Where should lighting be located? Should changes be made to lighting during an event? It is useful here to reflect on possible responses to these questions.

Lighting intensity has practical implications in event settings. For example, will attendees have sufficient light to see to take notes or to avoid potential injury such as when walking along an uneven path or downstairs. Intense beams of light, such as spotlights, can also be used to focus attendee attention on, for example, a speaker or performer, or an award winner on a table. Additionally, intensity is an issue when seeking to create a mood/feeling or to signify that a particular activity is about to start or finish. For example, low ambient light might serve to create a relaxed atmosphere, while increasing the intensity of lights might signal that an event has ended, such as is the case at theatres when a performance concludes.

Coloured lighting can serve to: suggest a mood (red for example can signify excitement or action, while purple has connotations of luxury and creativity); create zones within an event (for example, the green zone, red zone) where particular activities are to take place; and reflect an organisation's identity through the use of its brand colours or special effects gobos.

FIGURE 14.4 Example of an event site map (groundplan) for an outdoor festival

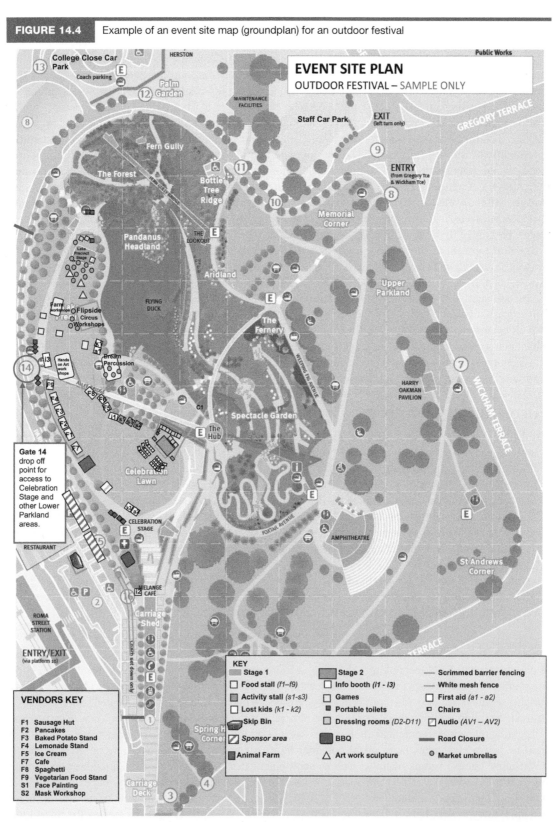

Source The State of Queensland 2019.

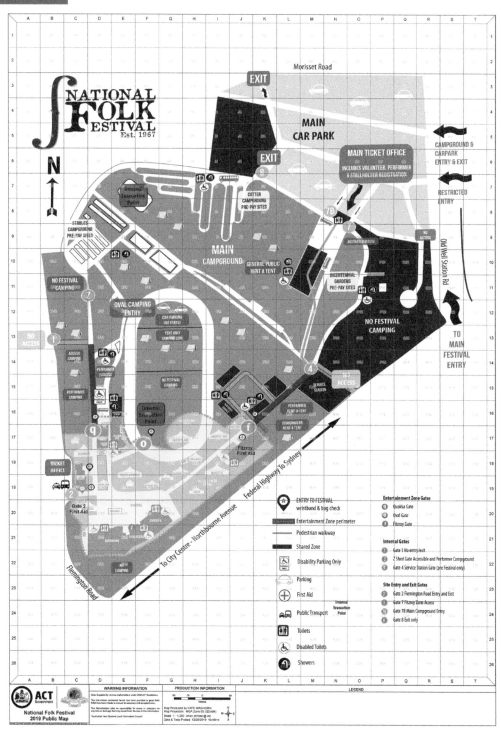

Source: National Folk Festival 2019.

Decisions as regards the distribution of lighting, and the locations of different types of lights (see figure 14.8) need to be worked through using the medium of a lighting design plan. It should also be kept in mind that sites/venues will have their own lighting and that this can be, and often is, part of such plans. While event organisers can develop their own plans, lighting can quickly become a complex area to manage, particularly when new and complex technologies are in use. For this reason, lighting designers are often contracted to undertake this task. For a more detailed description of event lighting options, see Peguero (2020) in the references list at the end of this chapter.

FIGURE 14.6 3D venue layout diagram

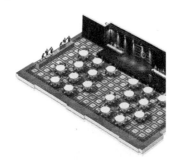

Source: Cast Group n.d.

FIGURE 14.7 Giant props

Source: Sydney Prop Specialists 2020.

Movement is another consideration with event lighting and has been alluded to previously. Light can be moved to cause attendees to focus on another area of a site/venue, a performer or speaker; and intensity can be moved up or down to signify a change in activity (for example, from eating dinner to listening to a guest speaker) or to fade one look into another while not breaking the flow of the event by being too abrupt.

In addition to these design considerations, lighting also plays other roles. It locates entry/exit points, toilets, evacuation pathways, and plays a major role in creating a sense of security and safety for event attendees.

Colour

Colour, as noted previously, can help create a mood or feeling and its selection should align with the nature of the event. For example, if the event is an extravagant evening celebration the use of metallic golds and silver combined with black will serve to reinforce its desired style and mood, while a corporate event will likely make use of its corporate colours to reinforce the association of the event with its brand and products/services. Whatever colour scheme is selected, it needs to flow through décor, furnishings, lighting, promotional materials, menus, table decorations and so on to create an overall integrated look to the event.

FIGURE 14.8 Basic types of event lighting

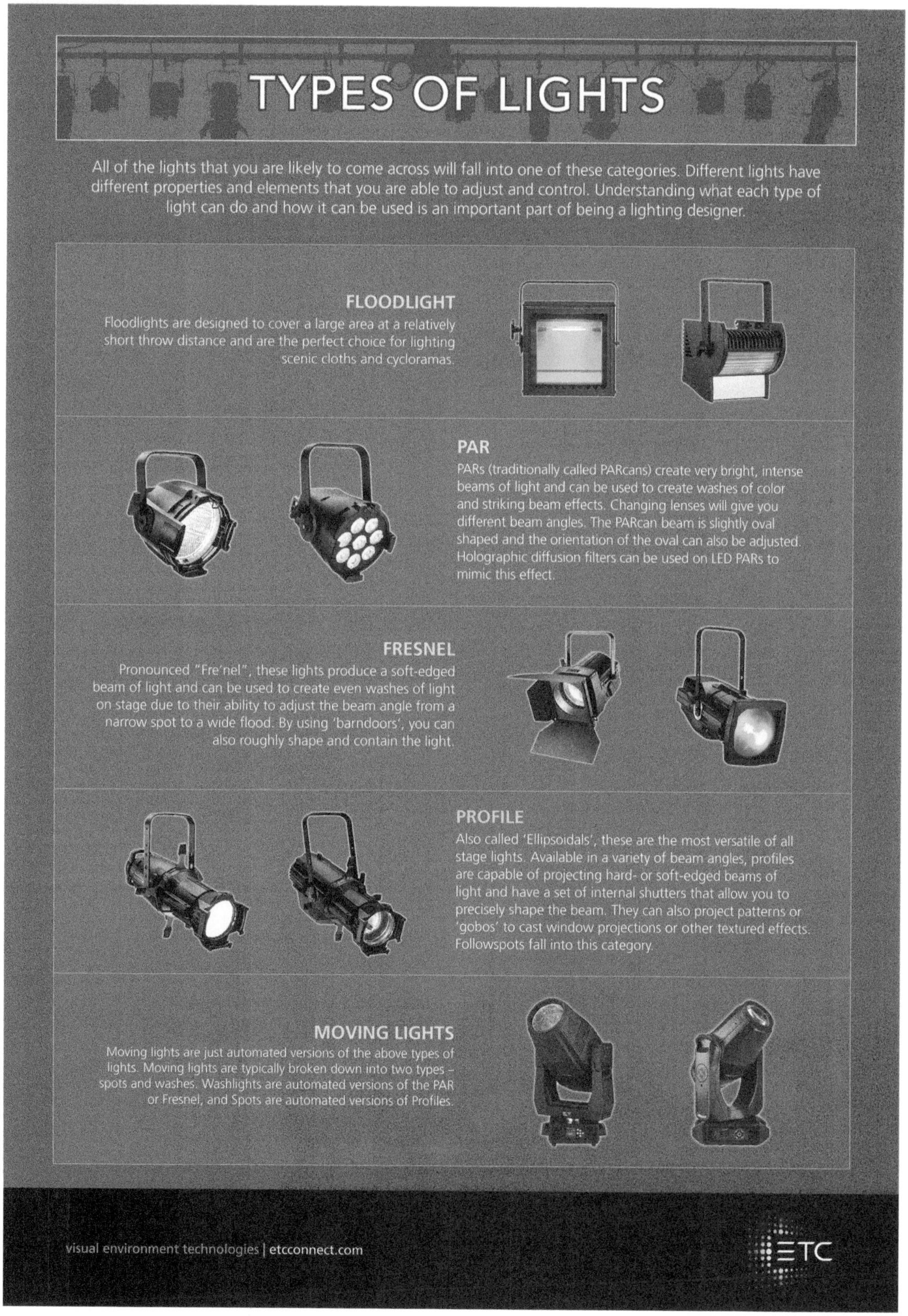

TYPES OF LIGHTS

All of the lights that you are likely to come across will fall into one of these categories. Different lights have different properties and elements that you are able to adjust and control. Understanding what each type of light can do and how it can be used is an important part of being a lighting designer.

FLOODLIGHT

Floodlights are designed to cover a large area at a relatively short throw distance and are the perfect choice for lighting scenic cloths and cycloramas.

PAR

PARs (traditionally called PARcans) create very bright, intense beams of light and can be used to create washes of color and striking beam effects. Changing lenses will give you different beam angles. The PARcan beam is slightly oval shaped and the orientation of the oval can also be adjusted. Holographic diffusion filters can be used on LED PARs to mimic this effect.

FRESNEL

Pronounced "Fre'nel", these lights produce a soft-edged beam of light and can be used to create even washes of light on stage due to their ability to adjust the beam angle from a narrow spot to a wide flood. By using 'barndoors', you can also roughly shape and contain the light.

PROFILE

Also called 'Ellipsoidals', these are the most versatile of all stage lights. Available in a variety of beam angles, profiles are capable of projecting hard- or soft-edged beams of light and have a set of internal shutters that allow you to precisely shape the beam. They can also project patterns or 'gobos' to cast window projections or other textured effects. Followspots fall into this category.

MOVING LIGHTS

Moving lights are just automated versions of the above types of lights. Moving lights are typically broken down into two types – spots and washes. Washlights are automated versions of the PAR or Fresnel, and Spots are automated versions of Profiles.

visual environment technologies | etcconnect.com

ETC

Source: ETC Connect n.d.

Music

Music has a role to play in influencing the mood and behaviour of event attendees. It can, for example, make people feel relaxed and laid back, or energised and buzzing. Certain genres of music might be leveraged to reinforce an event's efforts at creating a feeling of sophistication and elegance (for example, classical music), while others (for example, rock music) might energise an audience. Music can also be used to link attendees to a particular era (for example, roaring 20s), places (reggae — Caribbean), and create anticipation in the lead up to an award announcement, as well as excitement when the award is announced. The issue of music licensing arises (see the legal considerations in event planning and management chapter) when it is used in event settings, so event organisers need to keep this in mind.

Sound

The principal reason for having sound equipment at an event is so that all of the audience (including radio, television and streaming audiences) can clearly hear the music, speeches or audio effects. The type of equipment used needs to take account of the nature of, and the extent to which, sounds are to be amplified (for example, compare a rock concert to an intimate chamber music presentation) as well as the acoustic properties of the site/venue.

Sound, particularly for large-scale events, is a complex, and technical area, and as a result often requires experts to be employed to make decisions as to the needs of an event in this area, and to oversee this element of the event. For example, what will the event's requirements be for: microphones (for example, stage, lapel, radio); mixing desk; cabling; speakers; and backup equipment (for example, spare leads and microphones)? Considerable time can also be required with large-scale sound installations to tune the system to the site/venue's acoustic qualities, and to deal with any feedback issues (that is, unwanted, often high-pitched sound, that occurs when the sound coming out of the speakers is picked up by the microphones and comes out of the speakers again).

Volume and sound leakage during an event can become a major problem. Local councils can close an event if there are too many complaints from residents. At some venues, for example, there are volume switches that automatically turn off the power if the sound level is too high. At multi-venue events, sound can also leak between stages. This can be reduced by:

- thoughtful placement of stages
- careful positioning of all sound speakers
- constant monitoring of the volume level
- programming of activities on each stage in a way that avoids interference.

FIGURE 14.9 Staging considerations

Lighting requirements — will a lighting rig be required or is existing lighting sufficient?	Characteristics of planned performances/ceremonies/presentations and their associated space requirements
Stage layout — what stage type will best suit the event, for example, an arena stage, thrust stage, proscenium stage?	Is a backdrop (either digital or static) needed/wanted for such purposes as organisational branding?
Potential for noise bleed into surrounding areas	Construction considerations — for example, weight-bearing requirements
Nature of venue/site acoustics	Access — for example, one side or both? Is wheelchair access needed?
Access to power	What types, and what size, of screen technologies will be in use, for example, digital banners, LED screens and widescreen projections?

Sightlines — will additional screens be required to allow the stage to be viewed by some attendees?	Backstage requirements — for example, dressing rooms, chill-out area for performers and crew, equipment storage
Work health and safety requirements during setup and breakdown and engineering signoffs post-construction	Design requirements for stairs, skirting and fascia

Stage(s)

A stage is essentially an elevated platform that requires design and audiovisual elements in order for it to come to life and be integrated into an event. Stage(s) act as the/a focal point and as such they offer significant opportunities to connect with an audience in order to transfer ideas/information, feelings and messages. Business events, for example, often leverage this opportunity by using stage backdrops, LED screens, digital banners and widescreen projections to carry branding messages, and communicate information regarding products or services.

The placement, size and shape of a stage, is a major decision that requires multiple factors to be taken into account, many of which are listed in figure 14.9. Central among these is the layout of the stage itself. In this regard there is a range of options, each with its own strengths and weaknesses (see figure 14.10). Variations on these configurations can also be seen in use in events. For example, fashion shows employ a modified form of the thrust stage, employing a long rectangular runway. Once a stage layout option has been selected, the next task is to develop a stage plot — a diagram of what the onstage setup will look like along with the relative location of the equipment and so on to be placed there.

In some instances stages are already in place at sites/venues and simply need to be adapted to an event's requirements. In others, modular or mobile stages might need to be hired and assembled/installed at a site or venue. In the case of larger events, or events with significant budgets, stages are sometimes custom designed to accommodate the specific needs of contracted performer(s). In all cases, the time required to install a stage will need to be determined and integrated into an event's production schedule in order to avoid clashes with other site/venue preparatory work. Included in this time will need to be opportunities to test systems such as sound, lighting and screens, to undertake a rehearsal in association with performers/presenters. Coordinating what happens on a stage(s) is also a major concern for an event organiser. Depending on the scale and type of event, this task might be allocated to a stage manager who coordinates the flow of activities across a stage using a running sheet, and who works with contracted technical staff responsible for screens, lighting and sound.

FIGURE 14.10   Stage layout options

The pros and cons of stage layouts

Arena stage
Pros: The audience feel included. Creates an intimate atmosphere.
Cons: Sightlines might be an issue so there needs to be lots of movement around the space.

Proscenium theatre
Pros: Sightlines are excellent and work is easy to stage.
Cons: The audience can feel quite removed from the action.

Thrust stage
Pros: The audience feel included and an intimate atmosphere is created. Having one end which is visible to all provides a 'back' to the stage.
Cons: Sightlines can still be an issue.

Theatre in the round
Pros: An intimate and exciting atmosphere. Audience feel included.
Cons: Sightlines can be very tricky.

Traverse

Pros: The audience on either side can clearly see work that happens at two sides. The audience can see each other, creating intimacy.

Cons: The opposing sides of the audience might see two entirely different shows and sightlines are still an issue.

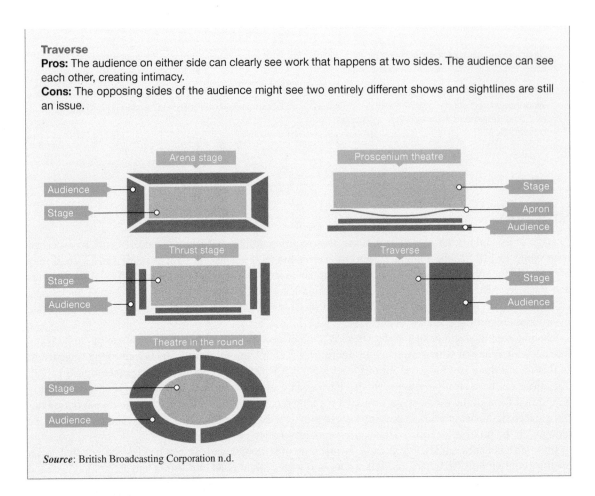

Source: British Broadcasting Corporation n.d.

Food and beverage

Food and beverage are often a major event element, and in many cases play a significant role in reinforcing an event's chosen theme. The choice of high-quality food and wine, for example, can reinforce an event's efforts to create a luxurious and sophisticated feeling. This feeling can be further reinforced through the use of celebrity chefs, formal table settings, and elaborate table centrepieces. WaitstaffWaitstaff can also play a role in creating the look and feel of an event. For example, an event based on a beach theme might choose to dress waitstaff in a 'beach casual' style, while an industry awards evening would likely require more formal attire.

The practicalities of arranging food and beverage need to be carefully considered. Often choice in this area can be constrained by the need to utilise a venue's own catering services or that of the caterers who are contracted to it. Where this is not the case, such as with non-traditional venues (for example, warehouses), or in situations where outdoor venues are used, event organisers have a free hand in this area. In these instances, a tender can be conducted, quotes can be called for, or a selection made based on past experience. When selecting caterers consideration must be given to their certifications and insurances. For example, in the Australian state of New South Wales, it should be established if a caterer has:

- NSW Restaurant & Caterers Gold Licence
- NSW Caterers Liquor Licence
- NSW Food Authority Number
- local council temporary food vendors licence
- current insurance certificates — public liability and workers compensation.

Once selected, an event organiser will need to supply a caterer with a range of information if they are to effectively integrate with their event. A detailed caterer brief, for example, might include:

- event objective(s), theme and style (catering service supplier will need to link to, and reinforce, these)
- budget, including estimated per-attendee spend (this might change as more people register/buy tickets, or if anticipated numbers are not achieved)

- number of people to be serviced, level of service to be provided (this will influence the number of waitstaff needed), menu/presentation style (for example, live cooking stations with a 'theatrical' element) and the level of 'customisation' likely to be required to accommodate guest dietary preferences
- waste management — need to integrate into event/site/venue waste management plan
- coordination (will the caterer be responsible for 'bump in' of equipment and oversight/management of other food and beverage suppliers?)
- what facilities/accommodation (for example, marquees) will be available to caterers on-site and what will need to be provided
- requirement to develop a schedule for food and beverage provision in association with the event organiser
- requirement to comply with responsible service of alcohol, and, especially regarding religious and cultural demands, food handling regulations and work health and safety legislation
- payment terms and conditions of the contractual relationship.

A particular concern in this element of event design is the provision of alcohol. If caterers are used, and they have the appropriate licence and trained staff, this responsibility can be outsourced to a large degree, and strategies established in association with the event organiser to manage this potentially troublesome area. These strategies can include: limiting the time bars are open at an event; making only a limited number of drinks available at no cost; allowing only a set number of bottles of alcohol to be provided to a table during an event and requiring attendees to purchase any further drinks.

Talent

The talent used at an event can range from music groups to motivational speakers to specially commissioned shows and can form a major part of the attendee experience. They can play many roles, including creating a mood in attendees, causing them, for example, to feel relaxed or energised; animate and add memorable moments to otherwise 'dead' event spaces, or event elements such as morning and afternoon tea or lunch; inject an element of excitement and fun into otherwise 'serious' events such as conferences; and change the rhythm and flow of an event by providing 'wow' moments.

When engaging and managing talent, the following factors need to be considered.
- Contact — at the outset, the person responsible for the employment of the talent (for example, agent, member of the band) needs to be determined so clear lines of communication and authority can be established.
- Staging requirements — a rock band, for example, will have more complex sound requirements than those of a solo singer or a motivational speaker. These requirements are usually listed on a document called the 'rider' or request sheet. Performance groups will also commonly have their own stage plot illustrating the stage area they require and their preferred lighting configuration.
- Availability for rehearsal, media interviews and presentation/performance — the available times given by talent management should include the period needed for stage setup and breakdown and rehearsal, and when media can engage with them (if required) so as to assist with event promotion.
- Accompanying personnel — some performers travel with an entourage that can include technicians, stagehands, cooks, stylists and bodyguards. It is important to establish their numbers and their roles and needs.
- Contracts and legal requirements — considerations here extend to union minimum rates and conditions, the legal structure of the talent (for example, sole trader/company), copyright, insurances and the presence of riders (these matters are discussed in detail in the legal considerations in event planning and management chapter).
- Payment — when is payment required, pre- or post-event? Is a partial payment required upon a contract being signed and is this amount refundable if the event is cancelled?
- On-site management — responsibility needs to be allocated to an event team member to manage talent from the time they arrive until their departure. In this regard, they might need to beprovided with stage running sheets; introduced to stage crew and technical staff (for example, lighting, sound desk coordinators/operators); provided with a work health and safety orientation; assigned security staff (if necessary); shown back-of-house facilities (for example, change areas); and assisted in removing equipment once their performance has been completed.

Talent come from a variety of professional and cultural backgrounds. This means different performers have different expectations about the facilities available to them, and how they are to be treated. Theatre performers and concert musicians, for example, expect professional guidelines to be provided by the event organiser. They might, for example, require a working script, or a musical score, and the credentials of the director or conductor with whom they will be working. Street and outdoor festival performers, on the other hand, can adjust to less formal conditions and to improvising during the event. However, every performer, no matter who they are, must always be treated in a professional manner by event organisers and their team.

When seeking to identify talent, reference can be made to such organisations as speakers bureaux, performer management agencies and directories such as TheBizBook (www.thebizbook.com.au).

Experience-enhancing technologies

Virtual reality and augmented realities

Virtual and augmented reality are technologies that are increasingly finding their way into both the planning and delivery stages of events. The technology can be used, for example, to:
- transport people to another location (for example, conference attendees can virtually attend an event and experience presenters and multimedia presentations live)
- provide event organisers with virtual tours of sites/venues and realistic renderings of event sites/venues so they can see what their events will appear like in real life
- provide entertainment for attendees (for example, simulations of climbing Everest, racing cars)
- showcase products/experiences (for example, explore and experience what it is like to drive a new car while at a car show).

Augmented reality (AR) essentially involves superimposing information — sounds, images and text — on real-world settings. For example, AR can be used to superimpose attendee location details on event maps uploaded onto smartphones. This facility can be an added element to an event's app.

While technologies of this nature can have a significant 'wow' factor, the issue of whether they contribute to an event's purpose, or provide added value to the attendee experience, needs to be given serious consideration.

Screen and projection technologies

A screen is simply a surface. Projections can be directed onto a surface (for example, a blank wall) or a surface can be digitised by using technologies such as LED screens. The use of screens, especially digitised ones, is now embedded not only in our daily lives but also in events. Everyone expects to see screens at an event.

By using the latest motion graphics and post-production techniques, screen content almost always uses imagery and sound that aims to be dynamic, eye-catching and (sometimes) ear bursting! However, unless the screen content directly relates to the event's purpose, it can have little meaning beyond entertainment. Creating high-quality content is time-consuming and costly, but the results can be breath-taking. Screen content can also be re-used by a client/organisation for other projects beyond the event.

Key advantages of using screens are that they are flexible in terms of the content that they can show (as opposed to static signs) and how quickly this content can be changed. For example, a last-minute program change resulting from a speaker cancellation can be quickly communicated, along with their photo and their bio.

Projection mapping technologies are another innovation that has increasingly found its way into event design adding textures, colours, interactivity and a 'wow' factor to an environment. The images they create are also highly shareable through social media, which greatly assists in, for example, creating brand/event/destination awareness. Lighting festivals that employ this technology are common in many cities (for example, Vivid Sydney) and larger towns (for example, White Night Ballarat) and allow virtually anything to be projected onto a building or structure's surface (see figure 14.11). Additionally, amazing indoor lighting projections are now appearing at events as varied as product launches and conferences. To better understand the effects projection mapping can have in indoor spaces, there are a number of YouTube videos that can be viewed (Visualpower 2013).

Theming

The elements of event design discussed previously are often combined to produce a consistent look, feel and/or focus to an event — its theme (see also the conceptualising the event chapter). An event's theme can be drawn from a variety of different sources. For example, current and topical issues in a particular industry sector (for example, Robotics), historical eras (for example, the Roaring 20s, Wild West), community celebrations (for example, Christmas, Easter), culture (for example, Indian, Chinese) and movies (for example, Star Wars). Themes can also be general in nature, for example, formal events such as black-tie dinners, or they can be very specific and based on a particular company's products/services (for example, product launches). In the area of theming, imagination is the only constraint, along with the purpose of the event. In figure 14.12, the relationship between the purpose of an event and an imaginative themed response by the event organising company Event Planet can be seen in the context of the fitness brand Fitbit.

| **FIGURE 14.11** | Architectural projections onto Australian Parliament House by The Electric Canvas for Enlighten Canberra 2020, presented by Events ACT. |

Source: Architectural projections onto Australian Parliament House by The Electric Canvas for Enlighten Canberra 2020, presented by Events ACT. Artwork 'Ngayuku ngura — My country' (Parliament House Art Collection) by Mick Wikilyiri (born c.1935), Sandra Ken (born 1968), Tjungkara Ken (born 1969), Marinka Tunkin (birthdate unknown), Yaritji Young (born 1955). Pitjantjatjara people. Image courtesy of Visabel. Photography by Photox.

| **FIGURE 14.12** | An example of the relationship between theming and an event's purpose |

Event brief

To design and produce a unique, youthful, fun and engaging health and fitness workout experience for Sydney-based consumers to encourage them to move confidently and freely with Fitbit and create the perfect environment to launch their new Versa Lite range.

The result

The leading event management company staged the event for the iconic fitness brand at Sydney's Luna Park on April 13.

Event Planet staged a 1980s aerobics workout experience for 150+ participants at Sydney's Luna Park for Fitbit. The aerobics class was led by Retrosweat, with DJ Feline setting the mood with 80s hits. Fitbit trainer Brittney Cutts hosted the event and took guests through a Fitbit inspired warm up and cool down.

In true Event Planet style, the fitness workout, held in the Crystal Ballroom, was amplified via user-generated content, as guests enjoyed a retro salon setting where hair and [make-up] artists paid homage to the 80s with crimping irons at the ready and the boldest of make-up colours available! Bright Fitbit-branded tank tops and sweatbands completed the look.

▶

A post-workout brunch bar featured branded coconuts and healthy treats before a group photo created memories for all who participated. All participants received a Fitbit tank top and 80s-style headband. One hundred per cent of proceeds of the nominal $15 ticket sales for this event went to Diabetes NSW and ACT.

Source: Event Planet n.d.

Themes, if executed successfully, can move people into 'alternate realities'; make an event memorable; add to, and reinforce, its narrative; draw attendees to a particular location within a site/venue (by using different sub-themes in different zones); and link the event to a client's brand or message. Examples of themes and their possible associated design elements have been provided in figure 14.13.

FIGURE 14.13 Themes and suggested design styles

- Formal — strict etiquette and dress for an official government dinner in a parliament house ballroom
    - Music — world-famous musician
    - Lighting — practical lighting throughout, table lighting
    - Decorations — floral arrangements
- Theatrical — exaggerated and dramatic like a themed ball set up in a film studio sound stage
    - Music — based around the theme, such as a 1920s jazz band
    - Lighting — moody, film studio lighting, films playing
    - Decorations — 1920s film set backdrops and props
- Elegant — graceful and stylish as with an outdoor garden party in the grounds of a historic house
    - Music — string quintet
    - Lighting — festoons, real fire pots and fireworks
    - Decorations — wind kinetics and flags
- Fun — light-hearted and enjoyable such as a pop-up retail launch unveiled in a CBD laneway
    - Music — cover band
    - Lighting — LED screens, festoons above, neons
    - Decorations — brand logos and graphics
- Casual — relaxed and laidback like a product demonstration given in a local shopping centre atrium space

- Music — pre-recorded tracks
- Mood — bright lights, LED screens with brand commercials
- Decorations — product graphics, block colours
- Playful — games and amusements as in an arcade built within a convention centre trade show
  - Music — soundscapes of games sound effects
  - Mood — flashing lights, LED neon, happy tubes
  - Decorations — game graphics enlarged and located overhead
- Chic — contemporary and stylish such as a catwalk fashion show in a disused warehouse
  - Music — latest YouTube music sensation
  - Mood — bright lighting above the catwalk, naked bulbs
  - Decorations — found industrial objects
- Celebratory — acknowledgement and pride as in an anniversary dinner held at a five-star hotel
  - Music — big band with guest singer
  - Mood — highlighted flags and bunting, follow spots
  - Decorations — projected historical photographs of the people being celebrated

Coordinating the event design experience

Many event organisers perform both the event organising and event designer function and are accomplished at both. Others prefer to employ specialist event designers/stylists who might have backgrounds in areas such as theatre design, interior design or floristry to undertake the task of creating the 'look' and feel of the event as they recognise their skill set does not extend into this area. These professionals can also assist with decisions as regards how light and sound can be integrated into an event, or these decisions might be made in association with separate companies that have been employed to provide equipment and oversee this aspect of an event. The task (if required) of recording the event in a video or audio format needs also to be part of these discussions. Some companies, it should be noted, can supply a fully integrated system of film, video, projections, audiovisual script, event recording and special effects.

Venues often have inhouse providers in the audiovisual area or have a limited number of suppliers from whom an event organiser can choose. This can be somewhat limiting, but there is little the event organiser can do if this is the case.

14.3 Selected event production considerations

LEARNING OBJECTIVE 14.3 Discuss selected event production processes and their significance in event experience delivery.

Queuing

Often, the first experience of an attendee at an event is queuing for entry, and once inside they can again confront queues for food, toilets and seating. As regards entry, queueing can be reduced through the pre-sale of tickets/registrations and the use of automated entry turnstiles or similar. However, when it is still possible to pay for tickets at the venue/on-site, significant queues can still arise.

Given that queues can significantly compromise the attendee experience, organisers need to consider how they can address both actual and perceived waiting times (the subjective time that attendees feel they have waited). This can be done by seeking answers to a range of questions, including:

- How many queues and possible bottlenecks are there likely to be?
- Has an adequate number of crowd controllers and security staff been allocated to manage queues?
- Should signage showing estimated waiting times at various points in queues be employed?
- Have queueing benchmarks been set that act as 'triggers' for additional gates/ticket aisles to be open, and have staff been given the responsibility for identifying when these benchmarks have been reached?
- When will queues form? Will they form at once (for example, during an event's opening) or over a period of time?
- Can perceived waiting times be reduced by, for example:
  - using entertainers/LED screens to distract attendees
  - employing zig-zag queue designs that make people believe they are closer to the end of a queue than they actually are
  - corralling attendees (as theatres and some corporate events do) in a bar area or similar space until the event begins?

- Is lighting, and sun and rain protection adequate?
- Are crowd-friendly barricades and partitions in place to structure queues?
- Can post-event entertainment/activities be used to stagger the flow of attendees (and resulting queues) from an event site and its car parks?

Transport

The selection of an event site/venue, as noted previously, needs to consider the availability and cost of transport to and from it. This consideration is relevant for attendees, as well as contractors, suppliers, VIPs and vendors, and so on. A lengthy (in distance or in time) and costly trip, involving multiple transport modes, for example, can both decrease its attractiveness and increase its input costs. Additionally, location raises other issues for some types of events (for example, marathons, marches, street markets, parades) that require access to a road. Commonly events in this situation need to supply a traffic management plan. An example, of how this process works in the context of New South Wales is provided in figure 14.14. As is evident from this diagram, an event organiser must first classify their event into one of four groups based on its impact on traffic and its surrounding area. Depending on this classification, different actions will need to be taken. For, example, a Class 1 event, such as a major car race through the streets of a city, would follow a process that includes preparing a detailed traffic management plan and advertising the traffic impacts of the event to the wider public (NSW Government 2018).

| FIGURE 14.14 | Actions required for different classifications of special events utilising roadways in New South Wales |

Source: NSW Government 2018, p. 21.

Consideration should also be given when working through traffic and transport management issues to the matter of sustainability. Encouraging people to use alternatives to private transport can significantly reduce an event's carbon footprint. With this goal in mind, key considerations in sustainable transport planning for events have been provided in figure 14.15.

FIGURE 14.15	Key considerations associated with sustainable transport planning for events		
	✓ Good	✓✓ Better	✓✓✓ Best
Virtual Events	Video conference speakers who live overseas	Live stream the event for distance attendees	Conduct the event entirely online
Active / Public Transport	Provide a shuttle service for large events	Provide public transport information to the venue	Encourage attendees to walk or cycle to your event
Logistics	Think about start and finish times	Provide suggested travel times and routes	Provide clear maps showing public transport options

Source: Sustainability Team, RMIT n.d.

Site/venue services and facilities

Prior to an event's commencement, decisions as to the type and number of various on-site service and facilities would have been made. In some instances, such as when using established venues, these might already be present (for example, toilets, electricity, water fountains, wi-fi, waste bins); in others, such as when using greenfield sites, they will need to be installed. During an event's delivery, these services and facilities will require monitoring to ensure they are of a suitable standard such that they meet user expectations. If they are not, the venue or the event organiser will need to take appropriate actions (for example, bring in additional toilets, require the waste contractor to provide additional bins). Waste bins that are overflowing, toilets that are in poor condition (or inadequate in number) are major sources of attendee complaints, and quickly impinge on the overall perception of the event experience.

Communication

The task of on-site communications prior to, during and post an event is an important one. Before an event commences, clear lines of communication/reporting must be established so that information flows where it needs to and when it needs to, and to ensure stakeholders (suppliers, attendees, sponsors, staff, volunteers etc.) have the information they require in order to engage with the event. In the case of attendees, event apps are increasingly performing a major role in this area. In addition to this tool, electronic notice boards, event signage, programs, event maps, SMS messaging, social media updates, stage sound systems, site public address systems and even 'old school' loud hailers can be used.

Staff and volunteers can be communicated with through the use of mobile phones, texts/email, two-way radios (different channels might be needed for different teams and protocols are required), and pre-event inductions and briefings. Increasingly, various apps are being employed to facilitate on-site communication between, and within, these groups (for example, Zoom and Google Hangouts). The issue of communication technology failure must also be planned for so that information can still flow under such circumstances (for example, failure of a local mobile phone tower).

One on-site and near-site communication tool that often comes in for criticism is that of signage. To deal with this issue, events should consider developing a detailed signage plan, that addresses issues such as:

- overall placement of signs — at decision points (for example, Do I get to the toilets by turning right or left), at danger spots (for example, uneven paths), on rows/seats/tables and near the venue/site (directional signage)

- types of signs needed — directional, entry/exit, statutory (legal and warning signs), operational (for example, supplier storage area), facility names (for example, stage one) and sponsor signage
- form — pictures/graphics/words (adhesive vinyl decal signs are now common at many events) and the signage size
- language requirements — single or multiple languages
- maintenance and removal
- accuracy — if changes to programming and so on are made, signs should be updated to reflect this (this is easy to do if signs are electronic).

In instances where near-site/venue signage is to be used, councils should be contacted, as they often have regulations as regards matters such as the quality of signs, their size, location, when they can be erected and so on. It is also the case that some councils have mobile billboards and banner poles that can be hired by event organisers.

Production team

The chapter on human resource management and events discussed the role of staff and volunteers at an event. It must also be kept in mind that there is a large contingent of other people (suppliers, contractors and stagehands etc.) that make up an event's entire production team. These people are central to an event's success, and many of them are skilled technical specialists looking after matters such as screens, sound, lighting, security, food and beverage. As specialists they have much to contribute to the event production process regarding matters such as scheduling, work health and safety, and the various ways their operational area (for example, lighting, sound) can enhance the attendee experience. As team members they need to understand their role in the event, so ensuring they receive the documentation they require (for example, site/venue plans, schedules, reporting lines) and are briefed prior to an event's commencement is important. It might also be necessary to undertake a 'walkthrough of the event' to ensure they are aware of their responsibilities. Identification of the production team (via clothing and/or passes), along with their degree of access to the various areas at a site/venue, must also be considered (see example in figure 14.16).

| FIGURE 14.16 | Use of clothing to identify event staff |

Production schedules, running sheets, risk management and contingency plans

These documents are integral to the event production process and have been discussed elsewhere (see the chapter on event project management and the chapter on risk management). Their role is to ensure an event is delivered as planned, is safe for all stakeholders and takes account of, and plans for, possible circumstances that might disrupt its conduct.

SUMMARY

Decisions regarding event design and production flow directly from its intended outcome(s). This outcome(s) in turn shapes the attendee experience and the decisions associated with it. These decisions extend to areas such as site/venue selection, programming, and the use of furniture and props, lighting, colour, music, sound, staging, food and beverage, talent and event experience–enhancing technologies. All of these elements need to be coordinated into a unified whole, commonly coalescing around a chosen theme.

This chapter also explored key considerations in the event production process, examining in doing so matters associated with the management of queues, transport, communication and site/venue services. It also stressed the importance of creating an effective event production team, along with considerations in the management of such teams and the types of contributions its members can make to an event's success.

QUESTIONS

1 What influence does programming have on event design decisions?

2 Identify and discuss major considerations in the layout of a festival site or a conference held at a five-star hotel.

3 Why is signage an important aspect of event design, and what types of signs might be relevant in the context of an indoor or an outdoor event?

4 If you were asked to select a venue for a conference of 500 doctors from around Australia and overseas, what factors would you consider when making your decision?

5 If you were trying to ensure you could communicate with your event staff and volunteers at an event, what communication technologies would you consider using?

6 Download a copy of the NSW Government's 'Guide to traffic and transport management for special events, version 3.5' (from www.rms.nsw.gov.au/documents/business-industry/event-management-gui delines/guide-traffic-transport-management-special-events.pdf). Assuming you were intending to hold a class 3 event (as defined by this publication), what would this mean in terms of the actions you would need to take?

7 Briefly discuss how colour and/or music can play a role in event design.

8 Explore (by way of a web search) how virtual reality is currently being employed in event settings. Provide three specific examples of its use.

9 Create an event layout diagram for a community market. Justify your placement of the various elements/zones you include.

10 What role(s) can talent play in an event? If you were conducting a product launch for an upmarket cosmetic brand, what type(s) of talent might you use?

CASE STUDY

BARANGAROO OPENING CELEBRATIONS

Barangaroo

Barangaroo is a large parcel of public land on the eastern shores of Cockle Bay, adjacent to Millers Point in Sydney. For several years, Barangaroo has been undergoing major redevelopment by the NSW State Government through the Barangaroo Delivery Authority (BDA). 'Barangaroo Reserve' and the 'Cutaway' — a harbourside reserve and a large, multi-use undercover space beneath the park — were the first components of the project to be opened to the public in July 2015, with other stages being completed over the following years. The site is part of the territory of the Gadigal people, and before colonisation, was a significant Indigenous area used for fishing and hunting. Barangaroo is named after a powerful Cammeraygal woman who played an important role in the early days of colonial Sydney and was also the wife of Bennelong. From the 1850s to the late 1990s the site was occupied by wharves and was a major port. During the Great Depression, Hickson Road, which runs alongside the site, became known as the 'Hungry Mile' as men would go to the wharves looking for work. It became synonymous with migration during the 1950s as many ships landed there full of largely European immigrants, ready to start a new life in Australia.

Event brief for the Opening Celebrations

In early 2015 the BDA awarded Gill Minervini Creative (GMC) the contract for the creative direction and delivery of the Opening Celebrations for Barangaroo Reserve and the Cutaway. These opening celebrations of stage one of the Barangaroo redevelopment took place over three months from September to the end of November 2015.

The main requirements for the opening events for Barangaroo Reserve and the Cutaway from the BDA were to produce three months of programming that:
- included 'occasions' and an extended form of activation over the span of twelve weeks
- introduced the people of Sydney and beyond to Barangaroo by producing civic-participatory public events with high impact
- included immersive event experiences that were memorable for participants and the community
- honoured the Indigenous history and contemporary significance of the site
- incorporated design that enhanced the reserve
- invited public participation in the reserve through a series of public events
- generated extensive public engagement and participation in the Cutaway.

Key stakeholders

The key stakeholders involved in the opening celebrations for Barangaroo Reserve and the Cutaway were:
- NSW State Government through the Barangaroo Delivery Authority
- the Indigenous community
- the Millers Point community
- local businesses
- tourists
- the media.

Constraints of the site

The main constraint in developing events for the opening celebrations was that the site was not completed until two months before the events took place, with considerable work still being done during the opening event period. The creative direction of the project and subsequent development and delivery of these ideas had to occur in a somewhat unknown environment — much of the site was under major construction and covered in scaffolding through most of the nine months of our engagement prior to the event opening. We were confirming event site plans, engaging artists for major public art commissions, securing performers for roving and staged performances, developing catering and other activations in an unfinished environment that had never been used for public events. This made creative direction and delivery very difficult and we relied heavily on our previous experience working in public spaces and our ability to operate flexibly to ensure the successful implementation of our ideas.

Structure

In order to meet the requirements of the BDA brief outlined above, GMC proposed the 'Welcome Celebrations', a program of events consisting of three months of programming that included:
- a 'Giant Picnic' event on the first Sunday of each of the three months
- 'Open Weekend' events — reduced programming on the following three weekends of each month
- event hours from 11 am to 5 pm with the exception of the first Giant Picnic that concluded at 8.30 pm with the Welcome Celebrations.

Narrative/themes

The program told the story of the Barangaroo site and its people through a thematic device for each month, celebrated the site's history and culture and introduced the audience to its new role as a major public space for Sydney. The themes were:
- 'Stone' (September)
  - the story of Indigenous history and ceremony, time and the cultural foundations of the site
- 'Sea' (October)
  - the story of the site's maritime history, including trade, labour, migration and multiculturalism
- 'Sky' (November)
  - the story yet to be written: the next generation and the future of the site

Content

The program of events proposed and delivered conveyed this story successfully through a variety of event elements that were programmed each month according to theme:

- programming
  - art installations by Brook Andrew (for 'Stone'), Esem Projects (for 'Sea') and James Dive & The Glue Society (for 'Sky')
  - performance — staged and roving, ceremony, talks, workshops, tours
  - activations — marine, fire, pyrotechnics, Welcome Walk, Opening Party
- design — enhanced natural environment and evoked themes
- food and beverage — bespoke menu and caterers, including well-known chefs, for each theme.

Key objectives and outcomes

The key objectives of the program outlined by GMC in the proposal to meet the BDA brief and the subsequent outcomes are outlined below.

- Showcase Barangaroo and the Cutaway
  - Programming directed around the site using natural elements as 'stages' and event platforms encouraged audiences to move around the site and experience its many assets and elements, ensuring the whole site was engaged in the event.
  - Design elements created were in harmony with the site, enhanced rather than detracted from it, and strengthened the themes of each month and therefore our narrative.
  - Program elements — such as the pyrotechnics display, use of fire, Indigenous dusk ceremony, welcome walk and party, art installations, talks series, tours, food and beverage stations, and entertainment — were designed to enhance, activate and experiment with the site.
- Accessible, inclusive, participatory and democratic
  - The structure of the events and the use of a picnic theme allowed an entry point for a broad audience demographic; it was easy to understand and inclusive of all cultures.
  - The events were free, with food and beverages available at affordable prices.
  - Event elements such as entertainment, food and art installations were selected for their broad appeal, high quality and artist profile.
  - Audience involvement and participation was a key element throughout the program with hands-on activities such as workshops, immersive elements of the art installations, ceremonies and participatory performances.
- Celebratory and fun
  - The program included many elements that celebrated the site and its story such as the dusk ceremony, Welcome to Country, opening party, art installations, the use of fire and the various maritime activations.
  - The aim of producing quality programming that had something for all audiences was achieved through providing quality cultural experiences that were enjoyable, uplifting, inclusive and educational.
- High quality
  - All aspects of the program were of the highest quality achievable within the budget and involved Australia's leading performers, visual artists, chefs, beverage producers and speakers.
  - All of these elements were provided to our audiences either free or at very reasonable prices (for food and beverages).
- Sydney/NSW focus
  - Over 90 per cent of the program elements — such as performers, chefs, artists and speakers — were from Sydney or NSW, to showcase the best that Sydney and NSW has to offer in Sydney's newest iconic venue.
- Memorable experiences
  - The program provided a range of unique experiences — such as the Stone ceremonies, pyrotechnics and fire displays, art installations, talks series, maritime activations and many of the performances — directed especially for this location.
- Safe, on budget and on time
  - The operational delivery of the event was generally very smooth considering it was a brand-new site and there were many unknowns. There were no serious incidents or injuries to audience or staff. All deadlines were met in planning and delivery and the project was delivered within the budget.

Summary

The Welcome Celebrations at Barangaroo Reserve and Cutaway were successful on a variety of levels. GMC met our objectives from a programming, management, financial, engagement and delivery perspective. Importantly, the events introduced 240 000 people to this new, iconic venue without any major safety or security issues and to the general delight of our audiences. In addition, media exposure was positive. We were pleased to be able to deliver the very best of NSW culture to the people of Sydney and beyond, and the GMC team worked incredibly hard with the BDA to deliver all of this to the highest standard. A great deal was learnt by all involved regarding how this new site worked and how people interacted with it.

The increased and return visitation experienced through the course of the three-month program and positive audience and media feedback was testament to the successful delivery of all of our aims and objectives. It was an incredible opportunity to be engaged to direct and deliver the opening celebrations for this new, iconic Australian site; it is an event that Gill Minervini Creative is very proud to have been a part of.

Prepared by Gill Minervini, Gill Minervini Creative

QUESTIONS

1 How do the themes of each month — 'Stone', 'Sea' and 'Sky' — help tell the narrative of the site?

2 Why were a variety of programming elements, such as visual art, performance and food, used throughout the Welcome Celebrations?

3 Why did the Creative Director choose to showcase Sydney and NSW suppliers for this event?

REFERENCES

British Broadcasting Corporation n.d., 'Creating and staging a devised performance', www.bbc.co.uk/bitesize/guides/zg9x34j/revision/7, viewed 22 April 2020.

Cast Group n.d., 'Vivien', https://cast-soft.com/vivien-event-designer, viewed 6 May 2020.

ETC Connect n.d., 'Types of lights', www.etcconnect.com/support/training-events/ltd/stage-lighting-essentials-poster-3.aspx, viewed 15 May 2020.

Event Planet n.d., '#freeyourfit Fitbit consumer event', www.eventplanet.com.au/case-study/freeyourfit-fitbit-consumer-event, viewed 26 April 2020.

Lovelock, C, Patterson, P & Wirtz, J 2015, *Services marketing*, 6th ed., Pearson, Australia.

National Folk Festival 2019, 'Site map', www.folkfestival.org.au/about-the-festival/festival-map, viewed 25 April 2020.

NSW Government 2018, 'Guide to traffic and transport management for special events Version 3.5', 1 July, www.rms.nsw.gov.au/documents/business-industry/event-management-guidelines/guide-traffic-transport-management-special-events.pdf, viewed 14 May 2020.

Peguero, M 2020, '20 types of light for your next event', *One Way Event Productions,* 4 March, www.onewayeventproductions.com/20-types-of-light-for-your-next-event, viewed 14 May 2020.

Silvers, J 2004, *Professional event coordination*, John Wiley & Sons Inc, Hoboken, New Jersey USA.

Sustainability Team, RMIT n.d., 'Sustainable events guide', http://mams.rmit.edu.au/go5yt43n3hf2.pdf, pp. 9–10, viewed 23 July 2020.

Sydney Prop Specialists n.d., 'Prop hire and event styling in Sydney', www.sydneyprops.com.au, viewed 24 April 2020.

The State of Queensland 2019, 'Help with running successful events' Event site plan template, www.qld.gov.au/about/events-awards-honours/events/running-events, viewed 18 August 2020.

Visualpower 2013, *Indoor 3 walls 3D building mapping — Visualpower* (video), YouTube, www.youtube.com/watch?v=kZcuO8lt-34, viewed 14 May 2020.

ACKNOWLEDGEMENTS

Photo: © Eugenio Marongiu / Shutterstock.com

Figure 14.4: © The State of Queensland 2019. Licensed under a Creative Commons Attribution 4.0 International Licence (licence available at www.creativecommons.org/licenses/by/4.0/legalcode).

Figure 14.5: © National Folk Festival, Canberra

Figure 14.6: © Cast Group

Figure 14.7: © Sydney Prop Specialists: www.sydneyprops.com.au, www.sydneypropsphotostudio.com.au, www.chaircoverscandelabra.com.au, www.customelements.com.au, www.sydneyeventservices.com

Figure 14.8: © ECT Connect

Figure 14.10: Copyright © 2020 BBC

Figure 14.11: Architectural projections onto Australian Parliament House by The Electric Canvas for Enlighten Canberra 2020, presented by Events ACT. Artwork 'Ngayukungura — My country' (Parliament House Art Collection) by Mick Wikilyiri (born c.1935), Sandra Ken (born 1968), Tjungkara

Ken (born 1969), Marinka Tunkin (birthdate unknown), Yaritji Young (born 1955). Pitjantjatjara people. Image courtesy of Visabel. Photography by Photox.

Figure 14.12: © Event Planet

Figure 14.14: © Transport for NSW

Figure 14.15: © Royal Melbourne Institute of Technology

Figure 14.16: © JoeFoxBelfast / Alamy Stock Photo

CHAPTER 15

Event evaluation and research

After studying this chapter, you should be able to:

15.1 describe the role of evaluation in the event management process and discuss the nature and purpose of pre-event, mid-event and post-event evaluation

15.2 identify the evaluation needs of event stakeholders and identify and utilise data sources relevant to the event evaluation process

15.3 discuss how knowledge gained through the event evaluation process can be applied to future events

15.4 describe the event evaluation process and analyse data gathered through the evaluation process.

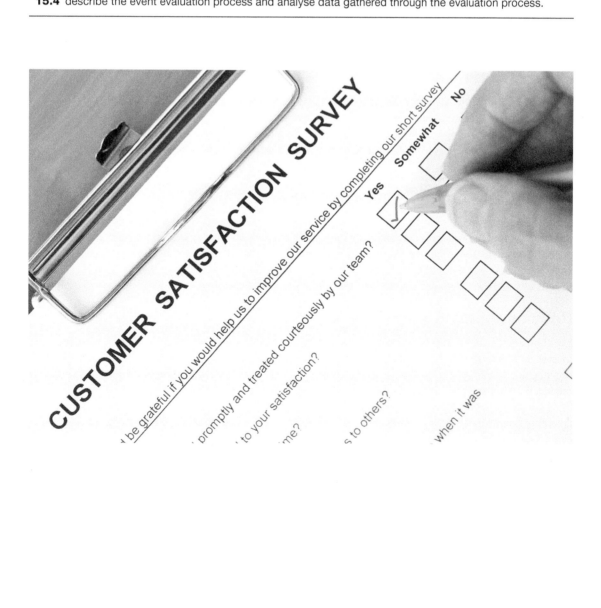

Introduction

The evaluation process is concerned with assessing the outcomes of an event against its stated goals and objectives. Information gained through this process allows event organisers to both report to their various stakeholders (for example, the client, the organising committee, granting bodies, government agencies) and assess the effectiveness of their own internal processes and systems. Insights gained serve to highlight areas where revisions/changes need to be made in subsequent event iterations, while also playing an organisational learning role for event organisers.

This chapter begins by examining the nature of event evaluation, along with the role this process plays over an event's planning and delivery cycle. The chapter then moves on to discuss those internal and external factors that might, depending on the event, be the subject of evaluative interest. The uses to which data resulting from the evaluative process is then discussed, before an overview of the steps involved in generating this information is provided. The chapter concludes with a case study of the evaluation of the Being Human Festival in the United Kingdom.

15.1 What is event evaluation?

LEARNING OBJECTIVE 15.1 Describe the role of evaluation in the event management process and discuss the nature and purpose of pre-event, mid-event and post-event evaluation.

Event evaluation can be defined as 'the holistic assessment of an event through the utilisation of a broad range of measures and approaches to determine its value and impacts in an agreed or prescribed context' (Brown et al. 2015, p. 136). The starting point for evaluation will differ depending on the nature of the event concerned. New public events, for example, may face initial evaluation through a feasibility study, while this task would be unnecessary for ongoing or simple events (for example, corporate product launch). All events, however, will benefit from evaluation during their planning and delivery, and upon their completion. These three phases of event evaluation are briefly discussed below.

Pre-event phase

In order to evaluate the potential capacity of some types of new events (particularly larger scale events) to achieve their intended outcomes, a feasibility study (see also the chapter on strategic event planning) is often conducted. It is important that these studies are conducted in an objective manner, and do not employ overly optimistic assumptions in areas such as projected ticket sales or tourism outcomes (Jago and Dwyer 2006).

Event planning and delivery phase

Various monitoring and control practices are available to event organisers (for example, regular budget reviews, assessments of progress against established schedules). These serve to ensure that an event's planning and delivery processes take place in line with forecasts and in ways that allow it to meet its stated goals and objectives. Should any divergence be observed as a result of applying these practices, remedial actions can then be taken (see also the chapter on event project management).

Post-event evaluation phase

Event outcomes, internal and/or external, are assessed during this phase, with the intention of both reporting to stakeholders (for example, clients, sponsors, organising committees, granting bodies, community organisations and police) regarding an event's outcomes in relation to its goals and objectives and obtaining feedback on current planning and operational practices. This information can then be used, among other things, to suggest changes or refinements in the way future events are planned and delivered, as well as to demonstrate the degree to which stakeholder outcomes have been met (see also the event planning context chapter).

Given that significant coverage has been given to the first two phases of event evaluation in prior chapters (see the chapters on the event planning context, strategic event planning and event project management), the following discussion will largely focus on post-event evaluation.

15.2 Post-event evaluation

LEARNING OBJECTIVE 15.2 Identify the evaluation needs of event stakeholders and identify and utilise data sources relevant to the event evaluation process.

In an event's initial planning phase, goals and objectives need to be developed to guide its organiser's subsequent actions. Progress towards these goals and objectives can be monitored through the use of benchmarks, often known as key performance indicators (KPIs). Each event will be unique in terms of the goals and objectives it seeks to pursue, and the associated KPIs it establishes to gauge its progress towards them. For example, a music festival is likely to have a goal, and associated objective(s), concerning revenue generation. This being the case, KPIs might be set for ticket sales, sponsorship signups, and food, beverage and merchandise sales. By way of another example, a conference might have a goal associated with quality of delivery, and this might be expressed in terms of an objective concerning attendee satisfaction levels. KPIs used to assess this outcome might then include the extent of satisfaction with speakers, overall program content, timeliness of delivery and satisfaction with the food and beverage provided. In general terms, factors that might be the subject of goals, objectives and associated KPIs are discussed in the following sections.

Factors of potential concern in post-event evaluation

Financial performance

Many events, both one-off and continuing, need to ensure they operate in a way that ensures their financial viability. This being the case, setting goals, objectives and KPIs in areas associated with their financial performance is important. For example, an event might seek to ensure its financial viability by establishing a set return on monies invested in it, which would then result in specific monetary targets (KPIs) for its various revenue streams (for example, ticket sales, registrations, merchandise sales and sponsorship) and the assessment of its performance against these.

Event management processes

Careful analysis of the processes employed in planning and delivering an event will enable potential refinements/changes to be made to current practices. Areas that might be the subject of such analysis include scheduling and programming practices, risk management, environmental sustainability, human resource management, and control and monitoring processes. KPIs relating to these factors can be diverse and extend to the extent of on-time delivery of event elements, number of incidents or injuries recorded, staff/volunteer satisfaction levels and volume of waste generated.

Attendee numbers, characteristics and perspectives

An event needs to have a clear understanding of its success in terms of the number of attendees it has attracted, along with their characteristics and perspectives on the event experience. This being the case measures associated with overall attendance, attendance by specific groups (along with characteristics of these groups) and matters such as satisfaction with various event elements are needed. This information, in turn, is used to determine the success or otherwise of marketing efforts, the degree to which programming was successful in meeting the needs of attendees, event delivery practices impacting the event experience (for example, poor signage, insufficient toilets) and the extent to which specific commitments to stakeholders have been met.

Economic impacts

Government agencies, as noted in previous chapters, often provide funds in support of events and, as a consequence of receiving such public funds, events need to include specific goals and objectives aligned with the purpose of these grants. Often these will concern increases in the number of out-of-area visitors. Additionally, government can be instrumental in supporting some events, such as large-scale sporting events, and may undertake their own evaluation of the economic impact of these as a way of assessing the return on their investment in both the short and long term. Further, it is common for governments — local, state and national — to create new events with primarily economic intent and to assess these on this criterion.

There was much criticism of early economic evaluations of events as providing inflated results due largely to exaggerated event participant numbers and/or their expenditure (Dwyer and Jago 2020). Much work has been done in recent times to agree upon guidelines for the conduct of these evaluations to ensure economically sound results.

The key variable that is needed to underpin the economic impact of an event is an estimate of the 'new money' that is attracted to the host region that would not have come had the event not taken place. This 'new money' is the spending that occurs by visitors to the event who come from outside the host region and would not have visited the area had the event not been staged. It does not include the spending of local residents as it is assumed that this spending would have occurred on other leisure activities in the host region had the event not been staged.

The most effective way to estimate the 'new money' generated by an event is to survey a sample of attendees to identify the average expenditure being made by those sampled that came from outside the host region. The types of questions commonly asked in order to determine this figure are:

- Do you live in the host region or are you from another region? (The expenditure of those from within the region is not counted as 'new money'.)
- Would you have come to this region if the event was not held? (If the respondent was coming anyway, their expenditure is not counted as 'new money'.)
- If you were coming to the region anyway, did you stay longer because of the event? (If they stayed longer, the spending on the extra days can be counted as 'new money'.)

Once this information has been obtained, an estimate is then made of total expenditure by out-of-area visitors by multiplying the average expenditure of survey respondents by the estimated number of all attendees from outside the region. In addition to the 'new spending' of event attendees, it is important to also capture the 'new spending' of the event organiser and any out-of-area exhibitors, stallholders or suppliers involved in the event.

The estimate of 'new money' that has been obtained through the survey process can also be put into an economic model of the local region so that the flow-on effects of this initial spending can be estimated. This is known as the multiplier effect, whereby the total impact on the economy is greater than the initial spending that occurred. There are various models that can be used for this purpose, with a summary of these appearing in figure 15.1. For a more detailed overview of the economic evaluation of the event process that is presented for non-economists, please consult Jago and Dwyer (2006).

FIGURE 15.1	Event economic evaluation models

Special events are widely recognised to have a range of impacts: economic, social and environmental. Increasingly, event assessment is used by policy evaluators such as public sector finance departments to inform policymakers whether allocating resources in support of an event is appropriate and, if so, to what extent. To make informed choices, public sector agencies increasingly demand greater rigour in evaluation techniques. When public funds are used to support an event, the cost of these funds must be compared to the expected benefits. Ideally, governments should fund events only if they create net benefits, especially if the event would not otherwise take place. The problem faced by researchers is to provide techniques that give accurate results, while at the same time having practical use for the different stakeholders.

Three main approaches to the economic evaluation of special events may be distinguished. These are standard economic impact analysis (EIA), computable general equilibrium (CGE) modelling and cost–benefit analysis (CBA).

Standard EIA takes event-related injected expenditure to generate direct and secondary (indirect and induced) effects, leading to estimates of increases in economic activity within the host destination. Standard EIA traces the flows of spending associated with tourism activity in an economy through business, households and government to identify the resulting changes in economic variables such as sales, output, government tax revenues, household income, value added and employment. The relationship between injected expenditure and output, income, value added and employment can be described by multipliers, the size of which will depend importantly upon the type of model used to estimate the impacts. Over the past decade, standard EIA approaches to the economic evaluation of special events have been heavily criticised for their use of input–output (I–O) models with unrealistic assumptions, narrow focus, exaggerated estimates of impacts, and their lack of a welfare measure to inform public policy.

Increasingly, event researchers now employ computable general equilibrium (CGE) models for event evaluation, particularly for larger events. CGE models represent best practice in assessing the economy-wide economic impacts of changes in visitor expenditure. Like standard EIA models, CGE models simulate the effects of an event-related expenditure shock on economic variables, such as GDP, prices, wages, income, employment and investment in the event destination. Unlike standard EIA, CGE models recognise that the greater resource requirements associated with event-related expenditure are likely to result in lower resource use, and output, in other areas of economic activity. Prices for goods and services used as inputs including wages, may be bid up, discouraging production of other goods and services. For open economies with flexible exchange rates, increased event-related spending by foreign visitors, puts upward pressure on the exchange rate, discouraging exports and economic activity in import-competing sectors. These effects on the wider economy need to be accounted for in an overall assessment of event impacts.

The third approach, cost–benefit analysis (CBA), is a comprehensive economic appraisal technique, which compares all the benefits associated with an event with the associated costs, present and expected in the future. The objective of CBA is to assess whether a destination economy is better or worse off because of hosting the event, estimating the community welfare effects in monetary terms (for example, dollar units). A welfare effect is simply any cost or benefit experienced by a member of the relevant community. CBA is concerned with measuring the change in all sources of economic welfare, whether occurring in markets or as implicit values. These include benefits and costs experienced by consumers and producers of the event(s), as well as by other members of the community who may be neither consumers nor producers of these events but who, as third-party participants, nevertheless experience the costs and benefits. CBA is particularly suited to valuing the social and environmental effects on the community that are associated with events. In contrast to EIA and CGE approaches, which, with few exceptions, treat resident expenditure as simply 'transferred money' having no economic effect, CBA takes serious account of community values. For a special event to be socially acceptable, the sum of the (social and private) benefits must exceed the sum of the (private and social) costs to society, and represent the best use of limited funds, when alternative calls on these funds exist.

To date, much event evaluation falls well short of 'best practice'. Researchers are now attempting to merge the best aspects of each of the three approaches in some 'hybrid' approach, which has greater flexibility and coverage than any single approach. While promising substantial gains in the process of event evaluation, 'hybrid' models need to be rigorously tested in valuing real-world events. An important expected outcome of the use of hybrid models is a narrowing of the divide between practitioners and theorists regarding best practice event evaluation to the benefit of all stakeholders.

If this attempt is successful, it promises to transform the event assessment literature both in its theoretical orientation and in stakeholder 'best practice' evaluation.

Prepared by: Professor Larry Dwyer PhD, Visiting Research Professor, Business School, University of Technology, Sydney; Adjunct Professor, Griffith Institute for Tourism (GIFT), Griffith University, Australia; Adjunct Professor, Faculty of Economics, University of Ljubljana, Slovenia

Social impacts

Prior to the development of event management as a field of study, a general view persisted that events brought only positive outcomes for the locations in which they took place, generally in the forms of spending in the local community, the creation of jobs and new facilities, the opportunity for local residents and business people to attend an event, the educative role of some events in facilitating the transfer of knowledge (for example, business events) and the 'psychic income' (for example, a sense of pride) derived from an event being conducted in the host community. Over time, however, with the increasing number and size of events, particularly large-scale sporting, cultural and music-based events, the social costs that events can generate have become more obvious (see example in figure 15.2). Examples of these social costs, or externalities, for host communities include congestion, noise, litter, vandalism and other forms of crime, and lack of access to local facilities during the period of the event. Given this, some host communities began to feel that these social costs outweighed the economic benefits that an event might generate. This concern was an important driver in the push to include an assessment of the social impact of hosting events within event evaluations.

The key problem in undertaking an evaluation of the social impact of an event is identifying the variables to assess and determining how these should be measured. While some of the variables can be measured objectively, such as the rise in reported crime during an event, many of the other variables are subjective and thus difficult to measure with any degree of accuracy. This does not mean, however, that they are not real and have serious consequences for the locations where they take place.

Many studies over the last decade have sought to identify the best approach to quantifying the social impacts of events. Social Exchange Theory was one of the early approaches used to explain how local residents perceive the social impacts on them by 'weighing up the individual and societal benefits generated against the societal costs of an event' (Andersson et al. 2016, p. 160). Another early approach that has proved popular with researchers uses the contingent valuation method (CVM) to estimate changes in social welfare by determining the willingness of local residents to pay (WTP) to attend an event or their willingness to avoid (WTA) the impacts of the event. As this is measured in monetary terms, it can be easily compared to an event's economic impact (Armbrecht 2012).

After considering the different approaches that could be used to measure the social impact of events, Fredline et al. (2003) proposed a scale based on resident perceptions. This scale seeks to determine local residents' views as to the impact of the event on their personal quality of life and on the quality of life of their community. Although clearly a subjective scale, it has been used in many studies to assess and compare the social impact of events across local communities.

It should be noted that event organisers can seek to drive social benefits and minimise social costs by including goals and objectives specifically intended to achieve this. For example, events can:

- encourage local cultural development by setting quotas for local performers, artists and school-based performance groups
- include donation targets for local groups/charities in financial plans
- establish a specific number of program elements that serve to encourage event participation and skill development in local youth and disadvantaged groups
- facilitate the development of professional and community networks and local community cultural development through incorporating a given number of program elements that encourage this.

FIGURE 15.2 Example of host community social impacts

How noise problems could impact Splendour & Falls Festival's future

Noise complaints have long been the scourge of the live music scene in Australia. This is certainly saying something, as it's seen more than its fair share of problems in the past, including everything from scuffles with the liquor licensing board, to seemingly unending council troubles. Music venues are on the front line when it comes to keeping both music fans and nearby residents happy, and sometimes neither party end up satisfied. But music festivals also see their fair share of problems when it comes to sound, and North Byron Parklands, the home of Splendour in the Grass and the Byron Bay leg of Falls Festival, is currently engaged in a battle with nearby residents. Last week we reported that Splendour in the Grass has copped its second fine in as many years for breaching noise limits during its 2015 event in June, a breach that has seen a local wildlife group call for the festival to be moved to a more suitable location.

The venue itself has admitted in its annual report released yesterday, which covers the 2015 Splendour in the Grass and the 2014/2015 Falls Festival, that 'there is still more work do be done in the area of noise management, particularly with regards to lower frequency emissions'. Compliance with strict noise restrictions is critical to both Splendour and Falls Festival continuing to use the site in the future, as the Department of Planning and Environment has only approved a five-year trial at the site, due for review by 31st December 2017. Noise restrictions already in place include:

1. Between 11 am and midnight, noise level measured at sensitive receivers must not exceed background +10dBA
2. Between midnight and 2 am, noise level measured outside the bedroom window(s) at sensitive receivers must not exceed background +5dBA
3. All stages must be shut down at midnight
4. Amplified music from bars, cafés and dance floor, are permitted to remain until 2 am, subject to the stricter noise limit
5. All amplified music must cease at 2 am

Organisers have done a remarkable job in reducing compliance issues across a number of key areas since first using the site for Splendour in 2013, including reducing phone calls to the community hotline regarding traffic problems to zero. However, noise remains a crucial and lingering problem. During Falls Festival 2014/2015, most breaches of noise requirements as measured by monitoring positions occurred between 9 pm and midnight, although these exceedences were also observed on days where the event was not operating (29 December 2014 and 3 January 2015).

In total 22 noise complaints were made to the community hotline, with a higher number of these calls being recorded on New Year's Day (Thursday Night). Only seven of those callers requested that the noise be measured at their residence. Reviews of those results indicate recorded levels were either significantly influenced by ambient noise in the locality of the residence rather than Falls Festival or compliant with the noise limits. An analysis of Splendour 2015 shows similar results, with recordings of breaches of noise limits occurring on days where the event was not even operating, suggesting that these exceedences are likely to be significantly influenced by local extraneous noise sources such as traffic.

Throughout the event a total of 127 complaints were received by the event community hotline, with 117 of those related to noise. In total, 98 different residences complained, with 18 residents lodging more

---

than one complaint (ranging from 2 to 7 complaints). Review of the data collated by the hotline operators indicated that noise related complaints were generally either described as the noise being too loud or specifically related to the low frequency noise content of the event noise. Interestingly enough, low level frequencies are not covered by the festival site's noise restrictions. In addition, the current noise criteria are based on 'backgroundCplus' limits that penalises events held during winter months.

During winter, background levels are up to 10dB lower than those recorded in summer. This seasonal differentiation in background levels has been repeatedly verified by way of multiple winter and summer background surveys undertaken by Parklands. So while front of house music levels have been consistent between Falls Festival (summer event) and Splendour in the Grass (winter event) only Falls festival has been able to comply with the existing project approval's noise limits, while Splendour in the Grass has not (due to the drop in ambient background noise levels). As a result Splendour in the Grass, which occurs in winter, is effectively prescribed a significantly lower noise limit than the Falls Festival held in the summer, with no material scientific or environmental basis. North Byron Parklands have since done their own assessment, and have applied to have low level frequency sounds included as part of their restrictions, in exchange for more flexibility on the higher frequency noise. The modification is currently being processed by the DP&E.

In the meantime, both residents and festival organisers are left frustrated by regulations that although well-intended, fail to properly address the needs of both parties. While residents should be able to get a good night's sleep, the festivals should not be unfairly burdened by factors that are simply outside of their own control. Although it might make residents happy, festival punters are unlikely to be friendly to simply turning the music down to almost inaudible levels. Moving forward, the concerns from residents will need to be carefully managed if there is to be a future of Splendour and Falls Festival at North Byron Parklands that keeps both the locals and festival punters happy.

Source: Jones 2015.

Environmental impacts

The main factors assessed in determining the environmental impacts of an event are water usage, energy consumed and waste produced. Although the components of the environmental impact of an event are more objective than most of the measures associated with the social impacts, it is not easy to bring them together into a single measure.

While it is possible to have a positive environmental impact as a result of conducting an event, such as the improvements to local transport systems that often result from the conduct of mega-events (for example, Olympic Games, Commonwealth Games), and the ability of some events to be leveraged for, or be specifically designed to result in, community environmental education (Collins et al. 2009; Harris 2005), the majority of environmental impacts from most events are negative. Given this, it is important that these impacts be measured so that strategies can be implemented to minimise them. Such strategies can have significant outcomes, as can be seen in the examples provided in the chapter on sustainable event planning. They can also result in innovative developments in the way events are conducted. Virtual conferences and exhibitions, which rely on online delivery, for example, can result in considerable reductions in environmental impacts. For example, one such event with over 9000 delegates claimed a 99.99 per cent reduction in its carbon footprint over that which would have resulted if it had been conducted in a face-to-face context (We Don't Have Time 2018).

One technique that has been employed to measure the environmental impacts of specific events is that of the 'Ecological Footprint' (Collins and Flynn 2015; Collins and Cooper 2017). This approach measures the area of land and water required to produce the goods and services consumed at an event and to assimilate the wastes generated. Another measurement approach that has emerged in recent years is that of assessing an event's carbon footprint using a carbon calculator. This tool, of which there are now a number of examples (for example, Carbonfund.org 2020) seeks to estimate the volume of carbon dioxide gas generated as a result of an event's conduct. It is noteworthy in this regard that attendee travel and other event-related transport account for the bulk of such emissions. One study, for example, of festival attendance–related travel in the UK concluded that this figure was close to two-thirds of the total carbon emissions resulting from these events (Julie's Bicycle 2009). In the context of large-scale business events, such as major international conferences, this amount has been estimated at an even higher amount, 90 per cent (Triplepundit 2014).

As with economic and social impacts, events seeking to achieve meaningful outcomes in this area need to set goals, objectives and associated KPIs against which their performance can be benchmarked. These might relate to matters such as energy usage (kilowatts of electricity, litres of fuel), waste generated (volume, weight, recyclable vs non-recyclable, compostable vs non-compostable), water usage (litres used, greywater and blackwater volumes) and overall carbon footprint.

Holistic evaluation — economic, social and environmental impacts

Prior discussion has demonstrated that while it is possible to measure the impact of events across economic, social and environmental dimensions, the measures used in each are quite different, which makes comparison, let alone aggregation, difficult. As a consequence, even when more comprehensive multi-dimensional evaluations have been undertaken, it is often the economic impact result that dominates as it is more tangible and uses measures that are more easily understood. Although this situation is changing as can be seen from the extract below from the Vivid Sydney (Australia's largest public event) where it can be seen that the issue of the event's environmental impact is being comprehensively embraced and assessed (Vivid Sydney 2020):

> In 2018, Vivid Sydney recorded more than 2.25 million people attending the festival and contributing over $172 million to the state's economy. In delivering such a successful international event, Destination NSW has committed to minimising its environmental impact by actively working towards the delivery of an efficient and sustainable event. In working towards this goal, Destination NSW continues to Partner with The Banksia Foundation, and in 2018, engaged Informed 365 to benchmark and track Vivid Sydney's Sustainability Performance.

> Destination NSW, as the Owner, Manager and Producer of Vivid Sydney, is committed to delivering a world class, sustainable, and efficient event. By working closely with all stakeholders, the Vivid Sydney Team are responsible for developing and communicating the annual sustainability program strategy, driving stakeholder engagement and defining the scope of Vivid Sydney's sustainability reporting objectives.

For comprehensive evaluations to be truly effective it is critical that methods be found to synthesise the evaluations of individual event impacts into an overall evaluation result. In this regard, Fredline, Raybould, Jago and Deery (2005) developed a holistic triple-bottom-line approach to the economic, social and environmental impacts of events. This study identified key performance indicators in each of the three domains and suggested a technique for examining them holistically by providing a framework for dealing with the inevitable trade-off between positive and negative impacts within them.

For economic impacts, they suggested using traditional indicators such as the net income as a ratio of the expenditure necessary to host the event, the financial yield of visitors and the net benefits per person of the event to the host community. For social impacts, they proposed using a range of indicators such as the percentage of locals who attend, volunteer for, or are employed by the event; the percentage of local businesses contracted to supply goods and services; the value of access to any new facilities that are developed, or access to facilities denied to locals during the event; crime reported linked to the event; crowd management incidents; traffic counts or dollar value of time lost in traffic; and the quantity and quality of media exposure generated. For environmental impacts, they suggested indicators such as the energy consumed at the venue/site and in transport to the event, water consumed and wastewater recycled, waste generated and waste recycling.

FIGURE 15.3   A measurement model describing the total impact from a sustainability perspective

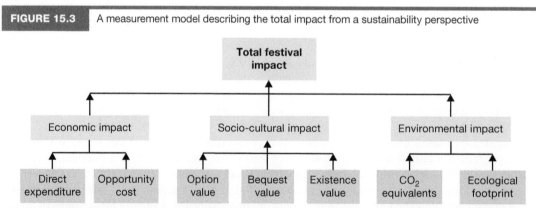

Source: Armbrecht and Andersson 2017, p. 52.

Fredline, Jago and Deery (2005) proposed a diagrammatic approach to combine the evaluations from each of the evaluation silos to provide an overall evaluation score. While this approach had substantial intellectual appeal, it was difficult to operationalise and did not proceed further. Some years later,

Andersson and Lundberg (2013) suggested a model that addressed the issue of commensurability of event evaluation by using monetary terms to measure economic, social and environmental impacts so that an overall assessment could be made by adding the impacts from each dimension (see figure 15.3). This method was trialled at a three-day music festival held in Gothenburg in Sweden, with the result being expressed as a monetary value (euros). This is an interesting approach that has significant potential to provide comprehensive overall evaluations. Nonetheless, it is still important that further exploratory work is done in this area if event evaluations are ever to be viewed as truly comprehensive.

15.3 How event evaluations should be used

LEARNING OBJECTIVE 15.3 Discuss how knowledge gained through the event evaluation process can be applied to future events.

Having gone to the trouble and expense of undertaking an event evaluation, be it of a very basic nature, or one that is more comprehensive, it is important that they are seen not as an end in themselves but as a means of driving future change in areas where current practices are not delivering on an event's goals, objectives and associated KPIs. Additionally, capturing and disseminating the achievements of an event can assist greatly in building its reputation and credibility. Some events, for example, make extensive use of their final reports to gain media exposure and support, while others use the reporting of event outcomes to gain public acceptance, as the Sydney Gay and Lesbian Mardi Gras has done by issuing frequent reports on the economic impacts of the event. It is also the case that governments commonly report on the economic impacts of the major events they financially support in order to gain political advantage by demonstrating to their respective communities the financial benefits they are receiving as a result of this investment and support.

Knowledge management

The event management process can be enhanced if event organisers actively seek to learn from their previous events, and so refine or change their operational systems and approaches they are using to achieve the outcomes they seek. In this way 'best practice' is constantly being advanced.

The owners of many large-scale mobile events (for example, Olympic and Commonwealth Games, FIFA World Cup and the FINA World Swimming Championships) and business events (for example, major association conferences, world expositions) have for some time sought to facilitate the transfer of knowledge between host organising committees. This is achieved through ensuring information (for example, manuals, operational plans, scheduling documents) are captured at the end of one event and subsequently made available (sometimes at a cost) to future organising committees. Additionally, individuals associated with the conduct of these events, also have the capacity to transfer knowledge, and for this reason are often sought out by host cities/countries. A number of Australians involved in the Sydney Olympic Games in 2000, for example, went on to work on the Athens, Beijing, London and Rio de Janeiro Games.

While the nature, types and forms of evaluation have been discussed so far in this chapter, the process itself has yet to be examined. It is to this matter that this chapter now turns its attention.

15.4 The event evaluation process

LEARNING OBJECTIVE 15.4 Describe the event evaluation process and analyse data gathered through the evaluation process.

The event evaluation process has five major stages:
1. planning and identification of event data requirements
2. data collection
3. data analysis
4. reporting
5. dissemination.

The evaluation process must be part of the initial event planning efforts and will involve the commitment of resources including staff, time and money. As the collection of data can be expensive, the availability of financial resources to commit to this task will sometimes be a limiting factor in the nature and type of evaluation that takes place.

Planning and identification of data requirements

The purposes that an evaluation is to serve must first be identified as these will determine what data needs to be collected. In this regard, it is important to identify the key stakeholders in an event along with their information requirements. Examples of the types of questions that events might seek to answer through the data they collect include the following.

- How well has the event performed against its stated goals and objectives and their associated KPIs?
- What were the personal characteristics of event attendees (for example, age, gender, home location)?
- To what extent did the event meet attendee expectations/needs?
- What level of attendee awareness and recall exists as regards sponsor products/services as a result of the event?
- What level of media coverage did the event achieve?
- How successful were marketing efforts in the various promotional channels used?
- How did event operational systems and processes perform?
- Were grant monies spent as required by the conditions associated with such funds?
- What community social, economic and environmental outcomes (both positive and negative) resulted from the conduct of the event?
- What impact did the event have on attracting visitors from out of the area to the host destination?

Once the purposes of the evaluation have been defined, the data that needs to be collected can be identified and listed. These can be grouped into matching areas or subsets; for example, one grouping may relate to attendance and demographic profile, another to audience response and satisfaction levels, another to media coverage and another to environmental outcomes. The fuller and more specific the identification of data required, the easier it will be to plan the collection of the information.

Qualitative and quantitative data

It is important at this stage to distinguish between two different types of data, both of which will often be involved in the event evaluation process.

Qualitative data are based on individual perceptions and responses and are often obtained through informal and in-depth interviews, focus groups, staff feedback and participant observation. Information of this nature can provide valuable insights but can suffer from being anecdotal and tend to be used more for descriptive purposes than for statistical analysis.

By contrast, quantitative data are measurable and can be analysed statistically. Data of this nature are often collected by drawing on box office receipts, registrations/ticket sales, financial records and surveys, and lend themselves to conclusions based on statistical analysis.

Both forms of data can play a valuable role in the event evaluation process, and their use needs to be carefully balanced in order to provide a total picture of an event.

Data collection

Potential sources of data will obviously be event dependent; however, in general they can be grouped into several main categories as outlined below (Silvers 2004; Veal 2006; Brown et al. 2015).

Event documentation

The process of organising an event will provide many opportunities for the collection of information on a variety of matters, including the following.

- *Financial performance.* An event's budget and final balance sheet will provide detailed information on income and expenditure, profit or loss. This data can be compared with the previous costs of staging an event and may require interpretation as regards any variances; for example, downturns in the economy, or currency exchange fluctuations can impact initial projections.
- *Attendee characteristics.* For a ticketed event, or an event requiring registration, box office reports or participant registration lists will provide general information on event attendees. Additionally, ticket and registration sales reports can provide other valuable information such as data on gender or attendee location (postcodes) breakdowns.
- *Crowd size.* For free-entry events, police crowd estimates, public transport and car park figures can be helpful in estimating attendance numbers. Other approaches can also be used for this purpose including judging the percentage of a venue/site filled in relation to its known capacity and undertaking photographic surveys at regular intervals in order to estimate attendance.

- *Performance statistics.* An examination of contracts will reveal numbers of performers engaged in, say, a multi-site festival over several days.
- *Merchandise sales.* Sales records will provide data on the sale of merchandise and the contribution of these sales to the income of the event.
- *Safety profiles.* Accurate recording of occurrences such as first-aid treatments and on-site incidents will help to establish risk management and safety profiles of the event. Police and security services in attendance can also be a source of this data.

Media monitoring

The extent of media coverage, in the context of some types of events, can be important in developing their brand, raising their profile within the markets they are interested in attracting, and in generating ticket and registration sales. This coverage can be either positive or negative, depending on the event outcomes, their impact on the community and the kind of relationship the event has built up with the media over time. It is important to monitor and record this coverage as part of the information-gathering process. If an event is local, it may be possible to do this by keeping a file of newspaper articles and by listening and being alert to any radio/television interviews or news coverage relating to the event. For larger events it may be necessary to employ a professional media-monitoring organisation that can track media coverage from a variety of sources. They will usually provide copies of print media stories and transcripts of radio/television interviews and news coverage, as well as social media exposure. Audiotapes and videotapes of electronic coverage can often be obtained for an additional charge. This information provides an excellent record of the event and can be used effectively in profiling it to potential sponsors and funding bodies.

Some media monitoring companies attempt to place a monetary value on positive media coverage, based on the cost of purchasing the equivalent amount of media space and/or time. These evaluations should be regarded as approximate only, but may provide a useful comparative assessment of media exposure. A media evaluation of Vivid Sydney in 2018, for example, valued its media coverage at approximately $75 million for a public-relations outlay of only $150 000 (Dawson 2018).

Given the meteoric growth in the use and importance of social media over the last decade in particular, it is important to require media-monitoring firms, or those charged with the media monitoring task by an event organiser, to also collect coverage appearing on social media platforms. Analysing this coverage can be critical in determining attendee satisfaction with an event, as well as providing insights on local community perspectives on its impact (Hudson and Hudson 2013; Hudson et al. 2015). Assessing social media feedback during an event should also be considered as it will allow service recovery strategies to be enacted before an issue escalates (for example, complaints about queues, sufficiency of food provided).

Observation

Another means of collecting data is by structured and detailed observation of an event. This may involve the event manager as well as staff, attendees and key stakeholders (for example, security staff, exhibitors, first aid providers, police, suppliers, stallholders). As senior event staff, for example, have detailed knowledge of an event's operation systems, processes and objectives, they are in an ideal situation to observe multiple aspects of it during its delivery. These matters might includeperformance/speaker quality; audience responses/mood; crowd behaviour and management; queue management; effectiveness of signage; and quality of service supply by caterers and stallholders. In some instances, observations can result in interventions to improve outcomes during an event, while in others, insights flowing from observations can be used to modify future practices or decision-making. The process of observation can also be aided by the use of checklists, which require staff to rate and comment on aspects of the event.

Debriefing meetings

A valuable opportunity for feedback on an event's planning and delivery processes is provided by the debriefing process. Meetings conducted for this purpose should be held as soon as practical after an event, while memory and impressions of it are still fresh. Depending on the event, these meetings might include staff members, volunteers, suppliers and contractors, venue management, speakers/performers, public authorities such as police and ambulance, and any other key stakeholders. In the case of large-scale events, a series of meetings might be needed involving individual stakeholder groups because of the number of people/organisations involved, and the many event elements that might need to be reviewed. To maximise the insights gained from these meetings an agenda should be prepared and circulated, and the meeting should be carefully chaired and not allowed to ramble or descend into blame or recrimination.

Focus groups

Focus groups can provide a useful opportunity to explore matters such as participant attitudes, opinions and motivations, non-attendee reasons for their lack of engagement with the event and community perspectives on an event. These information-gathering exercises usually involve directed discussions of eight to 12 people with similar demographics, or other specific characteristics (for example, resident of an event's host community) and are often conducted by professional interviewers in a relaxed environment. The event manager, or their representative, may be an observer but is often hidden behind a two-way mirror so as not to intrude on the process.

Questionnaires

It would be ideal to seek the opinions and responses of all attendees at an event, but for most events this task would be too costly and impractical. This being the case, questionnaires seek information from a representative sample of attendees. The better the design of the questionnaire, and the more rigorous the survey process, the more accurate will be the results obtained.

Questionnaires can range from simple feedback forms targeting event partners and stakeholders to detailed audience or visitor questionnaires undertaken by trained personnel. Various approaches can be used when employing questionnaires including face-to-face interviews, telephone interviews, participant-completed questionnaires and online self-complete forms. The latter has become increasingly popular with event organisers, with companies such as Survey Monkey providing the ability to customise questionnaires quickly, or use existing templates, with the resulting data being analysed automatically. These cloud-based tools can also be employed in face-to-face interview situations with data being directly entered into tablets, smartphones or other similar devices. Whatever approach is used, the issue of obtaining an adequate number of responses is always present. To this end, incentives such as prizes or small gifts (for example, movie tickets) can be used to increase the number of responses.

In the case of repeat events, event organisers may wish to use the same questionnaire each year in order to compare successive events and to establish trends, or they may want to embark on more ambitious research programs assessing different aspects of the event each year. Whatever information is sought through a questionnaire, the following basic factors should be kept in mind.

- Clarity of purpose — a clearly stated and defined purpose is most likely to lead to a well-targeted set of questions that provide an event with valuable managerial insights.
- Questionnaire design — keep it simple. If too much information is sought through a questionnaire, there is a danger that respondents will fail to complete it, or they will simply lose focus and provide minimal feedback to any open-ended questions. Questions also need to be clear and unambiguous and they should be tested by first piloting the questionnaire. For an example of the form these information-gathering instruments take see figure 15.4.
- Language — questions should use a suitable vocabulary and be grouped around topics. Avoid using both 'leading' questions that encourage preconceived answers and employing biased or emotive language.
- Open versus closed questions — an open question is one that invites the interviewee to answer in their own words without a predetermined range of responses. A closed question is one where the interview subject is offered a range of answers to choose from, such as rating an item on a scale of 1–5 or on a range of poor to excellent. Open questions can provide a greater opportunity for a respondent to express their opinion but are harder to quantify. Respondents are also less likely to answer open questions. Closed questions are more restrictive, however, they lend themselves to easier coding and analysis. A good questionnaire should seek an appropriate balance between open and closed questions.
- Size of sample — the number of participants must be large enough to provide a representative sample of the audience. The sample size will depend on the variability in the population to be sampled, the level of precision required and the available evaluation budget. There are various online tools that allow sample sizes to be determined for specific levels of confidence. Survey Monkey, for example, provides one on its website (Survey Monkey 2020).
- Randomness — the methodology employed in the selection of participants must avoid biases of age, sex and ethnicity. Procedures such as selecting every tenth person who passes by a specified point or sending every fifth registrant an online questionnaire, can help overcome the potential for bias. With multi-venue and multi-day events, care should also be taken that the survey process is spread evenly across venues and days in order to provide a truly random sample of participants.
- Support data — the calculation of some outcomes will depend on the collection of support data. The calculation of total visitor expenditure, for example, will require accurate data on the average expenditure of visitors as well as support data on the number of visitors to the event. This will allow the

spending pattern revealed by the survey to then be multiplied by the number of visitors to provide an estimate of the total visitor expenditure for the event (Jago and Dwyer 2006; Dwyer and Jago 2020).

Secondary data

In addition to the data collected from the previously cited sources, other data may be available that has been collected for another purpose, but which may be able to be drawn upon for event evaluation purposes. Examples of where this data can be found include event industry associations, government statistical bodies, convention bureax, academic journals and web searches.

Event industry associations

Various event industry representative bodies exist that commission or conduct studies on various matters germane to their industry sector. The International Congress and Convention Association, for example, collects and disseminates information on the international association meetings industry, while the International Festivals and Events Association does the same for the festival sector.

Government statistical bodies

The Australian Bureau of Statistics (ABS), for example, produces detailed information on a wide variety of topics, including Australian social trends, census statistics and how Australians spend their leisure time. The ABS directory of culture and leisure statistics provides useful information on topics such as attendance at cultural venues and arts festivals, and children's participation in cultural and leisure activities. Another government body that collects information potentially of interest to some events is Tourism Research Australia, which produces quarterly national and international visitor surveys. These provide accurate data on visitor patterns and their expenditure on a wide range of activities, including travel, accommodation and attendance at festivals and events.

Convention bureaux

Convention bureaux periodically commission studies on issues and trends impacting business meetings. In recent years, for example, the Melbourne Convention and Visitors Bureau has commissioned, or conducted studies on, delegate expenditure, the economic impacts of business events and the future of the business meetings industry (Melbourne Convention and Visitors Bureau 2020).

Academic journals

Various academic journals that focus specifically on the area of event management have emerged over the last 20 years. These include *Event Management, International Journal of Event and Festival Management, International Journal of Hospitality and Event Management* and the *International Journal of Event Management Research*. These publications contain a diverse range of articles of direct relevance to event managers including papers on sponsorship, event marketing, event attendee motivations and satisfaction, volunteering, risk management, event operations and evaluation. Access to these journals is by subscription, but it is also commonly the case that individual articles can be purchased.

Web searches

Web searches will often identify reports, articles or other material that can inform the event evaluation process. Some of this material, for example, can be found on the websites of events themselves, such as their annual reports, evaluations and strategy documents, while in other instances information can be located on non-government organisation websites that have an involvement in the event industry (for example, Sustainable Event Alliance, A Greener Festival) or on the websites of private businesses (for example, Event Training Australia).

FIGURE 15.4 Sample festival survey instrument

Hello. I am from the _____ festival. Could you spare a few minutes of your time to answer some questions to help us improve the festival?

Demographics
1. Gender: male / female
2. To which of the following age ranges do you belong?
   Under 15
   15–24
   25–44

▶

45–64

65+

3. Where do you live?
   Local (go to question 7)
   Elsewhere in the state
   Interstate
   Overseas (list country) _____
4. Who are you travelling with today?
   Travelling alone
   Couple
   Family/relatives
   Friends
   Club/society
   Business associates
   Other (specify) _____
5. How many nights are you staying in the local area?
6. Where are you staying?
   Hotel/motel
   B & B/guest house
   Caravan park/camping
   With friends/relatives
   Other (specify) _____

Marketing

7. How did you first hear about the festival?
   Brochures/posters
   Newspaper
   Radio
   TV
   Visitor information centre
   Web search
   Facebook
   Instagram
   Twitter
   Word of mouth
   Other (specify) _____

Activities/behaviour

8. How did you travel from your home or place of accommodation to the festival?
   Walked
   Car/motor bike
   Push bike
   Public transport
   Other (specify) _____
9. What activities have you participated in at the festival?
   Listening to bands
   Attending poetry readings
   Food stalls
   Workshops
   Speaker presentations
   Children's activities area
   Art exhibition

Attitude/motivation

10. What did you like most about the festival?
    _____

11. What aspects of the festival do you think could be improved?
    _____

12. Are there any additional comments that you wish to make about the festival?
    _____

    Thank you and I trust that you will enjoy the rest of your time at the festival.

Data analysis

Much of the data from the sources noted previously can be analysed manually, and resulting outcomes compared, for example, against event objectives and KPIs, or with data from previous iterations of the event concerned. The more voluminous data gathered through questionnaires will require the use of online survey platforms such as Survey Monkey or Zoho. These platforms (for which a subscription is required) act to create questionnaires, collect and collate resulting data, and produce customisable reports. These reports employ, as required, line graphs, bar charts and pie charts that make communicating the outcomes of a survey much easier. It should be noted that when open-ended questions are used in a questionnaire, they will likely need to be analysed separately and may be best reported on using a narrative rather than a statistical format.

Reporting

After relevant data have been collated and analysed, event evaluation report(s) can be prepared. For some events, a single report is all that might be required; in other instances, there might be a need for multiple reports that take account of the differing information needs of event stakeholders (for example, host organisation, government granting bodies, sponsors and the media). This being the case, different writing styles, levels of detail and approaches to overall report presentation might be required. It is nonetheless likely that the core aspects of the report will remain similar across these different groups.

Veal (2006) distinguishes between the report as narrative, telling the story of an event and its achievements, and the report as record, creating a formal and definitive account of the event process and outcomes. The narrative aspect of the report will need to be largely descriptive, focusing on key points and interpreting the data to create a cohesive picture of the event. It may be argued that all evaluation is to some degree subjective, but nonetheless the writer should try to reflect on the event as accurately as possible, quoting relevant data to support assumptions and conclusions. Quotations from attendees, media reports, photographs and copies of flyers, posters and programs may also help to communicate the flavour and atmosphere of an event.

The role of the report as the record of the event will lend itself to the use of statistics which serve to create an accurate profile of the event, supported by appropriate detail in the form of tables and graphs. Any economic, social or environmental outcomes noted should be supported by a description of the methodology used to evaluate them.

Both the narrative and record functions of the event report combine to present a useful basis for reporting to stakeholders and for planning the next event.

Dissemination

The final step in the post-event evaluation process is to disseminate the event report to relevant stakeholder groups. This may be done by face-to-face meetings with key stakeholders where the content of the report can be verbally communicated and discussed. For the host organisation, for example, this may represent an important closure and for sponsors it may give rise to a discussion on continued involvement with the event. It is worth considering preparing summaries of key evaluation outcomes for use in, for example, a PowerPoint presentation for any face-to-face stakeholder presentations, or for use in media releases that accompany distribution of the report to the media. If the event report is well written and carefully distributed, it can be an important tool for enhancing the reputation and future prospects of the event.

SUMMARY

Event evaluation is the process of measuring and assessing an event throughout its event planning and delivery cycle. Depending on the nature of the event concerned, it may involve pre-, mid- and post-event evaluation tasks or only the latter two.

Post-event evaluation serves a number of purposes, including measuring the success of an event in relation to its goals, objectives and associated KPIs. It also allows event organisers to feed lessons learnt back into any future iteration.

Good evaluation is planned and implemented from the beginning of the event planning and delivery process. It involves deciding on the purposes of an evaluation, and then identifying and collecting data from a number of sources including event documentation, observations, debrief meetings, focus groups and surveys. A good evaluation plan will strive to create the right balance between qualitative and quantitative data in order to provide a full and accurate picture of an event. Surveys are an important tool for providing quality data on an event and rely for their success on well-designed questionnaires and a rigorous survey process.

Once data have been gathered from all sources, an event evaluation report should be compiled and distributed to all stakeholders. This report should tell the story of the event and provide an accurate and enduring record of its outcomes and achievements. Once compiled, it should be distributed to all major stakeholders and be used to enhance the future reputation and success of the event.

QUESTIONS

1 Identify an event in your area with which you are familiar. Identify and list the purposes that the event might have in undertaking a post-event evaluation.

2 List and briefly describe sources of qualitative data that an event organiser might employ as part of the evaluation process.

3 If you were given the task of designing a questionnaire for a conference or a festival, what broad categories of information might you consider seeking data on?

4 Why is the concept of 'new money' so important when assessing an event's economic impact on its host city/region?

5 Discuss the key differences between, and roles of, debrief meetings and focus groups in event evaluation.

6 Why might an event produce several versions of its final report?

7 Develop a short evaluation questionnaire (maximum five questions) solely focused on attendee demographics using the free component of Survey Monkey. Send this questionnaire to three people by obtaining a link from the site and have them respond (it's acceptable for them to make up their responses), then analyse the results.

8 Secondary data sources can provide useful input into an event's evaluation efforts. What types of secondary data would you consider making use of if you were asked to evaluate a major conference or festival?

CASE STUDY

BEING HUMAN FESTIVAL, UNITED KINGDOM

Overview

Being Human is the UK's first and only national festival dedicated to the humanities. The inaugural Being Human festival ran over nine days, from 15th to 23rd November 2014. Led by the School of Advanced Study, University of London, in partnership with the Arts and Humanities Research Council and the British Academy, the 2014 festival encouraged universities and other cultural organisations to hold humanities-focussed events for the public. 163 events were held, attended by 15 000 to 20 000 people, and organised by 161 participating organisations, 57 of whom were registered as 'lead participants' for their festival events.

Evaluating the 2014 festival

In terms of evaluation, the festival team at the School of Advanced Study collected qualitative and quantitative data about people's experiences and perceptions of the first Being Human festival, via two questionnaire surveys and a series of 'vox pop' interviews. These data were then outsourced to an independent researcher (Dr Ruth Townsley) for analysis and reporting. Using data collected from 1254 festival attendees, 26 vox pop respondents and 45 lead participating organisations, the evaluation considered the success of the Being Human festival 2014 against its stated aims, which were:

- To inspire innovation in public engagement with leading research in the humanities.
- To foster collaboration between Higher Education Institutions (HEIs), independent research organisations and cultural and community partners.
- To make a significant and visible contribution to the national cultural life of the UK in November 2014.
- To demonstrate the need and desire for an annual national festival of the humanities.

Findings from the survey of attendees

- *Number of events attended*. Most people had attended just one event (89 per cent). A few (5 per cent) indicated they had attended two to four events, with just 1 per cent attending five events or more. A total of 1414 visits were made to festival events by the 1254 people who responded to the survey. The majority of attendees visited events in just one region of the UK, with a small proportion attending events in two or three regions.
- *Profile of festival attendees*. More women (53.6 per cent) than men (35.2 per cent) attended events and 10 per cent of all attendees described themselves as disabled. The age of attendees was mixed, with fairly equal representation across all age groups, with the exception of the youngest group of attendees (age 14 or less) where attendance was less than 1 per cent. The majority of festival attendees described themselves as White (76.4 per cent). The profile of festival attendees by ethnic group broadly matches national statistics for White, Mixed/Multiple, and Other ethnic groups. Proportionately, however, the festival is less consistent in reaching Asian and Black groups of the national population. More than three-quarters (77 per cent) of all attendees were graduates and of these, 70 per cent reported that they had a humanities degree.
- *Attendees' prior knowledge of festival events*. Most people heard about the festival by word of mouth, followed by web-based communication, email and social media. Paper-based communication (magazines, newspapers, newsletter and so on) were less successful in reaching people, with the national press playing a very minor role. Most attendees (86 per cent) felt that events had matched their expectations exactly, very closely or closely. Very few people (6 per cent) thought that events had not been as they had expected. When asked if they had visited the event venue before, 54 per cent said they had, 39 per cent had not and 7 per cent did not provide an answer.
- *Attendees' experiences of festival events*. Most people indicated that the events they attended had been 'excellent' (48 per cent) or 'very good' (33 per cent). Fewer described events simply as 'good' (18 per cent) and very few as 'not very good' (1 per cent). Just one person (less than 0.1 per cent) thought the event he had attended was 'terrible'. When asked if they would recommend the Being Human festival to others, the vast majority of attendees (85 per cent) said they would; 5 per cent did not know, and just 1 per cent said they would not.
- Attendees liked:
  - Speakers' knowledge, enthusiasm and expertise
  - The wide variety of presentations, talks, films, music, tours, exhibitions, readings, lectures, and other events on offer
  - Events that were different, engaging, free, friendly, informative, interactive, interesting and participative
  - Content and topics that prompted discussion, stimulated debate, were focussed on research, were academic but accessible, and involved the audience
  - Venues that were comfortable, had a good atmosphere and included refreshments.
- Attendees disliked:
  - Speakers who were hard to hear and spoke too fast; the fact there were no women speakers at some events
  - Events where the format was unclear in advance; that were too long or too short; had little discussion, debate or time for questions; did not involve the audience; had no activities; were difficult to book online; were fully booked in advance but not full on the day
  - Content and topics that lacked focus; where the central subject was unclear in advance; were not linked sufficiently to the festival theme
  - Venues that were too cold, too hot, difficult to find, lacked signage on site, had poor acoustics and did not include refreshments.

- *Attendees' perceptions of humanities research.* There was a small amount of qualitative evidence to suggest that attendance at festival events may have had an impact on people's perceptions of humanities research. Some attendees appeared mildly surprised that the academic events they attended were so accessible, relaxed and welcoming. Others described feeling inspired, informed and enthused by the content and delivery of events, possibly in ways that they had not expected. Some were now planning to do further research or reading on the topic and a few thought the festival had showcased the intrinsic value of humanities research for them personally, and for wider society.

Findings from the survey of lead participating organisations

- *Profile of lead participants.* All but one of the 45 respondents represented universities or other HEIs. Most (58 per cent) of these lead participants had organised one event as part of the Being Human festival 2014. Around a quarter (24.5 per cent) had organised between two and four events, whilst fewer (17.5 per cent) had put on five events or more, with 11 being the highest number of events organised (by two participants). A total of 121 separate events were organised by the lead participants who responded to the survey. Most of the lead participants (87 per cent) had taken part in some form of public engagement activities before and 47 per cent felt that centrally provided training in this area was not necessary. Just over a third (38 per cent) expressed an interest in training, whilst a few (9 per cent) thought it was something that was of 'possible' interest. Most participants had heard about the festival by word of mouth.
- *Visitor numbers.* The 45 lead participants who responded to the survey provided an estimated total audience of 18 881 people across the 121 events they organised, giving a mean average of 156 people per event (range: 4 to 10 000 people). Most events (84 per cent) averaged an audience of one to 100 people. Less events (16 per cent) catered for audiences of more than 100, and of these, only 4 per cent reached audiences of over 250.
- *Event partners.* Very few events (4 per cent) were run by one sole organisation. Most events were held by the lead participant plus one partner (33 per cent). Twenty-two per cent involved the lead plus two other organisations. Less than a quarter of events (21 per cent) were held by consortia of five or more organisations (including the lead). Most event partners were third sector organisations (40 per cent). Public sector organisations, other HEIs and private sector organisations or freelance individuals were significantly less likely to be involved in events. Forty-nine per cent of lead participants said that work on their festival events had helped to create new partnerships with other organisations, whilst 47 per cent felt their partnerships pre-dated the festival.
- *Funding for festival events.* Of the 57 lead organisations who took part in the 2014 festival, 36 received sponsorship of between £500 and £3000, totalling £58670 in direct funding for their events. In addition, nine lead participants were funded directly by AHRC with grants of £3000 and 175 drew on their own funds to finance their festival events. Using actual and estimated figures of additional sponsorship and indirect funding, it is suggested that the total resources leveraged by the festival team, HEIs and other sponsors for the 2014 festival was approximately £360479, five times the funding allocation for individual events administered by the festival team and the AHRC.
- *Staffing festival events.* In most cases (42 per cent), four to ten staff (including students and volunteers) were involved in helping to plan and run festival events. Around a third (31 per cent) of lead participating organisations involved one to three staff in their festival events, whilst a fifth (20 per cent) mobilised a larger number of 11 to 20 staff. In two cases, very large numbers of staff were involved from the lead organisation: one respondent cited 30 and another cited 33.
- *Extent and nature of media coverage gained by participants.* Sixty-nine per cent of participants had gained some media coverage for their events. Of the 73 examples given, the majority (31) were mentions in the regional press and local publications. There was also significant coverage online and via social media (21 mentions). Further media coverage included two mentions on national radio, ten on local radio, three on regional TV, four articles in trade and consumer publications and one mention each in the national press and an international media outlet.
- *Information, advice and support from the Being Human festival team.* Almost all lead participants (42 out of 45) were positive about the information, advice and support they had received from the festival team. Almost all centrally available festival resources were well-used by lead participants. Logos were used by almost all of the 45 respondents and two-thirds had used the evaluation guide or vox pop cameras.
- *Feedback on Being Human marketing and key messaging.* Most lead participants (78 per cent) provided 'excellent', 'very good' or 'good' feedback about central marketing and key messaging. Positive

feedback included: effective and professional marketing for the festival as a whole; excellent use of social media to market the festival, with visible results; clear and eye-catching marketing tools, including logo and branding materials; prompt, helpful and detailed responses from the festival team to individual marketing queries. Twenty-two per cent were less positive about the overall input on marketing and key messaging and highlighted the following issues as problematic from their perspective: festival logo and branding materials were perceived as old fashioned and corporate; online festival events listing was difficult to navigate; lack of a print version of the events programme for the festival as a whole; lack of online advertising outside of social media; too much expected of lead participants for the level of funding awarded.

- *Outcomes of festival events.* Analysis of open-ended data from lead participants about what they had gained from the festival highlighted that Being Human events had:
  - Provided experience of doing public engagement work
  - Created opportunities for innovation, experimentation and creativity
  - Led to the creation and development of new and existing partnerships
  - Promoted and validated humanities research.
- Outputs and legacy of festival events included:
  - Blog posts
  - Films of events
  - New websites and online content
  - Exhibition of photos and images from events
  - Technical developments and collection of new data
  - Sound-clips/podcasts
  - New research groups or working groups
  - Pinterest boards
  - Further joint work with event partners
  - Further showing or continued use of event outputs/materials
  - Learning resources for schools
  - Numerous other outputs including a conference paper, iTunes download, book, report, booklet, grant application, Twitter hashtag.

Website traffic, social media activity and media coverage

- *Website demographics.* Most users of the festival website were UK-domiciled (87 per cent) and based in London (42 per cent). Other main geographical areas represented were Nottingham, Oxford, Edinburgh and Newcastle-upon-Tyne. Men (54 per cent) were more likely to use the website than women (45 per cent) and two-thirds of users (60 per cent) were aged between 18 and 34.
- *Website traffic and referrals.* Thirty-eight per cent of new users and 33 per cent of all sessions originated directly by people typing in the URL or via a bookmark, indicating these users were led to the website by word of mouth or offline advertising. It would be good to explore these statistics further: they appear to validate a potential link with data from the surveys of attendees and lead participants where 'word of mouth' responses were highest in relation to the question 'where did you hear about the Being Human festival?' In terms of both sources and referrals, there were very significant levels of traffic via Twitter and Facebook. Time Out also played a key role in directing users to the website. Between them, Twitter, Facebook and Time Out were responsible for 51 per cent of referrals for all sessions, and 39 per cent of referrals of new users. Bounce rates for users visiting the website via Google, Twitter and Facebook were much higher (61–71 per cent) than those for users referred by Time Out and the School of Advanced Study (25–27 per cent). However, even the higher bounce rates were within average range for a site whose primary use appears to be for checking events listings.
- *Social media activity.* The festival team continued its active engagement with Twitter, Facebook and Pinterest and encouraged participating organisations and their partners to do the same. Data from website traffic and social media analytics show that Twitter and Facebook played a major role in advertising the 2014 festival and for directing new users towards the festival website. Pinterest was also useful both as a means for festival marketing and as a vehicle for displaying outputs and legacy projects. Despite this, the objectives for all social media channels are not clear at present and do not appear to have been adequately communicated to all festival participants. It would be helpful to clarify and restate if necessary the core purposes of using social media and set clear objectives for the 2015 festival so that participating organisations understand the rationale for their involvement, where requested.

- *Media coverage.* Two documents from the festival team showed that the festival had good media coverage and was referenced in nine national media outlets (print, online and radio) and in 23 regional media outlets (print, online, radio and TV). There was a slight mismatch between the details of some of the media coverage in the reports provided by the festival team; and not all of the media coverage mentioned by survey respondents appeared to have been logged centrally. For future festivals it is important to find an accurate and systematic means for recording media mentions both centrally, and via participants, so that the full regional, national (and international) impact of Being Human can be monitored. It may also be worth considering recording additional details such as whether the festival and/or events are directly named.

Conclusions

The evaluation has demonstrated that Being Human 2014 has been particularly successful in meeting all four of it stated aims. Analysis of the findings showed that the festival has inspired innovation in public engagement, fostered collaboration between event partners, and made a significant and visible contribution to the national cultural life of the UK. Feedback from attendees and lead participants highlighted that there is a strong desire for an annual national festival of the humanities and that the current festival team at the School of Advanced Study has the skills, knowledge and experience to continue to manage such a festival on a UK-wide basis.

'Distinctive, exciting, diverse — as it says — a festival of the humanities — what a treat!' (Lead participant)

Source: Townsley 2015.

QUESTIONS

1 To what extent does this event follow the steps in the event evaluation process outlined in this chapter?
2 Identify three to five insights that have resulted from the evaluation process evident in this case study. Discuss their implications for future iterations of this event.
3 What data sources have been used in this case study? Can you suggest any other potential data sources that might have assisted in the evaluation process?
4 Would you say that this event has been successful in achieving its stated aims? Why?
5 Given the feedback on the event program, how would you suggest modifying future deliveries of this event?

REFERENCES

Andersson, T, Armbrecht, J & Lundberg, E 2016, 'Triple impact assessments of the 2013 European athletics indoor championship in Gothenburg', *Scandinavian Journal of Hospitality and Tourism*, vol. 16, issue 2, pp. 158–79.

Andersson, T & Lundberg, E 2013, 'Commensurability and sustainability: Triple impact assessments of a tourism event', *Tourism Management*, vol. 37, pp. 99–109.

Armbrecht, J 2012, *The value of cultural institutions, measurement and description*, BAS, School of Business Economics and Law at University of Gothenburg.

Brown, S, Getz, D, Pettersson, R & Wallstam, M 2015, 'Event evaluation: definitions, concepts and a state of the art review', *International Journal of Event and Festival Management*, vol. 6, no. 2, pp. 135–57.

Carbonfund.org 2020, 'Event carbon calculator', www.carbonfund.org/take-action/businesses/business-calculators/event-carbon-calculator, viewed 3 March 2020.

Collins, A & Cooper, C 2017, 'Measuring and managing the environmental impact of festivals: the contribution of the Ecological Footprint', *Journal of Sustainable Tourism*, vol. 25, pp. 148–62.

Collins, A & Flynn, A 2015, *The ecological footprint: New developments in policy and practice*, Edward Elgar Publishing, Cheltenham.

Collins, A, Jones, C & Mundayac, M 2009, 'Assessing the environmental impacts of mega sporting events: Two options', *Tourism Management*, vol. 30, issue 6, pp. 828–37.

Dawson, A 2018, 'Vivid Sydney opens pitch for PR agencies with a "creative edge"', *Mumbrella*, 2 November, www.mumbrella.com.au/vivid-sydney-opens-pitch-for-pr-agencies-with-a-creative-edge-550227, viewed 3 March 2020.

Dwyer, L & Jago, L 2020, 'The economic contribution of special events', chapter in *Handbook of event studies*, eds J Connell & S Page, Routledge, London.

Fredline, L, Jago, L & Deery, M 2003, 'The development of a generic scale to measure the social impacts of events', *Event Management*, vol. 8, pp. 23–37.

Fredline, L, Jago, L & Deery, M 2005, 'Host community perceptions of the impacts of events: a comparison of different themes in urban and regional communities', in *The impacts of events: proceedings of international event research conference*, J Allen (ed.), Australian Centre for Event Management, Sydney.

Fredline, L, Raybould, M, Jago, L & Deery, M 2005, 'Triple bottom line event evaluation: a proposed framework for holistic event evaluation', in *The impacts of events: proceedings of international event research conference*, J Allen (ed.), Australian Centre for Event Management, Sydney.

Harris, R 2005, 'Approaches to community engagement by public events', in *The impacts of events: proceedings of international event research conference*, J Allen, Australian Centre for Event Management, Sydney.

Hudson, S & Hudson, R 2013, 'Engaging with consumers using social media: a case study of music festivals', *International Journal of Event and Festival Management,* vol. 4, no. 3, pp. 206–23.

Hudson, S, Roth, M, Madden, T & Hudson, R 2015, 'The effects of social media on emotions, brand relationship quality, and word of mouth: An empirical study of music festival attendees', *Tourism Management*, vol. 47, pp. 68–76.

Jago, L & Dwyer, L 2006, *Economic evaluation of special events: a practitioner's guide*, Common Ground Publishing, in association with Cooperative Research Centre for Sustainable Tourism, Melbourne.

Jones, N 2015, 'How noise problems could impact Splendour & Falls Festivals future', *Tone Deaf*, 15 December, https://tonedeaf.thebrag.com/noise-problems-splendour-falls-festival, viewed 23 June 2020.

Julie's Bicycle 2009, 'Jam packed part 1: audience travel emissions from festivals', www.juliesbicycle.com, viewed 3 March 2020.

Melbourne Convention and Visitors Bureau 2020, 'Articles: research', www.melbournecb.com.au/articles/category/research/5aa85 77740275007346e749e, viewed 3 March 2020.

Silvers, J 2004, *Professional event coordination*, John Wiley & Sons Inc, Hoboken, New Jersey.

Survey Monkey 2020, 'Sample size calculator', www.surveymonkey.com/mp/sample-size-calculator/?program, viewed 14 March 2020.

Townsley, R 2015, 'Being Human: a festival of the humanities: 2014 festival evaluation', report produced by Ruth Townsley Research and commissioned by Dr Michael Eades, Director of the Being Human Festival in the UK, for the School of Advanced Study, University of London, pp. 2–7.

Triplepundit 2014, 'Conferences and carbon: the impact behind the event', *Triple Pundit*, 18 December, www.triplepundit.com/story/2014/conferences-and-carbon-impact-behind-event/58101, viewed 3 March 2020.

Veal, A 2006, *Research methods for leisure and tourism: a practical guide*, Pearson Education Limited, Harlow, England.

Vivid Sydney 2020, 'Sustainability', www.vividsydney.com/sustainability, viewed 3 March 2020.

We Don't Have Time 2018, 'The World's first zero carbon Climate Conference saved 71.819 tonnes CO2e', *Medium*, www.medium.com/wedonthavetime/the-worlds-first-zero-carbon-climate-conference-9cf9b5353c31, viewed 3 March 2020.

ACKNOWLEDGEMENTS

Photo: © Pixsooz / Shutterstock.com

Figure 15.2: © The Brag Media

Extract: © Vivid Sydney 2020

Figure 15.3: © Armbrecht and Andersson 2017

Case study: © Ruth Townsley Research and the School of Advanced Study, University of London, 'Being Human: a festival of the humanities: 2014 festival evaluation', report commissioned by Dr Michael Eades, Director of the Being Human Festival in the UK for the School of Advanced Study, University of London. Reproduced with kind permission.

FUTURE SKILLS GUIDE

Preface

You are probably wondering what you need to do to gain and retain your dream job once your degree is completed. Industries and individuals have changed dramatically in recent years, in part due to COVID-19; so how do you differentiate yourself, and what can you do to get ahead?

In addition to the specialist knowledge and competencies that you are developing at university, there are certain general skills that are critical for any career you choose to pursue. We created the *Future Skills Guide* to capture and convey these skills, so that you can enter the workplace with confidence.

Here is an overview each of the authors that contributed to the *Future Skills Guide*.

- Steve Sammartino is Australia's leading futurist, an international keynote speaker and an author of three bestselling books on entrepreneurship and technology.
- Nicola Hazell is a technology expert. Hazell is among Australia's leading voices on women in leadership, gender equality and social innovation.
- Co-Director of the Bond Resolution Centre, Professor Rachael Field is internationally renowned for her research and service work in family mediation and student wellbeing.
- Clare Payne is globally recognised for her work in ethics in finance. She was named in the Australian '100 Woman of Influence' in 2016 and a World Economic Forum Young Global Leader in 2014 in recognition of her personal commitment to social issues.
- Swinburne University's Dean of Learning Innovation, Professor Angela Carbone is a passionate advocate and researcher on professional development and student employability skills.
- Michael Eales is the Partner of Business Models Inc and a Strategy Designer who specialises in business design and innovation capacity building.
- Mandy Johnson is an illustrious innovator whose bestselling books, keynote speeches and strategic advisory services provide innovative, evidence-based techniques to improve and transform both private and public organisations.

We hope that this practical handbook will support your wellbeing and help you build resilience and employability skills both now and into the future.

Future of work

QUESTIONS What changes do you anticipate to the way we work in the next five to ten years? How can we prepare for these changes now?

Professor Angela Carbone

During the recent COVID-19 disruption we have seen those organisations quick to adapt and adopt technology continue to operate and survive while the rest of the world was in shutdown. Advances in technology will continue to change the way we work. Concepts such as artificial intelligence (AI), machine learning, automation, globalisation and collaboration are infiltrating the workplace and will become the norm for the next generation entering the workforce. We are seeing organisations come together to solve extremely complex problems and address global challenges. Problems such as managing health pandemics and climate change are global concerns, not localised in one area. As we increasingly work together across international boundaries, whether to monitor weather patterns, rates of global warming or the spread of viruses, we will need global perspectives and a set of competencies to navigate cultural differences and manage the way we work.

Current and future generations will need to develop digital competencies and literacies so they can seamlessly adapt to the changing nature of work. Technology is capable of capturing, processing, storing and sharing huge volumes of data and information, and we need to prepare to be able to deal with this. The ability to manage and interpret data is becoming an important skill. Making sense of vast amounts of data often requires separating garbage from clean data. As you build these skills, it's a good idea to demonstrate your knowledge and competencies via an e-portfolio. Applying and critiquing models and predictions means working with others, so developing collaboration and communication skills is extremely important.

Participating in industry-based and cross-team projects throughout your university studies is a great way to build your interpersonal skills such as collaboration, negotiation and communication. To deal with the complexities of the global challenges that you will face during your career, you will need to develop more than just deep discipline knowledge; you will require an ability to work across disciplines and collaborate and communicate perceptively and effectively with others across a variety of fields.

Professor Rachael Field

It is clear that working in a post–COVID-19 world will look very different to our work life experiences up to 2020. While a five- to ten-year prediction might have been possible pre-COVID-19, it is now more difficult to anticipate what the future of work will be. However, there are three particular skills that we can develop now that will inevitably be important — whatever our future working environments look like. These are self-management skills, resilience and agility.

Self-management

Self-management skills support our self-regulation — that is, our ability to control our thoughts, feelings and actions. If we have strong self-management skills, we can set goals independently and take the initiative to achieve them, and this can enhance our achievements and career success.

Individual people have their own approaches to self-management that work for them. Generally, people with strong self-management skills will be positive and proactive thinkers who effectively manage their time, their stress levels and their emotional responses to issues and events. It is important to be aware of a range of self-management strategies and then choose ones that work best for you. In the Wellbeing section later in this guide you'll find three key wellbeing strategies that are also positive self-management strategies. Resilience is also a key element of effective self-management.

Resilience

Resilience skills help us to cope well with life and, in particular, with the stressors and challenges at work and in our personal lives. Life in general is naturally stressful — at least to some extent — and stress is something that we all experience, albeit at varying levels and in various contexts. Although stress is often thought of as a negative thing, it can have a positive side, and it is possible to experience healthy levels of stress.

The American Psychological Association has identified work as one of the top two causes of stress. When asked about their personal stressors, around six in ten adults (in the US) identified work and money as significant sources of stress, making them the most commonly mentioned personal stressors.[1] Despite this, developing our resilience skills can help us to use stress positively: as a motivator for achievement, as something that stimulates us to be active and engaged, and as a prompt to develop more effective and efficient ways of working.

Psychologists generally refer to resilience as our capacity to cope with stress, challenges and difficulties. Resilient people can better manage change or loss and deal with negative experiences or events. They can also harness resources (both internal resources within themselves and external resources) in order to steer their way effectively through a difficult time. Resilience is therefore a key predictor of success in life.

Some people are born with greater resilience than others, but everyone can develop and build their resilience and enhance their existing levels of resilience. Developing our resilience basically involves employing some common-sense wellbeing strategies. Some strategies that are easy to enact include:
- adopting a positive outlook
- reframing difficulties as challenges
- staying connected to and engaged with support networks of friends and family
- being prepared to ask for help
- managing goals and priorities
- developing a hobby or interest outside of work
- being organised and balanced
- avoiding procrastination
- sleeping and eating well
- exercising
- practising relaxation techniques (such as stretching, exercise, deep breathing, socialising and mindfulness meditation)
- having a sense of humour and perspective.

Agility

Change is stressful because our natural biological response to change is a stress reaction. The post-COVID-19 world and the future of work will inevitably involve a lot of change. Building our self-management skills can help us cope with these high levels of change. Along with self-management and resilience skills, agility is an important part of coping positively with change.

Dictionary definitions of agility tend to refer to an ability to move, think, understand and respond quickly and easily. Agile people are empowered and agentic. They remain calm when faced with the challenge of change, they process information quickly, they can be proactive and decisive and they take opportunities even if there is a level of potential risk.

So, how can we increase our agility? Generally, agility will follow a positive mindset. If you are proactive, problem-solving-oriented, keen to innovate and focused, this will help you to be agile. All of the approaches to building resilience referred to earlier are also relevant to our levels of agility, as are the wellbeing strategies discussed later.

Michael Eales

We have found ourselves at the epicentre of one of the biggest shifts in human history — that of shaping new systems for the future of human work with machines. To prepare for this future, we need to understand three of the biggest challenges to the way we work: automation and the future of human effort, adaptability and the future of human connection, and AI and the future of human expression.

Automation

Consider how a machine codifies human effort. Effort often manifests itself as jobs that require known and repetitive tasks, processes or calculations. These jobs will decline. The future we are moving towards will require people to work with machines to tackle complex challenges, making sense of nonlinear problems that do not come with a codified approach or guidebook. This is the VUCA world — volatile, uncertain, complex and ambiguous. Developing your skills for critical thinking and critical feeling will prepare you.

Adaptability

There is a future where technology supports our shared wellbeing, sense-making and ability to tackle complex challenges. In this future, trust, responsibility and accountability will be key characteristics to understand. As people continue to navigate work-life balance, the digital-physical divide will continue to widen. Your ability to communicate effectively, both online and offline, will be of increasing importance to navigating the bonds and bridges across individuals and groups, and their interests and intentions. Expect to see more jobs that require you to leverage your innately human attributes of care and compassion, communication and creativity. Developing your skills in managing uncertainty while facilitating individual and group connections will prepare you. Check out www.creative-capital.info and explore the value of the creative industries.

AI

We express ourselves in ways that machines are only just learning to replicate at the simplest level. Our intent to create and shape the world around us sees us make choices every day that shape the future of human expression in a more immersive digital world. These choices, whether they be via online communication or the workflow tools we use to manage our work and life, are pulling us towards a deeper digital-physical fusion. In this future your ability to interpret reality and help the machines you work with understand your interpretation will be key. This is the domain of the storyteller, the translator, the designer. You will choose to follow the programmed reality around you, or inform the programming itself. **Developing a curiosity for 'how you think', your intuitive intelligence, is key to preparing you for this future.** If you're interested in learning more, check out the field of speculative design and transmedia storyworlds.

The future of work is bright, provided we consciously design for humans at the centre.

Mandy Johnson

Predicting the future can be dangerous, as Microsoft's former CEO Steve Ballmer discovered after declaring in 2007: 'There's no chance that the iPhone is going to get any significant market share'. We can, however, confidently say that the world of work is morphing at lightning speed, through the combined power of technological and social forces. In 1950 the life expectancy of a company was around 75 years.

By 2001 it was less than 15 years, and today, the life cycle of any product or service is estimated to be about 5 to 7 years.[2] Given that Instagram, Netflix, Uber Eats, iPads, Google Home and Siri didn't even exist ten years ago, one wonders how we spent our hours before then!

With business evolving at warp speed, time is the victim, becoming an ever-shrinking commodity. Projects, meetings and emails are snowballing each year, and with mobile digital devices connecting us 24/7 there is a corporate expectation and social pressure to 'do it all'. Yet unlike most of history, when humans were hunter-gatherers, there are no natural 'off' times. We can no longer rely on the end of berry season or the annual buffalo migration to take a break.

Self-discipline, then, is a skill required in much greater measure than in past eras. In this new working paradigm, those who can channel their attention and concentrate on real achievement amid this mounting frenzy of activity and distraction — in effect, be thinking 'human beings' rather than mindless 'human doings' — will be the ultimate winners. Those who fail to make the transition — and there are many at present — will find the disruptive technology continually 'disrupts' themselves.

The way we work is also becoming much more fluid and flexible. Unlike employees of the past, who often held a single job for life, with set hours and fixed remuneration, future workers will have much more scope in their professional lives. They may be employees, contract or on-call workers, solo-preneurs, entrepreneurs, multiple job holders or a combination of these. They might work in a corporate office or as part of a collaborative virtual team, or be freelancing in their own business on the side. The hours they work will also be more elastic. Already some companies offer design-your-own shift times, four-day work weeks with three-day weekends, and more micro flexibility where people can have intermittent time off to pursue specific interests or hobbies.

As a result, there will be no predictable climb of the corporate ladder for young employees. This will create more uncertainty, but also more opportunities. Those who are just joining the workforce now will be better able to shape their own career path than previous generations. This self-directed career journey will be more challenging and exciting, and require some forethought in answering questions such as the following.

- What are the things you are good at/are passionate about/enjoy doing?
- What gives you purpose?
- What problems could you solve for companies?
- Where and when and how do you want to work?
- Who do you want to work with/for?

With youth unemployment on the rise, workers that give thought to these kinds of questions and come up with a deliberate, rational way forward will be the ones who flourish in the years ahead.

Another big shift in the future of work will be an increasing war for talent. Leadership surveys continually show that the number one issue keeping CEOs awake at night is finding and keeping great people. An enduring mismatch between skills and jobs means employers continue to struggle to fill positions with the right employees. The projections show this problem escalating. According to demographer Bernard Salt, Baby Boomers are exiting the workforce at a faster rate than the next generations are entering it.[3] Because we have had low birth rates for the last 20 years, we've had people exiting the workforce faster than new generations are entering — so the available labour pool is shrinking.

If forecasts are correct, the COVID-19 pandemic will have caused Australia's unemployment rate to double in the second quarter of 2020.[4] This will expand the talent pool; but for those insomniac CEOs, the battle for the *right* talent will continue to be the new long-term reality. For skilled future workers this creates a lot of incredible opportunities and even bidding wars for their services. For those with limited skills, or who don't constantly evolve, the future is less rosy.

Steve Sammartino

Non-linear work and careers

The infiltration of automation and AI in the workplace will increase the variety of work we do — both within our jobs themselves, and in terms of the variety of roles and positions we will take on over the decade. The number of tasks we need to take on within a job role will escalate. As automation increases, humans will need to become adept at adding skills to what they have learned in previous jobs or via their formal education.

AI will replace some of our previous tasks. Workers will need to take responsibility for ensuring they obtain new skills and knowledge so they can take on tasks that are not replaceable by machines. Many companies are already acknowledging this shift in managing human resources and are attempting to redeploy workers where possible, but smart career management means being proactive and pre-empting these changes to your industry. This is especially the case given automation is now headed for traditional white-collar sectors of employment, which have traditionally been immune to AI intervention.

The period of time we work in certain roles, jobs or industries will also truncate as the pace of change accelerates. **To be successful in your career you will need to develop transferable skills and become adept at moving sideways into related industries, especially given such a large number of industries will likely become disrupted and their business models will become less sustainable.** Climbing the corporate hierarchy vertically is now a far more difficult proposition. Companies are looking for skills outside of their industry — especially those facing changes to their revenue streams and operating models.

In the coming decade we will need to manage our own career rather than relying on traditional advancement and promotion within a single company or even a single industry. As AI becomes more prevalent, specialist skills will be outsourced to the machines. Humans will need to be generalists, providing insight, nuance and variety to the approach of how work is done. Efficiency will be left to the machines, while creativity and flexibility will be the skills in most demand. We'll need to be able to solve problems that haven't been solved before.

The shift to freelance and gig labour

Since industrialisation the place of work has been largely centralised: all the tools to do our jobs resided in factories and offices. Under this model it was difficult to find, train, organise and ratify the skills of people who weren't under a company's direct control. This is no longer the case.

The gig economy we're experiencing in the present day is just an indication of what is to come. The trend will extend beyond low-cost labour and into high-value-added corporate and white-collar roles. In the next five to ten years we will see more well-paid corporate freelancers emerge — modern-day digital craftspeople. Now that people can bring their reputations with them online and are connected, labour will become more fluent. Not only is it possible to have a workplace made up of freelancers, but it's a significant cost saving to employers: the on-costs of employing full-time staff are substantial — usually a minimum of 20 per cent of their salaries.

Both staff and companies can benefit from freelance staff working with more than one company simultaneously: it widens people's skill bases, and also reduces risk for both parties. Companies can contract and expand labour as needed, and employees will have a lower revenue risk by having multiple 'employers' from which they gain revenue. People will become 'projecteers', managing a number of complementary projects across more than one company at the same time.

The human element

Before industrialisation much of our labour was physical. In the past century the highest-paid labour was left-brain logic work. But in the next decade this will shift to emotional labour. With emotional labour, *how* we approach tasks and problems is even more important than *what* we are doing. It means that humans displaying the greatest amount of empathy, adaptability and creativity will become the most valued. **Emotions such as sincerity and authenticity will be valued most highly because they are human traits.** Even in situations where automation may be possible, much of the highest-paid work will be valued 'because a human is doing it' — even if this means it is imperfect. A classic example of this today is the fact that live performances of entertainment artists are worth more than the 'recorded version' of the same performance — it's because the human element is what we really value. Labour that is differentiated by its humanity will rise above automation as we find that our true purpose isn't just efficiency, but connection.

The machines will take care of volume and efficiency, and our ability to look someone in the eye and truly connect at a species level will be a core differentiator of us versus machines. The shift to remote work will also exacerbate the need for connection. People who can maintain a high level of humanity through digital channels and back that up in person will become indispensable. An era of quasi digital isolation will require us to find new ways to connect.

Self-education

The shelf life of any education is in flux. In the new economy, our formal education must be constantly upgraded. There is a wide gamut of learning opportunities available, from our most respected universities to independent YouTube channels. The new investment we need to make for our careers is in ourselves, and in our own time. Think of it as the career equivalent of maintaining your health and fitness. **Learning isn't something you do once and then forget about; you will need to practise it constantly to keep pace.** With self-education we can be nimble and quickly move up the learning curve, staying on the cutting edge of what is valued economically.

Personal branding

These days, your CV is not just the document you email to a prospective employer — it's whatever an internet search says about you. We need to become adept at displaying our proficiency in public forms. Smart career management will increasingly involve using social tools to display qualifications, industry experience and thought leadership. This doesn't just mean using traditional career tools such as LinkedIn; it means understanding that everything you publish online is accessible and fair game for any person or company looking to engage you economically. Everything we publish creates a permanent digital footprint that will work either for or against us in the job market. **To be a competitor in this space you need to manage your personal brand wisely; this means ensuring you present your best intellectual self and stay 'on brand' in all your digital communications channels.** The internet never forgets. Your digital social interactions should be kept to private channels.

The best place to announce your brand is on your personal website that you own and control. Your website is your modern CV, and if you are diligent about search engine optimisation you will be rewarded with having your website at the top of search results. This means you are in the best position to control your own narrative as much as possible.

Project management

Project management is a core skill of the future. Anyone who can lift their skillset above 'being a factor of production' into 'organising the factors of production' will be best placed for a future where AI is inexorably linked to work. Those who are good at managing changing situations and allocating resources, people and processes will be better placed than those undertaking production-based tasks.

Clare Payne

There has been much commentary about the future of work and how it will be different to what we know now. Through an ethical lens, the big changes to the way we work will be as follows.

More collaboration

We will see an increase in collaboration and partnerships across sectors that will help us devise solutions that bring us closer to a better world. The United Nations Sustainable Development Goal number 17, 'Partnerships for the goals', directs the global community to form partnerships for change.[5] The United Nations Sustainable Development Goals are a universal call to action to end poverty, protect the planet and ensure that all people enjoy peace and prosperity. The goals acknowledge that a successful sustainable development agenda requires partnerships between governments, the private sector and civil society. To achieve this, the United Nations promotes partnerships built upon sustainable principles and values, a shared vision, and shared goals that place people and the planet at the centre.

Throughout the COVID-19 crisis, we witnessed positive examples of collaboration for good. In Italy, a specialist scuba diving company worked with medical teams to adapt scuba masks to be used as ventilators. In Australia, the for-profit and not-for-profit sectors united to meet community needs. Supermarket chain Woolworths partnered with community-based not-for-profit Meals on Wheels to ensure the elderly had essential supplies. We also saw CEOs working together to determine how to manage workforce reductions by offering temporary employment in another business, such as CVS Pharmacies in the US taking on hotel staff from Hilton and Marriott. In Australia, companies such as Telstra, Woolworths and Rio Tinto publicly pledged to redeploy Qantas staff laid off due to COVID-19.[6]

These examples of collaboration and partnership for a common good are an indication of what is possible in the future.

Alignment of values and purpose

In recent years we've seen the rise of 'purpose' in business, where long-established businesses have redefined their purpose as providing value beyond the traditional, and often limited, measures of profit and shareholder returns. A purpose-led organisation strives to have a positive impact on society. This business trend was reinforced when the Business Roundtable, a group of 181 business leaders, declared in August 2019 their commitment to leading their companies for the benefit of all stakeholders.[7]

For many, this was long overdue, and the challenge will be for businesses to now ensure their actions match their promises. They would be wise to focus on getting this right, as individuals are increasingly seeking alignment between their own values and the organisation for which they work. Employees and customers expect businesses to take positions — to have a voice — on the big issues of the day that matter to them, such as climate change and human rights.

This drive for alignment between the values of individuals and their employer, and between customers and the products and services they choose, will only increase as new generations enter the workforce and progress to positions of power.

Technology for good

While we have already seen profound changes to our personal and professional lives due to innovations in technology, it is predicted that we will move to a more meaningful application of technology, particularly AI, that will change our lives and world for the better. For example, robots will be used in medicine to relieve medical staff from routine tasks.

Over the last decade, we have seen an increased focus on the ethics of AI and privacy issues related to data and social media. In some ways this process — where guidelines, formal councils and new regulations continue to be established over time — is 'ethics in practice'. While there is not a global consensus on how best to manage our interactions with technology to ensure all rights are protected, it remains on the agenda due to the promise of technology to change our lives for better.

Here are some ideas for how you can prepare for these changes now.

1. *'No-regret' actions.* There are some 'no-regret' actions that you can take to prepare yourself for the work of the future, and others that businesses can implement. For example, employers can accommodate flexible work arrangements to engage a broader workforce. As a new graduate, you can equip yourself to work away from traditional workplaces and become familiar with the technologies that facilitate your performance if you work from a home office or other work hub.

2. *Monitor and pilot.* Employers and individuals don't need to adopt every new technology or program that comes to market. Instead, they need to assess their own needs and determine what is right for them. For example, businesses can pilot the use of new technologies with one team or they can monitor the use of new technologies by competitors and involve stakeholders and staff in deciding what is appropriate for their business. In the spirit of collaboration for good, we've seen an increase in cross-functional teams in the workplace; this can also extend to cross-industry, with businesses working with their competitors in knowledge-sharing for the common good. Individuals should think about the connections and technology that might enhance their performance — for example, actively participating in webinars or joining groups and associations (online or in person).

3. *Investment.* There will be many new technologies and systems that businesses are not ready to implement for a variety of reasons, such as incompatibility with existing systems, lack of expertise or funding limitations. In order to prepare for changes that may become inevitable, businesses and individuals should invest in understanding developments, engaging experts and commissioning or keeping up-to-date with research and developments. Those that have the capacity can invest in innovation labs and collaborator programs that will help them adapt and select the right solutions. For example, in order for businesses to fully leverage customer data and insights they will need to have the right systems in place to extract value. **Those who are new to the world of work should look for opportunities such as emerging leader programs and 'hackathons'; these will allow you to grow your knowledge, impact and network.**

Nicola Hazell

In what has been dubbed the Fourth Industrial Revolution, change is happening at a more rapid pace than we've ever seen before. Amid this change, there are three key areas that will be transformed for the next generation: jobs, careers and skills.

Current estimates indicate around 40 per cent of jobs that exist today will be affected by automation by 2030.[8] This means some jobs will be transformed by technology and others will become obsolete.

The reality is, many of the jobs of the future don't even exist yet. Around 65 per cent of children entering primary school today will ultimately end up working in completely new job types that don't yet exist.[9] This phenomenon is already underway, as many of the most in-demand growth occupations today did not exist ten or even five years ago. The pace of change is predicted to accelerate.

So how do you figure out what your dream job is when that job might not yet exist? The answer is: you don't need to. Shifts in job mobility mean young people are predicted to have an average of 17 jobs across 5 different industries in their lifetime.[10] **It's no longer about 'a career for life', so building a plan to secure that dream job isn't really going to set you up for a long-term sustainable future.**

Not only will the jobs and careers young people experience be diverse, so too will the conditions of work, which are likely to become more fluid.[11] You are likely to hold portfolios of activities, including paid employment, unpaid employment (internships or volunteering), self-employment (including entrepreneurship), and caring for children or the elderly. These different conditions, as well as the different roles, will require a variety of skills — changing from one scenario to the next.

This is where a shift in approach to skills is required. To thrive in this new world of work, you will need more than a single specialist skillset or trade. You'll need to develop transferable 'enterprising skills' such as digital literacy, collaboration, creativity and resilience — which have already become vital assets in the quest to secure *any* job.[12] More than anything, you will need to be ready to hit the ground running.

To prepare for these shifts, you need to invest in skills, mindset and activation. The skills required can't be developed just by reading lots of textbooks. These are skills that have to be learned by *doing*.

So if you're learning about finance and business, be sure to put that learning to the test. **Team up with others and try turning your learnings into a business to see what happens when you apply your skills in the real world. If you're learning to code, don't just follow the study guide — try building something of your own.** Identify a problem that your friends or family members are struggling with and consider what role technology could play in solving that problem — then have a crack at creating the solution.

As you go through these scenarios, there will be other key skills that you develop along the way. How you communicate will be critical — can you listen to others to really understand the challenge they're facing before you set about solving it for them? Once you've built your first idea, can you tell a clear story to others so they understand why this idea is the right one to help them with their problem?

Throughout this process, you'll have moments when what you're working on falls in a heap. What you thought was the solution might not turn out how you planned. This feedback is where the magic sits; the chance to understand what doesn't work, so you can figure out what does. Building resilience is about knowing things will fail, embracing that failure, and using it to fuel you to try again and do better.

The final thing to remember is that no one person will have all the skills required to solve every problem. **You need to be able to collaborate and value the insights and knowledge of people who think differently to you and have diverse experiences or perspectives to share, and work with them to create something truly useful.** Success in the future of work will not be about the individual, it will be about the collective.

Technology

QUESTIONS What effect will future technology have on people entering the workforce over the next five to ten years? How can we prepare for these changes now?

Professor Angela Carbone

It is predicted that 50 per cent of today's jobs will disappear by 2030.[13] Technology will cause most, if not all, repetitive jobs to be automated. Many jobs that exist today will become obsolete, and the nature of work will change as innovation will cause new jobs to be created. As technology replaces jobs of a repetitive nature, people entering the workforce will focus less on job security but more on job opportunity. As technology continues to evolve, flexibility and mobility will matter more than stability and job loyalty. This means that you must prepare to be adaptable and able to transfer your skillset to new environments, as it is extremely unlikely you will have a single job title for your lifetime. Research to date already tells us that the current generation entering the workforce is likely to have 17 jobs and 5 careers over their lifetime.[14]

In the past, disciplines such as English and maths were the core units of study that most students needed to get a job. However, the next generation of students will need more than just deep disciplinary knowledge; they will need a complete set of employability skills — of which digital skills will be a high priority — to effectively operate in the future world of work.

Michael Eales

Technology is a key tool in facilitating personalised, unique and memorable experiences. A solution designed today without technology in mind neglects an integral component of life as we know it. Looking to the future, we will see changes and opportunities for exploration in the physical forms that technology takes, the evolving expectations of the user, and enabling accessibility for all members of society. We are all responsible for the design of responsible technology that realigns technology with humanity.

Check out the Centre for Humane Technology (https://humanetech.com) **to explore the emerging tensions between where technology and humans are going.**

Form — How will hardware be transformed?

As we become more creative in designing technologically enabled experiences, so too does the form in which technology takes in physical environments. From the family computer to the iPhone, we have transitioned from communal to individual technology consumption. We are currently in the process of transitioning from visible technology with set interfaces to technology that is embedded within environments with natural interfaces, presenting exciting challenges in manufacturing and customer experience design.

Expectations — How does technology transform customer expectations?

The uptake and acceptance of e-commerce has had flow-on effects to the expectations of the holistic user in daily life. Website checkouts are seamless — why aren't our local stores the same? No longer are digital channels operating in a complete vacuum; now, seamless experiences facilitated by digital technology are expected even in the real and organic world.

Accessibility — How can we create a world for all?

While participation in the physical world can be limited, the digital world provides exciting opportunities for accessibility. Until relatively recently, participating in sport was difficult for those not physically able; however, the digital sub world of esports now provides the opportunity for people of all abilities to collaborate, communicate and exchange value. The question is how we can further facilitate and embrace this new sub world.

Mandy Johnson

Even though humans have been making shoes for more than 40 000 years, a robot arm can now stitch a shoe together from scratch in just six minutes. This is not good news for all those wannabe cobblers out there, but with automation and AI the new reality, the first major impact is going to involve the kinds of jobs we do. This doesn't mean that there won't be *any* work: technology does threaten jobs that currently exist, but also leads to a whole host of roles that have never been envisaged. Social media managers, data scientists, Uber drivers and podcast producers didn't exist ten years ago.

Technology will, however, transform the types of skills required to get work. Machines remove repetitive tasks so there will be less need for manual labour and lower-level skills like data entry, but more requirement for human, intuitive input such as social and emotional skills. Innovative exploration will require abilities that haven't even been named yet. Elon Musk's Neuralink brain-computer interface, the Amazon Assistant that understands emotions and Li-Fi internet that can download at the speed of light are just a few cutting-edge ideas in development.

So what impact will all of this have on future workers? On average, most humans have a work life of 30-plus years, yet 42 per cent of all current job skills are predicted to be obsolete by 2022.[15] People will no longer be doing one or two jobs for life. In some fast-changing fields it's anticipated that skills taught in university courses will be obsolete before a person even graduates.[16] Lifelong learning, then, is the new way forward. Developing soft skills such as problem solving, communication and critical thinking and focusing on core high-demand technical skills such as data analytics will be key to future employment.

The way employees update and learn new skills will also change. Many organisations still offer training in cringe-worthy PowerPoint formats or tedious videos which, to the digital generation raised on touchscreens and powerful game technology, is like stepping back to the '80s and catching a ride in a DeLorean. More immersive education in things like virtual reality (VR) will see explosive growth, and it's already beginning. US retailer Walmart will VR-train over a million employees in 2020, and companies like Porsche, Boeing and UPS are all following suit.

How people work will also radically change. 'Going online' will be a thing of the past as smart, invisible technology effortlessly connects us everywhere and anywhere. Without the need to go into an office to access corporate IT systems, working from home will become one of the most efficient ways to work — and won't just be seen as a means to stay in one's pyjamas all day. Already over 50 per cent of Australians and New Zealanders do some work remotely and in shared co-working spaces, and future employees will have much more scope to work anywhere, any time.[17] **Consider getting a new desk and setting up an office in your spare room: the workplace of the future is coming to your home.**

Steve Sammartino

Artificial intelligence and automation

AI and automation are about to invade every pocket of our working lives. The cost of accessing software, hardware and data flows (cloud storage and uploads and downloads) is in rapid decline. Technology use in the workplace will be pushed beyond social media and basic software, entering the realm of machine learning and natural language processing (NLP). Computers will start to understand the work environment they are placed in. AI will adapt and change the things it is capable using data, feedback loops and interactions it has within the work context.

Machine learning is software that can learn to perform a task without specific instructions. It does this by using mathematical models that rely on patterns and inference instead of exacting instruction. The machine (AI) learns from the data it is exposed to, which is actually known as training data. So, in many ways, AI has a similar behaviour pattern to humans: it learns from what it sees and makes 'decisions' based on that data. As the data changes, the output changes, resulting in an increasing learning loop and accuracy.

NLP is related to computer languages that can synthesise and process natural human language and configure responses back in human-like form. NLP will become a bridge between people and machine-learning software and create a system where humans start to interact with computers in a collegiate way to solve business problems. We are already seeing this technology replace many of the keypad interactions we would traditionally have using software on the web and inside our homes (it is constantly evolving and improving its functionality). Current examples include voice commands on smartphones, in vehicles and via smart speakers. As NLP improves through these consumer interactions, it will progressively move up the hierarchy and into the workplace. In the coming five to ten years, many of our interactions in the workplace will be with machine-learning algorithms, and we will command these via our voice — much like we do with humans today. In the future, our 'colleagues' will be these new forms of androids.

Automation is the replacement of human activity via machine — in all its forms. Even the most intellectually complex tasks will be automated, and no career is immune. Lawyers, doctors and accountants will all be assisted by intelligent software systems. Technology that was once the reserve of only the largest organisations will become available to everyone as the costs of these services drop due to cloud computing, and ubiquitous low-cost hardware. Humans will need to learn to work with AIs, guiding machines and extracting answers and insight from their non-human partners.

Manufacturing returns to high-cost labour markets

Developed markets have seen a decline in local manufacturing since low-cost labour markets were opened to trading. In Australia, manufacturing as a percentage of the economy peaked in the mid 1960s at around 25 per cent of gross domestic product (GDP). It is now 6 per cent of our local economy.[18] We are about to see a reversal of this trend.

In the next decade, many firms currently relying on overseas manufacturing will re-localise manufacturing as labour becomes a reduced portion of manufacturing costs overall. Developed economies that have increasingly evolved into financial and service-based economies in the past 30 years will see manufacturing grow as a percentage of GDP. While it won't surpass the long-term trend towards services it will become a more important part of the economic mix.

Manufacturing's automation will be assisted by intelligent machinery, flexible manufacturing and advancements in 3D printing capability. Politically this process will be expedited by local firms' desire to reduce risk within global supply chains. Recent times have shown that trade wars and pandemics have exposed firms that are reliant on global suppliers to bring products to market. The next decade will see a shift towards deglobalisation as technology advances erode low labour cost advantage.

Dematerialisation and virtualisation

Software is increasingly replacing the functionality of things that used to be physical. This process is called dematerialisation. The beginnings of this phenomenon were seen in the office when email replaced physical mail, spreadsheets replaced physical ledgers and AutoCAD replaced physical blueprints.

Dematerialisation is the process that has caused the largest amount of disruption in the past two decades. It has reduced the cost of goods dramatically, and upended business models. For example, many hundreds of physical things now live inside smartphones. Many goods that used to require a separate physical item, purchase process and supply chain have become software. Think about it: when did you last use a physical torch, map, newspaper, music player, camera, video camera, GPS device, dictionary or photo album? Dematerialisation and virtualisation will continue as more goods are converted into software.

Digital twins will become a major part of the virtual economy. A digital twin is a virtual replica of any physical thing or process. Their implementation will become economical through the emergence of the Internet of Things (IoT) and advancements in augmented and virtual reality in the next decade. This pairing of the virtual and physical worlds allows analysis of data and monitoring of systems to head off problems before they even occur. Imagine a digital twin for a large industrial machine. Via the twin, anything that goes wrong with the physical version will immediately translate back to the virtual version. If any repairs, maintenance or changes are made to the physical version, the digital twin is automatically updated. Likewise, eventually we'll be able to change the physical version without actually touching it — it will all be done via the digital twin.

When a process starts to be affected by AI or dematerialisation we need to become alert to it immediately. We have to adopt the new virtual version of things, as the efficiency doctrine means that the former physical versions will eventually no longer be able to compete economically and they will be replaced. **It is best to lean into everything virtual as this is the long-term trajectory that can't be fought against.** We need to learn to operate the relevant software so we are not left behind using yesterday's methods; or, worse, seen as a luddite who is unable to adapt to the business world as it evolves.

We must also be prepared for large parts of our jobs — or even our entire jobs — to be replaced by software. Even high-paid roles such as radiography will be replaced by AI. In cases like this, humans need to learn to be able to move up the value chain within a work context — to a more human role where we organise things, rather than do things.

The other major preparation we can undertake is to become a student of business history and changing business models. Technology's trajectory is highly predictable, but the way most businesses react to technological upheavals is by resisting it. **If you closely study the mistakes disrupted industries and companies have made, you will see how certain patterns repeat and how business models can adapt to low-cost innovation, and this will help you prepare.**

By observing the shifts in business models our minds are trained to change and can adapt to disruption more fluidly. By observing history and being prepared for change, we don't suffer from shock when it arrives.

Clare Payne

While it's often tempting to focus on the exact skillset required for a certain job, it is the other skills, sometimes referred to as 'soft skills', that will become even more important as technology increasingly changes our workplaces and professional lives.

The skills most in demand could include the following.

1. *Relationship skills to complement technical skills.* While technology can assist us with our jobs, data still requires interpretation, systems require oversight and decisions need to be made and communicated. Having good communication and relationship skills will be very important in order to work effectively in teams and get the most out of the technology.

2. *Critical thinking and good decision making.* **We know we must remain vigilant in identifying fake news and being aware of the potential for manipulation through misinformation. It will be even more important in the future workplace to apply critical thinking to interpret and understand information and actions.** Individuals will increasingly be held accountable for their decisions and actions, so it is critical to develop good decision-making skills that bring you to conclusions that you can justify and defend.

3. *Openness to technology, rather than fear of it.* Many people fear advances in technology and have concerns for how it will affect our job security. Sometimes these concerns have overshadowed the complementary ways that technology can assist in making performance and work life better. In the future, it will be important to view technology as an enabler rather than being fearful of the changes it might bring. The full adoption of technology will require trust, and the large technology and social media providers will need to consistently demonstrate to us that they are worthy of our trust.

How can we prepare for these changes now?

The reality is that most of us now need a base level of competency in terms of understanding the digital world. We can no longer rely on an IT department to save us. We're fortunate that many programs and devices are designed for the novice and are accompanied by tutorials with the opportunity to ask questions and troubleshoot. Whether someone is 15 or 90 years old, they can learn how to use new technology that has the potential to make their life better.

Nicola Hazell

Technology is no longer a single industry; it has become the underpinning infrastructure and driver of almost *every* industry. This means that digital literacy — an understanding of how technology works, how it can be used and what its limitations are — will be critical for anyone entering the workforce over the next five to ten years.

This has never been so apparent as during the global crisis brought on by the spread of COVID-19 around the world in 2020. The most resilient businesses and organisations during the crisis have been those able to quickly shift their products or services to an online model. The digital maturity of a business has determined its capacity to continue operating and engaging with its customers. This is not just the case for big institutions such as banks; it has proven to be equally important for industries traditionally considered to be service industries defined by their in-person physical experience. For example, restaurants and gyms have had to quickly adapt their delivery and engagement models to an online experience in order to remain afloat. Some gyms have delivered equipment such as exercise bikes and weights to clients' homes to use during online workout sessions, while many restaurants have adopted online ordering and altered their menus to provide customers with produce that they can partially prepare at home, or can be enjoyed fully cooked and delivered to their door. Those without the capability or infrastructure to shift online have been forced to shut down. This is a critical example of the importance of technical knowledge coupled with the ability to *apply* it to solving problems as and when — let alone before — they arise.

Global crises aside, the rapid advancement of technology is making it possible for people with big ideas to conquer problems that have existed for centuries, but have previously been impossible to solve. Every day, the impossible is becoming possible — and this means the future can be seen as a world of possibility ready to be unlocked. But while technology can be a powerful vehicle for solving critical problems, that power is only unlocked by the ingenuity, creativity and empathy of a diverse range of people dedicated to solving those problems. This is why, even in a tech-driven future, it is our humanity that is the most critical factor.

In order to thrive in a tech-driven future of work, we need to understand and embrace the strength of diversity: diversity of thought, diversity of lived experience, diversity of perspective — all generated from ensuring you engage with the talents, insights and skills of people from a diverse range of backgrounds, genders and identities. Those who are curious, have a thirst for learning and a respect for the value that can be found in different perspectives will be best placed to thrive — collectively — in a tech-driven future of work.

Of course, all this is based on the premise of access to technology and the opportunity to use and understand it. Right now, just in Australia, more than one million households do not have access to the internet. While the global shutdown brought about by the rapid spread of COVID-19 has forced families and households around the world to work and study from home, the implications of this shift have not been felt equally. Those without access to internet connectivity, let alone without access to devices such as mobiles and laptops, have been left in the dark in this rapidly digitised world of work, learning and human connectivity.

This has cast a spotlight on one of the greatest challenges faced by many in the tech-driven future — that inequality of access means the impact of technical advancement will be felt asymmetrically across communities and countries around the world, presenting a risk of deepening inequality if the playing field is not levelled through structural intervention.

Wellbeing

QUESTIONS Why is mental wellbeing important? How can work negatively impact your mental wellbeing? What are some strategies for managing stress and maintaining wellbeing at work?

Professor Rachael Field

Mental wellbeing is critical to our success in the world of work. Taking a realistic perspective on the rigours and stressors of working life means that we can intentionally attend to our mental wellbeing. If we purposefully take action to prevent, or address, any decline in our wellbeing, this will improve our chances of being successful in our work-related endeavours, and also in our personal lives.

Professional working life can be rigorous and stressful. As we discussed earlier, the world of work post COVID-19 will incorporate a lot of change and change very often invokes a stress response in humans. Depending on the work context, people experience different stressors; however, some stressors are commonly experienced.

Most of us will feel stressed by the following scenarios:

- uncertainty about employment opportunities or job security
- high workloads
- long hours
- having to manage risk
- ethical dilemmas
- the pressure to stay up to date
- feeling out of our depth in terms of skills and expertise
- the competitive and adversarial nature of some work environments.

As noted earlier, being aware of the importance of mental wellbeing for our work success requires us to intentionally enact self-management skills. This is the key strategy for managing stress and maintaining mental wellbeing at work. Research tells us that up to 40 per cent of our happiness is within our personal control;[19] we need to harness our own agency to manage this 40 per cent through purposeful and informed approaches and activities. If we don't, we may become vulnerable to experiencing anxiety or depressive disorders, which in turn can put us at greater risk of physical and mental ill-health and at risk of adopting unhealthy coping strategies — such as abuse of alcohol.

The resilience and agility-building strategies identified earlier are relevant to maintaining wellbeing at work. Three additional ideas are mindfulness, harnessing hope theory and reflective practice.

Mindfulness

There are many approaches to relaxation and wellness, such as yoga and meditation, that support the development of self-management skills. Mindfulness meditation is a form of meditation that is particularly accepted as an effective approach to managing and coping with stress in professional work contexts. Research shows that mindfulness improves how we feel and enhances performance, as well as helping to unclutter our busy working minds so that there is increased capacity for idea generation, problem solving and engaging with broader and deeper perspectives. For these reasons, mindfulness can also support higher levels of personal satisfaction from work.

Meditation generally involves training the mind to be disciplined and contemplative. Mindfulness meditation involves being immersed in the moment and engaging with the idea of 'simply being'. **It involves taking time to sit quietly and be present, focusing on things such as breathing and cultivating a state of mind that is still — avoiding processes of evaluation, analysis and assessment.** It requires acceptance of thoughts, emotions and feelings, and engagement with our senses.

Mindfulness meditation can be practised anywhere and at any time — as long as there is a space to be quiet and still. While mindfulness meditation is only one of many wellbeing strategies and is not for everyone, it is definitely worth trying given the strong existing evidence base for its effectiveness in helping us cope with stress and pressure.

Harnessing hope theory

Charles Snyder was an expert in hope theory and wrote the book *Handbook of Hope*.[20] According to Snyder, hope is made up of agentic thinking, pathways thinking and goal setting. A person will have hope when they are motivated and have strong willpower (agentic thinking) to generate a range of strategies (pathways thinking) for achieving a goal (an endpoint). Hope theory suggests that hopeful people experience high levels of motivation and draw on their own capacity to control, or at least influence, their own circumstances. They actively work out potential viable strategies to achieve what they want, and are also open to using additional or alternative strategies on the pathway to achieving their goals if necessary.

Hope theory involves intentional approaches that anyone can enact to improve performance and wellbeing. Scholarly rigorous research has established that hope is an important predictor of success, happiness, resilience and motivation. Basically, hopeful people perform better, are more agile and better able to adjust to change and challenges, and they cope better with stressful circumstances. Hope also influences life satisfaction more generally. The research into hope indicates that hope can improve self-esteem and problem solving while supporting better mental health, and social competence and awareness. Hope has also been shown to result in higher pain tolerance thresholds and faster recovery from illness and injury.

So, how can we enact hope theory in our lives? We can do this by formulating goals, by being autonomous and adopting pathways thinking, and by practising agentic thinking.

The first element of hope theory involves goal setting. Setting goals is important for a range of self-management processes. According to the theory of hope, setting *appropriate* goals is the key. Appropriate goals help us to thrive. Inappropriate goals, on the other hand, tend to be unrealistic and unachievable and set us up for disappointment. Appropriate goals are connected to our intrinsic motivation. They are related to something we genuinely want to achieve, and care about. Appropriate goals are concrete, not abstract. A concrete goal is achievable — we can recognise when it has been accomplished, and it creates feelings of success and a sense of affirmation. Abstract goals are too vague to be achievable.

Pathways thinking is the next element of enacting hope theory and is related to our autonomy. Once goals have been set it is important to establish a realistic pathway that gives you a sense of control over achieving them. Pathways thinking involves generating a range of possible strategies for goal realisation — not just one strategy — so there is a back-up Plan B if Plan A doesn't work out. **Even in the most stressful circumstances, taking control of the situation by planning a range of ways to achieve a goal will support you to feel a sense of hope and wellbeing.**

The final element of engaging with hope theory is to adopt agentic thinking. Agentic thinking is the application of mental willpower, determination, motivation and energy. It involves a 'can-do' attitude to achieving success. Positive self-talk — that is, saying to ourselves that we believe in ourselves and backing ourselves to be successful — is a component of agentic thinking.

Reflective practice

Reflective practice is an important way of developing self-management skills such as resilience and agility and can help you to be psychologically well. Reflection involves thinking deeply and carefully in a structured and purposeful way — so that we can learn from experience (both successes and mistakes). Reflective practice is an important part of being successful in many professional work contexts.

Reflective practice is an important self-management skill because:
- it helps us to assess our strengths and weaknesses
- it aids in monitoring performance and interactions with others
- it supports a sense of self-direction
- it helps with processing feedback and assessing successes and failures
- it supports the generation of strategies for success
- it helps us take responsibility for our actions
- it allows us to live out our personal values, beliefs and principles.

Reflective practice is a critical skill for wellbeing in future work contexts because it is a means by which we can control feelings of helplessness, uncertainty, anxiety and stress. It supports the management of our mental processing of complicated or challenging issues. It can be used to help set goals and targets, and to engage in pathways and agentic thinking. Reflective practice can also help with:
- working through unstructured ideas
- solving dilemmas for which there are no obvious answers
- processing knowledge, concepts and emotions in order to make sense of them.

There is no one right or wrong way to do reflective practice. As individuals we can refine our own approach and create our own 'art' of reflective practice. There are, however, some established methods of effective reflective practice that can help with getting started.

Graham Gibbs' model of reflective practice[21] has the following six basic steps.
1. Identify an experience or situation that requires reflection.
2. Describe the experience or situation to yourself.
3. Explore your reactions and feelings in relation to the situation or experience.
4. Analyse and evaluate the situation or experience by asking questions like: 'What was good or bad about that experience?', 'What sense can be made of the situation?', 'What was really going on?', 'Was the experience similar or different to a previous experience?'. This process of evaluation and analysis involves making some value judgements about the experience and drawing on personal catalogues of experiences.
5. Make some conclusions about the situation or experience, starting with general conclusions and moving to conclusions that are more specific.
6. Use the reflections in the first five steps to create a personal action plan, using questions like: 'How will I manage a similar experience next time?', 'What will I do differently?', 'What will I do in the same way?', 'What have I learned from the situation?', 'What steps can I take to make the most of this learning experience?'.

Professor Angela Carbone

Mental wellbeing is extremely important to not just function, but to think clearly and have a positive impact on the world. **It is important to develop a 'professional purpose' mindset** — not only to navigate the complex world of work you'll face, but to have a more meaningful professional life. Professional purpose, as defined by Bates, Rixon, Carbone and Pilgrim, reflects a person's level of commitment to developing a professional future aligned with their personal values, professional aspirations and societal outlook.[22] People who have cultivated this mindset will become more self and socially aware, informed of the changing nature of work, connected through relevant global networks and prepared to pursue jobs that are meaningful to them. Having a professional purpose means that your personal interests and passion will align with your professional goals to shape the impact you have on the world.

Purpose in life has been defined as a central, self-organising life aim that organises and stimulates goals, manages behaviours and provides a sense of meaning.[23] We can think of purpose as operating as an overarching goal manager. The sense of purpose is not linked to the achievement of a designated goal, but operates as a mindset — motivating you to be oriented towards your goals.[24] Having a purpose in life allows you to pursue multiple goals and to generate new goals once a goal is attained, thereby experiencing personal growth. In contrast, having a specific goal that is not based on a sense of purpose makes new goals hard to identify after the goal is reached, and this makes it difficult to sustain the energy needed to pursue a goal.[25]

Here are some tips to manage stress and improve mental wellbeing in the workplace.

- When the pressures of work are demanding and stressful, it is important to have other interests in your life. Interests outside of work give you the chance to broaden your experiences and perhaps discover a new passion. Your interests or hobbies can also be a low-risk way to participate with new groups and cultures. A great way to do this is to join clubs and societies at university, if you haven't already. These provide a safe and fun space to learn about a new culture or skill.
- Make sure you incorporate regular physical activity, heathy food and eight hours of sleep per night into your daily routine. This will give you the energy and focus you need to deal with stress at work.

Michael Eales

Wellbeing is a fundamental aspect of an individual's overall health. Your mental wellbeing is just as important as your physical wellbeing. Mental wellbeing is more than the absence of mental health concerns; it is a dynamic state that encapsulates your social and emotional needs. When you take care of your mental wellbeing, you will have the mental, social and emotional capacity to get closer to your goals, creating a playground for thought, creativity and critical thinking.

Work can be a large part of our lives, playing a significant role in our mental wellbeing and subsequent capacity. It's normal to be busy at work sometimes, or to find yourself working on a project or in a role that wasn't your first choice. However, if your work is negatively impacting you to the point where you aren't able to foster social and emotional relationships or care for your mental wellbeing, it's important to take a step back and re-evaluate your options.

Check out www.healthdirect.gov.au/mental-health-and-wellbeing to explore the relevance of mental wellbeing, mindfulness and mental health issues further.

In managing stress and maintaining mental wellbeing at work, it's important to pinpoint what areas of work you find most beneficial, start a dialogue around mental wellbeing and create time to actively pursue activities that will support your mental wellbeing.

Areas of benefit

What gives you the most excitement in your current role or university studies? Think back to what tasks you do that excite you, or where the time seems to fly by; where you're able to get into a 'flow state'. Comparing these to activities where time seems to drag by can help you recognise which activities give you the most enjoyment or fulfilment. While it won't always be possible to only do the tasks you enjoy, recognising this can help you know when to make more time outside — or inside — work to focus on your mental wellbcing.

Start a dialogue

Are you having a bad day? Then tell your team. We aren't all going to be at the top of our game all the time. However, it's not up to your team to know when you have external concerns in your life — it's up to you to tell them. There's no need to go into detail about your concerns if you don't want to, but giving people a head's up will help reduce any additional pressure that you don't need to have.

Time for you

How are you getting fulfilment? From exercise to meditation to chatting with your friends, think about what makes you feel happy and fulfilled. Making sure you're creating time for these activities alongside your work life is important to support your mental wellbeing; meaning you won't burn out at work or at home, and can maintain a work-life balance that best fits your needs.

Mandy Johnson

'Choose a job you love, and you will never have to work a day in your life.' This may be an oft-repeated cliché, but it still holds true today. Managing mental wellbeing begins before you even have a job, because you'll be far happier working for a company with like-minded peers, and in a role that is the best 'fit' for you. If you are an apple working for a company that only values pears you will become stressed and unhappy, so finding an employer that needs, nurtures and appreciates apples will be essential for your personal wellbeing. **Don't be seduced by the job title. The choice of company is far more important than the initial job role, so find one that is a good fit for your talents, aligns with your personal values and has a track record of inspiring and rewarding its people.**

Once you have a started in a role or even set up your own business, the next strategy to maintain mental wellbeing is to manage your workload effectively. Over 2000 years ago the Greek philosopher, Socrates, warned us: 'Beware the barrenness of a busy life'. His message remains relevant today. New employees often believe that success means working themselves to the bone, wearing busyness as a badge of honour. Yet all the evidence contradicts this way of thinking. A Stanford University/IZA study showed that output falls sharply after a 50-hour work week, and declines even further after 55 hours — to the extent that someone who puts in 70 hours produces nothing more than the person who worked 55 hours.[26]

Setting healthy work boundaries allows you to avoid this pitfall and focus on achievement, not just activity. This is often easier said than done, especially for young or new employees. Working long hours is often necessary to meet an encroaching deadline or to help out on a vital team project. If you are forever feeling stretched thin, however, it's usually because you've over-committed, and this is especially true of 'people-pleasers'. Avoiding responding on the spot — for example, by telling your co-workers that you need to check your diary before agreeing to take on more work — is a good way to stop them using you as their 'go to' person for all their needs. **When it's your boss who is continually adding more work to your plate, a good diplomatic response is an enthusiastic, 'That looks like a great project. I'm currently working on A, B and C projects which are all due in the next few weeks — which one of these would you like me to put on hold, to enable me to do this new one for you?'.** As billionaire entrepreneur Warren Buffett famously said, 'The difference between successful people and really successful people is that really successful people say no to almost everything'.

Another strategy for managing stress and maintaining mental wellbeing is to actively develop social connections and satisfying hobbies outside of work. In other words, work to live, don't live to work. Every job is taxing at times but de-stressing in your personal life will enable you to cope better because once tension builds, even the smallest of incidents can lead to uncontrollable outbursts. Playing sport once a week, going out for dinner or just enjoying a laugh with friends — grasp whatever activities help to get you out of your work headspace and stop your work stress bucket overflowing. Those who prioritise themselves high up on their daily 'to-do' list will be the ones who survive and thrive in the future.

Steve Sammartino

For most of human history, our jobs included physical activity. Today, much of what we do is intellectual, and maintaining mental wellbeing is core to success. As our economy has become more complex, flexibility of mind and our ability maintain mental stability is inextricably linked to our ability to perform.

It is also worth remembering that this fact is even more important as work hours have become more fluid in our lives. Every year we do more work outside of traditional hours and our usual place of work. Mental wellbeing is now the bellwether for general wellbeing. In this sense many of us are never *not* working — we are almost always subconsciously working, even when we are not 'at work'. This is why we so often come up with solutions to a work problem at home, or randomly have a new idea we need to write down for work while we are engaged in non-work activities.

Mental wellbeing must be protected because in the modern economy as it is our most vital economic asset. We have to guard it like the bank vault to our future. There are a few main areas in which work can affect our mental wellbeing. The first is the interactions we have with people. Adversarial communication with colleagues, staff, managers or customers can have an impact on how we feel, long after the moment itself has passed. In many cases these interactions become a pattern of behaviour; the negative interactions become typical, so even the thought or expectation of such behaviours can impact our mental state. It becomes a negative cycle.

Stress around the specific tasks we have to do can have a similar impact on us mentally. When we are given a task load and deadline that is unrealistic, or asked to solve a problem without the required resources or that nobody else has been able to solve, the pressure mounts. Recurring patterns of this nature are dangerous for wellbeing if not well managed.

Another element that can impact wellbeing at work is the feeling of insecurity — that we may be dismissed, lose our job or the company might go under. Job insecurity can be an enormous source of stress.

Here are three tips to help you manage stress and improve mental wellbeing in the workplace.

1. *Ensure cultural fit.* Be sure you have a good cultural match with your company, work environment or clients. No amount of managing your career and personalities will ever fix a cultural misfit. It's not about what culture is right — it is about what culture is right for *you*. There is no such thing as the perfect culture, and this is evidenced by the fact there are many successful firms with many juxtaposed cultures. Some cultures are democratic, meritocratic, autocratic, scrappy, startup-like; there are no rules for success. The only rule that matters is finding a culture that matches how you like to operate, and your value system. **Keep switching companies until you find one that matches. If you can't find one, build your own company or work for yourself instead.**

2. *Maintain physical fitness.* Exercise and a healthy diet are key elements to maintaining mental wellbeing. Numerous studies show that exercise releases endorphins and serotonin which can have a positive impact on mood. In addition to this, regular exercise can help conditions including anxiety and depression and improve sleep. Being well rested is vital for work occurring in a high-stress environment.

3. *Invest more in yourself than you do in your job.* If we are constantly upgrading our skills and investing more in ourselves than our jobs, the companies we work for become the ultimate beneficiaries. In addition, this will ensure you have the skills needed to be valued by your next employer or client. This can radically reduce the tension associated with job insecurity.

Clare Payne

The Australian Psychological Society (APS) has found that problems at work can have an enormous impact on an individual's mental health and wellbeing.[27] We spend up to a third of our lives working, so it is crucial to our health and wellbeing that work is a positive and healthy experience.

We have seen a shift in our understanding of workplace health and safety to encompass a broader idea of wellbeing. Many businesses now offer workplace wellbeing programs that focus on work-life balance, support for parental and carer responsibilities and, importantly, mental health initiatives.

In a knowledge economy, people are considered the most valuable resource. For these people to contribute at their best and flourish we need to ensure their physiological wellbeing and safety, which are vital to living a good life.

There are many factors we encounter at work that can negatively impact our mental health and wellbeing, such as unfair pay or conditions, or harassment and bullying. We are also learning about the negative impact of workplace cultures that are psychologically unsafe. For example, cultures that promote a fear of failure and expect people to work with unclear direction, lack of job security or no recognition for a job well done can negatively impact individuals, and ultimately business outcomes as well.

Business in the Community, a UK-based organisation that is part of the Prince's Responsible Business Network, has called for employers to recognise the scale of poor mental health in the workplace.[28] Along with others, it has highlighted the duty of care of employers have to their employees, and the obligation employers have to respond to mental ill health just as they would to a physical illness.

Many organisations are now focusing on how to create positive, inclusive workplace cultures that help rather than harm the mental health of the people who work in them.

Here are some ways you can manage stress and improve mental wellbeing in the workplace.

1. *Understanding your rights.* It is essential for you to understand your rights at work, and also as a citizen. There are many online resources that will help you understand your rights, and the rights of others, so you can confidently protect and assert yourself.

2. *Taking time for what matters.* Many of us find that work can become overwhelming, particularly given that technology has increased expectations of availability and blurred the distinction between work and personal time. While employers should respect people's time, the reality is that we all need to be conscious of balancing our own lives — ensuring we prioritise things that are good for our mental health and wellbeing such as walking, a creative pursuit or just connecting with friends.

3. *Seeking clarification.* Seeking clarity on vision, goals and purpose can remove stress and provide a clear path for you to contribute to your organisation and reach your potential. When you are new to a workplace you will see things with 'fresh eyes'. This is a great advantage, as more experienced workers can slip into unthinking behaviours, which can lead to unethical practices. Asking questions is a powerful tool. For managers, removing ambiguity can drive employee satisfaction and performance.

Nicola Hazell

Stress has been described as the smoking of our generation. It costs the Australian economy more than $15 billion per year in work absenteeism and lost productivity.[29] In the US, that figure is more than $500 billion. Stress is a hidden epidemic, affecting the mental wellbeing — and, therefore, capacity and productivity — of not just our workforce, but our whole community. When there is widespread stress in a work environment, it creates toxic cultures, drives poor decision making and can lead to business failures.

On the flipside, those with strong mental wellbeing are in a far better position to do their best work in stressful situations. Not only do they have the energy and focus to generate great ideas and work well with others, they also develop an inbuilt resilience for the kinds of challenges a rapidly changing world of work can throw at us. Those who pay attention to their own mental health and put in place tools and habits to keep themselves mentally well are more likely to come up with great ideas, bounce back from rejection or failure and build sustainable, game-changing businesses and teams.

Here are some tips to manage stress and improve mental wellbeing in the workplace:[30]

1. *Monitor and manage your workload.* Be aware of what you are working on and how much you may have on your plate. Speak up at an early stage if you are feeling overwhelmed so you can seek guidance and support to share the load.

2. *Don't be afraid to address the hard topics.* You don't have to be the boss to encourage a culture of open communication about mental health and wellbeing so others know that it's okay to talk about stress at work. When people are able to be their authentic selves at work, it fosters positive mental wellbeing. As a member of a team, you can cultivate this within your own organisation by creating safe spaces for others to share, and being willing to do so yourself.

3. *Seek out and use emotional and mental health support tools.* Get to know the activities and tools that help you stay mentally well. Whether it's meditation, exercise, connection with loved ones, or one of the many online tools now available for improving mental wellbeing, it's essential to recognise the things that help you manage stress and keep you in a positive frame of mind and ensure you prioritise them as a consistent part of your routine.

4. *Be accountable.* You can't expect your workplace to help you manage stress and improve your wellbeing if you don't do the same for others. Be accountable for the way you behave and interact with your colleagues and managers, to ensure you're supporting them just as much as you'd like them to support you. Workplace wellbeing is a two-way street — everyone plays a role in creating a healthy environment where we all thrive.

Social intelligence

QUESTIONS What do you consider the biggest social challenge when entering the workforce? What are the traits of people who successfully navigate these challenges?

Nicola Hazell

Throughout childhood, and even during university, we spend most of our time outside the home with people our own age. Our peers may come from different neighbourhoods and backgrounds, but in many ways we have more in common than not. At university, you're exposed to the same learning and curriculum as your classmates, equipped with the same information and insights and tasked with many of the same challenges.

When you enter the workforce, this changes completely. Suddenly, your colleagues and managers come from different walks of life. They are different ages and have vastly different life experiences to you. Their stories are diverse and so, too, is the value they bring to an organisation.

Some of the greatest challenges in adapting to the workforce come in learning to work with such a diverse group of people; figuring out the value you add and when to add it in a much more complex environment; and understanding how to build relationships that are productive, healthy and respectful.

What's more, while you might think it is your technical skills and knowledge that will be the critical factor to your success, in reality, it is the transferable, interpersonal and social skills that will determine whether you thrive in the workforce. Research shows that the majority of modern employers looking to fill graduate positions are more interested in the non-technical skills a person has.[31] Your ability to communicate well, work with others, come up with ideas, solve problems, show resilience under pressure and to learn from your mistakes are the skills in demand. These skills don't just make great workers — they also make great leaders. If you can learn how to translate these skills into opportunities, you can significantly increase your employability.

The best companies to work for are those that create a healthy environment for ideas to be raised — and challenged. The best possible solutions can be found through debate and interrogation. To succeed in this kind of an environment requires a unique mix of skills:
- confidence, so you're not afraid to share your ideas, opinions and insights
- humility, so you recognise that your ideas, opinions and insights may and should be challenged
- collectivism, so you're willing to work together and support others to arrive at the best possible solution — whether it's your original idea or not.

To help develop these skills during your studies and early work experience, seek out opportunities to take part in extracurricular activities or projects that challenge you to develop and demonstrate new skills, allow you to connect and work with others, and provide the opportunity to learn from those who may have more experience or different perspectives. **When given the opportunity, seek feedback from managers, mentors and peers who can help you continue to grow these skills and attributes and offer additional opportunities to learn.**

These will be critical traits for navigating the challenges and opportunities that arise in any workplace of the future.

Professor Rachael Field

Social intelligence involves knowing ourselves and understanding others. High standards of professional performance and civil interaction are expected in the workforce, and this will continue into the future. Managing ourselves and engaging with others appropriately at work can be a big social challenge.

Effective communication is a fundamental skill-set for managing the social side of being in a workplace. Communication skills are important when it comes to professional conduct and building constructive working relationships with colleagues, and they are also critical to preventing, managing and resolving disputes. Conflict and disputes in the workplace can be damaging for productivity and your mental health. Workplace conflict can derive from relatively small matters (such as using all the milk in the fridge and not replacing it) to large, even legal, matters such as bullying.

Proactive leadership is an important element of creating healthy workplaces with low levels of disputation and conflict. Individuals, too, can manage the social challenges of working by building and enacting effective communication skills.

In dispute resolution and mediation training, the acronym LARSQ (listening, acknowledging, reframing, summarising and questioning) is used to describe the basic skills necessary for effective communication. Dispute resolution practitioners and mediators use these skills all the time in their professional practice. They are skills that you can employ as part of exercising social intelligence.

Effective listening involves listening actively and responsively, and letting the speaker know that they have not only been heard but also understood. This requires focus and attention. Acknowledging refers to the recognition of emotions, needs, interests, fears and priorities. When these things are acknowledged a person feels listened to and valued and they are then more likely to collaborate constructively and engage in positive problem solving. Reframing is a complex skill, but basically it involves taking negative words and sentiments and re-expressing them in a way that supports effective communication. For example, instead of saying 'I think you're lying', you might say 'I'm not sure about the accuracy of what you just said'. Summarising is a part of active listening involving repeating back to someone your understanding of what they have said to ensure the accuracy of that understanding and to demonstrate engagement in the communication. Finally, appropriate questioning is critical to effective communication. Effective questions are open and clarifying rather than closed or leading. The book *Mediation Skills and Techniques* by Laurence Boulle and Nadja Alexander is an excellent resource if you would like to learn more about effective communication and conflict resolution.[32]

Successfully navigating the challenges associated with being a socially intelligent work colleague and effective communicator in the workplace calls for a range of positive traits. Three important ones are emotional intelligence, awareness and responsiveness to others, and the ability to receive and give feedback appropriately.

Emotional intelligence

This involves an ability to engage with and use emotions logically and wisely. In order to do this, we need to be able to perceive emotions accurately, assimilate emotion-related feelings, understand emotions and manage them. Emotional intelligence is a form of intrapersonal intelligence involving emotional self-awareness and an ability to regulate your own emotions. It is also related to interpersonal intelligence, which is a person's ability to accurately detect the emotions of another person and to manage responses to those emotions.

Awareness of and responsiveness to others

This builds on emotional intelligence and is an important aspect of communicating effectively. Awareness and responsiveness can be realised through the skill of empathy. Empathy is the ability to understand another person's perspective — in other words, 'put yourself in their shoes'. It goes beyond simply recognising and understanding another person's feelings and experience to entering their world and acknowledging and valuing them as a person with their own individual needs, interests and concerns. Importantly, being empathic is not the same as agreeing with someone or feeling sorry for them. Empathy as a form of awareness and responsiveness can be shown through enacting all the elements of LARSQ — especially if you can incorporate empathic questions and acknowledgement. This approach will contribute to effective communication at work and can be a positive strategy in the prevention, management and resolution of workplace disputes and conflict.

The ability to give and receive feedback

This requires emotional intelligence and reflective practice. It is easy to feel criticised and upset by feedback you receive in the workplace. However, managing feedback (and also giving feedback) appropriately contributes to a socially healthy workplace and can positively support collegiality and your own wellbeing.

Responding to feedback appropriately requires an openness to the opinions of others and a willingness to improve. It is almost always nice to receive feedback on what you have done well; but not so easy to receive feedback that criticises what you have done, or that says something has been done incorrectly or should have been done differently. Building the skills of receiving and giving feedback well is an important aspect of professional self-management and self-regulation.

Some strategies for using the feedback process appropriately include:
- being open to receiving feedback
- valuing the time and effort of the person providing the feedback
- preparing for receiving feedback — having the right mindset to receive it with emotional intelligence
- avoiding taking feedback personally
- using feedback constructively to improve performance
- avoiding arguing with negative or critical feedback
- considering the big picture and keeping things in perspective
- building on the feedback by asking clarifying questions and asking for additional feedback on specific points.

Michael Eales

Having high social intelligence means you have the ability and capacity of knowing your true self, and understanding the core of others in your environment. Considering the dynamic and opportunistic course of a career, establishing and having a concrete and solid level of social intelligence will allow you to market yourself effectively to different audiences in your professional and personal life. This means having deep empathy for those you work with, understanding what makes you and others tick and translating the two as you work across company cultures. Mastering the relationship between social intelligence and empathy is key to better navigating the world around you.

Yourself

While it is important to be able to tailor your approach to different circumstances, your true self should never change. **Invest time in knowing what makes you tick, what your boundaries are and what motivates you, and use this knowledge as a parameter or criteria when presented with new opportunities.** Remember that what makes you, you is invaluable, and you are your best asset. If you're interested in exploring this further, check out https://businessmodelyou.com.

Culture

Having a solid understanding of yourself enables you to figure out how to work effectively in different environments. It's crucial to remember that each company culture is unique — pick and choose the parts you wish to emulate while remaining true to yourself. **Read the book *The Invincible Company* to learn more.**[33]

Relationships

Friction is a natural process of life that enables you to grow and develop as an individual. When confronted with the potential for conflict, embrace the opportunity to proactively manage the relationship through empathy in communication. It is a small world, after all, and if you maintain your relationships well there is decreased risk of 'burning bridges'.

Mandy Johnson

In 1913, the famous car manufacturer Henry Ford established a sociological department to control every aspect of his employees' lives. Investigators would turn up unannounced at employees' homes and if they failed the 'cleanliness evaluation' or were deemed to be consuming too much alcohol, they were sacked. We've come a long way from this kind of tyranny, however the first social challenge new employees face is understanding and dealing effectively with the many unspoken rules and operating norms within their organisation — what is known as workplace culture.

Every business has its own distinct culture, in the same way that people have their own distinct personalities, and this is expressed in daily practices that act as signals to workers. Can I joke around and have fun at work? Is it okay for people to make a mistake or do they try to cover it up? Are tattoos encouraged or frowned upon? Just to make things more confusing, in some cases the culture companies publicly proclaim can be the exact opposite of what happens in practice. Observing, asking questions of approachable co-workers and avoiding making assumptions are some tactics that can help new workers traverse this minefield.

Another area of social challenge for new employees is dealing with co-workers with vastly different personalities, experiences and cultural beliefs to their own. **Don't fall into the cloning trap, believing that everyone should think and communicate just like you.** Social assumptions and biases are also still rife in today's workplaces. Dog lovers like dog lovers, rugby players prefer other rugby players, and they'll often make unhelpful sweeping generalisations about those who don't like dogs or rugby.

Scenarios like these require effective social skills, such as asking questions rather than making assumptions. Compare: 'I know you people all hate loud music' to 'What is your opinion of heavy metal music?' which is far more diplomatic. Good conflict-handling skills are essential, too. These can include managing your emotions (taking deep breaths and keeping your tone of voice at normal levels) and listening and showing empathy ('That does sound frustrating'). Learning good techniques like these allows new workers to overcome natural defensiveness and reduces workplace arguments.

Yet perhaps the biggest factor that affects an employee's social success when entering a new workforce is their own mindset. Those who adopt a victim mentality — blaming others and denying that anything they do is a factor in the equation — bring about their own failure. Those who take responsibility, refuse to externalise and ask, 'How am I contributing to this?' and 'What can I do to change?' can overcome almost any hurdles. By paying attention, doing what you say you will do and being consistent and authentic, you will earn the respect from others that is necessary to achieve success. After all, who would you rather do something for — someone you like or someone you don't like?

Professor Angela Carbone

One of the biggest social challenges you will face when entering the workforce is building strong and trusting relationships with people that hold different cultural, spiritual and ethical values to you. People work well with those that they can trust; however, trust does not come instantaneously: it requires time, multiple interactions, and opportunities to engage in meaningful conversations and negotiate your position around challenging issues. Your values will be tested and questioned. You will encounter differences of opinions and approaches, which might lead to conflict. Being able to understand the sensitivities around an issue and appreciating and respecting the values of others — particularly those who have had different cultural and social experiences to you — will be instrumental in managing. Stellar negotiation, influencing and persuasion skills will be important, and you can hone all of these skills while at university.

Traits of people that can navigate such challenges include the following.

1. *Reliability and honesty.* Performing consistently well and being trustworthy enables you to develop strong relationships with your colleagues and stakeholders.
2. *Emotional intelligence.* Being self-aware and maintaining a positive attitude so that you can empathise with others and respond rather than react to conflict will enable you to successfully navigate relationships with others at work.
3. *Grit and tenacity.* You will need courage and strength to express your point of view when others might disagree and react in an unacceptable manner. It may take time and perseverance to achieve the outcome you want, as you will likely experience delays or difficulties in achieving success.
4. *Resilience.* You need to be able to recover quickly when faced with difficulties or when the outcome is different to what you expected.

Steve Sammartino

One of the biggest challenges you will face when entering the workforce is that workplaces are far less democratic than educational or social institutions. Over the past 20 years we have seen the emergence of a generation that has grown up without meritocracy. We've been taught that equality matters more than performance. But in the workforce, you don't get a ribbon just for participating. While social equality has certainly increased in the workplace, corporate hierarchies are still Darwinist in terms of who rises to the top. Not everyone gets to the 'next grade'.

Rapidly changing norms of acceptability mean that this is a new skill-base people must have to navigate a successful career. To avoid a clash of cultures (between people, media, industries and corporations) we need to understand belief systems outside of what we value personally, or grew up with socially or geographically.

Traits of people that can navigate such challenges include the following.

1. *Keen cultural observers.* People who are keen observers and students of the rapidly changing cultural landscape have a massive social advantage. As global cultures converge and people are more mobile physically and digitally, understanding different cultures and shifts in what is acceptable is now as valuable as being an observer of consumer trends.
2. *Listeners.* People who first want to understand someone else's point of view before they wish to have their viewpoint understood are particularly good at navigating and resolving conflict. As our tasks become more about managing projects and situations, this type of empathy is highly valued.
3. *Data enthusiasts.* In a digital society where algorithms determine what we all see, understanding bias in data is vital. People are increasingly exposed to more of what they already believe as they are served up news and opinions that match their existing viewpoints. It is becoming an important trait to be aware of this, and extend views outside of algorithmic wormholes so that we have a broad understanding of society.

Clare Payne

It can be a challenge to accept others who have different views, backgrounds and skills to your own. The focus on inclusion and diversity at work has been an important development, although there is still much progress to be made.

Recognising that others have a powerful contribution to make, even if their style or approach differs to your own, is an important concept to understand and practise. Looking for and being able to see the strengths in others is a good way to overcome this social challenge. You should take the time to get to know your colleagues and customers and seek to understand them. **Try to avoid using labels or stereotyping, which can be discriminatory and hinder effective connection and performance.**

You might find it helpful to think about the qualities of ethical leaders, as they are more likely to successfully navigate challenges. It's important to note that leaders can exist at all levels of an organisation — you don't necessarily need a title to be considered a leader.

In her book *Setting the Tone: Ethical Business Leadership*, Philippa Foster Back identified five key attributes of an ethical leader:[34]

1. openness
2. fair-mindedness
3. honesty
4. courage
5. the ability to listen.

These attributes set an ethical leader apart from others. We all possess these attributes in varying degrees, however they will be nurtured, developed and supported by an ethical leader.

Developing mental agility, such as the capacity to challenge your perspectives and evolve your opinions when presented with a variety of different perspectives or ideas, is important in developing as an ethical and inclusive worker and leader who is fit for the future.

Ethics

QUESTIONS How will ethics in the workplace evolve over the next five to ten years? What issues will emerge as top priority during this time? How can we prepare for these changes now?

Clare Payne

The issue of ethics will be front and centre as the next generation of leaders emerge — particularly as they question the outcomes that have arisen from past and current practices.

While laws and regulations will remain important, I believe we will see a continued move beyond mere compliance to an expectation of higher ethical standards. In January 2020, the annual credibility survey Edelman Trust Barometer declared that the battle for trust will be fought on the field of ethical behaviour.[35]

As global issues such an inequality and climate change become more pressing, ethics will only become more important. Individuals will look to their employer, in particular their CEO, to have a position and 'take a stand' on the issues of the day. Already, 92 per cent of employees expect their company's CEO to speak up on issues such as income inequality, diversity, ethical use of technology, climate change and immigration.[36] This expectation is predicted to continue to grow, propelling businesses and leaders to action and contribute to a better world.

Three issues that will emerge as a top priority during this time are as follows.

1. *The idea of moral money.* Until recently, morality and money were rarely paired. In June 2019 the *Financial Times* London launched a 'Moral Money' section. Now, one quarter of all investable assets globally, worth $31 trillion, are managed with an environmental, social and governance (ESG) mandate.[37] Our own Responsible Investment Association of Australasia has declared that responsible investment is 'mainstream', with 44 per cent of money managed (totalling $2.24 trillion) under a responsible investment mandate in 2019.[38] The increased focus on whether money is accumulated and spent morally will change investment, influence business practices and improve outcomes for society.

2. *Shifting from a short to long-term focus.* Much of our finance sector and business operations have been focused on short-term outcomes, such as quarterly profit cycles, rather than on the long-term viability and contribution of products and services to society. The COVID-19 pandemic has exposed many of the downfalls of focusing on short-term solutions rather than planning and preparing over a longer timeframe. For example, the drastic shortage of essential items exposed the vulnerability of just-in-time inventory systems, which are common to many businesses and often implemented by private equity in the quest to drive down costs and make a profit in the short term rather than ensuring a business can deliver to society over the longer term.

3. *Addressing inequity.* Inequity across society can't be ignored, in Australia or globally. It has become clear that traditional measures such as gross domestic product (GDP) do not tell us about the extent to which financial growth is shared across the population. Edelman has identified that a growing sense of inequity is undermining trust. It has found that the majority of those living in developed markets do not

believe they will be better off in five years' time, and more than half of globally believe that capitalism in its current form is doing more harm than good in the world. Our experiences during the COVID-19 crisis will likely reaffirm this position and propel us towards positive change.

In order to prepare for these changes, businesses and individuals will need to determine their role in society. Many businesses still remain focused on shareholder and financial returns without considering their impact. Those that work in the field of change and transformation have indicated that it can take a decade for businesses to truly transform their operations to be purpose-led.

As a society, we will need to determine measures and indicators, particularly non-financial, that signify a new idea of success and track progress towards a better world.

There are many ways that individuals can influence for good. Managers can ensure pay equity and fairness, and individuals can ensure they act with honesty and respect the contribution and individuality of those with whom they work and interact.

Professor Rachael Field

Ethics are foundational, fundamental principles on which professional work is based. Ethics in the workplace is about analysis and decision making in terms of what the right, moral or appropriate thing to do is. In the workplace you will be expected to act ethically at all times, and this will continue to be the case in the world post COVID-19 — although we may find that new ethical dilemmas arise in the future work environment that have not yet been anticipated.

Many professions have ethical codes of conduct, and membership of professions is often regulated by these codes. A breach of the ethical code can mean exclusion from the profession — which is generally regarded as a very shameful thing. Ethical decision making in workplaces requires more than simply abiding by a professional code of conduct, however. Ethical dilemmas are complex and don't always fit neatly into prescribed rules. This means that to be ethical at work, you will need an ability to apply ethical rules to real-life situations, a very clear personal commitment to taking the right path, as well as the skills to analyse, process and respond to ethical problems. Your capacity to manage the complexity of ethical challenges may take some time to develop. Even the most experienced professionals will say that they are challenged by ethical dilemmas in their daily work.

The evolution of workplace ethics in the future could force the emergence of three important issues. First, the need for individuals to have a well-developed moral compass; second, increased emphasis on the importance of an ability to exercise appropriate ethical judgement; and third, the critical nature of mentoring in workplaces.

A moral compass

Having a moral compass refers to a person's internal and innate ability to judge what is right and wrong and to act appropriately in accordance with that judgement. In the workplace a moral compass denotes honesty, propriety and competence.

Honesty refers to telling the truth and is related to integrity and candour. It also indicates an absence of deceit. To be ethical, communications and actions in the workplace must be honest and never intended to deceive or convey something known to be false. Propriety relates to the quality of a person's professional character; that is, a suitable and proper professional character. Reflective practice, emotional intelligence, communication skills and empathy are all important to maintaining our propriety in the workplace and behaving ethically. Competency concerns the ability (the knowledge, skills and expertise) to work accurately and effectively using appropriate levels of skill and expertise. An ethical person in the workplace will ensure that they have sufficient knowledge and experience to do the work that is asked of them. If they have concerns that they might not have sufficient competence for the task, they will ask for help and guidance.

An ability to make ethical judgements

Developing an ability to make ethical judgements is something that happens over time and through experience and lessons learned in practice, through reflective practice and through mentoring relationships. Ethical dilemmas in workplaces are hardly ever straightforward; they are messy and complex. 'Deliberative ethical decision making' is an approach that can help with ethical judgement. This approach is useful because it offers some logical steps for processing an ethical problem. It also provides evidence of a thoughtful and careful approach that — even if it isn't agreed with — is justifiable and based on logical reasoning.

The possible steps of a deliberative ethical decision-making process are:
1. identify the ethical issue
2. consider potential initial options for addressing the issue
3. identify the various interests of the relevant people involved in the problem
4. identify the relevant professional sources of authority such as the relevant rules of professional conduct that might apply to the situation
5. consider whether there are any broader ethical considerations
6. consult, seek help and guidance from someone not involved with the problem — possibly a mentor, professional counsellor or more experienced colleague
7. generate some possible courses of action and consider the consequences of each of them
8. on balance, in all the circumstances and informed by all the considerations in steps one to seven, make a decision about the most appropriate action to take
9. summarise a diary note of the decision and the reasons for it on the basis of the ethical deliberations.

Mentoring

Mentoring is an important part of developing a moral compass and the ability to make ethical judgments in professional contexts. A mentor is an experienced person in your workplace, industry or profession who helps and gives advice to you — a younger or less experienced person. Taking the initiative to find a mentor demonstrates an awareness of the importance of learning from peers and more experienced people; it shows a recognition of the complex nature of ethical judgement and the time it takes to develop. All young professionals need help with the development of their ethical and professional judgement, and it's important to know when to ask for help. Some workplaces establish formal mentoring relationships between staff. The most successful approaches to mentoring, however, are often the ones that develop organically.

Managing ethical challenges in future work environments requires intentional approaches to developing the skills discussed in this section. It also requires a positive attitude to developing self-regulation and self-management skills. This is because in the workplace a person who is well, emotionally balanced and coping is more likely to be able to make good ethical decisions.

Michael Eales

Ethics are reflected in the choices we make — both conscious and unconscious — for the greater good or individual rights. The ethical procedures of a company are now regarded as having the same importance as the products and services they deliver. As an employee, you will bear some responsibility for how ethics are upheld at the company you work for, while also needing to align your own personal ethics and values to your daily processes. Therefore, it is important to be aware of your own ethical principles, understand that transparency is the best policy, and regularly reflect on the world we live in today.

Principles

How you project yourself and what you actually do are two different things, and social responsibility is no exception. When reflecting on your own ethical principles, view yourself as if you were judging a company's corporate social responsibility program. Work out what you *say* you do versus what you *actually* do and go from there.

Transparency

As we become more aware and enlightened of human practices we must continually improve. This is only achieved based on true and evidenced information extracted from insights and observations we make of the world around us, and how this world works. To improve we must be aware of our preconceptions and assumptions we often carry around with us. **When in doubt, transparency and honesty is the best policy in both professional and personal circumstances.**

Reflect

With ongoing crises such as climate change, and humans increasing their roles in mitigating its effects, we all have some responsibility in enacting change in the world. **Remain up to date on global information to inform your ethical practices at home and work.** Many hands make light work.

Check out the work of the Ethics Centre — https://ethics.org.au.

Mandy Johnson

Ethics is one area that is changing exponentially and will offer some of the greatest challenges for employees entering the workforce in the next five to ten years. On the one hand, there is a lot of positive change. More companies are taking a public stance on ethical issues: Qantas publicly supported the Australian same-sex marriage bill, the big four banks refused to fund the Adani coalmine and Atlassian vocally supports climate change initiatives.

At the same time, the ethical line is blurring between personal and professional life. Employees can be sacked for posting articles and arguments on their private social media pages that contradict their employer's stance. In Australia, a sawmill worker was sacked after his company introduced a new fingerprint scanning system and he refused to hand over his biometric data, for fear of it being misused. A Chinese organisation even forces its employees to wear helmets with sensors that detect anger, depression and fatigue. A big ethical question in the future then will be where we draw the line between ourselves and our work, especially with employers that adopt Big Brother tactics.

The rise in the use of AI will also create new ethical issues. AI has many benefits such as reducing human error in fields such as weather forecasting, and decreasing risk for humans (think AI robots that defuse bombs in war zones). Yet unchecked, AI can be destructive. Amazon discovered this after it created an AI hiring tool that scored job applicants from one to five stars to automate the search process. It was eventually abandoned when Amazon realised the system was skewed towards male applicants and had been hiring far more men than women.

Decision making will also be more ambiguous in this rapidly changing world. Like pioneers in a new frontier, science is developing faster than ethics, meaning that front-line employees will be dealing with more complex ethical questions. For instance, if a corporation you work for uses neuromarketing to make children dependent on sugary products, is that okay with you? Or if your genetics company creates a cloning system that secretly selects embryos solely on intelligence, is it your duty to tell someone? If your software company uses AI algorithms to manipulate public and political debate in ways that make you uncomfortable, what do you do about that?

We are all dependent on employers for our jobs and salary so speaking up is easier said than done. Yet research shows that people regret *not* acting more than they regret actions not going well. This is certainly true of some General Motors workers who helped develop and install a cheap ignition switch that they knew to be faulty, even in the pre-production phase.[39] The defective part eventually led to over 153 deaths, multiple crashes and 10 million car recalls — all because no-one spoke up. This all goes to show that, even though we aren't taught much about ethics in schools or university, it can have a major impact on our future.

Steve Sammartino

In the coming years, ethics will extend well beyond selling products with ingredients and production histories that are ethically sound. Fair treatment of staff and animals and compliance with workplace health and safety are all now seen as the bare minimum. The next forms of evolution in ethics will pertain to the digital marketplace.

The first of these will be ethics around data. Globally, the regulations around using data for profit are very lax. Even where regulations exist, it is difficult to prove data is being accumulated or misused, and which jurisdiction the data actually resides in. It is also true that the large majority of data breaches remain unknown to the victims at a corporate and personal level.

Much of the data that is accumulated is gathered without the explicit approval of end users. While privacy and service agreements are usually presented prior to using digital services, this quasi-approval is done via legal obfuscation. That is, the agreements include a level of complexity that very few people understand, and most agreements are many thousands of words long — so the reality is, most of us click 'accept' without properly absorbing the information.

This is resulting in massive privacy impingements in consumer society we are yet to see or understand the long-term consequences of. This will be a new battleground for ethics in business in the coming decade. The accumulation of data, how secure it is and the privacy impacts will become a major issue for management.

Three issues that will emerge as a priority during this time are as follows.

1. *Data will become a liability.* Companies that currently gather data on end users do so by providing free services in exchange. Increasingly data is being seen as an asset that end users should own and control. There have even been calls for data to be treated as a form of labour, as those who supply data are essentially creating products for tech companies to use for advertising. Mitigation corporations will increasingly need to reward customers whose data they gather with something beyond free products. Data will need to be treated like a bank deposit, for which some form of interest is paid and that can be fully withdrawn at the request of the data depositor.

2. *Algorithms will be regulated.* Currently algorithms that decide how digital products are served up via advertising are completely unregulated. Algorithms can have a dramatic impact on how internet users behave and react, and what they believe to be true. They have an inordinate influence on civic society. In the future it will become vital to ensure any algorithms used are 'ethical in advance'. Corporations utilising algorithms for any business purpose should be prepared for them to be regulated in a similar way to packaged food. Consumers will eventually have access to information showing how digital decisions are made on their behalf. Dark patterns that are used in hidden algorithms (for example, racial or sexual preference profiling) are likely to be outlawed in any business context.

3. *Criminality of data breaches.* Data security is not taken very seriously by most corporations at this point because the consequences of a breach are so small. In most cases, the profit from misuse of data is greater than the fines most large corporations face when hacks occur. Legislators globally are becoming acutely aware of this flaw and will shift the focus from financial repercussions to hold directors and staff criminally liable for breaches. The focus for corporations will need to shift to securing data like money.

The number one strategy for corporations is to get ahead of the legislation; to act on what is likely to be legislated later, now. It can actually become a point of difference for brands and companies to be ethically proactive.

From a career management perspective, people need to align themselves with corporations that have data ethics — not just because it is the right thing to do, but because large digital brands are less likely to be dominant in a future where they have to have a greater corporate responsibility when the consumer marketplace becomes more aware of data ethics.

Nicola Hazell

Casualisation and the gig economy

Over the past decade, it has become increasingly difficult for young people to get a secure job in their chosen fields — to get that break as they are starting out their working lives.[40] In Australia, people are more in debt at a younger age than ever before; almost one in two are still relying on their parents financially at the age of 24, and one in four graduates are struggling to find full-time employment after completing secondary or tertiary studies.[41]

The under-employment factor is a critical issue that is likely to rise.[42] Already, despite 60 per cent of young Australians holding some form of post-school qualification, 50 per cent of them are unable to secure traditional employment scenarios of more than 35 hours of work per week. Even among those who can secure full-time hours, many are doing so in casual, insecure jobs. Compared to 30 years ago, twice the number of young people are now working full-time hours in casual jobs, and the majority are doing so by holding down multiple jobs at once.

For all the flexibility and opportunity the gig economy can offer, this emerging segment of our global workforce brings with it a great deal of vulnerability for young workers. They may have a job (or jobs) — as a casual barista, an Uber driver or a cleaner on AirTasker – but this work is not fulfilling their social or economic needs, nor creating pathways to quality, full-time employment. Already, there are concerns about the implications of this trend — that it could potentially create a working poor among younger generations.

The traditional social constructs that have been built to provide workplace safety nets — such as workplace rights, minimum wages, government benefits and collective bargaining — have not been built into the frameworks of this new way of working.

The ethical risks of this are significant, presenting serious challenges for government, companies, regulators and the public to confront. **As someone about to take the plunge into this environment, it's essential to be aware of your rights, to be cognisant of the risks, and to consider the flow-on effects of what you are individually willing to compromise on.** Human beings by nature crave and require security. In the middle ages, security was tribal. In the modern day, that sense of security comes from being part of a community, a town, a home or an organisation. In the gig economy, security doesn't really exist. And when a crisis hits, there is no safety net built into systems that sit around it.

In the future of work, the ethics of this model for commerce and work will be increasingly questioned. Just because it offers greater efficiency, independence and flexibility, does that outweigh the loss of security, community and accountability? Or does it instead serve to further deepen the inequalities that have long existed in the modern world of work?

The ethics of this new reality will come further into question in the years ahead. In a post-COVID-19 environment — where the implications of this lack of security will have been brought to light at greater scale — the debate as to how to create a future of work that is ethical, and that increases (not decreases) equality, human connection and security, will be brought to the fore.

The emergence of AI

The growth of AI presents one of the great ethical debates of our time. Ever since the idea of 'robots taking over' was introduced into the public discourse via film and television decades ago, questions of trust, privacy and control have been raised.

Now, as we see technology move rapidly into the realm of AI in ways that are already integrating deeply into our daily lives — think Google Home, Amazon's Alexa, Tesla's self-driven cars and even the way Facebook knows what ads to show you — the question of what constitutes ethical AI is an urgent and pressing issue.

In many ways, the horse has already bolted. Data rights and data privacy are issues that only the most dedicated technology advocates and regulators are deeply engaging with, while most of us simply enjoy the convenience these technologies bring into our lives without questioning what it is we are giving up. Without consumer-driven demand for, and comprehension of, the ethical treatment of data, it becomes increasingly difficult for regulators to challenge.

The implications of this go much further than what it means for our data today. If the algorithms that make up AI are being fed a baseline of knowledge that does not have ethics built in, the AI will continue to perpetuate that baseline. The same can be said of bias. If AI is built to see the world through the eyes of just one 'type' of person, then what AI recognises as true or false, right or wrong, will be intrinsically biased towards that point of view. We're already seeing the way this plays out, with indicators of racism and sexism in the behaviours and insights of some forms of AI.[43]

The ethics of this is critical. If action isn't taken to counter these biases and build a baseline that recognises and respects diversity, then the AI that will increasingly inform our work, our homes, our lives and the information we are fed will continue to perpetuate inequality, growing in a way that is inherently unethical.

Creating a better world

Now more than ever, companies are being forced to demonstrate and earn their social licence to operate. Community expectations of corporate social responsibility are stretching well beyond the charity arms of organisations, requiring businesses and individuals to increasingly look at their operations through a lens of impact. This consideration of impact is then informing and influencing the values of organisations, their business activities and the behaviour of their people.

This shift is not just being driven simply by a desire to 'do the right thing'; nor is it being driven by social causes succeeding in their advocacy. It's being driven in many ways by consumer behaviour and expectations. Therefore, companies that not only consider how to mitigate any negative impact they have, but in fact are built out of an intent to have a net positive impact, will be the ones that come out on top. If this utopian view does not come to fruition, the implications for humanity are perilous. Unless businesses recognise and value the qualities of community and connection, equality and environmental sustainability — and unless employees live out these qualities in the way they work and live their lives — the fabric of society in the future of work will be eroded.

For humanity to evolve, the future of work needs to be played out with a new human-centred model. The social contract of the industrial era will need to be challenged to focus on outcomes over hours, to value contribution in a less transactional way. And on an immediate, personal level, the next generation will need to take this opportunity to question what it means to be human, and what the role of 'work' should be within that greater human experience.

In the meantime, you don't need to worry about climbing ladders that have been put in place by previous generations. **Instead, focus on the impact you can make in the world, then create the path in front of you to get there.** And, importantly, take others along with you when you do.

Skills and development

QUESTIONS Why is staying sharp important? What can happen if you don't stay up to date and continually refine your skills? How will professional development evolve over the next five to ten years? Knowing this, what are some strategies you can use to stay at the top of your game?

Nicola Hazell

Perhaps the most critical attribute for any individual in the future of work is curiosity. Those who are curious and have a constant thirst for learning and growth will be best placed to have a meaningful career and an impactful life. It's no longer a case of studying one university degree or trade to set you up for life. Ongoing professional and personal development will be key over the next five to fifty years.

For those on the frontline of technology — even those who are driving the change — the need to learn and adapt as the tech evolves is constant. But being adaptable and curious will be critical whether you're working in a hands-on technology role or not. As technology shifts, so too do markets. And as our world becomes more and more politically unstable, the conditions we operate in are more volatile and uncertain. Job mobility — the fact we will all have diverse careers in changing roles across changing industries — means we'll constantly be placed in different environments and circumstances and required to upskill or re-skill for the changing scenario.

As we've seen off the back of the COVID-19 global crisis, many workers have already been forced to consider their skills and how they could apply them in a totally different context within a different industry and role. The confronting nature of this situation is an indication of further instability likely to come. The key here is that preparing for instability is not about simply acquiring *more* skills and knowledge — because in a world that is changing so fast, we can never accumulate all the knowledge we might need to confront every task and challenge we will be presented with. No amount of professional development or outside learning will ensure you have the answer to every problem. In this scenario, it's not about what you know; it's about how you respond. Being prepared to make a decision to do something risky, to put yourself out there and take on something you haven't done before when there is no guarantee it will work: this is the mindset you will need in the future of work.

You can't afford to wait for 'perfect'; to wait until you're sure you're making the right call. It's not about being flippant. You can still be considered and deliberate and thoughtful. But you've also got to take a leap of faith and trust your intuition when there is 'nothing but gut' to go on.

Mandy Johnson

Imagine you are sitting in on an executive meeting and the managing director (MD) asks each of her leaders what their plan is for the next 12 months. One worker who has just experienced his most successful year ever says he is going to do exactly what he did last year. The MD replies, 'Well, you're in trouble then!' The point she was making is that knowledge was king for past generations, but when the world of work is changing at a cyclonic pace, it is knowledge *by learning* that will determine someone's effectiveness. If you're just focused on doing the same thing each year, and others are constantly improving, within 12 months you will have gone backwards in comparison without even realising it.

The good news is that once you embrace the concept of lifelong learning you can make it a practical strategy. Start by focusing on aspects of your work you would like to investigate or develop, then ask yourself: 'How am I going to learn more this year?' This might be via bite-sized learning such as TED Talks or YouTube clips, or from observing an expert in the field or finding a mentor who can act as a sounding board.

Yet focusing just on improving technical job skills is a poor strategy if you want to achieve long-term success. Google discovered this when the corporation analysed the characteristics of its best employees.[44] The management team thought technical skills would be the primary driver, but they were wrong. Good communication, effective listening and building good relationships with co-workers were the top three. Despite all the hype about skills in STEM (science, technology, engineering and maths), occupations requiring people skills are growing the fastest, so improving these is a good way to prepare for the changes coming.

Improving your own self-awareness is another vital future skill. Top employees are always the ones with the most accurate understanding of their own abilities. **Assessing strengths and weaknesses, asking trusted colleagues and collaborators for feedback and then addressing these through targeted actions are all activities that can help you more effectively navigate future workplaces.**

Or as French novelist Marcus Proust put it: 'The real voyage of discovery consists not in seeking new landscapes, but in having new eyes'.

Professor Angela Carbone

Staying sharp means that you are quick to notice things; that you're keeping a careful watch for opportunities and possible danger or difficulties. Staying sharp is absolutely necessary to ensure we can realise opportunities for the betterment of society and avoid major disasters that could have a significant impact on our lives. During the COVID-19 crisis we saw actions from sharp-eyed ministers and politicians avoid an overburden of Australia's hospital system.

To succeed in the new world of work you must be sharp, show leadership, act effectively, address challenges and make decisions that contribute in a positive and impactful way. If we don't stay sharp and up to date, our ability to recognise economic and social opportunities will be diminished; in the worst scenarios, we could be faced with potential life-threatening situations. It is important to develop our professional skills and keep them relevant, so we can contribute to the world in a meaningful and positive way.

Over the next five to ten years professional development will evolve in three main ways.
1. Formal education will still be the leading way in which people will develop their knowledge and skills in preparation for work and life, but we may see a shift from multiple-year-long degrees to shorter, more specific training packages.
2. On-the-job training and development with a focus on work-integrated learning will become more prominent as a form of professional development. This will provide people with an additional insight into the nature of the business and why staying sharp is instrumental in decision making.
3. We will become more connected with experts, industry leaders, researchers and other key culturally diverse people that are exploring the same issues. This will help us engage more deeply with current issues and see them from different perspectives, enabling us to become more effective contributors.

To stay ahead of your game you will need to develop a lifelong learning attitude that fosters curiosity and collaboration, taking action and reflecting on processes and outcomes for improvement. **While you are at university, say 'yes' to any opportunities to begin building your professional network such as mentoring, leadership and work integrated learning programs.** These will help you learn about workplace realities and your intended profession.[45] Networking and mentoring activities can help you connect with people who have different personal backgrounds, mindsets or ideas, and this can challenge and inspire you. Networking and mentoring can also provide you will support to help you deal with stressful situations.[46]

Professor Rachael Field

Although it is hard to predict how future workplaces will be changed as a result of COVID-19, it seems inevitable that one development will involve an increased emphasis on individuals taking responsibility for staying current with the knowledge, skills and values that are relevant to their work environment. This means an increased expectation that people will be self-directed lifelong learners.

Lifelong learning involves the voluntary and self-directed pursuit of knowledge and expertise for personal and professional reasons over the course of a lifetime. Lifelong learners are autonomous and self-motivated.

Three possible strategies for staying on top of professional development are as follows.
1. Join a professional society that offers structured, credible and relevant continuing professional development programs.
2. Consider further advanced levels of university study such as a postgraduate degree.
3. Ensure that lifelong learning and continuing professional development are included in regular discussions with your mentor and in professional performance reviews with your supervisor.

Michael Eales

In this rapidly evolving world, the jobs of today do not represent the jobs of tomorrow. This increases the desirability and need for specific skills of unknown value. To prepare for the unknown, a shift in investment from learning processes to acquiring abilities or skills is required. This includes learning to navigate ambiguity, communicate complex information and understand people and contexts at the molecular level.

Ambiguity

The only thing in this world that is constant is the state of change itself. No longer can we rest on our laurels and be comfortable in processes and environments that rely on a state of homeostasis. Learning certain skills — such as the ability to be present in the moment, rapidly reframe problems in relation to new information and find patterns in information to forecast the future — will enable you to not only remain ahead of change, but learn to embrace it in everyday practices. To better understand the way our world is changing, check out the soon-to-be-released book by Business Models Inc and Wiley called *Business Model Shift*.

Communication

The power of information systems, databases and computing analysis has grown significantly in the last 20 years, with organisations now able to leverage unprecedented knowledge to inform day-to-day activities and strategy. Historically, most skills have focused on analysis and application to facilitate understanding of data within siloed teams. As we work in increasingly diverse and multidisciplinary teams, learning the ability to translate, communicate and visualise complex information in a timely manner continues to prove invaluable and transferable across time.

People

In the face of automation, once highly prized skills in analysis can now be achieved at the press of a button. However, the ability to observe, empathise and translate human behaviour remains essential and continues to grow in a world coming to understand the importance of human-centred design principles. Investing in learning the skills that unpack human behaviour and reasoning provides grounding to the only constant in this world: that we are all human. Check out the work of Vince Frost to find out more: https://designyourlife.com.au.

Steve Sammartino

A fundamental shift in work is occurring. In the past, our job was to know how to do something, or to know what the answer actually was. Today, in a world exploding with data, our role is to know where to look to find the answer. As the world increases in complexity there is simply too much for anyone to know in any role, career or industry. As we work with forms of AI, the grunt work will be outsourced to smart machines; the role of humans is to know which path to chose. We need to be able to navigate a territory, rather than choose a specific direction. This requires us to be sharp, to learn on the job and to look beyond what worked yesterday to find answers and efficiencies. The fundamental shift is away from memory towards exploration. This requires increased situational awareness and agility.

People who do not continually update their skills have an increased risk of redundancy, and could face career and income decline. It's also increasingly important to upgrade your skills given that lifelong positions are increasingly rare. We are now expected to hold a number of positions in several different companies to be seen as 'skilled'. Given this reality, it's incumbent upon people to have a CV that is in a constant state of readiness to undertake a new position elsewhere.

Professional development will increasingly become the responsibility of the individual over the next five to ten years. We will all need to upskill ourselves, outside of formal corporate training. This marries up with the emerging trend towards independent and freelance labour and reduced tenure at corporate workplaces. Because we will most likely be working for a number organisations — even simultaneously — corporations will be less likely to invest in employees who are employed on a project or casual basis.

Qualifications outside of formal learning institutions and universities will gain more respect than they have done traditionally. This is due to increased digital access, and the fact that topic-specific thought leaders are becoming educators. Evidence of self-directed learning will also become a sign of the personal qualities of individuals, such as having initiative and being a self-starter. Such qualities are highly desired by employers.

Three strategies that you can use to stay at the top of your game include the following.

1. *Take on a side project.* Don't wait for your company or current customers to provide opportunities. Be prepared to have a side project you launch, lead and complete independently to garner the skills you'll need in the future. Thoughtful design of side projects can build a skill base that can be brought into your work life, improve financial acumen or assist in your next career move. Side projects will also have a positive personal branding impact and show initiative.

2. *Invest in your skills.* In the new world order we will be paid for our skills — not our time on the job. We need to remove the 'punch clock' mentality of value being a time-based factor. This is where the lowest-paid workers are, and will remain. Being able to separate the time taken to do a task and the revenue or payment you receive for it is a fundamental aspect of earning a large income. This is a head's up for workaholics: the correlation people make between time spent at work and income is a false narrative. As labour becomes project-oriented, what we are paid will increasingly be based on outcomes, rather than hours.

3. *ABL.* ABL stands for 'always be learning'. **At least 30 minutes of each day should be allocated towards learning a new skill or concept related to your industry, current role or a career pivot you'd like to make.** This can be done through simple online methods. It could be reading up on emerging trends, listening to podcasts or watching instructional videos. This learning doesn't have to be formal, especially given that emerging trends and technologies take a while to enter formal learning institutions.

Clare Payne

Different people will take to change better than others. It's important to recognise your individual strengths and understand what drives you — your personal purpose — rather than just trying to fit in. The ideal situation is to find a workplace where your individualism is appreciated and benefits others.

We have already seen a shift in the idea of professional development from employer-led to individual-led. This will continue as more opportunities become available through online platforms with access to experts from all over the world and a lower cost barrier.

Three strategies you can use to stay at the top of your game include the following.

1. *Constant learning.* By reading and listening, we can constantly learn and develop, ensuring we stay sharp and up to speed with the state of the world and the role of business within society.

2. *Self-awareness.* Taking time to reflect on what you are seeing, learning and feeling can ensure that you are conscious of your actions and the path that you are taking, as well as your impact on others.

3. *Staying curious.* Asking questions is sometimes the quickest way to understanding. The classical Greek philosopher, Socrates, asked, 'What ought one to do?' It is a question for any situation where choice is being exercised, and propels us to reflect on what we *should* do rather than what we *can* do.

Entrepreneurship and venture design

QUESTIONS How do you see entrepreneurship and venture design changing in the future? What are some emerging trends that will impact the way people start their own businesses?

Michael Eales

Venture design is emerging as the battleground for true creative capital and a more equitable model for entrepreneurial effort. For entrepreneurs, this world continues to provide myriad opportunities for those willing to see it. More so, the fast-paced nature of this world creates both a launching pad and an obstacle to seeing a venture through to the next stage of maturity. Future entrepreneurs must see opportunity in a world of problems, iterate fast and view social responsibility as a core activity of their business.

Opportunity

Venture design is focused on solving a problem worth solving. The arbitrator of this equation is always the customer. When identifying where value is created, it can be tempting to focus on solving a problem you have. In the rear-view mirror, we can see that this is a well-trodden path to entrepreneurial success. However, true value is achieved when you turn a customer problem into an opportunity to add continued value to the customer's life. So think: yes, this solves a problem, but how can we further enhance this value proposition to continue to add value well into the future?

Speed

In this world, speed is the new intellectual property (IP) and it is important to note that lengthy reports don't generate high-speed impact. Let the inner workings of your business reflect the speed of the world around it and you will achieve the level of desired impact at market.

The customer's perception and evaluation of a company's social responsibility across business practices is of increasing importance. No longer are customers satisfied with a corporate social responsibility program; they want the products they are purchasing to contribute to positive change within the world. Entrepreneurs of the future should consider how their pipeline can create social change to, in turn, generate a more valuable product in the eyes of the consumer.

Want to learn more? Read the book *Design A Better Business*[47] and check out https://design abetterbusiness.tools to learn more.

Steve Sammartino

The Silicon Valley ethic that emerged after the dot-com crash has hijacked the perception of entrepreneurship. In the past 15 years, startups have focused on the venture-funded model. In this model, venture capital is used as an accelerant to grow quickly, establish and dominate a new or emerging digital market. Frequently this model is built around free or subsidised products to increase digital adoption rates. While other more traditional models of entrepreneurship continued to exist, the narrative of modern startups has focused on the potential of building digitally disruptive businesses that could financially displace a large, slow analogue incumbent.

This was strategically correct for the time, and has given birth to a tech sector for which three of the five largest companies by market capitalisation did not exist in a pre-internet world. But now that the internet is beyond its burgeoning phase, and most simple forms of digitisation have already come to market, we will see a return to a new kind of venture where an initial public offering (IPO) or market sale to a larger firm is no longer the objective.

This is in part due to increasing pressure on law makers to regulate powerful tech companies, and the fact that these same large tech firms have built platforms through which new forms of entrepreneurship can be built. These companies have in some part formed a digital infrastructure for new types of small and medium-sized businesses to emerge — businesses that are less likely to create a platform in themselves, but serve as a profit engine to their founders. A return to yield and profit-based business will shape the next decade of entrepreneurship,

An inordinate number of businesses in the past decade have lacked a sustainable business model and have been saved by a few dominant technology firms acquiring them. The evaporation of cheap capital in the form of venture funding as well as financial conservatism in a post-COVID-19 world will also turn future ventures to be more about profit and slow, sustainable growth.

Three emerging changes that will largely impact the way people start their own business are as follows.
1. *Self-funding.* People starting their own business will be far more likely to self-fund their ventures and be focused on profit from the beginning. As the nature of work becomes more short-term and project-oriented, people will become entrepreneurs in the micro sense — firstly, to generate an income; and secondly, to build out a firm bigger than themselves.
2. *Profit over growth.* The economic climate will result in entrepreneurs being focused on immediate profit and growth, which is built through retained profits rather than equity or debt financing. The low-cost production infrastructure that the web has enabled will facilitate this. We'll also see startups less likely to own their own infrastructure but to access it, making their operations more flexible and profitable.
3. *Beyond digital.* Most entrepreneurial ventures have been focused on digital. In the next decade we'll see a return to functional products and services that were seen as declining industries (such as fast-moving consumer goods) — but this time, they will be localised brands, reinventing the geographic-centricity that was destroyed by global conglomerates taking over local brands to grow via acquisition. The future of business will be a more fragmented marketplace of nimble, geographically isolated firms operating for profit.

Mandy Johnson

As 16-year-old environmental activist Greta Thunberg found when her climate change campaign exploded into a global movement, technology can be a great amplifier, connecting people with others outside of traditional structures. This is fuelling an upsurge in 'collaborator' and 'purpose-driven' entrepreneurs. Rather than being confined to jobs within standard organisations, collaborator entrepreneurs work with others, each contributing a component of the solution, yet operating as separate independent entities. Purpose-driven entrepreneurs balance profitability with mission and tackle challenges in areas such as health, the environment and social justice. Both purpose-driven and collaborator entrepreneurs use technology to connect with armies of like-minded peers, advocates and potential customers.

Technology is also the mechanism transforming venture design. Future entrepreneurs won't just be looking to improve features or benefits of an existing product, to outdo competitors. Complete paradigm shifts in an offering's form, transaction or engagement will become the norm, similar to the way movie live-streaming decimated traditional video stores: the product stayed the same, but the method of delivery underwent a radical transformation. Budding entrepreneurs will have to do all this on a shoestring budget. Finding investors is becoming harder, so those who require less cash at startup or are adept at crowdfunding have a real advantage.

For lasting success, elasticity will become an essential feature of venture design, especially in the wake of more frequent crises that impact business such as the global financial crisis (GFC) and the COVID-19 pandemic. Entrepreneurs who can easily ramp up and down in reaction to external events — such as 'dark kitchens' offering restaurant-quality delivery meals without the fixed costs of a traditional establishment — are the startups of the future. Elasticity can apply to all areas of a business, from staff numbers and warehouse goods through to cashflow. Even product offerings can be flexible, as demonstrated during the COVID-19 pandemic when gin distilleries redeployed their alcohol supplies to manufacture in-demand hand sanitiser, and car companies began mass-producing face masks.

Technology's ability to generate more meaningful, quality data will also affect venture design, especially when applied to specific target markets or community sectors. Retailer Lorna Jane uses data mining to determine what its clients really want and has grown into a global multi-million-dollar business for woman who want to wear active wear everywhere. Future entrepreneurs will be able to effectively track their target market's changing needs, and design, shape and alter their physical products to suit.

Those who don't will fail. Even though a Kodak employee invented digital photography, the company took 18 years to make the switch, well after its competitors, and it eventually went bankrupt in 2012. Nowadays some of the only people who use Kodak film canisters are African Masai men, who stuff them with snuff and wear them in their elongated ear holes.[48] It's a cautionary tale, and one that future entrepreneurs would do well to remember. As we know, the one thing that won't change in the workplace of the future is change itself. So enjoy the ride!

Clare Payne

It is now much easier to start a business, however securing funding remains difficult for some. The allocation of venture capital is predicted to become more diversified and fair in the future. For example, a focus on female entrepreneurship will see more female-led businesses come to market and, when matched with venture capitalists with a gender focus, we will see these leaders and businesses flourish. There is hope that having a greater mix of people that reflects our society will bring new solutions to old problems as they can operate outside the constraints of traditional business models.

Starting businesses will only get easier, however the challenge will be for businesses to become sustainable and achieve their purpose.

Emerging changes that will assist this transition are as follows.

1. *Lower-cost entry.* Cloud computing is already meaning the cost of entry capital is far lower than it was historically.
2. *Game changers.* With fewer barriers to entry and more global collaboration there is the possibility of 'game changers', such as new ideas or procedures that affect a significant shift in the current way of doing or thinking about something, rather than incremental innovation. Each new 'game changer' that emerges will likely inspire others to think differently.
3. *Pressing issues.* The pressing nature of big global issues such as health, poverty and climate change will propel new forms of business and partnerships, particularly by the young who are tech savvy and sceptical of the status quo. I believe young people and those who are new to the workforce will play a big role in leading us to a better future.

Nicola Hazell

While many new enterprises created in the tech and startup boom of the past two decades have been driven by what could grow the fastest, attract the most customers and make the most money, increasingly investors *and* customers are looking for more from new ventures. Today, purpose is becoming a core pillar of success. Not just because people are growing a conscience, but because purpose-driven businesses have the greatest potential for impact at scale.

Consider this: in a world where we face huge challenges affecting the future of humanity, those businesses and organisations set up to solve such challenges will be the ones with the largest addressable market and therefore the greatest opportunity to succeed at scale. This has played out clearly during the COVID-19 crisis. While the digital maturity and agility of businesses has been a critical factor in their ability to respond to physical restrictions in civic movement (enabling them to transition immediately to an online operation), the long-term resilience of those businesses will come down to their level of engagement with their community — whether there is a deep ethos of trust that ensures their customers stay with them through the period of transition and back again.

What's more, beyond survival, the businesses that are *thriving* are those with a mission of solving critical issues for humanity. This includes digital businesses focused on education, technology designed to improve access to health and essential services, platforms that enable people to connect and communicate, digital tools to improve workforce productivity and mental health, and technology that delivers insights on community wellbeing and economic resilience. Within Australia's startup community alone, these are the businesses that are growing through the crisis — because they are increasing their impact as they solve critical human-centred problems.

In the ultimate example of survival of the fittest, the businesses that are thriving and will continue to thrive are those driven by purpose, by creating positive impact, by a mission to solve real and tangible problems that will make the world a better place, and built on a framework of trust and ethics. For any young entrepreneur starting or joining a new venture in the years ahead, these will be the critical factors — for investors, for customers, for employees and for themselves.

ABOUT THE CONTRIBUTORS

Angela Carbone

Angela Carbone is a Professor and Dean (Learning Innovation) in the Faculty of Science, Engineering and Technology, Swinburne University, Australia. She has extensive teaching, leadership and research experience, and has held various educational leadership positions throughout her academic career. She was the inaugural Academic Director of Education Excellence for the Office of Learning and Teaching at Monash University. Prior to that she was the Associate Director of the Office of the Pro Vice-Chancellor (Learning and Teaching) and the Director of Education Quality in the Faculty of Information Technology at Monash University. Her teaching achievements have been recognised nationally, awarded the nation's highest teaching award, and securing two national teaching fellowships. Angela led a multi-institutional employability research project capturing innovative approaches to develop students' employability skills and is currently engaged in an externally funded project to support students' development of learner agency during work placement. She chaired the Embedding Employability into Teaching and Learning Conference 2016 and is a member of the International Education, Practice and Employability Network. She has presented her ideas at an international thinktank on graduate attributes and employability and is widely published in peer reviewed journals in the area of education and employability.

Michael Eales

Michael Eales is Managing Director of Business Models Inc. in Australia and New Zealand, an award-winning international business, design and innovation agency. Michael uses strategy design, system design and future-centred design to drive innovation across organisations and push the traditional boundaries of work.

As a design pioneer, Michael supports organisations of all sizes to think better, communicate more effectively and work faster — so their strategy can move as fast as their business. Michael has helped boards of directors, top leaders and innovation teams across government, for profits and not-for profits innovate their business model and design a future strategy. He also specialises in helping organisations navigate uncertainty through scenario planning, and is Good Design Australia's COVID-19 Design Taskforce lead.

Michael inspires people and organisations with his approach to future visioning, while grounding the design and execution of strategy with an evidence-based approach to look at their business (model) from a completely different perspective. In his projects he uses the new tools of business design, like the Business Model Canvas, Vision Canvas, Context Canvas and Value Proposition Designer, and co-creation techniques from the book produced by his team — *Design A Better Business*.

Rachael Field

Rachael is a Professor of Law in the Faculty of Law at Bond University, and Co-Director of the Bond University's Centre for Professional Legal Education. Her areas of research expertise include dispute resolution, legal education, family law and domestic violence. Rachael has received a number of national teaching awards including a national citation in 2008, a national teaching fellowship in 2010 (through which she developed curriculum practices for the promotion of law student wellbeing) and a national teaching excellence award in 2014. Rachael is an Australian Learning and Teaching Fellow, member of the Fellows Executive and a Senior Fellow of the Higher Education Academy. She co-chairs the annual STARS conference, which has a focus on student success in tertiary education. Rachael founded the Australian Wellness Network for Law in 2010 which is now expanding internationally. In 2010, Rachael contributed significantly to the drafting of the Threshold Learning Outcomes for law, which have had national and international impact. Rachael is also co-founder of the Australian Dispute Resolution Research Network. She has a portfolio of more than 100 scholarly publications many of which are legal education focussed, and is co-author of six books. Rachael has volunteered at Women's Legal Service, Brisbane, since 1993, and has been president of the Service since 2004. In 2013 Rachael was named Queensland Woman Lawyer of the Year.

Ideas and content for this piece were adapted from Nickolas James, Rachael Field and Jackson Walkden-Brown, *The New Lawyer* (Wiley, 2nd ed, 2020) and Rachael Field, James Duffy and Anna Huggins, *Lawyering and Positive Professional Identities* (LexisNexis, 2nd ed, 2020).

Nicola Hazell

Nicola Hazell is one of Australia's leading voices on gender equality, social innovation and the future of work. With a career spanning technology, politics, journalism, and civil society, Nicola has a track record of achieving social impact at scale. She has worked with organisations and sectors around the world — from global tech giants and intergovernmental organisations, to emerging start-ups and social enterprises — to design and accelerate new solutions to drive investment in inclusion, diversity and social innovation.

Nicola is a firm believer in collective impact and the power of giving back, acting as a mentor and judge for various leadership and development programs, and as a strategic advisor for a range of women-led start-ups and purpose-driven organisations. She is determined to continue growing the impact and influence of a new wave of leaders, ready to create a more inclusive future of work.

Mandy Johnson

With the world of work changing at lightning speed, Mandy Johnson speaks, writes and advises on the innovative people and leadership strategies that create remarkable workplaces and transform organisational results. A best-selling author, with 'in-the-trenches' experience as a start-up founder and director of global travel retailer Flight Centre's UK operation, she is renowned for her practical approach. Mandy has featured on Sky Business News, Qantas Radio with Alan Kohler and ABC Radio's Conversation Hour, and she's worked with companies from just about every industry. One of only a handful of Australians to present at the Asia–Pacific Talent Conference in Taipei, she also runs signature masterclasses, guest lectures MBA and incubate students and has delivered executive education courses for Bond University and the University of Queensland Business School. Mandy also facilitates the Australian Owner Manager Program and offers advice to global students from 193 countries as part of UQ Business School's edX MicroMasters program. Her goal is to challenge conventional thinking at every opportunity and spread the word that great people practices are the heart, soul *and* balance sheet of every future workplace.

Clare Payne

Clare Payne is the EY Fellow for Trust and Ethics and an Honorary Fellow of The University of Melbourne. Clare advises businesses and leaders on ethics, good governance and trust. She is a former employment lawyer who managed the integrity office of Macquarie Bank and founded The Banking and Finance Oath. Prior to the global financial crisis, Clare's paper titled, *'Ethics or Bust'* was awarded the inaugural Ethics & Trust in Finance Prize by the Observatoire de la Finance, Geneva. She then went on to co-author *A Matter of Trust — The Practice of Ethics in Finance* (Melbourne University Publishing). Clare is a World Economic Forum Young Global Leader and is recognised as an Australian '100 Women of Influence.' Clare has a Bachelor of Communications and Laws and is a Vincent Fairfax Fellow for Ethics in Leadership.

Steve Sammartino

Steve wrote his first lines of computer code at age 10, and is one of Australia's most respected business minds. After graduating from university majoring in economics, he worked in multiple Fortune 500 companies and held many senior positions culminating in directorships, before answering his true calling for independence from The System. Curious about why some people seemed to get richer, regardless of education and income, he delved deeply into the study of personal finance, informally. His experience means he intimately understands small and big business and how to play the game to get ahead and design your own future.

Steve has had multiple technology start-ups, including launching rentoid.com, one of the first 'sharing economy' startups, before Uber or Airbnb. Steve had a successful exit selling the start-up to a public company. He now invests in emerging technologies and has multiple advisory board positions in a variety of disruptive technologies across the airline, automotive, real estate and co-working industries, and the Internet of Things, quantified self, mobile applications, and 3D printing technologies.

A media commentator on technology and the future, Steve is a regular on the ABC and provides expert assessment on the rapidly evolving technology sector. He has also been featured on the BBC, The Smithsonian Institute, The Discovery Channel, Mashable, Wired, and has even had documentaries made about his projects.

ENDNOTES

1. American Psychological Association 2019, *Stress in America*, www.apa.org.
2. Deloitte Center for the Edge 2013, *Institutional innovation: Creating smarter organizations to scale learning*, Deloitte University Press, www2.deloitte.com.
3. Salt, Bernard 2011, 'Baby boom to baby bust', *The Australian*, 28 May, www.theaustralian.com.au.
4. Sullivan, Kath 2020, 'Unemployment rate predicted to reach 10 per cent amid coronavirus pandemic, pushing Australia into recession', *ABC News*, 13 April, www.abc.net.au.
5. The United Nations, 'Sustainable Development Goals', https://sustainabledevelopment.un.org.
6. Marin-Guzman, David and Baird, Lucas 2020, 'Woolworths offers jobs to laid-off Qantas workers', *The Australian Financial Review*, 19 March, www.afr.com.
7. Business Roundtable 2019, 'Business Roundtable Redefines the Purpose of a Corporation to Promote "An Economy That Serves All Americans"', 19 August, www.businessroundtable.org.
8. Committee for Economic Development of Australia (CEDA) 2015, *Australia's future workforce?*, www.ceda.com.au.
9. World Economic Forum 2016, *The Future of Jobs: Employment, Skills and Workforce Strategy for the Fourth Industrial Revolution*, www3.weforum.org.
10. McCrindle 2020, 'Job mobility in Australia', https://mccrindle.com.au.
11. Foundation for Young Australians 2015, *Backing Young Entrepreneurs*, www.pc.gov.au.
12. Foundation for Young Australians 2016, *The New Basics: Big data reveals the skills young people need for the New Work Order*, www.fya.org.au.
13. CBRE Group 2014, *Fast Forward 2030: The Future of Work and Workplace*, www.cbre.com.
14. Foundation for Young Australians 2018, *The New Work Order* report series, www.fya.org.au.
15. World Economic Forum 2018, *The Future of Jobs Report*, www3.weforum.org.
16. Zao-Sanders, Marc and Palmer, Kelly 2019, 'Why Even New Grads Need to Reskill for the Future', *Harvard Business Review*, 26 September, https://hbr.org.
17. McCrindle, 'Teleworking in Australia: Latest Trends and Perceptions', https://mccrindle.com.au; International Workplace Group 2019, *The IWG Global Workspace Survey*, http://assets.regus.com.
18. Reserve Bank of Australia 2020, 'Composition of the Australian Economy Snapshot', www.rba.gov.au.
19. Lyubomirsky, Sonja, Sheldon, Kennon M & Schkade, David 2005, 'Pursuing Happiness: The Architecture of Sustainable Change', *Review of General Psychology*, vol. 9, no. 2, pp. 111–131.
20. Snyder, Charles 2000, *Handbook of Hope : Theory, Measures, and Applications*, Academic Press.
21. Graham Gibbs 1988, *Learning by Doing: A Guide to Teaching and Learning Methods*, Oxford Centre for Staff and Learning Development.
22. Bates G, Rixon, A, Carbone, A & Pilgrim, C 2019, 'Beyond Employability Skills: Developing Professional Purpose', *Journal of Teaching and Learning for Graduate Employability*, vol. 10, no. 1.
23. McKnight, PE & Kashdan, TB 2009, 'Purpose in life as a system that creates and sustains health and well-being: An integrative, testable theory', *Review of General Psychology*, vol. 13, no. 3, pp. 242–251.
24. Elliott, A 2006, 'The hierarchical model of approach-avoidance motivation', *Motivation and Emotion*, vol. 30, no. 2, pp. 111–116.
25. McKnight, PE & Kashdan, TB 2009, *op. cit.*
26. Pencavel, John 2014, *The Productivity of Working Hours*, IZA Institute of Labor Economics, www.iza.org.
27. Australian Psychological Society, 'Stress & wellbeing - how Australians are coping with life', www.psychology.org.au.
28. Business in the Community 2019, *Mental Health at Work 2019*, www.bitc.org.uk.
29. Baldassarre, Gina 2018, 'Pioneera helps address employee stress and burnout with a chatbot', Startup Daily, 16 July, www.startupdaily.net.
30. Owen Whitford, Danielle, www.pioneera.com.
31. Foundation for Young Australians 2016, ibid.

32. Boulle, Laurence and Alexander, Nadja 2020, *Mediation Skills and Techniques*, 3rd edn, LexisNexis.

33. Osterwalder, Alexander et al. 2020, *The Invincible Company: How to Constantly Reinvent Your Organization with Inspiration From the World's Best Business Models*, Wiley.

34. Foster Back, Philippa 2005, *Setting the Tone: Ethical Business Leadership*, Institute of Business Ethics.

35. Edelman 2020, '2020 Edelman Trust Barometer Reveals Growing Sense of Inequality Is Undermining Trust in Institutions', www.edelman.com.

36. ibid.

37. 'A new revolution in finance: introducing Moral Money, the latest FT newsletter', *Financial Times*, https://subs.enterprise.ft.com.

38. Responsible Investment Association Australasia, *Responsible Investment Benchmark Report 2019 Australia*, https://responsibleinvestment.org.

39. Plumer, Brad 2015, 'The GM recall scandal of 2014', Vox, www.vox.com.

40. Organisation for Economic Co-operation and Development (OECD) 2019, 'OECD work on Youth', www.oecd.org.

41. Foundation for Young Australians, The New Work Order report series, www.fya.org.au.

42. Foundation for Young Australians 2018, *The New Work Reality*, www.fya.org.au.

43. Buranyi, Stephen 2017, 'Rise of the racist robots – how AI is learning all our worst impulses', *The Guardian*, 8 August, www.theguardian.com.

44. Strauss, Valerie 2017, 'The surprising thing Google learned about its employees — and what it means for today's students', *The Washington Post*, 21 December, www.washingtonpost.com.

45. Smith-Ruig, T 2014, 'Exploring the links between mentoring and work-integrated learning', *Higher Education Research & Development*, vol. 33, no. 4, pp. 769-782.

46. Stuart, M, Lido, C, Morgan, J & May, S 2009, *Student diversity, extra-curricular activities and perceptions of graduate outcomes*, York, UK: The Higher Education Academy.

47. Van der Pijl, Patrick et al. 2016, *Design A Better Business*, Wiley.

48. Roberts, David 1986, *Moments of Doubt and Other Mountaineering Writings*, Mountaineers Books.

INDEX